Visit classzone and get connected

Online resources for students and parents

ClassZone resources are linked together and provide instruction, practice, and learning support.

eEdition Plus ONLINE

This interactive version of the text encourages students to explore mathematics.

eWorkbook Plus ONLINE

Interactive practice, correlated to the text, provides support for key concepts and skills.

eTutorial Plus ONLINE

This interactive tutorial reinforces key skills and helps students prepare for tests.

Chapter-Based Support

Examples, state test practice, quizzes, vocabulary support, and activities help students succeed.

Now it all clicks!™

 CLASSZONE.COM

McDougal Littell

McDougal Littell Middle School

COURSE 2

Math

Larson   Boswell   Kanold   Stiff

McDougal Littell

A HOUGHTON MIFFLIN COMPANY

Evanston, Illinois   •   Boston   •   Dallas

About Middle School Math: Course 2

McDougal Littell Middle School Math will help you be successful in this course. The clearly written lessons with frequent step-by-step examples make even difficult math concepts and methods easier to understand. The number and variety of problems, ranging from basic to challenging, give you the practice you need to develop your math skills. This book will also help you develop your notetaking and problem-solving skills. Look for notetaking strategies and Help Notes that support problem solving, vocabulary, reading, homework, technology, and review. To help you get ready for tests, there are test-taking strategies and test-taking practice exercises throughout the book. Enjoy the Brain Games — they will challenge your thinking skills!

ISBN: 0-618-24974-5   456789–VJM–08 07 06 05 04

Internet Web Site: http://www.classzone.com

Ron Larson

Ron Larson is a professor of mathematics at Penn State University at Erie, where he has taught since receiving his Ph.D. in mathematics from the University of Colorado. Dr. Larson is well known as the author of a comprehensive program for mathematics that spans middle school, high school, and college courses. Dr. Larson's numerous professional activities keep him in constant touch with the needs of teachers and supervisors. He closely follows developments in mathematics standards and assessment.

Laurie Boswell

Laurie Boswell is the mathematics department chair at Profile Junior-Senior High School in Bethlehem, New Hampshire. A recipient of the Presidential Award for Excellence in Mathematics Teaching, she has also been a Tandy Technology Scholar. She serves on the National Council of Teachers of Mathematics Board of Directors. She speaks frequently on topics related to instructional strategies and course content.

Timothy Kanold

Timothy Kanold is the superintendent of Adlai E. Stevenson High School District 125, where he served as a teacher and the Director of Mathematics for 16 years. He recently received his Ph.D. from Loyola University Chicago. Dr. Kanold is a recipient of the Presidential Award for Excellence in Mathematics and Science Teaching and served on The Academy Services Committee for NCTM. He is a frequent speaker at mathematics meetings where he shares his in-depth knowledge of mathematics teaching and curriculum.

Lee Stiff

Lee Stiff is a professor of mathematics education in the College of Education of North Carolina State University at Raleigh. His extensive experience in mathematics education includes teaching at the middle school and high school levels. He has received the W. W. Rankin Award for Excellence in Mathematics Education, and was Fulbright Scholar to the Department of Mathematics of the University of Ghana. He served as President of the National Council of Teachers of Mathematics (2000–2002).

Advisers and Reviewers

Curriculum Advisers and Reviewers

Donna Foley
Curriculum Specialist for Math
Chelmsford Middle School
Chelmsford, MA

Barbara Nunn
Secondary Mathematics Specialist
Broward County Schools
Fort Lauderdale, FL

Wendy Loeb
Mathematics Teacher
Twin Groves Junior High School
Buffalo Grove, IL

Tom Scott
Resource Teacher
Duval County Public Schools
Jacksonville, FL

Teacher Panels

Florida Panel

Kathy Adams
Mathematics Teacher
Allapattah Middle School
Miami, FL

Micki Hawn
Mathematics Teacher
Pompano Beach Middle School
Pompano Beach, FL

Barbara Schober
Mathematics Department Chair
Okeeheelee Middle School
West Palm Beach, FL

Sue Carrico-Beddow
Mathematics Teacher
Bayonet Point Middle School
New Port Richey, FL

Pat Powell
Mathematics Department Chair
Stewart Middle School
Tampa, FL

Laurie St. Julien
Mathematics Teacher
Oak Grove Middle School
Clearwater, FL

Melissa Grabowski
Mathematics Teacher
Stone Middle School
Melbourne, FL

Kansas and Missouri Panel

Linda Cordes
Department Chair
Paul Robeson Middle School
Kansas City, MO

Rhonda Foote
Mathematics Department Chair
Maple Park Middle School
North Kansas City, MO

Jan Rase
Mathematics Teacher
Moreland Ridge Middle School
Blue Springs, MO

Linda Dodd
Mathematics Department Chair
Argentine Middle School
Kansas City, KS

Cas Kyle
District Math Curriculum Coordinator
Richard A. Warren Middle School
Leavenworth, KS

Dan Schoenemann
Mathematics Teacher
Raytown Middle School
Kansas City, MO

Melanie Dowell
Mathematics Teacher
Raytown South Middle School
Raytown, MO

Texas Panel

Judy Carlin
Mathematics Teacher
Brown Middle School
McAllen, TX

Judith Cody
Mathematics Teacher
Deady Middle School
Houston, TX

Lisa Hiracheta
Mathematics Teacher
Irons Junior High School
Lubbock, TX

Kay Neuse
Mathematics Teacher
Wilson Middle School
Plano, TX

Louise Nutzman
Mathematics Teacher
Sugar Land Middle School
Sugar Land, TX

Clarice Orise
Mathematics Teacher
Tafolla Middle School
San Antonio, TX

Wonda Webb
Mathematics Teacher
William H. Atwell Middle School
and Law Academy
Dallas, TX

Karen Young
Mathematics Teacher
Murchison Elementary School
Pflugerville, TX

Field Test Teachers

Kathryn Chamberlain
McCarthy Middle School
Chelmsford, MA

Sheree Daily
Canal Winchester Middle School
Canal Winchester, OH

Deborah Kebe
Canal Winchester Middle School
Canal Winchester, OH

Jill Leone
Twin Groves Junior High School
Buffalo Grove, IL

Wendy Loeb
Twin Groves Junior High School
Buffalo Grove, IL

Melissa McCarty
Canal Winchester Middle School
Canal Winchester, OH

Deb Mueth
St. Aloysius School
Springfield, IL

Gail Sigmund
Charles A. Mooney Middle School
Cleveland, OH

Teacher Reviewers

Susanne Artiñano
Bryn Mawr School
Baltimore, MD

Lisa Barnes
Bishop Spaugh Academy
Charlotte, NC

Beth Bryan
Sequoyah Middle School
Oklahoma City, OK

Jennifer Clark
Mayfield Middle School
Oklahoma City, OK

Lois Cole
Pickering Middle School
Lynn, MA

Louis Corbosiero
Pollard Middle School
Needham, MA

James Cussen
Candlewood Middle School
Dix Hills, NY

Kristen Dailey
Boardman Center Middle School
Boardman, OH

Shannon Galamore
Clay-Chalkville Middle School
Pinson, AL

Tricia Highland
Moon Area Middle School
Moon Township, PA

Myrna McNaboe
Immaculate Conception
East Aurora, NY

Angela Richardson
Sedgefield Middle School
Charlotte, NC

James Richardson
Booker T. Washington Middle School
Mobile, AL

Dianne Walker
Traverse City Central High School
Traverse City, MI

Stacey Wood
Cochrane Middle School
Charlotte, NC

CHAPTER

1

Number Sense, Patterns, and Algebraic Thinking

Notetaking and Student Help

Notetaking, 4, 10, 14, 18, 24, 27, 32, 39, 42
Reading, 5, 15, 26
Solving, 19, 39
Review, 6, 33
Technology, 23
Watch Out, 10

BRAIN GAME

Going for Gold, 2
Olympic Torch Run, 3
Number Jumble, 22
Shape Equations, 30

Internet Resources

- eEdition Plus Online
- eWorkbook Plus Online
- eTutorial Plus Online
- State Test Practice
- More Examples

Pre-Course Assessment

Pre-Course Test, xxvi
Pre-Course Practice, xxviii

Student Handbook, xx

Example 1, p. 38

Decimal Operations

BrAIN GAME

Internet Resources

- eEdition Plus Online
- eWorkbook Plus Online
- eTutorial Plus Online
- State Test Practice
- More Examples

EXPLORING
MATH IN SCIENCE

Earth Science
Describing Ocean Waves, 96

Example 3, p. 64

Data and Statistics

Notetaking and Student Help

BrAIN GAME

Internet Resources

- eEdition Plus Online
- eWorkbook Plus Online
- eTutorial Plus Online
- State Test Practice
- More Examples

Unit 1 Assessment

Exercises 14–15, p. 119

Number Patterns and Fractions

Notetaking and Student Help

Notetaking, 156, 173, 181, 185, 186, 194, 196
Reading, 158, 170, 185
Solving, 165, 169, 176, 192
Review, 158, 186, 190, 191
Technology, 195
Watch Out, 159, 165

BrAIN GAME

Coaster Commotion, 154
What am I?, 161
Missing Numerators, 189

Internet Resources

· eEdition Plus Online
· eWorkbook Plus Online
· eTutorial Plus Online
· State Test Practice
· More Examples

Problem Solving Strategies, p. 162

Fraction Operations

Internet Resources

· eEdition Plus Online
· eWorkbook Plus Online
· eTutorial Plus Online
· State Test Practice
· More Examples

Exercise 10, p. 213

Integers

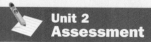

Exercise 10, p. 268

C H A P T E R
7

Equations, Inequalities, and Functions

Notetaking and Student Help
Notetaking, 316, 327, 328, 333, 334, 338, 360
Reading, 346
Solving, 318, 322, 323, 342, 354, 355
Review, 334, 344
Watch Out, 317, 328, 347, 355

BrAIN GAME
Deciphering Ancient Numbers, 314
Stone Tablet, 315
Orderly Words, 331
Fun with Functions, 358

Internet Resources
· eEdition Plus Online
· eWorkbook Plus Online
· eTutorial Plus Online
· State Test Practice
· More Examples

Exercise 22, p. 353

Ratios and Proportions

Notetaking and Student Help

BrAIN GAME

Internet Resources

- eEdition Plus Online
- eWorkbook Plus Online
- eTutorial Plus Online
- State Test Practice
- More Examples

EXPLORING

MATH in SCIENCE

Life Science

Example 3, p. 401

Notetaking and Student Help

BrAIN GAME

Internet Resources

- eEdition Plus Online
- eWorkbook Plus Online
- eTutorial Plus Online
- State Test Practice
- More Examples

Unit 3 Assessment

Percents

Example 1, p. 432

CHAPTER 10

Geometric Figures

Notetaking and Student Help

BrAIN GAME

Internet Resources

- eEdition Plus Online
- eWorkbook Plus Online
- eTutorial Plus Online
- State Test Practice
- More Examples

Example 1, p. 511

Measurement and Area

Notetaking and Student Help

BrAIN GAME

Internet Resources

- eEdition Plus Online
- eWorkbook Plus Online
- eTutorial Plus Online
- State Test Practice
- More Examples

EXPLORING MATH IN SCIENCE

Physical Science
Modeling the Motion of a
Pendulum, 578

Lesson 11.2, p. 540

Notetaking and Student Help
Notetaking, 582, 594, 598, 602, 607, 611, 616
Solving, 584, 588, 592, 594, 602
Review, 586, 612
Watch Out, 612

Basketball Blitz, 580
Face Painting, 599
Vocabulary Scramble, 617

· eEdition Plus Online
· eWorkbook Plus Online
· eTutorial Plus Online
· State Test Practice
· More Examples

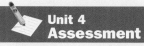

Unit 4 Assessment

Building Test-Taking Skills:
  Extended Response, 622
Practicing Test-Taking Skills, 624
Cumulative Practice, 626

Surface Area and Volume

Example 1, p. 583

Probability

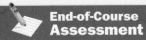

Example 2, p. 635

Contents of Student Resources

Student Handbook

Help with Taking Notes

One of the most important tools for success in mathematics is organizing what you have learned. Writing down important information in a notebook helps you remember key concepts and skills. You can use your notebook as a reference when you do your homework or when you study for a test.

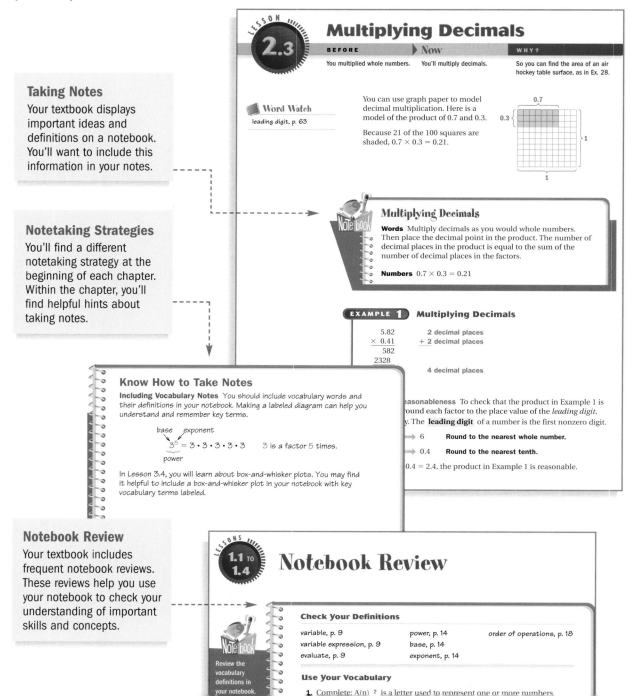

Taking Notes
Your textbook displays important ideas and definitions on a notebook. You'll want to include this information in your notes.

Notetaking Strategies
You'll find a different notetaking strategy at the beginning of each chapter. Within the chapter, you'll find helpful hints about taking notes.

Notebook Review
Your textbook includes frequent notebook reviews. These reviews help you use your notebook to check your understanding of important skills and concepts.

LESSON 2.3

Multiplying Decimals

BEFORE	Now	WHY?
You multiplied whole numbers.	You'll multiply decimals.	So you can find the area of an air hockey table surface, as in Ex. 28.

Word Watch

leading digit, p. 63

You can use graph paper to model decimal multiplication. Here is a model of the product of 0.7 and 0.3.

Because 21 of the 100 squares are shaded, $0.7 \times 0.3 = 0.21$.

Multiplying Decimals

Words Multiply decimals as you would whole numbers. Then place the decimal point in the product. The number of decimal places in the product is equal to the sum of the number of decimal places in the factors.

Numbers $0.7 \times 0.3 = 0.21$

EXAMPLE 1 **Multiplying Decimals**

5.82	2 decimal places
$\times$ 0.41	+ 2 decimal places
582	
2328	
	4 decimal places

...easonableness To check that the product in Example 1 is ...round each factor to the place value of the *leading digit*, ...y. The **leading digit** of a number is the first nonzero digit.

→ 6 **Round to the nearest whole number.**

→ 0.4 **Round to the nearest tenth.**

...0.4 = 2.4, the product in Example 1 is reasonable.

Know How to Take Notes

Including Vocabulary Notes You should include vocabulary words and their definitions in your notebook. Making a labeled diagram can help you understand and remember key terms.

base   exponent
$$3^5 = 3 \cdot 3 \cdot 3 \cdot 3 \cdot 3 \qquad 3 \text{ is a factor 5 times.}$$
power

In Lesson 3.4, you will learn about box-and-whisker plots. You may find it helpful to include a box-and-whisker plot in your notebook with key vocabulary terms labeled.

LESSONS 1.1 TO 1.4

Notebook Review

Review the vocabulary definitions in your notebook.

Check Your Definitions

variable, p. 9	power, p. 14	order of operations, p. 18
variable expression, p. 9	base, p. 14	
evaluate, p. 9	exponent, p. 14	

Use Your Vocabulary

1. Complete: A(n) ? is a letter used to represent one or more numbers.

Help with Learning Mathematics

Your textbook helps you succeed in mathematics. Keep your eye out for notes that help you with reading mathematics, learning vocabulary terms, solving problems, using technology, and doing your homework. Some examples of the types of notes you'll see are shown below.

Help Notes

These notes help you understand and apply what you've learned.

Watch Out!

These notes help you avoid common errors.

Help with Homework

These notes tell you which textbook examples may help you with homework exercises, and let you know where to find extra help on the Internet.

Using Prime Factorization Another way to find the greatest common factor of two or more numbers is to use the prime factorization of each number. The product of the common prime factors is the greatest common factor.

EXAMPLE 2 Using Prime Factorization to Find the GCF

HELP with **Solving**
Large numbers may have many factors, and it may be difficult to list all the factors. Sometimes it's easier to use prime factorization to find the greatest common factor of large numbers.

Find the greatest common factor of 180 and 126 using prime factorization.

Begin by writing the prime factorization of each number.

$$180$$
$$10 \times 18$$
$$2 \times 5 \times 2 \times 9$$
$$2 \times 5 \times 2 \times 3 \times 3$$

$$126$$
$$2 \times 63$$
$$2 \times 3 \times 21$$
$$2 \times 3 \times 3 \times 7$$

$$180 = 2 \times 2 \times 3 \times 3 \times 5$$
$$126 = 2 \times 3 \times 3 \times 7$$

ANSWER The common prime factors of 180 and 126 are 2, 3, and 3. So, the greatest common factor is $2 \times 3^2 = 18$.

Your turn now Find the greatest common factor of the numbers using prime factorization.

7. 90, 150   **8.** 84, 216   **9.** 120, 192   **10.** 105, 225

Relatively Prime Two or more numbers are **relatively prime** if their greatest common factor is 1.

EXAMPLE 3 Identifying Relatively Prime Numbers

Watch Out!
To say that two numbers are relatively prime does *not* mean that one of the numbers is prime.

Tell whether the numbers are relatively prime.

a. 28, 45   Factors of 28: 1, 2, 4, 7, 14, 28
                  Factors of 45: 1, 3, 5, 9, 15, 45   The GCF is 1.

ANSWER Because the GCF is 1, 28 and 45 are relatively prime.

b. 15, 51   Factors of 15: 1, 3, 5, 15
                  Factors of 51: 1, 3, 17, 51   The GCF is 3.

ANSWER Because the GCF is 3, 15 and 51 are not relatively prime.

HELP with **Homework**

Example	Exercises
1	15–23, 30–32
2	24–26
3	15–23, 30–32
4	15–23, 30–32
5	28–29

Online Resources
CLASSZONE.COM
· More Examples
· eTutorial Plus

Practice and Problem Solving

Evaluate the expression.

15. $12 + 2 \cdot 10$ **16.** $40 - 12 \div 6$ **17.** $7(14 - 9)$

18. $\dfrac{28}{7 - 3}$ **19.** $\dfrac{15 - 7}{3 + 1}$ **20.** $16 \div (3^2 - 1)$

21. $3^4 \div 9 \div 3$ **22.** $(8 - 2)^2 + 12 \div 6$ **23.** $35 - 15 - 5 + 10$

Algebra Evaluate the expression when $x = 3$, $y = 6$, and $z = 2$.

24. $18 \div x - z$ **25.** $\dfrac{x + y}{x}$ **26.** $4z^3 - y$

27. Critical Thinking Insert grouping symbols into the expression

Reading Your Textbook

You need special skills to read a math textbook. These skills include *identifying the main idea, learning new vocabulary,* and *focusing on the important concepts* in a lesson. Most important, you need to *be an active reader.* You need to practice and apply the ideas you read about.

Identify the Main Idea

Even before you begin reading a lesson, check to see what the lesson is about. Then you'll know what to focus on in the lesson. You can also assess how well you understand the lesson content when you've finished reading the lesson.

Lesson Opener Look at the lesson opener for information about the main idea of the lesson.

Example Heads Use other clues, such as the heads that appear above examples, to identify the main idea.

Understand the Vocabulary

Reading mathematics involves learning and using new vocabulary terms. Refer to diagrams and worked-out examples to clarify your understanding of new terms. If you forget what a term you've already learned means, look back at previous lessons or use the Glossary on pages 724–747.

Vocabulary New vocabulary terms are highlighted within a lesson. In addition, the *Word Watch* at the beginning of the lesson lists the important vocabulary terms in the lesson.

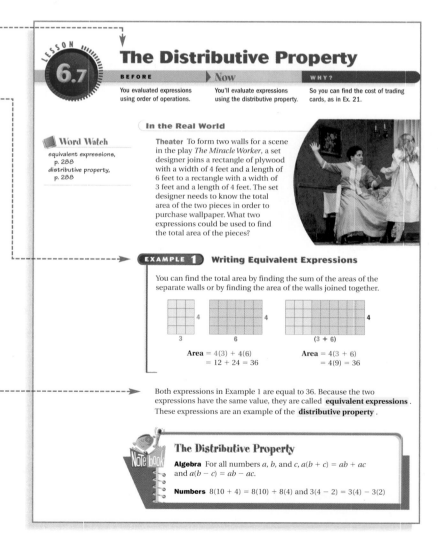

Know What's Important

Focus in on the important information in a lesson. Pay attention to highlighted vocabulary terms and definitions. Be on the lookout for definitions, properties, formulas, and other information displayed on a notebook. Make sure that you understand the worked-out examples.

Notebook Focus in on key ideas that are displayed on a notebook.

Worked-Out Examples Do the worked-out examples to make sure you know how to apply new concepts.

Be an Active Reader

As you read, keep a pencil in your hand and your notebook ready so that you can write down important information, practice new skills, and jot down questions to ask in class.

Use Your Notebook As you solve the examples yourself, you may find it helpful to describe the steps you follow. Write down any questions you have so you can ask them in class.

Your Turn Now Solve the *Your turn now* exercises to check your understanding.

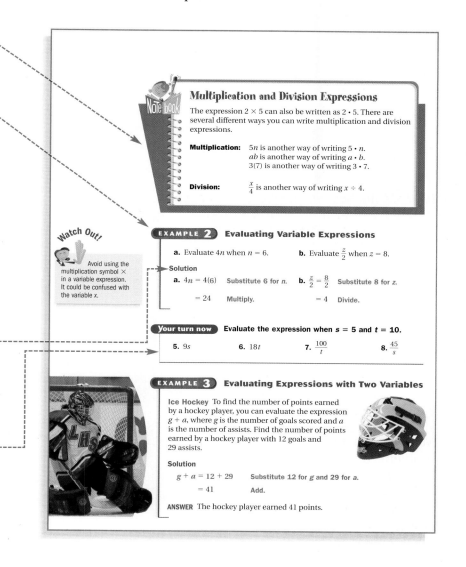

Notebook

Multiplication and Division Expressions

The expression 2×5 can also be written as $2 \cdot 5$. There are several different ways you can write multiplication and division expressions.

Multiplication: $5n$ is another way of writing $5 \cdot n$.
ab is another way of writing $a \cdot b$.
$3(7)$ is another way of writing $3 \cdot 7$.

Division: $\frac{x}{4}$ is another way of writing $x \div 4$.

Watch Out!

Avoid using the multiplication symbol $\times$ in a variable expression. It could be confused with the variable x.

EXAMPLE 2 Evaluating Variable Expressions

a. Evaluate $4n$ when $n = 6$. **b.** Evaluate $\frac{z}{2}$ when $z = 8$.

Solution

a. $4n = 4(6)$ Substitute 6 for n. **b.** $\frac{z}{2} = \frac{8}{2}$ Substitute 8 for z.

$= 24$ Multiply. $= 4$ Divide.

Your turn now Evaluate the expression when $s = 5$ and $t = 10$.

5. $9s$ **6.** $18t$ **7.** $\frac{100}{t}$ **8.** $\frac{45}{s}$

EXAMPLE 3 Evaluating Expressions with Two Variables

Ice Hockey To find the number of points earned by a hockey player, you can evaluate the expression $g + a$, where g is the number of goals scored and a is the number of assists. Find the number of points earned by a hockey player with 12 goals and 29 assists.

Solution

$g + a = 12 + 29$ Substitute 12 for g and 29 for a.

$= 41$ Add.

ANSWER The hockey player earned 41 points.

Reading and Problem Solving

The language in your math textbook is precise. When you do your homework, be sure to read carefully. For example, the direction line below asks you to do two different things for each exercise.

> **Find the greatest common factor of the numbers using prime factorization. Then tell whether the numbers are relatively prime.**
>
> **20.** 86, 154   **21.** 37, 93   **22.** 198, 216   **23.** 36, 168
>
> **24.** 34, 85   **25.** 75, 285   **26.** 144, 264   **27.** 65, 112

Reading Word Problems

Before you can solve a word problem, you need to read and understand it. You may find it useful to copy a word problem into your notebook. Then you can highlight important information, cross out unnecessary information, and organize your thinking.

You work 3 days in a row mowing lawns and babysitting. Your earn $12 for one lawn, $11 for a second lawn, and $18 for a third lawn. One lawn takes only 2 hours to mow. How much money do you earn mowing lawns?

Earned: $12
        $11
        $18

To find how much money you earn, add:
$12 + $11 + $18 = $41

Make sure that you've solved a word problem completely. For example, to solve the word problem at the right, you need to calculate how much ribbon you need. But to answer the question, you must determine how much money you will spend.

You buy ribbons for 5 costumes. Each costume needs 2 yards of ribbon. Ribbon costs $2.00 per yard. How much money will you spend?

How much ribbon: 5 × 2 yards = 10 yards
How much money: $2.00 × 10 = $20.00

Additional Resources in Your Textbook

Your textbook contains many resources that you can use for reference when you are studying or doing your homework.

Skills Review Handbook Use the Skills Review Handbook on pages 681–704 to review material learned in previous courses.

Tables Refer to the tables on pages 718–723 if you need information about mathematical symbols, measures, formulas, properties, and squares and square roots.

Glossary Use the Glossary on pages 724–747 to look up the meanings of math vocabulary terms. Each glossary entry also tells where in your book a term is covered in more detail.

Index Use the Index on pages 748–769 as a quick guide for finding out where a particular math topic is covered in the book.

Selected Answers Use the Selected Answers starting on page SA1 to check your work or to see whether you are on the right track in solving a problem.

Textbook Scavenger Hunt

Get some practice using your textbook. Use the additional resources described above to answer each question. Give page numbers to show where you found the answer to the question.

1 What formula can you use to find the volume of a rectangular prism?

2 On what page of the book can you find selected answers for Lesson 1.1?

3 On what page can you review the skill of using a compass?

4 What is a histogram?

5 Tell what each of these symbols means: $\sim$, $\cong$, $\neq$.

6 How many cups are there in 1 quart?

7 What is a straight angle?

8 What is the boiling point of water in degrees Fahrenheit? in degrees Celsius?

9 On what page or pages of the book is the distributive property first discussed?

Pre-Course Test

Number Sense

Whole Number Concepts *(Skills Review, pp. 681–685)*

Write the number in expanded form.

1. 5844   **2.** 11,933   **3.** 934,001   **4.** 6,016,009

Use a number line to order the numbers from least to greatest.

5. 6, 14, 2, 22, 9, 18   **6.** 19, 21, 16, 20, 14, 3   **7.** 31, 1, 16, 15, 27, 24   **8.** 99, 81, 79, 88, 92, 94

Round the number to the place value of the red digit.

9. 15,829   **10.** 3,286,188   **11.** 55,505,555   **12.** 137,999

Copy and complete the equation.

13. $\underline{\;?\;} + 9 = 18$ **14.** $9 \times \underline{\;?\;} = 45$ **15.** $15 - \underline{\;?\;} = 8$ **16.** $\underline{\;?\;} \div 6 = 6$

Test the number for divisibility by 2, 3, 5, 6, 9, and 10.

17. 918   **18.** 1155   **19.** 2860   **20.** 4077

Fraction Concepts *(Skills Review, p. 686)*

Write a fraction to represent the shaded part of the set or region.

21.    **22.**   **23.**   **24.**

Number Operations

Whole Number Operations *(Skills Review, pp. 687–690)*

Find the sum, difference, product, or quotient.

25. $12 + 7$ **26.** $919 - 899$ **27.** 4244×1000 **28.** $4858 \div 82$

Estimation *(Skills Review, pp. 691–694)*

Estimate the sum, difference, product, or quotient.

29. $449 + 481 + 512$ **30.** $66,109 - 12,674$ **31.** 712×45 **32.** $6667 \div 99$

Solving Real-World Problems *(Skills Review, pp. 695–696)*

33. At the start of a football game there were 41,516 people. During the game 2942 people left. How many people stayed the entire game?

34. A theater sells tickets for $5 and can seat an audience of 1152. If every seat is sold, what is the total revenue from ticket sales?

Measurement and Geometry

Time *(Skills Review, pp. 697–698)*

Copy and complete the statement using <, >, or =.

35. 5 d 8 h ? 128 h

36. 64 d ? 9 wk 4 d

37. 270 min ? 4 h 10 min

38. How long was a concert that began at 7:45 P.M. and ended at 10:15 P.M.?

Using Measurement Tools *(Skills Review, pp. 699–700)*

39. Use a metric ruler to draw a segment that is 2.7 centimeters long.

40. Use a compass to draw a circle with radius 4 inches.

Basic Geometric Figures *(Skills Review, p. 701)*

Draw and label the figure described. Then find its perimeter.

41. A square with sides 4 in. long

42. A rectangle with a length of 7 cm and a width of 5 cm

Data Analysis

Venn Diagrams and Logical Reasoning *(Skills Review, p. 702)*

43. Draw a Venn diagram of the whole numbers less than 15 where set A consists of numbers that are greater than 7 and set B consists of even numbers.

Data Displays *(Skills Review, pp. 703–704)*

44. In the bar graph, which city has the greatest average annual precipitation? Which city has the least average annual precipitation?

45. In a survey, 15 middle school students were asked how many pets they own. Their responses were 0, 3, 2, 1, 0, 1, 2, 4, 1, 0, 2, 2, 1, 3, 1. Make a line plot of the data and identify the most frequent response.

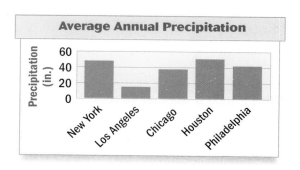

Average Annual Precipitation

Pre-Course Practice

Number Sense

Whole Number Concepts (*Skills Review, pp. 681–685*)

Write the number in expanded form.

1. 4966

2. 10,847

3. 821,004

4. 5,006,607

Write the number in standard form.

5. $5 \times 10{,}000 + 5 \times 1{,}000 + 8 \times 10 + 6 \times 1$

6. Nine million, four hundred sixty thousand, nine

Use a number line to order the numbers from least to greatest.

7. 5, 11, 3, 12, 9, 16

8. 24, 21, 19, 14, 2, 16

9. 9, 10, 31, 20, 12, 7

10. 23, 29, 17, 34, 10, 12

Use a number line to compare the numbers.

11. 8 and 9

12. 12 and 22

13. 2 and 0

14. 64 and 46

Round the number to the place value of the red digit.

15. 702

16. 4352

17. 28,856

18. 199,431

Copy and complete the number fact family.

19. $8 \times 4 = 32$ $\underline{?} \times 8 = 32$ $\underline{?} \div 8 = 4$ $32 \div \underline{?} = 8$

Copy and complete the equation.

20. $6 + \underline{?} = 13$

21. $\underline{?} \times 5 = 25$

22. $\underline{?} - 9 = 9$

23. $56 \div \underline{?} = 8$

Test the number for divisibility by 2, 3, 5, 6, 9, and 10.

24. 405

25. 900

26. 1986

27. 2050

Fraction Concepts (*Skills Review, p. 686*)

Write a fraction to represent the shaded part of the set or region.

28.

29.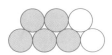

30.

31.

Write a mixed number to represent the shaded region.

32.

33.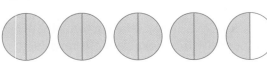

Number Operations

Whole Number Operations *(Skills Review, pp. 687–690)*

Use a number line to find the sum or difference.

34. $8 + 9$ **35.** $13 + 14$ **36.** $9 - 3$ **37.** $12 - 8$

Find the sum or difference.

38. $28 + 57$ **39.** $124 + 15$ **40.** $289 + 391$ **41.** $2441 + 626$

42. $188 - 149$ **43.** $2609 - 249$ **44.** $9079 - 2881$ **45.** $12{,}810 - 163$

Find the product.

46. 33×10 **47.** 81×81 **48.** 433×11 **49.** 851×35

50. 222×100 **51.** 1789×358 **52.** 4133×277 **53.** 1800×1000

Find the quotient.

54. $210 \div 7$ **55.** $273 \div 3$ **56.** $367 \div 9$ **57.** $371 \div 34$

58. $2282 \div 14$ **59.** $4393 \div 72$ **60.** $3018 \div 503$ **61.** $13{,}018 \div 181$

Estimation *(Skills Review, pp. 691–694)*

Estimate the sum.

62. $789 + 561 + 912$ **63.** $286 + 342 + 265$ **64.** $682 + 702 + 710$ **65.** $5417 + 2121 + 7456$

Estimate the difference.

66. $791 - 344$ **67.** $822 - 448$ **68.** $4024 - 1087$ **69.** $56{,}989 - 13{,}774$

Find a low and high estimate for the product.

70. 38×16 **71.** 44×78 **72.** 712×45 **73.** 928×65

Use compatible numbers to estimate the product.

74. 556×444 **75.** 888×559 **76.** 7088×88 **77.** 8011×66

Find a low and high estimate for the quotient.

78. $123 \div 4$ **79.** $8444 \div 84$ **80.** $22{,}675 \div 8$ **81.** $39{,}788 \div 74$

Use compatible numbers to estimate the quotient.

82. $438 \div 5$ **83.** $5332 \div 78$ **84.** $23{,}184 \div 6$ **85.** $68{,}899 \div 77$

Solving Real-World Problems *(Skills Review, pp. 695–696)*

86. A Web site received 6395 hits the first week. The next week it received 2768 hits. How many hits did the Web site receive in all?

87. An arena sold 12,217 tickets for a baseball game and 2250 tickets for a garden show. How many more tickets were sold for the game?

88. There are 62 windows on each story of a skyscraper that is 43 stories tall. How many windows are there altogether?

89. Tickets for a school production of a play sold for $9 each. The ticket sales for the play totaled $3213. How many tickets were sold?

Measurement and Geometry

Time *(Skills Review, pp. 697–698)*

Copy and complete.

90. 72 h = ? d　　**91.** 3 wk = ? d　　**92.** 300 min = ? h　　**93.** 15 min = ? sec

Copy and complete the statement using <, >, or =.

94. 4 wk 3 d ? 30 d

95. 5 h 50 min ? 500 min

96. 1455 sec ? 24 min 15 sec

97. 70 h ? 8 d 20 h

98. How long was a game that began at 2:15 P.M. and ended at 5:10 P.M.?

99. You talked on the phone with your aunt for 20 minutes, your friend for 29 minutes, and your math project partner for 48 minutes. Estimate how long you were on the phone.

100. It takes you about 115 minutes to mow 4 lawns. Estimate how long it takes you to mow each lawn.

Using Measurement Tools *(Skills Review, pp. 699–700)*

Use a ruler to draw a segment with the given length.

101. 5 centimeters　　**102.** $2\frac{1}{2}$ inches　　**103.** 6.5 centimeters　　**104.** $4\frac{15}{16}$ inches

105. Use a compass to draw a circle with radius 6 centimeters.

106. Use a compass to draw a circle with radius 3 inches.

107. Use a compass to draw a segment whose length is the sum of the lengths of the two given segments.

A ─────────────── B C ─────────── D

Basic Geometric Figures *(Skills Review, p. 701)*

Find the perimeter.

108.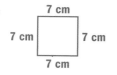

109.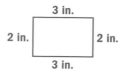

110.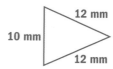

Draw and label the figure described. Then find its perimeter.

111. A square with sides 2 in. long

112. A rectangle with a length of 4 cm and a width of 2 cm

Data Analysis

Venn Diagrams and Logical Reasoning *(Skills Review, p. 702)*

113. Draw a Venn diagram of the whole numbers less than 12 where set *A* consists of numbers that are greater than 8 and set *B* consists of odd numbers.

114. Use the Venn diagram you drew in Exercise 113 to tell whether the following statement is *true* or *false*. Explain your reasoning. *There is only one odd number greater than 8 and less than 12.*

Data Displays *(Skills Review, pp. 703–704)*

In Exercises 115 and 116, use the bar graph, which shows the results of a survey on favorite ice cream flavors.

115. Which flavor is favored the most?

116. How many more people prefer chocolate than rocky road?

In Exercises 117 and 118, use the line graph, which shows the number of Atlantic hurricanes by year.

117. In which year were there 9 hurricanes?

118. Between which two years did the number of hurricanes decrease?

119. In a survey, 12 students were asked how many books they read over the summer. Their responses were 1, 2, 0, 4, 1, 2, 3, 1, 0, 6, 2, 3. Make a line plot of the data.

120. Use the line plot you made in Exercise 119 to determine how many students read more than 2 books.

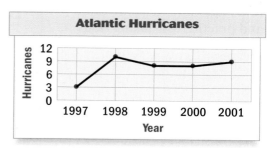

Content and Assessment

Course Content

The authors have developed a sequence of lessons that include all the concepts and skills you need in this course. What you learn is connected to prior knowledge and to your daily life.

LESSON 3.3
Stem-and-Leaf Plots

BEFORE	Now	WHY?
You displayed data using bar graphs and line graphs.	You'll display data using stem-and-leaf plots.	So you can analyze Olympic ski results, as in Ex. 15.

Word Watch

stem-and-leaf plot, p. 116

In the Real World

Speeds of Animals The table lists the maximum running speeds of various animals. How can the data be displayed to show the distribution of the speeds?

A **stem-and-leaf plot** is a data display that helps you to see the way data are distributed. You can use a stem-and-leaf plot to place data in increasing order.

Animal	Speed (miles per hour)
Elk	45
Cheetah	70
Greyhound	39
Wildebeest	50
Quarter horse	47
Zebra	40
Giraffe	32
Coyote	43

Test-Taking Practice

Each lesson includes test-taking practice that helps you become comfortable with different formats of test questions. Additional practice is provided on the Internet. There is also a chapter standardized test for each chapter.

Test-Taking Practice

INTERNET
State Test Practice
CLASSZONE.COM

46. Multiple Choice Which operation describes the numerical pattern 1, 3, 9, 27, . . . ?

  A. Add 3.   **B.** Subtract 3.   **C.** Multiply by 3.   **D.** Divide by 3.

47. Short Response Draw a visual pattern that is related to the numerical pattern 1, 3, 5, 7, ... Explain how the two patterns are related.

Chapter Standardized Test

Test-Taking Strategy **Be sure to avoid careless errors on easy questions.**

Multiple Choice

1. Round 5.8934 to the nearest thousandth.

  A. 5.8   **B.** 5.89   **C.** 5.893   **D.** 5.9

2. Which statement is true?

  F. $9.71 < 9.17$ **G.** $81.54 = 81.540$

  H. $3.09 > 3.19$ **I.** $5.64 < 5.24$

3. Which expression has a value of 6.2 when _____ $b = 14.8$?

    B. $b - a + 2.895$

    D. $b - a - 3.105$

_____ ifference of 15 and 10.769?

    4.331   **H.** 5.231   **I.** 5.331

_____ d estimate for the sum of 19.4

  A. 22   **B.** 23   **C.** 24   **D.** 25

9. Write 2.58×10^8 in standard form.

  A. 258   **B.** 2580

  C. 258,000   **D.** 258,000,000

10. Complete: The length of a ski could be __?__.

  F. 10 m   **G.** 80 mm   **H.** 150 cm   **I.** 175 m

11. Which measurements are equivalent?

  I. 34 cm   II. 3400 mm   III. 0.34 m

  A. I and II   **B.** I and III

  C. II and III   **D.** I, II, and III

12. Complete: 9800 kL = __?__ L.

  F. 0.98   **G.** 9.8

  H. 98   **I.** 9,800,000

Short Response

13. What is the area of the rectangle below? What is the perimeter?

3.7 ft

Test-Taking Skills and Strategies

At the end of each unit, you'll find pages that help you build and practice test-taking skills and strategies.

UNIT 2
Chapters 4–6

BUILDING **Test-Taking Skills**

Strategies for Answering
Short Response Questions

Scoring Rubric

Full credit
- answer is correct, *and*
- work or reasoning is included

Partial credit
- answer is correct, but reasoning is incorrect, *or*
- answer is incorrect, but reasoning is correct

No credit
- no answer is given, *or*
- answer makes no sense

A *short response* question should take about five minutes to answer. A solution should include the work or reasoning that leads to a correct answer. The three ways a solution can be scored are listed at the left.

Problem

You are organizing a karaoke night at your school. You allow an average of $3\frac{1}{2}$ minutes for each act to set up and $5\frac{1}{4}$ minutes for the song. How many acts can fit in a program that runs $1\frac{1}{2}$ hours?

_____ dship bracelets out of _____ ch bracelet, you need _____ ng. Each meter of _____ enough to buy the _____ bracelets? Explain

Full credit solution

The number of acts equals the total number of minutes - - - - - This reasoning
for the program divided by the sum of the set-up time and   is the key to
song time for each act.   choosing the
  operations you

The steps of the - - - - - - -   Acts = Total time ÷ (Set-up time + Song time)   need.
solution are
clearly written. $= 90 \div \left(3\frac{1}{2} + 5\frac{1}{4}\right) = 90 \div 8\frac{3}{4}$

  $= 90 \div \frac{35}{4} = 90 \times \frac{4}{35} = \frac{72}{7} = 10\frac{2}{7}$

Number Sense, Decimals, and Data

Chapter **1** Number Sense, Patterns, and Algebraic Thinking

- Describe and extend patterns to solve problems.
- Evaluate expressions and solve equations.
- Find perimeter and area.

Chapter **2** Decimal Operations

- Perform operations with decimals.
- Write numbers in scientific notation.
- Measure in the metric system and convert metric units.

Chapter **3** Data and Statistics

- Find the mean, median, and mode of a data set.
- Make and interpret different types of data displays.
- Choose an appropriate display for a data set.

From Chapter 1, p. 34
What is the perimeter of a basketball court?

Number Sense, Patterns, and Algebraic Thinking

BEFORE

In previous courses you've...

- Completed number fact families
- Performed whole number operations

Now

In Chapter 1 you'll study...

- Extending patterns
- Variable expressions and powers
- Order of operations
- Equations and mental math
- Formulas for area and perimeter
- Using a problem solving plan

WHY?

So you can solve real-world problems about...

- Hawaiian leis, p. 6
- ice hockey, p. 10
- dog pedigrees, p. 16
- video games, p. 20

Internet Preview
CLASSZONE.COM

- eEdition Plus Online
- eWorkbook Plus Online
- eTutorial Plus Online
- State Test Practice
- More Examples

Chapter Warm-Up Games

Review skills you need for this chapter in these quick games.

Going for Gold

BRAIN GAME

Key Skill:
Completing number fact families

- Each athlete above can only win gold medals whose sum, difference, product, or quotient is equal to the athlete's number.

- Find a way for each athlete to win two gold medals. Each medal can be won only one time.

Olympic Torch Run

START
4 —−3— [city] —+5— [city]

+6   +5   +3

[city] —+2— [city] —×4— [city]

÷2   ÷3   +8

[city] —×3— [city] —+8— [city]
FINISH

Key Skill:
Using whole number operations

Carry the Olympic torch from START to FINISH. Begin at the circle marked START. Move along a path to an adjacent city. Perform the indicated operation on the number 4. Remember the result.

- Then move to a new city. Perform the indicated operation on your result from the previous move.

- You may carry the torch through each city only one time. You do not need to visit all the cities.

- Your goal is to get the greatest possible result at the FINISH.

Stop *and* Think

1. **Writing** In *Going for Gold* is there more than one way that the athletes can each win two medals? Explain why or why not.

2. **Critical Thinking** Suppose you want to visit all the cities in *Olympic Torch Run*. Describe two different paths from START to FINISH. Give the result for each path.

Getting Ready to Learn

Word Watch

Review Words

whole number, p. 681
factor, p. 685
sum, p. 687
difference, p. 687
product, p. 689
quotient, p. 690

Review What You Need to Know

Using Vocabulary **Copy and complete using a review word.**

1. In the multiplication sentence 3 • 5 = 15, 3 and 5 are called ?
   and 15 is called the ? .

2. You subtract to find the ? of two numbers.

3. You divide to find the ? of two numbers.

4. You add to find the ? of two numbers.

Copy and complete the statement. (p. 684)

5. ? + 4 = 12   6. 6 − ? = 3   7. 7 × ? = 35   8. ? ÷ 5 = 4

Find the sum, difference, product, or quotient. (pp. 688–690)

9. 23 + 28   10. 523 + 49   11. 34 − 17   12. 201 − 158

13. 23 × 96   14. 392 × 105   15. 328 ÷ 8   16. 190 ÷ 5

NoTebook

You should include material that appears on a notebook like this in your own notes.

Know How to Take Notes

Keeping a Notebook Some useful items to put in your mathematics notebook include the following:

- vocabulary
- rules and properties
- worked-out examples

- symbols
- formulas
- assignments

When you write a rule in your notebook, also sketch any diagrams that help explain the rule. For example, a diagram can help you remember properties of rectangles and squares:

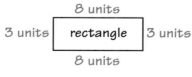

8 units

3 units | rectangle | 3 units

8 units

Opposite sides of a rectangle
are equal in length.

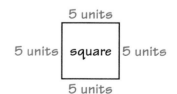

5 units

5 units | square | 5 units

5 units

All four sides of a square
are equal in length.

In Lesson 1.6, you will see how a diagram can help you remember the formula for finding the perimeter of a rectangle.

Describing Patterns

BEFORE	▶ Now	WHY?
You performed whole number operations.	You'll describe patterns using whole number operations.	So you can find the next number of basketball teams, as in Ex. 18.

Word Watch

Review Words

add, p. 687
subtract, p. 687
multiply, p. 689
divide, p. 690

> **In the Real World**

Summer Movie Club You are a member of a summer movie club at your local movie theater. The club meets every Wednesday in July to watch a movie. If the first meeting is on July 6, on what other dates in July will the club meet?

EXAMPLE 1 **Recognizing and Extending a Pattern**

To answer the question about the summer movie club above, start with July 6th and repeatedly add 7 days to the date.

Date of first meeting:	July 6	
Date of second meeting:	July 13	+ 7
Date of third meeting:	July 20	+ 7
Date of fourth meeting:	July 27	+ 7

Because July has only 31 days, July 27th is the date of the last club meeting in July.

Numerical Patterns To describe and extend a numerical pattern, try finding a relationship between the first and second numbers. Then see if the relationship is true for the second and third numbers, the third and fourth numbers, and so on.

EXAMPLE 2 **Extending a Numerical Pattern**

Describe the following pattern: 2, 7, 12, 17, ... Then write the next three numbers.

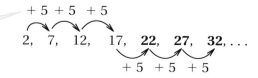

You *add 5* to the previous number to get the next number in the pattern.

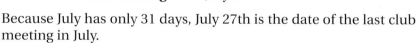

$$+5 +5 +5$$
$$2, \quad 7, \quad 12, \quad 17, \quad \mathbf{22}, \quad \mathbf{27}, \quad \mathbf{32}, \ldots$$
$$+5 \quad +5 \quad +5$$

> **HELP** with Reading
>
> The three dots at the end of a list of numbers mean that the numbers and the pattern continue without end.

 **with Review**

Need help with whole number operations? See pp. 688–690.

EXAMPLE 3 **Extending a Numerical Pattern**

Describe the following pattern: 2, 6, 18, 54, ... Then write the next three numbers.

You *multiply* the previous number *by 3* to get the next number in the pattern.

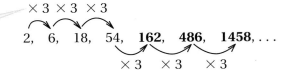

$\times 3 \times 3 \times 3$

2, 6, 18, 54, **162, 486, 1458**, . . .

$\times 3 \quad \times 3 \quad \times 3$

Your turn now **Describe the pattern. Then write the next three numbers.**

1. 28, 24, 20, 16, . . .   **2.** 256, 128, 64, 32, . . .

Visual Patterns To describe and extend a visual pattern, try looking for repeated colors and shapes, a change in the position of figures in the pattern, or a change in the number of figures in the pattern.

EXAMPLE 4 **Extending a Visual Pattern**

Hawaiian Leis A Hawaiian lei is a flower wreath that is sometimes given to symbolize friendship. What are the next three flowers that should be put on the lei shown?

yellow carnation   red carnation

orchids

Solution

Look for repeated flowers to find a pattern. The lei starts with a carnation, two orchids, another carnation, and then two orchids again. Notice that the carnations alternate between yellow and red.

ANSWER The last flower on the lei is a red carnation, so the next three flowers should be two orchids and then a yellow carnation.

Your turn now **Describe the pattern. Then draw the next figure.**

3.   **4.**

Getting Ready to Practice

Vocabulary **Match the pattern with its description.**

1. 0, 2, 4, 6, . . .   **A.** Subtract 5 from the previous number.

2. 30, 25, 20, 15, . . .   **B.** Divide the previous number by 10.

3. 1, 4, 16, 64, . . .   **C.** Add 2 to the previous number.

4. 10,000, 1000, 100, 10, . . .   **D.** Multiply the previous number by 4.

Describe the pattern. Then draw the next three figures.

5. 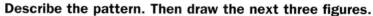   **6.**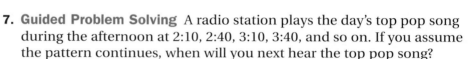

7. **Guided Problem Solving** A radio station plays the day's top pop song during the afternoon at 2:10, 2:40, 3:10, 3:40, and so on. If you assume the pattern continues, when will you next hear the top pop song?

   (**1** What is the relationship between the first time the song is played and the second time the song is played?

   (**2** Check that the relationship is true for all the other playing times.

   (**3** Use the relationship to find the next time the song will be played.

Practice and Problem Solving

HELP with Homework

Example	Exercises
1	17–18
2	8–16, 23–25
3	8–16, 23–25
4	19–21, 27

Online Resources
CLASSZONE.COM

· More Examples
· eTutorial Plus

Describe the pattern. Then write the next three numbers.

8. 1, 2, 4, 8, . . .   **9.** 100, 91, 82, 73, . . .   **10.** 640, 320, 160, 80, . . .

11. 2, 9, 16, 23, . . .   **12.** 0, 11, 22, 33, . . .   **13.** 4, 12, 36, 108, . . .

14. 80, 72, 64, 56, . . . **15.** 729, 243, 81, 27, . . . **16.** 1, 6, 36, 216, . . .

17. **Critical Thinking** Write the first four numbers in the pattern *start with 6 and repeatedly add 8.*

18. **Basketball** There are 64 teams in the first round of a college basketball tournament. In each round after the first, there are half as many teams as in the previous round. How many teams are in the next three rounds?

Describe the pattern. Then draw the next figure.

19.   **20.**

21. Bracelets Sketch the next three beads that will continue the pattern.

22. Writing Write a numerical pattern. Then describe the pattern.

Describe the pattern. Then write the next three numbers.

23. 45, 88, 131, 174, . . . **24.** 4, 28, 196, 1372, . . . **25.** 1458, 486, 162, 54, . . .

26. Writing Draw a visual pattern. Then describe the pattern.

27. The Moon The diagrams below show the different phases of the moon over time. Draw the next two phases of the moon.

Interpret **Describe the pattern. Then write the next three letters.**

28. A, C, E, G, . . .   **29.** A, Z, B, Y, . . .   **30.** Z, W, T, Q, . . .

Challenge **Describe the pattern. Then write the next three numbers.**

31. 2, 3, 6, 11, 18, . . .   **32.** 1, 3, 7, 15, 31, . . .   **33.** 1, 1, 2, 3, 5, 8, . . .

Mixed Review

Write the number in expanded form. *(p. 681)*

34. 55   **35.** 804   **36.** 2410   **37.** 3395

Round the number to the place value of the red digit. *(p. 683)*

38. 34   **39.** 382   **40.** 167   **41.** 9146

Basic Skills **Find the sum, difference, product, or quotient.**

42. 792 + 546   **43.** 301 − 148   **44.** 809 × 23   **45.** 168 ÷ 7

Test-Taking Practice

46. Multiple Choice Which operation describes the numerical pattern 1, 3, 9, 27, . . . ?

A. Add 3.   **B.** Subtract 3.   **C.** Multiply by 3.   **D.** Divide by 3.

47. Short Response Draw a visual pattern that is related to the numerical pattern 1, 3, 5, 7, ... Explain how the two patterns are related.

■ **The Moon**

The gravitational pull from the moon causes the water level on Earth to change. Such changes are called *tides*. A complete tide cycle takes about 12 hours. About how many tide cycles occur in one week?

Variables and Expressions

BEFORE	▶ Now	WHY?
You simplified numerical expressions.	You'll evaluate variable expressions.	So you can estimate bamboo growth, as in Ex. 35.

Word Watch

variable, p. 9
variable expression, p. 9
evaluate, p. 9

Activity   You can evaluate an expression by using a number strip.

1. Cut a long strip of paper. Write the numbers 1 through 9 on the strip.

1 2 3 4 5 6 7 8 9

2. Write "$n + 6$" on the remaining part of the paper. Cut two vertical slits (big enough for the number strip to fit through) on each side of the n.

n + 6

3. Slide the strip through the slits so that one number at a time shows. Write the resulting expression for each number. Then simplify.

5 + 6

Repeat the activity for the given expression.   1. $n - 1$ 2. $n \times 2$

In the activity, you substituted numbers for the *variable n.*
A **variable** is a letter that is used to represent one or more numbers.
A **variable expression** , like $n + 6$, consists of numbers, variables, and operations. To **evaluate** a variable expression, you substitute values for the variables and then simplify the resulting numerical expression.

EXAMPLE 1   **Evaluating Variable Expressions**

a. Evaluate $x + 4$ when $x = 9$.   **b.** Evaluate $y - 3$ when $y = 7$.

Solution

a. $x + 4 = 9 + 4$ Substitute 9 for *x.*

$ = 13$ Add.

b. $y - 3 = 7 - 3$ Substitute 7 for *y.*

$ = 4$ Subtract.

Your turn now   Evaluate the expression when $a = 3$ and $m = 9$.

1. $7 + m$ **2.** $a + 28$ **3.** $10 - a$ **4.** $m - 5$

Multiplication and Division Expressions

The expression 2×5 can also be written as $2 \cdot 5$. There are several different ways you can write multiplication and division expressions.

Multiplication: $5n$ is another way of writing $5 \cdot n$.
ab is another way of writing $a \cdot b$.
$3(7)$ is another way of writing $3 \cdot 7$.

Division: $\frac{x}{4}$ is another way of writing $x \div 4$.

Watch Out!

Avoid using the multiplication symbol $\times$ in a variable expression. It could be confused with the variable x.

EXAMPLE 2 **Evaluating Variable Expressions**

a. Evaluate $4n$ when $n = 6$.   **b.** Evaluate $\frac{z}{2}$ when $z = 8$.

Solution

a. $4n = 4(6)$ Substitute 6 for n.

$= 24$ Multiply.

b. $\frac{z}{2} = \frac{8}{2}$ Substitute 8 for z.

$= 4$ Divide.

Your turn now Evaluate the expression when $s = 5$ and $t = 10$.

5. $9s$ **6.** $18t$ **7.** $\frac{100}{t}$ **8.** $\frac{45}{s}$

EXAMPLE 3 **Evaluating Expressions with Two Variables**

Ice Hockey To find the number of points earned by a hockey player, you can evaluate the expression $g + a$, where g is the number of goals scored and a is the number of assists. Find the number of points earned by a hockey player with 12 goals and 29 assists.

Solution

$g + a = 12 + 29$ Substitute 12 for g and 29 for a.

$= 41$ Add.

ANSWER The hockey player earned 41 points.

Getting Ready to Practice

1. **Vocabulary** Give two examples of a variable expression.

Evaluate the expression when $x = 7$ and $y = 15$.

2. $y + 9$ 3. $x - 6$ 4. $4y$ 5. $8 + x$

6. $\dfrac{y}{5}$ 7. $3x$ 8. $20 - y$ 9. $\dfrac{14}{x}$

10. **Find the Error** Describe and correct the error in evaluating $2a$ when $a = 3$.

$$\times \quad 2a = 23$$

11. **Dance** You pay $8 to see a modern dance show. The expression $s + 8$, where s is the cost of snacks you buy at intermission, can be used to find the total cost of going to the show. Find the total cost if you buy snacks that cost $3.

Practice and Problem Solving

12. **Writing** Describe how to evaluate a variable expression.

13. Write the expression 4×8 in two other ways.

Evaluate the expression for the given value of the variable.

14. $x + 14$ when $x = 8$ 15. $y - 5$ when $y = 13$ 16. $7r$ when $r = 4$

17. $\dfrac{6}{s}$ when $s = 3$ 18. $\dfrac{t}{3}$ when $t = 18$ 19. $18 + a$ when $a = 17$

20. $y + 11$ when $y = 7$ 21. $8b$ when $b = 9$ 22. $24 - x$ when $x = 15$

23. **Television** A TV show is an hour long with commercials. To find how many minutes long the show is without commercials, you can evaluate the expression $60 - c$, where c is the number of minutes of commercials. If there are 12 minutes of commercials, how many minutes long is the show without commercials?

24. **Footbag** To play footbag, you kick a small bean bag to keep it in the air. The expression $3m$, where m is the number of minutes played, can be used to find the calories burned by a 100 pound person playing footbag. Find the calories burned by a 100 pound person playing footbag for 45 minutes.

with Homework

Example	Exercises
1	14–23
2	14–22, 24, 34
3	26–33, 35

Online Resources
CLASSZONE.COM
· More Examples
· eTutorial Plus

Bamboo

It's a good thing that bamboo grows so fast because pandas eat up to 83 pounds of bamboo a day! How many pounds of food do you estimate you eat in one day?

25. Critical Thinking Find the value of c that makes the expression $c + 12$ equal to 20.

Evaluate the expression when $x = 3$, $y = 9$, $m = 13$, and $p = 25$.

26. $p - m$ **27.** $y + p$ **28.** $m + p$ **29.** $m - y$

30. xy **31.** mx **32.** $\dfrac{y}{x}$ **33.** $m + y$

 34. Pluto The expression $\dfrac{w}{17}$, where w is weight in pounds on Earth, can be used to approximate weight in pounds on Pluto. If Tom weighs 153 pounds on Earth, find his approximate weight on Pluto.

35. Bamboo You can predict the growth for a stem of bamboo by evaluating the expression gn, where g is the average number of inches grown each day and n is the number of days. Predict the amount of growth in one week for bamboo that grows an average of 12 inches each day.

36. Compare Explain the difference between a number and a variable.

Challenge Evaluate the expression when $x = 20$, $y = 12$, and $z = 15$.

37. $9 + z + x$ **38.** $7yz$ **39.** xyz **40.** $x + y + z$

Mixed Review

Find the product. *(p. 689)*

41. 233×7 **42.** 546×8 **43.** 45×17 **44.** 330×42

Describe the pattern. Then write the next three numbers. *(Lesson 1.1)*

45. 1, 8, 15, 22, . . .   **46.** 7, 14, 28, 56, . . .   **47.** 99, 88, 77, 66, . . .

Basic Skills **Find a low and high estimate for the quotient.**

48. $28 \div 9$ **49.** $230 \div 6$ **50.** $5000 \div 22$ **51.** $7632 \div 5$

Test-Taking Practice

52. Multiple Choice Which of the following is *not* a variable expression?

A. $4n$ **B.** $n + m$ **C.** $n - 4$ **D.** $4 - 3$

53. Multiple Choice What is the value of the expression $x + y$ when $x = 15$ and $y = 21$?

F. 6   **G.** 30   **H.** 36   **I.** 42

Repeated Multiplication

There is a relationship between the number of times you fold a piece of paper and the number of sections formed by the folds.

Explore **Find the number of sections formed by folding a piece of paper 5 times.**

1 Fold a piece of paper in half. Open the paper and count the number of sections formed.

Fold. Open.

| 1 |
| 2 |

2 Copy the table at the right. Record the number of sections you counted from Step 1.

Folds	1	2	3	4	5
Sections	2	?	?	?	?

3 Close the paper. Then fold the paper in half again. Count the number of sections formed and record this in your table. Keep folding, counting, and recording until you have completed 5 folds.

Fold. Open.

| 1 | 2 |
| 3 | 4 |

Your turn now **Complete the following exercises.**

1. The number of sections you recorded in your table can be rewritten as a product of 2's. For example, 4 can be rewritten as $2 \cdot 2$. Add a *Rewritten form* row to your table and rewrite each number of sections as a product of 2's.

2. **Writing** What can you conclude about the relationship between the number of folds and the number of times 2 is a factor in the rewritten form?

Stop and Think

3. **Critical Thinking** How many sections would be formed if you folded a piece of paper 6 times? Extend and complete your table for 6, 7, and 8 folds.

Powers and Exponents

BEFORE — **Now** — **WHY?**

BEFORE	Now	WHY?
You multiplied pairs of numbers.	You'll write repeated multiplication using exponents.	So you can find the number of grandparents a dog has, as in Ex. 32.

In the Real World

Word Watch

power, p. 14
base, p. 14
exponent, p. 14

Biology All plants and animals are made up of tiny cells. A cell grows by dividing into two cells, each exactly like the original. This process continues, as shown below. What is another way to write the number of cells after the fourth division?

Division 1   **Division 2**   **Division 3**   **Division 4**

1   2 $2 \cdot 2$ $2 \cdot 2 \cdot 2$ $2 \cdot 2 \cdot 2 \cdot 2$

A **power** is a way of writing repeated multiplication. The **base** of a power is the factor, and the **exponent** of a power is the number of times the factor is used.

Powers and Exponents

base   exponent

Numbers $4^6 = 4 \cdot 4 \cdot 4 \cdot 4 \cdot 4 \cdot 4$

power   4 is a factor 6 times.

The power is read "four to the sixth power."

Algebra   If n is a nonzero whole number, then:

$$a^n = \underbrace{a \cdot a \cdot a \cdot \ldots \cdot a}$$

a is a factor n times.

The power is read "a to the nth power."

EXAMPLE 1   **Writing Powers**

After the fourth division described above, there are $2 \cdot 2 \cdot 2 \cdot 2$ cells.

$$\underbrace{2 \cdot 2 \cdot 2 \cdot 2} = 2^4$$

2 is a factor 4 times.

ANSWER There are 2^4 cells after the fourth division.

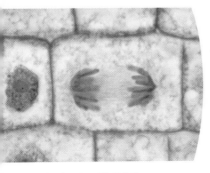

A plant cell dividing

HELP with **Reading**

You can read 7^2 as "7 to the second power" or as "7 squared."

You can read 4^3 as "4 to the third power" or as "4 cubed."

EXAMPLE 2 Evaluating Powers

Evaluate the power.

a. 7^2 **b.** 4^3 **c.** 3^1

Solution

a. $7^2 = 7 \cdot 7$ Write 7 as a factor 2 times.

     $= 49$ Multiply.

b. $4^3 = 4 \cdot 4 \cdot 4$ Write 4 as a factor 3 times.

     $= 64$ Multiply.

c. $3^1 = 3$ Write 3 as a factor 1 time.

Your turn now Write the product as a power.

1. $8 \cdot 8 \cdot 8$ **2.** $5 \cdot 5 \cdot 5 \cdot 5 \cdot 5 \cdot 5$ **3.** $6 \cdot 6 \cdot 6 \cdot 6 \cdot 6$

Evaluate the power.

4. 2^6 **5.** 6^2 **6.** 5^4

EXAMPLE 3 Evaluating Powers with Variables

 a. Evaluate x^2 when $x = 9$.   **b.** Evaluate b^3 when $b = 7$.

Solution

a. $x^2 = 9^2$ Substitute 9 for x.

     $= 9 \cdot 9$ Write 9 as a factor 2 times.

     $= 81$ Multiply.

b. $b^3 = 7^3$ Substitute 7 for b.

     $= 7 \cdot 7 \cdot 7$ Write 7 as a factor 3 times.

     $= 343$ Multiply.

Your turn now Complete the following exercises.

7. Evaluate m^8 when $m = 2$.   **8.** Evaluate p^3 when $p = 10$.

9. What number greater than zero is equal to itself when raised to any power?

Getting Ready to Practice

1. Vocabulary Name the base and the exponent in the power 9^4.

Write the product as a power.

2. $9 \cdot 9 \cdot 9$ **3.** $4 \cdot 4 \cdot 4 \cdot 4$ **4.** $x \cdot x$ **5.** $a \cdot a \cdot a$

Evaluate the power.

6. 6^3 **7.** 5^2 **8.** 2^7 **9.** 3^4

10. Find the Error Describe and correct the error in evaluating the expression b^4 when $b = 2$.

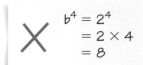

$$b^4 = 2^4$$
$$= 2 \times 4$$
$$= 8$$

11. Biology Every hour a cell divides into 2 cells. Write and evaluate an expression for the number of cells after 5 hours.

Practice and Problem Solving

HELP with **Homework**

Example	Exercises
1	16–23
2	24–32
3	34–36

Online Resources
CLASSZONE.COM

· More Examples
· eTutorial Plus

Write the power in words.

12. 6^2 **13.** 9^8 **14.** 5^1 **15.** x^3

Write the product as a power.

16. $3 \cdot 3 \cdot 3 \cdot 3 \cdot 3$ **17.** $10 \cdot 10$ **18.** $12 \cdot 12 \cdot 12$ **19.** $7 \cdot 7 \cdot 7 \cdot 7 \cdot 7$

20. $h \cdot h$ **21.** $t \cdot t \cdot t \cdot t \cdot t$ **22.** $g \cdot g \cdot g$ **23.** $s \cdot s \cdot s \cdot s$

Evaluate the power.

24. 3^2 **25.** 5^3 **26.** 8^4 **27.** 4^5

28. 0^8 **29.** 1^7 **30.** 6^4 **31.** 9^3

32. Dog Pedigrees A certificate of pedigree lists a dog's parents, grandparents, and so on. The power 2^6 describes the number of *great-great-great-great*-grandparents a dog has. How many is this?

33. Checkers A checkerboard has 8 rows of 8 squares. Write the number of squares on a checkerboard as a power. Use mental math to evaluate.

Algebra **Evaluate the expression for the given value of the variable.**

34. y^2 when $y = 12$ **35.** b^1 when $b = 18$ **36.** m^3 when $m = 10$

Write the number as a power.

37. 16 **38.** 81 **39.** 100 **40.** 49

Critical Thinking **Copy and complete the statement using <, >, or =.**

41. $2^5 \; \underline{?} \; 5^2$ **42.** $21 \; \underline{?} \; 3^7$ **43.** $1^9 \; \underline{?} \; 1$ **44.** $3^4 \; \underline{?} \; 4^3$

45. Use a number line to write the following numbers in order from least to greatest: $3, 6^2, 2^3, 9^2, 9, 6$.

46. **Green Goo** You make a big batch of green goo and split it into 3 parts. Then you split each of those parts into 3 parts. Again you split each of those parts into 3 parts. Write a power to describe the number of parts of goo you now have. Use mental math to evaluate the power.

47. **Writing** Given that $2^8 = 256$, describe how to find the value of 2^9 without multiplying nine 2's together.

48. **Challenge** Evaluate the following powers: $3^4, 3^3, 3^2,$ and 3^1. What happens to the value of the power as the exponent decreases? Based on this pattern, what do you think is the value of 3^0?

Mixed Review

49. An employee at a grocery store stacks soup cans as shown. Draw the next group of soup cans that will continue the pattern. *(Lesson 1.1)*

Evaluate the expression for the given value of the variable. *(Lesson 1.2)*

50. $7x$ when $x = 15$ **51.** $8y$ when $y = 11$ **52.** $12b$ when $b = 9$

Basic Skills **Find the quotient.**

53. $56 \div 7$ **54.** $108 \div 6$ **55.** $225 \div 15$

Test-Taking Practice

56. **Multiple Choice** Which two powers are equal?

     A. 1^2 and 2^1 **B.** 2^4 and 4^2 **C.** 2^3 and 3^2 **D.** 3^1 and 1^3

57. **Multiple Choice** What is the value of 8^3?

     F. 24 **G.** 64 **H.** 72 **I.** 512

Order of Operations

BEFORE	▶ Now	WHY?
You evaluated expressions involving one operation.	You'll evaluate expressions involving two or more operations.	So you can find the points scored in a video game, as in Example 5.

In the Real World

Music You buy a used guitar for $50. You then pay $10 for each of 5 guitar lessons. The total cost can be found by evaluating the expression $50 + 10 \times 5$. Is the total cost $100 or $300?

So that everyone gets the same result when evaluating an expression, a set of rules called the **order of operations** is always followed.

Order of Operations

1. Evaluate expressions inside grouping symbols.
2. Evaluate powers.
3. Multiply and divide from left to right.
4. Add and subtract from left to right.

EXAMPLE 1 Following Order of Operations

To find the guitar costs described above, evaluate $50 + 10 \times 5$.

$$50 + 10 \times 5 = 50 + 50 \qquad \text{First multiply 10 and 5.}$$
$$= 100 \qquad \text{Then add 50 and 50.}$$

ANSWER The total cost is $100.

EXAMPLE 2 Evaluating a Variable Expression

Evaluate $x - 3y^3$ when $x = 25$ and $y = 2$.

$$x - 3y^3 = 25 - 3(2^3) \qquad \text{Substitute 25 for } x \text{ and 2 for } y.$$
$$= 25 - 3(8) \qquad \text{Evaluate the power.}$$
$$= 25 - 24 = 1 \qquad \text{Multiply 8 and 3. Then subtract 24 from 25.}$$

1. $5 + 6 \times 5$ **2.** $20 - 4^2 \div 2$ **3.** $10 \times 3 + 3^3$

4. Evaluate $a + 4b^2$ when $a = 6$ and $b = 5$.

Left-to-Right Rule When an expression has a string of additions and subtractions or a string of multiplications and divisions, you need to perform the operations in order from left to right.

EXAMPLE 3 **Using the Left-to-Right Rule**

a. $12 - 7 + 3 - 6 = 5 + 3 - 6$ Subtract 7 from 12.

$= 8 - 6$ Add 5 and 3.

$= 2$ Subtract 6 from 8.

b. $54 \div 9 \div 3 = 6 \div 3$ Divide 54 by 9.

$= 2$ Divide 6 by 3.

Grouping Symbols Grouping symbols indicate operations that should be performed first. The most common grouping symbols are parentheses ( ) and brackets [ ]. A fraction bar is also a grouping symbol.

EXAMPLE 4 **Using Grouping Symbols**

a. $4(8 - 5) = 4(3)$ Subtract inside parentheses.

$= 12$ Multiply 4 and 3.

b. $\dfrac{13 + 7}{2 \cdot 5} = \dfrac{20}{10}$ Add 13 and 7. Multiply 2 and 5.

$= 2$ Divide 20 by 10.

c. $(4 + 1)^2 \cdot 3 = 5^2 \cdot 3$ Add inside parentheses.

$= 25 \cdot 3$ Evaluate the power.

$= 75$ Multiply 25 and 3.

HELP with Solving

Thinking of the letters PEMDAS might help you remember the order of operations:

Parentheses
Exponents
Multiplication
Division
Addition
Subtraction

Your turn now Evaluate the expression.

5. $18 - 10 - 5 - 1$ **6.** $(3 + 7)(6 - 3)^2$ **7.** $\dfrac{8 \cdot 3}{4 + 2}$

EXAMPLE 5 Using Order of Operations

Video Games The tricks and point values for a skateboarding video game are shown in the table. You complete one burntwist, three backflips, and four 360° flips. How many points did you score?

Trick	Points
Burntwist	500
Backflip	400
360° flip	150

Solution

You need to evaluate the expression $1 \cdot 500 + 3 \cdot 400 + 4 \cdot 150$.

$$1 \cdot 500 + 3 \cdot 400 + 4 \cdot 150 = 500 + 1200 + 600 \qquad \textbf{Multiply first.}$$
$$= 1700 + 600 \qquad \textbf{Add 500 and 1200.}$$
$$= 2300 \qquad \textbf{Add 1700 and 600.}$$

ANSWER You scored 2300 points.

Exercises

More Practice, p. 705

INTERNET
eWorkbook Plus
CLASSZONE.COM

Getting Ready to Practice

1. Vocabulary State the order of operations.

Evaluate the expression.

2. $6 + 7 \cdot 4$

3. $\dfrac{20 + 8}{4}$

4. $4 \cdot 3 \cdot 2^3$

5. $10 - 8 + 5 - 2$

6. $9(16 - 7)$

7. $45 \div 5 \div 3$

8. $\dfrac{12 + 6}{3 - 1}$

9. $(1 + 6)(5 - 2)^2$

xy Algebra Evaluate the expression when $x = 8$ and $y = 2$.

10. $4 + x \cdot y$

11. $(x + 12) \div 5$

12. $20 - y^4 + 6$

13. $x - y^2 - 2$

14. Guided Problem Solving Entrance to a museum costs $10 for adults and $7 for students. How much will it cost for 5 adults and 35 students to enter the museum?

(**1** Write an expression for the cost for the adults. Write an expression for the cost for the students.

(**2** Now write an expression for the total cost for adults and students.

(**3** Evaluate your expression using order of operations.

HELP with Homework

Example	Exercises
1	15–23, 30–32
2	24–26
3	15–23, 30–32
4	15–23, 30–32
5	28–29

Online Resources
CLASSZONE.COM
· More Examples
· eTutorial Plus

Sports

Practice and Problem Solving

Evaluate the expression.

15. $12 + 2 \cdot 10$

16. $40 - 12 \div 6$

17. $7(14 - 9)$

18. $\dfrac{28}{7 - 3}$

19. $\dfrac{15 - 7}{3 + 1}$

20. $16 \div (3^2 - 1)$

21. $3^4 \div 9 \div 3$

22. $(8 - 2)^2 + 12 \div 6$

23. $35 - 15 - 5 + 10$

Algebra Evaluate the expression when $x = 3$, $y = 6$, and $z = 2$.

24. $18 \div x - z$

25. $\dfrac{x + y}{x}$

26. $4z^3 - y$

27. Critical Thinking Insert grouping symbols into the expression $6 + 7 \cdot 5 + 8$ to make it equal to 73.

28. Magazine Web Site A magazine Web site has a $5 membership fee and charges $2 for each month. Write and evaluate an expression to find the cost to join for one year.

29. Weightlifting In the clean-and-jerk event in the 2000 Summer Olympics, Cheryl Haworth lifted a 15 kilogram bar, four plates that each weighed 25 kilograms, and 2 plates that each weighed 15 kilograms. Write and evaluate an expression to find the total weight that she lifted.

Match the given expression with an expression that has the same value.

30. $20 - 4^2 + 8$

31. $6(12 + 9)$

32. $21 - 6 \cdot 3 + 19$

 A. $(18 - 7) \cdot 2$

 B. $18 \cdot 2 \div 3$

 C. $8^2 \cdot 3 - 66$

Extended Problem Solving In Exercises 33–35, use the pricing information for Joe's Joke Shop.

Joe's Joke Shop	
Chattering teeth	$3
Hand buzzer	$4

33. Calculate You want to buy a present for each of 6 friends. If you have only $20, could you buy 6 chattering teeth or 6 hand buzzers?

34. Make a List Suppose you want to buy at least one of each item. Make a list of all the possible ways of buying 6 presents.

35. Critical Thinking Write and evaluate an expression to find the total cost of each combination you listed in Exercise 34. Which combinations of presents could you buy with $20?

Challenge Evaluate the expression.

36. $165 \div [(4 + 7) \cdot 5]$

37. $[(9 + 3^4) \div 30] \cdot 18$

38. $175 \div [35 \div (5 + 2)]$

■ **Weightlifting**

In the snatch event in the 2000 Summer Olympics, 17-year-old Cheryl Haworth lifted 125 kilograms. Given that 1 kilogram is equal to a little more than 2 pounds, about how many pounds did Haworth lift?

Mixed Review

39. To find the length of a theater production, you can use the expression $p + i$, where p is the length in minutes of the play and i is the length in minutes of the intermission. Find the length of a production where the play is 130 minutes long and the intermission is 15 minutes long. *(Lesson 1.2)*

Evaluate the power. *(Lesson 1.3)*

40. 12^1 **41.** 13^2 **42.** 5^4 **43.** 3^5

Basic Skills Find the difference.

44. $\begin{array}{r} 48 \\ -\ 29 \end{array}$ **45.** $\begin{array}{r} 126 \\ -\ 53 \end{array}$ **46.** $\begin{array}{r} 301 \\ -\ 164 \end{array}$ **47.** $\begin{array}{r} 357 \\ -\ 258 \end{array}$

Test-Taking Practice

INTERNET
State Test Practice
CLASSZONE.COM

48. **Multiple Choice** In what order should you perform the operations to correctly evaluate the expression $27 - 18 \div 3^2$?

A. Evaluate the power, subtract, and then divide.

B. Subtract, evaluate the power, and then divide.

C. Divide, evaluate the power, and then subtract.

D. Evaluate the power, divide, and then subtract.

49. **Short Response** Evaluate the expression $20 - 3^2 \cdot 2 + 8$. How could you insert parentheses to make the expression equal to 110?

BRAIN GAME

Number Jumble

Copy the expression below. How could you fill in the boxes with the numbers 1, 2, 3, and 4 to make the expression have the greatest possible value? the least possible value?

$$ \boxed{} + \boxed{} \cdot \boxed{} - \boxed{} $$

Using Order of Operations

GOAL Use a calculator to evaluate expressions using order of operations.

You can use the $($, $)$, and $\wedge$ keys to evaluate expressions.

Example 1 You buy 7 quarts of strawberries and 6 quarts of raspberries at a fruit stand. Each quart of fruit costs $3. What is the total cost?

Solution

To find the total cost, you need to evaluate the expression $3(7 + 6)$.

Keystrokes	Display
3 $($ 7 $+$ 6 $)$ $=$	39

ANSWER The total cost is $39.

Example 2 You can estimate the number of strawberries in one quart by evaluating 3^3. About how many strawberries are in 7 quarts?

Solution

To estimate the number of strawberries in 7 quarts, you need to evaluate the expression 7×3^3.

Keystrokes	Display
7 $\times$ 3 $\wedge$ 3 $=$	189

ANSWER There are about 189 strawberries in 7 quarts.

HELP with **Technology**

The keystrokes shown here may not be the same as on your calculator. See your calculator's instruction manual for alternative keystrokes.

Your turn now Use a calculator to evaluate the expression.

1. $3 + 4 \cdot 5$ **2.** $9^2 - 3^2$ **3.** $\dfrac{14 + 6}{4 + 1}$ **4.** $(4 + 2)^2 + 5^2$

5. Blueberries You can estimate the number of blueberries in one pint by evaluating 6^3. About how many blueberries are in 5 pints?

Notebook Review

Review the vocabulary definitions in your notebook.

Copy the review examples in your notebook. Then complete the exercises.

Check Your Definitions

variable, p. 9

variable expression, p. 9

evaluate, p. 9

power, p. 14

base, p. 14

exponent, p. 14

order of operations, p. 18

Use Your Vocabulary

1. Complete: A(n) _?_ is a letter used to represent one or more numbers.

1.1 Can you describe and extend patterns?

 EXAMPLE In the pattern 28, 25, 22, 19, . . . , you subtract 3 from the previous number to get the next number.

$$\overset{-3}{\frown}\ \overset{-3}{\frown}\ \overset{-3}{\frown}$$
28,   25,   22,   19,   **16,   13,   10,** . . .
$$\underset{-3}{\smile}\ \underset{-3}{\smile}\ \underset{-3}{\smile}$$

☑ **Describe the pattern. Then write the next three numbers.**

    2. 10, 20, 30, 40, . . .   **3.** 7, 14, 28, 56, . . .

1.2 Can you evaluate variable expressions?

 EXAMPLE Evaluate $8x$ when $x = 5$.

    $8x = 8(5)$ **Substitute 5 for x.**

    $\quad = 40$ **Multiply.**

☑ **4.** Evaluate $b - 8$ when $b = 19$.   **5.** Evaluate $m \div 6$ when $m = 30$.

1.3 Can you write and evaluate powers?

 EXAMPLE Evaluate 5^3.

    $5^3 = 5 \cdot 5 \cdot 5$ **Write 5 as a factor 3 times.**

    $\quad = 125$ **Multiply.**

☑ **6.** Write $8 \cdot 8 \cdot 8 \cdot 8$ as a power.   **7.** Evaluate 10^5.

1.4 Can you use order of operations?

EXAMPLE Evaluate the expression $3^3 + 14 \div 7$.

$$3^3 + 14 \div 7 = 27 + 14 \div 7 \qquad \text{Evaluate the power.}$$
$$= 27 + 2 \qquad \text{Divide 14 by 7.}$$
$$= 29 \qquad \text{Add 27 and 2.}$$

☑ **Evaluate the expression.**

8. $5^3 + 13 \cdot 2$ **9.** $15 - 3 + 7 - 2$ **10.** $(100 + 200) \div 4 + 3^2$

Stop *and* **Think**   about Lessons 1.1–1.4

11. Writing In your own words, describe how to extend a numerical pattern.

12. Critical Thinking Insert grouping symbols into the expression $3 + 9 \times 6 - 4$ to make it equal to 21.

Review Quiz 1

Describe the pattern. Then write the next three numbers.

1. 3, 6, 12, 24, . . .   **2.** 100, 95, 90, 85, . . .   **3.** 11, 15, 19, 23, . . .

4. Describe the pattern. Then draw the next three figures.

5. Soccer To find the number of points earned by a soccer player, you can evaluate the expression $2g + a$, where g is the number of goals scored and a is the number of assists. Find the number of points earned by a soccer player with 6 goals and 13 assists.

Write the product as a power.

6. $7 \cdot 7 \cdot 7 \cdot 7$ **7.** $3 \cdot 3 \cdot 3 \cdot 3 \cdot 3 \cdot 3 \cdot 3$ **8.** $11 \cdot 11$

Evaluate the expression.

9. $2 \cdot 6 \div 4 \cdot 10 \cdot 3$ **10.** $3 + 3^3 \div 3$ **11.** $5(12 - 6)^2 + 7$

Equations and Mental Math

LESSON 1.5

BEFORE

You used mental math to add, subtract, multiply, and divide.

▶ **Now**

You'll use mental math to solve an equation.

WHY?

So you can find the flying time for a homing pigeon, as in Example 3.

📓 **Word Watch**

equation, p. 26
solution, p. 26
solving an equation, p. 27

Activity You can use chips to find the value of a variable.

(1 Use chips to model the statement $n + 4 = 7$. Let each chip represent 1.

$n + \bullet\bullet\!\bullet\bullet = \bullet\bullet\bullet\bullet\!\bullet\bullet\bullet$

(2 Replace n with chips until you have the same number of chips on each side of the equal sign.

$\bullet\bullet\!\bullet + \bullet\bullet\!\bullet\bullet = \bullet\bullet\bullet\bullet\!\bullet\bullet\bullet$

(3 Replacing n with 3 chips gives a total of 7 chips on each side, so $n = 3$.

$\bullet\bullet\bullet\bullet\!\bullet\bullet\bullet = \bullet\bullet\bullet\bullet\!\bullet\bullet\bullet$

Model with chips to help you find the value of the variable.

1. $6 + x = 10$ **2.** $y + 2 = 9$ **3.** $8 = m + 3$

In the activity, you solved *equations* by modeling with chips. An **equation** is a mathematical sentence formed by setting two expressions equal. A **solution** of an equation is a number that you can substitute for a variable to make the equation true.

EXAMPLE 1   Checking Possible Solutions

Tell whether the value of the variable is a solution of $n + 5 = 12$.

  a. $n = 9$ **b.** $n = 7$

Solution

 **with Reading**

Symbol	Meaning
$=$	is equal to
$\stackrel{?}{=}$	is equal to?
$\neq$	is not equal to

  a. $n + 5 = 12$ Write original equation.

         $9 + 5 \stackrel{?}{=} 12$ Substitute 9 for n.

              $14 \neq 12$ The equation is not true, so 9 is not a solution.

  b. $n + 5 = 12$ Write original equation.

         $7 + 5 \stackrel{?}{=} 12$ Substitute 7 for n.

            $12 = 12$ ✓   The equation is true, so 7 is a solution.

Your turn now Tell whether the value of the variable is a solution of the equation.

1. $3x = 12; x = 4$ **2.** $7 = 13 - n; n = 5$ **3.** $6 \div y = 3; y = 2$

Solving an Equation Finding all solutions of an equation is called **solving the equation**. You can use mental math to solve simple equations by thinking of the equation as a question.

EXAMPLE 2 **Using Mental Math to Solve Equations**

	Equation	Question	Solution	Check
a.	$9 + x = 12$	9 plus what number equals 12?	3	$9 + 3 = 12$
b.	$n - 5 = 10$	What number minus 5 equals 10?	15	$15 - 5 = 10$
c.	$4t = 20$	4 times what number equals 20?	5	$4(5) = 20$
d.	$m \div 3 = 12$	What number divided by 3 equals 12?	36	$36 \div 3 = 12$

Your turn now Solve the equation using mental math.

4. $7x = 35$ **5.** $15 = n - 6$ **6.** $12 + a = 32$ **7.** $24 \div n = 6$

Distance Problems Some distance problems can be solved using an equation that relates distance, speed, and time. For example, if you travel on a moving walkway at a speed of 2 feet per second for 30 seconds, you can use the following formula to find the distance you travel.

Distance, Speed, and Time

Words Distance traveled is equal to the speed (rate of travel) times the travel time.

Algebra $d = rt$

Numbers distance = 2 feet per second · 30 seconds = 60 feet

EXAMPLE 3 **Using Mental Math to Solve an Equation**

Homing Pigeons A homing pigeon is a bird trained to fly back to its home. Homing pigeons can fly at a speed of about 50 miles per hour. About how long would it take for a homing pigeon to fly 300 miles?

Solution

$$d = rt$$ Write formula for distance.

$$300 = 50t$$ Substitute the values you know.

$$300 = 50 \cdot 6$$ Use mental math to solve equation.

ANSWER It would take a homing pigeon about 6 hours to fly 300 miles.

Your turn now Solve the following problem.

8. A car travels on a highway at a constant speed. If it takes the car 2 hours to drive 100 miles, at what speed is the car traveling?

 **Exercises**

More Practice, p. 705

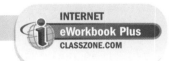
Getting Ready to Practice

1. **Vocabulary** What is the difference between an expression and an equation? Give an example of each.

Tell whether the given value of the variable is a solution of the equation.

2. $5x = 35; x = 7$ 3. $16 + y = 22; y = 8$ 4. $9 = z - 12; z = 20$

Mental Math Solve the equation using mental math.

5. $4a = 24$ 6. $b - 6 = 7$ 7. $\frac{z}{3} = 7$

8. $18 = 9 + y$ 9. $8 = 25 - t$ 10. $10x = 120$

11. **Skiing** A ski lift is advertised as being able to bring you to the top of a mountain in only 5 minutes. If the distance the ski lift travels to the top of the mountain is 3000 feet, about how many feet per minute does the ski lift travel?

Practice and Problem Solving

with Homework

Example	Exercises
1	12–14
2	15–27, 31–32
3	28–30, 35–36

Online Resources
CLASSZONE.COM

· More Examples
· eTutorial Plus

Tell whether the given value of the variable is a solution of the equation.

12. $40 = 8z; z = 5$ **13.** $s + 5 = 11; s = 7$ **14.** $24 - a = 13; a = 9$

Match the equation with the corresponding question. Then solve.

15. $t + 3 = 12$ **A.** 12 divided by what number equals 3?

16. $\dfrac{t}{12} = 3$ **B.** What number plus 3 equals 12?

17. $12 \div t = 3$ **C.** What number divided by 12 equals 3?

18. $3t = 12$ **D.** 3 times what number equals 12?

Mental Math Solve the equation using mental math.

19. $x + 8 = 15$ **20.** $\dfrac{36}{y} = 6$ **21.** $7t = 56$

22. $20 - b = 3$ **23.** $10 = x - 7$ **24.** $29 = 19 + p$

25. $a \div 6 = 8$ **26.** $11n = 44$ **27.** $54 = 9y$

Use the formula for distance to find the unknown value.

28. $d = 100$ miles, $r = 25$ miles per hour, $t = \underline{\ ?\ }$

29. $d = 72$ miles, $r = \underline{\ ?\ }$, $t = 8$ hours

30. $d = 9$ feet, $r = 3$ feet per second, $t = \underline{\ ?\ }$

31. Log Flumes You ride a log flume at an amusement park for 6 rotations in a row. According to your watch, you spent a total of 18 minutes on the ride. Solve the equation $6n = 18$ to find how long it takes to complete one rotation of the ride.

32. St. Louis Arch The elevator train inside the St. Louis arch can carry a total of 40 people, with 5 people in each of the cars. Solve the equation $\dfrac{40}{c} = 5$ to find the number of cars in the elevator train.

Critical Thinking Tell whether the equations have the same solution.

33. $x + 4 = 5$ and $x + 2 = 3$ **34.** $5y = 45$ and $6y = 48$

35. Cheetahs A cheetah can run at a top speed of about 100 feet per second. At this speed, find the approximate time it would take a cheetah to run the length of a football field that is 300 feet long.

36. Biking You bike at approximately the same speed for 2 hours. If you travel 24 miles, what is your speed?

What do you think?

Recreation

■ **Log Flumes**

Some log flumes hold as much as 90,000 gallons of water. An Olympic-size pool holds about 750,000 gallons of water. About how many log flumes could be filled with the water from an Olympic-size pool?

Challenge Solve the equation using mental math.

37. $2p + 0 = 6$ **38.** $4 - 2a = 0$ **39.** $10 - 3y = 1$ **40.** $2x + 1 = 5$

Mixed Review

Evaluate the expression when **x = 12** and **y = 3.** *(Lessons 1.3, 1.4)*

41. $2y^3$ **42.** $x^2 - y$ **43.** xy^2 **44.** $(x + y)^2$

Evaluate the expression. *(Lesson 1.4)*

45. $18 \div 9 + 5$ **46.** $42 \div 6 - 3$ **47.** $11 + 3 \cdot 8$ **48.** $12 + 10 \cdot 3$

Basic Skills Find the perimeter.

49.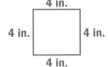

4 in.
4 in.   4 in.
4 in.

50.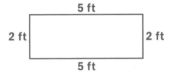

5 ft
2 ft   2 ft
5 ft

Test-Taking Practice

INTERNET
State Test Practice
CLASSZONE.COM

51. Multiple Choice What is the solution of the equation $\frac{21}{a} = 3$?

A. 3   **B.** 7   **C.** 18   **D.** 63

52. Multiple Choice Bats can fly at a speed of about 50 feet per second. Solve the equation $350 = 50t$ to estimate the time is takes a bat to fly 350 feet.

F. 6 seconds   **G.** 7 seconds   **H.** 70 seconds   **I.** 300 seconds

BRAIN GAME

Shape Equations

Find the number that each shape represents. Each square represents the same number.

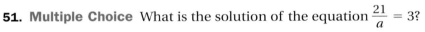

Hands-on Activity

GOAL
Develop formulas for finding the areas of rectangles and the areas of squares.

MATERIALS
· graph paper

Investigating Area

The *area* of a figure is the number of square units needed to cover it. You can use graph paper to develop formulas for the area of a rectangle and the area of a square.

Explore **Find the area of a rectangle with a length of 10 units and a width of 4 units.**

1 On graph paper, draw a rectangle that has a length of 10 units and a width of 4 units.

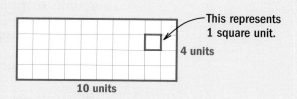

This represents 1 square unit.

4 units

10 units

2 Count the number of square units that cover the rectangle. The area is 40 square units.

Your turn now **Find the area of the rectangle or square.**

1.   **2.**   **3.**

Using graph paper, draw a rectangle or square with the given dimensions. Then find the area.

4. Rectangle:
length = 8 units
width = 7 units
area = _?_

5. Square:
side length = 6 units
area = _?_

6. Rectangle:
length = 9 units
width = 5 units
area = _?_

Stop and Think

7. Writing How can you use the length and the width of a rectangle to find its area? How can you use the side length of a square to find its area?

8. Critical Thinking Write an equation that relates the area A, length l, and width w of a rectangle. Similarly, write an equation that relates the area A and side length s of a square.

Perimeter and Area

BEFORE	▶ Now	WHY?
You used properties of rectangles and squares.	You'll use formulas to find perimeter and area.	So you can find the area of a theater's stage, as in Ex. 22.

📓 **Word Watch**

perimeter, p. 32
area, p. 32

The **perimeter** of a rectangle is the sum of the lengths of the sides. Perimeter is measured in linear units such as inches (in.), feet (ft), centimeters (cm), and meters (m).

The **area** of a rectangle is the number of square units needed to cover the rectangle. Area is measured in units such as square inches (in.²), square feet (ft²), square centimeters (cm²), and square meters (m²).

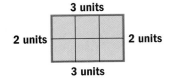

Perimeter = 3 + 3 + 2 + 2
= 10 units

Area = 6 square units

You can use formulas to find perimeter and area.

Perimeter and Area

	Rectangle	**Square**
	width w / length l	side length s
Perimeter P	$P = 2l + 2w$	$P = 4s$
Area A	$A = lw$	$A = s^2$

EXAMPLE 1 **Finding Perimeter**

HELP with Notetaking

If you forget the formula for the perimeter of a rectangle, you could draw and label a diagram like the one shown at the top of this page. Then just add the lengths of the sides.

Find the perimeter of the rectangle or square with the given dimensions.

a. $l = 5$ feet, $w = 2$ feet

b. $s = 3$ centimeters

Solution

a. $P = 2l + 2w$
$= 2(5) + 2(2)$
$= 10 + 4 = 14$

b. $P = 4s$
$= 4(3)$
$= 12$

ANSWER The perimeter is 14 ft.

ANSWER The perimeter is 12 cm.

with Review

Need help with rectangles and squares? See p. 701.

Your turn now Find the perimeter of the rectangle or square.

1.

7 in.
1 in.

2.

8 cm

EXAMPLE 2 **Finding Area**

Find the area of the rectangle or square with the given dimensions.

a. $l = 5$ inches, $w = 3$ inches   **b.** $s = 10$ feet

Solution

a. $A = lw$

$= 5(3)$

$= 15$

ANSWER The area is 15 in.^{2}.

b. $A = s^2$

$= 10^2$

$= 100$

ANSWER The area is 100 ft^2.

Your turn now Find the area of the rectangle or square.

3.

2 m

6 m

4.

11 ft

5. Find the perimeter and the area of a rectangle that has a length of 6 inches and a width of 4 inches.

EXAMPLE 3 **Using Perimeter and Area**

Wheelchair Slalom In a wheelchair slalom event, athletes weave around cones and race to the finish line. A diagram of the rectangular course is shown. Find the perimeter and the area of the course.

Start

16 m

30 m

Finish

Solution

$P = 2l + 2w$

$= 2(30) + 2(16)$

$= 60 + 32 = 92$

$A = lw$

$= 30(16)$

$= 480$

ANSWER The perimeter of the course is 92 m, and the area is 480 m^2.

INTERNET
eWorkbook Plus
CLASSZONE.COM

Getting Ready to Practice

Vocabulary **Copy and complete the statement.**

1. The sum of the lengths of the sides of a rectangle is the ? of the rectangle.

2. The number of square units needed to cover a rectangle is the ? of the rectangle.

Find the perimeter and the area of the rectangle or square with the given dimensions.

3. $l = 12$ inches, $w = 4$ inches

4. $l = 9$ meters, $w = 7$ meters

5. $s = 7$ centimeters

6. $s = 2$ centimeters

7. **Art** A rectangular painting has a width of 4 feet and a length of 7 feet. Find the perimeter and the area of the painting.

with Homework

Example	Exercises
1	8–17
2	8–17
3	18, 20, 22

Online Resources
CLASSZONE.COM
· More Examples
· eTutorial Plus

Practice and Problem Solving

Find the perimeter and the area of the rectangle or square.

8.
3 m
15 m

9.
20 in.

Find the perimeter and the area of the rectangle or square with the given dimensions.

10. $l = 20$ feet, $w = 2$ feet

11. $s = 4$ centimeters

12. $s = 9$ meters

13. $l = 11$ inches, $w = 6$ inches

14. $l = 15$ feet, $w = 4$ feet

15. $s = 12$ centimeters

16. $s = 13$ inches

17. $l = 8$ meters, $w = 5$ meters

18. **Gardening** You plant a rectangular garden that has a length of 20 feet and a width of 8 feet. Find the perimeter and the area of the garden.

19. **Compare** Which has the greater area: a rectangle with a length of 7 feet and a width of 5 feet, or a square with a side length of 6 feet? Explain how you know.

20. **Basketball** A high school basketball court is a rectangle with a length of 84 feet and a width of 50 feet. What is the perimeter of the court?

21. Measurement Measure the sides of the rectangle to the nearest inch. Use your measurements to find the perimeter and the area.

22. Globe Theatre William Shakespeare's plays were performed on the stage of the old Globe Theatre in London. The rectangular stage had a length of 43 feet and a width of 28 feet. Find the area.

Critical Thinking **Find the unknown dimension of the rectangle or square.**

23. $P = 24$ in., $s = \underline{\ ?\ }$

24. $A = 8$ ft^2, $l = 4$ ft, $w = \underline{\ ?\ }$

Challenge **The figures below can be broken into rectangles and squares. Find the perimeter and the area of each figure. Explain your method.**

25.
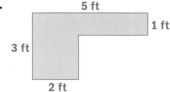

26.
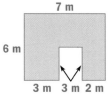

Mixed Review

27. You save $3 in September. The next three months you save $6, $12, and then $24. If this savings pattern continues, how much will you save in January? *(Lesson 1.1)*

Solve the equation using mental math. *(Lesson 1.5)*

28. $4c = 32$ **29.** $16 - a = 11$ **30.** $x + 18 = 25$

Basic Skills **Copy and complete the equation.**

31. $6 + \underline{\ ?\ } = 13$ **32.** $\underline{\ ?\ } - 8 = 19$ **33.** $14 \div \underline{\ ?\ } = 2$

Test-Taking Practice

34. Multiple Choice What is the area of a rectangular desktop that has a length of 5 feet and a width of 2 feet?

A. 10 in.^{2} **B.** 14 ft   **C.** 10 ft^2 **D.** 14 ft^2

35. Short Response Does a rectangular garden with a length of 6 feet and a width of 4 feet, or a square garden with side length 5 feet, have the greater area? Which requires more fencing? Explain.

Problem Solving Strategies

Make a Model
Draw a Diagram
Act it Out
Guess, Check, and Revise
Look for a Pattern
Make a List
Make a Table

Look for a Pattern

Problem What happens to the perimeter and the area of a rectangle if you double the length and the width?

① Read and Understand

Read the problem carefully.

You need to find how the perimeter and the area of a rectangle change when the dimensions of the rectangle are doubled.

② Make a Plan

Decide on a strategy to use.

Find the perimeter and the area of several rectangles, find the perimeter and the area when the dimensions are doubled, and then look for a pattern in how these measurements changed.

③ Solve the Problem

Reread the problem and look for a pattern.

Draw several rectangles and label the lengths and widths. Find the perimeter and the area of each rectangle. Organize your results in a table.

2 units
4 units

4 units
6 units

Make a second table that has the lengths and widths from the first table doubled. Find and record the perimeter and the area of each rectangle.

3 units
5 units

Original Dimensions			
Length l	Width w	Perimeter $2l + 2w$	Area lw
4	2	12	8
5	3	16	15
6	4	20	24

Dimensions Doubled			
Length l	Width w	Perimeter $2l + 2w$	Area lw
8	4	24	32
10	6	32	60
12	8	40	96

× 2

× 4

Look for a pattern in how the perimeters and the areas changed.

ANSWER Doubling the length and width of a rectangle makes the perimeter twice as great and the area four times as great.

④ Look Back

Test a few more rectangles to make sure the pattern holds.

Use the strategy _look for a pattern_.

1. **Swimming** Your swimming coach plans the number of meters you will swim in each practice. The number of meters for each of the first seven practices are 1000, 1250, 1000, 1500, 1000, 1750, and 1000. How many meters would you expect to swim in the eighth practice?

2. **Class Schedules** The schedule for your health, art, and physical education classes is shown below for the first 3 weeks of school. In which week will your schedule be the same as in the first week?

Week	M	T	W	Th	F
1	Health	Health	Art	Art	PE
2	PE	Health	Health	Art	Art
3	PE	PE	Health	Health	Art

3. **Rectangles** What happens to the perimeter and the area of a rectangle when the length and width are tripled? What happens when the length and width are quadrupled?

4. **Powers** Copy and complete the table for the powers of 3. Without actually calculating 3^9, how can you tell what its last digit is? What is the last digit?

Power	3^1	3^2	3^3	3^4	3^5	3^6
Value	3	9	27	?	?	?

5. **Concert Hall** The back section of a concert hall has 55 seats in the last row, 52 seats in the row before that, 49 seats in the row before that, 46 seats in the row before that, and so on. If the back section has 10 rows, how many seats are in the first row of the back section?

Mixed Problem Solving

Use any strategy to solve the problem.

6. **Height** Four friends stand in order from shortest to tallest for a photograph. Mary is taller than Jack. Harry is standing between Jack and Alicia. Jack is not the shortest. What is the order in which the friends are standing?

7. **Locker Combination** You forget the last number of your locker combination. You remember that it is a two digit number divisible by 9 and that the first digit is 2. What is the number?

8. **Carpeting** Your family is getting wall-to-wall carpeting installed in your living room and den, shown below. If the carpeting costs $10 per square yard, what is the total cost for the carpeting?

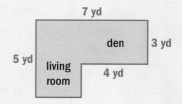

9. **Money** You are carrying a dollar's worth of change. Out of your piggy bank you take a nickel for each of 5 pennies you put in, a dime for each of 3 nickels you put in, and a quarter for each of 2 dimes you put in. How much money are you carrying now?

A Problem Solving Plan

BEFORE	▶ Now	WHY?
You used the problem solving strategy *look for a pattern*.	You'll use a 4-step plan to solve many kinds of problems.	So you can find when you need to start your homework, as in Ex. 5.

In the Real World

Word Watch

Review Words

sum, p. 687
difference, p. 687
product, p. 689
quotient, p. 690

Marching Band Your school's marching band can play for up to 14 minutes during halftime at a football game. The band must choose 3 songs from the table, and one of the songs must be the school song. What songs can the band play?

Marching Band Songs	Time (minutes)
School song	3
A	6
B	5
C	4
D	7

EXAMPLE 1　Understanding and Planning

To solve the marching band problem, you need to make sure you understand the problem. Then make a plan for solving the problem.

Read and Understand

What do you know?

The marching band can play for up to 14 minutes.

The table gives the playing times for songs.

The band must choose 3 songs, and one has to be the school song.

What do you want to find out?

What combinations of songs can the marching band play?

Make a Plan

How can you relate what you know to what you want to find out?

Find the time available for playing the two songs that are not the school song.

List all the possible combinations of two songs (excluding the school song) and the time it takes to play them.

Identify the combinations that fit within the available time.

Your turn now **Use the information at the top of the page.**

1. How many minutes long is the school song?

2. How many minutes does this leave for playing the other two songs?

with Solving

Notice the pattern of song pairings in the table:

A B C D

A B C D

A B C D

Using a pattern like this guarantees that you don't miss any song pairings.

EXAMPLE 2 **Solving and Looking Back**

To solve the marching band problem from the previous page, you need to carry out the plan from Example 1 and then check the answer.

Solve the Problem

Because of the school song requirement, there are $14 - 3 = 11$ minutes for playing the other two songs. Make a list of all the combinations of two songs, and the time it takes to play them.

Songs	Total Time
A: 6 min, B: 5 min	**11 min**
A: 6 min, C: 4 min	**10 min**
A: 6 min, D: 7 min	13 min
B: 5 min, C: 4 min	**9 min**
B: 5 min, D: 7 min	12 min
C: 4 min, D: 7 min	**11 min**

> Look for combinations that have a total playing time less than or equal to 11 minutes.

ANSWER The marching band can play the school song and either songs A and B, songs A and C, songs B and C, or songs C and D.

Look Back

Because song C is the shortest song and song D is the longest song, it makes sense that song C shows up most often in the answer and song D shows up least often in the answer. So, the answer seems reasonable.

Your turn now **Refer to Example 2.**

3. Suppose song C is 6 minutes long. Now what songs can the marching band play?

Problem Solving Plan

1. **Read and Understand** Read the problem carefully. Identify the question and any important information.

2. **Make a Plan** Decide on a problem solving strategy.

3. **Solve the Problem** Use the problem solving strategy to answer the question.

4. **Look Back** Check that your answer is reasonable.

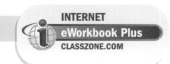

Getting Ready to Practice

1. **Vocabulary** What are the 4 steps of the problem solving plan?

2. **Guided Problem Solving** You are ordering whole pans of lasagna for a party. One pan of lasagna serves 8 people. You expect that there will be 52 people at the party. How many pans of lasagna should you order?

   1 What are you trying to find?

   2 What operation should you use to find an answer?

   3 Write an expression you could use to find an answer. Evaluate your expression.

   4 Make sure your answer is reasonable. You cannot order part of a pan of lasagna.

Practice and Problem Solving

3. **Find the Error** Describe and correct the error made in solving the following problem.

   You spent a total of $22 for you and a friend at the movies. If you spent $6 on snacks, how much did each movie ticket cost?

   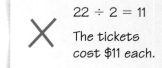

   $22 \div 2 = 11$
   The tickets cost $11 each.

4. **Writing** Why is it important to look back at the solution to a problem after you have solved the problem?

5. **Homework** Your favorite TV show starts at 9 P.M. Before you can watch the show, you have to complete 20 minutes of social studies homework, 30 minutes of math homework, and 15 minutes of science homework. What is the latest time you can start your homework and be done by 9 P.M.?

6. **Look for a Pattern** A marching band formation has 1 band member in the first row, 3 in the second row, 5 in the third row, and so on. How many band members are in the formation if it has 8 rows?

7. **Tiki Torches** You have a rectangular backyard with a length of 27 yards and a width of 9 yards. You want to place a tiki torch every 3 yards around the edge of the backyard. How many torches do you need?

8. **Number Sense** The sum of the digits of a two digit number is 7. The tens' digit is 3 more than the ones' digit. What is the number?

with Homework

Example	Exercises
1	5–10
2	5–10

Online Resources
CLASSZONE.COM

· More Examples
· eTutorial Plus

■ **Origami**

The origami-inspired dress above belongs to a set of dresses made by fashion designer Hiroaki Ohya. Each dress comes folded up in a book. The entire set of 21 books costs $6000. About how much does one book cost?

9. **Baseball Carpool** Brandon, Jeff, and Andrew are being driven to baseball practice. In how many different arrangements can they sit in the back seat of the car?

10. **Origami** Origami cranes are birds made out of folded paper. The number of cranes Jane folds on each of four days is given in the table. If she continues this folding pattern, on which day will Jane have a total of 70 cranes?

Day	Cranes
1	1
2	4
3	7
4	10

11. **Critical Thinking** You buy a 5 pound bag of apples for $2.50. Do you have enough information to find how much each apple costs? Explain your reasoning.

12. **Courtyards** A rectangular courtyard has a length of 21 feet and an area of 294 square feet. What is the perimeter of the courtyard? Use estimation to check the reasonableness of your answer.

13. **Challenge** Mary and Donata have lunch, and each agrees to pay half of the $30 cost (which includes tax and tip). Mary has two $10 bills, and Donata has a $20 bill and two $5 bills. Is there a way for them to pay the bill without getting change? Explain.

Mixed Review

Find the area of the rectangle with the given dimensions. *(Lesson 1.6)*

14. $l = 14$ inches, $w = 2$ inches

15. $l = 6$ feet, $w = 5$ feet

Choose a Strategy Use a strategy from the list to solve the following problem. Explain your choice of strategy.

> **Problem Solving Strategies**
> ■ Make a List
> ■ Draw a Diagram
> ■ Look for a Pattern

16. Karen, Ty, Mark, and Cindy are standing in line to buy movie tickets. Ty is directly behind Cindy. Mark is not last in line. Cindy is the first person in line. In what order are these four people standing?

Basic Skills **Use a number line to compare the numbers.**

17. 8 and 18

18. 10 and 7

19. 26 and 21

20. 34 and 38

Test-Taking Practice

21. **Extended Response** You are camping and have only a 3 cup container and a 5 cup container. You need to measure 12 cups of water into a pot. How can you do this? Is there more than one way? Explain.

Notebook Review

Review the vocabulary definitions in your notebook.

Copy the review examples in your notebook. Then complete the exercises.

Check Your Definitions

equation, p. 26   solving an equation, p. 27   area, p. 32
solution, p. 26   perimeter, p. 32

Use Your Vocabulary

1. **Writing** Describe in words how to find the perimeter and the area of a rectangle.

1.5 Can you solve equations using mental math?

EXAMPLE Solve the equation $n - 7 = 15$ using mental math.

Ask yourself "What number minus 7 equals 15?" Check 22 as a possible solution:

$$n - 7 = 15 \qquad \text{Write equation.}$$
$$22 - 7 \stackrel{?}{=} 15 \qquad \text{Substitute 22 for } n.$$
$$15 = 15 \checkmark \qquad \text{The equation is true.}$$

ANSWER So, 22 is a solution.

☑ **Solve the equation using mental math.**

2. $35 = 5t$ **3.** $y + 12 = 25$

1.6 Can you find perimeter and area?

EXAMPLE Your rectangular bedroom has a length of 11 feet and a width of 8 feet. Find the perimeter and the area of your bedroom.

$$P = 2l + 2w \qquad\qquad A = lw$$
$$= 2(11) + 2(8) \qquad\qquad = 11(8)$$
$$= 22 + 16 = 38 \text{ feet} \qquad = 88 \text{ square feet}$$

☑ **Find the perimeter and the area of the rectangle or square with the given dimensions.**

4. $l = 16$ inches, $w = 7$ inches   **5.** $s = 4$ meters

1.7 Can you use a problem solving plan?

EXAMPLE Your school is organizing a field trip for 81 students and 13 teachers. If a bus can hold a maximum of 40 people, how many buses do you need for the field trip?

Read and Understand You need to find the number of buses to transport 81 students and 13 teachers.

Make a Plan You can divide the total number of people by the number of people one bus can hold to find the number of buses needed.

Solve the Problem Find the total number of people: $81 + 13 = 94$. Divide the total number of people by 40: $94 \div 40 = 2$ R14.

ANSWER You need 3 buses for the field trip.

Look Back The answer is reasonable because 2 buses can hold only 80 people.

☑ 6. How many buses would you need for 150 students and 20 teachers?

Stop and Think about Lessons 1.5–1.7

7. Writing Describe a situation in which you might want to know the perimeter of a rectangle. Describe a situation in which you might want to know the area of a rectangle.

Review Quiz 2

Solve the equation using mental math.

1. $6 + m = 18$ **2.** $83 = 90 - b$ **3.** $16y = 32$ **4.** $\dfrac{32}{z} = 4$

Find the perimeter and the area of the rectangle or square.

5.
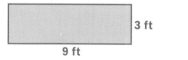
3 ft
9 ft

6.

15 cm

7. Travel To get to your grandparents' house, you could take a train that travels at a constant speed of 50 miles per hour for 150 miles, or you could take a bus that travels at a constant speed of 60 miles per hour for 240 miles. Which takes less time? (*Hint:* Use the formula $d = rt$.)

Chapter Review

Vocabulary

variable, p. 9
variable expression, p. 9
evaluate, p. 9
power, p. 14
base, p. 14

exponent, p. 14
order of operations,
  p. 18
equation, p. 26
solution, p. 26

solving an equation,
  p. 27
perimeter, p. 32
area, p. 32

Vocabulary Review

1. Copy and complete: A(n) _?_ of an equation is a number that you can substitute for the variable to make the equation true.

2. Copy and complete: The _?_ of a rectangle is the number of square units needed to cover the rectangle.

3. What does an equation have that an expression does not?

4. What are the two parts of a power? Give an example of a power and label these two parts.

Review Questions

Describe the pattern. Then write the next three numbers. *(Lesson 1.1)*

5. 1, 11, 21, 31, . . .

6. 50, 44, 38, 32, . . .

7. 25, 50, 100, 200, . . .

8. 320, 160, 80, 40, . . .

9. 100, 97, 94, 91, . . .

10. 8, 20, 32, 44, . . .

Describe the pattern. Then draw the next figure. *(Lesson 1.1)*

11.

12.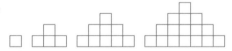

Evaluate the expression for the given value of the variable. *(Lesson 1.2)*

13. $9x$ when $x = 7$

14. $14 + s$ when $s = 12$

15. $\frac{y}{8}$ when $y = 40$

16. $t - 3$ when $t = 11$

17. $a + 19$ when $a = 13$

18. $10p$ when $p = 16$

19. Laundromat The cost of doing 4 loads of laundry can be found by evaluating the expression $4(w + d)$, where w is the cost of doing one load in the washer and d is the cost of doing one load in the dryer. Find the cost of doing 4 loads of laundry when $w = \$2$ and $d = \$1$. *(Lessons 1.2, 1.4)*

Write the product as a power. *(Lesson 1.3)*

20. $12 \cdot 12 \cdot 12 \cdot 12$ **21.** $9 \cdot 9$ **22.** $3 \cdot 3 \cdot 3 \cdot 3 \cdot 3 \cdot 3$ **23.** $15 \cdot 15 \cdot 15$

Evaluate the power. *(Lesson 1.3)*

24. 10^2 **25.** 7^3 **26.** 2^5 **27.** 3^5

Evaluate the expression. *(Lesson 1.4)*

28. $18 - 2 - 6 + 5$ **29.** $12 + 3 \cdot 6$ **30.** $50 - 2 \cdot 10 + 4$ **31.** $\dfrac{5 \cdot 6}{6 + 9}$

32. $3(15 \div 3)^2$ **33.** $14 + 4^2 \div 2$ **34.** $\dfrac{7 + 8}{9 - 4}$ **35.** $4 + 3(7 + 5)$

36. Target Game You are playing a game in which you try to hit a target with bean bags. You get 10 points for landing on a red zone and 5 points for landing on a blue zone. Write and evaluate an expression to find the total points you score for landing on a red zone 6 times and landing on a blue zone 4 times. *(Lesson 1.4)*

Solve the equation using mental math. *(Lesson 1.5)*

37. $x + 9 = 13$ **38.** $36 = 14 + a$ **39.** $w - 10 = 11$ **40.** $8 - r = 2$

41. $25 = 5t$ **42.** $11p = 110$ **43.** $\dfrac{m}{4} = 7$ **44.** $\dfrac{32}{n} = 16$

45. Ferry Boats You take a ferry boat a distance of 80 miles to get to an island. If the trip takes you 2 hours, at about what speed does the ferry boat travel? *(Lesson 1.5)*

Find the perimeter and the area of the rectangle or square with the given dimensions. *(Lesson 1.6)*

46. $l = 16$ feet, $w = 3$ feet   **47.** $l = 10$ meters, $w = 7$ meters   **48.** $s = 20$ inches

49. Rugs The area of a rectangular rug is 24 square feet. The perimeter of the rug is 20 feet. Find the length and the width of the rug. *(Lessons 1.6, 1.7)*

50. Karate A community recreation center is organizing karate classes. Each class can have a maximum of 22 people. If there are 130 people who are interested in taking one karate class, how many classes should the recreation center plan to have? *(Lesson 1.7)*

51. Vending Machines You put a dollar into a vending machine to get a $.65 bag of popcorn. How many different combinations of dimes, nickels, and quarters could you receive as change? *(Lesson 1.7)*

Chapter Test

Describe the pattern. Then write the next three numbers.

1. 10, 20, 40, 80, . . .　　　**2.** 99, 88, 77, 66, . . .　　　**3.** 16, 21, 26, 31, . . .

4. Wallpaper Describe the wallpaper pattern. Then draw the next three figures.

Evaluate the expression for the given value of the variable.

5. $28 - a$ when $a = 7$　　　**6.** $n + 14$ when $n = 19$　　　**7.** $8y$ when $y = 15$

Evaluate the power.

8. 4^3　　　**9.** 12^2　　　**10.** 5^5

Evaluate the expression.

11. $20 + 16 \div 4$　　　**12.** $15 - 3(5 - 3)^2$　　　**13.** $4 \cdot 8 + 8 \div 4$

14. Shopping A clothing store is having a sale. If you buy one sweater, you can get another sweater of equal or lesser value for half price. You buy a $38 sweater and a $42 sweater. Evaluate the expression $42 + 38 \div 2$ to find the total cost of the sweaters.

Solve the equation using mental math.

15. $13 + q = 27$　　　**16.** $7 = \dfrac{56}{w}$　　　**17.** $10r = 1000$

Find the perimeter and the area of the rectangle or square with the given dimensions.

18. $l = 7$ inches, $w = 5$ inches　　**19.** $s = 14$ centimeters　　　**20.** $l = 9$ meters, $w = 4$ meters

21. Arts and Crafts You have several rectangular photographs that are each 7 inches long and 5 inches wide. If you have 80 inches of yarn, how many photographs can you put yarn borders around?

22. Running A runner is following the training schedule below. How many miles do you predict the runner will run on each of the next 3 days?

Day	Su	M	T	W	Th	F	S	Su	M	T	W	Th
Miles	0	3	5	3	0	3	6	3	0	3	7	3

Chapter Standardized Test

Test-Taking Strategy Eliminate answer choices you know are wrong. This may improve your chances of answering a question correctly.

Multiple Choice

1. What is the next number in the pattern 5000, 1000, 200, 40, . . . ?

   A. 5   **B.** 8   **C.** 10   **D.** 20

2. What is the next figure in the pattern?

   F.   **G.**   **H.**   **I.**
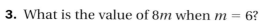

3. What is the value of $8m$ when $m = 6$?

   A. 2   **B.** 14   **C.** 24   **D.** 48

4. Which expression is *not* equivalent to the expression 5^2?

   F. 10   **G.** $5 \cdot 5$

   H. 25   **I.** 5 squared

5. What is the value of b^6 when $b = 2$?

   A. 8   **B.** 12   **C.** 32   **D.** 64

6. What is the first step in evaluating the expression $4 \cdot 5 + 2^3 - 18 \div 3$?

   F. Multiply 4 and 5.   **G.** Add 5 and 2.

   H. Evaluate 2^3.   **I.** Divide 18 by 3.

7. What is the value of the expression $6 \div 3 + 8(4 + 6)^2$?

   A. 1000   **B.** 802   **C.** 322   **D.** 100

8. What is the solution of the equation $3x = 36$?

   F. 12   **G.** 33   **H.** 39   **I.** 108

9. Which equation does *not* have 4 as a solution?

   A. $p + 5 = 9$ **B.** $14 - p = 10$

   C. $\dfrac{20}{p} = 4$ **D.** $9p = 36$

10. If you drive at a constant speed of 50 miles per hour, how long will it take you to travel 200 miles?

   F. 4 minutes   **G.** 2 hours

   H. 4 hours   **I.** 10 hours

11. A rectangle has a length of 8 inches and a width of 6 inches. What is its area?

   A. 14 in.^{2} **B.** 28 in.^{2}

   C. 48 in.^{2} **D.** 64 in.^{2}

Short Response

12. You buy 2 notebooks that cost $2 each, 4 pens that cost $3 each, and 2 erasers that cost $1 each. If you give the cashier $20, how much change will you receive?

Extended Response

13. You are trying to fit your family's home videos on two 2 hour videotapes. The table lists the lengths in minutes of the video clips. Which clips would you put on each videotape? Is there more than one way you could do this?

Clip	Minutes
A	40
B	60
C	10
D	80
E	20
F	30

2 Decimal Operations

BEFORE

In previous courses you've...

- Added, subtracted, multiplied, and divided whole numbers
- Compared whole numbers

Now

In Chapter 2 you'll study...

- Comparing and rounding decimals
- Adding, subtracting, multiplying, and dividing decimals
- Scientific notation
- The metric system

WHY?

So you can solve real-world problems about...

- earthquakes, p. 54
- gymnastics, p. 57
- comets, p. 66
- panda bears, p. 88

Internet Preview
CLASSZONE.COM

- eEdition Plus Online
- eWorkbook Plus Online
- eTutorial Plus Online
- State Test Practice
- More Examples

Chapter Warm-Up Game

Review skills you need for this chapter in this game. Work with a partner.

Key Skills:
- Comparing whole numbers
- Adding whole numbers

MALL MATH

MATERIALS

- *Mall Math* game board
- 1 number cube
- 2 place markers

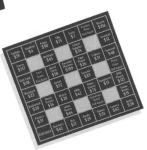

PREPARE Each player puts a place marker on the ENTRANCE space. Players take turns. On your turn, follow the steps on the next page.

Movie Tickets $16
$28 (Wat...)
Inline Skates $64
Video $33
Books $29
$20 (...ball)
Hat $17
Posters $37
Sneakers $42
Entrance

1. **ROLL** the number cube and move that many spaces. You cannot move diagonally or pass through the empty spaces.

HOW TO WIN The first player to spend at least $500 wins.

2. **BUY** the item in the space you have landed on. Cross out that space on the board. Players may land on that space on later turns, but they cannot purchase the item again.

3. **KEEP** a running tally of your spending by adding the price of the new item to your previous total.

42
+17
59

Stop *and* Think

1. **Writing** Suppose you are at the mall entrance. Describe how you could spend at least $500 in only 4 rolls. What would the rolls have to be, and what items would you buy?

2. **Critical Thinking** Suppose you are on the goldfish space and you know that your next two rolls will be a 2 and then a 3. Where should you move on each roll in order to spend the greatest possible amount of money on the next two turns?

CHAPTER 2 Getting Ready to Learn

Review What You Need to Know

Using Vocabulary **Copy and complete using a review word.**

Word Watch

Review Words

digit, p. 681
number line, p. 682
less than, p. 682
greater than, p. 682
round, p. 683
dividend, p. 690
divisor, p. 690
quotient, p. 690
estimate, p. 691

1. In the division equation $42 \div 6 = 7$, 42 is called the _?_, 6 is called the _?_, and 7 is called the _?_.

2. If you _?_ 1723 to the nearest hundred, you get 1700.

3. The _?_ in the tens' place of the number 637 is 3.

Round the number to the place value of the red digit. *(p. 683)*

4. 845   5. 12,047   6. 739,022   7. 2,993,438

Estimate the sum or difference. *(pp. 691–692)*

8. $\begin{array}{r} 905 \\ 782 \\ + 179 \\ \hline \end{array}$ 9. $\begin{array}{r} 54,036 \\ 13,987 \\ + 32,053 \\ \hline \end{array}$ 10. $\begin{array}{r} 2874 \\ - 1951 \\ \hline \end{array}$ 11. $\begin{array}{r} 26,780 \\ - 17,702 \\ \hline \end{array}$

Evaluate the expression. *(p. 18)*

12. $14 + 6 \times 7$ 13. $12 \div 2 + 4$ 14. $2 \times 4 + 5^2$ 15. $5 - 2 \times 2$

You should include material that appears on a notebook like this in your own notes.

Know How to Take Notes

Previewing the Chapter *Before you begin a chapter, make a list of the chapter's lesson titles in your notebook. Write down at least one fact you predict you will need to know in order to understand each lesson.*

Lesson 2.1 Comparing, Ordering, and Rounding Decimals

Prediction: I will need to know about place value.

Make similar predictions about the other lessons in Chapter 2.

This notetaking strategy will help you connect new topics with more familiar topics. It may make new concepts easier to understand.

GOAL
Use models to write equivalent decimals.

MATERIALS
· base-ten pieces

Modeling Decimals

You can use base-ten pieces to model decimals. The three types of base-ten pieces and their values are shown below.

1 one

1 tenth

1 hundredth

Explore **Model 26 hundredths using the fewest number of base-ten pieces possible.**

1 Model **26 hundredths**.

2 Use the fact that **10 hundredths** are equal to **1 tenth**.

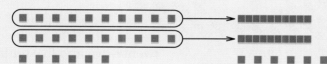

So, **26 hundredths = 2 tenths** and **6 hundredths**.

Your turn now **Copy and complete the statement. Use base-ten pieces as needed.**

1. 4 tenths = _?_ hundredths
2. 2 ones = _?_ tenths
3. 30 hundredths = _?_ tenths
4. 11 tenths = _?_ hundredths
5. 17 hundredths = _?_ tenth and _?_ hundredths
6. 25 tenths = _?_ ones and _?_ tenths

Stop and Think

7. **Compare** Explain how to use base-ten pieces to compare 74 hundredths and 8 tenths. Which is greater?

Comparing, Ordering, and Rounding Decimals

BEFORE	Now	WHY?
You compared, ordered, and rounded whole numbers.	You'll compare, order, and round decimals.	So you can order soapbox derby times, as in Ex. 34.

In the Real World

Word Watch

decimal, p. 52

Olympic Games In the 1968 Summer Olympics, Irena Szewinska of Poland won the women's 200 meter dash with a time of 22.5 seconds. In 1996, Marie-Jose Perec of France won the event with a time of 22.12 seconds. Whose time is faster?

The numbers 22.5 and 22.12 are *decimals*. A **decimal** is a number that is written using the base-ten place value system where a decimal point separates the ones' and tenths' digits. Each place value is 10 times the place value to its right.

Decimals and Place Value

hundred thousands	ten thousands	thousands	hundreds	tens	ones	tenths	hundredths	thousandths	ten-thousandths	hundred-thousandths	
				2	2	5					twenty-two and five tenths
				2	2	1	2				twenty-two and twelve hundredths

To compare decimals, write the numbers in a column, lining up the decimal points. If needed, write zeros as placeholders so that all decimals have the same number of digits. Then compare digits from left to right.

EXAMPLE 1 Comparing Decimals

To determine whose time is faster, compare 22.5 and 22.12.

The tens' and ones' digits are the same.

22.50 ← **Write a zero as a placeholder.**
22.12

The tenths' digits are different. 5 > 1, so 22.50 > 22.12.

ANSWER Because 22.5 > 22.12, Perec's time is faster.

Marie-Jose Perec

Your turn now Copy and complete the statement using <, >, or =.

1. 20.05 _?_ 20.1   **2.** 7.7 _?_ 7.70   **3.** 5.701 _?_ 5.699

EXAMPLE 2 Ordering Decimals

Order 2.11, 2.21, 2, 2.06, and 2.24 from least to greatest.

On a number line, mark tenths between 2.0 and 2.3. Mark hundredths by dividing each tenth into ten equal parts. Then graph each number.

ANSWER From least to greatest, the numbers are 2, 2.06, 2.11, 2.21, and 2.24.

with Solving

Remember that numbers on a number line increase from left to right.

Rounding Decimals

To round a decimal to a given place value, look at the digit in the place to the right.

• If the digit is less than 5, round down.

• If the digit is 5 or greater, round up.

EXAMPLE 3 Rounding a Decimal

Round 7.126 to the nearest tenth.

7.126

You want to round to the nearest tenth.

Because the hundredths' digit is less than 5, round down and drop the remaining digits.

ANSWER The decimal 7.126 rounded to the nearest tenth is 7.1.

Your turn now Order the numbers from least to greatest.

4. 3.84, 4.4, 4.83, 3.48, 4.38   **5.** 5.71, 5.8, 5.68, 5.79, 5.6

6. Round 34.0152 to the nearest hundredth.

Getting Ready to Practice

Vocabulary **Match the number with the place value of the red digit.**

1. 27.404

2. 3.579

3. 4.128

4. 15.26

A. ones

B. tenths

C. hundredths

D. thousandths

5. Name the numbers represented by the labeled points on the number line.

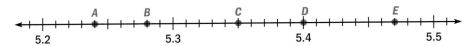

Copy and complete the statement using <, >, or =.

6. 6.5 _?_ 6.45

7. 12.8 _?_ 12.801

8. 30.650 _?_ 30.65

Round 21.6804 to the specified place value.

9. ones

10. tenths

11. hundredths

12. thousandths

13. **Earthquakes** Moment magnitude is a measure used by scientists to describe an earthquake's power. Order the moment magnitudes from least to greatest.

Earthquake Location	Year	Moment Magnitude
Ecuador	1906	8.8
Chile	1960	9.5
Alaska, U.S.	1965	8.7

Map showing an earthquake fault

Practice and Problem Solving

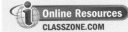

with Homework

Example	Exercises
1	18–27
2	28–34
3	35–42

Online Resources
CLASSZONE.COM
· More Examples
· eTutorial Plus

Match the decimal with its verbal description.

14. 7.086

15. 7.86

16. 78.06

17. 70.86

A. Seven and eighty-six hundredths

B. Seventy and eighty-six hundredths

C. Seventy-eight and six hundredths

D. Seven and eighty-six thousandths

Copy and complete the statement using <, >, or =.

18. 3.2 _?_ 2.3

19. 7.08 _?_ 7.03

20. 0.19 _?_ 0.20

21. 8.49 _?_ 8.48

22. 10.01 _?_ 10.10

23. 0.8 _?_ 1.3

24. 13.20 _?_ 13.2

25. 0.607 _?_ 0.66

26. 25.024 _?_ 26.023

■ **Soapbox Derby**

A soapbox derby is a downhill competition in which kids race homemade cars. If 3 cars race at a time, and 84 cars are entered in the derby, how many groups of 3 cars must there be?

27. Tents You and a friend are taking an overnight backpacking trip. You are both carrying lightweight tents. Your tent weighs 3.5 pounds, and your friend's tent weighs 3.25 pounds. Whose tent weighs less?

Order the numbers from least to greatest.

28. 1.2, 3.2, 0.2, 0.9   **29.** 6.6, 6.2, 6.8, 6.5   **30.** 2.2, 1.1, 2.01, 1.02

31. 0.86, 0.03, 0.91, 0.2   **32.** 4.3, 4.03, 4.27, 4.23   **33.** 8.56, 7.65, 8.65, 7.63

34. Soapbox Derby The winning times in each division for a soapbox derby are 29.15 seconds, 29.78 seconds, and 29.74 seconds. Order the times from fastest to slowest.

Round the decimal as specified.

35. 17.6 (nearest one)   **36.** 32.09 (nearest tenth)

37. 5.55 (nearest tenth)   **38.** 12.0092 (nearest thousandth)

39. 2.2949 (nearest hundredth)   **40.** 0.73 (nearest one)

41. 0.009 (nearest tenth)   **42.** 9.9999 (nearest hundredth)

43. Critical Thinking Write two numbers that round to 5.7.

Describe the pattern. Then write the next two numbers.

44. 10, 1, 0.1, 0.01, . . .   **45.** 2.01, 2.002, 2.0003, 2.00004, . . .

46. Challenge Write two numbers that are between 4.57 and 4.59.

Mixed Review

Evaluate the expression. *(Lesson 1.4)*

47. $5 + 12 - 2$ **48.** $4 \cdot 2 \cdot 3^2$ **49.** $52 - 12 \cdot 3$

50. One box of candy holds 50 pieces. How many boxes of candy do you need to make 16 goodie bags, each with 12 pieces of candy? *(Lesson 1.7)*

Basic Skills **Estimate the sum.**

51. $39 + 71 + 57$ **52.** $427 + 262 + 105$ **53.** $962 + 105 + 890$

Test-Taking Practice

54. Multiple Choice Which statement is true?

   A. $4.59 < 4.5$ **B.** $7.41 > 7.401$ **C.** $1.09 < 1.081$ **D.** $6.33 > 6.333$

55. Short Response Explain in words how to round 19.967 to the nearest tenth.

Make a List
Draw a Diagram
Act it Out
Work Backward
Estimate
Look for a Pattern
Make a Table

Estimate

Problem You are going bowling with friends, and you want to know how much money you should bring. You plan on bowling three games, renting shoes, and buying a slice of pizza and a bottle of soda. Use the prices in the flyer to find how much money should you bring to cover your costs.

Lakeside **Bowling Alley**

BOWLING $2.85 each game
SHOE RENTAL $1.90
PIZZA $2.75
SODA $1.25

① Read and Understand

Read the problem carefully.

- You know all of the individual costs.

- You want to determine how much money you should bring with you to cover these costs.

② Make a Plan

Decide on a strategy to use.

Because you only need to cover your costs, an estimate of the amount of money is sufficient. You can round each cost up to the next dollar and find the sum of the rounded costs.

③ Solve the Problem

Reread the problem and use estimation.

Round each cost up to the next dollar. Then find the sum of all of the costs.

Actual Cost	Rounded Cost	Sum of Rounded Costs
Bowling: $2.85 each game	Round up to $3.	$3 \times \$3 = \$9$
Shoe rental: $1.90	Round up to $2.	$1 \times \$2 = \$2$
Pizza: $2.75	Round up to $3.	$1 \times \$3 = \$3$
Soda: $1.25	Round up to $2.	$1 \times \$2 = \underline{\$2}$
		$16

ANSWER You should bring $16 to cover your costs.

④ Look Back

Because all of the costs were rounded *up*, $16 is an *overestimate*, so you have more than enough money to cover your costs.

Practice the Strategy

Use the strategy *estimate*.

1. **Flowers** You have $15 to spend at a flower shop. You want to buy a bouquet of tulips for $6.99 and a basket of assorted flowers for $7.50. Do you have enough money to buy both bouquets? Explain.

2. **Gymnastics** A gymnast's score in the women's all-around is calculated by adding her scores from four individual events. Prior to today's competition, Ann's personal best all-around score was 32.625. Her individual event results for today's competition are shown below. Is her all-around score in today's competition greater than her previous personal best score? Explain.

Event	Score
Balance beam	7.731
Floor exercise	8.625
Uneven bars	8.812
Vault	9.000

3. **Game Show** Contestants on a television game show are asked to choose 2 grocery items for which the sum of the prices is closest to $10. Without being told the prices, Jim chooses the batteries and cookies, and Cheryl chooses the detergent and cookies. Who is the winner? Explain.

Item	Batteries	Cookies	Detergent	Soup
Price	$4.59	$3.19	$6.29	$2.39

4. **Race Cars** You and a friend are racing remote controlled race cars on an indoor course. Your time for the course is 83.2 seconds. Your friend's time is 79.8 seconds. Before the race, your friend said that she was going to beat you by at least 5 seconds. Was she right? Explain.

Mixed Problem Solving

Use any strategy to solve the problem.

5. **Coins** You have 7 coins worth a total of $.72. You have at least one of each of the following coins: penny, nickel, dime, quarter. How many of each coin do you have?

6. **Class Survey** You take a survey of 30 students in your grade. In the survey, 12 students say they like math class, 13 students say they like science class, and 8 students say they like both math and science class. How many students do not like either math or science class?

7. **Movie Tickets** You plan to see a movie that starts at 7:10 P.M. You want to get to the theater 20 minutes early to buy tickets, and it takes 15 minutes to get to the theater. At what time should you leave your house?

8. **Video Game** In a video game, you need to score 50 points to pass Level 1, an additional 70 points to pass Level 2, an additional 90 points to pass Level 3, and so on. How many total points have you scored if you have just reached Level 7?

Adding and Subtracting Decimals

BEFORE ▶ **Now** **WHY?**

You added and subtracted whole numbers.

You'll add and subtract decimals.

So you can compare the areas of cornfield mazes, as in Ex. 24.

Activity You can use base-ten pieces to model decimal addition and subtraction.

1 Model the sum of 0.76 and 0.58 using base-ten pieces.

0.76   0.58

2 Combine and group the pieces.

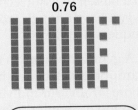

3 Trade **10 tenths** for **1 one** and **10 hundredths** for **1 tenth.** The sum of 0.76 and 0.58 is 1.34.

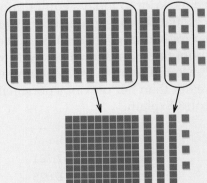

1.34

Use base-ten pieces to find the sum or difference.

1. 2.2 + 1.85   **2.** 2.77 − 1.47   **3.** 1.26 − 1.08

Use a vertical format to add or subtract decimals. Begin by lining up the decimal points. Then add or subtract as you would with whole numbers. Be sure to write the decimal point in the answer.

EXAMPLE 1 Adding and Subtracting Decimals

a. 6.047 + 13.46

$$
\begin{array}{r}
6.047 \\
+\ 13.460 \\
\hline
19.507
\end{array}
$$
←— **Write zero as a placeholder.**

b. 9 − 5.28

$$
\begin{array}{r}
9.00 \\
-\ 5.28 \\
\hline
3.72
\end{array}
$$
←— **Write zeros as placeholders.**

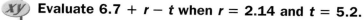

Watch Out!

Don't forget to add and subtract from left to right when evaluating expressions horizontally.

EXAMPLE 2 Evaluating a Variable Expression

Evaluate $6.7 + r - t$ when $r = 2.14$ and $t = 5.2$.

$$6.7 + r - t = 6.7 + 2.14 - 5.2 \quad \text{Substitute 2.14 for } r \text{ and 5.2 for } t.$$
$$= 8.84 - 5.2 \quad \text{Add.}$$
$$= 3.64 \quad \text{Subtract.}$$

Estimation When you do not need to find an exact sum, you can estimate. One type of estimation is *front-end estimation*. To use **front-end estimation** to estimate a sum, add the front-end digits, estimate the sum of the remaining digits, and then add the results.

EXAMPLE 3 Estimating a Sum

Video Games For your birthday you receive a $25 gift certificate. You want to buy 3 used video games whose prices are shown. Can you buy all 3 games using the gift certificate?

Solution

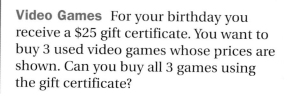

(1 Add the front-end digits: the dollars.

$8.79
$7.29
+ $7.89
———
$22

(2 Estimate the sum of the remaining digits: the cents.

$8.79
$7.29 → $1
+ $7.89 → $1
———
$2

(3 Add the results.

$22
+ $2
———
$24

ANSWER The estimated sum is less than $25, so you can buy all three games using the gift certificate.

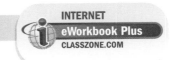

Getting Ready to Practice

1. **Vocabulary** Explain how to use front-end estimation to add decimals.

Find the sum or difference.

2. $6.04 + 12.51$ 3. $5.8 - 2.4$ 4. $16.5 - 3.675$ 5. $47.85 + 5.741$

6. **Guided Problem Solving** Is $20 enough money to buy the art supplies listed?

> Watercolor paints $8.69
> Paint brushes $3.78
> Canvas $6.32

    (1 Add the front-end digits: $8 + 3 + 6$.

    (2 Estimate the sum of the remaining digits: $0.69 + 0.78 + 0.32$.

    (3 Add the results. Is the sum greater than or less than $20?

Practice and Problem Solving

with Homework

Example	Exercises
1	13-21, 37-42
2	25-28, 43-45
3	29-34

Online Resources
CLASSZONE.COM
· More Examples
· eTutorial Plus

Write the decimal in expanded form. For example, 3.24 in expanded form is 3 + 0.2 + 0.04.

7. 6.912 8. 523.974 9. 43.07

Decide Would you *add* or *subtract* to find the answer? Explain.

10. How much does it cost to buy a pair of jeans and a shirt?

11. How much warmer is today's high temperature than yesterday's high?

12. How much more does a cheeseburger cost than a hamburger?

Find the sum or difference. Use estimation to check your answer.

13. $15.8 + 7.6$ 14. $124.6 + 47.01$ 15. $53.24 + 14.023$

16. $0.79 + 14.55$ 17. $90.2 - 7.5$ 18. $24.98 - 3.3$

19. $4.29 - 3.456$ 20. $168.42 - 5.608$ 21. $900 - 15.7$

22. **Stilts** Jared is 2.75 meters tall while on stilts and 1.6 meters tall without stilts. How far off the ground do the stilts raise Jared?

23. **Find the Error** Describe and correct the error in finding the sum of 3.8504 and 625.

$$\begin{array}{r} 3.8504 \\ +\ \ \ 625 \\ \hline 3.9129 \end{array}$$

Cornfield maze in Lindon, Utah

24. Cornfield Mazes The first cornfield maze, grown in Annville, Pennsylvania, in 1993, covered 3.3 acres. The largest cornfield maze, grown in Lindon, Utah, in 1999, covered 12.6 acres. How many acres larger was the Lindon maze than the Annville maze?

xy **Algebra** Evaluate the expression when $y = 26.3$ and $z = 12.28$.

25. $20.1 + y$　　**26.** $34 + z$　　**27.** $y - z$　　**28.** $30 - y + z$

Estimate the sum or difference using front-end estimation.

29. $5.24 + 9.79$　　**30.** $3.44 + 8.38$　　**31.** $4.11 + 5.90 + 8.02$

32. $5.78 + 9 + 2.2$　　**33.** $8.75 - 5.67$　　**34.** $6.6 - 4.45$

35. Rainfall A city had 3.57 inches of rain in April, 7.30 inches of rain in May, and 5.14 inches of rain in June. During this three-month period, did the city have more than 15 inches of rain? Explain why an estimate is sufficient in answering the question.

36. Critical Thinking When is the sum of two decimals a whole number? When is the difference of two decimals a whole number? Explain.

Evaluate the expression.

37. $467.2 + 5.63 + 11$　　**38.** $27 - 3.204 - 10.8$　　**39.** $8.55 + 20.4 - 15$

40. $0.032 + 0.29 + 1$　　**41.** $26.17 - 9.002 + 1.9$　　**42.** $3.876 + 2.2 - 4.10$

xy **Algebra** Evaluate the expression when $k = 5.874$ and $m = 123.1$.

43. $m - k - 6.401$　　**44.** $140 - (k + m)$　　**45.** $m - 6.78 - k + 28.3$

46. Directions Internet driving directions from Washington D.C.'s National Zoo to the White House Visitor Center are shown below. How much shorter is the shortest route than the fastest route?

Fastest Route	
Directions	**Distance**
Go SE on Connecticut Ave. NW	2.1 miles
Connecticut Ave. NW becomes 17th St. NW	0.2 mile
Turn left onto H St. NW	0.4 mile
Turn right onto 14th St. NW	0.3 mile
Turn right onto Pennsylvania Ave. NW	0.0 mile

Shortest Route	
Directions	**Distance**
Go SE on Connecticut Ave. NW	2.1 miles
Connecticut Ave. NW becomes 17th St. NW	0.5 mile
Turn left onto E St. NW	0.3 mile
E St. NW becomes Pennsylvania Ave. NW	0.0 mile

Challenge **Solve the equation using mental math.**

47. $w + 1.5 = 5$　　**48.** $6 + x = 8.8$　　**49.** $y - 2.4 = 0.6$　　**50.** $0.82 - z = 0.7$

Mixed Review

Order the numbers from least to greatest. *(Lesson 2.1)*

51. 2.46, 4.26, 4.06, 2.64, 2.42

52. 13.8, 8.3, 13.08, 8.31, 8.83

Choose a Strategy Use a strategy from the list to solve the following problem. Explain your choice of strategy.

> **Problem Solving Strategies**
> - Look for a Pattern
> - Draw a Diagram
> - Work Backward

53. On Monday, Jeff sold 3 raffle tickets. On Tuesday, he sold 6 tickets. On Wednesday, he sold 9 tickets. If the pattern continued through Friday, how many tickets did Jeff sell during the week?

Basic Skills **Find the product.**

54. 15×23

55. 21×5

56. 7×19

57. 11×29

Test-Taking Practice

58. Multiple Choice Which of the following numbers, when added to 8.43 using front-end estimation, results in an estimated sum of 15?

A. 6.59   **B.** 7.59   **C.** 8.04   **D.** 8.45

59. Multiple Choice What is the value of the expression
$15.2 + 9.8 - 7.12 - 2.07$?

F. 0.1581   **G.** 1.581   **H.** 15.81   **I.** 158.1

BRAIN GAME

Decode the Riddle

Find the values of **M**, **T**, **C**, **F**, and **Y** that make the sum and difference correct. Then replace the number in each box with its letter to find the answer to the riddle below.

$$
\begin{array}{r}
3.1\,T5 \\
+\ M.TC2 \\
\hline
11.61\,C
\end{array}
\qquad
\begin{array}{r}
0.3\,F1F \\
-\ 0.2C0F \\
\hline
0.091\,Y
\end{array}
$$

Why did the cookie go to the hospital?

I	4		6	E	L	4		7	R	U	8	8	0

Multiplying Decimals

LESSON 2.3

BEFORE	Now	WHY?
You multiplied whole numbers.	You'll multiply decimals.	So you can find the area of an air hockey table surface, as in Ex. 28.

Word Watch

leading digit, p. 63

You can use graph paper to model decimal multiplication. Here is a model of the product of 0.7 and 0.3.

Because 21 of the 100 squares are shaded, $0.7 \times 0.3 = 0.21$.

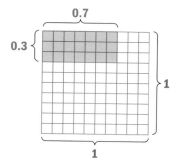

Multiplying Decimals

Words Multiply decimals as you would whole numbers. Then place the decimal point in the product. The number of decimal places in the product is equal to the sum of the number of decimal places in the factors.

Numbers $0.7 \times 0.3 = 0.21$

EXAMPLE 1 **Multiplying Decimals**

$$
\begin{array}{r}
5.82 \\
\times\ 0.41 \\
\hline
582 \\
2328 \\
\hline
2.3862
\end{array}
$$

2 decimal places
+ 2 decimal places

4 decimal places

with Notetaking

In previewing this lesson, you may have noticed that you need to know how to multiply whole numbers. Writing down what you know about multiplying whole numbers may help you understand how to multiply decimals.

Checking Reasonableness To check that the product in Example 1 is reasonable, round each factor to the place value of the *leading digit*, then multiply. The **leading digit** of a number is the first nonzero digit.

5.82 ⟶ 6 **Round to the nearest whole number.**

0.41 ⟶ 0.4 **Round to the nearest tenth.**

Because $6 \times 0.4 = 2.4$, the product in Example 1 is reasonable.

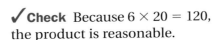

EXAMPLE 2 Multiplying Decimals

a.

$$\begin{array}{r} 6.45 \\ \times\ \ 18 \\ \hline 5160 \\ 645\ \ \ \\ \hline 116.10 \end{array}$$

2 decimal places
+ 0 decimal places

2 decimal places

> After you place the decimal point, you can drop any zeros at the end of an answer.

b.

$$\begin{array}{r} 1.273 \\ \times\ \ 0.06 \\ \hline 0.07638 \end{array}$$

3 decimal places
+ 2 decimal places

5 decimal places

> Write a zero before the 7 as a placeholder so that the number has five decimal places.

ANSWER $6.45 \times 18 = 116.1$

✓ **Check** Because $6 \times 20 = 120$, the product is reasonable.

ANSWER $1.273 \times 0.06 = 0.07638$

✓ **Check** Because $1 \times 0.06 = 0.06$, the product is reasonable.

Nature

Your turn now Find the product. Then check that your answer is reasonable.

1. 1.4×7.2 **2.** 0.98×0.21 **3.** 2.351×1.6

EXAMPLE 3 Multiplying Decimals to Find Area

Central Park Central Park is a rectangular park about 2.5 miles long and about 0.5 mile wide. What is the area of Central Park?

Solution

$A = lw$ Write formula for area of a rectangle.

$ = 2.5(0.5)$ Substitute 2.5 for l and 0.5 for w.

$ = 1.25$ Multiply.

ANSWER The area of Central Park is about 1.25 square miles.

■ **Central Park**

Central Park, in Manhattan, New York, is one of the world's most famous parks. If you walked around the entire perimeter of the 2.5 mile by 0.5 mile park, how far would you walk?

Your turn now Find the area of the rectangle.

4.
9.42 in.
2 in.

5.
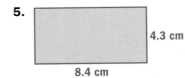
4.3 cm
8.4 cm

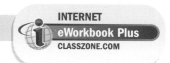

Getting Ready to Practice

1. Vocabulary What is the leading digit in the decimal 0.00462?

Find the product.

2. 0.4×0.6 **3.** 0.9×0.91 **4.** 0.8×3 **5.** 0.7×0.01

6. Find the Error Describe and correct the error in finding the product of 6.21 and 0.04.

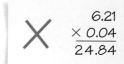

7. Nail Polish Laura has $10 to spend on nail polish. Including tax, each bottle of nail polish costs $2.89. Can Laura buy 3 bottles of nail polish? Explain.

Practice and Problem Solving

8. Writing How is placing the decimal point in decimal addition different than in decimal multiplication?

Find the product. Then check that your answer is reasonable.

9. 3.4×6.5 **10.** 9.3×8.1 **11.** 0.06×0.6 **12.** 0.05×8

13. 78.1×4.4 **14.** 3.9×21.8 **15.** 0.14×0.09 **16.** 0.086×0.007

17. 94.2×0.14 **18.** 0.045×1.20 **19.** 25×0.052 **20.** 16.34×1.001

Estimation Estimate the product by rounding each factor to the place value of the leading digit.

21. 3.45×90.2 **22.** 0.32×2.8 **23.** 4.57×199.4 **24.** 18.23×4.7

Geometry Find the area of the rectangle.

25.

3 mm

4.5 mm

26.

2.25 ft

8.23 ft

27.

8.76 yd

6.04 yd

28. Air Hockey The surface of a rectangular air hockey table is 7.04 feet long and 3.7 feet wide. Find the area of the surface of the air hockey table.

HELP with Homework

Example	Exercises
1	9–24
2	9–24
3	25–28

Online Resources
CLASSZONE.COM

· More Examples
· eTutorial Plus

 Algebra Evaluate the expression when $p = 2.29$ and $q = 0.034$.

29. $7.654p$ **30.** $4.41q$ **31.** pq **32.** $1.12pq$

33. Critical Thinking Copy and complete the table of products below. Then explain the pattern in the products.

×	0.001	0.01	0.1	1	10	100	1000
10.2	0.0102	0.102	?	?	?	?	?
5.31	?	?	?	?	?	?	?
0.006	?	?	?	?	?	?	?

34. Comets Halley's Comet takes about 23.06 times longer than Encke's Comet to orbit the Sun. Encke's Comet takes about 3.3 years. About how long does Halley's Comet take to orbit the Sun? Round to the nearest tenth.

Evaluate the expression.

35. $12.54 \times 0.023 \times 11$ **36.** $9.9 \times 9.9 \times 9.9$ **37.** $35.054 \times 12.3 \times 2.01$

38. $10.72 + 6.8 \times 9.08$ **39.** $0.34 \times (7.4 - 3.19)$ **40.** $18.62 - 1.04 \times 12.7$

41. Challenge What number(s) greater than zero can you multiply 2.3 by to make the product less than 2.3? greater than 2.3? equal to 2.3? Explain your reasoning.

Mixed Review

Solve the equation using mental math. *(Lesson 1.5)*

42. $d + 8 = 17$ **43.** $18 - f = 12$ **44.** $5g = 20$ **45.** $72 \div h = 9$

Find the sum or difference. *(Lesson 2.2)*

46. $34.2 + 84.6$ **47.** $424.1 + 63.5$ **48.** $630 - 25.7$ **49.** $24.42 - 9.69$

Basic Skills **Find the quotient.**

50. $156 \div 4$ **51.** $357 \div 7$ **52.** $96 \div 6$ **53.** $1752 \div 12$

Test-Taking Practice

54. Multiple Choice A marathon is 26.2 miles. If you average 8.5 minutes per mile, in how many minutes can you run a marathon?

A. 34.7 **B.** 222.7 **C.** 347 **D.** 2227

55. Multiple Choice What is the product of 7.24 and 0.9?

F. 6.516 **G.** 8.14 **H.** 65.16 **I.** 81.4

Dividing Decimals

BEFORE	▶ Now	WHY?
You divided whole numbers.	You'll divide decimals.	So you can find the price of a trading card, as in Example 3.

Word Watch

compatible numbers, p. 67

In the Real World

Ticket Prices The cost of 21 tickets to see Blue Man Group is $761.25. How much does each ticket cost?

You can use long division to divide a decimal by a whole number. Divide as with whole numbers. Then line up the decimal points in the quotient and the dividend.

© 2002 Blue Man Group/Photo by James Porto

EXAMPLE 1 Dividing a Decimal by a Whole Number

To find the cost of each ticket as described above, divide 761.25 by 21.

```
        36.25          Divide as you would with whole numbers.
    21)761.25
        63  ↑_____  Line up decimal point in quotient with
        131            decimal point in dividend.
        126
         52
         42
        105
        105
          0            Stop dividing when you get a zero remainder.
```

ANSWER Each ticket costs $36.25.

with Solving

You can also check your answer by multiplying the quotient and the divisor to see if you get the dividend: $36.25 \times 21 = 761.25$

To check the reasonableness of a quotient, use *compatible numbers*. **Compatible numbers** are numbers that make a calculation easier.

21	⟶	20	**Round divisor to place of leading digit.**
761.25	⟶	760	**Round dividend to nearest multiple of 20.**

Because $760 \div 20 = 38$, the quotient in Example 1 is reasonable.

Your turn now Find the quotient. Then check your answer.

1. $20.1 \div 3$ **2.** $64.35 \div 5$ **3.** $380.32 \div 4$

Dividing by a Decimal Notice the pattern in the equations below.

$$6 \div 3 = 2 \qquad 60 \div 30 = 2 \qquad 600 \div 300 = 2 \qquad 6000 \div 3000 = 2$$

The quotient remains the same when the divisor and the dividend are both multiplied by the same power of 10. You can use this fact to divide by a decimal.

Dividing by a Decimal

Words When you divide by a decimal, multiply both the divisor and the dividend by a power of ten that will make the divisor a whole number.

Numbers $12.5\overline{)8.75}$ ⟶ $125\overline{)87.5}^{\,0.7}$

EXAMPLE 2 **Dividing Decimals**

Divide: **a.** $3.804 \div 3.17$ **b.** $8 \div 1.6$ **c.** $0.114 \div 1.9$

Solution

a. $3.17\overline{)3.804}$ To multiply divisor and dividend by 100, move both decimal points 2 places to the right.

$$
\begin{array}{r}
1.2 \\
317\overline{)380.4} \\
\underline{317} \\
63\ 4 \\
\underline{63\ 4} \\
0
\end{array}
$$
— Line up decimal points.

b. $1.6\overline{)8.0}$ To multiply divisor and dividend by 10, move both decimal points 1 place to the right. Write a zero as a placeholder.

$$
\begin{array}{r}
5 \\
16\overline{)80} \\
\underline{80} \\
0
\end{array}
$$

Watch Out!

Don't forget to write zeros as placeholders in the quotient.

c. $1.9\overline{)0.114}$ To multiply divisor and dividend by 10, move both decimal points 1 place to the right.

$$
\begin{array}{r}
0.06 \\
19\overline{)1.14} \\
\underline{1\ 14} \\
0
\end{array}
$$

Find the quotient. Then check your answer.

4. $110.85 \div 1.5$ **5.** $0.234 \div 0.3$ **6.** $50.92 \div 1.9$

7. $7.2 \div 0.12$ **8.** $9 \div 0.3$ **9.** $0.208 \div 5.2$

EXAMPLE 3 **Rounding a Quotient**

Trading Cards You buy a pack of 8 trading cards for $1.49. Find the price of each card. Round to the nearest cent.

HELP with **Solving**

In Example 3, you are rounding to the nearest cent, or hundredth. Divide only until the quotient reaches the thousandths' place. Then round.

Solution

1 Divide $1.49 by 8.

```
      0.186
  8)1.490
      8
      69
      64
      50      Write zero as a placeholder.
      48
       2      Stop dividing when quotient
               reaches the thousandths' place.
```

2 Round the quotient to the nearest cent. $.186 ⟶ $.19

ANSWER The price of each card is about $.19.

2.4 **Exercises**

More Practice, p. 706

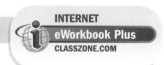

INTERNET
eWorkbook Plus
CLASSZONE.COM

Getting Ready to Practice

1. Vocabulary What two compatible numbers would you use to estimate the quotient $54.2 \div 6.7$?

Find the quotient. Then check your answer.

2. $3.45 \div 15$ **3.** $12.74 \div 2.6$ **4.** $9 \div 7.2$ **5.** $80.84 \div 9.4$

6. $0.201 \div 6.7$ **7.** $1.376 \div 21.5$ **8.** $8.7822 \div 3.57$ **9.** $0.3445 \div 6.5$

10. Knitting You are knitting a scarf using 4 balls of yarn. The yarn costs a total of $24.88. How much does 1 ball of yarn cost?

Practice and Problem Solving

with Homework

Example	Exercises
1	11–25
2	11–25
3	33–41

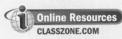

Online Resources
CLASSZONE.COM

· More Examples
· eTutorial Plus

Find the quotient. Then check your answer.

11. $342.4 \div 32$ **12.** $172.2 \div 82$ **13.** $2541.18 \div 41$

14. $1500.96 \div 16$ **15.** $7 \div 1.4$ **16.** $13 \div 6.5$

17. $367.7 \div 3.677$ **18.** $0.245 \div 4.9$ **19.** $1.387 \div 0.19$

20. $3.744 \div 11.7$ **21.** $30.94 \div 9.1$ **22.** $25.08 \div 4.56$

23. $4.03 \div 0.5$ **24.** $0.02997 \div 9.99$ **25.** $0.288 \div 3.6$

26. Number Sense Which quotients are equal? Explain your reasoning.

    A. $22.5 \div 18$ **B.** $22.5 \div 1.8$ **C.** $225 \div 1.8$ **D.** $2.25 \div 0.18$

27. Estimation Copy the division problem at the right. Then use estimation to place the decimal point in the quotient. Explain your reasoning.

$$9.76\overline{)31.232} \quad 32$$

Use compatible numbers to estimate the quotient.

28. $104.26 \div 4.98$ **29.** $1206.47 \div 29.2$ **30.** $1.90 \div 2.007$

31. Car Wash Your class is holding a car wash to raise money for a field trip. You earn \$4.75 for each car you wash. Estimate the number of cars you need to wash to reach your goal of \$750.

32. Critical Thinking If you divide 25.6 by a number and the quotient is 100, is the number *greater than 1* or *less than 1*? Explain your reasoning.

Find the quotient. Round your answer to the nearest hundredth.

33. $0.245 \div 6$ **34.** $12 \div 6.4$ **35.** $68 \div 3.1$

36. $37.857 \div 7.5$ **37.** $9.97 \div 2.9$ **38.** $18.01 \div 3.28$

39. $73.435 \div 3.8$ **40.** $23.5 \div 0.66$ **41.** $10.5 \div 0.37$

(xy) Algebra Evaluate the expression when $x = 8.5$ and $z = 39.1$.

42. $31.535 \div x + z$ **43.** $\dfrac{z}{x} - 0.23$ **44.** $50z \cdot 170.68 \div x$

45. Geometry Use the formula $w = \dfrac{A}{l}$, where w is width, l is length, and A is area, to find the width of the rectangle.

$A = 45.147 \text{ cm}^2$ w

$l = 8.94 \text{ cm}$

46. Decide If you want to find out how many times heavier an alligator is than an iguana, would you *multiply* or *divide*? Explain your reasoning.

Extended Problem Solving **In Exercises 47–49, use the following information.** In 1803, the United States purchased the Louisiana Territory, 828,000 square miles of land west of the Mississippi River, from France for $15,000,000. In 1867, the United States purchased Alaska from Russia for $7,200,000, about $.02 per acre.

47. About how many acres were acquired in the purchase of Alaska?

48. **Measurement** Use the fact that 1 mi^2 = 640 acres to find the number of square miles that were acquired in the purchase of Alaska.

49. **Critical Thinking** How much did the United States pay for each square mile of the Louisiana Territory? for each square mile of Alaska? Which was a better deal? Explain your reasoning.

HELP with **Review**

Need help with describing and extending patterns? See p. 5.

Describe the pattern. Then write the next three numbers.

50. 253.75, 50.75, 10.15, 2.03, . . .   **51.** 46.875, 18.75, 7.5, 3, . . .

52. **Challenge** A rectangle has a length of 12.3 feet and a width of 5.6 feet. Another rectangle has a length of 49.2 feet and a width of 22.4 feet. How many times greater is the perimeter of the larger rectangle than the perimeter of the smaller rectangle? How many times greater is the area of the larger rectangle than the area of the smaller rectangle?

Mixed Review

Evaluate the power. *(Lesson 1.3)*

53. 5^2 **54.** 4^3 **55.** 7^4 **56.** 3^5

Find the product. Then check that your answer is reasonable. *(Lesson 2.3)*

57. 2.14×78.5 **58.** 0.89×43 **59.** 31.2×7.4 **60.** 46.5×0.032

Basic Skills   **Write the number in standard form.**

61. One hundred thirty thousand, seven hundred sixteen

62. Eleven thousand, seven hundred twenty-four

Test-Taking Practice

INTERNET
State Test Practice
CLASSZONE.COM

63. **Multiple Choice** Which quotient is equal to 1.6?

   A. $0.008 \div 0.05$ **B.** $8 \div 0.05$ **C.** $0.8 \div 0.05$ **D.** $0.08 \div 0.05$

64. **Multiple Choice** What is the value of the expression $2.4 + 5.6 \div 0.02$?

   F. 4.282   **G.** 228.4   **H.** 282.4   **I.** 400

Notebook Review

Review the vocabulary definitions in your notebook.

Copy the review examples in your notebook. Then complete the exercises.

Check Your Definitions

decimal, p. 52

front-end estimation, p. 59

leading digit, p. 63

compatible numbers, p. 67

Use Your Vocabulary

1. Copy and complete: A(n) _?_ is a number that is written using the base-ten place value system.

2.1 Can you order decimals?

 EXAMPLE Order 6.29, 6.15, 6.2, 6.21, and 6.38 from least to greatest.

On a number line, mark tenths between 6.1 and 6.4. Mark hundredths by dividing each tenth into ten equal parts. Then graph each number.

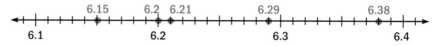

ANSWER In order, the numbers are 6.15, 6.2, 6.21, 6.29, and 6.38.

 Order the numbers from least to greatest.

2. 1.02, 1, 1.1, 1.008   **3.** 7.07, 0.77, 0.7, 7.7   **4.** 9.32, 9.3, 9.41, 9.04

2.2 Can you add and subtract decimals?

 EXAMPLE Find the sum or difference.

a. 26.37 + 4.685

$$\begin{array}{r} 26.370 \\ +\ 4.685 \\ \hline 31.055 \end{array}$$

b. 12 − 3.26

$$\begin{array}{r} 12.00 \\ -\ 3.26 \\ \hline 8.74 \end{array}$$

Find the sum or difference.

5. 6.51 + 1.874   **6.** 256 + 13.92   **7.** 15.1 − 10.987

2.3–2.4 Can you multiply and divide decimals?

 EXAMPLE Find the product or quotient.

a. 7.13×0.91

b. $6.5\overline{)0.52}$

$$
\begin{array}{r}
7.13 \\
\times\ 0.91 \\
\hline
713 \\
6417 \\
\hline
6.4883
\end{array}
$$

2 decimal places
+ 2 decimal places

4 decimal places

$$
\begin{array}{r}
0.08 \\
65\overline{)5.20} \\
5\ 20 \\
\hline
0
\end{array}
$$

To multiply divisor and dividend by 10, move both decimal points one place to the right.

ANSWER $7.13 \times 0.91 = 6.4883$

ANSWER $0.52 \div 6.5 = 0.08$

☑ **Find the product or quotient. Then check your answer.**

8. 32×0.012 **9.** 0.085×6.29 **10.** $253.59 \div 6.42$ **11.** $5.67 \div 0.09$

Stop and Think about Lessons 2.1–2.4

12. Critical Thinking Write three numbers that round to 19.23.

13. Writing Explain how dividing a decimal by a whole number is different than dividing two decimals. How is it the same?

Review Quiz 1

Copy and complete the statement using <, >, or =.

1. 7.6 ? 7.63   **2.** 14.09 ? 14.1   **3.** 5.26 ? 5.260   **4.** 0.32 ? 0.0327

5. Round 38.4985 to the nearest hundredth.

Find the sum or difference.

6. $20.62 + 9.58$ **7.** $8.56 + 16.4$ **8.** $9.505 - 3.44$ **9.** $80.1 - 17.95$

10. Shopping You decide to buy a novel that costs $15.89, including tax. You give the cashier a $20 bill. How much change should you receive?

Find the product or quotient. Then check your answer.

11. 9.58×6.19 **12.** 3.45×1.66 **13.** $3.374 \div 0.35$ **14.** $0.329 \div 28$

15. Chocolate In 1998, the average American consumed 12.2 pounds of chocolate. To the nearest hundredth, how much chocolate did the average American consume in one month?

Scientific Notation

BEFORE	Now	WHY?
You multiplied whole numbers by powers of 10.	You'll read and write numbers using scientific notation.	So you can compare the masses of Mars's moons, as in Example 3.

Word Watch

scientific notation, p. 74

In the Real World

Models Joseph King constructed a 23 foot model of the Eiffel Tower using 110,000 toothpicks. How can you use powers of 10 to write 110,000?

One way to write large numbers is to use *scientific notation*.

Using Scientific Notation

A number is written in **scientific notation** if it has the form $c \times 10^n$ where c is greater than or equal to 1 and less than 10 and n is a whole number.

Standard form	Product form	Scientific notation
2,860,000	$2.86 \times 1,000,000$	2.86×10^6

EXAMPLE 1 Writing Numbers in Scientific Notation

As described above, Joseph King used 110,000 toothpicks to construct his Eiffel Tower model. To write 110,000 in scientific notation, use powers of 10.

Standard form	Product form	Scientific notation
110,000	$1.1 \times 100,000$	1.1×10^5
5 decimal places	5 zeros	Exponent is 5.

ANSWER Joseph King used 1.1×10^5 toothpicks to make his model of the Eiffel Tower.

HELP with Vocabulary

Powers of ten:
$10^1 = 10$
$10^2 = 100$
$10^3 = 1000$
$10^4 = 10,000$
$10^5 = 100,000$
$10^6 = 1,000,000$

EXAMPLE 2 **Writing Numbers in Standard Form**

Write the number in standard form.

a. 7×10^3　　　　　　　　　　　**b.** 4.398×10^8

Solution

	Scientific notation	Product form	Standard form
a.	7×10^3	7×1000	7000
b.	4.398×10^8	$4.398 \times 100{,}000{,}000$	439,800,000

Your turn now Write the number in scientific notation.

1. 450,000　　　　　　**2.** 6,310,000　　　　　　**3.** 10,000,000,000

Write the number in standard form.

4. 3.71×10^4　　　　**5.** 9×10^7　　　　**6.** 4.652×10^{10}

EXAMPLE 3 **Comparing Numbers in Scientific Notation**

Mars Mars has two moons, Phobos and Deimos. Phobos has a mass of 1.06×10^{16} kilograms. Deimos has a mass of 2.4×10^{15} kilograms. Which moon has the greater mass?

Solution

To compare numbers written in scientific notation, first compare the exponents. If the exponents are equal, then compare the decimal parts.

　　Phobos: 1.06×10^{16}　　　**Deimos:** 2.4×10^{15}

Because $16 > 15$, $1.06 \times 10^{16} > 2.4 \times 10^{15}$.

ANSWER Phobos has a greater mass than Deimos.

✓**Check** Write the numbers in standard form and compare.

　　$1.06 \times 10^{16} = 10{,}600{,}000{,}000{,}000{,}000$

　　$2.4 \times 10^{15} = 2{,}400{,}000{,}000{,}000{,}000$

So, $1.06 \times 10^{16} > 2.4 \times 10^{15}$.

What do you think?
Astronomy

■ **Mars**

Mars is the fourth planet from the Sun. The distance between Mars and the Sun is about 1.416×10^8 miles. How can you write this distance in standard form?

Your turn now Copy and complete the statement using <, >, or =.

7. 9.74×10^{21} ? 2.1×10^{22}　　　　　**8.** 5.28×10^{12} ? 5.3×10^{12}

Getting Ready to Practice

Vocabulary Tell whether the number is written in *scientific notation*, *standard form*, or *neither*. If *neither*, explain why.

1. 7.2×10^4 **2.** 34.2×10^5 **3.** $70{,}231$

Write the number in scientific notation.

4. $75{,}000$ **5.** $284{,}500{,}000$ **6.** $3{,}001{,}000{,}000$

Write the number in standard form.

7. 3.41×10^6 **8.** 2.4×10^9 **9.** 5.0×10^1

10. Mathematicians Pythagoras, a Greek mathematician, was born about 2.6×10^3 years ago. Galileo, an Italian mathematician and astronomer, was born about 4.4×10^2 years ago. Who was born more recently?

Practice and Problem Solving

HELP with **Homework**

Example	Exercises
1	11–19, 36
2	20–28, 37
3	29–32

Online Resources
CLASSZONE.COM

· More Examples
· eTutorial Plus

Write the number in scientific notation.

11. $41{,}200$ **12.** 600 **13.** $29{,}200{,}000$

14. $12{,}000{,}000$ **15.** $154{,}000$ **16.** $90{,}000{,}000{,}000$

17. 102.4 **18.** 2000.1 **19.** 535

Write the number in standard form.

20. 7.1×10^5 **21.** 2×10^3 **22.** 8.29×10^4

23. 1.5×10^2 **24.** 3.52×10^5 **25.** 5.884×10^9

26. 3.5802×10^7 **27.** 6.07×10^1 **28.** 4.40044×10^6

Copy and complete the statement using $<$, $>$, or $=$.

29. 8.12×10^{15} ? 1.5×10^{17} **30.** 2.33×10^{10} ? 7.6×10^{10}

31. 4.4×10^7 ? $44{,}000{,}000$ **32.** $548{,}000{,}000$? 5.48×10^7

Order the numbers from least to greatest.

33. 3.25×10^5 3.5×10^5 7.98×10^4 2.61×10^6

34. 7.8×10^3 8.7×10^4 8.02×10^3 7.18×10^4

35. 1.101×10^8 1.1×10^8 1.01×10^9 1.11×10^8 1.10×10^7

Monster Trucks **In Exercises 36 and 37, use the following information.**
Bigfoot 5, the world's largest monster truck, is 15 feet 5 inches tall and weighs 38,000 pounds. Each tire is 10 feet tall and weighs 2.4×10^3 pounds.

36. Write the weight of the truck in scientific notation.

37. Write the weight of one tire in standard form.

Find the missing number(s).

38. $46,000 = 4.6 \times 10^{?}$

39. $2.\,?\,6 \times 10^6 = \,?\,,560,000$

40. **Critical Thinking** Multiply 3.6×10^4 by 1.4×10^6 by writing the numbers in standard form, then multiplying. Express the product in scientific notation. Look at the exponents in the factors and in the product. What do you notice?

41. **Challenge** Find the sum of 9.18×10^4 and 4.8×10^5. Express your answer in scientific notation.

42. **Light-Years** A *light-year*, the distance light travels in one year, is 5.88×10^{12} miles. The distance between Earth and the nearest star (other than the Sun) is 4.3 light-years. How many miles is this distance? Express your answer in standard form and in scientific notation.

Mixed Review

Evaluate the expression when $a = 14$ and $b = 7$. *(Lesson 1.2)*

43. $a + b$

44. $12 + b + 6$

45. $a + 28 + b$

Find the quotient. Then check your answer. *(Lesson 2.4)*

46. $19.44 \div 3.6$

47. $1.372 \div 0.28$

48. $0.38 \div 15.2$

Basic Skills **Find a low and high estimate for the product.**

49.
$$
\begin{array}{r}
62 \\
\times\ 31 \\
\hline
\end{array}
$$

50.
$$
\begin{array}{r}
23 \\
\times\ 59 \\
\hline
\end{array}
$$

51.
$$
\begin{array}{r}
514 \\
\times\ 94 \\
\hline
\end{array}
$$

52.
$$
\begin{array}{r}
7398 \\
\times\ 617 \\
\hline
\end{array}
$$

Test-Taking Practice

53. **Multiple Choice** In 2001, the population of the United States was about 278,000,000 people. Which choice expresses the population in scientific notation?

   A. 27.8×10^7 **B.** 2.78×10^8 **C.** 2.78×10^7 **D.** 278×10^6

54. **Short Response** Which is greater: 6.7263×10^7 or 68.763×10^6? Explain your reasoning.

Using Scientific Notation

GOAL Use a calculator to perform operations on numbers written in scientific notation.

The **EE** key on a calculator is used to enter numbers written in scientific notation.

Example 1 Earth has a mass of about 6×10^{21} metric tons. The mass of Neptune is about 17 times greater than the mass of Earth. What is the mass of Neptune?

Solution

To find the mass of Neptune, multiply the mass of Earth by 17.

HELP with Technology

The **EE** key on a calculator means "times 10 raised to the power of."

Keystrokes	Display
6 **EE** 21 **×** 17 **=**	$1.02_{\times 10}^{23}$

ANSWER Neptune has a mass of about 1.02×10^{23} metric tons.

Example 2 The distance between Earth and the Sun is about 9.3×10^7 miles. The distance between Neptune and the Sun is about 2.7931×10^9 miles. How many times farther is Neptune from the Sun than Earth is?

Solution

To find the number of times farther Neptune is from the Sun than Earth is, divide the distance between Neptune and the Sun by the distance between Earth and the Sun.

Keystrokes	Display
2.7931 **EE** 9 **÷** 9.3 **EE** 7 **=**	30.03333333

ANSWER Neptune is about 30 times farther from the Sun than Earth is.

Your turn now Use a calculator to evaluate the expression.

1. $(7.1 \times 10^9) + (2.0 \times 10^8)$ **2.** $(5.67 \times 10^5) - (1.23 \times 10^5)$

3. $(3.3 \times 10^7) \times (2.8 \times 10^{11})$ **4.** $(5.6 \times 10^9) \div (1.4 \times 10^4)$

5. Astronomy Earth's diameter is about 7.926×10^3 miles. Neptune's diameter is about 3.0775×10^4 miles. How many times greater is Neptune's diameter than Earth's diameter?

GOAL

Measure objects using a metric ruler.

MATERIALS

· metric ruler

Measuring Length

The *metric system* is a decimal system of measurement. Two units of length in the metric system are *centimeters* and *millimeters*. To measure the length of an object using centimeters and millimeters, use a metric ruler.

Explore **Measure the length of the tube of paint.**

1 To measure the length of the tube of paint, line up the ruler so that the top of the tube lines up with the 0 centimeter mark.

The distance between consecutive long tick marks is 1 centimeter.

The distance between consecutive short tick marks is 1 millimeter.

2 Look for the tick mark closest to the end of the tube. It is closest to the fourth tick mark after 8 centimeters. So, the length of the tube of paint is 8.4 centimeters, or 84 millimeters.

Your turn now **Find the length of the object in centimeters.**

1. Piece of chalk   **2.** Pencil   **3.** Staple

4. Piece of paper   **5.** Width of a belt   **6.** Your shoe

Stop and Think

7. Critical Thinking Measure the objects in Exercises 1–6 using millimeters instead of centimeters. What do you notice about the measurements?

8. Writing Explain why measuring to the nearest millimeter is more precise than measuring to the nearest centimeter.

LESSON 2.6

Measuring in Metric Units

BEFORE	▶ Now	WHY?
You used metric units.	You'll measure and estimate using metric units.	So you can estimate the mass of a bike, as in Ex. 20.

Word Watch

metric system, p. 80
length: meter, millimeter, centimeter, kilometer, p. 80
mass: gram, milligram, kilogram, p. 81
capacity: liter, milliliter, kiloliter, p. 82

The **metric system** is a decimal system of measurement. The metric system has units for length, mass, and capacity.

Length The **meter (m)** is the basic unit of length in the metric system. Three other metric units of length are the **millimeter (mm)**, **centimeter (cm)**, and **kilometer (km)**.

You can use the following benchmarks to estimate length.

1 millimeter
thickness of a dime

1 centimeter
width of a large paper clip

1 meter
height of the back of a chair

1 kilometer combined length of 9 football fields

EXAMPLE 1 Using Metric Units of Length

Estimate the length of the bandage by imagining paper clips laid next to it. Then measure the bandage with a metric ruler to check your estimate.

1 Estimate using paper clips.

> About 5 large paper clips fit next to the bandage, so it is about 5 centimeters long.

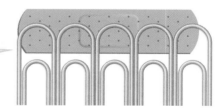

2 Measure using a ruler.

> Each centimeter is divided into tenths, so the bandage is 4.8 centimeters long.

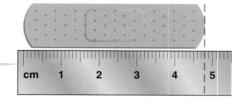

Watch Out!

A typical metric ruler allows you to measure only to the nearest tenth of a centimeter.

Mass Mass is the amount of matter that an object has. The **gram (g)** is the basic metric unit of mass. Two other metric units of mass are the **milligram (mg)** and **kilogram (kg)** .

EXAMPLE 2 Measuring Mass

Find the mass of the apples.

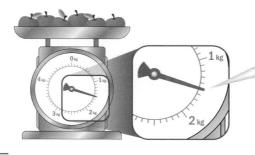

Each kilogram is divided into tenths, so the mass of the apples is 1.5 kilograms.

You can use the following benchmarks to estimate mass.

| **1 milligram** | **1 gram** | **1 kilogram** |
| grain of sugar | small paper clip | textbook |

EXAMPLE 3 Using Metric Units of Mass

Copy and complete using the appropriate metric unit: The mass of a CD is 16 ?.

The mass of a CD is greater than the mass of 16 grains of sugar (16 mg), and it is less than the mass of 16 textbooks (16 kg). Because a good estimate for the mass of a CD is 16 paper clips, the appropriate metric unit is grams.

ANSWER The mass of a CD is 16 grams.

Your turn now Complete the following exercise.

1. Estimate the thickness of this textbook in centimeters. Then use a metric ruler to check your estimate.

Copy and complete using the appropriate metric unit.

2. The mass of a baby is 4 ?.   **3.** The mass of a tack is 200 ?.

Capacity Capacity is a measure of the amount that a container can hold. The **liter (L)** is the basic metric unit of capacity. Two other metric units of capacity are the **milliliter (mL)** and **kiloliter (kL)** .

EXAMPLE 4 **Measuring a Liquid Amount**

Find the amount of liquid in the measuring cup.

400 mL
300 mL
200 mL

Each 100 mL is divided into fourths, so the liquid is at the 225 mL level.

ANSWER The measuring cup contains 225 milliliters of liquid.

You can use the following benchmarks to estimate capacity.

1 milliliter
eyedropper

1 liter
large water
bottle

1 kiloliter
8 large trash cans

EXAMPLE 5 **Using Metric Units of Capacity**

What is the most reasonable capacity of a bathtub?

  A. 750 mL   **B.** 14 L   **C.** 240 L   **D.** 5 kL

Solution

Both 750 mL (750 eyedroppers) and 14 L (14 water bottles) are too little to fill a bathtub. Using 5 kL (40 large trash cans) would overfill a bathtub. That leaves 240 L (240 large water bottles), which seems reasonable.

ANSWER The most reasonable capacity of a bathtub is (C) 240 L.

Your turn now Match the object with the appropriate capacity.

  4. Tube of toothpaste   **5.** Large trash can   **6.** Bottle cap

  A. 8 mL   **B.** 175 mL   **C.** 125 L

Getting Ready to Practice

1. **Vocabulary** Copy and complete: Milligrams, grams, and kilograms are metric units of _?_.

Copy and complete using the appropriate metric unit.

2. A tennis racket is 1.2 _?_ long.

3. A piece of paper is 0.1 _?_ thick.

4. The mass of a TV is 20 _?_.

5. The mass of a golf ball is 46 _?_.

6. A juice box contains 200 _?_.

7. A can of soup contains 0.4 _?_.

8. **Volleyball** Julia thinks that the mass of a volleyball is about 300 grams. Bailey thinks that its mass is about 3 kilograms. Who is right? Explain.

Practice and Problem Solving

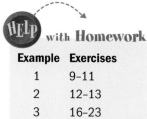

HELP with Homework

Example	Exercises
1	9–11
2	12–13
3	16–23
4	14–15
5	24–26

Online Resources
CLASSZONE.COM

· More Examples
· eTutorial Plus

Estimate the length of the object. Then measure the object using a metric ruler.

9. Your foot

10. Pencil eraser

11. This page

Find the mass of the object.

12.

13.

Find the amount of liquid in the measuring cup.

14.

15.

Copy and complete using the appropriate metric unit.

16. A building is 100 _?_ high.

17. The Hudson River is 507 _?_ long.

18. The width of a belt is 3 _?_.

19. The mass of a staple is 32 _?_.

20. The mass of a bike is 8 _?_.

21. The mass of a sock is 25 _?_.

22. A mug can hold 400 _?_.

23. A large bottle of soda holds 2 _?_.

Banana Pyramid

The world's largest banana pyramid was created using 5700 kilograms of bananas. If a typical bunch of bananas has a mass of about 1.2 kilograms, about how many bunches were used in the banana pyramid?

Choose the letter of the most reasonable measurement.

24. What is the perimeter of a doormat?

    A. 5 cm   **B.** 0.3 m   **C.** 2.5 m   **D.** 30 m

25. What is the mass of a toothpick?

    F. 1 mg   **G.** 100 mg   **H.** 10 g   **I.** 1 kg

26. What is the capacity of a birdbath?

    A. 90 mL   **B.** 2 L   **C.** 50 L   **D.** 2 kL

Copy and complete the statement using 3, 30, or 300.

27. Wheelbarrows An empty wheelbarrow has a mass of about ? kg.

28. Bananas Two bananas have a mass of ? g.

29. Stamps A postage stamp has a mass of about ? mg.

Match the object with the appropriate measurement.

30. Cell phone   **31.** Paper cup   **32.** Snowboard   **33.** Light bulb

    A. 20 g   **B.** 80 g   **C.** 100 cm   **D.** 240 mL

34. Challenge Name an object that has a large capacity and a small mass. Name an object that has a small capacity and a large mass.

Mixed Review

Copy and complete the statement using <, >, or =. *(Lesson 2.1)*

35. 4.2 ? 2.4   **36.** 1.08 ? 1   **37.** 2.07 ? 2.070

Write the number in scientific notation. *(Lesson 2.5)*

38. 12,500   **39.** 350,400   **40.** 10,600,000

Basic Skills **Use a number line to order the numbers from least to greatest.**

41. 59, 51, 9, 15, 19   **42.** 100, 101, 110, 10   **43.** 233, 322, 323, 232

Test-Taking Practice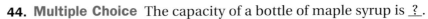

44. Multiple Choice The capacity of a bottle of maple syrup is ? .

    A. 500 L   **B.** 25 mL   **C.** 10 L   **D.** 250 mL

45. Short Response Use benchmarks to order the measurements from least to greatest: 1 kg, 5 g, 10 kg, 50 mg. Explain your reasoning.

Converting Metric Units

BEFORE

You used metric units of length, mass, and capacity.

▶ **Now**

You'll convert between metric units.

WHY?

So you can find the mass of a panda bear, as in Ex. 46.

In the Real World

Word Watch

Review Words

meter, p. 80
gram, p. 81
liter, p. 82

Running In the 4×800 meter relay race, four teammates each run 800 meters. The total length of the race is 3200 meters. How many kilometers long is the race?

The metric system is a base-ten system. Metric prefixes are associated with decimal place values.

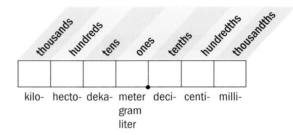

To convert between metric units n decimal places apart, multiply or divide as follows.

Multiply by 10^n.

larger unit ⟷ smaller unit

Divide by 10^n.

EXAMPLE 1 **Converting Metric Units of Length**

To find the length in kilometers of the relay race described above, convert 3200 meters to kilometers.

Solution

You are converting from a smaller unit (meters) to a larger unit (kilometers), so *divide* by a power of 10.

From meters to kilometers, the decimal point is moved **3 places** to the left, so divide by 10^3, or 1000.

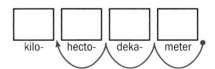

$3200 \div 1000 = 3.2$

3200 meters = 3.2 kilometers

ANSWER The 4×800 meter relay race is 3.2 kilometers long.

EXAMPLE 2 **Converting Units of Mass and Capacity**

Copy and complete the statement.

a. 15 g = _?_ mg

b. 590 mL = _?_ L

Solution

a. To convert from grams to milligrams, multiply by 1000.

$15 \times 1000 = 15{,}000$, so 15 g = 15,000 mg.

b. To convert from milliliters to liters, divide by 1000.

$590 \div 1000 = 0.59$, so 590 mL = 0.59 L.

Your turn now **Copy and complete the statement.**

1. 6800 m = _?_ km

2. 54 m = _?_ mm

3. 830 cm = _?_ m

4. 115 mm = _?_ cm

5. 9.25 kL = _?_ L

6. 100 g = _?_ kg

HELP with Solving

To compare two measurements that have different units, convert one of the measures so that both have the *same* units.

EXAMPLE 3 **Comparing Metric Measurements**

Copy and complete the statement using <, >, or =.

a. 320 cm _?_ 4 m

b. 0.2 kg _?_ 184 g

Solution

a. 320 cm _?_ 4 m   **Strategy: Convert meters to centimeters.**

320 cm _?_ 400 cm $4 \times 100 = 400$, so 4 m = 400 cm.

320 cm < 400 cm   **Compare.**

ANSWER 320 cm < 4 m

b. 0.2 kg _?_ 184 g   **Strategy: Convert kilograms to grams.**

200 g _?_ 184 g $0.2 \times 1000 = 200$, so 0.2 kg = 200 g.

200 g > 184 g   **Compare.**

ANSWER 0.2 kg > 184 g

Your turn now **Copy and complete the statement using <, >, or =.**

7. 1.4 kL _?_ 1400 L

8. 1.5 g _?_ 150 mg

9. 5.8 cm _?_ 580 mm

EXAMPLE 4 **Using Metric Units of Length**

Longest Submarine Sandwich In 1979, Chef Franz Eichenauer made a submarine sandwich that was 322.5 meters long. Suppose the sandwich was cut into pieces that each measured 25.8 centimeters. How many pieces would there be?

Solution

1. Convert 322.5 meters to centimeters by multiplying by 100.

    $322.5 \times 100 = 32{,}250$, so 322.5 m $= 32{,}250$ cm.

2. To find the number of pieces, divide the total length of the sandwich by the length of each piece.

    $32{,}250$ cm $\div 25.8$ cm $= 1250$

ANSWER The submarine sandwich would be divided into 1250 pieces.

2.7 Exercises

More Practice, p. 706

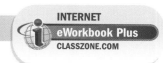

INTERNET
eWorkbook Plus
CLASSZONE.COM

Getting Ready to Practice

Vocabulary Copy and complete the statement with *millimeter(s)*, *centimeter(s)*, or *kilometer(s)*.

1. 1 meter = 1000 _?_
2. 1 meter = 100 _?_
3. 1 meter = 0.001 _?_

Copy and complete the statement.

4. 1.25 km = _?_ m
5. 890 mL = _?_ L
6. 4.7 kL = _?_ L
7. 3.75 kg = _?_ g
8. 1540 mg = _?_ g
9. 28 cm = _?_ m

10. **Paper Clips** A large paper clip is 5 centimeters long. About how many large paper clips do you need to make a chain of paper clips linked end to end that is 10 meters long?

11. **Guided Problem Solving** It is recommended that each day you drink eight glasses of water that are each 8 fluid ounces. One fluid ounce is about 30 milliliters. How many liters of water should you drink a day?

    1. How many fluid ounces of water should you drink each day?

    2. How many milliliters of water should you drink each day?

    3. Convert the result of Step 2 to liters.

Practice and Problem Solving

Tell whether you _multiply_ or _divide_ by a power of 10 to convert the units.

12. liters to milliliters

13. centimeters to meters

14. milligrams to grams

15. kilometers to millimeters

16. Find the Error Describe and correct the error in converting 50 milligrams to grams.

$$50 \times 1000 = 50{,}000$$
So, 50 mg = 50,000 g.

Copy and complete the statement.

17. 0.75 L = ? mL

18. 3528 m = ? km

19. 45,250 g = ? kg

20. 7.2 g = ? mg

21. 49 m = ? cm

22. 6.42 kL = ? L

23. 1.763 km = ? m

24. 8.95 L = ? mL

25. 840,000 mg = ? g

Copy and complete the statement using <, >, or =.

26. 160 mg ? 16 g

27. 740 L ? 0.74 kL

28. 2 km ? 2000 m

29. 4.1 g ? 410 mg

30. 6.5 m ? 65 cm

31. 8.9 mL ? 0.89 L

32. 2300 g ? 2 kg

33. 6.9 m ? 70 cm

34. 9.6 L ? 9600 mL

35. Leaky Faucet A leaky faucet drips 227 milliliters of water in one hour. How many liters of water does the leaky faucet drip in one day?

Copy and complete the statement.

36. 1.08 cm = ? mm

37. 2.42 kL = ? mL

38. 0.13 km = ? cm

39. 1300 mg = ? kg

40. 93.2 mm = ? km

41. 0.9 kg = ? mg

Find the sum or difference. Write your answer using the smaller unit of measurement.

42. 3 cm + 11 mm

43. 4 L − 35 mL

44. 6000 g − 3.5 kg

45. Lights Fifty mini-lights are equally spaced on a string of lights 7.5 meters long. There is a light at one end, and 15 centimeters between the last light and the plug at the other end. How many centimeters are between each light?

46. Panda Bears A baby panda has a mass of about 100 grams at birth. During the early stages of life, a panda gains about 57 grams each day. About how many kilograms is a 30-day-old panda?

HELP with **Homework**

Example	Exercises
1	17–25, 36–41
2	17–25, 36–41
3	26–34
4	35, 45–46

Online Resources
CLASSZONE.COM

· More Examples
· eTutorial Plus

Order the measurements from least to greatest.

47. 60 g, 69 mg, 9.5 mg, 0.04 kg, 45 g

48. 15 L, 1.5 mL, 1500 mL, 1.5 kL, 0.15 kL

49. 24 m, 42 km, 420 mm, 240 cm, 2.4 mm, 4.2 m, 0.24 km

50. Challenge A square has a side length of 10 millimeters. What is its area in square centimeters? Explain.

Mixed Review

Find the sum. *(Lesson 2.2)*

51. 2.1 + 3.02 + 7.59   **52.** 11.02 + 43.89 + 4   **53.** 0.034 + 0.34 + 3.4

54. What is the appropriate metric unit for the mass of a dog? *(Lesson 2.6)*

Basic Skills **Copy and complete.**

55. 8 h = _?_ min   **56.** 3 d = _?_ h   **57.** 32 min = _?_ sec

58. 120 min = _?_ h   **59.** 35 d = _?_ wk   **60.** 360 sec = _?_ min

Test-Taking Practice

61. Extended Response Show two different ways to find the area, in square centimeters, of a rectangle with a length of 4.5 meters and a width of 2.25 meters.

BRAIN GAME

The Case of the Missing Shoes

Melanie discovers her favorite pair of shoes missing. In their place is a mysterious note, written in her younger brother's handwriting. Melanie thinks that the directions will lead her in circles. Can you find a shorter route for Melanie to follow to find her shoes?

Your shoes are buried somewhere in the backyard. Follow these directions, or your shoes are gone for good! Start at the willow tree.

1. North 0.004 km
2. West 300 cm
3. South 2 m
4. East 6000 mm
5. South 100 cm
6. West 5000 mm
7. North 0.001 km

Notebook Review

Review the vocabulary definitions in your notebook.

Copy the review examples in your notebook. Then complete the exercises.

Check Your Definitions

scientific notation, p. 74	centimeter, p. 80	kilogram, p. 81
metric system, p. 80	kilometer, p. 80	liter, p. 82
meter, p. 80	gram, p. 81	milliliter, p. 82
millimeter, p. 80	milligram, p. 81	kiloliter, p. 82

Use Your Vocabulary

1. Name the basic metric units of length, mass, and capacity.

2.5 Can you write numbers using scientific notation?

 EXAMPLE

a. Write 83,000,000 in scientific notation.

b. Write 4.9×10^6 in standard form.

Solution

a. $83{,}000{,}000 = 8.3 \times 10{,}000{,}000 = 8.3 \times 10^7$

b. $4.9 \times 10^6 = 4.9 \times 1{,}000{,}000 = 4{,}900{,}000$

2. Write 902,400,000,000 in scientific notation.

3. Write 7.62×10^4 in standard form.

2.6 Can you use metric units?

 EXAMPLE Copy and complete using the appropriate metric unit: The capacity of a sandbox is 1.2 _?_ .

One kiloliter is equal to the capacity of 8 large trash cans. A sandbox holds more than 1 kiloliter, so kiloliters is the appropriate unit.

ANSWER The capacity of a sandbox is 1.2 kL.

Copy and complete using the appropriate metric unit.

4. The width of a standard sized postage stamp is 18 _?_ .

5. The mass of a paperback novel is 250 _?_ .

2.7 Can you convert between metric units?

 EXAMPLE Convert 834 centimeters to meters.

Because you move 2 decimal places to the left to go from centimeters to meters, *divide* by 10^2, or 100.

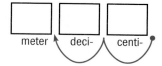

ANSWER $834 \div 100 = 8.34$, so 834 cm = 8.34 m.

☑ **Copy and complete the statement.**

6. 4.6 kg = _?_ g   **7.** 8923 mm = _?_ m   **8.** 95 L = _?_ kL

Stop and Think about Lessons 2.5–2.7

9. Critical Thinking Is 35.89×10^3 written in scientific notation? Explain why or why not.

10. Writing Describe how to compare two lengths measured in different metric units.

Review Quiz 2

1. Write 987,000 in scientific notation.

2. Earth's Core Beneath Earth's crust, there are 3 layers. The *mantle* is 1.8×10^3 miles thick, the *outer core* is 1.4×10^3 miles thick, and the *inner core* is 8×10^2 miles thick. Which layer is the thickest?

Copy and complete using the appropriate metric unit.

3. A skateboard is 85 _?_ long.   **4.** The mass of a pencil is 10 _?_.

Copy and complete the statement.

5. 3200 mg = _?_ g   **6.** 16 L = _?_ mL   **7.** 57 cm = _?_ mm

8. Pumpkin Contest A pumpkin contest is held at a county fair. The pumpkin with the greatest mass is declared the winner. Which pumpkins will be awarded first, second, and third place?

Name	Orange 1	Stumpy	Pie Guy	Pumped Up	Miss P.
Mass	18,000 g	45 kg	6300 g	37.5 kg	40,000 g

2 Chapter Review

 **Vocabulary**

decimal, p. 52
front-end estimation,
　p. 59
leading digit, p. 63
compatible numbers,
　p. 67

scientific notation, p. 74
metric system, p. 80
meter, p. 80
millimeter, p. 80
centimeter, p. 80
kilometer, p. 80

gram, p. 81
milligram, p. 81
kilogram, p. 81
liter, p. 82
milliliter, p. 82
kiloliter, p. 82

Vocabulary Review

1. Give three examples of decimals.

2. In your own words, explain how to use front-end estimation to estimate a sum.

3. What is the leading digit of 0.0398?

4. What is the difference between scientific notation and standard form?

5. Copy and complete: Milliliters, liters, and kiloliters are metric units of　?　.

Review Questions

Copy and complete the statement using <, >, or =. *(Lesson 2.1)*

6. 8.54 　?　 8.55

7. 6.11 　?　 6.01

8. 0.051 　?　 0.006

9. Order 1.11, 1.01, 0.01, 1.1, 0.11, and 0.1 from least to greatest. *(Lesson 2.1)*

10. Explain how to round a decimal to the nearest hundredth. *(Lesson 2.1)*

Find the sum or difference. *(Lesson 2.2)*

11. $54.2 + 19.25$

12. $1.295 + 24.6$

13. $100 - 16.574$

14. $35.002 - 9.9$

Evaluate the expression when $x = 2.75$ and $y = 16.2$. *(Lesson 2.2)*

15. $x + 10.32$

16. $5 + y + x$

17. $y - 3.909$

18. $22.02 - y + x$

19. **Racing Event** You are in a 3-part racing event. Your friend's total time is 80.63 seconds. Your times for each part of the race are 22.34 seconds, 25.8 seconds, and 30.15 seconds. Is your total time faster than your friend's total time? Explain. *(Lessons 2.1, 2.2)*

Find the product. Then check that your answer is reasonable. *(Lesson 2.3)*

20. 54×18.4

21. 2.5×34.6

22. 10.21×6.74

23. 0.002×9.009

24. **Baseball** Cal Ripken, Jr., played major league baseball for 21 years. He played about 142.9 games each year. How many games did he play in his career? Round to the nearest whole number. *(Lesson 2.3)*

Find the quotient. Then check your answer. *(Lesson 2.4)*

25. $71 \div 0.5$ **26.** $7434.44 \div 98.6$ **27.** $1.4568 \div 6.07$ **28.** $0.7866 \div 8.74$

29. Find the quotient of $5 \div 9.5$. Round to the nearest hundredth. *(Lesson 2.4)*

30. **Silver Platter** Mike gives his parents an engraved silver platter for their anniversary. The engraving says "Happy Anniversary" and costs $13.60 total. How much does each letter cost to engrave? *(Lesson 2.4)*

Write the number in scientific notation. *(Lesson 2.5)*

31. 3,356,000   **32.** 5600   **33.** 780,000   **34.** 40,200

Write the number in standard form. *(Lesson 2.5)*

35. 4.06×10^8 **36.** 9.3×10^6 **37.** 1.25×10^2 **38.** 3.887×10^5

Find the value of the exponent. *(Lesson 2.5)*

39. $24{,}500 = 2.45 \times 10^{?}$ **40.** $6.301 \times 10^{?} = 63{,}010{,}000{,}000$

Tell whether the measurement is of *length*, *mass*, or *capacity*. *(Lesson 2.6)*

41. 6 kg   **42.** 1.5 L   **43.** 17 mL   **44.** 3600 m

Copy and complete using the appropriate metric unit. *(Lesson 2.6)*

45. The length of a coffee table is 1.2 ? .

46. The mass of a football is 0.8 ? .

47. The capacity of a kitchen sink is 20 ? .

Copy and complete the statement. *(Lesson 2.7)*

48. 7 cm = ? m   **49.** 802 L = ? mL   **50.** 9.4 mg = ? kg

Copy and complete the statement using <, >, or =. *(Lesson 2.7)*

51. 240 cm ? 24 m   **52.** 9800 mg ? 9.798 g   **53.** 4.302 kL ? 4320 L

Order the measurements from least to greatest. *(Lesson 2.7)*

54. 37 L, 48,000 mL, 0.039 kL, 34 L, 42,000 mL, 0.035 kL

55. 0.8 km, 6 cm, 97 mm, 2.5 m, 256 cm, 0.08 m

2 Chapter Test

Copy and complete the statement using <, >, or =.

1. 12.01 ? 12.101

2. 34.05 ? 34.04

3. 6.29 ? 6.3

4. Currency The exchange rates for several currencies are shown below. Write the values in order from least to greatest.

E.U. euro	U.S. dollar	Canadian dollar	Mexican peso	Japanese yen
0.9942	1	0.6399	0.1034	0.008561

Find the sum, difference, product, or quotient.

5. $4.88 + 219.405$

6. $6.67 + 2.36$

7. $6 - 2.65$

8. $30.105 - 9.9$

9. 0.94×0.63

10. 0.009×0.9

11. 0.16×8

12. 0.72×0.146

13. $60.25 \div 5$

14. $53.756 \div 8.9$

15. $0.291 \div 9.7$

16. $0.084 \div 0.2$

17. School Supplies You are shopping for school supplies. If you have $12, can you buy everything on the list? Assume that there is no sales tax.

Notebook	$1.99
Pen	$1.15
Pencil	$.65
Stapler	$6.29

18. Evaluate $5.7 + 2.8 \div x$ when $x = 0.04$.

19. Write 786,000 in scientific notation.

20. Write 8.2×10^6 in standard form.

In Exercises 21 and 22, copy and complete using the appropriate metric unit.

21. The mass of a crayon is 25 ? .

22. The height of a giraffe is 5 ? .

23. Find the length of the eraser shown.

| cm | 1 | 2 | 3 | 4 | 5 | 6 |

Copy and complete the statement.

24. 8.7 cm = ? mm

25. 28 kL = ? L

26. 1.7 g = ? kg

27. Nutrition It is recommended that a teenager's diet include 1.2 grams of calcium each day. Will eating the foods listed in the table meet the recommended daily amount? Explain.

Food	Calcium
1 cup of milk	300 mg
1 cup of cooked broccoli	70 mg
1 slice of cheese	200 mg

Chapter Standardized Test

Test-Taking Strategy Be sure to avoid careless errors on easy questions.

Multiple Choice

1. Round 5.8934 to the nearest thousandth.

   A. 5.8   **B.** 5.89   **C.** 5.893   **D.** 5.9

2. Which statement is true?

   F. $9.71 < 9.17$ **G.** $81.54 = 81.540$

   H. $3.09 > 3.19$ **I.** $5.64 < 5.24$

3. Which expression has a value of 6.2 when $a = 5.495$ and $b = 14.8$?

   A. $a + 1.205$ **B.** $b - a + 2.895$

   C. $b - 7.6$ **D.** $b - a - 3.105$

4. What is the difference of 15 and 10.769?

   F. 4.231   **G.** 4.331   **H.** 5.231   **I.** 5.331

5. What is a good estimate for the sum of 19.4 and 3.652?

   A. 22   **B.** 23   **C.** 24   **D.** 25

6. What is the product of 0.32 and 1.9?

   F. 0.608   **G.** 6.08   **H.** 60.8   **I.** 608

7. Which quotient is *not* equal to 5.44?

   A. $0.1088 \div 0.02$ **B.** $10.88 \div 2$

   C. $0.01088 \div 0.2$ **D.** $1.088 \div 0.2$

8. What is 97,634,100 written in scientific notation?

   F. 9.76341×10^6 **G.** 97.6341×10^6

   H. 9.76341×10^7 **I.** 97.6341×10^7

9. Write 2.58×10^8 in standard form.

   A. 258   **B.** 2580

   C. 258,000   **D.** 258,000,000

10. Complete: The length of a ski could be _?_ .

   F. 10 m   **G.** 80 mm **H.** 150 cm **I.** 175 m

11. Which measurements are equivalent?

   I. 34 cm   II. 3400 mm   III. 0.34 m

   A. I and II   **B.** I and III

   C. II and III   **D.** I, II, and III

12. Complete: 9800 kL = _?_ L.

   F. 0.98   **G.** 9.8

   H. 98   **I.** 9,800,000

Short Response

13. What is the area of the rectangle below? What is the perimeter?

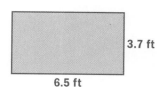

6.5 ft   3.7 ft

Extended Response

14. You are making friendship bracelets out of colored string. For each bracelet, you need 75 centimeters of string. Each meter of string costs $.49. Is $5 enough to buy the string needed for 12 bracelets? Explain your reasoning.

DESCRIBING

OCEAN WAVES

Properties of Waves

Waves form on the ocean when wind blows across the surface of the water. The top of a wave is the *crest*, and the bottom is the *trough*. The *height* of a wave is the vertical distance between the crest and trough. For a series of waves, the *wavelength* is the horizontal distance between one crest and the next. The *period* is the time it takes for one wavelength to pass a fixed point.

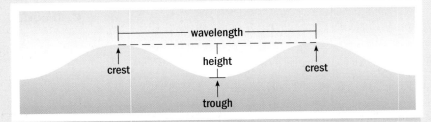

In deep water, the speed v and wavelength l of a series of waves are related to the period T by the equations

$$v = 1.56T \quad \text{and} \quad l = 1.56T^2$$

where v is measured in meters per second, l is measured in meters, and T is measured in seconds.

1. Copy and complete the table.

Period T (seconds)	1	2	4	8	16	32
Wave Speed v (meters per second)	?	?	?	?	?	?
Wavelength l (meters)	?	?	?	?	?	?

2. Based on your completed table from Exercise 1, what effect does doubling the period have on wave speed? on wavelength?

Identifying Rogue Waves

As shown below, some waves are unusually large when compared to a wave of typical height. Such waves are called *rogue waves*.

Wave of typical height	About 1 out of 23 waves are at least twice the typical height.	About 1 out of 1175 waves are at least three times the typical height.

Suppose the period for a series of waves is 10 seconds.

3. Use the verbal model to find the number of seconds in one day.

$$\begin{array}{ccccc}
\text{Seconds in} & = & \text{Hours in} & \times & \text{Minutes in} & \times & \text{Seconds in} \\
\text{one day} & & \text{one day} & & \text{one hour} & & \text{one minute}
\end{array}$$

4. Use your answer from Exercise 3 and the given wave period to find the number of waves that pass a fixed point in one day.

5. Approximately how many of the waves in Exercise 4 are at least twice the typical height? at least three times the typical height?

Project IDEAS

- **Illustrate** Draw a diagram of waves with wavelength l and height h. Draw a second diagram with wavelength $2l$ and height h, and a third diagram with wavelength l and height $2h$.

- **Report** Write a report on rogue waves. Discuss their causes, where they most often occur, and the danger they pose to ships.

- **Research** Find out about waves called *tsunamis*. Describe how a tsunami is like a rogue wave and how it is different.

- **Career** An *oceanographer* is a scientist who studies the ocean. Find out the types of work oceanographers do and the kind of education they need. Present your findings to your class.

INTERNET
Project Support
CLASSZONE.COM

Data and Statistics

BEFORE

In previous chapters you've...

- Performed whole number operations
- Ordered decimals

Now

In Chapter 3 you'll study...

- Mean, median, mode, and range
- Bar graphs and line graphs
- Stem-and-leaf plots
- Box-and-whisker plots
- Histograms

WHY?

So you can solve real-world problems about...

- tornadoes, p. 112
- skiing, p. 119
- roller coasters, p. 123
- music, p. 131

Internet Preview
CLASSZONE.COM

- eEdition Plus Online
- eWorkbook Plus Online
- eTutorial Plus Online
- State Test Practice
- More Examples

Chapter Warm-Up Games

Review skills you need for this chapter in these quick games. Work with a partner.

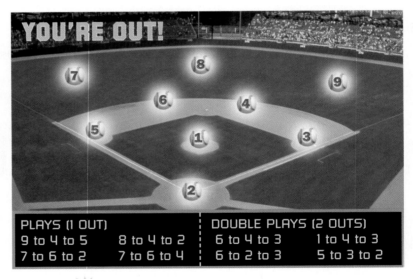

PLAYS (1 OUT)		DOUBLE PLAYS (2 OUTS)	
9 to 4 to 5	8 to 4 to 2	6 to 4 to 3	1 to 4 to 3
7 to 6 to 2	7 to 6 to 4	6 to 2 to 3	5 to 3 to 2

 Key Skill:
Using whole number operations

You and your partner each represent a baseball team that is on the field. You are in a race to get three outs.

- Each position on the field is associated with a number. A play or a double play is described using these numbers.

- Choose a play or a double play. Use the numbers to write a true statement using = and one of the following: +, −, ×, or ÷. If you can write a true statement, you get the out(s). Each play or double play can be used only once. The first player to get three outs wins.

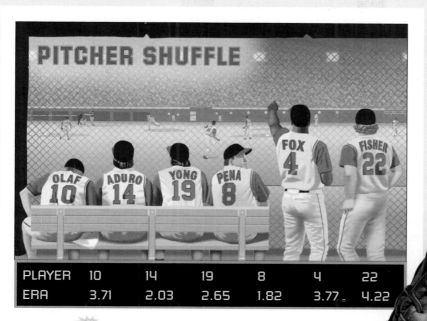

PITCHER SHUFFLE

PLAYER	10	14	19	8	4	22
ERA	3.71	2.03	2.65	1.82	3.77	4.22

BRAIN GAME

Key Skill:
Ordering decimals

A pitcher's earned run average (ERA) indicates how successful the pitcher is at preventing players from scoring runs. In general, the lower the ERA, the better the pitcher.

• Order the ERAs of the pitchers from least to greatest. Then write the names of the pitchers in the same order.

• The first letters of the pitchers' names spell out the answer to the question below.

What is the name of the pitch that follows a three-ball, two-strike count?

Stop *and* Think

1. **Critical Thinking** In *You're Out!*, suppose the following numbers describe a triple play: 9 to 6 to 2 to 3. Use these numbers to write a true statement using = and one or more of the following: +, −, ×, or ÷.

2. **Critical Thinking** In *Pitcher Shuffle*, make up a last name and an ERA for a seventh pitcher so that you can spell out the word PLAYOFF with the first letters of all seven pitchers' names.

Getting Ready to Learn

Review What You Need to Know

Using Vocabulary Copy and complete using a review word.

1. You can use a(n) ? to order and compare numbers.

2. A(n) ? uses a number line to show how often data values occur.

The bar graph shows the average swimming speeds for some common fish. *(p. 703)*

3. What is the average swimming speed for carp?

4. What fish swims at an average speed of 8 kilometers per hour?

5. Which of the fish has the fastest average swimming speed?

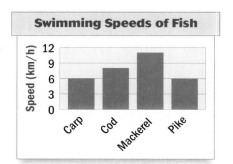

Make a line plot of the data. *(p. 704)*

6. 10, 9, 8, 8, 9, 7, 11, 10, 8, 9, 8

7. 6, 7, 9, 5, 7, 9, 6, 5, 5, 7, 9, 7, 7

Order the numbers from least to greatest. *(p. 52)*

8. 11.6, 5.4, 22, 18.4, 13.8, 9.9

9. 12.1, 11.2, 13.8, 9.4, 13.4, 12

10. 4.2, 1.5, 5.31, 4.4, 6.2, 5.2

11. 6.28, 6.4, 6.2, 6.15, 6.6, 6, 6.5

Know How to Take Notes

Including Vocabulary Notes You should include vocabulary words and their definitions in your notebook. Making a labeled diagram can help you understand and remember key terms.

base   exponent

$$3^5 = 3 \cdot 3 \cdot 3 \cdot 3 \cdot 3$$ 3 is a factor 5 times.

power

In Lesson 3.4, you will learn about box-and-whisker plots. You may find it helpful to include a box-and-whisker plot in your notebook with key vocabulary terms labeled.

Mean, Median, and Mode

BEFORE	▶ Now	WHY?
You compared and ordered whole numbers and decimals.	You'll describe data using mean, median, and mode.	So you can find average auto racing speeds, as in Ex. 21.

In the Real World

Word Watch

mean, p. 101
median, p. 101
mode, p. 101
range, p. 102

Geysers Over a span of 12 hours, Old Faithful Geyser in Yellowstone National Park erupted 10 times. The lengths, in minutes, of the eruptions are shown below.

2.8   4.5   4.1   3.7   3.5   4.5   2.2   4.9   2.6   4.2

What is the average length of the eruptions?

Averages

The **mean** of a data set is the sum of the values divided by the number of values.

The **median** of a data set is the middle value when the values are written in numerical order. If a data set has an even number of values, the median is the mean of the two middle values.

The **mode** of a data set is the value that occurs most often. A data set can have no mode, one mode, or more than one mode.

EXAMPLE 1 Finding a Mean

To find the mean length of the eruptions of Old Faithful listed above, divide the sum of the 10 lengths by 10.

$$\text{Mean} = \frac{2.8 + 4.5 + 4.1 + 3.7 + 3.5 + 4.5 + 2.2 + 4.9 + 2.6 + 4.2}{10}$$

$$= \frac{37}{10}$$

$$= 3.7$$

ANSWER The mean length of the eruptions is 3.7 minutes.

Range To describe how spread out data are, you can find the *range*. The **range** of a data set is the difference between the greatest value and the least value.

HELP with **Review**

Need help with ordering whole numbers? See p. 682.

EXAMPLE 2 Finding Median, Mode, and Range

Find the median, mode(s), and range of the numbers below.

64   60   64   38   52   65   61   48

Write the numbers in order from least to greatest.

38   48   52   60   61   64   64   65

Median: Because there is an even number of data values, the median is the mean of the two middle values.

$$\text{Median} = \frac{60 + 61}{2} = \frac{121}{2} = 60.5$$

Mode: The number that occurs most often is 64.

Range: Find the difference between the greatest and the least values.

Range = 65 − 38 = 27

Your turn now Find the mean, median, mode(s), and range.

1. 9, 13, 19, 14, 16, 11, 7, 6, 13   **2.** 18, 52, 23, 79, 66, 17, 20, 10

EXAMPLE 3 Choosing the Best Average

Dance-a-Thon You receive the pledge amounts listed below for your participation in a dance-a-thon. Which average best represents the pledge amounts?

$1 $8 $12 $10 $45 $9 $1 $7 $6

Solution

Compare the mean, median, and mode.

Mean: $\dfrac{1 + 8 + 12 + 10 + 45 + 9 + 1 + 7 + 6}{9} = \$11$

> The mean suggests that the pledges are greater than they actually are.

Median: 1   1   6   7   **8**   9   10   12   45

The median is $8.

> The mode suggests that the pledges are less than they actually are.

Mode: The pledge that occurs most often is $1.

ANSWER The median best represents the pledge amounts.

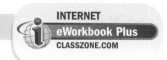

INTERNET
eWorkbook Plus
CLASSZONE.COM

Getting Ready to Practice

Vocabulary **Tell whether the statement is *true* or *false*.**

1. The value that occurs the most often in a data set is the mode.

2. The range of a data set is the sum of the greatest and the least values.

Televisions **The data below are the number of televisions that 11 students have in their homes.**

3   2   1   1   1   5   3   1   2   1   2

3. Find the mean.

4. Find the median.

5. Find the mode(s).

6. Find the range.

7. **Find the Error** Describe and correct the error in finding the median of the data set.

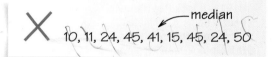

10, 11, 24, 45, 41, 15, 45, 24, 50 — median

Practice and Problem Solving

HELP with Homework

Example	Exercises
1	8–18
2	8–18
3	19, 21, 25–26

Online Resources
CLASSZONE.COM

· More Examples
· eTutorial Plus

Find the mean, median, mode(s), and range of the data.

8. 17, 30, 38, 38, 42

9. 4, 4, 8, 11, 12, 16, 22

10. 108, 490, 502, 502, 502, 518

11. 20, 26, 31, 42, 44, 47, 51, 75

12. 46, 23, 63, 23, 81, 75, 46

13. 9, 63, 87, 45, 8, 87, 25, 12

14. 1.1, 0, 3, 2.8, 4.6

15. 7.6, 7.6, 6.1, 6, 14.3

16. 5.1, 5.3, 5.1, 5.2, 5.2, 5.3, 5.2

17. 68.4, 65.7, 63.9, 79.5, 52.5

Earrings **In Exercises 18 and 19, use the following information.** Sixteen 12-year-old girls were asked how many pairs of earrings they own. The results are listed below.

23, 27, 12, 20, 11, 9, 5, 10, 16, 32, 14, 31, 13, 8, 37, 32

18. Find the mean, median, and mode(s) of the data.

19. Which average best represents the data? Explain your reasoning.

20. **Critical Thinking** Is it possible for the mean, median, and mode of a data set to be the same number? If so, give an example.

21. Indy 500 The table shows the speeds of the fastest qualifiers in the Indy 500 each year for 1996–2001. Find the median and mean rounded to the nearest thousandth. Which average better represents the speeds?

Year	Name	Speed (miles per hour)
1996	Scott Brayton	236.986
1997	Arie Luyendyk	218.263
1998	Billy Boat	223.503
1999	Arie Luyendyk	225.179
2000	Greg Ray	223.471
2001	Scott Sharp	226.037

22. Find the mode(s) of the following words: red, yellow, red, blue, blue, yellow, red, blue, yellow, red. Why is only the mode appropriate?

23. School Newspaper Use the excerpt from a school newspaper to identify the mean, mode(s), and range of hours spent on homework.

Survey Says!

The student council surveyed students about the number of hours they spend on homework each night. The responses spanned 3 hours, falling between 0 hours and 3 hours. The typical response was 1.5 hours, and the most frequent response was 1 hour. ■

■ **Indy 500**

In 1911, it took Ray Harroun about 6 hours 42 minutes to win the first Indy 500. In 2000, it took Juan Montoya, pictured above, about 2 hours 59 minutes to win. About how much longer did it take Harroun than Montoya to win?

Comic Book Club **The line plot at the right shows the ages of students in a comic book club.**

24. Find the mean, median, and mode(s) of the data.

25. Which average best represents the data? Explain your reasoning.

Test Scores **Sally's scores on her science quizzes are listed below.**

86 78 70 68 95 81 85 89 95

26. Which average best represents Sally's scores? Explain your reasoning.

27. Sally receives a score of 100 on the next quiz. How does this score affect the mean, median, and mode(s) of Sally's scores?

with Review

Need help with reading line plots? See p. 704.

xy **Algebra** **Find the value of x that makes the mean the given number.**

28. $5, 8, 9, 4, 1, x$; mean = 5

29. $12, 7, 18, 15, 11, 9, x$; mean = 12

30. Challenge Find five numbers with a mean of 16, a median of 15, a mode of 21, and a range of 11.

Copy and complete the statement. *(Lesson 2.7)*

31. $5 \text{ kg} = \underline{?} \text{ g}$ **32.** $3.7 \text{ m} = \underline{?} \text{ cm}$ **33.** $480 \text{ mL} = \underline{?} \text{ L}$

Choose a Strategy Use a strategy from the list to solve the following problem. Explain your choice of strategy.

Problem Solving Strategies
▪ Look for a Pattern
▪ Estimate
▪ Work Backward

34. You are buying art supplies to make signs for a car wash. Each piece of poster board costs $1.20, and a package of markers costs $3.88. Will $15 cover the cost of 10 pieces of poster board and 2 packages of markers?

Basic Skills **Find the product or quotient.**

35. 65×19 **36.** $729 \div 9$ **37.** $583 \div 11$

Test-Taking Practice

38. Multiple Choice The amount of money you earned each week from baby-sitting is listed below. Find the mean of the data.

$15 $20 $10 $15 $20 $15 $15 $10

A. $10   **B.** $15   **C.** $20   **D.** $25

39. Short Response The ages of the players on your baseball team are as follows: 10, 11, 11, 12, 12, 12, 13, 13, 13, 13. Your friend says the mean age of the players is 11.5 years because $\frac{13 + 10}{2} = 11.5$.

Do you agree with your friend? Explain your reasoning.

BRAIN GAME

What's my age?

Use the following clues to find the age of each member of a family of five.

The median is 12.   **The mean is 21.**   **The mode is 41.**

The age of one of the family members is the median divided by 3.

Samples

GOAL Identify biased samples and surveys.

Word Watch

population, p. 106
sample, p. 106
random sample, p. 106
biased sample, p. 106

A common way to gather data is through a survey. A **population** is the entire group of people or objects that you want information about. When it is difficult to survey an entire population, a **sample**, or a part of the group, is surveyed.

In a **random sample**, each person or object has an equally likely chance of being selected. A non-random sample can result in a **biased sample** that is not representative of the population.

EXAMPLE 1 **Identifying Potentially Biased Samples**

School Spending The athletic department at a school has been given a donation. Administrators want students to help decide how to spend the money by having students choose one of the options listed at the right.

Surveying all of the students will take too long, so a sample will be surveyed. Tell whether the survey method could result in a biased sample. Explain.

a. Survey girls as they leave gym class.

b. Survey students as they wait in line to buy school lunch.

c. Survey the students who are on the baseball team.

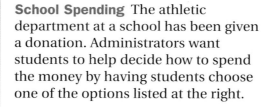

How $hould we $pend the money?

$ $ $ $ $ $ $ $ $ $ $ $ $ $

Choose one:
❏ Buy new baseball team uniforms.
❏ Add more bleachers in the gym.
❏ Put new lockers in the girls' locker room.

Solution

a. This method could result in a biased sample because the girls are more likely to favor new lockers in the girls' locker room.

b. This method is not likely to result in a biased sample because a wide range of students will be surveyed.

c. This method could result in a biased sample because the baseball players are more likely to favor new baseball team uniforms.

Survey Questions When you conduct a survey, you should phrase the questions in such a way that the responses of the people surveyed accurately reflect their opinions or actions. If not, claims based on the survey results may be biased.

EXAMPLE 2 **Identifying Potentially Biased Questions**

Tell whether the question could produce biased results. Explain.

a. Do you, like most people your age, dislike listening to boring classical music?   ❏ yes   ❏ no

b. Do you agree with your town's policy for skateboarding on public property?   ❏ yes   ❏ no

Solution

a. A response of "no" implies that the person responding disagrees with most people his or her age and likes listening to "boring" classical music. Therefore, the question encourages a response of "yes." So, the question could produce biased results.

b. This question assumes that the person responding knows the town's policy. Without information about the policy, the response may not be an accurate opinion. So, the question could produce biased results.

Exercises

Libraries In Exercises 1–3, a town wants to know whether residents will favor an increase in taxes to fund an addition for the library. Tell whether the method could result in a biased sample. Explain.

1. Ask people as they leave the library.

2. Ask every fifth person who enters the bookstore in town.

3. Ask every tenth person listed in the phone book.

4. **Music** A radio station wants to know what type of music its audience would prefer to hear. Describe a survey method that the radio station can use so that is not likely to result in a biased sample.

Tell whether the question could produce biased results. Explain.

5. Would you rather spend a Friday night with your friends at an exciting movie or baby-sitting a crying baby?

6. How often do you read the school newspaper?

7. The fewer trash cans that a city has, the more litter the city has. Should our city include money in its budget for more trash cans?

8. Do you agree with this state's process for getting a driver's license?

Bar Graphs and Line Graphs

LESSON 3.2

BEFORE	▶ Now	WHY?
You used a line plot to display data.	You'll make and interpret bar graphs and line graphs.	So you can display data, such as wingspans of birds in Ex. 5.

In the Real World

Word Watch

bar graph, p. 108
line graph, p. 109

Space Shuttle Missions In the 1990s, four space shuttles were used for various missions. The number of missions taken by each shuttle during this time are shown in the table. How can you represent the data visually?

One way to represent data visually is to use a *bar graph*. In a **bar graph**, the lengths of the bars are used to represent and compare data. The bars can be vertical or horizontal.

Shuttle	Missions
Atlantis	16
Columbia	18
Discovery	17
Endeavour	13

EXAMPLE 1 Making a Bar Graph

You can use a bar graph to represent the space shuttle data above.

(1 Choose a scale.

The largest data value is 18. So, start the scale at 0 and extend it to a value greater than 18, such as 20. Use increments of 4.

(2 Draw and label the graph.

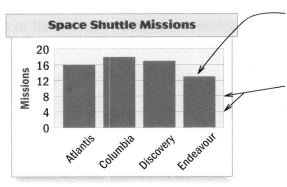

Use the scale to determine the lengths of the bars.

Include horizontal gridlines.

All of the bars should have the same width.

Astronaut Mae Jemison

Your turn now Make a bar graph of the data.

1.

Weekday Museum Visitors					
Day	Monday	Tuesday	Wednesday	Thursday	Friday
Visitors	115	113	133	56	84

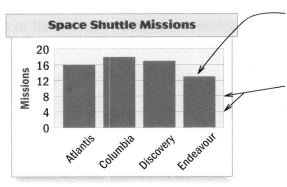

EXAMPLE **2** **Making a Double Bar Graph**

Sports The table shows the sports participation of students at a school.

To make a *double bar graph* of the data, start by drawing bars for the boys. Then draw bars for the girls.

Sport	Boys	Girls
Soccer	26	20
Basketball	17	21
Track and field	25	25
Volleyball	11	15

A *legend* tells you what each bar represents.

Line Graphs Another way to represent data visually is to use a *line graph*. In a **line graph**, points that represent data pairs are connected using line segments. Line graphs often show a change in data over time.

EXAMPLE **3** **Interpreting a Line Graph**

Hot Air Balloons The line graph shows the number of entries in the Albuquerque Balloon Fiesta from 1995 to 2000. What conclusions can you make about the line graph?

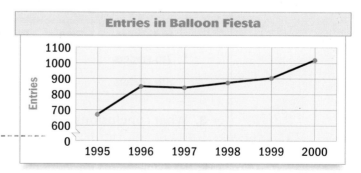

HELP with **Solving**

In the line graph, the break in the vertical axis allows you to focus on the data values between 600 and 1100.

ANSWER The line graph shows that the number of entries remained relatively steady between 1996 and 1999, but there were sharp increases from 1995 to 1996 and from 1999 to 2000.

EXAMPLE 4 Making a Line Graph

Cell Phones Use the table to make a line graph of the number of cellular phone subscribers from 1994 through 1999.

Solution

(1) Choose horizontal and vertical axes.

Years from 1994 through 1999 will be shown on the horizontal axis.

The greatest number of millions of subscribers is 86. So, start the vertical axis at 0 and end with 100, using increments of 20.

(2) Draw and label the graph.

Year	Subscribers (millions)
1994	24
1995	34
1996	44
1997	55
1998	69
1999	86

Cellular Phone Subscribers

Plot a point for each year. Then connect the points with line segments.

Include evenly spaced horizontal and vertical gridlines.

Your turn now Complete the following exercises.

2. Make a double bar graph of the data.

Students in the School Band					
Instrument	**Flute**	**Clarinet**	**Saxophone**	**Trumpet**	**Drums**
7th graders	5	7	2	2	1
8th graders	8	4	2	1	2

3. What conclusions can you make about the line graph in Example 4?

4. Make a line graph of the data.

Number of People in Line at a Fast Food Restaurant						
Time	**8 A.M.**	**10 A.M.**	**Noon**	**2 P.M.**	**4 P.M.**	**6 P.M.**
People	11	4	18	6	9	12

Getting Ready to Practice

1. **Vocabulary** How do bar graphs and line graphs differ?

Student Lunch The double bar graph shows the number of beverages purchased by students during lunch.

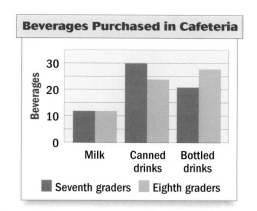

Beverages Purchased in Cafeteria

(Bar graph with y-axis labeled "Beverages" ranging 0 to 30, x-axis showing Milk, Canned drinks, Bottled drinks; legend: Seventh graders, Eighth graders)

2. About how many bottled drinks were purchased by eighth graders?

3. What type of beverage did seventh graders buy the most?

4. **Guided Problem Solving** The table shows the average cost of a movie ticket over time. Make a conclusion about the data.

Average Cost of a Movie Ticket							
Year	1940	1950	1960	1970	1980	1990	2000
Average Cost	$.24	$.53	$.69	$1.55	$2.69	$4.23	$5.39

(1 Draw a line graph to represent the data visually.

(2 Compare the steepness of the line segments. Write a statement that describes the change in cost over time.

Practice and Problem Solving

HELP with Homework

Example	Exercises
1	5–6
2	7
3	8–9
4	10–11

Online Resources
CLASSZONE.COM
· More Examples
· eTutorial Plus

Make a bar graph of the data.

5.

Wingspans of Birds	
Bird	Wingspan
White pelican	3.6 m
Andean condor	3.2 m
Golden eagle	2.5 m
Grey heron	1.7 m
Gannet	1.7 m

6.

School Days per Year	
Country	School Days
Belgium	175
Japan	243
Nigeria	190
South Korea	220
United States	180

7. State Parks Make a double bar graph of the data.

Workers on Duty at a State Park					
Month	May	June	July	August	September
Park Rangers	32	41	55	59	40
Lifeguards	13	19	28	29	21

Weather The line graph shows the number of tornadoes in the United States each year for 1991–1997.

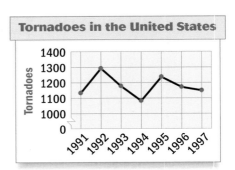

Tornadoes in the United States

8. Between which years was the decrease in the number of tornadoes greater: 1992–1993 or 1995–1996? Explain your answer.

9. Make a conclusion about the graph.

Make a line graph of the data.

10.

Temperature During a Day						
Time	7 A.M.	10 A.M.	1 P.M.	4 P.M.	7 P.M.	10 P.M.
Temperature	45°F	52°F	63°F	59°F	55°F	47°F

11.

CDs Sold at a Store During a Week							
Day	Sun.	Mon.	Tues.	Wed.	Thurs.	Fri.	Sat.
CDs	123	51	98	62	49	71	142

Newspapers The table shows the circulation of daily newspapers each year for 1994–1999, grouped by morning and evening papers.

12. Make a double line graph of the data. Use different colors for the morning and the evening papers.

13. Make a conclusion about the data.

14. Make a prediction about the circulation of morning and evening papers for 2000 and beyond.

Circulation of Newspapers (millions)		
Year	Morning	Evening
1994	43.4	15.9
1995	44.3	13.9
1996	44.8	12.2
1997	45.4	11.3
1998	45.6	10.5
1999	46.0	10.0

15. **Decide** Is it more appropriate to make a double bar graph or a double line graph to display the populations of two countries over time? Explain.

What do you think?

Science

■ **Extreme Weather**

Many storm chasing tours pursue *supercells*. These rotating thunderstorms tend to produce the most tornadoes. If a storm chasing tour has room for 7 guests on each of their 3 vans, how many guests can they take on their search for a supercell?

16. Collect Data Ask the same number of seventh and eighth graders in your school what kind of pet(s) they have. Display the data in a double bar graph. Make a conclusion about your data.

17. Critical Thinking Can the data collected in Exercise 16 be displayed in a double line graph? Explain.

18. Challenge The table shows the number of medals won by three countries at the 2002 Winter Olympics. Make a multiple bar graph of the data.

Country	Bronze	Silver	Gold
Austria	10	4	2
Canada	8	3	6
Norway	6	7	11

Mixed Review

Copy and complete the statement using <, >, or =. *(Lesson 2.1)*

19. 5.15 ? 5.5

20. 1.78 ? 1.708

21. 2.01 ? 2.0100

22. Find the mean of the following data: 6, 5, 11, 7, 9, 4. *(Lesson 3.1)*

Basic Skills **Use a number line to order the numbers from least to greatest.**

23. 29, 5, 23, 19, 0, 9

24. 32, 47, 40, 38, 34

25. 48, 47, 54, 60, 51

Test-Taking Practice

26. Multiple Choice The graph shows the average heights of boys and girls at specific ages. Which conclusion is supported by the graph?

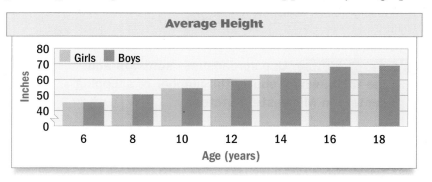

A. Girls are taller than boys until the age of 14.

B. Girls and boys grow the same amount each year.

C. After the age of 14, boys grow faster than girls.

D. Boys are always taller than girls.

Technology Activity

Making Data Displays

GOAL Use spreadsheet software to display data in bar graphs and line graphs.

Example 1 The prices of the merchandise at a concert are shown at the right. Use spreadsheet software to make a vertical bar graph of the data.

	A	B
1	Merchandise	Price (dollars)
2	Hat	15
3	Long-sleeve shirt	35
4	Poster	10
5	Sweatshirt	40
6	T-shirt	25

Solution

1 Enter the data in the first two columns of a spreadsheet, as shown above.

2 Highlight the data in cells A2:B6. The expression A2:B6 refers to the rectangular array of cells that has A2 and B6 at the corners.

3 Use the Insert menu to insert a graph. Select a vertical bar graph, or column chart, as the type of graph. Then choose the options for your graph, such as the titles and labels.

4 To change other features of your graph after it has been created, double click on the part of the graph that you wish to change and adjust the formatting.

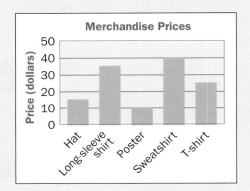

Your turn now Use spreadsheet software and the table, which shows the number of shopping centers in Midwestern states.

1. Make a vertical double bar graph of the data. Follow the steps for a single bar graph, but highlight three columns of data. Adjust the scale on the vertical axis so that it starts at 600.

2. Make a conclusion about the number of shopping centers in the states listed.

Shopping Centers		
State	1999	2000
Illinois	2146	2175
Indiana	918	926
Michigan	1039	1056
Ohio	1716	1741
Wisconsin	629	637

Example 2 Search the Internet to find the daily mean temperatures for each month in Chicago. Then make a line graph of the data.

Solution

① Search the Internet for the following:

Search the Internet for:

| normal daily mean temperatures Chicago | **Search** |

② Enter the data in the first two columns of a spreadsheet, as shown below.

	A	**B**
1	Month	Temperature (°F)
2	Jan.	22
3	Feb.	27
4	Mar.	37.3
5	Apr.	47.8
6	May	58.7
7	Jun.	68.2
8	Jul.	73.3
9	Aug.	71.7
10	Sep.	63.8
11	Oct.	52.1
12	Nov.	39.3
13	Dec.	27.4

③ Use the steps for making a bar graph, but select line graph instead.

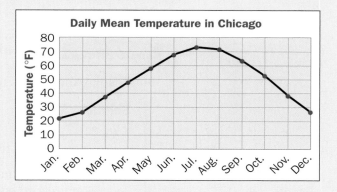

Your turn now Use the Internet and spreadsheet software to complete the following exercises.

3. Find the daily mean temperatures for each month of the year in San Diego, California. Then make a line graph of the data.

4. Writing Compare the daily mean temperatures for Chicago with those for San Diego.

5. Sports Find the number of medals awarded to the country of your choice in the past five Winter Olympics. Use the phrase "International Olympics Committee Winter Olympics" to search for the data. Then make a line graph of the data.

Stem-and-Leaf Plots

BEFORE	▶ Now	WHY?
You displayed data using bar graphs and line graphs.	You'll display data using stem-and-leaf plots.	So you can analyze Olympic ski results, as in Ex. 15.

In the Real World

Word Watch

stem-and-leaf plot, p. 116

Speeds of Animals The table lists the maximum running speeds of various animals. How can the data be displayed to show the distribution of the speeds?

A **stem-and-leaf plot** is a data display that helps you to see the way data are distributed. You can use a stem-and-leaf plot to place data in increasing order.

Animal	Speed (miles per hour)
Elk	45
Cheetah	70
Greyhound	39
Wildebeest	50
Quarter horse	47
Zebra	40
Giraffe	32
Coyote	43

EXAMPLE 1 **Making a Stem-and-Leaf Plot**

Display the speeds of the animals given above in a stem-and-leaf plot.

Solution

(1) The numbers vary from 32 to 70, so let the **stems** be the tens' digits from 3 to 7. Let the **leaves** be the ones' digits.

(2) Write the stems first. Draw a vertical line segment next to the stems. Then record each speed by writing its ones' digit on the same line as its corresponding tens' digit.

(3) Make an ordered stem-and-leaf plot.

Unordered Plot

```
3 | 9 2
4 | 5 7 0 3
5 | 0
6 |
7 | 0
```

Key: 4|7 = 47

Ordered Plot

```
3 | 2 9
4 | 0 3 5 7
5 | 0
6 |
7 | 0
```

Key: 4|7 = 47

> In the ordered plot, the leaves for each stem are listed in order from least to greatest.

> Include a key to show what the stems and leaves represent.

■ **Bicycle Stunt Competition**

Each point total in Example 2 is the mean of the scores given by three judges. If the judges give scores of 89, 90, and 88 to a rider, what is his point total?

EXAMPLE **2** **Interpreting a Stem-and-Leaf Plot**

Bicycle Stunt Competition The point totals (rounded to the nearest tenth) for the 20 participants in a bicycle stunt competition are listed below. The rider with the highest point total out of 100 points wins.

89.4 90 87.5 84.3 89.7 90.3 91.4 91 86.7 84.1

89.2 86 89.1 88.2 89.5 85.6 90.5 90.2 91.1 88.9

Use a stem-and-leaf plot to order the data. Then make a conclusion about the data.

Solution

Begin by making an unordered stem-and-leaf plot. Because the point totals range from 84.1 to 91.4, the stems are the digits in the tens' and ones' places. The leaves are the digits in the tenths' place.

Then make an ordered stem-and-leaf plot.

Unordered Plot		Ordered Plot
84 │ 3 1		84 │ 1 3
85 │ 6		85 │ 6
86 │ 7 0		86 │ 0 7
87 │ 5		87 │ 5
88 │ 2 9		88 │ 2 9
89 │ 4 7 2 1 5		89 │ 1 2 4 5 7
90 │ 0 3 5 2		90 │ 0 2 3 5
91 │ 4 0 1		91 │ 0 1 4
Key: 87│5 = 87.5		Key: 87│5 = 87.5

ANSWER More than half of the participants finished near the top, with 12 participants having point totals greater than 89.

Your turn now **Complete the following exercises.**

1. The test scores for the students in a social studies class are listed below. Make an ordered stem-and-leaf plot of the scores.

   92 78 73 89 98 89 83 75 83 100
   69 71 96 67 81 73 88 86 82 94

2. Use the stem-and-leaf plot from Exercise 1 to determine the number of test scores greater than 84.

3. Use the stem-and-leaf plot from Exercise 1 to make a conclusion about the test scores.

Getting Ready to Practice

1. **Vocabulary** The key for a stem-and-leaf plot is $10|5 = 10.5$. Which number in the key is the stem? the leaf?

U.S. Presidents **The ages of recent U.S. Presidents at the time of their inaugurations are listed below.**

54   46   64   69   52   61   56   55   43   62   60   51   54   51

2. Make an ordered stem-and-leaf plot of the data.

3. **Writing** Use the stem-and-leaf plot from Exercise 2 to make a conclusion about the data.

Practice and Problem Solving

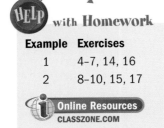
HELP with Homework

Example	Exercises
1	4–7, 14, 16
2	8–10, 15, 17

Online Resources
CLASSZONE.COM
· More Examples
· eTutorial Plus

Make an ordered stem-and-leaf plot of the data.

4. Students in each class: 22, 29, 12, 27, 15, 19, 13, 27, 12, 9, 26, 10

5. Numbers of volunteers: 12, 11, 34, 11, 35, 29, 9, 30, 15, 10, 13, 11

6. Miles walked: 2.2, 4.1, 2.5, 0.5, 5.8, 6.6, 2, 3, 2.4, 1.1

7. Hours spent on the Internet: 4.3, 5.9, 4.1, 1.5, 0.8, 2.8, 1.1, 1.2, 2.4, 1.5

Family Reunion **The ages of the people at your family reunion are given in the stem-and-leaf plot.**

```
0 | 2 5 5 7 9
1 | 1 1 3 4 7 9
2 | 2 5 7 8
3 | 2 3 4 4 9
4 | 0 2
5 | 3 7
6 | 0 1          Key: 5|3 = 53
```

8. How many people attended the reunion?

9. How old was the oldest person there?

10. Make a conclusion about the data.

11. Suppose that your 98 year old great-grandfather attended the reunion. Why do you think his age is an *outlier*?

12. **Video Game Sales** The stem-and-leaf plot shows the number of video games sold at a store each day over two weeks. Find the mean, median, mode(s), and range of the data.

```
0 | 3
1 | 0 0 2
2 | 3 8 9
3 | 0 2 5 5 7 9
4 | 1          Key: 2|8 = 28
```

13. **Critical Thinking** When using a stem-and-leaf plot to find the median of a data set, why is it important to use an ordered stem-and-leaf plot?

**Daniela Ceccarelli,
2002 Winter Olympics super
giant slalom gold medalist**

Skiing The times, in seconds, for the women's super giant slalom event at the 2002 Winter Olympics are listed below.

73.86   74.08   73.95   74.44   74.28   73.99   73.59   74.99
74.73   74.89   75.13   73.64   74.84   74.83   75.17

14. Make an ordered stem-and-leaf plot of the data.

15. Make a conclusion about the data.

Extended Problem Solving In Exercises 16–18, use the heights, in inches, of plants grown using two different fertilizers.

Organic fertilizer: 23, 18, 38, 52, 46, 9, 36, 39, 40, 49, 50, 42, 47

Chemical fertilizer: 42, 51, 36, 29, 12, 46, 30, 9, 18, 16, 23, 28, 24

16. Display Make an ordered stem-and-leaf plot for each fertilizer.

17. Interpret Make a conclusion about each stem-and-leaf plot.

18. Compare Which of the two fertilizers is more effective? Explain.

19. Challenge Explain how rounding the numbers below will make it easier to make a stem-and-leaf plot of the data.

5716   5944   4764   1750   3811   1940   5650   7982   5203   9393   3256

Mixed Review

Find the quotient. Then check your answer. *(Lesson 2.4)*

20. $19.95 \div 7$ **21.** $25.9 \div 4$ **22.** $242 \div 2.2$ **23.** $1925 \div 5.5$

Find the mean, median, mode(s), and range of the data. *(Lesson 3.1)*

24. 12, 31, 26, 39, 11, 15, 18, 22   **25.** 1.6, 1.9, 1.2, 3.2, 2.7, 1.1, 2.3

Basic Skills **Find the sum or difference.**

26. $45 + 187$ **27.** $2851 + 979$ **28.** $155 - 68$ **29.** $964 - 892$

Test-Taking Practice

30. Multiple Choice What is the greatest number in the stem-and-leaf plot?

A. 2.71   **B.** 23.5

C. 27.5   **D.** 275

```
23 | 4 5
24 | 4 7 9
25 | 0 4 8 8
26 | 3 8 9
27 | 1 2 5     Key: 24|7 = 24.7
```

31. Multiple Choice What is the median of the data in Exercise 30?

F. 25.4   **G.** 25.8   **H.** 254   **I.** 258

Notebook Review

Review the vocabulary definitions in your notebook.

Copy the review examples in your notebook. Then complete the exercises.

Check Your Definitions

mean, p. 101
median, p. 101
mode, p. 101

range, p. 102
bar graph, p. 108
line graph, p. 109

stem-and-leaf plot, p. 116

Use Your Vocabulary

1. Writing Describe how to find the median of a data set.

3.1 Can you find the mean, median, mode, and range?

 EXAMPLE Find the mean, median, mode(s), and range of the data.

5, 6, 11, 11, 16, 18, 19, 21, 21, 23, 24, 29

Mean: $\dfrac{5 + 6 + 11 + 11 + 16 + 18 + 19 + 21 + 21 + 23 + 24 + 29}{12} = 17$

Median: $\dfrac{18 + 19}{2} = 18.5$ **Modes:** 11 and 21 **Range:** $29 - 5 = 24$

☑ **2.** Find the mean, median, mode(s), and range of the data.

10, 5, 25, 23, 21, 28, 15, 39, 16, 17, 5, 14, 29

3.2 Can you make line graphs and bar graphs?

 EXAMPLE The table and the line graph show the price of a snowboard at the same time each day during a five-day Internet auction.

Day	Price (dollars)
1	50
2	57
3	76
4	103
5	145

Snowboard Auction Price

☑ **3.** Make a bar graph of the lengths of the rivers listed in the table.

Lengths (in miles) of the Longest Rivers in the United States				
Mississippi	Missouri	Rio Grande	St. Lawrence	Yukon
2340	2540	1900	1900	1980

3.3 Can you make stem-and-leaf plots?

 EXAMPLE An ordered stem-and-leaf plot of the data below appears at the right.

38, 36, 10, 23, 19, 30, 6,
16, 39, 12, 12, 5, 27

```
0 | 5 6
1 | 0 2 2 6 9
2 | 3 7
3 | 0 6 8 9
```

Key: 1 | 6 = 16

☑ **4.** Make an ordered stem-and-leaf plot of the data below.

10, 13, 41, 55, 38, 22, 12, 55, 17, 27, 13, 19, 48, 25, 36

Stop and Think about Lessons 3.1–3.3

5. Critical Thinking Which of the averages in Exercise 2 best represents the data? Explain.

Review Quiz 1

Find the mean, median, mode(s), and range of the data.

1. 42, 16, 21, 34, 25, 28, 30, 20   **2.** 8.4, 8.9, 8.5, 8.5, 8, 7.9, 9.3

In Exercises 3 and 4, use the table, which shows the responses of students at a school when asked to name their favorite type of music.

Music Type	Responses
Country	27
Hip-hop	36
Pop	58
Rock	34
Other	12

3. Decide whether to display the data in a bar graph or a line graph. Then make the data display.

4. Make a conclusion about the data.

5. Make an ordered stem-and-leaf plot of the data below.

9.7, 10.6, 7.8, 7.2, 6.4, 8.3, 10.3, 7.7, 11.9, 10.1, 11.5, 6.4, 7.2

Hands-on Activity

GOAL
Organize data using the median.

MATERIALS
· paper
· pencil

Organizing Data Using the Median

Explore Use the median to divide your class into groups according to the number of letters in students' first and last names.

1 Count the number of letters in your first and last name. Write the total on a piece of paper.

2 Hold up your paper and form a line with your classmates so that the numbers are arranged from least to greatest.

3 Determine the median number of letters.

4 Use the median to divide the line into a lower half and an upper half. If there is an odd number of students, the median is not included in either the lower or upper half.

5 Repeat Steps 3 and 4 for each half. The original line should be divided into 4 parts.

Your turn now Answer the following questions about your class.

1. What is the median of your entire class?

2. What is the median of the lower half?

3. What is the median of the upper half?

4. What are the least and greatest numbers?

Stop and Think

5. Critical Thinking About what fraction of the class should have numbers of letters that are greater than or equal to the median of the lower half and less than or equal to the median of the upper half? Count the number of students that fall in this range and compare it with the total number of students to check your answer.

Box-and-Whisker Plots

BEFORE | ▶ **Now** | **WHY?**

You displayed data using bar graphs and line graphs.

You'll display data using box-and-whisker plots.

So you can compare heights of redwood trees, as in Exs. 14–15.

In the Real World

Word Watch

box-and-whisker plot, p. 123
lower quartile, p. 123
upper quartile, p. 123
lower extreme, p. 123
upper extreme, p. 123

Roller Coasters The heights, in feet, of suspended roller coasters in the United States are given below. How can the data be displayed so that it is divided into quarters?

35   42   42.5   60   60   70   76   78   81   100

A **box-and-whisker plot** is a data display that divides data values into four parts. Ordered data are divided into a lower and an upper half by the median. The median of the lower half is the **lower quartile**. The median of the upper half is the **upper quartile**. The **lower extreme** is the least data value. The **upper extreme** is the greatest data value.

EXAMPLE 1 **Making a Box-and-Whisker Plot**

To make a box-and-whisker plot of the roller coaster heights given above, first find the median. Then find the lower and upper quartiles.

HELP with Solving

If a data set has an odd number of values, the median value is not included in either the lower half or the upper half.

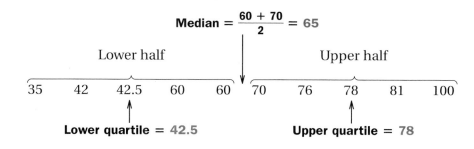

$$\text{Median} = \frac{60 + 70}{2} = 65$$

Lower half | Upper half

35   42   42.5   60   60 | 70   76   78   81   100

Lower quartile = 42.5 | Upper quartile = 78

Plot the lower extreme, lower quartile, median, upper quartile, and upper extreme using a number line.

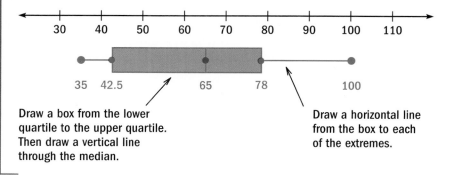

Draw a box from the lower quartile to the upper quartile. Then draw a vertical line through the median.

Draw a horizontal line from the box to each of the extremes.

Interpreting a Box-and-Whisker Plot A box-and-whisker plot helps to show how varied, or spread out, the data are.

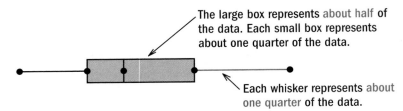

The large box represents about half of the data. Each small box represents about one quarter of the data.

Each whisker represents about one quarter of the data.

EXAMPLE 2 **Interpreting a Box-and-Whisker Plot**

Watches The prices of the watches at a store are displayed in the box-and-whisker plot below.

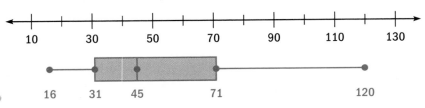

a. If all of the watches under $31 are on clearance, then about what fraction of the watches are on clearance?

b. If all of the watches from $31 to $71 are on sale, then about what fraction of the watches are on sale?

Solution

a. The watches **less than $31** are about the same as the number in one of the whiskers, which represents **about one quarter** of the watches.

b. The watches between **$31 and $71** are about the same as the number in the large box of the plot, which represents **about half** of the watches.

Your turn now **Complete the following exercises.**

1. A movie theater recorded the number of tickets sold for each showing of a movie during its opening weekend. Make a box-and-whisker plot of the ticket data listed below.

    497 429 746 469 504 464 326 302 509 467 401 499

2. Use the box-and-whisker plot from Exercise 1 to make a conclusion about the data.

3. In Example 2, is the number of watches between $71 and $120 greater than the number of watches between $16 and $31?

EXAMPLE 3 **Comparing Box-and-Whisker Plots**

Football The box-and-whisker plots below represent the number of points scored in each game of the 2001–2002 season for the New England Patriots and the St. Louis Rams. What conclusions can you make about the data?

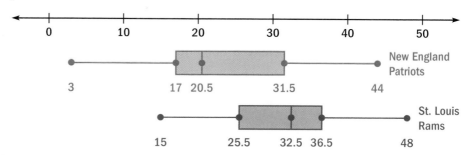

Solution

In general, the Rams scored more points per game than the Patriots. There is more variability in the points scored by the Patriots than by the Rams, with the range for the Patriots being $44 - 3 = 41$ and the range for the Rams being $48 - 15 = 33$.

3.4 **Exercises**
More Practice, p. 707

INTERNET
eWorkbook Plus
CLASSZONE.COM

Getting Ready to Practice

Vocabulary In Exercises 1–4, tell whether the statement about the box-and-whisker plot is *true* or *false*.

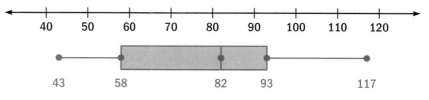

1. The upper extreme is 93.

2. The median is 82.

3. The lower quartile is 58.

4. The upper quartile is 117.

5. DVD Rentals The number of DVDs rented each day over two weeks at a video rental store are given. Make a box-and-whisker plot of the data.

38 42 50 65 82 91 88 40 34 41 71 93 87 94

6. Writing Use the box-and-whisker plot from Exercise 5 to make a conclusion about the data.

Practice and Problem Solving

with Homework

Example	Exercises
1	7–10, 14, 17
2	11–12
3	13, 18

Online Resources
CLASSZONE.COM
· More Examples
· eTutorial Plus

7. Choose the set of data that is displayed in the box-and-whisker plot.

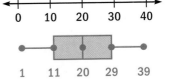

   A. 1, 30, 39, 12, 13, 20, 11, 22, 29

   B. 12, 28, 13, 10, 1, 39, 30, 20, 22

Make a box-and-whisker plot of the data.

8. Hourly rates of pay: 8.75, 7.50, 9, 8, 6.50, 8, 6.50, 7, 6, 7, 6.25

9. Pages per chapter in a book: 21, 25, 20, 14, 15, 19, 14, 14, 10, 25

10. Ages of roller rink employees: 24, 22, 30, 18, 29, 38, 33, 17, 22, 25, 16, 41

Fuel Economy The box-and-whisker plots show the average miles per gallon of gasoline used in city driving for 2002 models of small cars and sport utility vehicles.

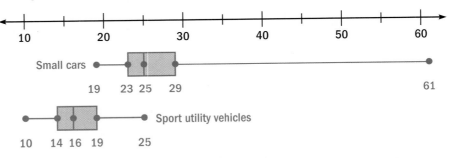

11. Compare the number of small cars that get less than 25 miles per gallon with those that get more than 25 miles per gallon.

12. About what fraction of the sport utility vehicles get less than 14 miles per gallon?

13. Writing Make a conclusion comparing the two groups of vehicles.

Trees In Exercises 14 and 15, use the heights, to the nearest foot, of coastal redwood trees known to be over 340 feet tall listed below.

   359, 361, 363, 358, 368, 361, 366, 360, 358, 359, 358, 366, 363, 364, 358, 363

14. Make a box-and-whisker plot of the data.

15. Suppose the tallest tree is struck by lightning and its height is reduced to 352 feet. Make a box-and-whisker plot for the new data. How does this plot differ from the one that you made in Exercise 14?

16. Critical Thinking Suppose you have to make a box-and-whisker plot for an unordered data set with 50 values. Explain how a stem-and-leaf plot of the data can help you make the box-and-whisker plot.

What do you think?

Science

■ **Redwood Trees**

Suppose the arch in a redwood tree is 2.1 meters high. Can a truck that is 260 centimeters tall pass through the arch?

Golf The distances, in yards, that Julia and Ty hit 14 golf balls at a driving range are listed below.

Julia: 116, 147, 167, 157, 88, 130, 155, 161, 118, 144, 220, 213, 222, 52

Ty: 62, 129, 103, 217, 230, 160, 151, 63, 133, 203, 159, 142, 185, 201

17. Using the same number line, make a box-and-whisker plot for each person.

18. Interpret Make a conclusion about the data.

Challenge Tell whether the statement is *always*, *sometimes*, or *never* true.

19. When a data set has 13 items, the lower quartile is one of the items.

20. Exactly half of the items in a data set are greater than the median.

21. The upper extreme and the upper quartile are not the same number.

Mixed Review

Write the number in scientific notation. *(Lesson 2.5)*

22. 25,500,000   **23.** 700,000,000   **24.** 9999   **25.** 326,700

26. Make a stem-and-leaf plot of the data listed below. *(Lesson 3.3)*

6.6, 6.4, 4.1, 5.5, 5, 4.2, 8.1, 6.8, 8.5, 4.2, 9.5, 8.7, 5.3, 4.2

Basic Skills Use a number line to order the numbers from least to greatest.

27. 14, 9, 10, 1, 7, 13, 3   **28.** 27, 32, 22, 25, 36, 29, 39

Test-Taking Practice

29. Multiple Choice The box-and-whisker plot shows the heights, in feet, of waves at a beach during one day. What is the lower quartile?

A. 5   **B.** 7   **C.** 9.5   **D.** 11

30. Multiple Choice Which statement about the plot above is *not* true?

F. The smallest wave measured was 5 feet high.

G. About one quarter of the data lie between 9.5 feet and 11 feet.

H. About half of the data lie between 7 feet and 11 feet.

I. The range in heights is 4 feet.

Draw a Diagram

Look for a Pattern

Guess, Check, and Revise

Estimate

Make a Table

Solve a Related Problem

Work Backward

Make a Table

Problem The students planning a comedy show need to determine how many programs to print for the one show. They survey 40 students, asking them how many tickets they are planning to purchase for the show. The results are listed below.

2, 3, 2, 2, 3, 2, 2, 4, 3, 1, 1, 5, 2, 0, 1, 3, 0, 1, 2, 1,
2, 4, 2, 0, 0, 1, 2, 1, 1, 2, 1, 2, 3, 2, 0, 3, 2, 2, 2, 5

Use the fact that there are 312 students in the school to determine an estimate for the number of programs that they need to print.

❶ Read and Understand

Read the problem carefully.

- You need to find an estimate for the number of people who will attend the comedy show.

- The problem assumes that each person attending the show will receive one program.

❷ Make a Plan

Decide on a strategy to use.

One way to understand the situation is to make a table. To solve this problem, you can organize the results of the survey in a table to see the most frequent response.

❸ Solve the Problem

Reread the problem and make a table.

First, set up the table. For each data value, make a tally mark next to the corresponding number of tickets. Next, find the total number of tally marks in each row.

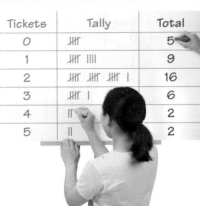

Tickets	Tally	Total
0	JHT	5
1	JHT IIII	9
2	JHT JHT JHT I	16
3	JHT I	6
4	II	2
5	II	2

The most frequent response, the mode, is 2 tickets. To find an estimate for the number of people who will attend the show, multiply the number of students in the entire school by 2.

Number of programs to print = 312 × 2 = 624

❹ Look Back

Find the mean of the data in the statement of the problem to make sure that 2 tickets per student is a good estimate.

Use the strategy _make a table._

1. **Dolphins** A wild dolphin resort has a nightly feeding for the dolphins that visit the resort. The calendar below shows how many dolphins were present for the feeding session each day for one month. What is the most common number of dolphins that attended the feeding sessions?

		8	4	4	6	6
6	7	6	7	6	7	8
3	3	5	2	3	4	5
4	6	6	6	8	8	6
6	8	6	3	4		

2. **Siblings** You and a friend survey students in your school to see how many siblings they have. What is the most common number of siblings that students have?

   2, 1, 1, 0, 3, 1, 2, 4, 5, 1, 0, 0, 1, 3, 1, 0, 2, 1, 1, 0, 1, 3, 1, 1, 0

3. **Jogging** You go jogging every other day. Your friend goes jogging every third day. If you both go jogging on Monday, when will you both go jogging together again?

4. **Daycare Center** A daycare center has three-legged stools and four-legged chairs for the children to sit on. The total number of stools and chairs is 20, and the total number of legs is 72. Use the table below to determine the number of chairs in the daycare center for the children to sit on.

Stools	1	2	3	?
Chairs	19	18	17	?
Legs	79	78	77	?

Mixed Problem Solving

Use any strategy to solve the problem.

5. **Concert** You are going to a concert. You want to buy a concert ticket, two souvenir T-shirts, a CD, and a beverage. How much money should you bring with you to cover your costs?

Price List	
Concert ticket	$49.50
T-shirt	$22.25
CD	$15.99
Beverage	$1.50

6. **Sunrise** During one week in February the sun rose at the times shown in the table below. At what times would you expect the sun to rise during the weekend?

Mon.	Tues.	Wed.	Thurs.	Fri.	Sat.	Sun.
7:18	7:17	7:15	7:14	7:12	?	?

7. **Walking** Justin decides to go for a walk to become familiar with his new neighborhood. Starting from his house, he walks 1 block north, 1 block east, 1 block north, 2 blocks east, 4 blocks south, 2 blocks west, 2 blocks south, 4 blocks west, 2 blocks north, 1 block east, and 2 blocks north. How far should he walk and in which direction to get home?

Histograms

BEFORE	▶ Now	WHY?
You made bar graphs.	You'll make and interpret histograms.	So you can display trail lengths in a histogram, as in Ex. 10.

Word Watch

frequency table, p. 130
frequency, p. 130
histogram, p. 131

You can use a *frequency table* to help organize and interpret data. A **frequency table** is used to group data values into intervals. The **frequency** of an interval is the number of values that lie in the interval.

Data Values

Calendars Sold in Mr. Moore's Homeroom

1, 7, 12, 2, 3, 22, 7, 5, 10, 1, 15, 9, 8, 2, 7, 17, 24, 14, 5, 4

Frequency Table

Interval	Tally	Frequency
1–5	⦀⦀ ⦀⦀⦀	8
6–10	⦀⦀ ⦀	6
11–15	⦀⦀⦀	3
16–20	⦀	1
21–25	⦀⦀	2

A tally mark, |, represents one data value. The mark ⦀⦀ represents five data values.

EXAMPLE 1 **Making a Frequency Table**

Science The number of named stars in a group of 34 constellations are listed below. Make a frequency table of the data.

7, 5, 4, 10, 5, 7, 2, 6, 8, 1, 5, 1, 3, 1, 12, 11, 2, 11, 2, 5, 0, 6, 14, 8, 3, 1, 15, 10, 0, 2, 0, 15, 9, 1

Solution

(1 Choose intervals of equal size that cover all the data values, which range from 0 to 15. In the table, each interval covers 4 whole numbers. The first interval is 0–3 and the last interval is 12–15.

(2 Make a tally mark next to the interval containing a given number of named stars.

(3 Write the frequency for each interval by totaling the number of tally marks for the interval.

Interval	Tally	Frequency
0–3	⦀⦀ ⦀⦀ ⦀⦀⦀⦀	14
4–7	⦀⦀ ⦀⦀⦀⦀	9
8–11	⦀⦀ ⦀⦀	7
12–15	⦀⦀⦀⦀	4

The three bright stars in a row are part of the Orion constellation.

Histograms A **histogram** is a graph that displays data from a frequency table. A histogram has one bar for each interval that contains data values. The length of the bar indicates the frequency for the interval.

EXAMPLE 2 Making a Histogram

Music Every Sunday morning, a radio station plays a countdown of the top 30 requested songs from the previous week.

The table shows the number of weeks that each of the songs on this week's top 30 have been on the countdown.

Make a histogram of the data.

Weeks	Tally	Frequency
1–5	IIII	4
6–10	JHT JHT I	11
11–15	JHT IIII	9
16–20	IIII	4
21–25		0
26–30	II	2

Solution

(**1** Draw and label the horizontal and vertical axes.

List each interval from the frequency table on the horizontal axis.

The greatest frequency is 11. So, start the vertical axis at 0 and end at 12, using increments of 2.

(**2** Draw a bar for each interval. The bars should have the same width.

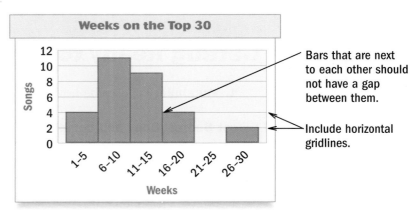

Bars that are next to each other should not have a gap between them.

Include horizontal gridlines.

Watch Out!

Make sure that your histogram includes all of the intervals in the table, even the intervals that have a frequency of 0.

Your turn now Complete the following exercises.

1. The number of words that students in a typing class can type in a minute are listed below. Make a frequency table of the data.

25, 19, 23, 29, 34, 26, 30, 40, 33, 20, 35, 35, 25, 29, 36, 22, 31

2. Make a histogram of the data in Exercise 1.

EXAMPLE **3** Interpreting a Histogram

Butterflies The histogram shows the butterflies spotted in a butterfly garden between 8 A.M. and 8 P.M. Make a conclusion about the data.

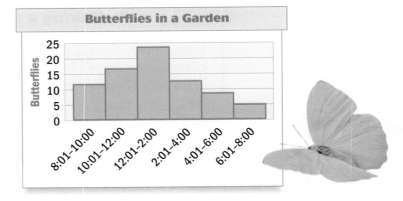

Butterflies in a Garden

ANSWER The number of butterflies increased during the morning, with the most butterflies in the garden between 12:01 P.M. and 2:00 P.M. After 2:00 P.M., the number of butterflies decreased.

3.5 Exercises
More Practice, p. 707

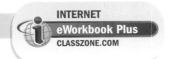

INTERNET
eWorkbook Plus
CLASSZONE.COM

Getting Ready to Practice

1. **Vocabulary** Describe how a histogram differs from a bar graph.

Test Scores **Copy and complete the frequency table using the data.**

2. **Math test scores for class 1:**
   70, 78, 68, 82, 91, 98, 76, 97, 89, 79, 88, 90, 85, 77, 84, 82, 90, 86, 93, 64, 94, 68, 86, 87

Interval	Tally	Frequency
61–70	?	?
71–80	?	?
81–90	?	?
91–100	?	?

3. **Math test scores for class 2:**
   90, 96, 87, 64, 74, 95, 87, 76, 88, 65, 83, 71, 74, 84, 95, 97, 81, 72, 80, 74, 97, 88, 100, 92

Interval	Tally	Frequency
61–70	?	?
71–80	?	?
81–90	?	?
91–100	?	?

4. Make a histogram of the test scores for each class in Exercises 2 and 3.

5. **Writing** Make a conclusion about each histogram in Exercise 4.

Practice and Problem Solving

with Homework

Example	Exercises
1	6-7, 9
2	10, 14
3	11, 15

Online Resources
CLASSZONE.COM

· More Examples
· eTutorial Plus

Copy and complete the frequency table using the data.

6. Ages of camp counselors:
19, 23, 26, 23, 16, 20, 26, 19, 21,
24, 21, 17, 27, 25, 22, 17, 16, 25

Interval	Tally	Frequency
?	?	?
19-21	?	?
22-24	?	?
?	?	?

7. Minutes spent on phone daily:
9, 19, 9, 13, 20, 8, 9, 19, 6, 12,
6, 18, 20, 10, 13, 17, 9, 5, 16, 5

Interval	Tally	Frequency
5-8	?	?
?	?	?
13-16	?	?
?	?	?

8. Find the Error The prices of televisions at a store are given below. Describe and correct the error(s) in the frequency table of the prices.

170, 135, 120, 175,
200, 260, 275, 160,
230, 165, 280, 150,
180, 280, 125, 100

Interval	Tally	Frequency
100–150	ЖII	5
150–200	ЖII II	7
200–250	II	2
250–300	IIII	4

9. Alligators Which intervals can be used to make a frequency table of the lengths, in inches, of alligators at an alligator farm?

140, 127, 103, 140, 118, 100, 117, 101, 116, 129, 130, 105, 99, 143

A. 90–110, 111–130, 131–150
B. 91–110, 111–130, 131–150
C. 90–110, 110–130, 130–150
D. 81–100, 101–120, 121–140

Walking Trails The frequency table below groups the lengths, in miles, of historical walking trails in the United States.

10. Make a histogram of the data.

11. Make a conclusion about the data.

12. Critical Thinking Is it possible to determine the data values by looking at the frequency table or histogram? Explain.

13. Use the frequency table to make a new frequency table with the following intervals: 3–6.9, 7–10.9, 11–14.9. How does changing the intervals affect the histogram?

Length	Frequency
3-4.9	4
5-6.9	5
7-8.9	17
9-10.9	2
11-12.9	6
13-14.9	1

Freedom Trail in Boston, Massachusetts

Canoe Racing In Exercises 14–16, use the point totals for each team in a Hawaiian canoe racing regatta, which are listed below. The team with the most points wins.

72, 69, 65, 54, 45, 44, 37, 36, 34, 33, 32, 32, 29, 27, 24, 21,
20, 18, 14, 14, 14, 13, 12, 11, 10, 10, 9, 8, 7, 7, 4, 4, 1, 0

14. Make a histogram of the data.

15. Make a conclusion about the data.

16. **Describe** Make a stem-and-leaf plot of the data. Then compare the stem-and-leaf plot with the histogram from Exercise 14. What information does each data display show?

17. **Challenge** Write a survey question whose results can be displayed in a histogram. Make a prediction about your results. Then survey your class and display the results in a histogram. How does your prediction compare with your results?

Mixed Review

Multiply. Then check that your answer is reasonable. *(Lesson 2.3)*

18. 6.283×7 **19.** 0.2×5.8 **20.** 9.2×4.99 **21.** 1.01×4.4

22. Make a box-and-whisker plot of the data, which are the number of tracks on 20 CDs. *(Lesson 3.4)*

21, 10, 11, 11, 17, 10, 17, 9, 13, 9, 13, 19, 20, 14, 12, 8, 9, 15, 10, 13

Basic Skills **Test the number for divisibility by 2, 3, 5, 6, 9, and 10.**

23. 35   **24.** 72   **25.** 468   **26.** 134

Test-Taking Practice

27. **Multiple Choice** The histogram shows the years that the 50 states were admitted to the Union. How many states were admitted during the years 1781–1810?

A. 2   **B.** 8

C. 17   **D.** 18

28. **Short Response** Make a conclusion about the data displayed in the histogram.

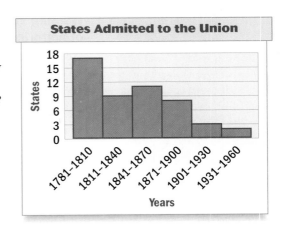

States Admitted to the Union

Appropriate Data Displays

BEFORE	Now	WHY?
You displayed data using several types of graphs.	You'll choose an appropriate display for a data set.	So you can choose a data display for phone data, as in Ex. 6.

Activity You can collect data and choose an appropriate display.

① Word Watch

Review Words

bar graph, p. 108
line graph, p. 109
stem-and-leaf plot, p. 116
box-and-whisker plot, p. 123
histogram, p. 131

(1 Have someone time you for 5 seconds as you write as many letters of the alphabet as you can in order. Record your result. Combine your result with those of your classmates.

a b c d e f g h i j

(2 Work with a group to decide how to display the data for the class. Then display the data and make a conclusion about the data. Compare your data display and conclusions with other groups.

Using appropriate data displays helps you make meaningful conclusions.

Appropriate Data Displays

Use a *bar graph* to display data in distinct categories.

Use a *line graph* to display data over time.

Use a *stem-and-leaf plot* to group data into ordered lists.

Use a *box-and-whisker plot* to display the lower extreme, lower quartile, median, upper quartile, and upper extreme of a data set.

Use a *histogram* to compare the frequencies of data that fall in equal intervals.

EXAMPLE 1 Choosing an Appropriate Data Display

Manatees A marine biologist wants to display the lengths of manatees living in a Florida waterway. What data display(s) should he use to see how the data are distributed, without displaying individual data?

ANSWER Either a *box-and-whisker plot* or a *histogram* will show how the data are distributed without showing individual data.

Misleading Data Displays You need to be able to identify potentially misleading data displays so that you interpret them correctly. Examples of potentially misleading data displays are shown below.

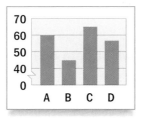

Broken Vertical Axis

The break in the axis exaggerates differences in bar lengths.

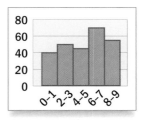

Large Increments

The large increments compress the graph vertically.

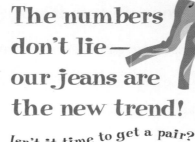

Small Intervals

The small intervals make it difficult to see the clustering of data.

EXAMPLE 2 **Identifying Misleading Data Displays**

Advertising Is the advertisement potentially misleading? Explain.

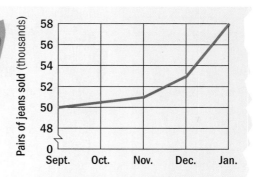

Watch Out!

Make sure that you read the scale on the vertical axis of the data display in Example 2 carefully. Notice the break in the scale.

Solution

The graph could be misleading because there is a break in the scale on the vertical axis, as it jumps from 0 to 48. The graph indicates a significant rise in sales. However, this rise would look less impressive if the vertical axis did not have a break in the scale.

Your turn now **Complete the following exercises.**

1. A car dealership sells seven makes of cars. Which data display should be used to compare sales for each make of car during last month?

2. Redraw the line graph in Example 2 without a break in the scale. Compare the two graphs. What do you notice?

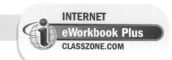
Getting Ready to Practice

1. **Vocabulary** List five data displays that you have learned.

2. **Restaurants** Should a bar graph or a line graph be used to compare the number of restaurants of different types in a city? Explain.

3. **Donations** The graph shows the donations collected each year for a charity. Choose a reason why the graph could be misleading.

   A. Break in the vertical axis

   B. Large increments on the vertical axis

   C. Small intervals on the horizontal axis

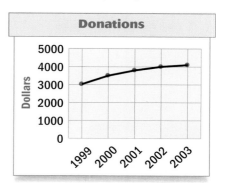

Practice and Problem Solving

with Homework

Example	Exercises
1	4–7
2	8, 16

Online Resources
CLASSZONE.COM
· More Examples
· eTutorial Plus

Tell which of the two given types of data displays would be appropriate for the set of data. Then make the data display.

4. A line graph or a stem-and-leaf plot

Price for a Gallon of Gasoline at Different Gas Stations						
$1.45	$1.25	$1.50	$1.31	$1.28	$1.46	$1.41
$1.29	$1.37	$1.19	$1.50	$1.27	$1.39	$1.44

5. A bar graph or a histogram

Ages of Students in a CPR Class						
Interval	10–19	20–29	30–39	40–49	50–59	60–69
Frequency	5	11	9	7	7	5

Explain **Choose an appropriate data display for the data. Explain your choice.**

6. You want to display the lengths of the long distance phone calls that you made last month so that the lengths are in four equal groups.

7. You want to display the results of a survey that asked people to name their favorite basketball team.

8. Test Grades The test grades for a science class are displayed in the histogram. Explain why the graph could be misleading.

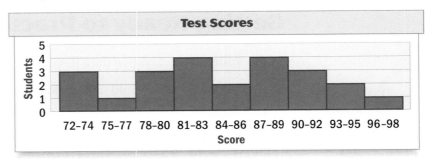

Test Scores

9. Collect Data Ask at least 20 students how many CDs they own. Choose a data display for the data and explain your choice. Then display the data and make conclusions about the data.

Favorite Meals The graph shows the results of a survey that asked students to choose their favorite type of meal. Tell whether the statement is *true* or *false*. Explain your reasoning.

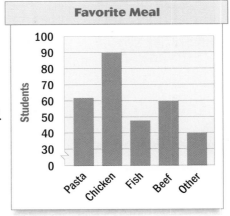

Favorite Meal

10. Chicken is twice as popular as beef.

11. Chicken is twice as popular as fish.

12. Pasta is twice as popular as fish.

13. Students chose Beef twice as often as Other.

Extended Problem Solving In Exercises 14–16, use the graph below, which shows the amounts of waste recycled in the United States.

14. Interpret About how many times more waste was recycled in 2000 than in 1990?

15. Analyze About how many times greater is the area of the recycle bin for 2000 than the area of the recycle bin for 1990? Does this agree with your answer to Exercise 14?

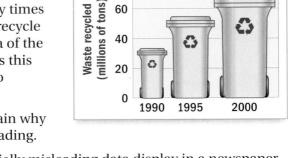

Recycling in the United States

16. Make Conclusions Explain why the graph could be misleading.

17. Challenge Find a potentially misleading data display in a newspaper or a magazine. Explain why the display could be misleading.

Find the sum or difference. *(Lesson 2.2)*

18. $3.7 + 0.58$ **19.** $0.413 + 8.07$ **20.** $7.29 - 2.12$

21. A city's daily high temperatures, in degrees Fahrenheit, over 18 days are listed below. Make a histogram of the data. *(Lesson 3.5)*

76, 84, 78, 83, 77, 83, 85, 80, 72, 68, 76, 89, 90, 91, 86, 78, 72, 75

Basic Skills **Copy and complete the statement.**

22. $3 \text{ min} = \underline{?} \text{ sec}$ **23.** $540 \text{ min} = \underline{?} \text{ h}$ **24.** $21 \text{ d} = \underline{?} \text{ wk}$

Test-Taking Practice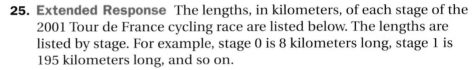

25. **Extended Response** The lengths, in kilometers, of each stage of the 2001 Tour de France cycling race are listed below. The lengths are listed by stage. For example, stage 0 is 8 kilometers long, stage 1 is 195 kilometers long, and so on.

8, 195, 219, 198, 215, 67, 211, 163, 223, 185, 209,
32, 167, 193, 145, 233, 228, 194, 61, 150, 160

What data display should be used to determine whether there is a pattern in the kilometers traveled in the stages of the race? Make the data display. Then make a conclusion about the data.

BrAIN GAME

Get your tickets!

The graph represents all of the ticket sales for the first 5 shows on a band's tour. How many shows were sold out? Would you consider this a good start to the tour?

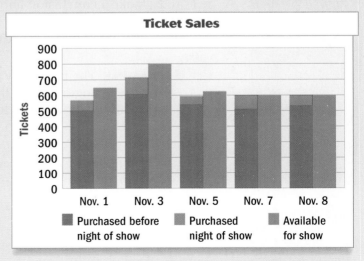

Ticket Sales

Tickets

■ Purchased before night of show ■ Purchased night of show ■ Available for show

Notebook Review

Review the vocabulary definitions in your notebook.

Copy the review examples in your notebook. Then complete the exercises.

Check Your Definitions

box-and-whisker plot, p. 123

lower quartile, p. 123

upper quartile, p. 123

lower extreme, p. 123

upper extreme, p. 123

frequency table, p. 130

frequency, p. 130

histogram, p. 131

Use Your Vocabulary

1. Describe how to find the lower quartile and upper quartile of a data set.

3.4 Can you make box-and-whisker plots?

 EXAMPLE Make a box-and-whisker plot of the data below.

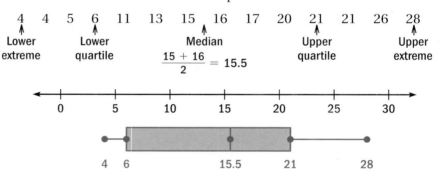

2. Make a conclusion about the box-and-whisker plot above.

3.5 Can you make histograms?

 EXAMPLE The frequency table and the histogram show the prices of the different styles of shoes in a store.

Price (dollars)	Frequency
10–19	10
20–29	22
30–39	16
40–49	11

Chapter 3 Data and Statistics

3. The number of students in each math class at a school is listed below. Organize the data in a frequency table. Then make a histogram of the data.

22, 28, 17, 9, 15, 30, 26, 18, 19, 31, 29, 20, 24, 8, 18, 17

3.6 Can you identify misleading data displays?

Review

EXAMPLE Explain why the data display could be misleading.

The graph could be misleading because there is a break in the scale on the vertical axis. The rise in the value of the baseball card would not appear as impressive if there was no break in the scale.

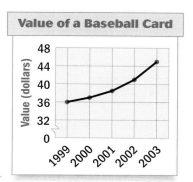

Value of a Baseball Card

 4. You want to display the number of visits to a company's Web site each day over a week. Should you use a line graph or a histogram?

Stop and Think about Lessons 3.4–3.6

5. Writing Describe a way that a data display could be misleading.

Review Quiz 2

1. Make a box-and-whisker plot of the data below.

90, 102, 104, 120, 114, 95, 118, 105, 107, 106, 110, 109, 112

In Exercises 2 and 3, use the hours worked during a week by each employee at a music store, which are listed below.

29, 26, 23, 10, 17, 42, 38, 9, 29, 22, 16, 11, 39, 38, 26, 14

2. Make a histogram of the data with the following intervals: 0–9, 10–19, 20–29, 30–39, 40–49.

3. Make a conclusion about the data.

4. You want to display the number of points scored during the season by each player on a basketball team. What display should you use to group the points into ordered lists?

Chapter Review

Vocabulary

mean, p. 101	line graph, p. 109	lower extreme, p. 123
median, p. 101	stem-and-leaf plot, p. 116	upper extreme, p. 123
mode, p. 101	box-and-whisker plot, p. 123	frequency table, p. 130
range, p. 102	lower quartile, p. 123	frequency, p. 130
bar graph, p. 108	upper quartile, p. 123	histogram, p. 131

Vocabulary Review

1. What data display is most appropriate for displaying data that are in distinct categories?

2. What data display is most appropriate for comparing data grouped into equal intervals?

3. What numbers do you plot to make a box-and-whisker plot?

Copy and complete the statement.

4. The ? of a data set is the sum of the values divided by the number of values.

5. The ? of a data set is the value that occurs most often.

6. An ordered ? is used to group data into ordered lists.

Review Questions

In Exercises 7–10, find the mean, median, mode(s), and range of the data. *(Lesson 3.1)*

7. 0, 1, 2, 4, 4, 5, 7, 8, 10, 12, 13

8. 151, 183, 184, 163, 201, 162

9. 5.5, 6.3, 4.7, 4.6, 4.6, 7.1, 6.3, 7.4, 6, 7.5

10. 67.5, 70.7, 67.3, 71.2, 72.1, 71.2, 69.7, 70.3

11. **Reading** The number of books read by each of 20 students in 3 months is listed below. Which average best represents the number of books read? Explain your reasoning. *(Lesson 3.1)*

    13, 19, 5, 9, 7, 8, 6, 2, 6, 5, 5, 7, 6, 2, 2, 8, 9, 7, 5, 9

12. **Movies** Students at a school were asked to name their favorite type of movie. Make a double bar graph of the results given below. *(Lesson 3.2)*

	Drama	Comedy	Action	Science Fiction	Animated	Other
Boys	53	62	33	15	16	11
Girls	85	60	14	2	10	12

In Exercises 13–15, use the table at the right, which shows Holly's weekly allowance for each month last year. *(Lesson 3.2)*

Month	Allowance	Month	Allowance
Jan.	$15.00	July	$18.00
Feb.	$15.00	Aug.	$18.50
Mar.	$16.00	Sep.	$19.00
Apr.	$16.00	Oct.	$19.00
May	$16.00	Nov.	$20.00
June	$18.00	Dec.	$20.00

13. Make a line graph of the data.

14. Between which two months did Holly's allowance increase the most?

15. Make a conclusion about the data.

Make an ordered stem-and-leaf plot of the data. *(Lesson 3.3)*

16. Test scores: 98, 96, 83, 85, 89, 72, 84, 73, 88, 93, 89, 67, 83, 79, 83, 78, 75

17. Ages: 38, 38, 17, 23, 36, 35, 20, 12, 19, 39, 27, 36, 41, 30, 18, 22, 37, 25, 13

Speed Limits In Exercises 18 and 19, use the stem-and-leaf plot, which shows the speeds, in miles per hour, of cars on a highway. *(Lesson 3.4)*

18. Make a box-and-whisker plot of the data.

19. If a police officer decides to pull over anyone traveling at 65 miles per hour or faster, about what fraction of the cars would get pulled over?

```
5 | 5 8 7 6
6 | 0 1 2 8 7 5 5 2 8
7 | 2 0 5 0 5 2

Key: 6|2 = 62
```

Swimming In Exercises 20 and 21, use the data below, which are the number of seconds that students in a swimming class can hold their breath underwater. *(Lesson 3.5)*

65, 29, 38, 50, 60, 43, 27, 48, 29, 79, 37, 45, 48, 32, 57, 35, 54, 53, 37, 47

20. Make a frequency table of the data, using the following intervals: 20–29, 30–39, 40–49, 50–59, 60–69, 70–79.

21. Use the frequency table that you made in Exercise 20 to make a histogram of the data.

22. School Lunches The line graph at the right shows the number of school lunches purchased during the lunch period at a school. Explain why the graph could be misleading. *(Lesson 3.6)*

23. Pizza You want to display the results of a survey that asked students to name their favorite pizza topping. Choose an appropriate data display. Explain your choice. *(Lesson 3.6)*

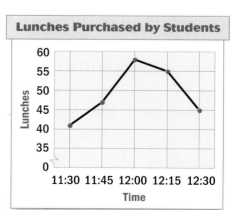

Lunches Purchased by Students

Chapter Test

In Exercises 1 and 2, find the mean, median, mode(s), and range.

1. 2, 7, 2, 7, 13, 7, 11, 9, 6, 5, 8

2. 48, 67, 88, 82, 41, 66, 72, 64, 49, 53

3. Find the missing values in the data below so that the mean is 28 and the mode is 15.

20, 40, 36, _?_, 15, 38, _?_, 30, 41

Baseball **In Exercises 4–6, use the bar graph at the right, which shows the wins and losses for the Baltimore Orioles over three seasons.**

4. In which season did the Orioles lose 14 more games than they won?

5. About how many more games did the Orioles win in 1999 than in 2000?

6. Which of the three seasons would you consider the most successful? Explain.

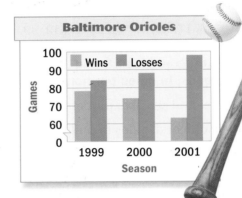

7. **Computers** The table shows a computer's price over time. Make a line graph of the data. Then make a conclusion about the data.

Date	October 15	November 15	December 15	January 15	February 15	March 15
Price	$699	$699	$649	$629	$599	$499

Fundraising **In Exercises 8 and 9, use the data below, which are the numbers of tins of popcorn sold by members of a school band.**

40, 32, 16, 14, 11, 16, 11, 12, 26, 1, 15, 9, 6, 3, 27, 5, 12, 18, 23, 33, 17, 50

8. Make a stem-and leaf-plot of the data.

9. Use the stem-and-leaf plot to make a histogram of the data.

10. **Pets** The miles covered while walking your dog each day over two weeks are listed below. Make a box-and-whisker plot of the data.

1.8, 2.6, 0.4, 2, 0.9, 2.5, 2, 1.9, 1.5, 1.5, 0.5, 0.8, 1.3, 1.6

11. **Restaurants** What data display should a restaurant owner use to display the number of customers served on each Saturday night during the past year? Explain your choice.

Chapter Standardized Test

Test-Taking Strategy Think positively during the test. This will help you keep up your confidence and let you focus on each question.

Multiple Choice

1. The points you scored in the last seven basketball games are listed below. Which statement about the data is false?

$$11, 15, 6, 10, 7, 22, 6$$

- **A.** The range is 11.
- **B.** The median is 10.
- **C.** The mode is 6.
- **D.** The mean is 11.

2. Which data set has a median of 16?

- **F.** 16, 21, 26, 29, 32
- **G.** 0, 4, 7, 10, 16, 16
- **H.** 4, 15, 18, 20, 23
- **I.** 0, 8, 10, 22, 26, 31

3. The graph shows the number of campsites being used at a campground each night. Which statement about the graph is true?

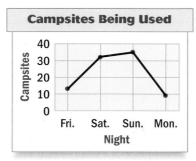

- **A.** The number of campsites being used increased each day from Friday to Monday.
- **B.** The number of campsites being used increased from Sunday to Monday.
- **C.** The number of campsites being used decreased each day from Friday to Monday.
- **D.** The number of campsites being used decreased from Sunday to Monday.

4. What is the median of the data shown in the stem-and-leaf plot?

- **F.** 2
- **G.** 3
- **H.** 6.2
- **I.** 62

5	2 4 5 8
6	0 1 3
7	1 1 1
8	8 9

Key: $7\,|\,1 = 7.1$

5. The number of lifts at 10 ski resorts are listed below. What is the lower quartile of the data set?

$$8, 9, 11, 11, 11, 13, 17, 18, 19, 25$$

- **A.** 8
- **B.** 11
- **C.** 12
- **D.** 18

6. Which intervals would be most appropriate for making a histogram of the data below?

$$0, 1, 1.3, 2.4, 5, 3.1, 2.2, 3, 1.2, 2.4$$

- **F.** 0–1, 1–2, 2–3, 3–4, 4–5
- **G.** 0–1.9, 2–3.9, 4–5
- **H.** 0–1.9, 2–3.9, 4–5.9
- **I.** 0.1–2, 2.1–4, 4.1–6

Short Response

7. Make a box-and-whisker plot of the data.

$$25, 19, 29, 24, 15, 24, 17, 20,$$
$$7, 5, 30, 22, 18, 39, 9, 21$$

Extended Response

8. Students' scores on a science quiz are listed below. Find the mean, median, and mode(s). Then decide which average best represents the data. Explain your reasoning.

$$98, 100, 91, 64, 74, 98, 75, 68,$$
$$82, 97, 95, 77, 93, 71, 92$$

Strategies for Answering
Multiple Choice Questions

You can use the problem solving plan on page 39 to solve any problem. If you have difficulty solving a problem involving multiple choice, you may be able to use one of the strategies below to choose the correct answer. You may also be able to use these strategies and others to check whether your answer to a multiple choice question is reasonable.

Strategy: Estimate the Answer

Problem 1

You need to add the cost of renting 3 DVDs to the cost of renting 1 video game.

At a video rental store, it costs \$3.80 to rent a DVD and \$3.15 to rent a video game. How much will it cost to rent 3 DVDs and 1 video game?

A. \$6.95

B. \$11.97

C. \$14.55 — — — — Estimate: $3(3.80) + 3.15 \approx 3(4) + 3 = 15$,

D. \$19.99

so the correct answer is C .

Strategy: Use Visual Clues

Problem 2

You need to compare the two bars that represent the number of students with times in the two specified intervals.

The histogram shows the times, in minutes, that it took students at a school to run 1 mile. How many more students had times in the 9–10.9 minute interval than in the 7–8.9 minute interval?

F. 10   G. 19

H. 22   I. 41

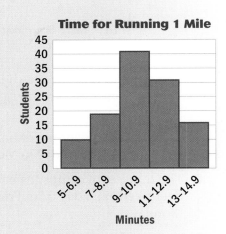

Time for Running 1 Mile

The scale on the vertical axis uses increments of 5. Because there are slightly more than 4 increments of 5 separating the bars, the difference between the bars is slightly more than 20. So, the correct answer is H .

Strategy: Use Number Sense

Problem 3

Use the fact that the number of decimal places in the product is equal to the sum of the number of decimal places in the factors.

Evaluate 0.9×0.7.

A. 0.063

B. 0.63 — The sum of the decimal places in the factors is 2 and the last digit of the product is not 0, so the correct answer is B.

C. 6.3

D. 63

Eliminating Unreasonable Choices The strategies used to find the correct answers for Problems 1–3 can also be used to eliminate answer choices that are unreasonable or obviously incorrect.

Problem 4

Read the problem carefully. Notice that the width of the canvas is $61 - 15.3 = 45.7$ cm, not 15.3 cm. Use the formula $A = lw$ to find the area.

The length of an artist's rectangular canvas is 61 centimeters. The width is 15.3 centimeters less than the length. What is the area?

F. 106.7 cm — Not the correct answer; area is measured in *square* units.

G. 933.3 cm^2 — Not the correct answer; $61 \times 45.7 \approx 60 \times 46 = 2760$.

H. 2700 cm^2 — Not the correct answer; the product 61×45.7 has one decimal place.

I. 2787.7 cm^2

Watch Out!

Some answers may appear correct at first glance, but they may be incorrect answers you would find by making common errors.

Your turn now

Explain why the selected answer choice is unreasonable.

1. A rectangular garden has a length of 5 feet and a perimeter of 16 feet. What is the width of the garden?

   A. 2 ft   B. 3 ft   ✗ C. 6 ft^2 D. 11 ft

2. Which of the quotients is equivalent to $16.7 \div 1.3$?

   F. $16.7 \div 13$ ✗ G. $1.67 \div 1.3$ H. $167 \div 13$ I. $1.67 \div 0.13$

3. The numbers of goals scored by a soccer team in each game over a season are listed below. What is the mean number of goals?

   6, 2, 1, 2, 5, 1, 3, 4, 4, 3, 7, 2, 1, 3, 0, 4

   A. 0   B. 2   C. 3   ✗ D. 8

GO ON   147

Multiple Choice

1. Which operation describes the numerical pattern 160, 80, 40, 20, . . . ?

   A. Add 20. **B.** Subtract 80.

   C. Multiply by 2. **D.** Divide by 2.

2. What is the value of the expression $j \div (k - 5)$ when $j = 11$ and $k = 6$?

   F. 1 **G.** 5 **H.** 11 **I.** 12

3. The dimensions of a rectangular soccer field are shown below. If one bag of fertilizer will cover 15,000 square feet, how many bags are needed to cover the soccer field?

   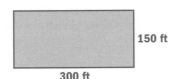

   150 ft

   300 ft

   A. 2 bags **B.** 3 bags

   C. 5 bags **D.** 10 bags

4. Which decimal has a verbal description of "sixty and thirty-two hundredths"?

   F. 6.32 **G.** 60.32

   H. 63.02 **I.** 6032

5. What is the value of $6.84 - 5.12 + 1.68$?

   A. 0.04 **B.** 1.72

   C. 3.4 **D.** 6.8

6. What is the value of $0.4st$ when $s = 4.3$ and $t = 5.55$?

   F. 1.72 **G.** 9.546

   H. 10.25 **I.** 23.865

7. The prices for making copies at a self-service copy center are listed in the table below. How much will it cost you to make 7 copies of a 30 page report?

Copies	Price for one copy
1–100	$.08
101–200	$.06
over 200	$.05

   A. $2.40 **B.** $10.50

   C. $12.60 **D.** $16.80

8. The weights of the dogs, in pounds, that visited a veterinarian's office during one day are listed below. What is the median weight?

   34, 65, 20, 13, 11, 40, 18, 12, 6, 30, 71, 66

   F. 20 lb **G.** 25 lb **H.** 29 lb **I.** 30 lb

9. The stem-and-leaf plot lists the ages of people who work at a park. Which statement is *not* true?

   ```
   1 | 6 7 8 7 8 7 7 9
   2 | 0 8 8 2 1 4 7 3
   3 | 2 4 8 6
   4 | 5 2 0
   5 | 6 0    Key: 3|2 = 32
   ```

   A. The mode is 17 years.

   B. The median is 24 years.

   C. The range of ages is 34 years.

   D. The youngest worker is 16 years old.

10. You want to display the number of students in the lunch line in the cafeteria every 15 minutes during a lunch period. Which data display is most appropriate?

   F. Line graph **G.** Bar graph

   H. Histogram **I.** Stem-and-leaf plot

Short Response

11. Carlene makes greeting cards. She spends $.30 for the materials to make one card. She sells the cards for $1.50 each. How many cards does she need to sell to make a profit of $36?

12. You bought a spool of ribbon that contains 1.5 meters of ribbon. You use 35 centimeters of the ribbon for a craft project. How many meters of ribbon are left on the spool?

13. You and 5 of your friends are going to an ice skating rink. The cost for admission is $8, and the cost for renting ice skates is $2.50. How much will it cost for all of you to go ice skating if only 4 of you need to rent ice skates?

14. Students who have summer jobs were surveyed. As part of the survey, the students were asked to name their employers. The results are shown in the table. Make a bar graph of the data.

Summer Jobs	
Employer	**Students**
Grocery store	12
Amusement park	9
Day camp	8
Department store	7
Restaurant	11
Other	9

Extended Response

15. Paula is starting an exercise program on April 13. On the first day she wants to do 24 sit-ups. Each day she will increase the number of sit-ups by 4. On which day will Paula have to do 100 sit-ups? Explain.

16. A city wants to build a patio around a rectangular reflecting pool in a park, as shown. The landscaper's estimates are $11.25 for each square foot of a flagstone surface and $9.75 for each square foot of a concrete paver surface. If the city has budgeted $3500 for the patio, can they afford either surface, one surface, or neither surface? Explain.

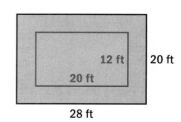

17. The average costs, in dollars, for one ticket to a professional football game at each of the stadiums in the National Football League are listed below. Make a frequency table of the data. Use 6 equal intervals, starting with 30–39. Use the frequency table to make a histogram of the data. Then make a conclusion about the data.

50, 52, 55, 46, 48, 38, 52, 59, 43, 45, 71, 82, 60, 61, 39, 50, 50, 57, 46, 56, 77, 63, 56, 54, 50, 62, 39, 45, 50, 56, 53

Cumulative Practice for Chapters 1–3

Chapter 1

Multiple Choice In Exercises 1–9, choose the letter of the correct answer.

1. What is the next figure in the pattern below? *(Lesson 1.1)*

A. B. C. D.

2. What is the value of $a + b$ when $a = 14$ and $b = 22$? *(Lesson 1.2)*

 F. 7   G. 14   H. 26   I. 36

3. What is the value of 6^3? *(Lesson 1.3)*

 A. 18   B. 36   C. 63   D. 216

4. What is the first step in evaluating $6(5 - 4) + 6^2 \div 2 - 1$? *(Lesson 1.4)*

 F. Subtract 1 from 2.

 G. Evaluate 6^2.

 H. Divide 6 by 2.

 I. Subtract 4 from 5.

5. What is the value of the expression $3x^2 + 5y - 2$ when $x = 2$ and $y = 5$? *(Lesson 1.4)*

 A. 20   B. 35   C. 83   D. 98

6. What is the solution of the equation $6z = 30$? *(Lesson 1.5)*

 F. 5   G. 6   H. 24   I. 180

7. If a train travels at a constant speed of 50 miles per hour, how long will it take for the train to travel 150 miles? *(Lesson 1.5)*

 A. 3 minutes   B. 2 hours

 C. 3 hours   D. 6 hours

8. A square has a side length of 13 inches. What is its area? *(Lesson 1.6)*

 F. 13 in.^{2} G. 26 in.^{2} H. 62 in.^{2} I. 169 in.^{2}

9. On a 3 day hiking trip, you hiked the same amount on the first and second days, and 5 miles on the third day. If you hiked a total of 17 miles, how many miles did you hike on the first day? *(Lesson 1.7)*

 A. 4   B. 6   C. 12   D. 17

10. **Short Response** Insert grouping symbols into the expression $6 + 12 \div 4 \times 3$ to make it equal to 7. *(Lesson 1.4)*

11. **Extended Response** Your family wants to carpet the rectangular floor at the right. *(Lesson 1.6)*

16 ft

11 ft

 a. How many square feet of carpet are needed?

 b. The carpet that your family picked out at a flooring store costs $2 for a square foot. If the store also charges $85 for installation, how much will the carpet and installation cost?

 c. A second store charges $3 for a square foot of the same carpet, but it offers free installation. Should your family purchase the carpet at this store instead of the store in part (b)? Explain.

Chapter 2

Multiple Choice In Exercises 12–20, choose the letter of the correct answer.

12. Which statement is true? *(Lesson 2.1)*

A. $0.24 > 0.136$ **B.** $0.56 > 0.89$

C. $0.37 > 0.73$ **D.** $0.52 < 0.46$

13. What is 158.3627 rounded to the nearest hundredth? *(Lesson 2.1)*

F. 158.36   **G.** 158.363

H. 158.4   **I.** 200

14. The table shows the amount of money raised by each of the 3 groups of seventh graders at a school fair. How much money did the 3 groups raise? *(Lesson 2.2)*

Group	7A	7B	7C
Money raised	$133.88	$148.59	$122.77

A. $271.36   **B.** $282.47

C. $405.24   **D.** $424.35

15. What is the value of $1.6k$ when $k = 2.2$? *(Lesson 2.3)*

F. 0.352   **G.** 3.52   **H.** 3.8   **I.** 35.2

16. Which quotient is equal to 1.31? *(Lesson 2.4)*

A. $6.55 \div 0.05$ **B.** $65.5 \div 50$

C. $6.55 \div 0.5$ **D.** $655 \div 50$

17. Which choice expresses 188,650,000 in scientific notation? *(Lesson 2.5)*

F. 1.8865×10^6 **G.** 1.8865×10^7

H. 1.8865×10^8 **I.** 1.8865×10^9

18. About how long is an unsharpened pencil? *(Lesson 2.6)*

A. 20 mm   **B.** 20 cm

C. 50 cm   **D.** 200 cm

19. Which statement is *not* true? *(Lesson 2.7)*

F. $500 \text{ mL} < 5 \text{ L}$ **G.** $6 \text{ g} = 6000 \text{ mg}$

H. $3.5 \text{ m} > 350 \text{ km}$ **I.** $17 \text{ cm} > 17 \text{ mm}$

20. What is the value of 22 cm − 16 mm? *(Lesson 2.7)*

A. 8 mm   **B.** 8 cm

C. 204 mm   **D.** 204 cm

21. Short Response The table shows the batting averages of the starting infielders on a softball team. Order the averages from least to greatest. Which infielder has the greatest batting average? *(Lesson 2.1)*

Player	Average
Mary	0.322
Leah	0.224
Emily	0.314
Erica	0.289

22. Extended Response You bring five 2-liter bottles of soda to a dance. It will be sold at the refreshment table. *(Lessons 2.3, 2.7)*

a. You bought 5 bottles of the same kind of soda. If 1 bottle cost $1.29, how much did 5 bottles cost?

b. The soda will be served in plastic cups. If one cup holds 250 milliliters of soda, how many cups of soda can be served?

c. Students can purchase a cup of soda for $.50. Find the amount of money collected by selling all of the cups of soda.

Chapter 3

Multiple Choice In Exercises 23–27, choose the letter of the correct answer.

23. Which data set has a median of 28?
(Lesson 3.1)

A. 17, 29, 28, 38, 31   **B.** 17, 38, 27, 15, 34, 29

C. 38, 21, 17, 19, 28   **D.** 34, 38, 15, 17, 30, 28

24. The longest drops for each of the three highest waterfalls in the world are shown in the bar graph. Which question cannot be answered by looking at the graph?
(Lesson 3.2)

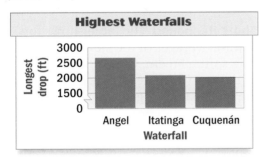

F. Which waterfall has a longest drop of 2648 feet?

G. About how much longer is the drop of the Angel waterfall than the Cuquenán waterfall?

H. What is the length of the longest drop of the Itatinga waterfall?

I. In what country is the Angel waterfall located?

25. What is the least number in the stem-and-leaf plot?
(Lesson 3.3)

```
11 | 2 9 4 5
12 | 6 7 0
13 | 8 3 5 6
14 | 8 4 6

Key: 12 | 6 = 1.26
```

A. 1.12   **B.** 1.46

C. 11.2   **D.** 11.5

26. The box-and-whisker plot shows the scores for the balance beam event at a gymnastics meet. Which statement about the plot is *not* true? *(Lesson 3.4)*

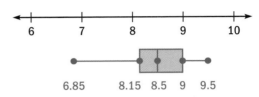

F. The least score is 6.85.

G. The greatest score is 9.5.

H. About half of the scores fall between 8.5 and 9.

I. The median score is 8.5.

27. You want to display the results of a survey that asked students to name their favorite type of music. Which data display is most appropriate? *(Lesson 3.6)*

A. Bar graph   **B.** Line graph

C. Histogram   **D.** Stem-and-leaf plot

28. Short Response The data below are the times, in minutes, it takes students in your class to get to school. Which average best represents the data? Explain. *(Lesson 3.1)*

14, 40, 47, 37, 15, 8, 27, 24, 40, 5, 10, 9

29. Extended Response A radio station gave away concert tickets. The ages of the ticket winners are listed below. *(Lesson 3.5)*

30, 36, 28, 26, 29, 21, 43, 15, 16, 24, 31, 18

a. Make a frequency table of the data using the intervals 10–19, 20–29, 30–39, 40–49.

b. Use the frequency table to make a histogram of the data.

c. Use your histogram to make a conclusion about the ages of the ticket winners.

Chapter **4** **Number Patterns and Fractions**

- Find greatest common factors and least common multiples.
- Identify equivalent fractions and write fractions in simplest form.
- Compare and convert between fractions, mixed numbers, and decimals.

Chapter **5** **Fraction Operations**

- Add and subtract fractions and mixed numbers.
- Multiply and divide fractions and mixed numbers.
- Measure in the U.S. customary system and convert customary units.

Chapter **6** **Integers**

- Perform operations with integers and rational numbers.
- Use the distributive property to rewrite and evaluate expressions.
- Identify and plot points in a coordinate plane.

From Chapter 5, p. 236

How much does a humpback whale weigh?

Number Patterns and Fractions

BEFORE

In previous chapters you've...

- Compared and ordered decimals
- Performed operations on whole numbers and decimals

Now

In Chapter 4 you'll study...

- Finding greatest common factors and least common multiples
- Comparing and ordering fractions and mixed numbers
- Writing fractions as decimals and decimals as fractions

WHY?

So you can solve real-world problems about...

- Chinese New Year, p. 160
- Rose Bowl floats, p. 167
- flying insects, p. 178
- Rainbow Bridge, p. 192

Internet Preview
CLASSZONE.COM

- eEdition Plus Online
- eWorkbook Plus Online
- eTutorial Plus Online
- State Test Practice
- More Examples

Chapter Warm-Up Game

Review skills you need for this chapter in this quick game.

Key Skill:
Whole number division

COASTER COMMOTION

HOW TO PLAY

Did you know that there are more roller coasters in the United States than in any other country? In this game, you'll use division to find out how many roller coasters there are in the United States.

1 **COPY** the lists below. Each list corresponds to one of the roller coaster facts on page 155, and each roller coaster fact includes a trivia number. Determine whether each number in a list is a factor of its corresponding trivia number. If a number is a factor, cross it off the list.

 2, 8, 10   4, 6, 8   3, 6, 9

2 **MULTIPLY** the remaining numbers to find the total number of roller coasters in the United States as of 2002.

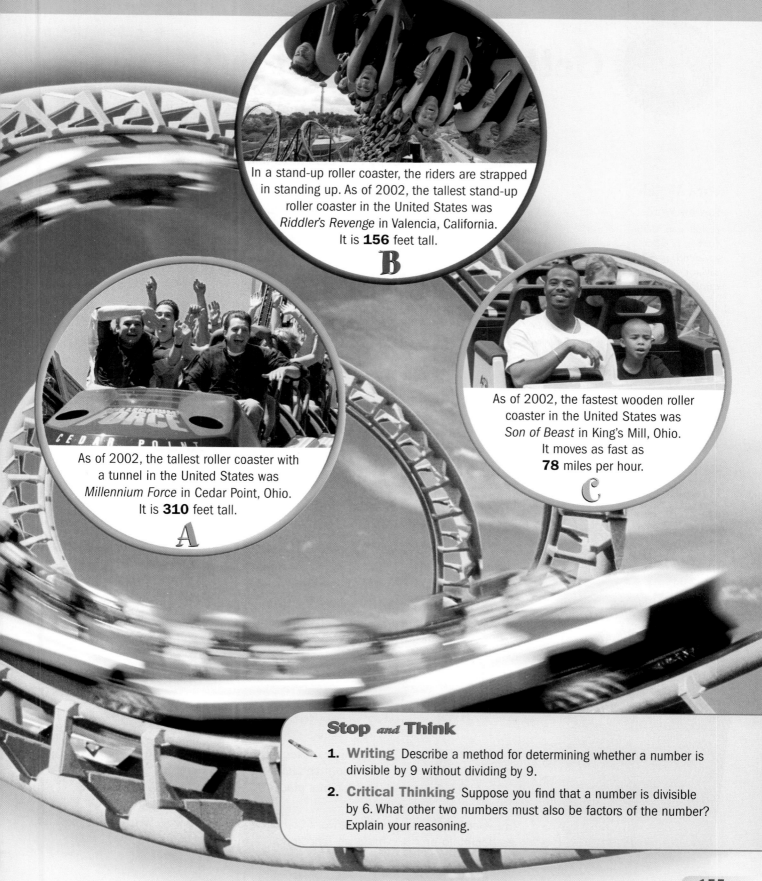

In a stand-up roller coaster, the riders are strapped in standing up. As of 2002, the tallest stand-up roller coaster in the United States was *Riddler's Revenge* in Valencia, California. It is **156** feet tall.

B

As of 2002, the tallest roller coaster with a tunnel in the United States was *Millennium Force* in Cedar Point, Ohio. It is **310** feet tall.

A

As of 2002, the fastest wooden roller coaster in the United States was *Son of Beast* in King's Mill, Ohio. It moves as fast as **78** miles per hour.

C

Stop *and* Think

1. **Writing** Describe a method for determining whether a number is divisible by 9 without dividing by 9.

2. **Critical Thinking** Suppose you find that a number is divisible by 6. What other two numbers must also be factors of the number? Explain your reasoning.

Getting Ready to Learn

Review What You Need to Know

Using Vocabulary **Copy and complete using a review word.**

1. The number 12 is said to be __?__ by 4 because 4 divides evenly into 12.

2. In the expression 144 ÷ 3, 144 is called the __?__.

Write a fraction to represent the shaded part of the set or region. *(p. 686)*

3.   **4.**    **5.**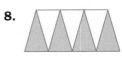

6.   **7.**   **8.**

Find the product or quotient. *(pp. 689–690)*

9. 356 × 79 **10.** 592 ÷ 16 **11.** 960 ÷ 12

12. 827 × 654 **13.** 1590 ÷ 15 **14.** 562 × 308

15. 1544 × 290 **16.** 3672 ÷ 9 **17.** 1479 × 567

You should include material that appears on a notebook like this in your own notes.

Know How to Take Notes

Using Your Homework Write a question mark next to a homework exercise you did incorrectly. Get help from your teacher or another student, and write down what you learned. Review homework corrections when you study for a test.

~~1.07~~
~~× 0.03~~   **?**
~~0.321~~

      1.07
    × 0.03   Number of decimal places in product
    ———   is equal to the sum of the number
    0.0321 ◄——— of decimal places in the factors.

In Lesson 4.7, use your homework to help you learn how to write fractions as decimals and decimals as fractions.

Prime Factorization

BEFORE	▶ Now	WHY?
You multiplied whole numbers to find their product.	You'll write a number as a product of prime numbers.	So you can tell whether a Chinese New Year is prime, as in Ex. 51.

Word Watch

prime number, p. 157
composite number, p. 157
prime factorization, p. 158
factor tree, p. 158

Activity You can make a list of *prime numbers*.

1 Write the whole numbers from 2 through 50.

2 Cross out all multiples of 2 other than 2. (The first row in the list below has been done for you.) Then go to the next remaining number after 2 and cross out all its multiples other than itself. Repeat until you can no longer cross out numbers.

```
 2   3   X̶   5   X̶   7   X̶   9   X̶
11  12  13  14  15  16  17  18  19  20
21  22  23  24  25  26  27  28  29  30
31  32  33  34  35  36  37  38  39  40
41  42  43  44  45  46  47  48  49  50
```

In the activity, the numbers that are not crossed out are called *prime numbers*. A **prime number** is a whole number greater than 1 whose only whole number factors are 1 and itself. A **composite number** is a whole number greater than 1 that has positive factors other than 1 and itself. For example, 5 is a prime number while $6 = 2 \times 3$ is a composite number. The number 1 is neither prime nor composite.

EXAMPLE 1 Writing Factors of a Number

Field Trip A class of 36 students is on a field trip at the zoo. The teacher wants to break the class into groups of the same size. Find all the possible group sizes by writing all the factors of 36.

Solution

$$36 = 1 \times 36$$
$$= 2 \times 18$$
$$= 3 \times 12$$
$$= 4 \times 9 \qquad \text{36 isn't divisible by 5. Skip to 6.}$$
$$= 6 \times 6 \qquad \text{36 isn't divisible by 7 and 8. Skip to 9.}$$
$$= 9 \times 4 \qquad \text{Stop when the factors repeat.}$$

ANSWER The possible group sizes are 1, 2, 3, 4, 6, 9, 12, 18, and 36.

Poison dart frog from a zoo in New York City

with Review

Need help with divisibility rules? See p. 685.

EXAMPLE 2 Identifying Prime and Composite Numbers

Tell whether the number is *prime* or *composite*.

a. 56

b. 11

Solution

a. The factors of 56 are 1, 2, 4, 7, 8, 14, 28, and 56. So, 56 is composite.

b. The only factors of 11 are 1 and 11. So, 11 is prime.

Prime Factorization Expressing a whole number as a product of prime numbers is called **prime factorization**. You can use a diagram called a **factor tree** to write the prime factorization of a number. Use an exponent when a prime factor appears more than once in the prime factorization.

with Reading

To *factor* a number means to write the number as a product of its factors.

EXAMPLE 3 Using a Factor Tree

Use a factor tree to write the prime factorization of 54.

One possible factor tree:

Write original number.

Factor 54 as 2 × 27.

Factor 27 as 3 × 9.

Factor 9 as 3 × 3.

Another possible factor tree:

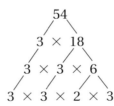

Write original number.

Factor 54 as 3 × 18.

Factor 18 as 3 × 6.

Factor 6 as 2 × 3.

Both factor trees give the same result: $54 = 2 \times 3 \times 3 \times 3 = 2 \times 3^3$.

ANSWER The prime factorization of 54 is 2×3^3.

Your turn now Use a factor tree to write the prime factorization of the number.

1. 30   **2.** 48   **3.** 44   **4.** 75

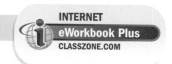
Getting Ready to Practice

1. **Vocabulary** In your own words, describe the difference between a prime number and a composite number.

Tell whether the number is *prime* or *composite*. Explain your reasoning.

2. 5   **3.** 10   **4.** 15   **5.** 43   **6.** 22

7. **Guided Problem Solving** You are a tour guide and want to divide 90 people into the same size tour groups. The ideal tour group size is between 11 and 15 people. How many people should be in each tour group?

  (1) Find all the factors of 90.

  (2) Use the factors of 90 to find all the possible group sizes.

  (3) Is more than one answer possible? Explain your reasoning.

Watch Out!
A number may be divisible by the same prime number multiple times.

Practice and Problem Solving

Write all the factors of the number.

8. 20   **9.** 45   **10.** 24   **11.** 13   **12.** 21

13. 18   **14.** 16   **15.** 54   **16.** 100   **17.** 60

Tell whether the number is *prime* or *composite*. Explain your reasoning.

18. 88   **19.** 23   **20.** 61   **21.** 39   **22.** 51

23. 67   **24.** 41   **25.** 99   **26.** 87   **27.** 201

28. List the first 10 prime numbers.

29. Critical Thinking What is the only even prime number?

30. Souvenir Pouches As a volunteer at a museum, you fill souvenir pouches with semi-precious stones. Each pouch has the same number of stones, and there are no leftover stones. Is the total number of stones in the souvenir pouches *prime* or *composite*? Explain your reasoning.

with Homework

Example	Exercises
1	8–17, 52
2	18–27, 51
3	32–44

Online Resources
CLASSZONE.COM
· More Examples
· eTutorial Plus

31. Find the Error Describe and correct the error in writing the prime factorization of 36.

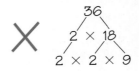

The prime factorization of 36 is $2^2 \times 9$.

Copy and complete the factor tree. Then write the prime factorization.

32.

$$12$$
$$2 \times ?$$
$$? \times 2 \times 3$$

33.

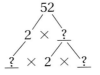

$$52$$
$$2 \times ?$$
$$? \times 2 \times ?$$

34.

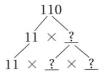

$$110$$
$$11 \times ?$$
$$11 \times ? \times ?$$

Use a factor tree to write the prime factorization of the number.

35. 26   **36.** 49   **37.** 68   **38.** 50   **39.** 64

40. 144   **41.** 225   **42.** 588   **43.** 612   **44.** 864

45. Writing Explain the difference between finding the factors of a number and finding the prime factorization of a number.

Algebra Tell whether the value of the variable expression is *prime* or *composite*.

46. $6p - 2$ when $p = 5$ **47.** $3x + 1$ when $x = 6$

48. $7n^2 + 3$ when $n = 2$ **49.** $r^3 + 17$ when $r = 4$

50. Goldbach's Conjecture A conjecture is a statement believed to be true but not proved to be true. Christian Goldbach (1690–1764) made this conjecture about prime numbers: Every even number greater than 2 can be written as the sum of two prime numbers. Show that Goldbach's conjecture is true for every even number between 3 and 11.

51. Chinese New Year The year 2019 is the Year of the Pig. Is 2019 prime or composite? Explain your reasoning.

52. Desks in a Classroom A classroom in your school contains 32 desks, and another classroom contains 35 desks. Which classroom allows for more rectangular desk arrangements if you use all the desks? Explain your answer.

Use a factor tree to write the prime factorization of the number.

53. 1764   **54.** 1089   **55.** 1232   **56.** 2310   **57.** 2205

58. Challenge Identify which columns of the table mostly contain composite numbers. Explain why.

	2	3	4	5	6
7	8	9	10	11	12
13	14	15	16	17	18
19	20	21	22	23	24

Find the mean, median, mode(s), and range of the data. *(Lesson 3.1)*

59. 4, 6, 4, 7, 8, 3, 9, 4, 3, 2

60. 12, 15, 14, 20, 25, 13, 18, 19, 8

Choose a Strategy Use a strategy from the list to solve the following problem. Explain your choice of strategy.

> **Problem Solving Strategies**
> - Look for a Pattern
> - Estimate
> - Make a Table

61. A family of 2 adults and 2 children buys a family season pass to a water park for $249.99. A single adult ticket costs $39.99, and a single child ticket costs $27.99. How many times must the entire family go to the water park for the pass to be worth its cost?

Basic Skills Test the number for divisibility by 2, 3, 5, 6, 9, and 10.

62. 144 **63.** 345 **64.** 2040 **65.** 2514

Test-Taking Practice

66. Short Response Give two different factor trees for 348.

67. Multiple Choice What is the prime factorization of 72?

A. $2^2 \times 3 \times 6$ **B.** $3^3 \times 2^2$ **C.** $2^3 \times 3^2$ **D.** $2^3 \times 9$

What am I?

If a number in the list below is a factor of 2,343,750, write its corresponding letter on a piece of paper. Unscramble the letters to answer the riddle.

2	3	4	5	6	7	8	9	10
C	A	E	H	M	L	N	R	T

Riddle: Take me out and scratch my head,
I am now black, but once was red.
What am I?

Answer: I am a(n) __?__ .

4.2 Problem Solving Strategies

- Draw a Diagram
- Look for a Pattern
- Guess, Check, and Revise
- Estimate
- **Make a List**
- Make a Table
- Work Backward

Make a List

Problem Tamia is building a rectangular kennel for her dog. She wants the kennel to have an area of 24 square yards. What is the least amount of fencing Tamia needs to enclose the kennel? (Use whole numbers only.)

❶ Read and Understand

Read the problem carefully.

You know that the kennel must be rectangular and have an area of 24 square yards.

You want to determine the least amount of fencing Tamia could use to enclose the kennel.

❷ Make a Plan

Decide on a strategy to use.

One way to solve this problem is to make a list. You can list all the possible dimensions for a rectangular kennel that has an area of 24 square yards.

❸ Solve the Problem

Reread the problem and make a list.

Because the area of a rectangle is the product of the length and width, list all the whole number products equal to 24 to find the possible lengths and widths.

$$24 \times 1, 12 \times 2, 8 \times 3, 6 \times 4$$

Now use the formula for the perimeter of a rectangle to calculate the perimeters.

Area = 24 yd² | w
l

Length	Width	2l + 2w	Perimeter
24	1	2(24) + 2(1)	50
12	2	2(12) + 2(2)	28
8	3	2(8) + 2(3)	22
6	4	2(6) + 2(4)	20

ANSWER The 6 × 4 kennel has the least perimeter. So, it uses the least amount of fencing, 20 yards.

❹ Look Back

The greater the difference between a rectangle's length and width, the greater its perimeter. So, it seems reasonable that a rectangular kennel with a length of 6 yards and a width of 4 yards uses the least amount of fencing.

Use the strategy *make a list*.

1. **Camp** A counselor divides 30 campers into teams with the same number of campers on each team. Each team will participate in a scavenger hunt. How many different team sizes are possible?

2. **Best of Five** In a best-of-five series the first team to win three games wins the series. One way that a team can win a best-of-five series is represented by WWLW (first two games won, third game lost, and fourth game won). List all possible ways a team can win a best-of-five series.

3. **Wardrobe** You are going on a trip and have packed 2 pairs of pants (P1 and P2), 3 T-shirts (T1, T2, and T3), and 2 sweaters (S1 and S2). If you wear pants, a T-shirt, and a sweater, how many different outfits can you make with these clothes?

4. **Lunch Menu** If you can select 1 sandwich, 1 side dish, and 1 dessert from the menu below, how many different combinations do you have to choose from for lunch?

LUNCH MENU		
SANDWICHES	**SIDE DISHES**	**DESSERTS**
TURKEY CLUB	SALAD	COOKIE
HAMBURGER	FRUIT	BROWNIE
GRILLED CHEESE	FRIES	APPLE PIE

5. **Perfect Numbers** A *perfect number* is a number that equals the sum of its factors not including itself. For example, the factors of 28 are 1, 2, 4, 7, 14, and 28. Because $1 + 2 + 4 + 7 + 14 = 28$, 28 is a perfect number. What are the perfect numbers between 1 and 10?

Mixed Problem Solving

Use any strategy to solve the problem.

6. **Number Patterns** Describe the following pattern: 1, 3, 7, 15, 31, 63, ... What are the next three numbers?

7. **Pottery** The prices at a paint-your-own pottery store are listed below. If you have $16, do you have enough money to spend an hour in the studio and paint a ceramic dog bowl and a vase?

Price List	
Studio time: $6.00 each hour	
Ceramics: Dog bowl	$5.00
Vase	$4.50
Flower pot	$6.00

8. **Bird Watching** On a nature hike, Bob was the first to see 3 sparrows, 1 robin, and 2 finches. Sean saw 2 sparrows, 2 robins, and 1 finch. Marcus pointed out 2 sparrows, 3 robins, and 1 finch. Which type of bird was seen the most?

9. **Movies** You and a friend together have $18 to spend at the movies. After the movie there is $1.25 left in change. What did you and your friend spend your money on?

Item	Ticket	Soda	Popcorn	Candy
Price	$6.25	$1.15	$1.95	$.75

Greatest Common Factor

BEFORE	▶ **Now**	**WHY?**
You found all the factors of a whole number.	You'll find the greatest common factor of two or more numbers.	So you can decorate Rose Bowl floats, as in Ex. 38.

In the Real World

Word Watch

common factor, p. 164
greatest common factor
(GCF), p. 164
relatively prime, p. 165

Orchestra An orchestra conductor divides 48 violinists, 24 violists, and 36 cellists into ensembles. Each ensemble has the same number of each instrument. What is the greatest number of ensembles that can be formed? How many violinists, violists, and cellists will be in each ensemble?

A whole number that is a factor of two or more nonzero whole numbers is called a **common factor**. The greatest of the common factors is called the **greatest common factor (GCF)**. One way to find the greatest common factor of two or more numbers is to make a list of all the factors of each number and identify the greatest number that is on every list.

EXAMPLE 1 Making a List to Find the GCF

In the orchestra problem above, the greatest number of ensembles that can be formed is given by the greatest common factor of 48, 24, and 36.

Factors of 48: **1, 2, 3, 4, 6**, 8, **12**, 16, 24, 48
Factors of 24: **1, 2, 3, 4, 6**, 8, **12**, 24
Factors of 36: **1, 2, 3, 4, 6**, 9, **12**, 18, 36

The common factors are 1, 2, 3, 4, 6, and 12. The GCF is 12.

ANSWER The greatest common factor of 48, 24, and 36 is 12. So, the greatest number of ensembles that can be formed is 12. Then each ensemble will have 4 violinists, 2 violists, and 3 cellists.

Your turn now Find the greatest common factor of the numbers by listing factors.

1. 16, 28   2. 21, 42   3. 60, 96

4. 12, 33, 39   5. 14, 35, 63   6. 32, 40, 64

Using Prime Factorization Another way to find the greatest common factor of two or more numbers is to use the prime factorization of each number. The product of the common prime factors is the greatest common factor.

 with **Solving**

Large numbers may have many factors, and it may be difficult to list all the factors. Sometimes it's easier to use prime factorization to find the greatest common factor of large numbers.

EXAMPLE 2 Using Prime Factorization to Find the GCF

Find the greatest common factor of 180 and 126 using prime factorization.

Begin by writing the prime factorization of each number.

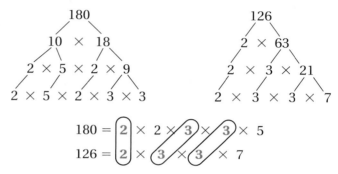

ANSWER The common prime factors of 180 and 126 are 2, 3, and 3. So, the greatest common factor is $2 \times 3^2 = 18$.

Your turn now Find the greatest common factor of the numbers using prime factorization.

7. 90, 150 **8.** 84, 216 **9.** 120, 192 **10.** 105, 225

Relatively Prime Two or more nonzero whole numbers are **relatively prime** if their greatest common factor is 1.

Watch Out!

To say that two numbers are relatively prime does *not* necessarily mean that one of the numbers is prime.

EXAMPLE 3 Identifying Relatively Prime Numbers

Tell whether the numbers are relatively prime.

a. 28, 45   Factors of 28: 1, 2, 4, 7, 14, 28
           Factors of 45: 1, 3, 5, 9, 15, 45   **The GCF is 1.**

ANSWER Because the GCF is 1, 28 and 45 are relatively prime.

b. 15, 51   Factors of 15: 1, 3, 5, 15
           Factors of 51: 1, 3, 17, 51   **The GCF is 3.**

ANSWER Because the GCF is 3, 15 and 51 are not relatively prime.

Getting Ready to Practice

1. Vocabulary Copy and complete: The numbers 35 and 36 are _?_ because their _?_ is 1.

Find the greatest common factor of the numbers by listing factors.

2. 14, 21   **3.** 24, 32   **4.** 20, 55, 65   **5.** 42, 72, 84

Find the greatest common factor of the numbers using prime factorization. Then tell whether the numbers are relatively prime.

6. 98, 140   **7.** 27, 117   **8.** 56, 88   **9.** 72, 169

10. Science Class A science class with 15 girls and 12 boys is divided into groups where each group has the same number of boys and the same number of girls. What is the greatest number of groups that can be formed? How many boys and girls are in each group?

Practice and Problem Solving

with Homework

Example	Exercises
1	11–18
2	20–28, 30–35, 38
3	20–27

Online Resources
CLASSZONE.COM

· More Examples
· eTutorial Plus

Find the greatest common factor of the numbers by listing factors.

11. 56, 81   **12.** 39, 52   **13.** 24, 63   **14.** 45, 76

15. 75, 90, 105   **16.** 48, 64, 96   **17.** 18, 30, 60   **18.** 36, 54, 135

19. Writing In your own words, describe how to find the greatest common factor of two numbers given their prime factorizations.

Find the greatest common factor of the numbers using prime factorization. Then tell whether the numbers are relatively prime.

20. 86, 154   **21.** 37, 93   **22.** 198, 216   **23.** 36, 168

24. 34, 85   **25.** 75, 285   **26.** 144, 264   **27.** 65, 112

28. Fruit Baskets A school is preparing fruit baskets for a local nursing home. There are 162 apples, 108 oranges, and 180 bananas. If the baskets are identical and there is no leftover fruit, what is the greatest number of baskets that can be made? How many apples, oranges, and bananas are in each basket?

Recreation

Rose Bowl Floats

Every square inch of a Rose Bowl float must be covered by something natural like flowers, seeds, and leaves. Suppose it takes 25 roses to cover one square foot. How many square feet do 20,000 roses cover?

29. Critical Thinking The lesser of two numbers is a factor of the greater number. What can you say about the GCF of the numbers?

Find the GCF of the numbers using prime factorization.

30. 63, 84, 126   **31.** 39, 65, 182   **32.** 110, 132, 176

33. 168, 210, 238   **34.** 70, 147, 175, 280   **35.** 68, 102, 136, 153

Tell whether the statement is *always*, *sometimes*, or *never* true.

36. The greatest common factor of two odd numbers is 2.

37. The greatest common factor of two even numbers is 2.

38. Rose Bowl Floats You are decorating a Rose Bowl float. There are 108 red roses, 144 white roses, 48 yellow roses, and 72 purple roses. If bunches of roses are identical and there are no leftover roses, what is the greatest number of bunches that can be made? How many roses of each color are in each bunch?

39. Challenge The GCF of a number and 96 is 32. The sum of the number's digits is 13. Find two numbers that satisfy these conditions.

Mixed Review

Find the quotient. Then check your answer. *(Lesson 2.4)*

40. $113.24 \div 7.6$ **41.** $27.44 \div 1.4$ **42.** $10.352 \div 1.6$ **43.** $15.67 \div 2.5$

Tell whether the number is *prime* or *composite*. *(Lesson 4.1)*

44. 41   **45.** 290   **46.** 57   **47.** 63

Basic Skills   **Solve the following problems.**

48. A tube contains 18 lead refills for a mechanical pencil. If you buy 4 tubes, how many lead refills do you have?

49. You and a friend baked 54 brownies for a bake sale. The recipe says that each batch yields 9 brownies. How many batches did you make?

Test-Taking Practice

50. Multiple Choice Identify which number pairs are relatively prime.

    I. 21, 32   II. 30, 36   III. 49, 72

A. I and II   **B.** I and III   **C.** II and III   **D.** I, II, and III

51. Multiple Choice Find the greatest common factor of 180 and 225.

F. 9   **G.** 15   **H.** 25   **I.** 45

Hands-on Activity

GOAL
Use area models
to find equivalent
fractions.

MATERIALS
• paper
• colored pencils

Modeling Equivalent Fractions

You can use area models to find equivalent fractions.

Explore **Find two fractions equivalent to $\frac{4}{6}$.**

1 Draw a rectangle on a piece of paper. Divide the rectangle into 6 equal parts, and shade 4 of the parts.

2 Look for other ways of dividing the rectangle into equal parts.

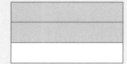 There are 3 parts, and 2 are shaded.

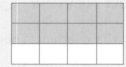 There are 12 parts, and 8 are shaded.

3 Write the equivalent fractions.

The fractions $\frac{2}{3}$ and $\frac{8}{12}$ are equivalent to $\frac{4}{6}$.

Your turn now **Draw a model of the given fraction. Then find two equivalent fractions.**

1. $\frac{9}{18}$ **2.** $\frac{2}{14}$ **3.** $\frac{4}{5}$ **4.** $\frac{15}{20}$

Stop and Think

5. Writing How could you show that $\frac{3}{4}$ is equivalent to $\frac{18}{24}$?

Equivalent Fractions

BEFORE   ▶ **Now**   **WHY?**

You factored whole numbers.   You'll write equivalent fractions.   So you can compare the numbers of bones in a skeleton, as in Ex. 38.

 **Word Watch**

fraction, p. 169
numerator, p. 169
denominator, p. 169
equivalent fractions, p. 169
simplest form, p. 170

In the Real World

Aquarium There are 10 fish in an aquarium, and 2 of them are goldfish. What *fraction* of the fish in the aquarium are goldfish?

A **fraction** is a number of the form $\frac{a}{b}$ ($b \neq 0$) where a is called the **numerator** and b is called

the **denominator** . A fraction is used to describe equal parts of a whole. Fractions that represent the same part-to-whole relationship are called **equivalent fractions** .

EXAMPLE 1   **Identifying Equivalent Fractions**

The fish in the aquarium described above are arranged in the diagram. Using the diagram, you can write two equivalent fractions:

$$\frac{\text{Number of goldfish}}{\text{Number of fish}} = \frac{2}{10}$$

$$\frac{\text{Number of groups of 2 goldfish}}{\text{Number of groups of 2 fish}} = \frac{1}{5}$$

The fractions $\frac{2}{10}$ and $\frac{1}{5}$ are equivalent fractions because they represent the same part-to-whole relationship.

EXAMPLE 2   **Writing Equivalent Fractions**

Write two fractions that are equivalent to $\frac{6}{8}$.

Multiply or divide the numerator and denominator by the same nonzero number to find an equivalent fraction.

$$\frac{6}{8} = \frac{6 \times 3}{8 \times 3} = \frac{18}{24}$$ **Multiply numerator and denominator by 3.**

$$\frac{6}{8} = \frac{6 \div 2}{8 \div 2} = \frac{3}{4}$$ **Divide numerator and denominator by 2, a common factor of 6 and 8.**

HELP with Solving

For any fraction, if you tried to list all the equivalent fractions, the list would continue without end. This is because you can multiply the numerator and denominator by *any* nonzero number.

Simplest Form A fraction is in **simplest form** if its numerator and denominator have 1 as their greatest common factor. Writing a fraction in simplest form is called *simplifying* the fraction. To simplify a fraction, you divide its numerator and denominator by their GCF.

HELP with **Reading**

The fraction $\frac{8}{28}$ is read "eight twenty eighths."

EXAMPLE 3 Simplifying Fractions

Write the fraction in simplest form.

a. $\frac{8}{28}$

b. $\frac{8}{15}$

Solution

a. $\frac{8}{28} = \frac{2 \cdot \overset{1}{\cancel{4}}}{7 \cdot \cancel{4}_{1}}$ Divide out GCF of 8 and 28.

$= \frac{2}{7}$

b. $\frac{8}{15}$ The GCF is 1.

The fraction is in simplest form.

Your turn now Write two fractions that are equivalent to the given fraction.

1. $\frac{1}{6}$

2. $\frac{3}{10}$

3. $\frac{8}{18}$

4. $\frac{30}{36}$

Write the fraction in simplest form.

5. $\frac{12}{16}$

6. $\frac{15}{35}$

7. $\frac{7}{28}$

8. $\frac{14}{34}$

EXAMPLE 4 Using Fractions in Simplest Form

Basketball At a girls' basketball game, the home team made 14 out of 22 free throw attempts. The away team made 10 out of 25 free throw attempts. Write the number of free throws made by each team as a fraction. Are the fractions equivalent?

Home Team

$$\frac{\text{Free throws made}}{\text{Free throws attempted}} = \frac{14}{22} = \frac{7 \cdot \overset{1}{\cancel{2}}}{11 \cdot \cancel{2}_{1}} = \frac{7}{11}$$

Away Team

$$\frac{\text{Free throws made}}{\text{Free throws attempted}} = \frac{10}{25} = \frac{2 \cdot \overset{1}{\cancel{5}}}{5 \cdot \cancel{5}_{1}} = \frac{2}{5}$$

ANSWER No, $\frac{7}{11}$ and $\frac{2}{5}$ are not equivalent fractions.

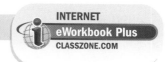

Getting Ready to Practice

1. **Vocabulary** How can you tell if a fraction is in simplest form?

Tell whether the fractions are equivalent.

2. $\dfrac{5}{6}, \dfrac{15}{18}$

3. $\dfrac{20}{24}, \dfrac{5}{8}$

4. $\dfrac{14}{15}, \dfrac{21}{24}$

5. $\dfrac{4}{6}, \dfrac{8}{12}$

6. $\dfrac{12}{18}, \dfrac{8}{32}$

7. **Find the Error** Describe and correct the error in simplifying $\dfrac{24}{42}$.

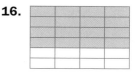

Write the fraction in simplest form.

8. $\dfrac{32}{72}$

9. $\dfrac{6}{21}$

10. $\dfrac{15}{21}$

11. $\dfrac{12}{35}$

12. $\dfrac{28}{48}$

13. **Reading Books** You read 35 pages of a chapter in a book and have 15 pages left. What fraction of the chapter have you read? Write the fraction in simplest form.

Practice and Problem Solving

HELP with **Homework**

Example	Exercises
1	14–16
2	17–21, 33–37
3	22–27
4	28–32, 38

Online Resources
CLASSZONE.COM
· More Examples
· eTutorial Plus

Write two equivalent fractions that describe the model.

14.

15.

16.

Write two fractions that are equivalent to the given fraction.

17. $\dfrac{25}{120}$

18. $\dfrac{18}{21}$

19. $\dfrac{14}{34}$

20. $\dfrac{30}{52}$

21. $\dfrac{28}{32}$

Write the fraction in simplest form.

22. $\dfrac{30}{45}$

23. $\dfrac{24}{32}$

24. $\dfrac{22}{27}$

25. $\dfrac{33}{81}$

26. $\dfrac{49}{105}$

27. **U.S. Presidents** During the 1800s, there were 22 different Presidents of the United States, and 6 of them were born in Virginia. Write a fraction comparing the number of Presidents born in Virginia with the total number of Presidents in the 1800s.

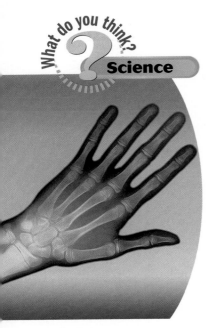
■ **Skeletons**

There are about 206 bones in an adult's skeleton. There are 62 bones in the lower limbs and 64 bones in the upper limbs. How many bones in the body are *not* in the upper and lower limbs?

Write the fractions in simplest form. Tell whether they are equivalent.

28. $\frac{14}{21}, \frac{24}{36}$ **29.** $\frac{45}{54}, \frac{8}{18}$ **30.** $\frac{15}{36}, \frac{40}{96}$ **31.** $\frac{56}{196}, \frac{132}{462}$ **32.** $\frac{34}{44}, \frac{136}{144}$

Write two fractions that are equivalent to the given fraction.

33. $\frac{84}{96}$ **34.** $\frac{95}{126}$ **35.** $\frac{54}{168}$ **36.** $\frac{92}{115}$ **37.** $\frac{39}{169}$

38. Skeletons Use the table to write the number of bones in the wrists as a fraction of the number of bones in the upper limbs, and to write the number of bones in the ankles as a fraction of the number of bones in the lower limbs. Are the fractions equivalent?

Body Region	Bones
Lower limbs	62
Upper limbs	64
Ankles	14
Wrists	16

39. Challenge You are burning music onto a CD. There are 74 minutes available on a CD. You have used 36 minutes. Write a fraction for the part of the CD that is unused.

Mixed Review

Write the product as a power. *(Lesson 1.3)*

40. $3 \cdot 3 \cdot 3 \cdot 3$ **41.** $7 \cdot 7 \cdot 7 \cdot 7$ **42.** $y \cdot y \cdot y \cdot y \cdot y \cdot y$

Find the greatest common factor of the numbers. *(Lesson 4.2)*

43. 64, 88, 144 **44.** 42, 70, 112 **45.** 81, 108, 117

Basic Skills **Copy and complete.**

46. 55 min = _?_ sec **47.** 2 h = _?_ min **48.** 98 d = _?_ wk

Test-Taking Practice

49. Multiple Choice Three ninths of the students in your class have brown eyes. Which fraction pairs are equivalent to three ninths?

A. $\frac{9}{10}, \frac{1}{3}$ **B.** $\frac{3}{19}, \frac{6}{38}$ **C.** $\frac{1}{3}, \frac{5}{20}$ **D.** $\frac{6}{18}, \frac{2}{6}$

50. Multiple Choice The U.S. highway speed limit in 20 states is 55 miles per hour. In simplest form, what fraction of states have a speed limit of 55 miles per hour?

F. $\frac{2}{8}$ **G.** $\frac{2}{5}$ **H.** $\frac{4}{10}$ **I.** $\frac{10}{25}$

Notebook Review

4.1 TO 4.3

Review the vocabulary definitions in your notebook.

Copy the review examples in your notebook. Then complete the exercises.

Check Your Definitions

prime number, p. 157

composite number, p. 157

prime factorization, p. 158

factor tree, p. 158

common factor, p. 164

greatest common factor (GCF), p. 164

relatively prime, p. 165

fraction, p. 169

numerator, p. 169

denominator, p. 169

equivalent fractions, p. 169

simplest form, p. 170

Use Your Vocabulary

Tell whether the statement is *true* or *false*.

1. The numerator and denominator of a fraction in simplest form are relatively prime.

2. A prime number is a whole number greater than 1 whose only whole number factors are 1 and itself.

4.1–4.2 Can you find the GCF using prime factorization?

Review

EXAMPLE Use a factor tree to write the prime factorization of 72 and 84. Then find the greatest common factor of 72 and 84.

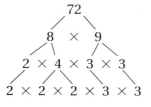

$$72 = \boxed{2} \times \boxed{2} \times 2 \times \boxed{3} \times 3 = 2^3 \times 3^2$$
$$84 = \boxed{2} \times \boxed{2} \times \boxed{3} \times 7 = 2^2 \times 3 \times 7$$

ANSWER The common prime factors of 72 and 84 are 2, 2, and 3. So, the greatest common factor is $2^2 \times 3 = 12$.

☑ **Find the greatest common factor of the numbers using prime factorization.**

3. 18, 32   **4.** 16, 49   **5.** 90, 135   **6.** 96, 112

4.3 Can you tell whether fractions are equivalent?

 EXAMPLE Write $\frac{36}{42}$ and $\frac{48}{64}$ in simplest form. Tell whether they are equivalent.

$$\frac{36}{42} = \frac{6 \cdot \overset{1}{\cancel{6}}}{7 \cdot \cancel{6}_{1}} = \frac{6}{7} \qquad\qquad \frac{48}{64} = \frac{3 \cdot \overset{1}{\cancel{16}}}{4 \cdot \cancel{16}_{1}} = \frac{3}{4}$$

ANSWER Because $\frac{6}{7} \neq \frac{3}{4}$, $\frac{36}{42}$ and $\frac{48}{64}$ are not equivalent fractions.

☑ **Write the fractions in simplest form. Tell whether they are equivalent.**

7. $\frac{6}{10}, \frac{9}{15}$ **8.** $\frac{6}{15}, \frac{4}{16}$ **9.** $\frac{14}{22}, \frac{10}{35}$ **10.** $\frac{15}{33}, \frac{25}{55}$

Stop *and* **Think** about Lessons 4.1–4.3

11. Writing Describe two different ways you can find the greatest common factor of 45 and 56.

Review Quiz 1

Tell whether the number is *prime* or *composite*. Explain your reasoning.

1. 75 **2.** 53 **3.** 61 **4.** 98

5. Quilt Squares You are making a quilt. You made 36 squares to be sewn together. How many different rectangular arrangements can you make?

Find the greatest common factor of the numbers using prime factorization. Then tell whether the numbers are relatively prime.

6. 12, 30 **7.** 10, 21 **8.** 28, 50 **9.** 117, 195

Write the fractions in simplest form. Tell whether they are equivalent.

10. $\frac{15}{28}, \frac{45}{84}$ **11.** $\frac{7}{56}, \frac{12}{84}$ **12.** $\frac{27}{72}, \frac{36}{90}$ **13.** $\frac{45}{75}, \frac{81}{180}$

14. Critical Thinking A number is a common factor of 96 and 144. The sum of the number's digits is 7. Find the number.

Least Common Multiple

LESSON **4.4**

BEFORE	▶ Now	WHY?
You found the GCF of two or more numbers.	You'll find the LCM of two or more numbers.	So you can find when the Mayan calendars coincide, as in Ex. 37.

In the Real World

Word Watch

multiple, p. 175
common multiple, p. 175
least common multiple (LCM), p. 175

Model Trains You visit a model train shop that has two working model trains. The trains share a station, but they run on separate tracks. One of the trains returns to the station every 4 minutes. The other returns every 6 minutes. Both trains just left the station. When will they both return to the station?

A **multiple** of a number is the product of the number and any nonzero whole number. A multiple that is shared by two or more numbers is a **common multiple** . The least of the common multiples is the **least common multiple (LCM)** .

EXAMPLE 1 Using the Least Common Multiple

You can determine when the model trains described above will return to the station by finding the least common multiple of 4 and 6. Begin by writing the multiples of 4 and 6. Then identify any common multiples.

Multiples of 4: 4, 8, 12, 16, 20, **24**, 28, 32, **36**, . . .

Multiples of 6: 6, 12, 18, **24**, 30, **36**, . . .

12, 24, and 36 are common multiples. The LCM is 12.

ANSWER The trains will both return to the station in 12 minutes.

EXAMPLE 2 Finding the Least Common Multiple

Find the least common multiple of 7 and 8.

Multiples of 7: 7, 14, 21, 28, 35, 42, 49, 56, . . .

Multiples of 8: 8, 16, 24, 32, 40, 48, 56, . . .

ANSWER The least common multiple of 7 and 8 is 56.

Using Prime Factorization Another way to find the least common multiple of two or more numbers is to use prime factorization.

HELP with Solving

Use the prime factorization method to find the least common multiple of large numbers.

EXAMPLE 3 **Using Prime Factorization to Find the LCM**

Find the LCM of 84 and 360 using prime factorization.

Begin by writing the prime factorization of each number.

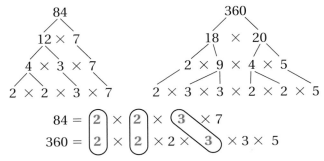

$$84 = \boxed{2} \times \boxed{2} \times \boxed{3} \times 7$$
$$360 = \boxed{2} \times \boxed{2} \times 2 \times \boxed{3} \times 3 \times 5$$

Circle the common factors. Then multiply the common factors (one for each pair) and all the uncircled factors.

$$2 \times 2 \times 2 \times 3 \times 3 \times 5 \times 7 = 2^3 \times 3^2 \times 5 \times 7 = 2520$$

ANSWER The least common multiple of 84 and 360 is 2520.

Your turn now **Find the LCM of the numbers by listing multiples.**

1. 3, 5   **2.** 12, 16   **3.** 9, 10   **4.** 2, 6, 14

Find the LCM of the numbers using prime factorization.

5. 36, 72   **6.** 24, 30   **7.** 54, 126   **8.** 20, 22, 55

EXAMPLE 4 **Using the Least Common Multiple**

Tour Bus Schedules Three tour buses leave the visitor's center at 9:00 A.M. Bus A returns to the visitor's center every 60 minutes, Bus B returns every 40 minutes, and Bus C returns every 75 minutes. What is the next time the buses will all return to the visitor's center?

Solution

Find the least common multiple of 60, 40, and 75.

$$60 = 2^2 \times 3 \times 5 \qquad 40 = 2^3 \times 5 \qquad 75 = 3 \times 5^2$$

The least common multiple is $2^3 \times 3 \times 5^2 = 600$.

ANSWER The buses all return in 600 minutes, or 10 hours, after 9:00 A.M., which is 7:00 P.M.

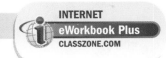

Getting Ready to Practice

1. **Vocabulary** What is the difference between finding the least common multiple and finding the greatest common factor of two numbers?

Match the number pairs with their least common multiple.

2. 4, 18   **3.** 8, 9   **4.** 6, 21   **5.** 5, 12

A. LCM = 60   **B.** LCM = 72   **C.** LCM = 36   **D.** LCM = 42

Find the LCM of the numbers using prime factorization.

6. 28, 60   **7.** 49, 56   **8.** 25, 70   **9.** 22, 64

10. **Find the Error** Describe and correct the error in finding the least common multiple of 6 and 16.

$6 \times 16 = 96$

So, the LCM of 6 and 16 is 96.

11. **Running Laps** David and James are running laps on a quarter mile track. It takes James 3 minutes and David 4 minutes to run once around the track. They both start running from the starting line at the same time. When will they both be at the starting line again?

Practice and Problem Solving

with Homework

Example	Exercises
1	12–19
2	12–19
3	20–27, 29–36
4	37

Online Resources
CLASSZONE.COM

· More Examples
· eTutorial Plus

Find the LCM of the numbers by listing multiples.

12. 9, 24   **13.** 12, 18   **14.** 16, 20   **15.** 30, 33

16. 5, 8, 12   **17.** 6, 11, 18   **18.** 9, 14, 21   **19.** 7, 20, 35

Find the LCM of the numbers using prime factorization.

20. 34, 52   **21.** 28, 46   **22.** 36, 81   **23.** 27, 48

24. 42, 56, 140   **25.** 39, 52, 169   **26.** 28, 40, 144   **27.** 16, 25, 27

28. **Choose a Strategy** You want to find the LCM of 32 and 49. Would you list multiples or use prime factorization? Explain your choice.

Find the GCF and the LCM of the numbers using prime factorization.

29. 90, 165   **30.** 34, 66   **31.** 54, 132   **32.** 72, 168

33. 288, 405   **34.** 42, 81, 105   **35.** 55, 88, 220   **36.** 78, 96, 174

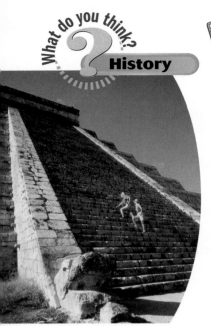

What do you think?

History

■ **Mayan Calendars**

Some people believe that the Temple of Kukulcan, a Mayan ruin, is a representation of the solar calendar. The temple has 4 sides. Each side has 91 steps that lead up to the top. Counting the top as 1 step, how many steps are there altogether?

37. Mayan Calendars The Mayans used more than one calendar system. One calendar had 365 days. Another calendar, considered sacred to the Mayans, had 260 days. If both calendars began on the same day, in how many years would they next begin on the same day?

Extended Problem Solving In Exercises 38–40, use the following information. Cicadas, which are flying insects, live underground until they are fully developed. It takes 13 years for one type of cicada and 17 years for another type of cicada to fully develop. In 1998, the two types of cicadas emerged together.

38. Evaluate In how many years will the two types emerge together again?

39. Analyze How is the answer found in Exercise 38 related to 13 and 17?

40. Predict Between the years 1998 and 2998, how many times will the two cicadas emerge together? Identify in which years they will emerge.

Algebra Find the LCM of the variable expressions.

41. w^2, w^3 **42.** $3d, 9d$ **43.** $4s^2, 2s^4$ **44.** $12x^2, 16x$

45. Challenge The greatest common factor of two numbers is 1. Is the least common multiple of the numbers always the product of the numbers? Give examples to explain your reasoning.

Mixed Review

46. Find the perimeter and the area of a rectangle with a width of 8 centimeters and a length of 12 centimeters. *(Lesson 1.6)*

Write two fractions that are equivalent to the given fraction. *(Lesson 4.3)*

47. $\dfrac{16}{24}$ **48.** $\dfrac{12}{20}$ **49.** $\dfrac{10}{25}$ **50.** $\dfrac{6}{7}$

Basic Skills Write the number in standard form.

51. one hundred twenty-three   **52.** four hundred one

53. sixteen hundred forty   **54.** twenty-two thousand, forty-five

Test-Taking Practice

55. Extended Response Sarah and Jen are swimming laps. Sarah swims 7 laps in 5 minutes, and Jen swims 11 laps in 6 minutes. If they start swimming and stop swimming at the same time and they swim a whole number of laps, what is the least possible amount of time they could have been swimming? In this amount of time, how many laps did each girl swim? Explain how you found the numbers of laps.

Hands-on Activity

Comparing Fractions

You can use area models to compare fractions with different denominators.

Explore 1 Use models to compare $\frac{3}{4}$ and $\frac{5}{6}$.

1 Draw two rectangles of the same size. Divide one rectangle vertically into 4 equal parts and shade 3 of the parts. Divide the other rectangle horizontally into 6 equal parts and shade 5 of the parts.

$\frac{3}{4}$ 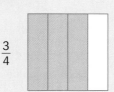 $\frac{5}{6}$

2 Divide the two rectangles into the same number of equal parts by dividing the model for $\frac{3}{4}$ horizontally into 6 equal parts and dividing the model for $\frac{5}{6}$ vertically into 4 equal parts.

$\frac{3}{4} = \frac{18}{24}$  $\frac{5}{6} = \frac{20}{24}$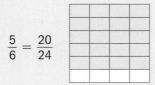

Now both rectangles have 24 equal parts.

3 Because both rectangles are divided into the same number of equal parts, you can compare the fractions: $\frac{18}{24} < \frac{20}{24}$, so $\frac{3}{4} < \frac{5}{6}$.

Your turn now Model the two fractions. Then copy and complete the statement using <, >, or =.

1. $\frac{1}{3}$? $\frac{3}{8}$ **2.** $\frac{5}{6}$? $\frac{3}{5}$ **3.** $\frac{4}{7}$? $\frac{1}{2}$ **4.** $\frac{2}{9}$? $\frac{1}{4}$

On the previous page you compared $\frac{3}{4}$ and $\frac{5}{6}$ using models to write equivalent fractions with a common denominator of 24.

$$\frac{3}{4} = \frac{3 \times 6}{4 \times 6} = \frac{18}{24} \qquad \frac{5}{6} = \frac{5 \times 4}{6 \times 4} = \frac{20}{24}$$

Notice that the 18 in $\frac{18}{24}$ is a result of multiplying the 3 in $\frac{3}{4}$ by the 6 in $\frac{5}{6}$.

Similarly, the 20 in $\frac{20}{24}$ is a result of multiplying the 5 in $\frac{5}{6}$ by the 4 in $\frac{3}{4}$.

These observations suggest a way to compare fractions using *cross products*.

Explore 2 Compare $\frac{5}{8}$ and $\frac{7}{12}$ using cross products.

1 Multiply the denominator of the first fraction by the numerator of the second fraction.

$$8 \times 7 = 56$$
$$\frac{5}{8} \nearrow \frac{7}{12}$$

> When you divide a model of $\frac{7}{12}$ into 8 equal parts, you get 56 shaded parts out of 96 total parts.

2 Multiply the denominator of the second fraction by the numerator of the first fraction.

> When you divide a model of $\frac{5}{8}$ into 12 equal parts, you get 60 shaded parts out of 96 total parts.

$$12 \times 5 = 60 \qquad 8 \times 7 = 56$$
$$\frac{5}{8} \quad \frac{7}{12}$$

3 Compare the two products. Because $60 > 56$, $\frac{5}{8} > \frac{7}{12}$.

Your turn now Compare the fractions using cross products. Then copy and complete the statement using $<$, $>$, or $=$.

5. $\frac{1}{6} \underline{\ ?\ } \frac{2}{9}$ **6.** $\frac{1}{4} \underline{\ ?\ } \frac{3}{10}$ **7.** $\frac{3}{7} \underline{\ ?\ } \frac{2}{3}$ **8.** $\frac{4}{7} \underline{\ ?\ } \frac{6}{11}$

Stop and Think

9. Writing If you were comparing $\frac{31}{36}$ and $\frac{24}{27}$, which method is easier: drawing models or using cross products?

LESSON 4.5

Comparing and Ordering Fractions

BEFORE	Now	WHY?
You compared and ordered decimals.	You'll compare and order fractions.	So you can determine the greater fraction of games won, as in Ex. 36.

Word Watch

least common denominator (LCD), p. 181

In the Real World

Kayaking Julie and Seth are kayaking down a river. Julie kayaks a distance of $\frac{7}{10}$ mile, and Seth kayaks $\frac{3}{4}$ mile. Who kayaked the greater distance?

You can compare fractions by using the *least common denominator*. The **least common denominator (LCD)** of two or more fractions is the least common multiple of the denominators.

Comparing Two or More Fractions

1. Find the LCD of the fractions.

2. Use the LCD to write equivalent fractions.

3. Compare the numerators.

EXAMPLE 1 Comparing Fractions Using the LCD

To find who kayaked the greater distance, as described above, you need to compare $\frac{7}{10}$ and $\frac{3}{4}$.

1. Find the LCD of the fractions.

   Because the LCM of 10 and 4 is 20, the LCD is 20.

2. Use the LCD to write equivalent fractions.

   Julie: $\frac{7}{10} = \frac{7 \times 2}{10 \times 2} = \frac{14}{20}$ **Seth:** $\frac{3}{4} = \frac{3 \times 5}{4 \times 5} = \frac{15}{20}$

3. Compare the numerators: $\frac{14}{20} < \frac{15}{20}$, so $\frac{7}{10} < \frac{3}{4}$.

ANSWER Seth kayaked the greater distance.

EXAMPLE 2 **Ordering Fractions Using the LCD**

Order the fractions $\frac{2}{3}$, $\frac{3}{8}$, $\frac{1}{6}$, and $\frac{3}{4}$ from least to greatest.

1 Find the LCD of the fractions.

Because the LCM of 3, 8, 6, and 4 is 24, the LCD is 24.

2 Use the LCD to write equivalent fractions.

$$\frac{2}{3} = \frac{2 \times 8}{3 \times 8} = \frac{16}{24} \qquad \frac{3}{8} = \frac{3 \times 3}{8 \times 3} = \frac{9}{24}$$

$$\frac{1}{6} = \frac{1 \times 4}{6 \times 4} = \frac{4}{24} \qquad \frac{3}{4} = \frac{3 \times 6}{4 \times 6} = \frac{18}{24}$$

3 Compare the numerators: $\frac{4}{24} < \frac{9}{24} < \frac{16}{24} < \frac{18}{24}$, so $\frac{1}{6} < \frac{3}{8} < \frac{2}{3} < \frac{3}{4}$.

ANSWER From least to greatest, the fractions are $\frac{1}{6}$, $\frac{3}{8}$, $\frac{2}{3}$, and $\frac{3}{4}$.

Your turn now **Copy and complete the statement using <, >, or =.**

1. $\frac{5}{8} \underline{\ ?\ } \frac{7}{12}$

2. $\frac{5}{6} \underline{\ ?\ } \frac{9}{10}$

3. $\frac{3}{14} \underline{\ ?\ } \frac{1}{4}$

Order the fractions from least to greatest.

4. $\frac{2}{3}, \frac{5}{6}, \frac{1}{2}, \frac{1}{6}$

5. $\frac{9}{14}, \frac{5}{7}, \frac{3}{4}, \frac{5}{28}$

6. $\frac{5}{48}, \frac{1}{2}, \frac{1}{6}, \frac{7}{12}$

EXAMPLE 3 **Comparing Fractions Using Approximation**

Use approximation to tell which fraction is greater, $\frac{13}{24}$ or $\frac{15}{34}$.

Notice that $\frac{13}{24}$ and $\frac{15}{34}$ are both approximately equal to $\frac{1}{2}$ because the numerator of each fraction is about half the denominator.

Because $\frac{1}{2} = \frac{12}{24}$, you know that $\frac{13}{24} > \frac{1}{2}$.

Because $\frac{1}{2} = \frac{17}{34}$, you know that $\frac{15}{34} < \frac{1}{2}$.

ANSWER So, $\frac{13}{24} > \frac{15}{34}$.

Getting Ready to Practice

1. **Vocabulary** Copy and complete: The <u>?</u> of two or more fractions is the least common multiple of the denominators of the fractions.

Copy and complete the statement using <, >, or =.

2. $\frac{9}{16}$ <u>?</u> $\frac{3}{4}$

3. $\frac{17}{34}$ <u>?</u> $\frac{9}{18}$

4. $\frac{6}{13}$ <u>?</u> $\frac{2}{5}$

Order the fractions from least to greatest.

5. $\frac{1}{3}, \frac{2}{5}, \frac{3}{10}, \frac{11}{30}$

6. $\frac{3}{4}, \frac{2}{5}, \frac{5}{8}, \frac{7}{10}$

7. $\frac{5}{18}, \frac{7}{9}, \frac{1}{2}, \frac{3}{4}$

Use approximation to tell which fraction is greater.

8. $\frac{9}{17}, \frac{8}{16}$

9. $\frac{10}{21}, \frac{15}{28}$

10. $\frac{15}{31}, \frac{27}{50}$

11. **Pies** After Thanksgiving dinner, $\frac{1}{4}$ of an apple pie and $\frac{3}{10}$ of a pumpkin pie are left uneaten. Which pie has the greater portion left?

Practice and Problem Solving

with Homework

Example	Exercises
1	12–20, 36
2	21–27
3	28–35

Online Resources
CLASSZONE.COM
· More Examples
· eTutorial Plus

Copy and complete the statement using <, >, or =.

12. $\frac{5}{6}$ <u>?</u> $\frac{7}{8}$

13. $\frac{11}{15}$ <u>?</u> $\frac{2}{3}$

14. $\frac{11}{12}$ <u>?</u> $\frac{7}{9}$

15. $\frac{7}{10}$ <u>?</u> $\frac{5}{12}$

16. $\frac{13}{14}$ <u>?</u> $\frac{26}{28}$

17. $\frac{15}{56}$ <u>?</u> $\frac{2}{7}$

18. $\frac{5}{24}$ <u>?</u> $\frac{1}{6}$

19. $\frac{28}{81}$ <u>?</u> $\frac{7}{24}$

20. **Carousels** Carousel horses that move up and down are called jumpers. The Broadway Flying Horses carousel in San Diego has 28 jumpers out of 40 horses. The carousel at the San Francisco Zoo has 24 jumpers out of 36 horses. Which carousel has the greater fraction of jumpers?

Order the fractions from least to greatest.

21. $\frac{3}{8}, \frac{9}{32}, \frac{1}{4}, \frac{5}{16}$

22. $\frac{3}{7}, \frac{1}{3}, \frac{1}{2}, \frac{9}{14}$

23. $\frac{17}{81}, \frac{5}{9}, \frac{13}{27}, \frac{2}{3}$

24. $\frac{13}{20}, \frac{11}{15}, \frac{5}{8}, \frac{7}{12}$

25. $\frac{5}{12}, \frac{3}{4}, \frac{19}{36}, \frac{7}{8}$

26. $\frac{7}{9}, \frac{32}{45}, \frac{20}{27}, \frac{2}{3}$

27. Wrenches The sizes, in inches, of several wrenches are as follows: $\frac{11}{16}, \frac{3}{8}, \frac{3}{4}, \frac{1}{2}, \frac{5}{8}$, and $\frac{7}{16}$. Order the wrenches from smallest to largest.

Use approximation to tell which fraction is greater.

28. $\frac{15}{56}, \frac{8}{35}$ **29.** $\frac{40}{79}, \frac{23}{48}$ **30.** $\frac{13}{30}, \frac{10}{19}$ **31.** $\frac{19}{30}, \frac{16}{33}$

32. $\frac{55}{108}, \frac{35}{72}$ **33.** $\frac{47}{100}, \frac{38}{75}$ **34.** $\frac{37}{70}, \frac{57}{120}$ **35.** $\frac{223}{500}, \frac{28}{54}$

36. Tennis At a summer tennis camp, Veronica won 13 games and lost 15 games. Audrey won 17 games and lost 20 games. Write a fraction for the number of games won to the total number of games played by each girl. Did Veronica or Audrey win the greater fraction of games?

37. Challenge Write a fraction that is exactly halfway between $\frac{3}{7}$ and $\frac{3}{5}$. Explain how you found the fraction.

Mixed Review

Order the numbers from least to greatest. *(Lesson 2.1)*

38. 1.02, 1.2, 1.202, 1.12 **39.** 9.07, 9.17, 9.71, 9.7 **40.** 0.54, 0.5, 0.546, 0.55

Find the least common multiple of the numbers. *(Lesson 4.4)*

41. 15, 27   **42.** 36, 48   **43.** 21, 84, 126

Basic Skills **Estimate the difference.**

44. $\begin{array}{r} 4766 \\ -\ 2581 \end{array}$ **45.** $\begin{array}{r} 43,027 \\ -\ 17,985 \end{array}$ **46.** $\begin{array}{r} 124,017 \\ -\ 78,143 \end{array}$

Test-Taking Practice

47. Multiple Choice Which fractions are in order from least to greatest?

   A. $\frac{8}{15}, \frac{5}{9}, \frac{3}{5}$ **B.** $\frac{7}{18}, \frac{2}{9}, \frac{5}{12}$ **C.** $\frac{5}{6}, \frac{13}{18}, \frac{16}{27}$ **D.** $\frac{3}{8}, \frac{5}{16}, \frac{15}{32}$

48. Short Response Jon and Anne raised money for a school fundraiser. Jon's fundraising goal was $225. Anne's fundraising goal was $175. Jon raised $150, and Anne raised $90. Write a fraction for how much money each student raised compared with each student's fundraising goal. Who raised the greater fraction of his or her goal?

Mixed Numbers and Improper Fractions

BEFORE	▶ Now	WHY?
You compared and ordered fractions.	You'll compare and order fractions and mixed numbers.	So you can compare long jump distances, as in Ex. 40.

Word Watch

mixed number, p. 185
proper fraction, p. 185
improper fraction, p. 185

A **mixed number** has a whole number part and a fraction part.

The number $2\frac{3}{4}$ is a mixed number.

Model A represents $2\frac{3}{4}$.

A fraction whose numerator is less than its denominator is called a **proper fraction**. A fraction is called an **improper fraction** if its numerator is greater than or equal to its denominator. The mixed number $2\frac{3}{4}$ can be written as an improper fraction by dividing each of the 2 wholes into 4 equal sized parts, then counting the number of fourths. This is shown in Model B.

Model A

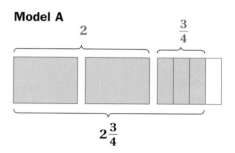

Model B

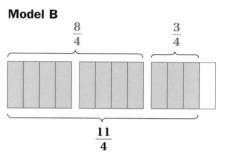

Writing Mixed Numbers as Improper Fractions

Words To write a mixed number as an improper fraction, multiply the whole number part and the denominator, add the numerator, and write the sum over the denominator.

Numbers $2\frac{3}{4} = \frac{2 \cdot 4 + 3}{4} = \frac{11}{4}$

HELP with **Reading**

The mixed number $2\frac{3}{4}$ is read "two and three fourths."

EXAMPLE 1 **Writing Improper Fractions**

Write (a) $3\frac{5}{6}$ and (b) $2\frac{3}{8}$ as improper fractions.

Solution

a. $3\frac{5}{6} = \frac{3 \cdot 6 + 5}{6} = \frac{23}{6}$

b. $2\frac{3}{8} = \frac{2 \cdot 8 + 3}{8} = \frac{19}{8}$

Writing Improper Fractions as Mixed Numbers

Words To write an improper fraction as a mixed number, divide the numerator by the denominator and write any remainder as a fraction.

Numbers $\frac{7}{3}$ ⟶ $7 \div 3 = 2 \text{ R1}$, or $2\frac{1}{3}$

HELP with **Review**

Need help with dividing whole numbers? See p. 690.

EXAMPLE 2 **Writing Mixed Numbers**

Write $\frac{23}{6}$ as a mixed number.

$$6\overline{)23} \quad 3 \text{ R5, or } 3\frac{5}{6}$$
$$\underline{18}$$
$$5$$

You can write a remainder as a fraction: $\frac{\text{remainder}}{\text{divisor}}$.

ANSWER $\frac{23}{6} = 3\frac{5}{6}$

Your turn now Write the number as an improper fraction.

1. $1\frac{2}{5}$ **2.** 2 **3.** $4\frac{1}{2}$ **4.** $3\frac{3}{4}$

Write the improper fraction as a mixed number.

5. $\frac{17}{11}$ **6.** $\frac{13}{6}$ **7.** $\frac{17}{3}$ **8.** $\frac{15}{7}$

EXAMPLE 3 **Comparing Mixed Numbers and Fractions**

Compare $\frac{17}{6}$ and $2\frac{1}{4}$.

① Write $2\frac{1}{4}$ as an improper fraction: $2\frac{1}{4} = \frac{9}{4}$.

② Rewrite $\frac{17}{6}$ and $\frac{9}{4}$ using the least common denominator of 12.

$$\frac{17}{6} = \frac{17 \times 2}{6 \times 2} = \frac{34}{12} \qquad\qquad \frac{9}{4} = \frac{9 \times 3}{4 \times 3} = \frac{27}{12}$$

③ Compare the fractions: $\frac{34}{12} > \frac{27}{12}$, so $\frac{17}{6} > 2\frac{1}{4}$.

EXAMPLE 4 Ordering Mixed Numbers and Fractions

Fitness The Presidential Physical Fitness Award involves a flexibility test called the V-sit reach. The distances, in inches, that four students were able to reach are listed below. Order the distances from least to greatest.

$$3\frac{5}{8} \qquad 3 \qquad \frac{17}{4} \qquad 3\frac{1}{2}$$

Solution

The denominators are 8, 1 $\left(\text{because } 3 = \frac{3}{1}\right)$, 4, and 2. Write the numbers as improper fractions using the least common denominator of 8.

$$3\frac{5}{8} = \frac{29}{8} \qquad\qquad\qquad 3 = \frac{3}{1} = \frac{3 \times 8}{1 \times 8} = \frac{24}{8}$$

$$\frac{17}{4} = \frac{17 \times 2}{4 \times 2} = \frac{34}{8} \qquad\qquad 3\frac{1}{2} = \frac{7}{2} = \frac{7 \times 4}{2 \times 4} = \frac{28}{8}$$

ANSWER From least to greatest, the distances are 3, $3\frac{1}{2}$, $3\frac{5}{8}$, and $\frac{17}{4}$.

4.6 **Exercises**

More Practice, p. 708

INTERNET
eWorkbook Plus
CLASSZONE.COM

Getting Ready to Practice

Vocabulary Tell whether the number is a *mixed number*, a *proper fraction*, or an *improper fraction*.

1. $\frac{12}{12}$ **2.** $\frac{12}{17}$ **3.** $8\frac{3}{8}$ **4.** $\frac{21}{20}$

5. Find the Error Describe and correct the error in writing $5\frac{2}{3}$ as an improper fraction.

$$5\frac{2}{3} = \frac{(5+3)\cdot 2}{3} = \frac{16}{3}$$

6. Write $\frac{12}{7}$ as a mixed number.

Copy and complete the statement using <, >, or =.

7. $\frac{3}{2}$? $3\frac{1}{2}$ **8.** $\frac{8}{3}$? $2\frac{2}{3}$ **9.** $\frac{22}{3}$? $7\frac{1}{4}$ **10.** $\frac{29}{5}$? $6\frac{3}{5}$

11. Walking to School You walk to and from school five days a week. You live a quarter mile away from the school. Write the total distance you walk in a week as an improper fraction and as a mixed number.

Practice and Problem Solving

 **with Homework**

Example	Exercises
1	14–23
2	24–33
3	36–38, 40
4	36–38, 40

 **Online Resources**
CLASSZONE.COM
· More Examples
· eTutorial Plus

Write an improper fraction and a mixed number to describe the model.

12. 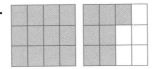   **13.**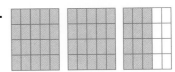

Write the mixed number as an improper fraction.

14. $5\frac{1}{3}$ **15.** $4\frac{2}{7}$ **16.** $2\frac{4}{9}$ **17.** $3\frac{3}{11}$ **18.** $4\frac{1}{8}$

19. $3\frac{4}{15}$ **20.** $10\frac{2}{5}$ **21.** $11\frac{3}{8}$ **22.** $8\frac{6}{7}$ **23.** $4\frac{5}{16}$

Write the improper fraction as a mixed number.

24. $\frac{27}{5}$ **25.** $\frac{45}{8}$ **26.** $\frac{67}{8}$ **27.** $\frac{24}{11}$ **28.** $\frac{95}{6}$

29. $\frac{99}{4}$ **30.** $\frac{149}{10}$ **31.** $\frac{58}{21}$ **32.** $\frac{107}{13}$ **33.** $\frac{159}{16}$

34. Critical Thinking Which number is greater, an improper fraction or a proper fraction? Explain your reasoning.

35. Bubbles You are filling 5 bottles with bubble solution. To fill one bottle, you need $1\frac{1}{4}$ cups of water. You can find only a quarter-cup measure. How many quarter-cups of water do you need?

Order the numbers from least to greatest.

36. $\frac{22}{2}, 2\frac{2}{3}, \frac{22}{11}, 2\frac{20}{33}$ **37.** $\frac{40}{40}, \frac{49}{42}, \frac{22}{20}, 1\frac{1}{9}$ **38.** $7\frac{1}{5}, 7, \frac{38}{5}, \frac{20}{7}$

39. Writing How could you order $3\frac{1}{4}$, $3\frac{3}{4}$, $3\frac{2}{7}$, and $3\frac{1}{8}$ from least to greatest without writing them as improper fractions? Explain your reasoning.

40. Long Jumps The top four long jumps at a track meet are $18\frac{7}{12}$ feet, $18\frac{2}{3}$ feet, $18\frac{3}{4}$ feet, and $18\frac{1}{3}$ feet. Order the numbers from least to greatest. What is the distance of the longest jump?

Challenge Order the numbers from least to greatest.

41. $9\frac{4}{9}, 9\frac{11}{20}, 9\frac{21}{40}, \frac{19}{2}, \frac{28}{3}$ **42.** $11\frac{2}{7}, \frac{34}{3}, \frac{147}{13}, 11\frac{3}{11}, \frac{45}{4}$

43. The table shows the number of households, in millions, with cable television for the years from 1996 through 2000. Use the information in the table to graph the data in an appropriate data display. Explain your choice. *(Lesson 3.6)*

Year	Households
1996	63
1997	64
1998	66
1999	67
2000	69

Order the fractions from least to greatest. *(Lesson 4.5)*

44. $\dfrac{11}{18}, \dfrac{17}{24}, \dfrac{7}{12}, \dfrac{3}{4}$

45. $\dfrac{13}{25}, \dfrac{2}{5}, \dfrac{11}{20}, \dfrac{7}{15}$

46. $\dfrac{15}{28}, \dfrac{7}{14}, \dfrac{3}{8}, \dfrac{5}{7}$

Basic Skills **Find the sum or difference.**

47. $\begin{array}{r} 624 \\ -\ 359 \end{array}$

48. $\begin{array}{r} 2008 \\ +\ 1333 \end{array}$

49. $\begin{array}{r} 3258 \\ -\ 1699 \end{array}$

Test-Taking Practice

50. Multiple Choice Write thirteen sevenths numerically.

A. $\dfrac{3}{17}$ **B.** $\dfrac{7}{13}$ **C.** $\dfrac{13}{7}$ **D.** 137

51. Multiple Choice Which mixed number is equivalent to its paired improper fraction?

F. $5\dfrac{1}{7}, \dfrac{35}{7}$ **G.** $5\dfrac{1}{5}, \dfrac{5}{1}$ **H.** $3\dfrac{2}{5}, \dfrac{22}{5}$ **I.** $3\dfrac{10}{11}, \dfrac{43}{11}$

Missing Numerators

Copy and complete the fractions using 2, 3, 4, 6, and 8. Each number should be chosen so that the fractions are in order from least to greatest, and each number can be used only once.

$$\dfrac{?}{24} \qquad \dfrac{?}{12} \qquad \dfrac{?}{16} \qquad \dfrac{?}{20} \qquad \dfrac{?}{18}$$

LESSON 4.7

Fractions and Decimals

BEFORE	Now	WHY?
You wrote decimals and fractions.	You'll write fractions as decimals and decimals as fractions.	So you can compare the lengths of marsupials, as in Ex. 45.

Word Watch

terminating decimal, p. 191
repeating decimal, p. 191

In the Real World

Geography The map gives the areas of the four largest states as fractions of the total area of the United States. What is the order of the states from greatest to least area? This question will be answered in Example 4.

EXAMPLE 1 Writing Fractions as Decimals

Write (a) $\frac{7}{20}$ and (b) $3\frac{5}{8}$ as decimals.

with Review

Need help with dividing decimals? See p. 67.

Solution

a.
$$\begin{array}{r} 0.35 \\ 20\overline{)7.00} \\ \underline{60} \\ 100 \\ \underline{100} \\ 0 \end{array}$$ ◄—— Write zeros in dividend as placeholders.

◄—— Remainder is zero.

b.
$$\begin{array}{r} 0.625 \\ 8\overline{)5.000} \\ \underline{48} \\ 20 \\ \underline{16} \\ 40 \\ \underline{40} \\ 0 \end{array}$$ ◄—— Write zeros in dividend as placeholders.

◄—— Remainder is zero.

ANSWER $\frac{7}{20} = 0.35$

ANSWER $3\frac{5}{8} = 3 + 0.625 = 3.625$

Your turn now Write the fraction or mixed number as a decimal.

1. $\frac{3}{10}$ **2.** $\frac{17}{200}$ **3.** $3\frac{4}{5}$ **4.** $2\frac{7}{8}$

Terminating and Repeating Decimals When a long division problem results in a remainder of 0, the quotient is a **terminating decimal**. Sometimes, long division gives a **repeating decimal**, where one or more digits repeat without end. Repeating decimals can be written with a bar over the digit(s) that repeat.

$$0.4444\ldots = 0.\overline{4} \qquad \text{One digit repeats.}$$
$$3.0505\ldots = 3.\overline{05} \qquad \text{Two digits repeat.}$$

EXAMPLE 2 **Writing Fractions as Repeating Decimals**

Write (a) $\dfrac{5}{3}$ and (b) $\dfrac{13}{33}$ as decimals.

Solution

a.
$$\begin{array}{r} 1.666\ldots \\ 3\overline{)5.000} \\ \underline{3} \\ 20 \\ \underline{18} \\ 20 \\ \underline{18} \\ 20 \\ \underline{18} \\ 2 \end{array}$$

←— The digit 6 keeps repeating.

←— Remainder will never be zero.

b.
$$\begin{array}{r} 0.3939\ldots \\ 33\overline{)13.0000} \\ \underline{99} \\ 310 \\ \underline{297} \\ 130 \\ \underline{99} \\ 310 \\ \underline{297} \\ 13 \end{array}$$

←— The digits 3 and 9 keep repeating.

←— Remainder will never be zero.

ANSWER $\dfrac{5}{3} = 1.\overline{6}$

ANSWER $\dfrac{13}{33} = 0.\overline{39}$

Need help with place value? See p. 52.

To write a decimal as a fraction, use the place value of the last digit of the decimal to determine the denominator. For example, to write 0.45 as a fraction, use the fact that 5 is in the hundredths' place and write $\dfrac{45}{100}$.

EXAMPLE 3 **Writing Decimals as Fractions**

Write (a) 0.85 and (b) 4.375 as a fraction or mixed number.

Solution

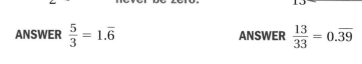

a. $0.85 = \dfrac{85}{100}$

5 is in the hundredths' place.

$= \dfrac{17 \cdot \cancel{5}^{1}}{20 \cdot \cancel{5}_{1}}$

$= \dfrac{17}{20}$

b. $4.375 = 4\dfrac{375}{1000}$

5 is in the thousandths' place.

$= 4\dfrac{3 \cdot \cancel{125}^{1}}{8 \cdot \cancel{125}_{1}}$

$= 4\dfrac{3}{8}$

HELP with Solving

Only the digit(s) under the bar should be repeated. In Example 4, Alaska's area compared with the area of the U.S. is as a decimal, $0.1\overline{6} = 0.1666...$, *not* $0.1616...$

EXAMPLE 4 **Ordering Numbers**

To order the four largest states from page 190, you can write the fractions as decimals and then compare the decimals.

Alaska: $\frac{1}{6} = 0.1\overline{6}$ **California:** $\frac{17}{400} = 0.0425$

Montana: $\frac{1}{25} = 0.04$ **Texas:** $\frac{9}{125} = 0.072$

ANSWER Because $0.1\overline{6} > 0.072 > 0.0425 > 0.04$, the states are, from greatest to least area, Alaska, Texas, California, and Montana.

Your turn now Write the fraction or mixed number as a decimal.

5. $\frac{7}{9}$ **6.** $\frac{13}{6}$ **7.** $2\frac{5}{11}$ **8.** $4\frac{3}{22}$

Write the decimal as a fraction or mixed number in simplest form.

9. 0.4   **10.** 2.65   **11.** 1.0025   **12.** 0.735

4.7 **Exercises**

More Practice, p. 708

INTERNET
eWorkbook Plus
CLASSZONE.COM

Getting Ready to Practice

1. Vocabulary What is the difference between a terminating decimal and a repeating decimal?

Write the fraction or mixed number as a terminating or repeating decimal.

2. $\frac{1}{2}$ **3.** $1\frac{1}{4}$ **4.** $1\frac{1}{3}$ **5.** $\frac{5}{6}$

6. $2\frac{2}{3}$ **7.** $2\frac{2}{5}$ **8.** $\frac{3}{4}$ **9.** $3\frac{4}{9}$

Write the decimal as a fraction or mixed number in simplest form.

10. 0.6   **11.** 1.25   **12.** 0.2   **13.** 0.125

14. Rainbow Bridge At 88.4 meters, Rainbow Bridge in Utah is the highest natural bridge in the world. Write the height as a mixed number in simplest form.

Practice and Problem Solving

with Homework

Example	Exercises
1	19–26, 47–50
2	19–30, 47–50
3	31–38
4	40–43

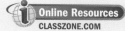
Online Resources
CLASSZONE.COM

· More Examples
· eTutorial Plus

Match the number with its graph on the number line.

15. 1.75   **16.** $2\frac{1}{4}$ **17.** $\frac{6}{5}$ **18.** $1.\overline{3}$

Write the fraction or mixed number as a decimal. Then tell whether the decimal is a *terminating decimal* or *repeating decimal*.

19. $\frac{3}{5}$ **20.** $\frac{7}{6}$ **21.** $\frac{5}{18}$ **22.** $7\frac{7}{8}$

23. $7\frac{9}{20}$ **24.** $2\frac{1}{9}$ **25.** $\frac{7}{12}$ **26.** $5\frac{4}{25}$

Rewrite the repeating decimal using bar notation.

27. 0.7777...   **28.** 5.2121...   **29.** 3.5888...   **30.** 2.358358...

Write the decimal as a fraction or mixed number.

31. 0.8   **32.** 0.12   **33.** 0.475   **34.** 1.375

35. 6.24   **36.** 4.175   **37.** 2.245   **38.** 1.78

39. Writing If you were comparing $5\frac{3}{5}$ and 5.75, would you change the mixed number to a decimal or the decimal to a mixed number? Why?

Order the numbers from least to greatest.

40. $\frac{2}{7}$, 0.25, $\frac{5}{2}$, 0.2, $0.\overline{2}$ **41.** 3.67, $3\frac{4}{5}$, $3\frac{2}{3}$, $\frac{16}{5}$, $3.6\overline{7}$

42. $\frac{8}{3}$, 1.9, 1.94, $\frac{9}{4}$, $1\frac{4}{9}$ **43.** $\frac{9}{10}$, 0.89, $\frac{6}{7}$, $0.\overline{90}$, $\frac{15}{20}$

44. Critical Thinking If you are using division to write a fraction as a decimal, how do you know when to stop dividing?

45. Marsupials Koalas, numbats, and wombats are marsupials. A koala is about $\frac{5}{2}$ feet long. A numbat is about $\frac{4}{3}$ feet long. A wombat is about $\frac{63}{20}$ feet long. Write the three lengths as decimals.

Numbat

Koala

46. Surface Area of Earth The total surface area of Earth (including land and water) is about 510,000,000 square kilometers. The total land area is about 150,000,000 square kilometers. Write a fraction that compares the land area with the total surface area of Earth. Write the fraction as a decimal to the nearest thousandth.

Write the fraction or mixed number as a decimal. Then tell whether the decimal is a *terminating decimal* or *repeating decimal*.

47. $5\frac{16}{37}$ **48.** $\frac{29}{25}$ **49.** $\frac{55}{32}$ **50.** $9\frac{7}{111}$

51. Number Sense Find the decimal forms of $\frac{1}{9}$, $\frac{2}{9}$, and $\frac{3}{9}$. Predict the decimal forms of $\frac{4}{9}$, $\frac{5}{9}$, and $\frac{6}{9}$. Explain how you made your predictions.

52. Challenge What is true about the denominator of any fraction whose decimal form terminates rather than repeats?

with Notetaking

If you find that you are having trouble writing a fraction as a decimal, write a question mark next to the problem and remember to ask someone to explain it to you.

Mixed Review

Write the number in standard form. *(Lesson 2.5)*

53. 4.9×10^5 **54.** 5.358×10^2 **55.** 3.7743×10^8

Write the improper fraction as a mixed number. *(Lesson 4.6)*

56. $\frac{16}{5}$ **57.** $\frac{56}{9}$ **58.** $\frac{23}{12}$

Basic Skills Solve the following problem.

59. Find how much time has elapsed between 12:44 P.M. and 9:36 P.M.

Test-Taking Practice

60. Multiple Choice There were 60 students who tried out for the school play. Only 0.7 of the students were selected to be in the play. What fraction of the students were *not* selected to be in the play?

  A. $\frac{1}{20}$ **B.** $\frac{7}{60}$ **C.** $\frac{3}{10}$ **D.** $\frac{7}{10}$

61. Multiple Choice You collect stamps from all over the world, and $\frac{3}{5}$ of your stamps are from the United States. What decimal represents the portion of stamps from the United States?

  F. 0.25 **G.** 0.35 **H.** 0.4 **I.** 0.6

Fraction and Decimal Conversion

GOAL Use a calculator to write fractions and mixed numbers as decimals and decimals as fractions and mixed numbers.

Some calculators allow you to work with fractions. You can use the [▶F] key to change decimals into fractions or mixed numbers. Use the [▶D] key to change fractions and mixed numbers into decimals.

Example 1 Write the decimal as a fraction or mixed number.

a. 2.125   **b.** 0.85

Solution

Keystrokes	Display
a. 2.125 [▶F] [=]	2⊔1/8
b. 0.85 [▶F] [=]	17/20

> The ⊔ in the display separates the whole number part from the fraction part of the mixed number.

Example 2 Write the fraction or mixed number as a decimal.

a. $1\frac{3}{4}$ **b.** $\frac{23}{9}$

> The [UNIT] key is used to write a mixed number. The display for the key is ⊔.

Solution

Keystrokes	Display
a. 1 [UNIT] 3 [/] 4 [▶D] [=]	1.75
b. 23 [/] 9 [▶D] [=]	2.555555556

HELP with Technology

Calculators have a limit on how many digits they can display, so it may not be possible to tell whether a decimal is terminating or repeating when the display is full.

Your turn now Write the decimal as a fraction or mixed number.

1. 0.375   **2.** 1.825   **3.** 2.56   **4.** 0.9375

Write the fraction or mixed number as a decimal.

5. $15\frac{5}{6}$ **6.** $\frac{128}{11}$ **7.** $\frac{20}{3}$ **8.** $\frac{123}{200}$

4.4 TO 4.7

Notebook Review

Review the vocabulary definitions in your notebook.

Copy the review examples in your notebook. Then complete the exercises.

Check Your Definitions

multiple, p. 175

common multiple, p. 175

least common multiple (LCM), p. 175

least common denominator (LCD), p. 181

mixed number, p. 185

proper fraction, p. 185

improper fraction, p. 185

terminating decimal, p. 191

repeating decimal, p. 191

Use Your Vocabulary

1. Copy and complete: The __?__ of $\frac{3}{4}$ and $\frac{1}{3}$ is 12.

4.4 Can you find the LCM of two or more numbers?

 EXAMPLE Find the LCM of 56 and 126 using prime factorization.

$$56 = \boxed{2} \times 2 \times 2 \times \boxed{7} = 2^3 \times 7$$
$$126 = \boxed{2} \times 3 \times 3 \times \boxed{7} = 2 \times 3^2 \times 7$$
$$2 \times 2 \times 2 \times 3 \times 3 \times 7 = 2^3 \times 3^2 \times 7 = 504$$

Write common factors only once.

ANSWER The least common multiple of 56 and 126 is 504.

☑ **Find the LCM of the numbers using prime factorization.**

2. 32, 40 **3.** 54, 110 **4.** 45, 189

4.5–4.6 Can you compare fractions and mixed numbers?

 EXAMPLE Compare the fractions $\frac{4}{7}$ and $\frac{5}{8}$.

The LCM of 7 and 8 is 56, so the LCD is 56.

$$\frac{4}{7} = \frac{4 \times 8}{7 \times 8} = \frac{32}{56} \qquad \frac{5}{8} = \frac{5 \times 7}{8 \times 7} = \frac{35}{56}$$

ANSWER Compare the numerators: $\frac{32}{56} < \frac{35}{56}$, so $\frac{4}{7} < \frac{5}{8}$.

☑ **Copy and complete the statement using <, >, or =.**

5. $\frac{29}{8}$ __?__ $3\frac{5}{8}$ **6.** $\frac{17}{3}$ __?__ $6\frac{7}{9}$ **7.** $\frac{9}{5}$ __?__ $\frac{13}{6}$

4.7 Can you convert between fractions and decimals?

 Review

EXAMPLE

a. Write $\frac{13}{25}$ as a decimal.

$$\begin{array}{r} 0.52 \\ 25\overline{)13.00} \\ \underline{12\,5} \\ 50 \\ \underline{50} \\ 0 \end{array}$$ ← Write zeros in dividend as placeholders.

← Remainder is zero.

b. Write 0.825 as a fraction.

$$0.825 = \frac{825}{1000} = \frac{33 \cdot \cancel{25}^{1}}{40 \cdot \cancel{25}_{1}} = \frac{33}{40}$$

☑ **8.** Write $2\frac{1}{8}$ as a decimal.

9. Write 7.65 as a mixed number.

Stop *and* **Think** about Lessons 4.4–4.7

10. Writing Is the product of two whole numbers always a common multiple of the numbers? Is the product always the least common multiple of the numbers? Explain your reasoning.

Review Quiz 2

Find the LCM of the numbers using prime factorization.

1. 15, 27
2. 16, 18
3. 24, 50
4. 72, 147

Copy and complete the statement using <, >, or =.

5. $\frac{7}{12}$? $\frac{2}{3}$
6. $4\frac{7}{12}$? $\frac{29}{6}$
7. $\frac{5}{7}$? $\frac{1}{3}$
8. $\frac{22}{27}$? $\frac{55}{72}$

If the given number is a fraction or mixed number, write it as a decimal. If the given number is a decimal, write it as a fraction or mixed number.

9. $\frac{25}{6}$
10. 0.8125
11. $8\frac{7}{11}$
12. $\frac{52}{12}$

13. Snowfall During the winter of 1976–1977, Buffalo, New York, accumulated a record $16\frac{7}{12}$ feet of snow during a single season for a United States city. Write the number as an improper fraction and as a decimal.

4

Chapter Review

 **Vocabulary**

prime number, p. 157	fraction, p. 169	least common
composite number,	numerator, p. 169	denominator (LCD),
p. 157	denominator, p. 169	p. 181
prime factorization,	equivalent fractions,	mixed number, p. 185
p. 158	p. 169	proper fraction, p. 185
factor tree, p. 158	simplest form, p. 170	improper fraction, p. 185
common factor, p. 164	multiple, p. 175	terminating decimal,
greatest common factor	common multiple, p. 175	p. 191
(GCF), p. 164	least common multiple	repeating decimal,
relatively prime, p. 165	(LCM), p. 175	p. 191

Vocabulary Review

Copy and complete the statement.

1. The number 71 is a(n) ? because its only factors are 1 and itself.

2. The ? of 24 and 36 is 12.

3. The fraction $\frac{13}{8}$ is a(n) ? .

4. The ? of 2, 4, and 7 is 28.

5. The fractions $\frac{3}{10}$ and $\frac{4}{5}$ have a(n) ? of 10.

6. The decimal $1.\overline{63}$ is a(n) ? because the digits of the decimal repeat without end.

Review Questions

Tell whether the number is *prime* or *composite*. Then write all the factors of the number. *(Lesson 4.1)*

7. 27   **8.** 68   **9.** 43   **10.** 72

Use a factor tree to write the prime factorization of the number. *(Lesson 4.1)*

11. 116   **12.** 425   **13.** 459   **14.** 726

Find the greatest common factor of the numbers by listing factors. *(Lesson 4.2)*

15. 12, 18   **16.** 35, 42   **17.** 28, 90   **18.** 70, 84

Find the greatest common factor of the numbers using prime factorization. *(Lesson 4.2)*

19. 72, 136   **20.** 99, 363   **21.** 144, 192   **22.** 93, 248

23. Friendship Bracelets You have 280 green beads, 200 yellow beads, and 240 blue beads to make friendship bracelets. If you use all the beads, what is the greatest number of identical bracelets that you can make? How many beads of each color are on each bracelet? *(Lesson 4.2)*

Write two fractions that are equivalent to the given fraction. *(Lesson 4.3)*

24. $\dfrac{3}{5}$ **25.** $\dfrac{6}{9}$ **26.** $\dfrac{4}{8}$ **27.** $\dfrac{2}{7}$

28. Test Scores On the first test in math class you earned 46 out of a possible 50 points. On the second test, you earned 54 out of a possible 60 points. For each test, write the number of points earned as a fraction of possible points. Are the fractions equivalent? *(Lesson 4.3)*

Find the least common multiple of the numbers by listing multiples. *(Lesson 4.4)*

29. 8, 20   **30.** 4, 15   **31.** 15, 30   **32.** 14, 21

Find the least common multiple of the numbers using prime factorization. *(Lesson 4.4)*

33. 45, 81   **34.** 12, 25   **35.** 144, 156   **36.** 75, 225

Order the fractions from least to greatest. *(Lesson 4.5)*

37. $\dfrac{3}{4}, \dfrac{49}{52}, \dfrac{25}{26}, \dfrac{11}{13}$ **38.** $\dfrac{8}{15}, \dfrac{1}{2}, \dfrac{7}{10}, \dfrac{2}{3}$ **39.** $\dfrac{5}{21}, \dfrac{1}{3}, \dfrac{3}{7}, \dfrac{2}{9}$ **40.** $\dfrac{6}{13}, \dfrac{25}{39}, \dfrac{5}{6}, \dfrac{17}{26}$

Copy and complete the statement using <, >, or =. *(Lesson 4.6)*

41. $\dfrac{9}{2} \; \underline{?} \; \dfrac{23}{5}$ **42.** $1\dfrac{4}{11} \; \underline{?} \; 1\dfrac{2}{9}$ **43.** $4\dfrac{3}{8} \; \underline{?} \; 4\dfrac{5}{14}$ **44.** $12\dfrac{3}{16} \; \underline{?} \; \dfrac{195}{16}$

45. Toddlers The weights, in pounds, of five 2-year-olds are as follows: $\dfrac{59}{2}$, $26\dfrac{2}{5}$, $\dfrac{187}{7}$, $26\dfrac{1}{3}$, and $\dfrac{121}{4}$. Order the weights from least to greatest. *(Lesson 4.6)*

Write the decimal as a fraction or mixed number. *(Lesson 4.7)*

46. 0.75   **47.** 0.06   **48.** 5.125   **49.** 3.3125

Write the fraction or mixed number as a decimal. *(Lesson 4.7)*

50. $\dfrac{11}{6}$ **51.** $5\dfrac{7}{8}$ **52.** $\dfrac{12}{25}$ **53.** $4\dfrac{7}{9}$

Chapter Test

Tell whether the number is *prime* or *composite*. Then write all the factors.

1. 51   **2.** 63   **3.** 49   **4.** 67

Use a factor tree to write the prime factorization of the number.

5. 96   **6.** 128   **7.** 168   **8.** 260

Find the GCF and the LCM of the numbers by making lists. Then tell whether the numbers are relatively prime.

9. 9, 16   **10.** 12, 15   **11.** 10, 25   **12.** 7, 13

Find the GCF and the LCM of the numbers using prime factorization. Then tell whether the numbers are relatively prime.

13. 42, 66   **14.** 64, 120   **15.** 49, 84   **16.** 72, 144, 192

17. Marching Band A marching band has 81 trombonists, 36 flutists, 54 saxophonists, and 27 drummers. For a parade, the band is arranged into rows of equal size with one type of instrument in a row. What is the greatest number of musicians in each row? How many rows are there for each instrument?

Write the fraction in simplest form.

18. $\dfrac{15}{80}$ **19.** $\dfrac{13}{78}$ **20.** $\dfrac{54}{81}$ **21.** $\dfrac{76}{135}$

Copy and complete the statement using <, >, or =.

22. $\dfrac{6}{7} \; \underline{?} \; \dfrac{9}{11}$ **23.** $\dfrac{5}{9} \; \underline{?} \; \dfrac{60}{108}$ **24.** $3\dfrac{2}{7} \; \underline{?} \; \dfrac{16}{5}$ **25.** $5\dfrac{5}{6} \; \underline{?} \; \dfrac{59}{10}$

Order the numbers from least to greatest.

26. $\dfrac{7}{4}, \dfrac{23}{12}, 1\dfrac{5}{6}, \dfrac{5}{3}$ **27.** $\dfrac{5}{6}, \dfrac{7}{9}, \dfrac{23}{27}, \dfrac{13}{18}$ **28.** $\dfrac{1}{2}, \dfrac{17}{42}, \dfrac{16}{21}, \dfrac{5}{7}$ **29.** $\dfrac{8}{5}, 1\dfrac{8}{15}, \dfrac{8}{3}, \dfrac{22}{15}$

Write the fraction or mixed number as a decimal.

30. $\dfrac{11}{5}$ **31.** $\dfrac{29}{11}$ **32.** $\dfrac{14}{15}$ **33.** $5\dfrac{9}{16}$

Write the decimal as a fraction or mixed number.

34. 2.68   **35.** 0.56   **36.** 0.286   **37.** 3.048

Chapter Standardized Test

Test-Taking Strategy When you are taking a test, concentrate on what you are doing. Don't worry about what everyone else is doing. It will only distract you.

Multiple Choice

1. Which value of x makes the value of the expression $11x + 1$ prime?

A. 1   **B.** 2   **C.** 3   **D.** 4

2. Which expression is the prime factorization of 132?

F. $2^2 \times 3 \times 11$ **G.** $2 \times 3^2 \times 11$

H. $2 \times 3 \times 11$ **I.** $2^2 \times 3^2 \times 11$

3. Which number is a common factor of 30 and 72?

A. 2   **B.** 5   **C.** 9   **D.** 12

4. What is the GCF of 108 and 156?

F. 4   **G.** 12   **H.** 132   **I.** 1404

5. Which numbers are relatively prime?

A. 13, 39   **B.** 48, 49   **C.** 54, 99   **D.** 21, 49

6. Which fraction is in simplest form?

F. $\frac{21}{56}$ **G.** $\frac{12}{26}$ **H.** $\frac{15}{32}$ **I.** $\frac{26}{39}$

7. Which number is *not* a common multiple of 16, 30, and 36?

A. 720   **B.** 2160   **C.** 3360   **D.** 17,280

8. What is the LCM of 72 and 105?

F. 105   **G.** 840   **H.** 2520   **I.** 7560

9. What is the LCD of $\frac{225}{56}$ and $4\frac{3}{14}$?

A. 7   **B.** 8   **C.** 28   **D.** 56

10. Which fractions are in order from least to greatest?

F. $\frac{7}{12}, \frac{5}{6}, \frac{1}{2}, \frac{3}{8}$ **G.** $\frac{3}{8}, \frac{5}{6}, \frac{7}{12}, \frac{1}{2}$

H. $\frac{3}{8}, \frac{1}{2}, \frac{7}{12}, \frac{5}{6}$ **I.** $\frac{7}{12}, \frac{1}{2}, \frac{3}{8}, \frac{5}{6}$

11. Which number is *not* equal to the others?

A. 2.375   **B.** $\frac{19}{8}$ **C.** $2\frac{3}{8}$ **D.** $\frac{37}{24}$

12. Which decimal is equal to $\frac{4}{9}$?

F. 0.4   **G.** $0.\overline{4}$ **H.** 0.5   **I.** 2.25

13. Which decimal and fraction are *not* equal?

A. $3.2, \frac{4}{25}$ **B.** $1.\overline{3}, \frac{4}{3}$

C. $0.55, \frac{11}{20}$ **D.** $1.25, \frac{10}{8}$

Short Response

14. Suzie rode a go-cart for $\frac{7}{9}$ mile. Tom rode a go-cart for $\frac{5}{6}$ mile, Nikki rode a go-cart for $\frac{2}{3}$ mile, and Lisa rode a go-cart for $\frac{1}{2}$ mile. Order the fractions from least to greatest. Who rode the farthest?

Extended Response

15. You are using a rectangular pan 9 inches by 12 inches to bake brownies. You want to cut out the largest possible square brownies of equal size. What size should the brownies be? How many brownies will you have? Explain your work.

5

Fraction Operations

BEFORE

In previous chapters you've...

- Found the GCF and LCM of two or more numbers
- Written equivalent fractions

Now

In Chapter 5 you'll study...

- Adding and subtracting fractions and mixed numbers
- Multiplying and dividing fractions and mixed numbers
- Customary units

WHY?

So you can solve real-world problems about...

- music, p. 209
- baseball, p. 211
- stained glass windows, p. 219
- pyramids, p. 238

Internet Preview
CLASSZONE.COM

- eEdition Plus Online
- eWorkbook Plus Online
- eTutorial Plus Online
- State Test Practice
- More Examples

Chapter Warm-Up Games

Review skills you need for this chapter in these quick games.

 Brain Game

Key Skill:
Finding the least common multiple

- The number on each acrobat above the bottom row is the least common multiple of the numbers on the two acrobats supporting the acrobat.

- Copy the number triangle and fill in the missing numbers.

Trapeze Math

2 / 8
3 / 12

5 / 15
6 / 24
8 / 27
9 / 32

BrAIN GAME

Key Skill:
Writing equivalent fractions

- The numbers on the four trapeze artists shown above form a pair of equivalent fractions.

- Arrange the eight trapeze artists standing on the ground into two teams of four, so that each team forms two equivalent fractions.

Stop *and* Think

1. **Writing** Is the number at the top of the *Acrobat Triangle* a multiple of all the numbers below it? Is it the least common multiple? Explain your reasoning.

2. **Critical Thinking** Take one of your teams from *Trapeze Math* and see if you can rearrange the numbers to form other equivalent fractions. How many can you form?

Getting Ready to Learn

Review What You Need to Know

Using Vocabulary **Copy and complete using a review word.**

Word Watch

Review Words

greatest common factor
(GCF), p. 164
equivalent fractions, p. 169
simplest form, p. 170
least common denominator
(LCD), p. 181
mixed number, p. 185
improper fraction, p. 185

1. Fractions that represent the same part-to-whole relationship are called $\underline{?}$.

2. A(n) $\underline{?}$ is a number that has a whole number part and a fraction part.

Write the fractions in simplest form. Tell whether they are equivalent. *(p. 169)*

3. $\frac{14}{28}, \frac{12}{21}$ **4.** $\frac{8}{12}, \frac{10}{15}$ **5.** $\frac{15}{24}, \frac{25}{40}$ **6.** $\frac{24}{27}, \frac{36}{42}$

Write an improper fraction and a mixed number to describe the model. *(p. 185)*

7.    **8.**

You should include material that appears on a notebook like this in your own notes.

Know How to Take Notes

Taking Notes in Class Take notes about examples that your teacher discusses. If you don't understand something, write a question in your notebook. Discuss questions with a friend or your teacher and write down what you learn.

Example: Write the mixed number $6\frac{2}{5}$ as an improper fraction.

$$6\frac{2}{5} = \frac{6 \cdot 5 + 2}{5}$$ Question: Why do you multiply 6 and 5, then add 2?

$$= \frac{32}{5}$$

Answer: Think of 6 as $\frac{30}{5}$ and combine that with $\frac{2}{5}$ to get $\frac{32}{5}$.

In Lesson 5.3, asking questions may help you understand the process of dividing out common factors.

Adding and Subtracting Fractions

BEFORE	**Now**	WHY?
You added and subtracted whole numbers and decimals.	You'll add and subtract fractions.	So you can find the length of an alligator, as in Ex. 22.

Word Watch

Review Words

least common denominator (LCD), p. 181

 **Activity** You can use models to add and subtract fractions.

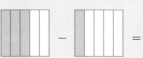

$$\frac{1}{3} + \frac{1}{3} = \frac{2}{3} \qquad \frac{3}{5} - \frac{1}{5} = \frac{2}{5}$$

Use a model to find the sum or difference.

1. $\frac{2}{3} + \frac{1}{3}$ **2.** $\frac{1}{5} + \frac{1}{5}$ **3.** $\frac{7}{9} - \frac{3}{9}$ **4.** $\frac{3}{4} - \frac{1}{4}$

The activity suggests the following rules about adding and subtracting fractions with common denominators.

Fractions with Common Denominators

Words To add or subtract two fractions with a common denominator, write the sum or difference of the numerators over the denominator.

Numbers $\frac{1}{5} + \frac{2}{5} = \frac{3}{5}$ **Algebra** $\frac{a}{c} + \frac{b}{c} = \frac{a+b}{c}$ $(c \neq 0)$

$\frac{4}{7} - \frac{1}{7} = \frac{3}{7}$ $\frac{a}{c} - \frac{b}{c} = \frac{a-b}{c}$ $(c \neq 0)$

EXAMPLE 1 Adding Fractions

$\frac{2}{9} + \frac{5}{9} = \frac{2+5}{9}$ Add numerators.

$= \frac{7}{9}$ Simplify numerator.

 with **Review**

Need help with simplifying fractions? See p. 169.

EXAMPLE 2 **Subtracting Fractions**

$\dfrac{7}{8} - \dfrac{3}{8} = \dfrac{7-3}{8}$ Subtract numerators.

$= \dfrac{4}{8}$ Simplify numerator.

$= \dfrac{1}{2}$ Simplify fraction.

Your turn now **Add or subtract. Simplify if possible.**

1. $\dfrac{3}{8} + \dfrac{1}{8}$ **2.** $\dfrac{3}{5} + \dfrac{4}{5}$ **3.** $\dfrac{4}{5} - \dfrac{2}{5}$ **4.** $\dfrac{11}{12} - \dfrac{5}{12}$

Different Denominators When adding or subtracting fractions with different denominators, rewrite the fractions so they have the same denominator. Then add or subtract the numerators as before.

Fractions with Different Denominators

1. Rewrite the fractions using the LCD.

2. Add or subtract the numerators.

3. Write the result over the LCD.

4. Simplify if possible.

 with **Solving**

Need help with writing improper fractions as mixed numbers? See p. 185.

EXAMPLE 3 **Adding Fractions**

$\dfrac{3}{4} + \dfrac{2}{3} = \dfrac{9}{12} + \dfrac{8}{12}$ Rewrite fractions using the LCD of $\dfrac{3}{4}$ and $\dfrac{2}{3}$.

$= \dfrac{9+8}{12}$ Add numerators.

$= \dfrac{17}{12}$, or $1\dfrac{5}{12}$ Simplify.

✓**Check** You can use estimation to check that your answer is reasonable. Because $\dfrac{3}{4}$ is greater than $\dfrac{1}{2}$ and $\dfrac{2}{3}$ is greater than $\dfrac{1}{2}$, the sum of $\dfrac{3}{4}$ and $\dfrac{2}{3}$ should be greater than 1.

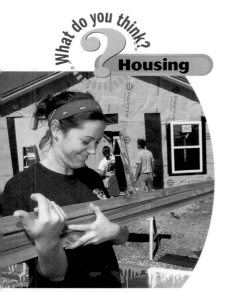
EXAMPLE 4 **Subtracting Fractions**

Construction Before a rough piece of wood can be used in building a house, it needs to be squared off and sanded. During this process, the thickness of a rough piece of wood $\frac{5}{8}$ inch thick is always reduced to $\frac{7}{16}$ inch. How much thinner is the wood now?

Solution

To find how much thinner the wood is, subtract $\frac{7}{16}$ from $\frac{5}{8}$.

$$\frac{5}{8} - \frac{7}{16} = \frac{10}{16} - \frac{7}{16}$$ Rewrite $\frac{5}{8}$ using the LCD of the fractions.

$$= \frac{10 - 7}{16}$$ Subtract numerators.

$$= \frac{3}{16}$$ Simplify numerator.

ANSWER The wood is now $\frac{3}{16}$ inch thinner.

■ **Construction**

From 1976 to 2001, the volunteers of Habitat for Humanity have built more than 100,000 houses in more than 80 countries, including about 30,000 houses across the United States. How many houses do you think they build in a year?

Your turn now Add or subtract. Simplify if possible.

5. $\frac{3}{4} + \frac{1}{12}$ **6.** $\frac{3}{5} + \frac{1}{2}$ **7.** $\frac{7}{8} - \frac{2}{3}$ **8.** $\frac{5}{6} - \frac{1}{10}$

5.1 **Exercises**
More Practice, p. 709

INTERNET
eWorkbook Plus
CLASSZONE.COM

Getting Ready to Practice

1. **Vocabulary** Copy and complete: To add fractions with different denominators, first rewrite the fractions using the ? .

Find the sum or difference. Simplify if possible.

2. $\frac{5}{7} + \frac{1}{7}$ **3.** $\frac{7}{9} - \frac{4}{9}$ **4.** $\frac{11}{12} - \frac{3}{4}$ **5.** $\frac{3}{5} + \frac{7}{10}$

6. **Swimming** In a $\frac{1}{2}$ mile relay swimming event, Brad swims $\frac{1}{8}$ mile. What is the total distance that his teammates have left to swim?

with Homework

Example	Exercises
1	8–19, 28–33
2	8–19, 28–33
3	8–19, 28–34
4	8–19, 22, 28–33

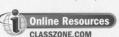

Online Resources
CLASSZONE.COM

· More Examples
· eTutorial Plus

Practice and Problem Solving

 7. Writing Describe how $\frac{1}{4} + \frac{1}{3}$ is related to $\frac{3}{12} + \frac{4}{12}$.

Find the sum or difference.

8. $\frac{1}{10} + \frac{8}{10}$

9. $\frac{4}{7} + \frac{5}{7}$

10. $\frac{9}{20} + \frac{7}{20}$

11. $\frac{3}{5} - \frac{1}{5}$

12. $\frac{7}{12} - \frac{5}{12}$

13. $\frac{8}{9} - \frac{2}{9}$

14. $\frac{11}{12} - \frac{3}{4}$

15. $\frac{4}{5} - \frac{3}{10}$

16. $\frac{7}{12} - \frac{5}{18}$

17. $\frac{1}{6} + \frac{3}{4}$

18. $\frac{1}{9} + \frac{5}{6}$

19. $\frac{2}{3} + \frac{1}{4}$

xy **20. Algebra** Evaluate $\frac{1}{2} + x$ when $x = \frac{1}{7}$.

21. School Day From the time you wake up, you need 43 minutes to get ready for school and 24 minutes to travel from home to school. Using fractions of an hour, approximate the time it takes for you to get to school from the time you wake up.

22. Alligators A recently hatched alligator is $\frac{3}{4}$ foot long and grows $\frac{5}{12}$ foot over the next 5 months. How long is the alligator at 5 months old?

23. Look for a Pattern Describe the following pattern: $\frac{1}{16}, \frac{1}{8}, \frac{3}{16}, \frac{1}{4}, \ldots$. Then write the next three fractions.

xy **Algebra** **Use mental math to solve the equation.**

24. $\frac{5}{7} = \frac{3}{7} + x$

25. $x + \frac{4}{8} = \frac{5}{8}$

26. $\frac{3}{11} - x = \frac{1}{11}$

27. Critical Thinking Can the sum of three fractions greater than zero and less than 1 be greater than 1? Explain your reasoning with an example.

Find the sum or difference.

28. $\frac{11}{12} - \frac{5}{12} + \frac{1}{12}$

29. $\frac{4}{9} + \frac{5}{9} - \frac{2}{9}$

30. $\frac{3}{4} + \frac{5}{16} + \frac{7}{8}$

31. $\frac{13}{15} - \frac{2}{15} - \frac{6}{15}$

32. $\frac{5}{6} - \frac{7}{30} - \frac{2}{5}$

33. $\frac{2}{3} + \frac{3}{4} - \frac{2}{5}$

34. Trail Mix A recipe for trail mix calls for $\frac{3}{4}$ cup dried mixed fruit, $\frac{1}{2}$ cup mixed nuts, and $\frac{1}{3}$ cup granola. How many cups of trail mix does this recipe make? Estimate to check your answer.

Music In music, a $\frac{4}{4}$ time signature means that there are 4 beats per measure. The beats for seven musical notes with this time signature are in the table below. In Exercises 35 and 36, tell whether the measure contains 4 beats. Explain your reasoning.

Note							
Beats	4	2	1	$\frac{3}{4}$	$\frac{1}{2}$	$\frac{3}{8}$	$\frac{1}{4}$

35.

36.

37. **Challenge** When you find $\frac{5}{6} + \frac{3}{8}$, what advantage does using the LCD of the two fractions have over any other common denominator?

Mixed Review

Find the sum or difference. *(Lesson 2.2)*

38. $32.8 + 4.25$ **39.** $13.6 + 7.07$ **40.** $400 - 29.1$ **41.** $240.24 - 0.533$

Write the decimal as a fraction or mixed number. *(Lesson 4.7)*

42. 0.6 **43.** 0.17 **44.** 5.375 **45.** 10.34

Basic Skills **Use long division to find the quotient.**

46. $547 \div 8$ **47.** $6552 \div 5$ **48.** $387 \div 12$ **49.** $8284 \div 16$

Test-Taking Practice

50. Multiple Choice Which of the following numbers, when added to $\frac{1}{4}$, results in a number greater than $\frac{1}{2}$?

A. $\frac{1}{8}$ **B.** $\frac{1}{6}$ **C.** $\frac{1}{4}$ **D.** $\frac{1}{3}$

51. Multiple Choice What is the value of the expression $\frac{5}{6} + \left(\frac{2}{3} - \frac{1}{8}\right)$?

F. $\frac{6}{11}$ **G.** $\frac{31}{30}$ **H.** $\frac{11}{8}$ **I.** 6

William Eddins, Resident Conductor of the Chicago Symphony Orchestra

5.2 Hands-on **Activity**

GOAL
Use area models to add mixed numbers.

MATERIALS
- paper
- pencil

Modeling Addition of Mixed Numbers

You can use area models to add mixed numbers.

Explore Find the sum of $2\frac{3}{5}$ and $1\frac{4}{5}$.

1 Draw area models for $2\frac{3}{5}$ and $1\frac{4}{5}$.

2 Combine the two models. Group the whole parts together and group the fractional parts together.

$$2\frac{3}{5} + 1\frac{4}{5} = 3\frac{7}{5}$$

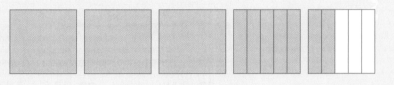

3 Simplify. Because $\frac{5}{5}$ is equivalent to 1, $2\frac{3}{5} + 1\frac{4}{5} = 4\frac{2}{5}$.

Your turn now Draw area models to find the sum. Simplify if possible.

1. $5\frac{1}{5} + 2\frac{3}{5}$ **2.** $3\frac{2}{3} + 1\frac{2}{3}$ **3.** $1\frac{2}{5} + 3\frac{4}{5}$ **4.** $7\frac{1}{4} + 2\frac{1}{4}$

Stop and Think

5. Writing How would you model subtracting $1\frac{1}{4}$ from $4\frac{3}{4}$? Explain your reasoning and draw an area model.

6. Critical Thinking Is it possible to have a whole number answer when you add two mixed numbers together? Explain your reasoning and give an example.

Adding and Subtracting Mixed Numbers

LESSON 5.2

BEFORE	Now	WHY?
You added and subtracted fractions.	You'll add and subtract mixed numbers.	So you can find how much a baby has grown, as in Ex. 24.

In the Real World

World Series In the playoffs leading up to the 2001 World Series, Curt Schilling pitched $48\frac{1}{3}$ innings and his teammate Randy Johnson pitched $41\frac{1}{3}$ innings.

What is the total number of innings they pitched?

To find the total number of innings, you will need to add two mixed numbers, using the rules below.

Word Watch

Review Words

least common denominator (LCD), p. 181
mixed number, p. 185
improper fraction, p. 185

Adding and Subtracting Mixed Numbers

1. Find the LCD of the fractions, if necessary.

2. Rename the fractions, if necessary. Then add or subtract the fractions.

3. Add or subtract the whole numbers.

4. Simplify if possible.

EXAMPLE 1 Adding with a Common Denominator

To solve the problem above, you need to find the sum of $48\frac{1}{3}$ and $41\frac{1}{3}$.

Add the whole numbers. $\qquad$ Add the fractions.

$$
\begin{array}{r}
48\frac{1}{3} \\
+\ 41\frac{1}{3} \\
\hline
89\frac{2}{3}
\end{array}
$$

ANSWER Schilling and Johnson pitched a total of $89\frac{2}{3}$ innings.

EXAMPLE **2** **Subtracting with a Common Denominator**

$$6\frac{7}{9} - 4\frac{1}{9} = 2\frac{6}{9} \quad \text{Subtract fractions and whole numbers.}$$

$$= 2\frac{2}{3} \quad \text{Simplify.}$$

Your turn now Add or subtract. Simplify if possible.

1. $3\frac{1}{8} + 2\frac{5}{8}$ **2.** $7\frac{1}{5} + 1\frac{2}{5}$ **3.** $8\frac{5}{7} - 4\frac{1}{7}$ **4.** $12\frac{5}{6} - 9\frac{5}{6}$

HELP with **Solving**

In Example 3, you can estimate the answer by rounding each mixed number to the nearest whole number. By doing so, you have $5 + 4 = 9$, so the answer is reasonable.

EXAMPLE **3** **Adding with Different Denominators**

$$4\frac{5}{6} + 3\frac{3}{4} = 4\frac{10}{12} + 3\frac{9}{12} \quad \text{Rewrite fractions using LCD of } \frac{5}{6} \text{ and } \frac{3}{4}.$$

$$= 7\frac{19}{12} \quad \text{Add fractions and whole numbers.}$$

$$= 7 + 1\frac{7}{12} \quad \text{Write improper fraction as a mixed number.}$$

$$= 8\frac{7}{12} \quad \text{Add whole numbers.}$$

Renaming When subtracting mixed numbers, you may have to *rename* the first mixed number so that you can subtract the fractional parts.

EXAMPLE **4** **Renaming to Subtract Mixed Numbers**

$$6\frac{1}{6} - 3\frac{2}{3} = 6\frac{1}{6} - 3\frac{4}{6} \quad \text{Rewrite fractions using LCD of } \frac{1}{6} \text{ and } \frac{2}{3}.$$

$$= 5\frac{7}{6} - 3\frac{4}{6} \quad \text{Rename } 6\frac{1}{6} \text{ as } 5\frac{7}{6}.$$

$$= 2\frac{3}{6} \quad \text{Subtract fractions and whole numbers.}$$

$$= 2\frac{1}{2} \quad \text{Simplify.}$$

Your turn now Add or subtract. Simplify if possible.

5. $7\frac{1}{4} + 3\frac{1}{2}$ **6.** $1\frac{3}{4} + 4\frac{3}{8}$ **7.** $8 - 5\frac{1}{8}$ **8.** $8\frac{1}{6} - 6\frac{3}{4}$

Getting Ready to Practice

1. Vocabulary When is it necessary to rename a mixed number when subtracting?

Find the sum or difference. Then estimate to check the answer.

2. $8\frac{4}{9} - 5\frac{2}{9}$ **3.** $7\frac{3}{5} - 3\frac{1}{5}$ **4.** $22\frac{2}{7} + 17\frac{4}{7}$ **5.** $8\frac{7}{12} + 4\frac{5}{12}$

6. $8\frac{1}{3} - 5\frac{4}{9}$ **7.** $4\frac{3}{4} + 6\frac{2}{3}$ **8.** $5\frac{1}{4} + 2\frac{5}{6}$ **9.** $7\frac{1}{5} - 3\frac{3}{10}$

10. Running At track practice, you run $5\frac{1}{2}$ miles and cool down by walking $1\frac{1}{3}$ miles. What is your total distance?

Practice and Problem Solving

HELP with **Homework**

Example	Exercises
1	12–23
2	12–23
3	12–23
4	12–24

Online Resources
CLASSZONE.COM
· More Examples
· eTutorial Plus

11. Writing Describe what steps you would take to find $2\frac{3}{4} - 1\frac{1}{4}$.

Find the sum or difference. Then estimate to check the answer.

12. $3\frac{2}{3} - 2\frac{1}{3}$ **13.** $12\frac{3}{5} + 5\frac{1}{5}$ **14.** $6\frac{4}{7} + 5\frac{5}{7}$ **15.** $2\frac{3}{8} + 5\frac{5}{8}$

16. $8\frac{6}{7} + 2\frac{4}{7}$ **17.** $13\frac{5}{6} - 9\frac{1}{6}$ **18.** $4\frac{1}{4} + 3\frac{3}{8}$ **19.** $7\frac{5}{6} + 3\frac{1}{9}$

20. $12\frac{3}{4} - 9\frac{1}{6}$ **21.** $6\frac{2}{5} + 11\frac{1}{6}$ **22.** $5\frac{1}{4} - 3\frac{3}{4}$ **23.** $9\frac{1}{3} - 7\frac{4}{9}$

24. Child Development Anastasia was $19\frac{1}{4}$ inches long at birth. At her 3 month checkup, she measures $23\frac{1}{2}$ inches. How much has she grown?

25. Mental Math Explain how you can use mental math to find $4\frac{1}{5} + 7\frac{4}{5}$.

xy **Algebra** **Evaluate the expression when** $x = 7\frac{2}{5}$, $y = 5\frac{1}{3}$, **and** $z = 3\frac{3}{7}$.

26. $y + x$ **27.** $y - z$ **28.** $x - y + z$ **29.** $z + y - x$

30. Critical Thinking Can you subtract two fractions with common denominators and get an answer with a different denominator? Explain your reasoning and provide an example.

31. Cars Can two cars that measure $14\frac{4}{5}$ feet and $15\frac{5}{6}$ feet fit in a parking space that is $31\frac{1}{2}$ feet long? Use estimation to answer the question.

Coins In Exercises 32 and 33, use the table below.

Coin	Dime	Penny	Nickel	Quarter	Half-dollar
Mass (grams)	$2\frac{1}{2}$	$3\frac{1}{8}$	5	$6\frac{1}{4}$	$12\frac{1}{2}$

32. What is the difference in mass between a half-dollar and two dimes?

33. What is the sum of the masses of a penny, a dime, and a quarter?

34. Challenge Find the missing side length if the perimeter of the figure is $9\frac{7}{15}$ inches.

$1\frac{1}{3}$ in.   ? $1\frac{3}{5}$ in. $3\frac{1}{5}$ in.

Mixed Review

35. Find the area of a rectangle that has a length of 6.2 feet and a width of 5.3 feet. *(Lesson 2.3)*

Find the sum or difference. *(Lesson 5.1)*

36. $\frac{7}{8} - \frac{3}{8}$ **37.** $\frac{4}{11} + \frac{9}{11}$ **38.** $\frac{3}{8} + \frac{1}{2}$ **39.** $\frac{11}{12} - \frac{3}{8}$

Basic Skills Find the product or quotient.

40. $326 \cdot 12$ **41.** $53 \cdot 487$ **42.** $225 \div 5$ **43.** $392 \div 28$

Test-Taking Practice

44. Multiple Choice Find the difference $8\frac{1}{4} - 3\frac{5}{6}$.

   A. $4\frac{1}{12}$ **B.** $4\frac{1}{4}$ **C.** $4\frac{5}{12}$ **D.** $5\frac{7}{12}$

45. Multiple Choice At the beginning of a trip, a boat's gasoline tank contained $14\frac{1}{5}$ gallons of gasoline. At the end of the trip, it contained $8\frac{2}{3}$ gallons. How many gallons of gasoline did the boat use?

   F. $5\frac{8}{15}$ **G.** $6\frac{1}{4}$ **H.** $6\frac{7}{15}$ **I.** $22\frac{13}{15}$

5.3 **Hands-on Activity**

GOAL
Use models to multiply fractions.

MATERIALS
· paper
· colored pencils

Multiplication of Fractions

To model the product $\frac{3}{4} \times \frac{1}{3}$, you need to find $\frac{3}{4}$ of $\frac{1}{3}$.

Explore Use a model to find $\frac{3}{4} \times \frac{1}{3}$.

1 Draw a unit square and divide it into 3 equal horizontal sections. Shade one of the sections to model $\frac{1}{3}$.

 $\frac{1}{3}$

2 Divide the unit square into **4** equal vertical sections so you can select $\frac{3}{4}$ of the shaded part of the model.

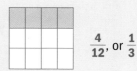 $\frac{4}{12}$, or $\frac{1}{3}$

3 Now select $\frac{3}{4}$ of $\frac{1}{3}$. The product of $\frac{3}{4}$ and $\frac{1}{3}$ is $\frac{3}{12}$, or $\frac{1}{4}$.

 $\frac{3}{12}$, or $\frac{1}{4}$

Your turn now Use the given model to find the product.

1. $\frac{1}{2} \times \frac{3}{5}$

2. $\frac{1}{4} \times \frac{2}{3}$

Use a model to find the product.

3. $\frac{1}{2} \times \frac{3}{4}$ **4.** $\frac{1}{6} \times \frac{2}{3}$ **5.** $\frac{3}{5} \times \frac{1}{3}$ **6.** $\frac{2}{3} \times \frac{2}{3}$

Stop and Think

7. Writing When using a model to find the product of two fractions, what do you notice about the number of sections the model is divided into and the product of the denominators of the fractions?

LESSON 5.3

Multiplying Fractions and Mixed Numbers

BEFORE	Now	WHY?
You added and subtracted fractions and mixed numbers.	You'll multiply fractions and mixed numbers.	So you can determine the height of a horse, as in Ex. 10.

Word Watch

Review Words

greatest common factor (GCF), p. 164
mixed number, p. 185
improper fraction, p. 185

In the Real World

Ice Cream Neapolitan ice cream is made up of one third chocolate, one third vanilla, and one third strawberry. How many gallons of strawberry ice cream are in a half gallon container?

To find a fraction *of* an amount, you *multiply*.

For the problem above, you need to find $\frac{1}{3}$ of $\frac{1}{2}$, or $\frac{1}{3} \cdot \frac{1}{2}$.

Multiplying Fractions

Words The product of two or more fractions is equal to the product of the numerators over the product of the denominators.

Numbers $\frac{1}{5} \cdot \frac{3}{8} = \frac{3}{40}$ **Algebra** $\frac{a}{b} \cdot \frac{c}{d} = \frac{a \cdot c}{b \cdot d}$ $(b, d \neq 0)$

EXAMPLE 1 **Multiplying Fractions**

To find the amount of strawberry ice cream described above, find $\frac{1}{3} \cdot \frac{1}{2}$.

$\frac{1}{3} \cdot \frac{1}{2} = \frac{1 \cdot 1}{3 \cdot 2}$ Use rule for multiplying fractions.

$= \frac{1}{6}$ Multiply.

ANSWER A half gallon container has $\frac{1}{6}$ gallon of strawberry ice cream.

Your turn now Find the product. Simplify if possible.

1. $\frac{2}{3} \cdot \frac{4}{5}$ **2.** $\frac{1}{6} \cdot \frac{7}{9}$ **3.** $\frac{5}{7} \cdot \frac{1}{2}$ **4.** $\frac{3}{4} \cdot \frac{3}{10}$

Dividing Out Common Factors When multiplying fractions, you can divide out common factors from the product's numerator and denominator so that the product will be in simplest form.

HELP with **Notetaking**

If you don't understand the process of dividing out common factors, write a question down in your notebook and discuss the question with a friend or teacher. Then write down what you learn.

EXAMPLE 2 **Multiplying Whole Numbers and Fractions**

Election The winner for class president got $\frac{3}{5}$ of the vote. If 200 students voted, how many students voted for the winner?

Solution

$$\frac{3}{5} \times 200 = \frac{3}{5} \times \frac{200}{1} \qquad \text{Write 200 as } \frac{200}{1}.$$

$$= \frac{3 \times \overset{40}{\cancel{200}}}{\underset{1}{\cancel{5}} \times 1} \qquad \text{Use rule for multiplying fractions. Divide out GCF of 200 and 5.}$$

$$= \frac{120}{1}, \text{ or } 120 \qquad \text{Multiply.}$$

ANSWER There were 120 students who voted for the winner.

Multiplying Mixed Numbers When multiplying mixed numbers, you should first rewrite them as improper fractions. Then use the rule for multiplying fractions.

EXAMPLE 3 **Multiplying Mixed Numbers**

$$5\frac{1}{4} \times 4\frac{2}{3} = \frac{21}{4} \times \frac{14}{3} \qquad \text{Write } 5\frac{1}{4} \text{ and } 4\frac{2}{3} \text{ as improper fractions.}$$

$$= \frac{\overset{7}{\cancel{21}} \times \overset{7}{\cancel{14}}}{\underset{2}{\cancel{4}} \times \underset{1}{\cancel{3}}} \qquad \text{Use rule for multiplying fractions. Divide out GCF of 21 and 3 and GCF of 14 and 4.}$$

$$= \frac{49}{2} \qquad \text{Multiply.}$$

$$= 24\frac{1}{2} \qquad \text{Write as a mixed number.}$$

Your turn now Find the product. Simplify if possible.

5. $12 \times \frac{3}{8}$ **6.** $\frac{2}{3} \times 6$ **7.** $2\frac{3}{4} \times 3\frac{1}{6}$ **8.** $4\frac{4}{5} \times 1\frac{1}{9}$

Getting Ready to Practice

1. **Vocabulary** Copy and complete: When multiplying two mixed numbers, you first write them as   ? .

Find the product. Simplify if possible.

2. $\frac{1}{4} \times \frac{3}{4}$

3. $\frac{3}{7} \times \frac{5}{6}$

4. $\frac{1}{3} \times 4$

5. $\frac{5}{6} \times 12$

6. $5 \times \frac{2}{11}$

7. $8 \times \frac{3}{4}$

8. $1\frac{1}{2} \times 5\frac{1}{2}$

9. $1\frac{2}{5} \times 4\frac{2}{7}$

10. **Horses** Trainers measure horses in *hands*, the distance across an adult's palm. The average height of a horse is $15\frac{1}{2}$ hands. If a hand is about $\frac{1}{3}$ foot, about how tall is an average horse in feet?

Practice and Problem Solving

HELP with Homework

Example Exercises
1   12–23
2   12–24
3   12–23, 33

Online Resources
CLASSZONE.COM

· More Examples
· eTutorial Plus

11. **Mental Math** Explain how you can use mental math to find $1\frac{1}{2} \cdot \frac{1}{2}$.

Find the product.

12. $\frac{1}{10} \times \frac{1}{12}$

13. $\frac{2}{5} \times \frac{1}{9}$

14. $\frac{1}{8} \times \frac{3}{4}$

15. $\frac{1}{3} \times 6$

16. $5 \times \frac{1}{5}$

17. $\frac{1}{6} \times 2$

18. $\frac{1}{4} \times 50$

19. $4\frac{1}{8} \times \frac{2}{11}$

20. $\frac{4}{9} \times 1\frac{1}{8}$

21. $3\frac{1}{3} \times 2\frac{7}{10}$

22. $8\frac{4}{5} \times 5\frac{5}{11}$

23. $7\frac{1}{2} \times 4\frac{2}{5}$

24. **Water Cooler** A water cooler contains 5 gallons of water. If you drink $\frac{3}{5}$ gallon for each of the next 6 days, how many gallons will be left in water cooler at the end of the sixth day?

Algebra **Evaluate the expression when x = 3 and y = 6.**

25. $\frac{3}{4}x$

26. $\frac{1}{4} \cdot \frac{1}{x} + \frac{5}{6}$

27. $3 - \frac{1}{5}y$

28. $\frac{1}{y} \cdot \frac{2}{5}$

Estimation **Estimate the product by rounding each factor to the nearest whole number.**

29. $\frac{9}{10} \times 1\frac{7}{9}$

30. $\frac{1}{5} \times 3\frac{11}{13}$

31. $1\frac{7}{8} \times 2\frac{2}{5}$

32. $5\frac{1}{4} \times 1\frac{6}{7}$

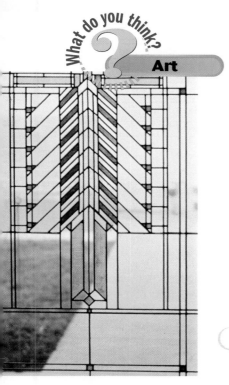

What do you think?

Art

■ **Stained Glass Windows**

Frank Lloyd Wright
(1867–1959) was an
architect who designed
decorative windows for more
than half of his buildings.
From 1885 to 1923, Wright
designed 4365 stained glass
windows for 97 houses.
Estimate how many windows
were in a typical house.

INTERNET

State Test Practice
CLASSZONE.COM

33. Stained Glass Windows The Darwin D. Martin house, built by Frank
Lloyd Wright, has a rectangular stained glass window with a length of
$41\frac{1}{2}$ feet and a width of $26\frac{1}{4}$ feet. What is the area of the window?

Critical Thinking Copy and complete the statement using *always*,
sometimes, or *never*.

34. Multiplying a mixed number by a proper fraction $\underline{\ ?\ }$ results in
a number greater than 1.

35. The product of two proper fractions is $\underline{\ ?\ }$ equal to 1.

Challenge Order the values of the expressions from least to
greatest when $s = \frac{3}{4}$ and $t = 6$.

36. $2\frac{1}{4} \cdot t,\ 2\frac{1}{3} \cdot s,\ 2t$ **37.** $st,\ 3s,\ \frac{1}{2}s$ **38.** $\frac{1}{3}s,\ 2s,\ \frac{1}{8}t$

Mixed Review

Copy and complete the statement using <, >, or =. *(Lesson 4.5)*

39. $\frac{1}{4}\ \underline{?}\ \frac{5}{6}$ **40.** $\frac{1}{2}\ \underline{?}\ \frac{9}{30}$ **41.** $\frac{7}{48}\ \underline{?}\ \frac{11}{12}$

Find the sum or difference. *(Lesson 5.2)*

42. $6\frac{1}{3} - 2\frac{1}{4}$ **43.** $5\frac{1}{3} - 2\frac{4}{5}$ **44.** $3\frac{2}{9} + 2\frac{7}{18}$

Basic Skills   Estimate the quotient.

45. $77 \div 19$ **46.** $38 \div 4$ **47.** $197 \div 24$

Test-Taking Practice

48. Multiple Choice Which of the following numbers, when multiplied by
$4\frac{1}{3}$, results in a number greater than $4\frac{1}{3}$?

A. 0   **B.** $\frac{1}{4}$ **C.** $\frac{7}{10}$ **D.** $1\frac{1}{3}$

49. Short Response Jen wrote a book report that is 4 pages long. It took
her $\frac{3}{4}$ hour to write each page. She also spent 1 hour proofreading
the report. How much time, in all, did she spend on the report? Write
and evaluate an expression to describe the situation. Explain how you
got your answer.

Lesson 5.3   Multiplying Fractions and Mixed Numbers   **219**

Draw a Diagram

- Estimate
- Act it Out
- Guess, Check, and Revise
- Look for a Pattern
- Draw a Diagram
- Make a List
- Make a Table

Problem A ball, dropped from a height of 6 feet, begins bouncing. The height of each bounce is $\frac{3}{4}$ of the height of the previous bounce. When will the ball bounce to a height less than $\frac{1}{2}$ of its initial height?

❶ Read and Understand

Read the problem carefully.

You need to find when the ball bounces to a height of less than $\frac{1}{2}$ of its initial height. Because the ball's initial height is 6 feet, you need to find when it bounces to a height of less than 3 feet.

❷ Make a Plan

Decide on a strategy to use.

You could draw a diagram to keep track of the number of bounces and the heights of the bounces. Then you can use your diagram to see on which bounce the ball reaches a height of less than 3 feet.

❸ Solve the Problem

Reread the problem and draw a diagram.

Calculate the ball's height for each bounce by finding $\frac{3}{4}$ of the height of the previous bounce. Draw a diagram that shows each bounce height.

First: $\frac{3}{4} \cdot 6 = \frac{3}{4} \cdot \frac{6}{1} = \frac{3 \cdot \overset{3}{\cancel{6}}}{\cancel{4} \cdot 1} = \frac{9}{2}$, or $4\frac{1}{2}$

Second: $\frac{3}{4} \cdot \frac{9}{2} = \frac{3 \cdot 9}{4 \cdot 2} = \frac{27}{8}$, or $3\frac{3}{8}$

Third: $\frac{3}{4} \cdot \frac{27}{8} = \frac{3 \cdot 27}{4 \cdot 8} = \frac{81}{32}$, or $2\frac{17}{32}$

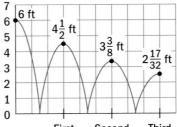

ANSWER The ball will reach a height less than $\frac{1}{2}$ of its initial height on the third bounce.

❹ Look Back

You could also find the height of the ball on the third bounce by finding $\frac{3}{4} \cdot \frac{3}{4} \cdot \frac{3}{4}$ of the initial height. Because $\frac{27}{64} < \frac{1}{2}$, the answer is reasonable.

Use the strategy *draw a diagram*.

1. **Locker Decorations** You are decorating your locker at school with pictures. Your locker is 32 inches tall and 14 inches wide. You have 6 pictures that are 4 inches long and 7 inches wide and 3 pictures that are 8 inches long and 10 inches wide. Can you fit them all in your locker? Explain why or why not.

2. **Woodworking** You are making a picture frame in a woodworking class. You have 8 pieces of wood. Their lengths are listed in the table below. Can you make a frame that has a width of 7 inches and a length of 10 inches without cutting any of the pieces? Explain why or why not.

Length (inches)	8	6	4	3	2	1
Pieces of Wood	1	2	2	1	1	1

3. **Directions** Your neighborhood is laid out as a grid. You need to go to the video rental store to return a video and to the grocery store to buy some milk. You need to walk 6 blocks north and 4 blocks east to get to the video rental store from your house. The grocery store is 3 blocks north and 7 blocks west of the video rental store. What directions will get you home from the grocery store?

4. **Number Line** Use the statements below about points *A*, *B*, *C*, and *D* on a number line to determine how far apart points *B* and *D* are.

   Point *B* is 6 units to the right of point *A*.

   Point *C* is 12 units to the left of point *A*.

   Point *D* is halfway between *A* and *C*.

Mixed Problem Solving

Use any strategy to solve the problem.

5. **Trading Cards** Suppose that you buy a baseball card for $12, sell it for $15, buy it back for $18, and sell it again for $20. How much money have you made in buying and selling the card?

6. **Vending Machine** You have 3 quarters, 7 nickels, and 4 dimes in your pocket. A carton of juice costs $1 from a vending machine. What are the different combinations of coins that add up to $1 that you could use to buy the juice?

7. **Cameras** As a gift for Teri's summer trip, her parents gave her $90.00 to spend on a camera and some film. If she buys the camera for $69.99, about how many rolls of film can she buy if each roll costs $4.99?

8. **Smoothies** You work at a smoothie shop. A customer asks for a jumbo strawberry smoothie. You notice that the jumbo column on the recipe card has been smudged. Use the measures for the other sizes to determine the amounts of frozen yogurt and strawberries needed to make the jumbo smoothie.

Ingredients	S	M	L	Jumbo
Frozen yogurt (fluid ounces)	2	4	8	?
Strawberries (scoops)	1	2	4	?

LESSON 5.4

Dividing Fractions and Mixed Numbers

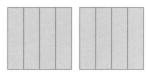

BEFORE	▶ Now	WHY?
You multiplied fractions and mixed numbers.	You'll divide fractions and mixed numbers.	So you can set up a slalom skiing course, as in Ex. 35.

Word Watch

reciprocal, p. 222

You can use a model to find the quotient $2 \div \frac{1}{4}$.

First draw two unit squares. Then divide each square into fourths.

There are 8 fourths in the model. So, $2 \div \frac{1}{4} = 8$. Notice that there are 4 fourths in each square and there are 2 squares, so $2 \times 4 = 8$. The numbers $\frac{1}{4}$ and 4 are *reciprocals*. Two nonzero numbers whose product is 1 are **reciprocals**.

$$\frac{2}{3} \text{ and } \frac{3}{2} \text{ are reciprocals, because } \frac{2}{3} \cdot \frac{3}{2} = 1.$$

$$5 \text{ and } \frac{1}{5} \text{ are reciprocals, because } 5 \cdot \frac{1}{5} = 1.$$

As you saw above, $2 \div \frac{1}{4} = 2 \times 4$, which suggests the following rule.

Using Reciprocals to Divide

Words To divide by any nonzero number, multiply by its reciprocal.

Numbers $\frac{3}{4} \div \frac{2}{3} = \frac{3}{4} \cdot \frac{3}{2} = \frac{9}{8}$ **Algebra** $\frac{a}{b} \div \frac{c}{d} = \frac{a}{b} \cdot \frac{d}{c} = \frac{ad}{bc}$

$(b, c, d \neq 0)$

EXAMPLE 1 **Dividing a Fraction by a Fraction**

$\dfrac{5}{9} \div \dfrac{2}{3} = \dfrac{5}{9} \cdot \dfrac{3}{2}$ **Multiply by reciprocal.**

$= \dfrac{5 \cdot \cancel{3}^{\,1}}{\cancel{9}_{3} \cdot 2}$ **Use rule for multiplying fractions. Divide out common factor.**

$= \dfrac{5}{6}$ **Multiply.**

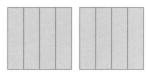

 with **Solving**

In Example 2, you can check your answer by multiplying the quotient and the divisor and comparing the result with the dividend:

$\frac{2}{5} \times 2 = \frac{2}{5} \times \frac{2}{1} = \frac{4}{5}$.

EXAMPLE 2 **Dividing a Fraction by a Whole Number**

$\frac{4}{5} \div 2 = \frac{4}{5} \cdot \frac{1}{2}$ Multiply by reciprocal.

$= \frac{\overset{2}{\cancel{4}} \cdot 1}{5 \cdot \cancel{2}_{1}}$ Use rule for multiplying fractions.
Divide out common factor.

$= \frac{2}{5}$ Multiply.

Your turn now   **Find the quotient. Simplify if possible.**

1. $\frac{5}{6} \div \frac{7}{9}$ **2.** $\frac{9}{2} \div \frac{3}{2}$ **3.** $\frac{1}{6} \div 3$ **4.** $\frac{2}{3} \div 4$

EXAMPLE 3 **Drawing a Diagram to Solve a Problem**

In-line Skating You set up an in-line skating course 21 feet long to practice weaving around cones. You want a cone every $3\frac{1}{2}$ feet, but not at the start or end of the course. How many cones will you need?

Solution

Method 1 Draw a diagram on graph paper. Make the course 21 grid boxes long. Draw a point to mark the location of a cone every $3\frac{1}{2}$ grid boxes.

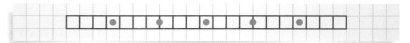

Method 2 Use division.

$21 \div 3\frac{1}{2} = 21 \div \frac{7}{2}$ Write $3\frac{1}{2}$ as an improper fraction.

$= \frac{21}{1} \times \frac{2}{7}$ Multiply by reciprocal.

$= \frac{\overset{3}{\cancel{21}} \times 2}{1 \times \cancel{7}_{1}}$ Use rule for multiplying fractions.
Divide out common factor.

$= 6$ Multiply.

The quotient 6 gives you the number of $3\frac{1}{2}$ foot *spaces*, not the number of *cones*. You have to subtract 1 to get the number of cones: $6 - 1 = 5$.

ANSWER You will need 5 cones.

HELP with Solving

In Example 4, you can estimate the answer by rounding each mixed number to the nearest whole number. By doing so, you have $9 \div 3 = 3$, so the answer is reasonable.

EXAMPLE 4 **Dividing Two Mixed Numbers**

$$8\frac{3}{4} \div 2\frac{5}{8} = \frac{35}{4} \div \frac{21}{8}$$ Write $8\frac{3}{4}$ and $2\frac{5}{8}$ as improper fractions.

$$= \frac{35}{4} \cdot \frac{8}{21}$$ Multiply by reciprocal.

$$= \frac{\overset{5}{\cancel{35}} \cdot \overset{2}{\cancel{8}}}{\underset{1}{\cancel{4}} \cdot \underset{3}{\cancel{21}}}$$ Use rule for multiplying fractions. Divide out common factors.

$$= \frac{10}{3}, \text{ or } 3\frac{1}{3}$$ Multiply.

Your turn now Find the quotient. Then estimate to check the answer.

5. $3 \div \frac{6}{11}$ **6.** $12 \div 2\frac{2}{5}$ **7.** $5\frac{2}{3} \div \frac{3}{5}$ **8.** $4\frac{1}{2} \div 1\frac{1}{4}$

5.4 Exercises

More Practice, p. 709

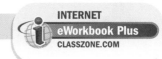

INTERNET
eWorkbook Plus
CLASSZONE.COM

Getting Ready to Practice

1. **Vocabulary** Copy and complete: The reciprocal of $\frac{3}{7}$ is _?_.

2. **Writing** Explain in your own words how to divide a fraction by a fraction.

Write the reciprocal of the number.

3. $\frac{1}{7}$ 4. 8 5. $1\frac{4}{9}$ 6. $3\frac{3}{4}$

Match the division expression with the related multiplication expression.

7. $\frac{3}{20} \div \frac{4}{9}$ 8. $\frac{7}{8} \div \frac{3}{13}$ 9. $1\frac{1}{7} \div 4\frac{1}{3}$ 10. $6\frac{2}{3} \div 2\frac{1}{4}$

A. $\frac{8}{7} \times \frac{3}{13}$ B. $\frac{3}{20} \times \frac{9}{4}$ C. $\frac{20}{3} \times \frac{4}{9}$ D. $\frac{7}{8} \times \frac{13}{3}$

11. **Sandwiches** To surprise the guests at a party, the host prepares a $5\frac{1}{2}$ foot long submarine sandwich. The sandwich is cut into 11 equal pieces. How long is each piece?

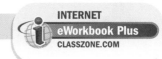

Practice and Problem Solving

with Homework

Example	Exercises
1	16–27
2	16–27
3	35–36
4	16–27

Online Resources
CLASSZONE.COM

· More Examples
· eTutorial Plus

Write the reciprocal of the number.

12. $\frac{5}{6}$ **13.** $1\frac{3}{4}$ **14.** $5\frac{2}{5}$ **15.** 1

Find the quotient. Then check the answer.

16. $\frac{3}{8} \div \frac{1}{4}$ **17.** $\frac{6}{7} \div \frac{5}{14}$ **18.** $\frac{8}{9} \div 1\frac{2}{15}$ **19.** $\frac{7}{12} \div 4$

20. $\frac{9}{10} \div 6$ **21.** $8 \div 2\frac{3}{4}$ **22.** $10 \div 4\frac{1}{6}$ **23.** $4\frac{1}{5} \div \frac{3}{10}$

24. $2\frac{5}{6} \div 7$ **25.** $5 \div \frac{2}{3}$ **26.** $9\frac{4}{5} \div 1\frac{1}{13}$ **27.** $7\frac{1}{6} \div 2\frac{7}{12}$

 Algebra Evaluate the expression when $x = \dfrac{5}{8}$ and $y = 3$.

28. $x \div y$ **29.** $y \div x$ **30.** $4\frac{1}{6} \div y$

31. Cooking Making pasta requires boiling 6 cups of water, but your measuring cup holds only $1\frac{1}{2}$ cups. How many times do you need to fill the measuring cup?

Evaluate the expression.

32. $\left(2\frac{3}{5} \div 3\frac{9}{10}\right) \times 3\frac{5}{8}$ **33.** $\left(5\frac{2}{3} - 3\frac{1}{2}\right) \div 8\frac{3}{5}$ **34.** $\left(6\frac{2}{7} + 3\frac{2}{3}\right) \div 5\frac{3}{4}$

35. Slalom Skiing On a slalom skiing course, the distance from the start to the first gate is 15 meters, and the distance from the last gate to the finish is 20 meters. If the slalom course is 635 meters long and the distance between gates is $1\frac{1}{2}$ meters, how many gates are needed for the course?

36. Draw a Diagram You are an editor for your school yearbook. Each row of photos is $8\frac{5}{8}$ inches wide, including the margins. Each photo is $1\frac{1}{4}$ inches wide, the space between each photo is $\frac{1}{8}$ inch, and each margin is $\frac{1}{4}$ inch. How many photos can fit in one row?

37. Challenge Choose a nonzero number and divide it by a series of fractions, each less than the one before, such as $\frac{3}{4}, \frac{2}{3}, \frac{1}{2}, \ldots$. Describe what happens to the corresponding series of quotients.

Mixed Review

In Exercises 38 and 39, copy and complete the statement using the appropriate metric unit. *(Lesson 2.6)*

38. The capacity of a vase is 325 __?__.   **39.** A basketball has a mass of 0.62 __?__.

40. Find the product of $\frac{5}{12}$ and $7\frac{3}{5}$. *(Lesson 5.3)*

Basic Skills   **Use a ruler to draw a segment with the given length.**

41. 5 inches   **42.** $3\frac{1}{2}$ inches   **43.** $\frac{3}{4}$ inch   **44.** $2\frac{5}{8}$ inches

Test-Taking Practice

45. Extended Response A CD case is $\frac{3}{8}$ inch wide. A cassette case is $\frac{5}{8}$ inch wide. If you want to put 8 cassettes on a shelf that is 20 inches wide, how many CDs would fit in the remaining space? Explain your reasoning.

BRAIN GAME

Mix and Match

Play this game with a partner. Take turns doing the following:

1. Choose two fractions from the clothesline. (Fractions cannot be used more than once.)

2. Let one fraction be the dividend and the other be the divisor.

3. Find the quotient. (Your partner should check your answer.)

4. Add the quotient to your score. (You both start with a score of zero.)

Once all the fractions have been used, the player with the higher score wins.

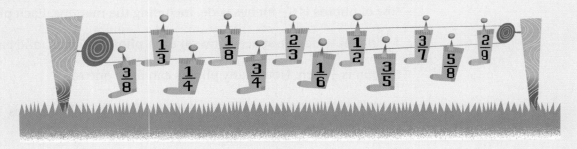

Fraction Operations

GOAL Use a calculator to perform operations on fractions and mixed numbers.

Some calculators allow you to perform operations with fractions and mixed numbers. If you have such a calculator, be sure it is set to display answers as mixed numbers in simplest form.

Example How many $\frac{1}{2}$ minute commercials can a television station run during a $2\frac{1}{2}$ minute break?

Solution

To find the number of commercials, you need to find the quotient $2\frac{1}{2} \div \frac{1}{2}$.

Keystrokes	Display
2 [UNIT] 1 [/] 2 [÷] 1 [/] 2 [=]	5

ANSWER The television station can run 5 commercials during the break.

HELP with Technology

The [UNIT] key is used to separate the whole number part of a mixed number from the fractional part of a mixed number. A ⊔ is displayed on the screen when [UNIT] is pressed.

Your turn now Use a calculator to evaluate the expression.

1. $\frac{5}{11} + \frac{7}{9}$

2. $\frac{2}{5} + \frac{5}{7}$

3. $\frac{19}{20} - \frac{3}{4}$

4. $\frac{2}{3} - \frac{2}{5}$

5. $5\frac{4}{7} \times \frac{1}{2}$

6. $\frac{3}{4} \times 10\frac{1}{15}$

7. $5\frac{11}{12} \div \frac{5}{20}$

8. $8\frac{1}{7} \div \frac{5}{9}$

9. $\frac{13}{20} \times \frac{7}{10} \times \frac{2}{5}$

10. $2\frac{1}{3} + 9\frac{8}{15} - \frac{2}{5}$

11. $\frac{13}{25} \div \left(\frac{1}{3} + \frac{2}{7}\right)$

12. $\left(17\frac{9}{10} - 7\frac{5}{8}\right) \times 4\frac{1}{6}$

13. **Posters** A standard movie poster is $2\frac{1}{4}$ feet wide. The width of a wall is $13\frac{1}{2}$ feet. How many standard movie posters can you fit across the wall without overlapping? If each poster sells for $12.95, how much will it cost to put posters across the wall?

Review the vocabulary definitions in your notebook.

Copy the review examples in your notebook. Then complete the exercises.

Notebook Review

Check Your Definitions

greatest common factor (GCF), p. 164

least common denominator (LCD), p. 181

mixed number, p. 185
improper fraction, p. 185
reciprocal, p. 222

Use Your Vocabulary

1. What is the product of a nonzero number and its reciprocal?

5.1–5.2 Can you add and subtract fractions and mixed numbers?

 EXAMPLE

a. $\dfrac{1}{5} + \dfrac{3}{10} = \dfrac{2}{10} + \dfrac{3}{10}$

$= \dfrac{5}{10} = \dfrac{1}{2}$

b. $10\dfrac{5}{6} - 4\dfrac{1}{4} = 10\dfrac{10}{12} - 4\dfrac{3}{12}$

$= 6\dfrac{7}{12}$

✓ **Find the sum or difference.**

2. $\dfrac{3}{7} + \dfrac{1}{4}$ **3.** $6\dfrac{4}{21} + 16\dfrac{1}{6}$ **4.** $\dfrac{1}{2} - \dfrac{1}{5}$ **5.** $9\dfrac{13}{14} - 8\dfrac{3}{7}$

5.3 Can you multiply fractions and mixed numbers?

 EXAMPLE

$3\dfrac{3}{4} \times 4\dfrac{2}{5} = \dfrac{15}{4} \times \dfrac{22}{5}$ Write $3\dfrac{3}{4}$ and $4\dfrac{2}{5}$ as improper fractions.

$= \dfrac{\overset{3}{\cancel{15}} \times \overset{11}{\cancel{22}}}{\underset{2}{\cancel{4}} \times \underset{1}{\cancel{5}}}$ Use rule for multiplying fractions. Divide out common factors.

$= \dfrac{33}{2}$, or $16\dfrac{1}{2}$ Multiply.

✓ **Find the product.**

6. $10 \times \dfrac{5}{8}$ **7.** $\dfrac{7}{12} \times 18$ **8.** $5\dfrac{5}{6} \times 2\dfrac{2}{7}$ **9.** $4\dfrac{7}{8} \times 2\dfrac{4}{9}$

5.4 Can you divide fractions and mixed numbers?

 Review **EXAMPLE**

$$\frac{5}{6} \div \frac{4}{9} = \frac{5}{6} \times \frac{9}{4} \qquad \text{Multiply by reciprocal.}$$

$$= \frac{5 \times \overset{3}{\cancel{9}}}{\underset{2}{\cancel{6}} \times 4} \qquad \text{Use rule for multiplying fractions.}$$
$$\text{Divide out common factor.}$$

$$= \frac{15}{8}, \text{ or } 1\frac{7}{8} \qquad \text{Multiply.}$$

✓ **Find the quotient.**

10. $\dfrac{7}{8} \div \dfrac{1}{12}$ **11.** $\dfrac{3}{5} \div 6$ **12.** $36 \div 6\dfrac{3}{4}$ **13.** $10\dfrac{1}{8} \div 1\dfrac{7}{20}$

Stop and Think about Lessons 5.1–5.4

14. Writing How can you check an answer to a division problem that involves fractions? Give an example.

15. Critical Thinking Without dividing, tell whether the quotient $\dfrac{3}{4} \div 1\dfrac{1}{2}$ is *greater than* or *less than* $\dfrac{3}{4}$. Explain your reasoning.

Review Quiz 1

Find the sum or difference.

1. $\dfrac{2}{3} + \dfrac{1}{6}$ **2.** $\dfrac{5}{6} - \dfrac{5}{12}$ **3.** $11\dfrac{7}{18} + 24\dfrac{5}{12}$ **4.** $21\dfrac{3}{4} - 5\dfrac{9}{14}$

5. Hiking At Mount Monadnock in New Hampshire, the distance from the parking lot to the top of the mountain along Red Spot Trail is $2\dfrac{3}{4}$ miles. If you hike to the top and back down, how far have you traveled?

Find the product or quotient.

6. $13 \times \dfrac{17}{26}$ **7.** $2\dfrac{5}{8} \times 1\dfrac{5}{9}$ **8.** $3\dfrac{1}{3} \div \dfrac{1}{9}$ **9.** $5\dfrac{1}{2} \div 1\dfrac{3}{4}$

10. Books If Ryan gives away $\dfrac{1}{3}$ of his books and sells $\dfrac{3}{4}$ of the remaining books, how many of his 180 books has he sold?

Measuring in Customary Units

LESSON 5.5

BEFORE	▶ Now	WHY?
You measured and estimated using metric units.	You'll measure and estimate using customary units.	So you can estimate the weight of an elephant, as in Ex. 22.

📓 **Word Watch**

U.S. customary system, p. 230
length: inch, foot, yard, mile, p. 230
weight: ounce, pound, ton, p. 231
capacity: fluid ounce, cup, pint, quart, gallon, p. 232

The units of measurement for length, weight, and capacity commonly used in the United States are part of the **U.S. customary system** .

Length The **inch (in.)** is a unit of length in the customary system. Three other customary units of length are the **foot (ft)** , **yard (yd)** , and **mile (mi)** . You can use the following benchmarks to estimate length.

1 inch
length of a small paper clip

1 foot
distance from shoulder to elbow

1 yard
width of a door

1 mile combined length of 15 football fields

EXAMPLE 1 **Using Customary Units of Length**

To estimate the length of a barrette, think of small paper clips laid next to it. Then measure the barrette with a ruler to check your estimate.

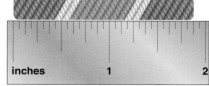

About $1\frac{1}{2}$ paper clips fit alongside the barrette, so it is about $1\frac{1}{2}$ inches long.

The ruler shows sixteenths of an inch, so the barrette is $1\frac{14}{16}$, or $1\frac{7}{8}$, inches long.

Weight The weight of an object tells you how heavy the object is. Three customary units of weight are the **ounce (oz)** , **pound (lb)** , and **ton (T)** . You can measure the weight of an object using a scale.

EXAMPLE 2 **Measuring Weight**

Find the weight of the bananas.

Each pound is divided into sixteenths, so the arrow is at the $1\frac{14}{16}$ lb or $1\frac{7}{8}$ lb mark.

ANSWER The bananas weigh $1\frac{7}{8}$ pounds.

You can use the following benchmarks to estimate weight.

1 ounce	**1 pound**	**1 ton**
slice of bread	soccer ball	walrus

EXAMPLE 3 **Using Customary Units of Weight**

Copy and complete the statement using the appropriate customary unit: The weight of a bowling ball is 14 _?_.

The weight of a bowling ball is greater than the weight of 14 slices of bread (14 oz), and it is certainly less than the weight of 14 walruses (14 T). Because a good estimate for the weight of a bowling ball is the weight of 14 soccer balls, the appropriate customary unit is pounds.

ANSWER The weight of a bowling ball is 14 pounds.

Your turn now **Complete the following exercises.**

1. Estimate the length of an unsharpened pencil in inches. Then use a ruler to check your estimate.

2. The weight of a baseball bat is 33 _?_ .

Watch Out!

A fluid ounce is not the same as an ounce. Fluid ounces are a measure of the capacity of a container holding liquid, while an ounce measures the weight of the container.

Capacity Capacity is a measure of the amount that a container can hold. Five customary units of capacity are the **fluid ounce (fl oz)**, **cup (c)**, **pint (pt)**, **quart (qt)**, and **gallon (gal)**.

EXAMPLE 4 **Measuring a Liquid Amount**

Find the amount of liquid in the measuring cup.

| 4 cups |
| 3 cups |
| 2 cups |

Each cup is divided into fourths, so the liquid is at the $3\frac{3}{4}$ cup level.

ANSWER There are about $3\frac{3}{4}$ cups of liquid in the measuring cup.

You can use the benchmarks shown to estimate capacity.

1 fluid ounce

EXAMPLE 5 **Using Customary Units of Capacity**

What is the most reasonable capacity of a lemonade pitcher?

A. 8 fl oz   **B.** 2 qt   **C.** 10 gal   **D.** 3 c

Solution

Both 8 fluid ounces and 3 cups of water are too little to fill the pitcher. A pitcher couldn't hold more than a gallon, so 10 gallons is too much. That leaves 2 quarts of water, which seems an appropriate capacity.

ANSWER The most reasonable capacity of a lemonade pitcher is (B) 2 qt.

Your turn now **Match the object with the appropriate capacity.**

3. Juice glass   **4.** Paint can   **5.** Ice cube tray

A. 1 gal   **B.** 1 pt   **C.** 7 fl oz

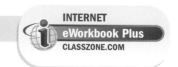
Getting Ready to Practice

1. Vocabulary Which unit measures capacity: *yard*, *cup*, or *pound*?

Copy and complete using the appropriate customary unit.

2. A dictionary is $2\frac{1}{2}$? thick.

3. A marathon is $26\frac{1}{5}$? long.

4. A stapler weighs 8 ? .

5. A swimming pool holds 15,000 ? .

6. Sunglasses Dave thinks that the weight of a pair of sunglasses is 7 oz. Mary thinks that the weight is about 2 lb. Who is right? Explain.

Practice and Problem Solving

Estimate the length of the object in inches. Then measure the object using a ruler.

7. Your shoe

8. Calendar

9. Picture frame

Find the weight of the object.

10.

11.

Find the amount of liquid in the measuring cup.

12.

4 cups	3 cups
3 cups	2 cups
2 cups	1 cup
1 cup	

13.

4 cups	3 cups
3 cups	2 cups
2 cups	1 cup
1 cup	

Copy and complete using the appropriate customary unit.

14. Mount Everest is $5\frac{1}{2}$? high.

15. A tennis racket weighs $9\frac{1}{2}$? .

16. A shampoo bottle holds 12 ? .

17. A teakettle holds 10 ? .

Tell what measurement tool would be appropriate for the given unit.

18. fluid ounce

19. inch

20. pound

HELP with Homework

Example	Exercises
1	7–9, 14–17, 21–22
2	10–11
3	14–17, 21–22
4	12–13
5	14–17

Online Resources
CLASSZONE.COM
· More Examples
· eTutorial Plus

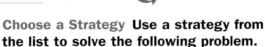

In Exercises 21 and 22, choose the letter of the most reasonable measurement.

21. **Travel** What is the distance between Austin, Texas, and Tallahassee, Florida?

    A. 1760 yd   **B.** 7000 ft   **C.** 600 in.   **D.** 800 mi

22. **Elephants** What is the weight of an Indian bull elephant?

    F. $3\frac{1}{2}$ T   **G.** 600 lb   **H.** 2000 oz   **I.** 100 lb

23. **Critical Thinking** If one scale has each pound divided into fourths and another scale has each pound divided into halves, which scale will give you a more precise measurement? Explain your reasoning.

Tell whether an *exact answer* or an *estimate* is needed for the given situation.

24. Sawing wood to build a deck   **25.** Distance from home to the park

26. The amount of weight you lost   **27.** Your finish time in a track race

28. **Challenge** Is it possible for two containers, when filled, to have the same weight but different capacities? If so, give an example. If not, explain why not.

■ **Elephants**

An Indian bull elephant's footprint has a width of about $1\frac{1}{2}$ feet. How many of your footprints would fit across the footprint of an Indian bull elephant?

Mixed Review

Choose a Strategy Use a strategy from the list to solve the following problem. Explain your choice of strategy.

Problem Solving Strategies

■ Make a List
■ Estimate
■ Look for a Pattern

29. Jackie, Sean, Tim, and Katie have four seats in a row at a basketball game. In how many different ways can they sit?

Basic Skills Copy and complete the statement.

30. 120 min = ? h   **31.** 90 sec = ? min   **32.** 3 wk = ? d

Test-Taking Practice

33. **Multiple Choice** What is a reasonable capacity for a fish aquarium?

    A. 18 fl oz   **B.** 7 pt   **C.** 16 qt   **D.** 14 gal

34. **Multiple Choice** Which is the greatest length?

    F. 30 in.   **G.** 3 ft   **H.** $\frac{1}{2}$ mi   **I.** 1 yd

Converting Customary Units

LESSON 5.6

BEFORE You measured objects using customary units.

▶ **Now** You'll convert between customary units.

WHY? So you can determine the tallest pyramid, as in Ex. 25.

In the Real World

Word Watch

Review Words

U.S. customary system, p. 230

length: inch, foot, yard, mile, p. 230

weight: ounce, pound, ton, p. 231

capacity: fluid ounce, cup, pint, quart, gallon, p. 232

Art In 1976, the artist Christo built a $24\frac{1}{2}$ mile long fabric fence in California. He and his team joined pieces of fabric, each 63 feet long, together to form the fence. How many yards long was each piece?

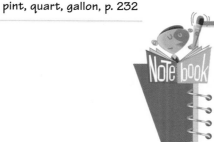

Customary Units of Measure

Length	Weight	Capacity
1 ft = 12 in.	1 lb = 16 oz	1 c = 8 fl oz
1 yd = 3 ft = 36 in.	1 T = 2000 lb	1 pt = 2 c
1 mi = 1760 yd = 5280 ft		1 qt = 2 pt
		1 gal = 4 qt

Converting Units To convert units, multiply by a convenient form of 1. Some useful facts are:

- To convert inches to feet, multiply by $\frac{1 \text{ ft}}{12 \text{ in.}}$.

- To convert feet to inches, multiply by $\frac{12 \text{ in.}}{1 \text{ ft}}$.

EXAMPLE 1 Converting Customary Units of Length

To find the length, in yards, of each piece of fabric described above, convert 63 feet to yards.

with Solving

Because 1 yd = 3 ft, the fraction $\frac{1 \text{ yd}}{3 \text{ ft}}$ is equivalent to 1.

$$63 \text{ ft} \times \frac{1 \text{ yd}}{3 \text{ ft}} = \frac{\overset{21}{\cancel{63 \text{ ft}}} \times 1 \text{ yd}}{\underset{1}{\cancel{3 \text{ ft}}}}$$

Use rule for multiplying fractions.
Divide out common factor and unit.

$$= 21 \text{ yd}$$

Multiply.

ANSWER Each piece of fabric was 21 yards long.

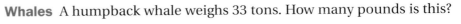

EXAMPLE 2 **Converting Customary Units of Weight**

Whales A humpback whale weighs 33 tons. How many pounds is this?

Solution

Use the fact that 1 T = 2000 lb.

$$33 \text{ T} \times \frac{2000 \text{ lb}}{1 \text{ T}} = \frac{33 \text{ T}}{1} \times \frac{2000 \text{ lb}}{1 \text{ T}}$$ Write 33 T as $\frac{33 \text{ T}}{1}$.

$$= \frac{33 \cancel{\text{T}} \times 2000 \text{ lb}}{1 \times 1 \cancel{\text{T}}}$$ Use rule for multiplying fractions. Divide out common unit.

$$= 66,000 \text{ lb}$$ Multiply.

ANSWER The humpback whale weighs 66,000 pounds.

EXAMPLE 3 **Converting Customary Units of Capacity**

Convert 25 fluid ounces to pints. Use the fact that 1 c = 8 fl oz and 1 pt = 2c.

$$25 \text{ fl oz} \times \frac{1 \text{ c}}{8 \text{ fl oz}} \times \frac{1 \text{ pt}}{2 \text{ c}} = \frac{25 \cancel{\text{fl oz}} \times 1 \cancel{\text{c}} \times 1 \text{ pt}}{8 \cancel{\text{fl oz}} \times 2 \cancel{\text{c}}}$$ Use rule for multiplying fractions. Divide out common units.

$$= \frac{25}{16} \text{ pt, or } 1\frac{9}{16} \text{ pt}$$ Multiply.

Your turn now Copy and complete the statement.

1. 3000 lb = ? T   **2.** 10 yd = ? in.   **3.** 6 c = ? fl oz

EXAMPLE 4 **Writing Measurements in Mixed Units**

Convert 26 fluid ounces to cups and fluid ounces.

(1 Convert 26 fluid ounces to cups.

$$26 \text{ fl oz} \times \frac{1 \text{ c}}{8 \text{ fl oz}} = \frac{\overset{13}{\cancel{26}} \cancel{\text{fl oz}} \times 1 \text{ c}}{\underset{4}{\cancel{8}} \cancel{\text{fl oz}}}$$

$$= \frac{13}{4} \text{ c, or } 3\frac{1}{4} \text{ c}$$

(2 Convert the fractional part from cups to fluid ounces.

$$\frac{1 \text{ c}}{4} \times \frac{8 \text{ fl oz}}{1 \text{ c}} = \frac{1 \cancel{\text{c}} \times \overset{2}{\cancel{8}} \text{ fl oz}}{\underset{1}{\cancel{4}} \times 1 \cancel{\text{c}}}$$

$$= 2 \text{ fl oz}$$

ANSWER So, 26 fluid ounces = 3 cups 2 fluid ounces.

Your turn now Copy and complete the statement.

4. 35 oz = ? lb ? oz

5. 5 pt = ? qt ? pt

Mixed Units When adding or subtracting measures given in mixed units, you may need to convert between units.

EXAMPLE 5 Adding and Subtracting with Mixed Units

Wakeboards One type of wakeboard weighs 7 pounds 6 ounces. Another type of wakeboard weighs 6 pounds 14 ounces.

a. Find the sum of the weights.

b. Find the difference of the weights.

Solution

a. Add. Then rename the sum.

$$
\begin{array}{r}
7 \text{ lb} \quad 6 \text{ oz} \\
+ \ 6 \text{ lb} \ 14 \text{ oz} \\
\hline
13 \text{ lb} \ 20 \text{ oz}
\end{array}
$$

13 lb 20 oz = 13 lb + 1 lb 4 oz

ANSWER The sum is 14 lb 4 oz.

b. Rename. Then subtract.

$$
\begin{array}{r}
7 \text{ lb} \quad 6 \text{ oz} \\
- \ 6 \text{ lb} \ 14 \text{ oz}
\end{array}
\longrightarrow
\begin{array}{r}
6 \text{ lb} \ 22 \text{ oz} \\
- \ 6 \text{ lb} \ 14 \text{ oz} \\
\hline
8 \text{ oz}
\end{array}
$$

ANSWER The difference is 8 oz.

5.6 Exercises
More Practice, p. 709

INTERNET
eWorkbook Plus
CLASSZONE.COM

Getting Ready to Practice

Vocabulary Copy and complete the statement with *feet*, *inches*, or *yards*.

1. 1 mi = 1760 ?

2. 1 mi = 63,360 ?

3. 1 mi = 5280 ?

Copy and complete the statement.

4. 24 oz = ? lb

5. 15 pt = ? c

6. 35 in. = ? ft

Find the sum or difference.

7.
$$
\begin{array}{r}
3 \text{ c} \ 5 \text{ fl oz} \\
+ \ 8 \text{ c} \ 6 \text{ fl oz}
\end{array}
$$

8.
$$
\begin{array}{r}
6 \text{ lb} \ 7 \text{ oz} \\
+ \ 8 \text{ lb} \ 9 \text{ oz}
\end{array}
$$

9.
$$
\begin{array}{r}
10 \text{ ft} \ 3 \text{ in.} \\
- \ 4 \text{ ft} \ 9 \text{ in.}
\end{array}
$$

10. Water Bottles A water bottle contains 20 fluid ounces. Convert this to cups and fluid ounces.

Practice and Problem Solving

HELP with Homework

Example	Exercises
1	13–18, 25–31, 35–37
2	13–18, 26–31, 35–37
3	13–18, 26–31, 35–37
4	19–21
5	22–24

Online Resources
CLASSZONE.COM

· More Examples
· eTutorial Plus

11. Writing Explain in your own words how to convert from feet to yards.

12. Critical Thinking When converting from pounds to ounces, will the number of ounces be greater than the number of pounds? Explain.

Copy and complete the statement.

13. 5 ft = _?_ in.

14. 16,320 ft = _?_ mi

15. $4\frac{5}{8}$ lb = _?_ oz

16. $1\frac{1}{4}$ T = _?_ lb

17. $3\frac{3}{4}$ c = _?_ fl oz

18. 25 c = _?_ pt

19. 96 in. = _?_ yd _?_ ft

20. 9 qt = _?_ gal _?_ qt

21. 70 oz = _?_ lb _?_ oz

Find the sum or difference.

22.
```
   12 mi   500 ft
 + 27 mi  5250 ft
```

23.
```
   6 ft   2 in.
 - 2 ft  11 in.
```

24.
```
   45 lb   9 oz
 - 17 lb  13 oz
```

25. Pyramids The three great pyramids in Giza, Egypt, and their original heights are listed in the table. Determine which pyramid was the tallest.

Pyramid	Khafre	Menkaure	Khufu
Height	157 yd	2580 in.	481 ft

Copy and complete the statement using <, >, or =.

26. 36 in. _?_ 3 ft

27. 10 pt _?_ 2 gal

28. 10 lb _?_ 64 oz

29. 3 yd _?_ 10 ft

30. 10 c _?_ 20 fl oz

31. 2 T _?_ 5000 lb

Extended Problem Solving In Exercises 32–34, use the following information. You are building a wall-mounted CD rack with 3 shelves that are each 1 foot 3 inches long. Each end piece is 2 inches long.

32. Calculate How many feet of wood will you need to buy for the shelves and the end pieces?

33. Predict Each CD has a width of $\frac{3}{8}$ inch.

Estimate the number of CDs in one inch. Predict the number of CDs that will fit on a shelf. Calculate to check your prediction.

34. Interpret Your friend asks you to build a wall-mounted CD rack for him. He has a collection of 100 CDs. How long should you make each of the 3 shelves?

What do you think?

History

■ **Pyramids**

The pyramids no longer reach their original heights because thieves have stripped the outer coating of white limestone. If Khufu's original height was 481 feet and is presently $451\frac{2}{5}$ feet, what is the difference in the heights?

Find the product. Express the answer in the given unit.

35. 27 in. × 4; yards **36.** 13 gal × 3; pints **37.** 320 oz × 200; tons

38. Backpacks The weight of a school backpack should not exceed 25 pounds. The following items are in your backpack. Does it exceed 25 pounds? If not, how much more weight can you add without exceeding 25 pounds? If so, by how much is it over 25 pounds?

Item	Math book	Notebook	Calculator	History book	Gym clothes and shoes
Weight	3 lb 14 oz	24 oz	9 oz	4 lb 10 oz	1 lb 9 oz

Challenge Order the measurements from least to greatest.

39. $\frac{1}{4}$ lb, 7 oz, $\frac{5}{8}$ lb, 0.5 lb, $\frac{32}{3}$ oz **40.** 0.75 ft, 8.7 in., $\frac{37}{5}$ in., $\frac{5}{6}$ ft, $7\frac{3}{4}$ in.

 Algebra Copy and complete the statement.

41. There are ? miles in f feet. **42.** There are ? hours in m minutes.

Mixed Review

Find the LCM of the numbers using prime factorization. *(Lesson 4.4)*

43. 112, 168 **44.** 99, 77 **45.** 36, 40, 60

Tell whether the measurement is a *length*, *weight*, or *capacity*. *(Lesson 5.5)*

46. 124 lb **47.** 16 qt **48.** 34 mi

Basic Skills Complete the number fact family.

49. 15 + 3 = 18 3 + ? = 18 18 − ? = 15 18 − ? = 3
50. 24 + 7 = 31 ? + 24 = 31 ? − 24 = 7 31 − ? = 24

Test-Taking Practice

51. Multiple Choice One lap of the Indy 500 is $2\frac{1}{2}$ miles long. How many feet are in three complete laps?

A. 1250 feet **B.** 13,200 feet **C.** 39,600 feet **D.** 79,200 feet

52. Short Response You have 2 hours before you have to go to bed. You ask permission to watch a movie that lasts 115 minutes. Do you have enough time to watch the movie? Explain.

Notebook Review

Review the vocabulary definitions in your notebook.

Copy the review examples in your notebook. Then complete the exercises.

Check Your Definitions

U.S. customary system, p. 230
inch, p. 230
foot, p. 230
yard, p. 230

mile, p. 230
ounce, p. 231
pound, p. 231
ton, p. 231
fluid ounce, p. 232

cup, p. 232
pint, p. 232
quart, p. 232
gallon, p. 232

Use Your Vocabulary

1. Which unit measures length: *pint*, *ounce*, or *yard*?

5.5 Can you measure and estimate in customary units?

EXAMPLE Copy and complete the statement using the appropriate customary unit: The weight of a fire extinguisher is 8 _?_ .

Using the benchmarks from Lesson 5.5, you know that the weight of a fire extinguisher is greater than the weight of 8 slices of bread (8 oz) and is less than the weight of 8 walruses (8 T). A good estimate for the weight of a fire extinguisher is the weight of 8 soccer balls (8 lb).

ANSWER The weight of a fire extinguisher is 8 pounds.

☑ **Copy and complete using the appropriate customary unit.**

2. An apple weighs 8 _?_ .   **3.** The length of a chopstick is 9 _?_ .

5.6 Can you convert between customary units?

EXAMPLE Convert 5720 yards to miles by using 1760 yd = 1 mi.

$$\frac{5720 \text{ yd}}{1} \times \frac{1 \text{ mi}}{1760 \text{ yd}} = \frac{\overset{13}{\cancel{5720 \text{ yd}}} \times 1 \text{ mi}}{1 \times \underset{4}{\cancel{1760 \text{ yd}}}}$$

Use rule for multiplying fractions. Divide out common factor and unit.

$$= \frac{13}{4} \text{ mi, or } 3\frac{1}{4} \text{ mi}$$

Simplify.

☑ **Copy and complete the statement.**

4. 8500 lb = _?_ T   **5.** 19 yd = _?_ in.   **6.** 48 c = _?_ qt

7. **Writing** Explain how to convert from gallons to pints.

8. **Critical Thinking** The capacity of container A is $2\frac{3}{4}$ pints, and the capacity of container B is 36 fluid ounces. Which container has a greater capacity? Explain.

Review Quiz 2

Tell what the measurement describes about a bottle of mouthwash.

1. 17 oz   **2.** 1 pt   **3.** 9 in.

Copy and complete the statement.

4. $46\frac{2}{3}$ yd = _?_ ft   **5.** 11 qt = _?_ c   **6.** 22 qt = _?_ gal _?_ qt

Find the sum or difference.

7.   6 gal 3 qt
   + 2 gal 2 qt

8.   52 lb   8 oz
   − 27 lb 13 oz

9.   12 yd 2 ft
   + 4 yd 1 ft

10. **Cooking** You are making soup that requires 4 cups of water. How many *fluid ounces* of water do you need?

BRAIN GAME

Convert Alert

With a partner, copy the given chart and take turns doing the following.

30 ft	6 yd	8 yd	108 in.
3 ft	15 ft	54 in.	12 ft
18 in.	36 in.	24 ft	15 ft
144 in.	72 in.	9 ft	5 ft
6 ft	4 yd	1 ft	5 yd

1. Choose any two measurements from the chart, convert them to inches, and find their sum. This will be your score for the round.

2. Cross off the measurements that have been used. When the last measurement has been crossed off, total your scores. The player with the higher score wins.

Chapter Review

Vocabulary

reciprocal, p. 222
U.S. customary system, p. 230
inch, p. 230
foot, p. 230

yard, p. 230
mile, p. 230
ounce, p. 231
pound, p. 231
ton, p. 231

fluid ounce, p. 232
cup, p. 232
pint, p. 232
quart, p. 232
gallon, p. 232

Vocabulary Review

1. Copy and complete: The __?__ of $\frac{3}{10}$ is $\frac{10}{3}$.

2. Which unit measures length: *pound, yard,* or *quart*?

3. Which unit measures capacity: *ounce, pound,* or *fluid ounce*?

4. How many inches are in a yard?

Review Questions

Find the sum or difference. *(Lesson 5.1)*

5. $\frac{3}{11} + \frac{5}{11}$

6. $\frac{1}{6} + \frac{1}{12}$

7. $\frac{7}{15} - \frac{4}{15}$

8. $\frac{5}{9} - \frac{1}{12}$

9. $\frac{7}{8} - \frac{5}{6}$

10. $\frac{2}{7} + \frac{3}{4}$

11. $\frac{5}{6} + \frac{1}{9}$

12. $\frac{17}{18} - \frac{5}{12}$

13. Diamonds A diamond's weight is measured in carats. If a ring has one $\frac{1}{4}$-carat diamond and two $\frac{1}{8}$-carat diamonds, what is the total weight of the diamonds on the ring? *(Lesson 5.1)*

Find the sum or difference. *(Lesson 5.2)*

14. $1\frac{1}{12} + 4\frac{1}{2}$

15. $2\frac{1}{5} + 3\frac{3}{5}$

16. $10\frac{5}{8} - 8\frac{7}{8}$

17. $16\frac{1}{3} - 12\frac{5}{12}$

18. $9\frac{3}{4} - 7\frac{5}{9}$

19. $28\frac{1}{6} - 17\frac{11}{12}$

20. $5\frac{16}{27} + 2\frac{2}{3}$

21. $31\frac{12}{21} + 48\frac{9}{14}$

22. Height Records The tallest known human was $107\frac{1}{10}$ inches tall (almost 9 feet). The shortest known human was about $22\frac{5}{16}$ inches tall. Find the difference of these heights. *(Lesson 5.2)*

Find the product or quotient. *(Lessons 5.3, 5.4)*

23. $\frac{3}{4} \times \frac{1}{6}$

24. $\frac{5}{7} \times \frac{1}{15}$

25. $\frac{5}{8} \times 4$

26. $7 \times \frac{9}{56}$

27. $1\frac{1}{2} \div 3\frac{1}{2}$

28. $4\frac{4}{9} \div \frac{8}{15}$

29. $\frac{7}{10} \div 5\frac{3}{5}$

30. $7\frac{1}{2} \div 1\frac{1}{4}$

31. Orchestra One half of an orchestra plays brass instruments. The horn section makes up $\frac{1}{7}$ of the brass instruments. What fraction of the whole orchestra is in the horn section? *(Lesson 5.3)*

32. Skating The surface of the Olympic Oval's ice skating rink in Salt Lake City, Utah, was created by repeatedly spraying water to make 24 layers of ice for a total thickness of $\frac{3}{4}$ inch. How thick is each layer of ice? *(Lesson 5.4)*

33. Find the length of the pencil to the nearest quarter inch. *(Lesson 5.5)*

Copy and complete using the appropriate customary unit. *(Lesson 5.5)*

34. The height of a cereal box is $10\frac{3}{4}$? .

35. A male white-tailed deer weighs 400 ? .

36. The capacity of a bathtub is 55 ? .

37. An airplane weighs 455 ? .

Copy and complete the statement. *(Lesson 5.6)*

38. 180 in. = ? yd

39. 3 qt = ? c

40. 3 T = ? oz

41. 50 oz = ? lb

42. 16 pt = ? gal

43. 2 mi = ? ft

44. Fruit Punch You need to make 16 one-cup servings of punch for a party. How many quarts of punch do you need to make? *(Lesson 5.6)*

Find the sum or difference. *(Lesson 5.6)*

45. $\begin{array}{r} 7 \text{ gal } 3 \text{ qt} \\ + 3 \text{ gal } 1 \text{ qt} \\ \hline \end{array}$

46. $\begin{array}{r} 9 \text{ ft } 2 \text{ in.} \\ - 3 \text{ ft } 11 \text{ in.} \\ \hline \end{array}$

47. $\begin{array}{r} 3 \text{ T } 654 \text{ lb} \\ - 1 \text{ T } 1541 \text{ lb} \\ \hline \end{array}$

Order the measurements from least to greatest. *(Lesson 5.6)*

48. 82 in., $5\frac{1}{2}$ ft, $\frac{27}{4}$ ft, 67.5 in., 68 in.

49. 24 pt, 1.2 qt, 0.48 qt, 3840 fl oz, $1\frac{1}{2}$ gal

Chapter Test

Find the sum or difference.

1. $\frac{4}{5} + \frac{2}{15}$

2. $\frac{1}{2} + \frac{8}{9}$

3. $\frac{2}{3} - \frac{4}{7}$

4. $\frac{3}{4} - \frac{3}{10}$

5. $9\frac{3}{8} - 5\frac{1}{8}$

6. $14\frac{1}{6} + 12\frac{5}{6}$

7. $6\frac{2}{3} + 4\frac{3}{8}$

8. $7\frac{3}{4} - 5\frac{4}{5}$

9. **Apple Pie** You have $2\frac{1}{3}$ pounds of apples, and your friend has $2\frac{1}{6}$ pounds. A pie recipe calls for $4\frac{1}{2}$ pounds of apples. Do you and your friend have enough apples to make a pie? Explain.

10. **Rain** A rain gauge is used to collect rainfall data. During a rainstorm, a gauge reads $1\frac{3}{8}$ inches after the first three hours and $2\frac{1}{3}$ inches two hours later. How much rain has fallen in the last two hours?

Find the product or quotient.

11. $\frac{1}{5} \cdot \frac{1}{8}$

12. $\frac{4}{9} \cdot \frac{3}{16}$

13. $10 \cdot \frac{3}{4}$

14. $5\frac{1}{2} \cdot 2\frac{7}{9}$

15. $\frac{9}{17} \div \frac{3}{34}$

16. $\frac{7}{8} \div \frac{7}{12}$

17. $8\frac{2}{3} \div 5\frac{1}{6}$

18. $3\frac{6}{7} \div 1\frac{2}{7}$

19. **Population** A middle school has 900 students. If 7th grade students make up $\frac{2}{5}$ of all the students, how many of the students are in the 7th grade?

20. **Necklaces** You want to make a necklace with beads $1\frac{1}{4}$ inches apart. If the necklace needs to be 20 inches long and there are no beads at the ends of the necklace, how many beads do you need?

Copy and complete using the appropriate customary unit.

21. The weight of an empty wallet is 3 _?_ .

22. The length of a toothbrush is 7 _?_ .

23. The capacity of a kitchen sink is 20 _?_ .

24. A lawn mower weighs 76 _?_ .

Copy and complete the statement.

25. 20 lb = _?_ oz

26. 2 gal = _?_ pt

27. 5 yd = _?_ in.

28. 34 oz = _?_ lb _?_ oz

Chapter Standardized Test

Test-Taking Strategy Put a mark next to unanswered questions in your test booklet so you can find them faster when you go back.

Multiple Choice

1. Find the difference $\frac{1}{3} - \frac{2}{15}$.

   A. $\frac{1}{45}$ **B.** $\frac{1}{15}$ **C.** $\frac{1}{5}$ **D.** $\frac{1}{3}$

2. Which expression is equal to $\frac{1}{3}$?

   F. $\frac{5}{6} - \frac{1}{3}$ **G.** $\frac{1}{6} + \frac{1}{12}$ **H.** $\frac{5}{18} - \frac{1}{9}$ **I.** $\frac{3}{4} - \frac{5}{12}$

3. What is the sum of $\frac{3}{5}$ and $\frac{1}{6}$?

   A. $\frac{2}{15}$ **B.** $\frac{4}{11}$ **C.** $\frac{7}{10}$ **D.** $\frac{23}{30}$

4. Find the difference $8\frac{5}{6} - 3\frac{9}{10}$.

   F. $4\frac{2}{16}$ **G.** $4\frac{14}{15}$ **H.** $5\frac{1}{10}$ **I.** $5\frac{14}{15}$

5. You ran $\frac{1}{4}$ of a $\frac{1}{4}$-mile relay race. Which expression could you use to find how many miles you ran?

   A. $\frac{1}{4} \div \frac{1}{4}$ **B.** $\frac{1}{4} \times \frac{1}{4}$ **C.** $1 \times \frac{1}{4}$ **D.** $\frac{1}{4} + \frac{1}{4}$

6. What is the product of $\frac{2}{3}$ and $\frac{6}{7}$?

   F. $\frac{8}{21}$ **G.** $\frac{4}{7}$ **H.** $\frac{4}{5}$ **I.** $1\frac{11}{21}$

7. What is the value of $4\frac{3}{4} \div x$ when $x = \frac{5}{8}$?

   A. $\frac{5}{38}$ **B.** $2\frac{1}{2}$ **C.** $5\frac{1}{5}$ **D.** $7\frac{3}{5}$

8. Which expression is equal to $\frac{4}{5}$?

   F. $\frac{4}{5} \times \frac{4}{5}$ **G.** $4 \div \frac{1}{5}$ **H.** $\frac{1}{5} \times 1\frac{3}{5}$ **I.** $1\frac{1}{4} \times \frac{16}{25}$

9. Which of the following measurements is longer than 10 feet?

   A. 50 in.   **B.** 1 yd   **C.** 9 ft   **D.** 7 yd

10. How many feet long is a $5\frac{1}{2}$ inch nail?

   F. $\frac{11}{24}$ ft   **G.** $\frac{1}{2}$ ft   **H.** $1\frac{5}{6}$ ft   **I.** 66 ft

11. Which measurement is *not* a capacity?

   A. 5 qt   **B.** 7 fl oz   **C.** 2 pt   **D.** 3.5 T

12. Which measurement could be a car's weight?

   F. 2.6 lb   **G.** 26 lb   **H.** 260 lb   **I.** 2600 lb

Short Response

13. You and three friends buy $\frac{3}{4}$ lb of roast beef and $\frac{1}{2}$ lb of turkey. Did you buy enough meat so that everyone has $\frac{1}{3}$ lb of meat for a sandwich? Explain your reasoning.

Extended Response

14. The table below gives the lengths, in feet, of 6 red pandas. Find the mean, median, mode(s), and range of the lengths.

Panda	A	B	C	D	E	F
Length (feet)	$1\frac{2}{3}$	$1\frac{7}{8}$	$2\frac{1}{3}$	$1\frac{3}{4}$	$2\frac{1}{8}$	$2\frac{1}{2}$

Comparing Planets

Diameters of Planets

Scientists often describe the size of a planet by giving its *diameter* (the width of the planet at its widest point). For example, the diameter of Jupiter is about 1.4×10^5 kilometers, while the diameter of Earth is about 1.3×10^4 kilometers.

To compare the sizes of Jupiter and Earth, find the quotient of their diameters.

$$\frac{\text{Diameter of Jupiter}}{\text{Diameter of Earth}} = \frac{1.4 \times 10^5}{1.3 \times 10^4}$$

$$= \frac{1.4}{1.3} \times \frac{10^5}{10^4}$$

$$\approx 1.1 \times \frac{\overset{1}{\cancel{10}} \cdot \overset{1}{\cancel{10}} \cdot \overset{1}{\cancel{10}} \cdot \overset{1}{\cancel{10}} \cdot 10}{\underset{1}{\cancel{10}} \cdot \underset{1}{\cancel{10}} \cdot \underset{1}{\cancel{10}} \cdot \underset{1}{\cancel{10}}}$$

$$= 1.1 \times 10$$

$$= 11$$

So, the diameter of Jupiter is about 11 times the diameter of Earth. The diagram at the right shows the relative sizes of the two planets.

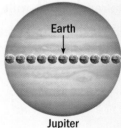

Earth

Jupiter

1. **Critical Thinking** In the calculation above, notice that $\frac{10^5}{10^4} = 10^1$.

   How are the exponents in this equation related?

2. Use your result from Exercise 1 to complete this equation: $\frac{10^7}{10^3} = 10^?$.

3. **Applying the Method** Pluto's diameter is about 2.4×10^3 kilometers. Use a quotient to compare the diameters of Jupiter and Pluto.

Masses of Planets

You can also use mass to describe a planet's size. The table below shows the mass of each planet in the solar system.

Planet	Mass (kg)	Mass Relative to Pluto
Mercury	3.3×10^{23}	?
Venus	4.9×10^{24}	?
Earth	6.0×10^{24}	?
Mars	6.4×10^{23}	?
Jupiter	1.9×10^{27}	?
Saturn	5.7×10^{26}	?
Uranus	8.7×10^{25}	?
Neptune	1.0×10^{26}	?
Pluto	1.3×10^{22}	1

4. Copy the table. In the last column, enter the quotient of the mass of each planet and the mass of Pluto.

5. **Critical Thinking** The mass of a large buffalo is about 900 kilograms. The mass of a house mouse is about 0.02 kilogram. In terms of mass, the relationship between a large buffalo and a house mouse is most like the relationship between which planet and Pluto? Explain.

Project IDEAS

- **Illustrate** The diameters of Jupiter, Earth, and Pluto are given on page 246. Find out the diameters, in kilometers, of the other planets in the solar system. Draw nine circles that show the relative sizes of the nine planets.

- **Report** Choose one of the nine planets and write a report on it. Discuss the planet's size, location relative to Earth and the sun, surface temperature, and other characteristics.

- **Research** Find out the mean distance, in kilometers, of each planet from the sun. Also find information about the *asteroid belt*, including its distance from the sun.

- **Career** A scientist who studies planets or other objects in space is called an *astronomer*. Find out what types of work astronomers do. What kind of education is required to be an astronomer? Present your findings to your class.

INTERNET
Project Support
CLASSZONE.COM

6

Integers

Chapter Warm-Up Game

Review skills you need for this chapter in this game. Work with a partner.

Key Skills:
• Using order of operations
• Writing expressions

BEFORE

In previous chapters you've...

• Performed operations on whole numbers, decimals, and fractions
• Used order of operations

Now

In Chapter 6 you'll study...

• Comparing and ordering integers
• Performing integer operations
• Rational numbers
• Graphing in a coordinate plane

WHY?

So you can solve real-world problems about...

Internet Preview
CLASSZONE.COM

• eEdition Plus Online
• eWorkbook Plus Online
• eTutorial Plus Online
• State Test Practice
• More Examples

OPERATION SCRAMBLE

MATERIALS

• 1 deck of *Operation Scramble* cards

• a pencil and paper for each player

PREPARE Deal four cards face up between you and your partner. The numbers on the cards are expression numbers. Deal a fifth card face up. The number on this card is the target number. For each round, both players should follow the directions on the next page.

Expression cards   **Target card**

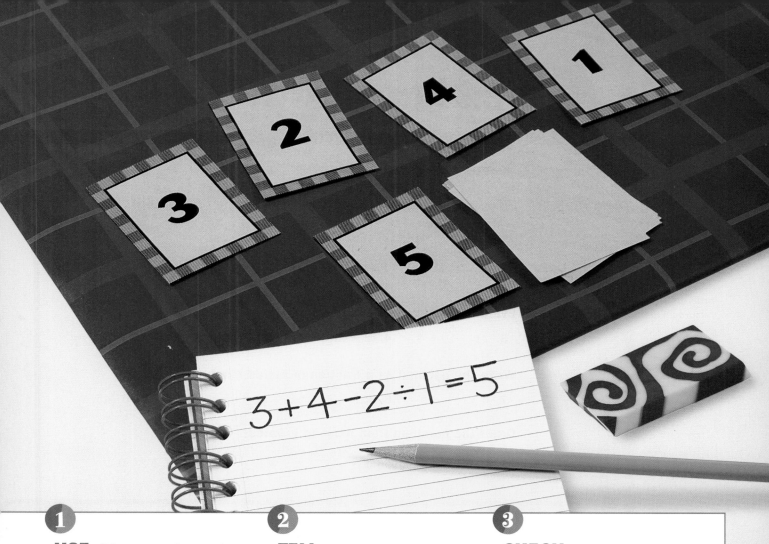

①

USE all four expression numbers in any order and any of the operation symbols +, −, ×, or ÷ to write an expression that equals the target number. You may also use parentheses.

HOW TO WIN Be the first player to get three points.

②

TELL your partner when you are finished writing your expression. Both players must stop working if one person is finished. If both players agree that an expression cannot be written, turn over a new target number card.

③

CHECK the work of the player who finished writing an expression first. If the expression is correct, that player gets one point. If it is incorrect, deal new cards and try again.

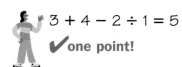

$3 + 4 - 2 \div 1 = 5$

✔ **one point!**

Stop *and* **Think**

1. **Writing** In *Operation Scramble*, suppose you have only even numbers on the expression cards. The target number is odd. Give an example of a correct expression and a target number that fit this description. Explain which operations you had to use.

2. **Critical Thinking** Use the numbers 5, 4, 3, and 2 as expression numbers. Show how you can write expressions equal to the whole numbers from 1 through 10.

Getting Ready to Learn

Review What You Need to Know

Using Vocabulary **Copy and complete using a review word.**

1. The _?_ of 5 is $\frac{1}{5}$.

2. When a power is expressed as a product, the _?_ is the repeated factor and the _?_ is the number of times the factor is used.

Evaluate the expression. *(p. 18)*

3. $21 - 10 + 1$ 4. $(2 + 5)(6 - 4)^2$ 5. $13(2) - 4^2$ 6. $\frac{3^2}{4 + 9 - 4}$

Write the decimal as a fraction or mixed number. *(p. 190)*

7. 0.35 8. 4.5 9. 2.85 10. 0.745

Order the numbers from least to greatest. *(p. 190)*

11. $9, 7\frac{1}{3}, 8.9, 7.5, 0, 0.4$ 12. $\frac{5}{6}, \frac{3}{4}, 0.25, 0.5, 1.23, 0$

You should include material that appears on a notebook like this in your own notes.

Know How to Take Notes

Recording the Process You should record and summarize in your notebook the key steps that you take in performing a multi-step calculation. Referring to these steps can help you perform similar calculations.

Calculations	Key Steps
$6\frac{2}{3} \cdot 1\frac{4}{5} = \frac{20}{3} \cdot \frac{9}{5}$	Write mixed numbers as improper fractions.
$= \frac{\overset{4}{\cancel{20}} \cdot \overset{3}{\cancel{9}}}{\underset{1}{\cancel{3}} \cdot \underset{1}{\cancel{5}}}$	Use rule for multiplying fractions. Divide out common factors.
$= \frac{12}{1}$, or 12	Multiply.

In Lesson 6.6, you will see how recording the process can help you evaluate expressions.

Comparing and Ordering Integers

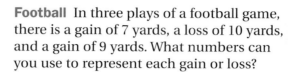

BEFORE	Now	WHY?
You compared and ordered whole numbers and fractions.	You'll compare and order integers.	So you can order historic dates, as in Ex. 41.

In the Real World

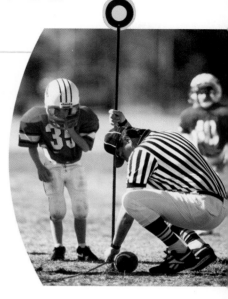

Football In three plays of a football game, there is a gain of 7 yards, a loss of 10 yards, and a gain of 9 yards. What numbers can you use to represent each gain or loss?

The following numbers are **integers** :
$\dots, -4, -3, -2, -1, 0, 1, 2, 3, 4, \dots$

Negative integers are integers that are less than zero. **Positive integers** are integers that are greater than 0. Zero is neither positive nor negative.

HELP with Reading

The integer -4 is read "negative four." A number other than 0 that has no sign is considered to be positive, so the integer 4 is read "positive four" or "four."

Integers and Their Opposites

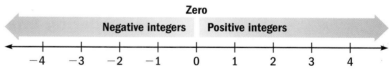

Two numbers are **opposites** if they are the same distance from 0 on a number line but are on opposite sides of 0. For example, -3 is the opposite of 3. The opposite of 0 is 0.

EXAMPLE 1 Writing Integers

You can use integers to represent the gains and losses described above.

7 yard gain: 7   10 yard loss: -10 9 yard gain: 9

Your turn now Write the opposite of the integer.

1. 15   **2.** -8 **3.** -35 **4.** 100

Comparing Integers You can use a number line to compare and order integers. Remember that numbers decrease as you move to the left on a number line and increase as you move to the right.

EXAMPLE 2 **Comparing Integers Using a Number Line**

a. Compare -2 and -5.

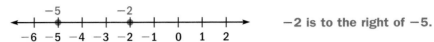

-2 is to the right of -5.

ANSWER $-2 > -5$ or $-5 < -2$.

b. Compare -6 and 1.

-6 is to the left of 1.

ANSWER $-6 < 1$ or $1 > -6$.

Your turn now **Copy and complete the statement using < or >.**

5. $0 \underline{\ ?\ } -7$ **6.** $-9 \underline{\ ?\ } 4$ **7.** $-5 \underline{\ ?\ } -4$ **8.** $-3 \underline{\ ?\ } -13$

EXAMPLE 3 **Ordering Integers Using a Number Line**

Weather The table shows the average temperatures, in degrees Celsius, for six months in the Gobi Desert of Mongolia. Which of these months has the least average temperature?

Month	Nov.	Dec.	Jan.	Feb.	Mar.	Apr.
Average Temperature	$-6°C$	$-14°C$	$-15°C$	$-12°C$	$-3°C$	$6°C$

Solution

You can graph each integer on a number line to order the temperatures.

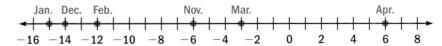

The temperatures from least to greatest are: $-15, -14, -12, -6, -3, 6$.

ANSWER At $-15°C$, January has the least average temperature.

Getting Ready to Practice

1. Vocabulary Which of the following numbers are integers?

$$2675, 0, -56, \frac{3}{4}, 75, 0.65$$

Write the integer that represents the situation. Then write the opposite of that integer.

2. 1333 feet above sea level   **3.** Sixteen degrees below zero

4. A nine million dollar loss   **5.** A $15 account withdrawal

Copy and complete the statement using < or >.

6. -2 ? 5 **7.** -8 ? -12 **8.** -36 ? -25 **9.** 1 ? -5

Order the temperatures from least to greatest.

10. $-7°C, -2°C, 4°C, -8°C$ **11.** $-5°F, 9°F, -2°F, 3°F, -1°F$

HELP with Homework

Example	Exercises
1	12-17, 41
2	18-23, 33-40
3	24, 29-32, 41

Online Resources
CLASSZONE.COM
· More Examples
· eTutorial Plus

Practice and Problem Solving

Draw a number line and graph the integer. Then give a real-world situation that the integer could represent.

12. -5 **13.** 0 **14.** The opposite of -7

15. -9 **16.** 4 **17.** The opposite of 3

Copy and complete the statement using < or >.

18. 34 ? -43 **19.** -17 ? -13 **20.** 42 ? 37

21. -18 ? 3 **22.** -7 ? 4 **23.** 26 ? -26

24. Miniature Golf In miniature golf, *par* is the expected number of strokes to finish a hole. Your score for the game is the sum of your number of strokes above or below par for each hole. The player with the least score wins. Order the scores given in the table from least to greatest to determine the order of finish.

Player	Score
Andrew	-5
Mandy	$+3$
Mitchell	0
Pedro	-4

Algebra **Name two integer values of the variable that make the statement true.**

25. $0 < d$ **26.** $c < 23$ **27.** $-10 > k$

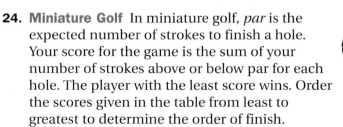

28. Writing Is the fraction $\frac{5}{6}$ an integer? Explain your reasoning.

Order the integers from least to greatest.

29. $-28, 18, 7, -17, 0, -12$

30. $99, -42, 13, -2, 11, -49$

31. $-150, 235, -435, 345, -75$

32. $-66, 21, 9, -10, -22, 44$

Tell whether the statement is *true* or *false*. Explain your reasoning.

33. $-3 < 2$ **34.** $-6 > -8$ **35.** $6 > -1$ **36.** $0 > -10$

37. $-7 > -5$ **38.** $-50 < -55$ **39.** $100 > 0$ **40.** $-67 < -68$

41. Roman Battles The location and date of five Roman battles are listed in the table. Use a number line to order the battles from earliest in time to most recent. Let positive integers represent the years A.D. and negative integers represent the years B.C. (for example, 89 B.C. = -89).

Location	Date
Alexandria	47 B.C.
Byzantium	196 A.D.
Carthage	147 B.C.
Jerusalem	70 A.D.
Syracuse	211 B.C.

42. Challenge If the missing integer in the list of numbers below is the median of the numbers, what could the missing integer be?

$$-44, 23, -11, 12, -27, \underline{\ ?\ }, -4, 0, 1$$

Mixed Review

Find the sum or difference. *(Lesson 2.2)*

43. $12.7 + 87.35$ **44.** $98.6 + 5.01$ **45.** $300 - 11.3$ **46.** $254.65 - 9.202$

Find the sum or difference. *(Lesson 5.6)*

47. 4 gal 3 qt
     + 5 gal 1 qt

48. 8 yd 10 in.
     − 1 yd 11 in.

49. 5 ft 9 in.
     + 4 ft 10 in.

50. 13 ft 5 in.
     − 2 ft 7 in.

Basic Skills **Find the sum or difference.**

51. $63 + 49$ **52.** $109 + 57$ **53.** $46 - 27$ **54.** $513 - 24$

Test-Taking Practice

55. Multiple Choice Which statement is true?

   A. $-56 < -58$ **B.** $1 < -112$ **C.** $-7 > -5$ **D.** $-9 > -11$

56. Short Response The integers $17, -10, 32, -29,$ and 0 are temperature readings in degrees Fahrenheit. Graph the integers on a number line and find the median temperature.

Negative and Zero Exponents

GOAL Evaluate powers with negative and zero exponents.

 **Word Watch**

Review Words

power, p. 14
exponent, p. 14
scientific notation, p. 74
reciprocal, p. 222

In Lesson 1.3, you wrote powers using positive exponents. You can also use negative integers and zero as exponents.

When you look down the table at the right, notice that as the exponents for the powers of 2 decrease by 1, the values of the powers are halved. This pattern suggests that

$$2^0 = 2 \cdot \frac{1}{2} = 1, \, 2^{-1} = 1 \cdot \frac{1}{2} = \frac{1}{2} = \frac{1}{2^1},$$

$$2^{-2} = \frac{1}{2} \cdot \frac{1}{2} = \frac{1}{4} = \frac{1}{2^2}, \text{ and } 2^{-3} = \frac{1}{4} \cdot \frac{1}{2} = \frac{1}{8} = \frac{1}{2^3}.$$

This in turn suggests the following definitions.

Power	Value
2^3	8
2^2	4
2^1	2
2^0	?
2^{-1}	?
2^{-2}	?
2^{-3}	?

Negative and Zero Exponents

Negative Exponent For any integer n and any nonzero number a, a^{-n} is the reciprocal of a^n. That is, $a^{-n} = \frac{1}{a^n}$.

Zero Exponent For any nonzero number a, $a^0 = 1$.

EXAMPLE 1 **Evaluating Powers**

Evaluate the power.

a. 5^{-3}

b. 10^{-5}

Solution

a. $5^{-3} = \frac{1}{5^3}$ **Definition of negative exponent**

$\phantom{5^{-3}} = \frac{1}{125}$ **Evaluate the power.**

b. $10^{-5} = \frac{1}{10^5}$ **Definition of negative exponent**

$\phantom{10^{-5}} = \frac{1}{100,000}$ **Evaluate the power.**

$\phantom{10^{-5}} = 0.00001$ **Write fraction as a decimal.**

Special Topic Continued

with Review

Need help with powers and scientific notation? See pp. 14 and 74.

Scientific Notation In Lesson 2.5, you wrote numbers in scientific notation using positive integers as exponents. You can also write numbers in scientific notation using 0 and negative integers as exponents. To change between scientific notation and standard form, you can first write the number as a product with the power of 10 written as a decimal in standard form.

Power	Standard Form
10^0	1
10^{-1}	0.1
10^{-2}	0.01
10^{-3}	0.001
10^{-4}	0.0001
10^{-5}	0.00001
10^{-6}	0.000001
10^{-7}	0.0000001

EXAMPLE 2 Writing Numbers in Standard Form

Scientific notation	Product form	Standard form
a. 6×10^{-3}	6×0.001	0.006
b. 3.781×10^{-5}	3.781×0.00001	0.00003781

EXAMPLE 3 Writing Numbers in Scientific Notation

Standard form	Product form	Scientific notation
a. 0.00059	5.9×0.0001	5.9×10^{-4}
4 decimal places	Write product.	Exponent is −4.
b. 0.0000678	6.78×0.00001	6.78×10^{-5}
5 decimal places	Write product.	Exponent is −5.

Exercises

Evaluate the power.

1. 6^{-2} **2.** 4^{-4} **3.** 2^{-5} **4.** 10^{-6}

Write the number in standard form.

5. 2.1×10^{-2} **6.** 6.54×10^0 **7.** 8.92×10^{-3} **8.** 7.8×10^{-6}

9. Art A microscopic sculpture of a bull is about 0.00076 mm wide. A virus has a width of about 3.6×10^{-4} mm. Which is greater, the width of the sculpture or the width of the virus?

Write the number in scientific notation.

10. 0.004567   **11.** 0.0001   **12.** 0.00078   **13.** 0.0000932

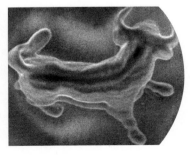

Microscopic bull sculpture

6.2 **Hands-on Activity**

GOAL
Model integer addition on a number line.

MATERIALS
· paper
· pencil

Modeling Integer Addition

You know from your earlier work that you can use a number line to model the addition of two positive numbers. You can use a similar approach when adding integers. Adding a positive integer indicates movement to the right along the number line. Adding a negative integer indicates movement to the left.

Explore **Find the sum 3 + (−2).**

1 Draw a number line on a sheet of paper, or use a row of tiles on the classroom floor to represent a number line. Choose the edge of one tile to represent 0.

2 Start at 0. Move **3** units to the **right**.

3 Next, move **2** units to the **left**.

Final position

−2

3

−2   −1   0   1   2   3   4   5

Start at 0.

4 Find your final position on the number line. You are 1 unit to the right of 0. So, 3 + (−2) = 1.

Your turn now **Use a number line to find the sum.**

1. $1 + 6$ **2.** $2 + 5$ **3.** $-3 + (-3)$ **4.** $-2 + (-3)$

5. $-7 + 3$ **6.** $-5 + 8$ **7.** $2 + (-5)$ **8.** $6 + (-2)$

Stop and Think

9. Critical Thinking Does order matter when adding integers? Explain your reasoning and give an example to support your answer.

10. Writing Can the sum of a negative integer and a positive integer be positive? Explain your reasoning.

11. Critical Thinking What is the sum of two integers that are opposites?

Adding Integers

BEFORE ▶ **Now** **WHY?**

You compared and ordered integers.

You'll add integers.

So you can find the depth of a scuba diver, as in Ex. 34.

In the Real World

Science Atoms, the building blocks of all matter, are made up of protons that each have a charge of 1, neutrons that each have a charge of 0, and electrons that each have a charge of -1. Suppose an atom has 11 protons and 10 electrons. What is its total charge?

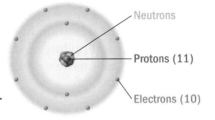

You can use a number line to add integers. Always start at 0 on the number line. Adding a positive integer indicates movement to the right. Adding a negative integer indicates movement to the left.

EXAMPLE 1 Using a Number Line to Add Integers

Find the sum $-5 + (-3)$ using a number line.

Start at 0. Move **5** units to the **left**.
Then move **3** more units to the **left**.

ANSWER The final position is -8, so $-5 + (-3) = -8$.

EXAMPLE 2 Using Integer Addition

You can find the total charge of the atom described above by finding the sum $11 + (-10)$ using a number line.

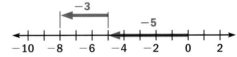

Start at 0. Move **11** units to the **right**.
Then move **10** units to the **left**.

ANSWER The final position is 1, so $11 + (-10) = 1$. The total charge of the atom is 1.

Your turn now Use a number line to find the sum.

1. $-9 + (-5)$ **2.** $-7 + 4$ **3.** $6 + (-13)$ **4.** $12 + (-9)$

Absolute Value The **absolute value** of a number is the distance between the number and 0 on a number line. The absolute value of a number a is written $|a|$.

with Solving

Because distance cannot be negative, the absolute value of a number cannot be negative.

EXAMPLE 3 **Finding Absolute Value**

Find the absolute value of the number.

a. 8   **b.** -7 **c.** 0

Solution

a. The distance between 8 and 0 is 8. So, $|8| = 8$.

b. The distance between -7 and 0 is 7. So, $|-7| = 7$.

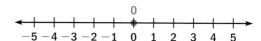

c. The distance between 0 and 0 is 0. So, $|0| = 0$.

Your turn now Find the absolute value of the number.

5. 100   **6.** -9 **7.** -45 **8.** 22

You can use absolute value to add integers without drawing a number line.

Adding Integers with Absolute Value

Words	Numbers
Same Sign Add the absolute values and use the common sign.	$10 + 14 = 24$ $-7 + (-5) = -12$
Different Signs Subtract the lesser absolute value from the greater absolute value and use the sign of the integer with the greater absolute value.	$13 + (-9) = 4$ $-11 + 6 = -5$
Opposites The sum of an integer and its opposite is 0.	$-4 + 4 = 0$

EXAMPLE 4 **Adding Two Integers Using Absolute Value**

a. Find the sum $-3 + (-12)$.

These integers have the same sign.

$$-3 + (-12) = -15$$

— Add $|-3|$ and $|-12|$.

— Both integers are negative, so the sum is negative.

b. Find the sum $-7 + 9$.

These integers have different signs.

$$-7 + 9 = 2$$

— Subtract $|-7|$ from $|9|$.

— Because $|9| > |-7|$, the sum has the same sign as 9.

Your turn now **Use absolute values to find the sum.**

9. $-5 + (-11)$ **10.** $-9 + 6$ **11.** $0 + (-7)$

12. $-13 + 15$ **13.** $15 + (-8)$ **14.** $-12 + 12$

EXAMPLE 5 **Adding Three or More Integers**

Personal Finance Aaron has kept track of his earnings and expenses for one week. Find the sum of his earnings and expenses.

Allowance: $12
School field trip: −$3
Pay from mowing lawns: $13
Repaid sister: −$5

Solution

You can find the sum by adding the integers two at a time.

$$12 + (-3) + 13 + (-5) = 9 + 13 + (-5)$$ Add 12 and −3.

$$= 22 + (-5)$$ Add 9 and 13.

$$= 17$$ Add 22 and −5.

ANSWER The sum of Aaron's earnings and expenses is $17.

Your turn now **Refer to Example 5.**

15. During the next week, Aaron records these earnings and expenses:

$11, −$13, −$9, $3, $6

Find the sum of his earnings and expenses for the week.

Getting Ready to Practice

1. **Vocabulary** Tell whether the following statement is *true* or *false*, and explain your reasoning: The absolute value of an integer is its opposite.

Find the absolute value of the number.

2. 6   **3.** -13 **4.** -98 **5.** 43

Find the sum.

6. $-11 + 0$ **7.** $10 + (-7)$ **8.** $-5 + (-2)$ **9.** $-8 + 4$

10. **Board Games** You are playing a board game with a friend. You draw one card each turn. If you draw a positive integer, you move forward, and if you draw a negative integer, you move backward. You draw the following cards on your first five turns: 3, -3, 5, 1, -4. How far and in what direction have you moved along the board after these five turns?

Practice and Problem Solving

Write the addition expression modeled on the number line. Then find the sum.

11.
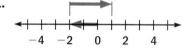

12.

13.

14.
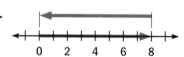

Find the absolute value of the number.

15. -12 **16.** 0   **17.** 54

18. -37 **19.** -567 **20.** 47

Find the sum.

21. $23 + 6$ **22.** $9 + (-9)$ **23.** $-13 + (-1)$

24. $-20 + 5$ **25.** $0 + (-145)$ **26.** $-4 + (-15)$

27. $-27 + 17$ **28.** $-25 + (-5)$ **29.** $-18 + (-7)$

30. $-37 + (-43)$ **31.** $-4 + (-1) + (-5)$ **32.** $-7 + 2 + (-1)$

HELP with **Homework**

Example	Exercises
1	11-14
2	11-14
3	15-20
4	21-32
5	21-32, 34

Online Resources
CLASSZONE.COM

· More Examples
· eTutorial Plus

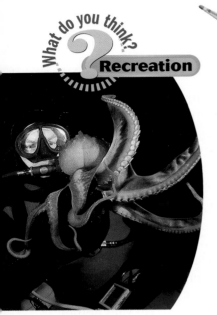

33. Writing Explain why the absolute value of a number is never negative.

34. Scuba Diving A scuba diver dives to a depth of 60 feet, then rises 25 feet, sinks 10 feet, then rises 25 feet. Write an addition expression involving integers that you could use to find the diver's final depth. Then evaluate the expression.

Copy and complete the statement using <, >, or =.

35. $|-5|$? 4

36. 0 ? $|-1|$

37. $|7|$? $|-7|$

38. -6 ? $|2|$

39. $|-9|$? $|-2|$

40. $|-12|$? 12

Algebra Evaluate the expression when $a = 6$ and $b = -3$.

41. $-2 + a$

42. $b + (-6)$

43. $b + a + (-1)$

44. $7 + a + b$

Copy and complete the statement using <, >, or =.

45. $(-2) + 3 + (-10)$? $(-6) + 12$

46. $(-9) + 13$? $11 + (-7) + (-10)$

47. $5 + (-8) + (-4)$? $2 + (-9)$

48. Critical Thinking The absolute value of x is 10. What two values can x be? Explain your reasoning.

Mental Math Use mental math to solve the equation.

49. $-2 + d = 2$

50. $-7 = a + 10$

51. $c + (-5) = 0$

52. $8 = -8 + g$

53. $-17 = -9 + d$

54. $w + (-2) = -12$

Extended Problem Solving In Exercises 55–57, use the following information.
Disc golf is a version of golf played with discs that are thrown at a target on each hole. *Par* is the expected number of throws needed to hit the target. Your score for each hole is the number of throws you make above or below par, and the player with the least total score wins. The table gives the scores of two players for 9 holes of disc golf.

Hole	Par	Kyra	Mark
1	2	+3	+1
2	4	−1	0
3	4	+1	−1
4	3	−1	+2
5	2	0	+1
6	2	+1	+1
7	3	−1	−1
8	2	?	?
9	4	?	?

55. Compute What was each player's total score after the 7th hole?

56. Calculate Mark scored −1 on the 8th hole. If the score was tied after the 8th hole, what did Kyra score?

57. Compare Kyra scored +2 on the 9th hole, and Mark scored 0. Who won the game?

Critical Thinking Copy and complete the statement using *always*, *sometimes*, or *never*.

58. The sum of a positive integer and a negative integer is _?_ positive.

59. The sum of three negative integers is _?_ negative.

60. The sum of three positive integers is _?_ negative.

61. The sum of a negative integer and a positive integer is _?_ negative when the negative integer has the greater absolute value.

62. Challenge A local bike shop keeps track of each day's income and expenses by hand. The sum of all of the transactions for the day was $20. What amount should have been recorded for the new wrench set?

Transactions	
$95	bicycle sold
$5	flat tire repaired
?	new wrench set
$35	cycling jersey sold
−$40	newspaper ad

Mixed Review

Copy and complete the statement using < or >. *(Lesson 6.1)*

63. −32 _?_ 23   **64.** 0 _?_ −10   **65.** −1 _?_ −8   **66.** −24 _?_ −18

Choose a Strategy Use a strategy from the list to solve the following problem. Explain your choice of strategy.

67. Amanda placed candles around the edge of a rectangular cake that was 6 inches wide and 8 inches long. She placed one candle on each corner and then placed one candle every 2 inches along each side. How many candles did she place on the cake?

> *Problem Solving Strategies*
> - Draw a Diagram
> - Make a Table
> - Estimate

Basic Skills Estimate the sum.

68. 16 + 24   **69.** 82 + 45   **70.** 270 + 503   **71.** 4511 + 2608

Test-Taking Practice

72. Multiple Choice What is the value of $|-4|$?

   A. −4   **B.** 0   **C.** 4   **D.** 8

73. Multiple Choice Which number makes the statement _?_ + (−5) > −2 true?

   F. −8   **G.** −5   **H.** −1   **I.** 4

Hands-on Activity

GOAL
Model integer subtraction on a number line.

MATERIALS
• paper
• pencil

Modeling Integer Subtraction

You have already used number lines to add integers. You can also use a number line to model the subtraction of integers.

To find $a - b$ using a number line, follow these steps.

1 Draw a number line on a sheet of paper, or use a row of tiles on the classroom floor to represent a number line. Choose the edge of one tile to represent 0.

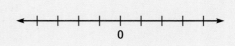

2 Start at 0. Move $|a|$ units forward if $a > 0$ or backward if $a < 0$.

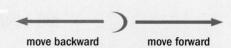

move backward   move forward

3 The subtraction sign tells you to turn and face the opposite direction.

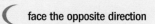

face the opposite direction

4 Move $|b|$ units forward if $b > 0$ or backward if $b < 0$.

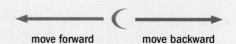

move forward   move backward

Explore 1 **Find the difference 3 − 2.**

1 Start at 0. Because $3 > 0$, move $|3|$ units forward.

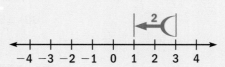

2 The subtraction sign tells you to turn and face the opposite direction.

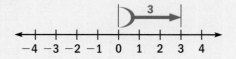

3 Because $2 > 0$, move $|2|$ units forward. Now find your position on the number line. You are 1 unit to the right of 0, so $3 - 2 = 1$.

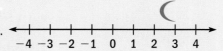

Your turn now **Use a model to find the difference.**

1. $7 - 4$ **2.** $3 - 6$ **3.** $2 - 8$ **4.** $0 - 5$

Explore 2   **Find the difference −2 − (−5).**

1   Start at 0. Because $-2 < 0$, move $|-2|$ units backward.

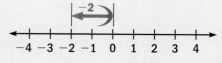

2   The subtraction sign tells you to turn and face the opposite direction.

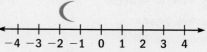

3   Because $-5 < 0$, move $|-5|$ units backward. Now find your final position on the number line. You are 3 units to the right of 0, so $-2 - (-5) = 3$.

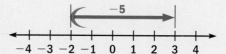

Your turn now   **Use a model to find the difference.**

5. $0 - 4$ **6.** $1 - (-3)$ **7.** $-1 - 6$ **8.** $-2 - (-8)$

Write the subtraction expression modeled by the figure. Then evaluate the expression.

9.

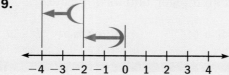

10.

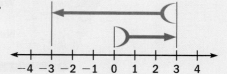

11.

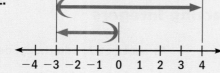

12.

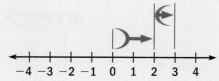

Stop and Think

13. Critical Thinking Evaluate $-5 - (-4)$. Is there an addition expression with the same integers or their opposites that gives the same result? If so, what is it?

14. Writing Can the difference of two negative integers be positive? Can the difference of two negative integers be negative? Explain your reasoning and give examples to support your claims.

15. Critical Thinking Evaluate $2 - 5$ and $5 - 2$. Does the order of the integers in a subtraction expression affect the difference?

Subtracting Integers

BEFORE	▶ Now	WHY?
You added integers.	You'll subtract integers.	So you can compare elevations in South America, as in Ex. 20.

Word Watch

Review Words

opposite, p. 251

Number line models of the subtraction expression $5 - 2$ and the addition expression $5 + (-2)$ are shown below.

Subtraction Model: $5 - 2$

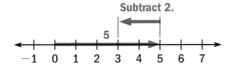

Addition Model: $5 + (-2)$

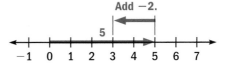

Notice that the model for $5 - 2 = 3$ is identical to the model for $5 + (-2) = 3$. This suggests the following rule for subtracting integers.

Subtracting Integers

Words To subtract an integer, add its opposite.

Numbers $5 - 7 = 5 + (-7)$ **Algebra** $a - b = a + (-b)$

EXAMPLE 1 **Subtracting Integers**

with Review

Need help with finding opposites? See p. 251.

a. $2 - 7 = 2 + (-7)$ To subtract 7, add its opposite, -7.

       $= -5$ Use rule for adding integers.

b. $-6 - 8 = -6 + (-8)$ To subtract 8, add its opposite, -8.

       $= -14$ Use rule for adding integers.

c. $12 - (-9) = 12 + 9$ To subtract -9, add its opposite, 9.

       $= 21$ Use rule for adding integers.

d. $-10 - (-5) = -10 + 5$ To subtract -5, add its opposite, 5.

       $= -5$ Use rule for adding integers.

Your turn now **Find the difference.**

1. $4 - 6$ **2.** $-7 - (-8)$ **3.** $-2 - 1$ **4.** $15 - (-3)$

Geography

■ The Dead Sea

The water in the Dead Sea is so dense with salt and minerals that people float easily. The water in oceans and seas is usually $\frac{7}{200}$ salt. The Dead Sea has about 10 times this amount. About what fraction of the water in the Dead Sea is salt?

EXAMPLE 2 **Using Integer Subtraction**

Geography The highest point in Asia is Mount Everest at 8850 meters. The shore of the Dead Sea, the lowest point in Asia, is about 410 meters below sea level. What is the difference between these elevations?

Solution

(1 Use integers to represent the two elevations.

Mount Everest: 8850 m   **Dead Sea:** −410 m

(2 Find the difference of 8850 and −410 meters.

$$8850 - (-410) = 8850 + 410 \qquad \text{Rule for subtracting integers}$$
$$= 9260 \qquad \text{Add.}$$

ANSWER The difference between the elevations is 9260 meters.

Change Subtraction can be used to find a change in a variable such as temperature or elevation. To find the change, subtract the old or start value of the variable from the new or end value of the variable.

EXAMPLE 3 **Finding a Change in Temperature**

Weather In Fairfield, Montana, on December 24, 1924, the air temperature dropped a record amount. At noon, the temperature was 63°F. Twelve hours later, the temperature was −21°F. What was the change in temperature?

Solution

Change in temperature = **end temperature − start temperature**
$$= -21 - 63 \qquad \text{Substitute values.}$$
$$= -21 + (-63) \qquad \text{Rule for subtracting integers}$$
$$= -84 \qquad \text{Add.}$$

ANSWER The change in temperature was −84°F, so the temperature dropped 84°F.

Your turn now **Solve the following problems.**

5. Find the difference between an elevation of 535 feet above sea level and an elevation of 8 feet below sea level.

6. The temperature at 6 A.M. was −12°F. At 3 P.M. the temperature was 32°F. What was the change in temperature?

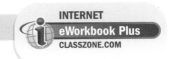
Getting Ready to Practice

1. **Vocabulary** Copy and complete: To simplify the expression $8 - (-9)$, you can add the _?_ of -9 to 8.

Match the subtraction expression with the equivalent addition expression.

2. $-7 - 3$ 3. $7 - (-3)$ 4. $-7 - (-3)$ 5. $7 - 3$

A. $-7 + 3$ B. $7 + (-3)$ C. $-7 + (-3)$ D. $7 + 3$

Find the difference.

6. $13 - (-4)$ 7. $-9 - 3$ 8. $10 - 12$ 9. $-16 - (-2)$

10. **Guided Problem Solving** A professional cliff diver dives from a ledge 65 feet above the surface of the water. The diver reaches an underwater depth of 15 feet before returning to the surface. What was the diver's change in elevation from the highest point of the dive to the lowest?

    ① What operation do you use to find a change in elevation?

    ② What integer represents the highest elevation of the dive? the lowest elevation of the dive?

    ③ Write and evaluate an expression to find the change in elevation.

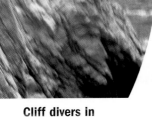

Cliff divers in Acapulco, Mexico

Practice and Problem Solving

with Homework

Example	Exercises
1	11–19
2	20, 27
3	21, 28

Online Resources
CLASSZONE.COM
· More Examples
· eTutorial Plus

Find the difference.

11. $-17 - 9$ 12. $15 - (-18)$ 13. $13 - 24$

14. $25 - 5$ 15. $7 - (-7)$ 16. $-5 - (-25)$

17. $-54 - (-7)$ 18. $-56 - 28$ 19. $33 - (-27)$

20. **Geography** The highest point in South America is Mount Aconcagua at 22,834 feet above sea level. The lowest point in South America is the Valdes Peninsula at 131 feet below sea level. Find the difference between these elevations.

21. **Death Valley** If you were to travel from the lowest point to the highest point in Death Valley, California, you would begin at 282 feet below sea level in Badwater and end up at 11,049 feet above sea level on Telescope Peak. What would your change in elevation be?

22. **Compare** How is integer subtraction related to integer addition?

 Algebra **Evaluate the expression for the given value(s) of the variable(s).**

23. $m - 5$ when $m = 4$

24. $-22 - x + 4$ when $x = -16$

25. $10 + t - (-63)$ when $t = -17$

26. $x - y$ when $x = 9$ and $y = -11$

27. Planet Temperatures A temperature expressed using the Kelvin (K) unit can be converted to degrees Celsius (°C) by subtracting 273. For example, $300\ K = (300 - 273)°C = 27°C$. Convert the mean surface temperatures of the planets given in the table to degrees Celsius.

Planet	Temperature
Mercury	452 K
Earth	281 K
Jupiter	120 K
Saturn	88 K
Pluto	37 K

28. Hiking A group of hikers on a mountain began at an elevation of 3350 feet above sea level and stopped for a break at an elevation of 2160 feet above sea level. What was their change in elevation between these two points? How can you tell from the change in elevation whether the hikers were going up or down the mountain?

29. Critical Thinking Describe the following pattern: $2, -1, -4, -7, \ldots$. Then write the next three integers.

30. Challenge Find two integers whose sum is 2 and whose difference is 8.

Mixed Review

Find the product. *(Lesson 2.3)*

31. 5.4×2.8　**32.** 7.3×1.9　**33.** 0.15×0.28　**34.** 0.08×0.7

Copy and complete the statement using <, >, or =. *(Lesson 6.2)*

35. $\left| -7 \right| \ \underline{?}\ 6$　**36.** $\left| -7 \right| \ \underline{?}\ \left| 6 \right|$　**37.** $\left| -3 \right| \ \underline{?}\ \left| 3 \right|$　**38.** $0 \ \underline{?}\ \left| 8 \right|$

Basic Skills **Find a low and high estimate for the product.**

39. 12×48　**40.** 24×47　**41.** 63×49　**42.** 116×64

Test-Taking Practice

43. Multiple Choice Find the difference $-14 - (-7)$.

　A. -21　　**B.** -7　　**C.** -2　　**D.** 7

44. Short Response Write and evaluate the addition expression that is equivalent to the subtraction expression $-1 - (-4)$. Then give a real-world situation that the expression could represent.

Notebook Review

Check Your Definitions

Review the vocabulary definitions in your notebook.

Copy the review examples in your notebook. Then complete the exercises.

integer, p. 251

negative integer, p. 251

positive integer, p. 251

opposite, p. 251

absolute value, p. 259

Use Your Vocabulary

1. Copy and complete: The _?_ of 10 is −10, and the _?_ of 10 is 10.

6.1 Can you compare and order integers?

EXAMPLE Order the integers −3, 1, 3, 0, and −1 from least to greatest.

Graph the integers on a number line.

From least to greatest, the integers are −3, −1, 0, 1, and 3.

Copy and complete the statement using < or >.

2. 11 _?_ −10   **3.** −4 _?_ −8   **4.** −29 _?_ −28   **5.** −6 _?_ 5

6.2 Can you add integers?

EXAMPLE Find the sum.

a. −15 + 8

b. −21 + (−6)

Solution

a. These integers have different signs.

$$-15 + 8 = -7 \longleftarrow \text{Subtract } |8| \text{ from } |-15|.$$

Because $|-15| > |8|$, the sum has the same sign as −15.

b. These integers have the same sign.

$$-21 + (-6) = -27 \longleftarrow \text{Add } |-21| \text{ and } |-6|.$$

Both integers are negative, so the sum is negative.

Find the sum.

6. −7 + 8   **7.** −3 + (−8)   **8.** −20 + 7   **9.** −16 + (−12)

6.3 Can you subtract integers?

 EXAMPLE Find $-27 - 21$.

$$-27 - 21 = -27 + (-21) \qquad \text{To subtract 21, add its opposite, } -21.$$
$$= -48 \qquad \text{Use rule for adding integers.}$$

☑ **Find the difference.**

10. $3 - (-2)$ **11.** $34 - 43$ **12.** $-46 - 22$ **13.** $-14 - (-31)$

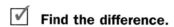 **about Lessons 6.1–6.3**

14. Writing If one integer is negative and a second integer is positive, when is the sum of the two integers positive? When is the sum negative? Explain your reasoning.

15. Critical Thinking What integer is less than all positive integers and greater than all negative integers?

Review Quiz 1

1. Name two different integers that have an absolute value of 25.

Write the integer that represents the situation.

2. 140 feet below sea level   **3.** A loss of 7 yards

4. A profit of $85   **5.** 12 degrees below 0

Order the integers from least to greatest.

6. $0, -7, 6, -3, 2$ **7.** $-9, -7, -8, -5, -6$

8. $-1, 3, -3, 0, -5$ **9.** $11, -11, 3, -3, -7$

Find the sum or difference.

10. $-7 + (-4)$ **11.** $21 + (-15)$ **12.** $-11 + 5$ **13.** $-25 + (-8)$

14. $-16 - 10$ **15.** $30 - 63$ **16.** $-9 - (-17)$ **17.** $17 - (-17)$

18. Temperature At dawn this morning, the temperature was $-3°F$. By noon, the temperature was $25°F$. What was the change in temperature?

19. Personal Finance Find the sum of the following transactions recorded for a bank account over a one week period: $25, -$35, $12, $14, -$43.

Multiplying Integers

BEFORE	▶ Now	WHY?
You multiplied whole numbers, decimals, and fractions.	You'll multiply integers.	So you can find how deep a seal dives, as in Ex. 33.

Word Watch

Review Words

product, p. 689

 Activity **You can use patterns to find rules for multiplying integers.**

① Copy and complete Table 1.

② What pattern do you see as you read down the *Product* column in Table 1? Extend Table 1 using this pattern to find the next two products, $3 \cdot (-1)$ and $3 \cdot (-2)$.

③ What do you notice about the product of a positive integer and a negative integer?

④ Copy Table 2. Then use your answer from Step 3 to complete the table.

⑤ What pattern do you see as you read down the *Product* column in Table 2? Extend Table 2 using this pattern to find the next two products, $-3 \cdot (-1)$ and $-3 \cdot (-2)$.

⑥ What do you notice about the product of two negative integers?

Table 1

Expression	Product
$3 \cdot 3$	9
$3 \cdot 2$	?
$3 \cdot 1$	?
$3 \cdot 0$	?

Table 2

Expression	Product
$-3 \cdot 3$	?
$-3 \cdot 2$	?
$-3 \cdot 1$	?
$-3 \cdot 0$	?

HELP with **Review**

Need help describing and extending patterns? See p. 5.

In the activity, you may have found three rules for multiplying integers.

Multiplying Integers

Words	Numbers
Same Sign The product of two integers with the same sign is positive.	$4 \cdot 2 = 8$ $-4 \cdot (-2) = 8$
Different Signs The product of two integers with different signs is negative.	$4 \cdot (-2) = -8$ $-4 \cdot 2 = -8$
Zero The product of an integer and 0 is 0.	$4 \cdot 0 = 0$ $-4 \cdot 0 = 0$

EXAMPLE 1 **Multiplying Integers**

a. $-5(-7) = 35$ The product of two integers with the same sign is positive.

b. $-8(2) = -16$ The product of two integers with different signs is negative.

c. $-12(0) = 0$ The product of an integer and 0 is 0.

Your turn now **Find the product.**

1. $9(2)$ **2.** $-3(-4)$ **3.** $5(-5)$ **4.** $-7(7)$ **5.** $0(-14)$

EXAMPLE 2 **Evaluating Variable Expressions**

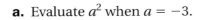

a. Evaluate a^2 when $a = -3$.

b. Evaluate xyz when $x = 2$, $y = -4$, and $z = 6$.

Solution

a. $a^2 = (-3)^2$ Substitute -3 for a.

$= -3(-3)$ Write -3 as a factor 2 times.

$= 9$ Multiply -3 and -3.

b. $xyz = 2(-4)(6)$ Substitute 2 for x, -4 for y, and 6 for z.

$= -8(6)$ Multiply 2 and -4.

$= -48$ Multiply -8 and 6.

EXAMPLE 3 **Using Integer Multiplication**

Greenland Most of Greenland is covered with ice that in some places is almost two miles thick. Scientists estimate that 3 feet of this ice melts each year. Find the change in the thickness of the ice after 10 years.

Solution

You can find the total change in the ice thickness by multiplying the yearly change by the number of years. Use -3 for the yearly change because the thickness of the ice decreases by 3 feet each year.

Change in ice thickness $= -3(10) = -30$

ANSWER The thickness of the ice will decrease 30 feet after 10 years.

What do you think?

Geography

■ **Greenland**

One hotel in Greenland is made entirely of ice. The temperature inside a guest room is usually $-10°C$. If the outside temperature is $-35°C$, what is the difference between the inside and outside temperatures?

Getting Ready to Practice

Vocabulary Copy and complete using *positive* or *negative*.

1. The product of two negative integers is ___?___.

2. The product of a positive integer and a negative integer is ___?___.

Find the product.

3. $4(8)$ 4. $-3(11)$ 5. $5(-6)$ 6. $-2(-12)$

 Algebra Evaluate the expression when $k = -9$.

7. $6k$ 8. k^2 9. $-2k$ 10. $5k$

11. **Guided Problem Solving** The lowest temperature recorded in May at McMurdo Station, Antarctica, is 3 times the average low temperature for May. In degrees Fahrenheit, the average low temperature for May is 16 below zero. What is the lowest temperature recorded in May?

   (1 What operation is needed to solve this problem?

   (2 What integer represents the average low temperature for May?

   (3 Write and evaluate an expression to find the lowest temperature recorded in May at McMurdo Station.

 **with Homework**

Example	Exercises
1	12-23
2	25-32
3	33-34

 **Online Resources**
CLASSZONE.COM

· More Examples
· eTutorial Plus

Practice and Problem Solving

Find the product.

12. $11(10)$ 13. $0(-15)$ 14. $-9(-7)$ 15. $-8(5)$

16. $6(-6)$ 17. $15(-2)$ 18. $-5(7)$ 19. $-4(-7)$

20. $-13(0)$ 21. $-4(-4)(-2)$ 22. $10(0)(-7)$ 23. $5(-1)(9)$

24. **Writing** Explain how to use addition to find the product of 6 and -8.

 Algebra Evaluate the expression when $a = -5$, $b = -2$, and $c = -7$.

25. $7c$ 26. b^4 27. a^2 28. ab

29. $-12b$ 30. $0c^2$ 31. $-ab$ 32. $2bc$

33. **Diving Seals** Antarctic Weddell seals can dive to extraordinary depths by collapsing their lungs. If a seal is diving at a speed of 2 meters every second, what integer represents the seal's change in position after 30 seconds?

34. Airplane Landing Suppose an airplane descends 4 feet every second prior to landing. Write and simplify an expression to represent the change in the altitude of the airplane after 10 seconds.

Mental Math **Solve the equation using mental math.**

35. $-25s = -100$ **36.** $2n = -10$ **37.** $-6m = -60$

38. $-9p = 36$ **39.** $4a = -32$ **40.** $-5x = 65$

41. Panama Canal In the Panama Canal, a system of locks releases water from upper chambers into lower chambers so that ships can move through the canal. The water level in an upper chamber begins at 72 feet and falls about 3 feet every minute for 9 minutes. Write and evaluate an expression that represents the change in the water depth after 9 minutes. Then find the depth of the water after 9 minutes.

42. Challenge Would you expect the product of the numbers listed below to be positive or negative? Explain your reasoning.

$$-4300, 5000, -2100, -1500$$

Panama Canal

Mixed Review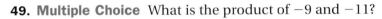

43. Find the median and the lower and upper quartiles of the following set of data. Then make a box-and-whisker plot of the data. *(Lesson 3.4)*

$$28, 23, 25, 29, 16, 21, 26, 21, 13$$

Find the difference. *(Lesson 6.3)*

44. $-8 - 3$ **45.** $21 - 27$ **46.** $-39 - (-9)$ **47.** $18 - (-31)$

Basic Skills **Solve the following problem.**

48. You distribute a 500 sheet package of printer paper evenly among 4 printers. How many sheets of paper do you load into each printer?

Test-Taking Practice

49. Multiple Choice What is the product of -9 and -11?

A. -99 **B.** -20 **C.** 2 **D.** 99

50. Short Response Your bank account had a balance of $36. You made a $3 withdrawal from the account each day for 5 days. Write and evaluate an expression to find the account balance after the 5 days. If you continue to make the same daily withdrawal, when will the balance reach $0?

Work Backward

Draw a Diagram

Look for a Pattern

Guess, Check, and Revise

Solve a Related Problem

Make a List

Make a Table

Solve a Related Problem

Problem In a magic square, the row, column, and diagonal sums are all equal. You are trying to complete a magic square using each of the numbers 1, 2, 3, 4, 5, 6, 7, 8, and 9 only once. Where should you place the numbers?

① Read and Understand

Read the problem carefully.

The row, column, and diagonal sums in the magic square must all be equal. Each of the given numbers can be used only once.

② Make a plan

Decide on a strategy to use.

You can replace the given numbers with a related set of numbers that is easier to work with.

③ Solve the Problem

Reread the problem and solve a related problem.

Because opposites have a sum of 0, consider subtracting the same number from each of the numbers 1 through 9 so that the new set of numbers includes opposites. The best number to subtract is 5 because it produces the greatest number of opposites.

1, 2, 3, 4, 5, 6, 7, 8, 9　　**Subtract 5.**　　$-4, -3, -2, -1, 0, 1, 2, 3, 4$

If 0 is placed in the center of the magic square and the opposites are arranged in pairs around it, the sums will all be equal to 0. Once done, 5 can be added back to each number to reinstate the original numbers.

Magic square with opposites

3	−2	−1
−4	0	4
1	2	−3

Magic square with original numbers

8	3	4
1	5	9
6	7	2

④ Look Back

To check your answer, look at the magic square to make sure that you used each number only once and that all row, column, and diagonal sums are equal.

Use the strategy *solve a related problem*.

1. **Sailboats** A triangular piece of fabric is needed to make a sail for a sailboat. The triangle has a right angle, and the two sides that form the right angle have lengths of 10 feet and 15 feet. How much material is needed for the sail? Consider the area of the rectangle formed by two sails of this size.

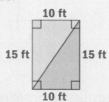

2. **Magic Square** Complete the magic square using each of the numbers 2, 4, 6, 8, 10, 12, 14, 16, and 18 only once. Place the numbers so that all the row, column, and diagonal sums are 30.

?	?	?
?	?	?
?	?	?

3. **Movie Attendance** In a recent year, the population of the United States was about 268,000,000. In the same year, Americans spent almost $7,600,000,000 on movie tickets. What was the mean amount each American spent on movie tickets? Think of 268,000,000 as 268 million and $7,600,000,000 as $7,600 million. How does this help you find the mean amount spent to the nearest dollar?

4. **Page Numbers** A chapter that begins on page 1 and ends on page 20 is 20 pages long. How long is a chapter that begins on page 470 and ends on page 527? To answer this question, think about what number you would subtract from 470 to get 1.

Mixed Problem Solving

Use any strategy to solve the problem.

5. **Soccer** Bryan is conditioning for the upcoming soccer season. An 8 day running schedule is shown below. What distance would you expect him to run on day 10?

Day	1	2	3	4	5	6	7	8
Distance (miles)	1	1.5	1	2	1	2.5	1	3

6. **Survey** You survey your class to find out how many hours each student slept last night. The results are shown below. What is the mode?

Survey Results:

7.5	8.5	8	5.5	10	7.5
8.5	8	8.5	11	7.5	11.5
8.5	8.5	8.5	10	8	8.5
10	10.5				

7. **Traveling** Scott and Dan are traveling together. First Scott drives one fifth of the way. Then Dan drives one third of the remaining distance. Next Scott drives one half of the remaining distance, and finally Dan drives the last 80 miles. What is the total distance traveled? How far does each person drive?

Dividing Integers

BEFORE	Now	WHY?
You multiplied integers.	You'll divide integers.	So you can find a squirrel's body temperature, as in Example 3.

Word Watch

Review Words
mean, p. 101

Activity   You can evaluate a division equation by solving the related multiplication equation.

(1   Copy and complete the table.

Division Equation	Related Multiplication Equation	Quotient
$18 \div 9 = \underline{?}$	$\underline{?} \cdot 9 = 18$	2
$-15 \div 5 = \underline{?}$	?	?
$-14 \div 7 = \underline{?}$	?	?
$10 \div (-2) = \underline{?}$	?	?
$-12 \div (-4) = \underline{?}$	?	?

Copy and complete the statement using _positive_ or _negative_.

(2   A negative integer divided by a positive integer is $\underline{?}$.

(3   A negative integer divided by a negative integer is $\underline{?}$.

In the activity, you saw that the rules for dividing integers are similar to the rules for multiplying integers.

Dividing Integers

Words	Numbers
Same Sign The quotient of two integers with the same sign is positive.	$10 \div 2 = 5$ $$\frac{-24}{-3} = 8$$
Different Signs The quotient of two integers with different signs is negative.	$15 \div (-3) = -5$ $$\frac{-18}{6} = -3$$
Zero The quotient of 0 and any nonzero integer is 0.	$0 \div 17 = 0$ $$\frac{0}{-9} = 0$$

Watch Out!

You cannot divide a number by 0. Any number divided by 0 is _undefined_. For example, $8 \div 0 = \underline{?}$ can be rewritten as $\underline{?} \cdot 0 = 8$. No number times 0 will result in a nonzero product.

EXAMPLE 1 **Dividing Integers**

a. $28 \div (-4) = -7$
The quotient of two integers with different signs is negative.

b. $\dfrac{-60}{-12} = 5$
The quotient of two integers with the same sign is positive.

c. $0 \div (-13) = 0$
The quotient of 0 and any nonzero integer is 0.

Your turn now Find the quotient.

1. $-24 \div 6$ **2.** $\dfrac{0}{-2}$ **3.** $\dfrac{-39}{-13}$ **4.** $19 \div (-1)$

What do you think?

Geography

■ Bangor, Maine

Bangor, Maine, is home to the statue of mythical lumberman Paul Bunyan. Standing 31 feet tall and weighing 3700 pounds, the statue greets visitors entering Bangor. What is the statue's mean weight per foot of height?

EXAMPLE 2 **Finding the Mean**

Bangor, Maine The table shows the high temperatures for four days in January in Bangor, Maine. Find the mean of the temperatures.

Day	Temperature
Monday	−7°C
Tuesday	−4°C
Wednesday	−7°C
Thursday	−2°C

Solution

(1 Find the sum of the temperatures.

$$-7 + (-4) + (-7) + (-2) = -20$$

(2 Divide the sum by the number of temperatures, 4.

$$-20 \div 4 = -5$$

ANSWER The mean high temperature for the four days was −5°C.

Your turn now Solve the following problem.

5. A submarine's elevations over several hours are -284 ft, -245 ft, -372 ft, -356 ft, and -343 ft. Find the mean of the elevations.

Temperature Conversions Operations with positive and negative numbers are needed to convert temperatures between degrees Celsius C and degrees Fahrenheit F.

- To convert Celsius to Fahrenheit, use the formula $F = \dfrac{9}{5}C + 32$.

- To convert Fahrenheit to Celsius, use the formula $C = \dfrac{5}{9}(F - 32)$.

EXAMPLE 3 **Converting a Temperature**

Biology During hibernation, an Arctic ground squirrel can decrease its body temperature to $-30°C$. Convert this temperature to degrees Fahrenheit.

Solution

$F = \dfrac{9}{5}C + 32$ Write formula for degrees Fahrenheit.

$= \dfrac{9}{5}(-30) + 32$ Substitute -30 for C.

$= \dfrac{9 \cdot (\overset{-6}{\cancel{-30}})}{\underset{1}{\cancel{5}} \cdot 1} + 32$ Use rule for multiplying fractions. Divide out common factor.

$= -54 + 32$ Multiply.

$= -22$ Add.

ANSWER The temperature $-30°C$ is equal to $-22°F$.

Your turn now Convert the temperature from degrees Fahrenheit to degrees Celsius or from degrees Celsius to degrees Fahrenheit.

6. $0°C$ **7.** $-4°F$ **8.** $-45°C$ **9.** $77°F$

 **6.5 Exercises**
More Practice, p. 710

INTERNET
eWorkbook Plus
CLASSZONE.COM

Getting Ready to Practice

 **HELP with Review**

Need help with finding the mean? See p. 101.

Vocabulary **Tell whether the statement is *true* or *false*. Explain.**

1. The quotient of a negative integer and a positive integer is positive.

2. The mean of 10, -2, and 7 is -5.

3. The expressions $\dfrac{-5}{0}$ and $0 \div (-5)$ are both equal to 0.

Find the quotient.

4. $6 \div (-2)$ **5.** $-6 \div 2$ **6.** $-6 \div (-2)$

7. $36 \div (-12)$ **8.** $-26 \div 13$ **9.** $-42 \div (-7)$

10. Boiling Point The boiling point of water is $100°C$. What is this temperature in degrees Fahrenheit?

Practice and Problem Solving

with Homework

Example	Exercises
1	11-22
2	23-28, 33
3	29-32, 34-35

Online Resources
CLASSZONE.COM

· More Examples
· eTutorial Plus

Find the quotient.

11. $-44 \div 11$ **12.** $-64 \div 32$ **13.** $70 \div (-10)$ **14.** $34 \div (-17)$

15. $-76 \div (-19)$ **16.** $-84 \div (-7)$ **17.** $63 \div (-9)$ **18.** $-52 \div 13$

19. $-24 \div 8$ **20.** $72 \div (-9)$ **21.** $0 \div (-121)$ **22.** $-96 \div (-12)$

Find the mean of the integers.

23. $-10, -6, 3, 9$ **24.** $-46, -33, 0, 11$

25. $10, -27, 4, -9$ **26.** $8, -11, 18, -8$

27. $7, -9, 9, -7, 0$ **28.** $-17, -4, 5, 21, 30$

Convert the temperature from degrees Fahrenheit to degrees Celsius or from degrees Celsius to degrees Fahrenheit.

29. $-50°C$ **30.** $32°F$ **31.** $-13°F$ **32.** $-1°C$

33. Bowling Alley A bowling alley's gains and losses over 5 months are $450, −$675, $1230, −$776, and −$95. Find the mean of the monthly gains and losses for the bowling alley.

34. Bathing Monkeys During the winter in Japan, macaque monkeys find warmth in a hot spring that is fed by the Shirane Volcano. The water temperature is typically around 39°C, while the air temperature can reach −5°C. Convert these temperatures to degrees Fahrenheit.

35. Cooking A recipe says to preheat your oven to 160°C. Your oven has temperature settings in degrees Fahrenheit. At what temperature should you set your oven?

 Algebra Evaluate the expression when *s* = 16 and *t* = −5.

36. $t \div (-1)$ **37.** $s \div (-8)$ **38.** $-64 \div s$ **39.** $-45 \div t$

40. $0 \div s$ **41.** $s \div (-4) + 2$ **42.** $25 \div t - 7$ **43.** $10 \div t + s$

44. Critical Thinking What can you tell about two integers when their quotient is positive? negative? zero?

45. Estimate Explain why the expression $2C + 30$ can be used to estimate the value of a Celsius temperature in degrees Fahrenheit. Then use the expression to estimate the value of $-15°C$ in degrees Fahrenheit.

Copy and complete the statement using <, >, or =.

46. $4 \div (-2) - 1 \underline{\ ?\ } 4 \div 2 - 1$ **47.** $46 \div (-23) \underline{\ ?\ } -46 \div 23$

48. $0 \div 4 + 9 \underline{\ ?\ } 0 \div 7 + 9$ **49.** $-25 \div (-5) \div (-1) \underline{\ ?\ } 5$

50. Astronomy Find the mean of the following average temperatures of four of Saturn's moons: $-328°F$, $-330°F$, $-289°F$, $-305°F$.

Use the number line to complete the statement using <, >, or =.

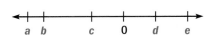

51. $a \div c \ \underline{?}\ 0$ **52.** $d \div c \ \underline{?}\ 0$ **53.** $e \div d \ \underline{?}\ a$

54. $0 \div a \ \underline{?}\ 0 \div e$ **55.** $e \div a \ \underline{?}\ e \div d$ **56.** $c \div d \ \underline{?}\ a \div b$

57. Challenge The mean of four integers is 0. Three of the integers are -9, 7, and -3. What is the fourth integer?

Mixed Review

Find the quotient. *(Lesson 5.4)*

58. $5 \div \dfrac{3}{4}$ **59.** $7 \div \dfrac{9}{10}$ **60.** $\dfrac{7}{12} \div \dfrac{49}{60}$ **61.** $\dfrac{8}{13} \div \dfrac{11}{26}$

Find the product. *(Lesson 6.4)*

62. $-13(5)$ **63.** $29(-6)$ **64.** $-41(-52)$ **65.** $67(80)$

Basic Skills Write a fraction to represent the shaded part of the set or region.

66.   **67.**   **68.**   **69.**

Test-Taking Practice

70. Extended Response The temperature was $-5°C$ at 6:15 A.M., 49°F at noon, and 5°C at 6:15 P.M. Make a line graph of the temperature data in degrees Fahrenheit. What was the change in temperature, in degrees Fahrenheit, between 6:15 A.M. and noon? What was the change in temperature, in degrees Fahrenheit, between noon and 6:15 P.M.?

BrAIN GAME

Same Numbers, Different Answers

Copy and complete each statement using the numbers -3, -2, 4, and 5. Use all four numbers in each statement.

$$\underline{?} \cdot \underline{?} \cdot \underline{?} - \underline{?} = 26 \qquad \underline{?} \div \underline{?} + \underline{?} - \underline{?} = 6$$

Rational Numbers

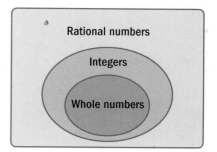

BEFORE

You performed operations on positive fractions and decimals.

Now

You'll perform operations on rational numbers.

WHY?

So you can find the area of a volleyball court, as in Ex. 28.

Word Watch

rational number, p. 283
additive inverse, p. 285
multiplicative inverse, p. 285
additive identity, p. 285
multiplicative identity, p. 285

A **rational number** is a number that can be written as $\frac{a}{b}$ where a and b are integers and $b \neq 0$.

The Venn diagram at the right shows the relationship among rational numbers, integers, and whole numbers. Notice that integers include whole numbers and rational numbers include integers.

EXAMPLE 1 Identifying Rational Numbers

Show that the number is rational by writing it in $\frac{a}{b}$ form.

a. $6 = \frac{6}{1}$ **b.** $-\frac{3}{5} = \frac{3}{-5}$ **c.** $0.75 = \frac{3}{4}$ **d.** $-2\frac{1}{3} = \frac{-7}{3}$

The negative sign in a negative fraction usually appears in front of the fraction bar. However, it can also appear in the numerator, as in part (d), or in the denominator, as in part (b).

EXAMPLE 2 Ordering Rational Numbers

Order -1, -1.6, $\frac{2}{5}$, $-1\frac{1}{4}$, and $-\frac{3}{8}$ from least to greatest.

Graph each number on a number line.

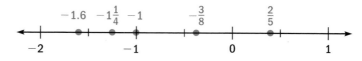

ANSWER From least to greatest, the numbers are: -1.6, $-1\frac{1}{4}$, -1, $-\frac{3}{8}$, $\frac{2}{5}$.

Your turn now Show that each number is rational by writing it in $\frac{a}{b}$ form. Then order the numbers from least to greatest.

1. 2.5, -1, $-\frac{5}{8}$, -0.8

2. $4\frac{1}{5}$, -3.6, $-3\frac{8}{9}$, 0

Commutative and Associative Properties The commutative and associative properties can help you add or multiply rational numbers.

Commutative and Associative Properties	
Commutative Property of Addition **Words** In a sum, you can add terms in any order. **Numbers** $5 + (-6) = -6 + 5$ **Algebra** $a + b = b + a$	**Commutative Property of Multiplication** **Words** In a product, you can multiply factors in any order. **Numbers** $4(-7) = -7(4)$ **Algebra** $ab = ba$
Associative Property of Addition **Words** Changing the grouping of terms will not change the sum. **Numbers** $(9 + 8) + 6 = 9 + (8 + 6)$ **Algebra** $(a + b) + c = a + (b + c)$	**Associative Property of Multiplication** **Words** Changing the grouping of factors will not change the product. **Numbers** $(2 \cdot 3) \cdot 4 = 2 \cdot (3 \cdot 4)$ **Algebra** $(ab)c = a(bc)$

HELP with **Vocabulary**

To remember the commutative property, remember that *commuters* are people who *move* or travel.
To remember the associative property, remember that the people you *associate* with are the friends in your *group*.

EXAMPLE 3 Using Commutative, Associative Properties

Evaluate the expression. Justify each step you take.

a. $-10.6 + 3 + (-4.4)$

$= 3 + (-10.6) + (-4.4)$ Commutative property of addition

$= 3 + [-10.6 + (-4.4)]$ Associative property of addition

$= 3 + (-15) = -12$ Add -10.6 and -4.4, then 3 and -15.

b. $-25(7)(-4)$

$= 7(-25)(-4)$ Commutative property of multiplication

$= 7[(-25)(-4)]$ Associative property of multiplication

$= 7(100) = 700$ Multiply -25 and -4, then 7 and 100.

HELP with **Notetaking**

Remember that recording the steps you take in a multi-step calculation can help you perform similar calculations.

Your turn now Evaluate the expression. Justify each step you take.

3. $3.5 + [(-3) + 6.5]$ **4.** $5(-9)(-4)$ **5.** $-6(3)(-5)$

6. $2.8 + 7 + (-1.8)$ **7.** $0.5(7)(8)$ **8.** $0.9 + [9.1 + (-2)]$

Inverse and Identity Properties The inverse and identity properties can help you use mental math to evaluate expressions.

Inverse and Identity Properties	
Inverse Property of Addition **Words** The sum of a number and its **additive inverse** , or opposite, is 0. **Numbers** $5 + (-5) = 0$ **Algebra** $a + (-a) = 0$	**Inverse Property of Multiplication** **Words** The product of a nonzero number and its **multiplicative inverse** , or reciprocal, is 1. **Numbers** $\frac{3}{4} \cdot \frac{4}{3} = 1$ **Algebra** For nonzero integers a and b, $\frac{a}{b} \cdot \frac{b}{a} = 1.$
Identity Property of Addition **Words** The sum of a number and the **additive identity** , 0, is the number. **Numbers** $-7 + 0 = -7$ **Algebra** $a + 0 = a$	**Identity Property of Multiplication** **Words** The product of a number and the **multiplicative identity** , 1, is the number. **Numbers** $9 \cdot 1 = 9$ **Algebra** $a(1) = a$

I wish
I were feeling
more positive
today.

EXAMPLE 4 **Using Inverse and Identity Properties**

Evaluate the expression. Justify each step you take.

$$\frac{2}{3} + \frac{7}{10} + \left(-\frac{2}{3}\right) = \frac{2}{3} + \left(-\frac{2}{3}\right) + \frac{7}{10} \qquad \text{Commutative property of addition}$$

$$= 0 + \frac{7}{10} \qquad \text{Inverse property of addition}$$

$$= \frac{7}{10} \qquad \text{Identity property of addition}$$

Your turn now Evaluate the expression. Justify each step you take.

9. $94 + 87 + (-94)$ **10.** $-\frac{3}{4} + \frac{5}{6} + \frac{3}{4}$ **11.** $\frac{1}{9} \cdot 91 \cdot 9$

12. $\frac{1}{3} \cdot \frac{5}{6} \cdot 3$ **13.** $-53 + (-25) + 53$ **14.** $\frac{1}{6} \cdot 310 \cdot 6$

Getting Ready to Practice

Vocabulary **Write the number described.**

1. The multiplicative identity of 23   **2.** The additive inverse of -2

3. The additive identity of -17 **4.** The multiplicative inverse of 3

Show that the number is rational by writing it in $\frac{a}{b}$ form.

5. 0.4 **6.** $-3\frac{5}{8}$ **7.** $-\frac{7}{9}$ **8.** -12

Mental Math **Evaluate the expression. Justify each step you take.**

9. $3 \cdot \frac{1}{2} \cdot \frac{1}{3}$ **10.** $-\frac{3}{4} + \frac{5}{6} + \frac{3}{4}$ **11.** $7 \cdot 13 \cdot \frac{1}{7}$ **12.** $4 + 17 + (-4)$

13. **Rainfall** The table shows the amount of rainfall, in inches, above or below the mean for four regions of Oklahoma during a recent drought. Order the numbers from least to greatest to determine which region's rainfall was the most above the mean and which region's rainfall was the most below the mean.

Region	Departure from Mean
Panhandle	-5.87
Northeast	$-\frac{631}{100}$
Southwest	$-8\frac{4}{25}$
Southeast	1.97

Practice and Problem Solving

HELP with Homework

Example	Exercises
1	14–17
2	18–21
3	22–27
4	22–27

Online Resources
CLASSZONE.COM

· More Examples
· eTutorial Plus

Show that the number is rational by writing it in $\frac{a}{b}$ form. Then give the multiplicative inverse and the additive inverse of the number.

14. $-\frac{2}{3}$ **15.** $5\frac{3}{7}$ **16.** 0.7 **17.** 21

Order the rational numbers from least to greatest.

18. $-3.1,\ -4,\ -\frac{10}{3},\ -3\frac{3}{4},\ -3.7$ **19.** $3,\ -2\frac{2}{3},\ 0,\ -\frac{5}{4},\ -0.85$

20. $\frac{3}{10},\ -1\frac{1}{3},\ 0.02,\ 1,\ -0.5$ **21.** $-4.25,\ 1,\ -\frac{22}{5},\ -4\frac{7}{8},\ -3$

Mental Math **Evaluate the expression. Justify each step you take.**

22. $43 + 68 + 57$ **23.** $7(-8)(5)$ **24.** $-2.4 + [7 + (-0.6)]$

25. $\frac{1}{2} + \frac{4}{7} + \left(-\frac{1}{2}\right)$ **26.** $14 \cdot \frac{2}{3} \cdot \frac{1}{14}$ **27.** $2(3)(35)$

28. Volleyball Court A volleyball court is a rectangle that is 9 m wide and 18 m long. Which property allows you to find the area using either the product 18×9 or the product 9×18? What is the area of the court?

Algebra Evaluate the expression for the given values of the variables. Justify each step you take.

29. $a + (4.8 + b)$ when $a = -2.5$ and $b = -6.5$

30. $x \cdot \left(-\dfrac{2}{3}\right) \cdot y$ when $x = -\dfrac{8}{9}$ and $y = -\dfrac{9}{8}$

Copy and complete the statement using <, >, or =.

31. $-\dfrac{9}{11} + \dfrac{9}{11} \underline{\ ?\ } 1$ **32.** $-0.85 \underline{\ ?\ } -\dfrac{3}{4}$ **33.** $7 \cdot \dfrac{1}{7} \underline{\ ?\ } -1$

34. Critical Thinking Use the properties of addition to show that the expression $a + b + (-a) + (-b)$ is equal to 0. Justify each step you take.

35. Challenge Copy and complete the following statement: The multiplicative inverse of 0.25 is $\underline{\ ?\ }$.

Mixed Review

Evaluate the expression. *(Lesson 1.4)*

36. $\dfrac{32}{4+4}$ **37.** $54 + 3 \cdot 9$ **38.** $35 - 28 \div 4$ **39.** $5(23 - 11)$

Find the quotient. *(Lesson 6.5)*

40. $-180 \div 12$ **41.** $-112 \div 7$ **42.** $84 \div (-14)$ **43.** $-220 \div (-11)$

Basic Skills **Use compatible numbers to estimate the product.**

44. 6429×43 **45.** 27×13 **46.** 386×293 **47.** 252×53

Test-Taking Practice

48. Multiple Choice What is the multiplicative inverse of $1\dfrac{1}{3}$?

A. $\dfrac{3}{4}$ **B.** $\dfrac{4}{3}$ **C.** $\dfrac{3}{1}$ **D.** 4

49. Multiple Choice Which equation illustrates the associative property of addition?

F. $5 + 22 = 22 + 5$ **G.** $(15 + 3) + 67 = 15 + (3 + 67)$

H. $5(-17) = -17(5)$ **I.** $(6 \cdot 8) \cdot 10 = 6 \cdot (8 \cdot 10)$

The Distributive Property

LESSON 6.7

BEFORE	▶ Now	WHY?
You evaluated expressions using order of operations.	You'll evaluate expressions using the distributive property.	So you can find the cost of trading cards, as in Ex. 21.

Word Watch

equivalent expressions, p. 288
distributive property, p. 288

In the Real World

Theater To form two walls for a scene in the play *The Miracle Worker*, a set designer joins a rectangle of plywood with a width of 4 feet and a length of 6 feet to a rectangle with a width of 3 feet and a length of 4 feet. The set designer needs to know the total area of the two pieces in order to purchase wallpaper. What two expressions could be used to find the total area of the pieces?

EXAMPLE 1 **Writing Equivalent Expressions**

You can find the total area by finding the sum of the areas of the separate walls or by finding the area of the walls joined together.

$$\textbf{Area} = 4(3) + 4(6)$$
$$= 12 + 24 = 36$$

$$\textbf{Area} = 4(3 + 6)$$
$$= 4(9) = 36$$

Both expressions in Example 1 are equal to 36. Because the two expressions have the same value, they are called **equivalent expressions**. These expressions are an example of the **distributive property**.

The Distributive Property

Algebra For all numbers a, b, and c, $a(b + c) = ab + ac$ and $a(b - c) = ab - ac$.

Numbers $8(10 + 4) = 8(10) + 8(4)$ and $3(4 - 2) = 3(4) - 3(2)$

EXAMPLE 2 **Writing Equivalent Expressions**

Use the distributive property to write an equivalent expression. Check your answer.

   a. $-4(5 + 8)$ **b.** $4(50 - 3)$ **c.** $7(9) + 7(5)$

Solution

HELP with **Solving**

The *symmetric property of equality* lets you read an equation from left to right or from right to left, so if $a(b + c) = ab + ac$, then $ab + ac = a(b + c)$.

  a. Expression: $-4(5 + 8) = -4(5) + (-4)(8)$ Distributive property

        Check: $-4(13) \stackrel{?}{=} -20 + (-32)$ Simplify.

                  $-52 = -52 \checkmark$ Answer checks.

  b. Expression: $4(50 - 3) = 4(50) - 4(3)$ Distributive property

        Check: $4(47) \stackrel{?}{=} 200 - 12$ Simplify.

                $188 = 188 \checkmark$ Answer checks.

  c. Expression: $7(9) + 7(5) = 7(9 + 5)$ Distributive property

        Check: $63 + 35 \stackrel{?}{=} 7(14)$ Simplify.

                $98 = 98 \checkmark$ Answer checks.

Your turn now   Use the distributive property to write an equivalent expression. Check your answer.

  1. $6\left(\dfrac{1}{7}\right) + 6\left(\dfrac{6}{7}\right)$ **2.** $-6(12 + 3)$ **3.** $8(12 - 5)$ **4.** $3(11) - 3(4)$

EXAMPLE 3 **Using the Distributive Property**

Lava Lamps You are buying 8 small lava lamps as door prizes for a disco party that your school is having. Each lava lamp costs $15.95. Use the distributive property to find the total cost of the lamps.

Solution

$8(15.95) = 8(16.00 - 0.05)$ Write 15.95 as a difference of a whole number and a decimal.

        $= 8(16.00) - 8(0.05)$ Distributive property

        $= 128.00 - 0.40 = 127.60$ Multiply. Then subtract.

ANSWER The total cost of the lava lamps is $127.60.

Getting Ready to Practice

1. **Vocabulary** Copy and complete: You can use the distributive property to write _?_ expressions.

Match the expression with an equivalent expression.

2. $3(4 + 3)$
3. $3(-4 + 3)$
4. $4(3 + 3)$
5. $4(3 - 3)$

A. $4(3) + 4(3)$
B. $3(-4) + 3(3)$
C. $4(3) - 4(3)$
D. $3(4) + 3(3)$

6. **Find the Error** Describe and correct the error in using the distributive property to evaluate the expression $-8(5 + 4)$.

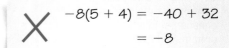

$$-8(5 + 4) = -40 + 32$$
$$= -8$$

7. **Pumpkins** You buy 2 pumpkins to carve for Halloween. The pumpkins weigh 10 pounds and 6 pounds, and cost $.70 per pound. Use the distributive property to write two equivalent expressions to represent the total amount that you pay for the pumpkins.

Practice and Problem Solving

Use the distributive property to write an equivalent expression. Check your answer.

8. $5(3 + 7)$
9. $4(4 + 5)$
10. $7(3) + 7(4)$

11. $8(100 - 4)$
12. $6\left(\dfrac{5}{12}\right) - 6\left(\dfrac{1}{12}\right)$
13. $4\left(\dfrac{3}{5}\right) + 4\left(\dfrac{2}{5}\right)$

Use the distributive property to evaluate the expression.

14. $3(7.3) + 3(2.7)$
15. $4(8.1) + 4(2.9)$
16. $9(13.2) + 9(6.8)$

17. $11\left(\dfrac{5}{8}\right) + 11\left(\dfrac{3}{8}\right)$
18. $13\left(\dfrac{3}{7}\right) - 13\left(-\dfrac{4}{7}\right)$
19. $3(10.4)$

20. **Writing** One meaning of the word *distribute* is to supply or deliver to each individual in a group. How can this meaning help you remember the distributive property?

21. **Trading Cards** A friend is selling his collection of trading cards. He is selling each card for $.95, and you want to purchase 20 cards. Write an expression for the total cost of 20 cards. Then use the distributive property and mental math to evaluate the expression.

HELP with **Homework**

Example	Exercises
1	8–19, 25
2	8–19
3	21–22

Online Resources
CLASSZONE.COM
· More Examples
· eTutorial Plus

22. Talent Show At a talent show, each performer has 2 minutes to set up, 3 minutes for an introduction, and 5 minutes for the act. There are 20 people performing. How long will the talent show be in minutes?

xy **Algebra** **Use the distributive property to find the missing number or variable.**

23. $n \cdot 30 + n \cdot 40 = n(30 + \underline{?})$ **24.** $18 \cdot 4 + 18 \cdot \underline{?} = 18(4 + a)$

25. Quilting A rectangular section of a quilt is made up of two smaller rectangles. The larger of the two rectangles is 8 inches long and 4 inches wide. Its dimensions are twice the dimensions of the smaller rectangle. Write two equivalent expressions for the area of the entire quilt section.

26. Technology You want to find the product 5×215, but the "2" button on your calculator is broken. How can you use the distributive property and your calculator to find the product?

27. Challenge The expression $2l + 2w$ is used to find the perimeter of a rectangle. Use the distributive property to write an equivalent expression for the perimeter. Show that both formulas work for finding the perimeter of a rectangle that is 14 cm long and 12 cm wide.

Mixed Review

Order the integers from least to greatest. *(Lesson 6.1)*

28. $4, -4, 3, -3, 5, -6$ **29.** $7, -8, -9, 10, -5, 8, 9$

Order the rational numbers from least to greatest. *(Lesson 6.6)*

30. $-\frac{1}{2}, 0.2, \frac{2}{5}, -\frac{8}{7}, -2$ **31.** $-\frac{22}{5}, -5, -\frac{21}{4}, -\frac{16}{3}, -4.8$

Basic Skills **Use a ruler to draw a segment with the given length.**

32. $\frac{1}{4}$ inch **33.** $\frac{3}{4}$ inch **34.** $1\frac{5}{16}$ inches **35.** $\frac{7}{16}$ inch

Test-Taking Practice

36. Multiple Choice What is the value of the expression $-9(7 - 2)$?

A. -81 **B.** -65 **C.** -61 **D.** -45

37. Multiple Choice Which expression represents the perimeter of a rectangle with a width of 2 units and a length of 7 units?

F. $2 \cdot 5 + 2$ **G.** $5(2 + 2)$ **H.** $2(7 + 2)$ **I.** $2(2 + 5)$

Making a Scatter Plot

A *scatter plot* is a way to represent paired data visually. Each point on a scatter plot represents one data pair.

Explore Working in a group of six people, make a scatter plot that shows the relationship between height and lower-arm length.

1 Make a table like the one shown. Measure and record the height and lower-arm length of each person in your group to the nearest centimeter. Your lower-arm length is the distance between your elbow and your fingertips.

Name	Height (cm)	Lower-Arm Length (cm)
Damon	155	40
?	?	?

2 Make a scatter plot of your group's data by plotting each person's height and lower-arm length as a data pair. Label the axes and plot the points as shown.

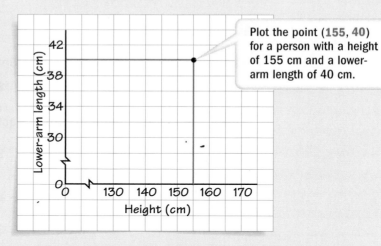

Plot the point (**155, 40**) for a person with a height of 155 cm and a lower-arm length of 40 cm.

Stop and Think

1. **Look for a Pattern** What do you notice about the points on the scatter plot? What tends to happen to a person's lower-arm length as height increases?

2. **Predict** Suppose a student is 170 centimeters tall. Use your scatter plot to predict the student's lower-arm length. Explain your reasoning.

The Coordinate Plane

BEFORE ▸ **Now** **WHY?**

You graphed and compared numbers on a number line.

You'll identify and plot points in a coordinate plane.

So you can find locations in a broadcast area, as in Ex. 41.

Word Watch

coordinate plane, p. 293
x-axis, p. 293
y-axis, p. 293
origin, p. 293
quadrant, p. 293
ordered pair, p. 293
x-coordinate, p. 293
y-coordinate, p. 293
scatter plot, p. 295

A **coordinate plane** is formed by the intersection of a horizontal number line, called the **x-axis**, and a vertical number line, called the **y-axis**. The x-axis and the y-axis meet at a point called the **origin** and divide the coordinate plane into four **quadrants**.

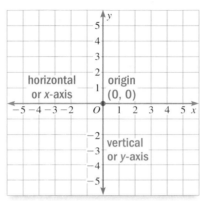

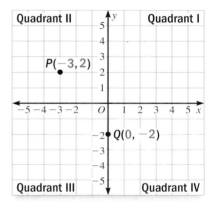

Points in a coordinate plane are represented by **ordered pairs** in which the first number is the **x-coordinate** and the second number is the **y-coordinate**. For example, in the graph at the right above, point P is represented by the ordered pair $(-3, 2)$ and lies in Quadrant II. Point Q is represented by the ordered pair $(0, -2)$ and lies on the y-axis. A point on an axis is not in any quadrant.

EXAMPLE 1 Naming Ordered Pairs

Name the ordered pair that represents the point.

a. A **b.** B

Solution

a. Point A is 3 units to the right of the origin and 4 units up. So, the x-coordinate is 3 and the y-coordinate is 4. Point A is represented by the ordered pair $(3, 4)$.

b. Point B is 2 units to the left of the origin and 3 units down. So, the x-coordinate is -2 and the y-coordinate is -3. Point B is represented by the ordered pair $(-2, -3)$.

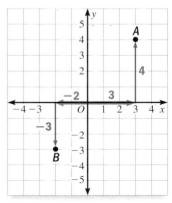

EXAMPLE 2   Plotting Points in a Coordinate Plane

Plot the point and describe its location.

a. $P(3, -4)$ **b.** $Q(-1, -3)$ **c.** $R(0, 2)$

Solution

a. Begin at the origin. Move 3 units to the right, then 4 units down. Point P is located in Quadrant IV.

b. Begin at the origin. Move 1 unit to the left, then 3 units down. Point Q is located in Quadrant III.

c. Begin at the origin. Move 2 units up. Point R is located on the y-axis.

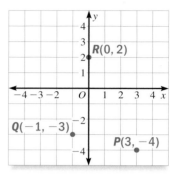

Your turn now   **Plot the point and describe its location.**

1. $A(2, 3)$ **2.** $B(0, 0)$ **3.** $C(-2, 0)$ **4.** $D(-1, -4)$

EXAMPLE 3   Finding Segment Lengths and Area

Find the length, width, and area of rectangle *ABCD* shown.

The length of the rectangle is the *horizontal* distance between A and B. To find this distance, find the absolute value of the difference between the x-coordinates of A and B.

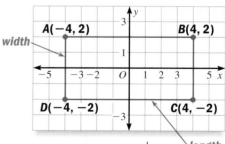

$$\textbf{Length} = \left| x\text{-coordinate of } A - x\text{-coordinate of } B \right|$$

$$= \left| -4 - 4 \right| = \left| -8 \right| = \textbf{8 units}$$

The width of the rectangle is the *vertical* distance between A and D. To find this distance, find the absolute value of the difference between the y-coordinates of A and D.

$$\textbf{Width} = \left| y\text{-coordinate of } A - y\text{-coordinate of } D \right|$$

$$= \left| 2 - (-2) \right| = \left| 4 \right| = \textbf{4 units}$$

The area of the rectangle is found by multiplying the length and width.

$$\textbf{Area} = lw = 8(4) = \textbf{32 square units}$$

Scatter Plots You can use a coordinate plane to make a **scatter plot** of paired data. Each data pair is plotted as a point, and from the collection of plotted points you can recognize patterns and make predictions.

EXAMPLE 4 **Making a Scatter Plot**

Pine Trees The table gives the ages and heights of 10 pine trees. Make a scatter plot of the data. Then make a conclusion about the data.

Age (years)	0	1	6	10	13	18	21	32	36	39
Height (feet)	0	2	4	8	14	16	23	31	34	34

Solution

Make a scatter plot of the data pairs. Use the first quadrant of a coordinate plane, and show age on the *x*-axis and height on the *y*-axis.

Because the points tend to rise from left to right, you can conclude that as the age of a pine tree increases, its height tends to increase as well.

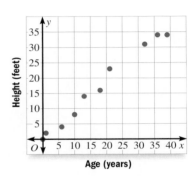

■ **Pine Trees**

Only $\frac{1}{100}$ to $\frac{3}{100}$ of short leaf pine tree seeds become seedlings. If one bushel of short leaf pine cones produces 34,000 seeds, what is the greatest number of seedlings that could be produced from the bushel?

6.8 Exercises
More Practice, p. 710

INTERNET
eWorkbook Plus
CLASSZONE.COM

Getting Ready to Practice

1. Vocabulary Copy and complete: In a coordinate plane, the horizontal number line is called the __?__.

Plot the point and describe its location.

2. $L(-3, 3)$ **3.** $M(0, -3)$ **4.** $N(-2, -4)$ **5.** $P(4, 1)$

6. Make a conclusion about the data shown in the scatter plot.

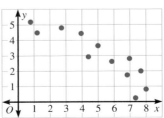

Practice and Problem Solving

with Homework

Example	Exercises
1	7–16, 25
2	17–24
3	26–28
4	29–30, 40

Online Resources
CLASSZONE.COM

· More Examples
· eTutorial Plus

Name the ordered pair that represents the point.

7. A

8. B

9. C

10. D

11. E

12. F

13. G

14. H

15. J

16. K

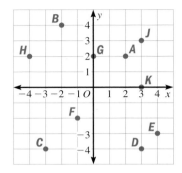

Plot the point and describe its location.

17. $R(-2, 5)$

18. $S(7, 0)$

19. $T(-1, -8)$

20. $U(6, 3)$

21. $V(4, -2)$

22. $W(-4, -5)$

23. $X(0, -4)$

24. $Y(5, -7)$

25. **Shipwrecks** Suppose a researcher uses a coordinate plane where each unit is equal to 1 mile to record the location of a shipwreck. The research station is the origin. The shipwreck is 4 miles to the east and 8 miles south of the station. What ordered pair can the researcher use to represent the location of the shipwreck?

Plot and connect the points to form a rectangle. Then find the length, width, and area of the rectangle.

26. $A(0, 0)$, $B(6, 0)$, $C(6, 2)$, $D(0, 2)$

27. $W(3, -4)$, $X(-1, -4)$, $Y(-1, -5)$, $Z(3, -5)$

28. $E(3, 4)$, $F(-5, 4)$, $G(-5, 2)$, $H(3, 2)$

Fuel Economy In Exercises 29 and 30, use the table below showing the engine size, in liters, and highway mileage, in miles per gallon, for 12 cars.

Engine Size (liters)	3	5	1	6	2	2	4	3	3	2	4	5
Highway Mileage (mi/gal)	28	23	47	19	33	31	25	24	25	37	24	22

29. Make a scatter plot of the data. Then make a conclusion about the data.

30. What would you predict the highway mileage to be for a 5.5 liter engine?

xy **Algebra** **Tell what you know about the numbers *x* and *y*, given the location of the point (*x*, *y*).**

31. The point is in Quadrant I.   **32.** The point is in Quadrant IV.

33. The point is on the *x*-axis.   **34.** The point is on the *y*-axis.

35. The point is in Quadrant II.   **36.** The point is in Quadrant III.

Extended Problem Solving **In Exercises 37–39, use the following information.** Suppose a computerized drill follows instructions that are given as ordered pairs in which the first number in the ordered pair determines horizontal movement and the second number determines vertical movement. For example, given the instruction (−3, −4), the drill would move 3 units left and 4 units down from (0, 0), drill a hole, and return to (0, 0).

37. Compare Compare the movements made by the drill given the instructions (6, −7) and (−7, 6).

38. Predict What movement would the drill make given the instruction (0, 9)?

39. Apply Give the instructions the drill would need in order to make each hole shown on the graph.

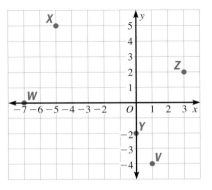

40. Red Foxes Suppose a group of scientists are recording information on a population of red foxes in a geographic region. The ordered pairs show the length, in feet, and the weight, in pounds, of 15 red foxes. Make a scatter plot of the data. Then make a conclusion about the data.

(3, 8), (3.4, 11), (3.1, 8.5), (3.5, 13), (3.5, 12.5), (3, 9), (3.7, 15), (3.7, 14.5), (3.4, 10), (3.3, 12), (3.2, 9), (3.2, 11.5), (3.6, 14.5), (3.6, 15), (3.5, 14)

Radio Broadcasting **In Exercises 41 and 42, use the coordinate plane, which shows the broadcast area of a radio station as a circle and its interior.**

41. Determine whether houses located at the following points are in the station's broadcast area.

A(9, 9), *B*(−6, −6), *C*(4, −5), *D*(−3, 9)

42. Challenge How far does the radio station's broadcast reach in every direction if the scale on the coordinate plane is in miles? Explain your reasoning.

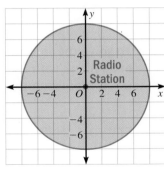

Mixed Review ⟳

Use the distributive property to evaluate the expression. *(Lesson 6.7)*

43. $6(10.21) - 6(8.21)$ **44.** $12(3.4) + 12(2.6)$ **45.** $6(2.3)$

Choose a Strategy Use a strategy from the list to solve the following problem. Explain your choice of strategy.

46. A square piece of plywood with a side length of 6 inches can be cut into 9 squares of equal size. What are the dimensions of each small square?

Problem Solving Strategies

- Look for a Pattern
- Solve a Related Problem
- Draw a Diagram
- Estimate

Basic Skills Solve the following problem.

47. There are 8 snack cakes in one box. How many boxes do you need so you can give one snack cake to each of 32 students?

Test-Taking Practice ✎

48. Multiple Choice In which quadrant is the point $K(-4, 2)$ located?

  A. I   **B.** II   **C.** III   **D.** IV

49. Multiple Choice What is the length of a line segment with endpoints $G(3, 3)$ and $H(3, -4)$?

  F. -7 units   **G.** 0 units   **H.** 3 units   **I.** 7 units

BRAIN GAME

The more there is, the less you **Sẽẽ!**

To solve the riddle given in the title, fill in each blank with the letter located at the point represented by the ordered pair.

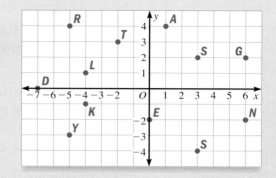

_____   _____   _____   _____   _____   _____   _____   _____

$(-7, 0)$ $(1, 4)$ $(-5, 4)$ $(-4, -1)$ $(6, -2)$ $(0, -2)$ $(3, 2)$ $(3, -4)$

Graphing in a Coordinate Plane

GOAL Graph ordered pairs using a graphing calculator.

A graphing calculator allows you to graph ordered pairs in a coordinate plane.

Example **Graph the ordered pairs (4, −1) and (2, 3).**

Solution

① Clear Lists 1 and 2 (L1 and L2) on your calculator. Then enter the *x*-coordinates of the ordered pairs in L1 and the *y*-coordinates of the ordered pairs in L2.

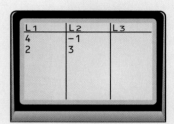

Keystrokes

2nd [STAT] ▶ 3 2nd [STAT] 1 , 2nd [STAT] 2 ENTER

LIST 4 ENTER 2 ENTER ▶ (−) 1 ENTER 3 ENTER

② Prepare the calculator to graph the ordered pairs.

Keystrokes

2nd [PLOT] ENTER

Select the options as shown on the screen at the right. To select an item, put the cursor on the item and press ENTER.

③ Graph the ordered pairs by pressing ZOOM 6.

HELP with **Technology**

Many calculator keys have two uses. The use shown by the label above the key is called the *second function*. To use the second function of a key, press 2nd before pressing the key. In Step 2, use [PLOT], the second function of Y=.

Your turn now **Graph the ordered pair and describe its location.**

1. (6, 8)   **2.** (−4, 8)   **3.** (7, −8)   **4.** (−4, −4)

Notebook Review

Review the vocabulary definitions in your notebook.

Copy the review examples in your notebook. Then complete the exercises.

Check Your Definitions

rational number, p. 283
additive inverse, p. 285
multiplicative inverse, p. 285
additive identity, p. 285
multiplicative identity, p. 285

equivalent expressions, p. 288
distributive property, p. 288
coordinate plane, p. 293
x-axis, p. 293
y-axis, p. 293

origin, p. 293
quadrant, p. 293
ordered pair, p. 293
x-coordinate, p. 293
y-coordinate, p. 293
scatter plot, p 295

Use Your Vocabulary

1. Copy and complete: In a coordinate plane, the point represented by the ordered pair (0, 0) is the called the ? .

6.4–6.5 Can you multiply and divide integers?

 EXAMPLE Find the product or quotient.

a. $5(-4) = -20$ The product of two integers with different signs is negative.

b. $-36 \div (-12) = 3$ The quotient of two integers with the same sign is positive.

 Find the product or quotient.

2. $-4(-10)$ 3. $-3(16)$ 4. $0 \div (-6)$ 5. $56 \div (-7)$

6.6–6.7 Can you use properties to evaluate expressions?

 EXAMPLE Evaluate the expression. Justify each step you take.

$$-12(7)(-5) = -12(-5)(7)$$ Commutative property of multiplication

$$= 60(7) = 420$$ Multiply −12 and −5, then 60 and 7.

 Evaluate the expression. Justify each step you take.

6. $\dfrac{5}{8} \cdot \dfrac{3}{16} \cdot \dfrac{8}{5}$ 7. $-3(1.2)$ 8. $-4(7)(-5)$

9. $4(3.2) + 4(0.8)$ 10. $12(10.2)$ 11. $-3.7 + 8 + (-4.3)$

EXAMPLE Plot the point $A(-2, -1)$ and describe its location.

Start at the origin. Move 2 units to the left and 1 unit down. The point lies in Quadrant III.

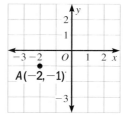

☑ **Plot the point and describe its location.**

12. $H(4, -5)$ **13.** $J(0, 3)$

14. $K(-6, -2)$ **15.** $L(-7, 0)$

Stop and Think about Lessons 6.4–6.8

16. Writing Is division associative? Use the expressions $[(-12) \div 6] \div (-2)$ and $(-12) \div [6 \div (-2)]$ to support your answer.

Review Quiz 2

Find the product or quotient.

1. $-18 \div 9$ **2.** $3(-25)$ **3.** $-3(-12)$ **4.** $-21 \div (-3)$

5. Stock Market A newspaper reports these changes in the price of a stock over five days: $-1, -3, 5, -8, 2$. Find the mean daily change.

Evaluate the expression. Justify each step you take.

6. $(-5)(9)\left(-\dfrac{1}{5}\right)$ **7.** $\dfrac{1}{16}(-4)(16)$ **8.** $-3.4 + 7 + (-3.6)$

Use the distributive property to evaluate the expression.

9. $20(2) + 20(7)$ **10.** $12(9) - 12(3)$ **11.** $4(6.9)$

12. Car Wash The members of a club hold a car wash and earn $4.25 for each car they wash and $3.75 for each car they wax. The club washes and waxes 16 cars. Use the distributive property to write and evaluate an expression for the total amount of money the club earned.

13. Plot the points $K(4, -5)$ and $L(-7, 0)$ and describe the location of each point.

14. Plot and connect the points $A(-5, 4)$, $B(2, 4)$, $C(2, -2)$, and $D(-5, -2)$ to form a rectangle. Then find the length, width, and area of the rectangle.

Chapter Review

 Vocabulary

integer, p. 251
negative integer, p. 251
positive integer, p. 251
opposite, p. 251
absolute value, p. 259
rational number, p. 283
additive inverse, p. 285
multiplicative inverse,
    p. 285

additive identity, p. 285
multiplicative identity,
    p. 285
equivalent expressions,
    p. 288
distributive property,
    p. 288
coordinate plane, p. 293
x-axis, p. 293

y-axis, p. 293
origin, p. 293
quadrant, p. 293
ordered pair, p. 293
x-coordinate, p. 293
y-coordinate, p. 293
scatter plot, p. 295

Vocabulary Review

1. Which of the following numbers are both integers and opposites?

$$2.3, -4, 5, -2.3, -2, 4$$

2. Define absolute value in your own words.

3. Define a rational number.

4. Explain the difference between additive inverse and additive identity.

5. How is the multiplicative inverse of a number different from the additive inverse of the number?

6. Draw a coordinate plane. Label the x-axis, the y-axis, and the origin.

Review Questions

Copy and complete the statement using < or >. *(Lesson 6.1)*

7. $12 \underline{\ ?\ } -23$

8. $-44 \underline{\ ?\ } 7$

9. $-21 \underline{\ ?\ } -19$

10. $-4 \underline{\ ?\ } -7$

Order the integers from least to greatest. *(Lesson 6.1)*

11. $7, 9, 8, -8, -10, 11$

12. $45, 53, -17, 42, -22, -68$

13. Finance Write the integer that corresponds to a bank withdrawal of $350. *(Lesson 6.1)*

Find the sum or difference. *(Lessons 6.2, 6.3)*

14. $1 - 8$

15. $-14 + 29$

16. $11 - (-2)$

17. $-7 - 3$

18. $31 + (-73)$

19. $34 - (-41)$

20. $-47 + (-13)$

21. $-16 + (-22)$

Algebra Evaluate the expression when $x = -19$ and $s = 7$. *(Lessons 6.2, 6.3)*

22. $s - 29$

23. $18 - x$

24. $x + (-6)$

25. $x - s$

26. Lowest Points The lowest point in Europe is 28 meters below sea level. The lowest point in Australia is 16 meters higher than the lowest point in Europe. Write an addition expression involving integers that you could use to find the elevation of the lowest point in Australia. Then evaluate the expression. *(Lesson 6.2)*

27. Freeze-Dried Ice Cream During the freeze-drying process, all of the water content is removed from the food item. To freeze-dry ice cream, regular ice cream is frozen at a temperature of $-40°F$ and then dried in a vacuum. Convert this temperature to degrees Celsius. *(Lesson 6.5)*

Find the product or quotient. *(Lessons 6.4, 6.5)*

28. $-88 \div 22$ **29.** $-10(10)$ **30.** $-27(0)$ **31.** $96 \div (-32)$

32. $-6(-3)$ **33.** $0 \div (-37)$ **34.** $-87 \div (-29)$ **35.** $-9(-2)(-3)$

Show that the numbers are rational by writing each number in $\frac{a}{b}$ form. Then order the numbers from least to greatest. *(Lesson 6.6)*

36. $-3.7, 3\frac{5}{8}, -3.1, -\frac{16}{5}, 3$ **37.** $2.4, -2.1, -2\frac{4}{5}, 2, 2\frac{1}{9}$

Evaluate the expression. Justify each step you take. *(Lesson 6.6)*

38. $-\frac{2}{3} + \left(-\frac{2}{3}\right) + \frac{2}{3}$ **39.** $12 \cdot (-27) \cdot \frac{1}{12}$ **40.** $\frac{3}{7} \cdot (-1) \cdot \frac{7}{3}$ **41.** $-\frac{1}{4} \cdot 1 \cdot (-4)$

Use the distributive property to write an equivalent expression. Then evaluate the expression. *(Lesson 6.7)*

42. $9\left(\frac{5}{12}\right) + 9\left(\frac{7}{12}\right)$ **43.** $4(0.38)$ **44.** $4(7) + 4(6)$ **45.** $9(2.6) + 9(5.4)$

Plot the point and describe its location. *(Lesson 6.8)*

46. $A(0, -5)$ **47.** $V(5, -3)$ **48.** $X(-4, 3)$ **49.** $G(1, 4)$

50. Plot the points $P(-6, -7)$ and $Q(3, -7)$. Then find the distance between the two points. *(Lesson 6.8)*

51. Butter Clams The ordered pairs show the widths and lengths, in centimeters, of nine butter clam shells. Make a scatter plot of the data. Then make a conclusion about the data. *(Lesson 6.8)*

     $(2.1, 2.7), (3.1, 4.1), (3.0, 4.0), (2.8, 3.8), (2.8, 3.5), (2.6, 3.5),$
     $(2.4, 3.2), (2.9, 3.8), (2.6, 3.4)$

Chapter Test

Order the integers from least to greatest.

1. $16, -17, 34, 7, -15$ **2.** $38, -120, 201, -12, -422$ **3.** $-72, -54, 102, 33, 16$

4. Elevation Write the integer that represents an elevation of 36 feet below sea level.

5. Coldest Temperature The coldest recorded temperature in South Carolina is $-28°C$, and the coldest recorded temperature in North Carolina is $-37°C$. Which state has the lower recorded temperature?

Find the sum, difference, product, or quotient.

6. $-12 + 10$ **7.** $11 + (-8)$ **8.** $-9 + (-9)$ **9.** $-4 - (-6)$

10. $7 - (-27)$ **11.** $36 - 56$ **12.** $15(-3)$ **13.** $-20(-4)$

14. $-12(-3)$ **15.** $-54 \div (-27)$ **16.** $-46 \div (-23)$ **17.** $54 \div (-9)$

18. Hot Air Balloons A hot air balloon descends 210 feet each minute when landing. What is the change in the altitude of the balloon after 3 minutes?

Show that the numbers are rational by writing each number in $\frac{a}{b}$ form. Then order the numbers from least to greatest.

19. $9.6, -\frac{7}{9}, -5, -4\frac{5}{6}, 9\frac{1}{2}$ **20.** $2\frac{5}{6}, 0, -2.3, -3\frac{3}{4}, 2.4$

Evaluate the expression. Justify each step you take.

21. $\frac{2}{9} + \frac{8}{13} + \left(-\frac{2}{9}\right)$ **22.** $9 \cdot 16 \cdot \frac{1}{9}$ **23.** $5\left(\frac{5}{6}\right) - 5\left(-\frac{1}{6}\right)$ **24.** $4(8.5)$

25. Baby-Sitting You baby-sit for 5 hours at $7.75 an hour. Use the distributive property to write and evaluate an expression to find the amount you earn.

26. Glitter Pens You buy three glitter pens. Each pen costs $.95. Use the distributive property to write and evaluate an expression to find the total cost of the pens.

27. Plot and connect the points $C(-6, 0)$, $D(-6, -3)$, $E(-1, -3)$, and $F(-1, 0)$ to form a rectangle. Then find the length, width, and area of the rectangle.

Chapter Standardized Test

Test-Taking Strategy If you find yourself frustrated by a question on a test, move on to the next question. Return to the question you were having trouble with later.

Multiple Choice

1. Which integer is less than -13?

    A. -14 **B.** -12 **C.** -9 **D.** -6

2. Which set of integers is in order from least to greatest?

    F. $-3, -5, -7, -9$ **G.** $-3, 5, 7, 9$

    H. $-9, -7, 5, -3$ **I.** $5, 7, 9, -13$

3. Which statement is true when $x = -3$ and $y = |-3|$?

    A. $y < x$ **B.** $0 > y$ **C.** $x < y$ **D.** $x > 0$

4. Which expression has a value greater than -3?

    F. $4 + (-9)$ **G.** $3 + (-8) + 1$

    H. $-10 + 8$ **I.** $-1 + (-5) + 2$

5. Find $38 - (-16)$.

    A. -16 **B.** -6 **C.** 16 **D.** 54

6. The product of two integers is ? .

    F. always positive   **G.** never zero

    H. sometimes negative   **I.** always zero

7. What is the mean of the following set of numbers?

$$8, -13, -9, 4, 2, -16$$

    A. -24 **B.** -4 **C.** -3.5 **D.** 4

8. The temperature of a room is 68°F. What is the temperature in degrees Celsius?

    F. $-20°C$ **G.** $20°C$ **H.** $36°C$ **I.** $154.4°C$

9. Which property states that the value of the sum $-7 + 9 + (-3)$ is the same as the value of the sum $9 + (-7) + (-3)$?

    A. Associative property of addition

    B. Commutative property of addition

    C. Distributive property

    D. Additive identity property

10. What is the product of -2 and its multiplicative inverse?

    F. -1 **G.** $-\frac{1}{2}$ **H.** 1 **I.** 2

11. You buy two DVDs on sale for \$14.09 each. Which expression represents the total cost of the two DVDs?

    A. $2(14) + 2(0.09)$ **B.** $14(2 + 0.09)$

    C. $2(14 - 0.09)$ **D.** $2(14) + 0.09$

12. Which point is located in Quadrant IV?

    F. $(-4, 7)$ **G.** $(0, 0)$ **H.** $(1, -1)$ **I.** $(-3, -5)$

Short Response

13. Describe the pattern below. Then write the next three numbers.

$$2, -4, 8, -16, \ldots$$

Extended Response

14. A city planner uses a coordinate plane to design a new rectangular park. The four corners of the park are represented by the ordered pairs $(2, 2)$, $(6, 2)$, $(2, 0)$, and $(6, 0)$. Graph the ordered pairs. Then find the perimeter and the area of the new park if each unit on the graph represents 20 feet.

Strategies for Answering
Short Response Questions

A *short response* question should take about five minutes to answer. A solution should include the work or reasoning that leads to a correct answer. The three ways a solution can be scored are listed at the left.

Problem
You are organizing a karaoke night at your school. You allow an average of $3\frac{1}{2}$ minutes for each act to set up and $5\frac{1}{4}$ minutes for the song. How many acts can fit in a program that runs $1\frac{1}{2}$ hours?

Full credit solution

The steps of the solution are clearly written.

The number of acts equals the total number of minutes for the program divided by the sum of the set-up time and song time for each act.

This reasoning is the key to choosing the operations you need.

Acts = Total time ÷ (Set-up time + Song time)

$$= 90 \div \left(3\frac{1}{2} + 5\frac{1}{4}\right) = 90 \div 8\frac{3}{4}$$

$$= 90 \div \frac{35}{4} = 90 \times \frac{4}{35} = \frac{72}{7} = 10\frac{2}{7}$$

The question is answered correctly.

Because there is not enough time for 11 acts, the program can have 10 acts.

Partial credit solution

Divide the total amount of time, 90 minutes, by the time needed for each act, $8\frac{3}{4}$ minutes.

The reasoning and calculations are correct.

Acts $= 90 \div \frac{35}{4} = 90 \times \frac{4}{35} = \frac{72}{7} = 10\frac{2}{7}$

The answer makes no sense. You cannot have a fractional number of acts.

The program can have $10\frac{2}{7}$ acts.

Partial credit solution

The problem does not call for an estimated answer.

The total amount of time for each act is about 9 minutes.

You can have 10 acts.

The answer is correct, but there is no evidence of work or calculations.

No credit solution

The units are not equivalent. Hours should be converted to minutes.

$$1\frac{1}{2} \div (3\frac{1}{2} + 5\frac{1}{4}) = 1\frac{1}{2} \div 8\frac{3}{4}$$

$$= \frac{3}{2} \times \frac{35}{4} = \frac{105}{8} = 13\frac{1}{8}$$

The student did not multiply by the reciprocal.

The answer is incorrect.

You can have 13 acts.

Watch Out!

Remember to think about positive and negative numbers when working with deposits and withdrawals.

Your turn now

Score each solution to the short response question as _full credit_, _partial credit_, or _no credit_. Explain your reasoning.

Problem Derek had $57 in his checking account. He wrote a check for $45 to buy sneakers. Then he remembered that he had withdrawn $20 the day before. How much must Derek deposit to avoid a service fee for insufficient funds?

1. $57 + $45 − $20 = $82. Derek must deposit $82 to avoid a service fee.

2. $57 − $20 = $37; $37 − $45 = −$8. After the $20 withdrawal, Derek had $37 in his account. He spent $45, which was $8 more than he had. Derek must deposit $8 to avoid a service fee.

3. Derek had $57. He spent $45 on sneakers. He had $12 left. Then he remembered the $20 withdrawal. So he had $8. Derek needs to deposit $8 to avoid a service fee.

GO ON

Short Response

1. Alice has two rolls of streamers to use in decorating the school gym for a dance. One roll is 64 feet long, and the other roll is 72 feet long. If she wants to cut the streamers into strips of equal length and have no leftover materials, what is the greatest length each strip can be?

2. Jan is making gift baskets. She has 104 jars of jam, 26 boxes of chocolate, and 65 scented candles. If the gift baskets are identical and there are no leftovers, what is the greatest number of gift baskets that can be made? How many jars of jam, boxes of chocolate, and scented candles would be in each gift basket?

3. At the town fair, George sold glasses of lemonade for 60 cents each. With the money he earned, he bought several bags of popcorn for 75 cents each. If he didn't have any change after buying the popcorn, what is the fewest number of glasses of lemonade he could have sold?

4. Mrs. Willis and Mr. Roberts gave the same test to their seventh-grade classes. Which class had the greater fraction of students who passed the test? Explain.

Mrs. Willis's Class		Mr. Robert's Class	
Passed	Failed	Passed	Failed
28	8	26	6

5. In the last 4 days, Rachel walked $1\frac{1}{4}$ miles, 2 miles, $3\frac{1}{2}$ miles, and $2\frac{3}{4}$ miles. Her goal was to walk a total of 9 miles by the end of the fourth day. Did she meet her goal? Explain your reasoning.

6. When you asked 12 of your friends what they did over the weekend, $\frac{1}{4}$ of them said they went bowling. Of your remaining friends, $\frac{2}{3}$ of them went roller skating. The rest of your friends stayed home. How many of your friends stayed home? Explain your reasoning.

7. You make 3 gallons of iced tea. Do you have enough iced tea to fill 16 bottles that each hold 20 fluid ounces? If so, how many fluid ounces will you have left? If not, how many more fluid ounces will you need? Explain your reasoning.

8. The integers 12, -20, -7, 22, -6, and 2 are temperature readings in degrees Celsius. Graph the integers on a number line and find the median temperature.

9. During halftime at a basketball game, your parents go to the concession stand to buy a sandwich and a drink for everyone. Each sandwich costs \$3.75, and each drink costs \$1.25. Your parents order 4 sandwiches and 4 drinks. Use the distributive property to write and evaluate an expression for the total amount of money your parents spend.

10. Graph the first three points in the table in a coordinate plane. To form a rectangle, what must the ordered pair be that represents point D? Then find the length, width, and perimeter of rectangle $ABCD$.

Point	Ordered Pair
A	$(-4, 2)$
B	$(3, 2)$
C	$(3, -3)$
D	$(?, ?)$

Multiple Choice

11. Which number is a common factor of 56 and 84?

A. 3   **B.** 6   **C.** 7   **D.** 8

12. What is the least common multiple of 81 and 105?

F. 105   **G.** 945   **H.** 2835   **I.** 8505

13. Find the difference $\frac{4}{5} - \frac{3}{10}$.

A. $\frac{1}{10}$ **B.** $\frac{1}{5}$ **C.** $\frac{1}{2}$ **D.** $\frac{3}{5}$

14. What is the value of $3\frac{1}{3} \div x$ when $x = \frac{5}{6}$?

F. $\frac{1}{4}$ **G.** $2\frac{1}{2}$ **H.** $2\frac{7}{9}$ **I.** 4

15. Which of the following measurements is the greatest?

A. 3 qt   **B.** 5 pt   **C.** 11 c   **D.** 90 fl oz

16. The table shows the highest and lowest temperatures ever recorded in 4 states. Which state has the greatest range?

State	High	Low
California	135°F	−45°F
Florida	109°F	−2°F
Illinois	117°F	−36°F
Nevada	125°F	−50°F

F. Nevada   **G.** Illinois

H. Florida   **I.** California

17. What is the mean of the following set of numbers?

$$-1, -2, -1, 0, 1, -1, -2, -2$$

A. −2   **B.** −1   **C.** 0   **D.** 1

18. Which ordered pair represents a point located in Quadrant IV?

F. $(-2, 2)$ **G.** $(2, -2)$ **H.** $(2, 2)$ **I.** $(-2, -2)$

Extended Response

19. There are 200 girls and 250 boys being placed on coed basketball teams. Each team will have the same number of girls and the same number of boys. What is the greatest number of teams that can be formed? How many players would be on each team? Write the number of girls on a team to the number of boys on the team as a fraction.

20. The corner points for a rectangular garden are plotted in a coordinate plane as shown. Name the ordered pair that represents each point. Then find the area and perimeter of the garden if each unit in the coordinate plane represents 5 feet.

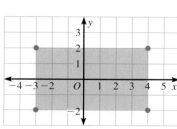

21. Mrs. Martin bought $27\frac{1}{4}$ yards of material. She used $22\frac{1}{2}$ yards to make 5 bridesmaid dresses. She used half of the remaining material to make 1 flower girl dress. How much material was used for each bridesmaid dress? How much material was used for the flower girl dress?

Cumulative Practice for Chapters 4–6

Chapter 4

Multiple Choice **In Exercises 1–8, choose the letter of the correct answer.**

1. What is the prime factorization of 126? *(Lesson 4.1)*

   A. $2 \times 7 \times 9$ **B.** $2 \times 3^2 \times 7$

   C. 2×63 **D.** 7×18

2. What is the GCF of 28 and 36? *(Lesson 4.2)*

   F. 2   **G.** 4   **H.** 7   **I.** 9

3. Which fraction is in simplest form? *(Lesson 4.3)*

   A. $\frac{50}{100}$ **B.** $\frac{18}{27}$ **C.** $\frac{21}{25}$ **D.** $\frac{32}{34}$

4. What is the LCM of 6 and 21? *(Lesson 4.4)*

   F. 18   **G.** 21   **H.** 42   **I.** 84

5. The graph shows the number of songs on each of 4 CDs and the number of songs Juan liked on each CD. On which CD did Juan like the greatest fraction of songs? *(Lesson 4.5)*

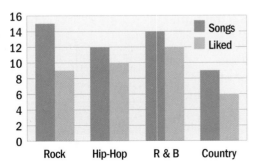

   A. Rock   **B.** Hip-Hop

   C. R & B   **D.** Country

6. What is $5\frac{1}{8}$ written as an improper fraction? *(Lesson 4.6)*

   F. $\frac{13}{8}$ **G.** $\frac{14}{8}$ **H.** $\frac{41}{8}$ **I.** $\frac{42}{8}$

7. What is $\frac{22}{9}$ written as a mixed number? *(Lesson 4.6)*

   A. $1\frac{4}{9}$ **B.** $2\frac{2}{9}$ **C.** $2\frac{4}{9}$ **D.** $22\frac{1}{9}$

8. Which decimal is equivalent to $\frac{2}{5}$? *(Lesson 4.7)*

   F. 0.2   **G.** 0.25   **H.** 0.4   **I.** 0.6

9. **Short Response** Habib has 42 postcards from around the world. He wants to arrange them in his scrapbook in groups that each have an equal number of postcards. How many ways can he do this? Explain your answer. *(Lesson 4.1)*

10. **Extended Response** The animals on a family farm are listed in the table. *(Lessons 4.3, 4.5)*

Animal	Number
Hen	4
Pig	12
Sheep	10
Horse	8
Cow	6

   a. What fraction of the farm animals are pigs?

   b. What fraction of the farm animals are sheep or horses?

   c. What fraction of the farm animals are cows?

   d. Write your answers from parts (a), (b), and (c) in order from least to greatest.

Chapter 5

Multiple Choice In Exercises 11–20, choose the letter of the correct answer.

11. The Chen family spends $\frac{1}{3}$ of their budget on housing costs and $\frac{2}{5}$ of their budget on food and clothing. What fraction of their budget is spent on these items combined? *(Lesson 5.1)*

A. $\frac{3}{8}$ **B.** $\frac{1}{2}$ **C.** $\frac{11}{15}$ **D.** $1\frac{5}{12}$

12. What is the sum of $\frac{3}{4}$ and $\frac{2}{3}$? *(Lesson 5.1)*

F. $\frac{1}{12}$ **G.** $\frac{3}{8}$ **H.** $\frac{1}{2}$ **I.** $1\frac{5}{12}$

13. Find the difference $8\frac{1}{8} - 3\frac{1}{4}$. *(Lesson 5.2)*

A. $2\frac{5}{6}$ **B.** $4\frac{7}{8}$ **C.** $5\frac{1}{3}$ **D.** $9\frac{11}{16}$

14. What is $2\frac{5}{8} \times 7\frac{1}{3}$? *(Lesson 5.3)*

F. $4\frac{17}{24}$ **G.** $9\frac{23}{24}$ **H.** $14\frac{5}{24}$ **I.** $19\frac{1}{4}$

15. How many times must you run around a $\frac{1}{4}$ mile track to run $2\frac{1}{2}$ miles? *(Lesson 5.4)*

A. $2\frac{1}{2}$ **B.** 8   **C.** 10   **D.** 12

16. Find the quotient $\frac{5}{8} \div \frac{3}{4}$. *(Lesson 5.4)*

F. $\frac{15}{32}$ **G.** $\frac{5}{9}$ **H.** $\frac{5}{6}$ **I.** 3

17. Which is the greatest length? *(Lesson 5.5)*

A. 44 in.   **B.** $\frac{1}{4}$ mi   **C.** 6 yd   **D.** 4334 ft

18. What is a reasonable capacity for a yogurt container? *(Lesson 5.5)*

F. 1 gal   **G.** 3 qt   **H.** 10 c   **I.** 8 fl oz

19. How many quarts are there in 40 fluid ounces? *(Lesson 5.6)*

A. $1\frac{1}{4}$ qt   **B.** 2 qt   **C.** $2\frac{1}{4}$ qt   **D.** 3 qt

20. The square tile shown is measured in feet. What is the perimeter of the tile in *inches*? *(Lesson 5.6)*

3 ft

3 ft

F. 9 in.   **G.** 12 in.   **H.** 108 in.   **I.** 144 in.

21. **Short Response** At a fish market, a pound of salmon costs \$6 and a pound of shrimp costs \$12. Mr. Hart wants to buy $2\frac{1}{3}$ pounds of salmon and $3\frac{1}{2}$ pounds of shrimp. If he has \$55, can he buy the amounts of salmon and shrimp he wants? Explain. *(Lesson 5.3)*

22. **Extended Response** The table gives the triple jump attempts made by 2 athletes in a track meet. Use the table to answer the questions below. *(Lessons 5.2, 5.4)*

Athlete	1st Jump	2nd Jump	3rd Jump
Leslie	$41\frac{3}{5}$ ft	$39\frac{5}{6}$ ft	$40\frac{2}{3}$ ft
Jade	$40\frac{1}{12}$ ft	$38\frac{2}{3}$ ft	$42\frac{1}{4}$ ft

a. Out of all the jumps, which girl jumped the farthest?

b. Find the difference between the longest jump distance and the shortest jump distance for each girl.

c. Which girl has the greater mean jump distance?

d. How does your answer from part (c) compare with your answer from part (a)? How can you account for the similarity or difference?

Chapter 6

Multiple Choice In Exercises 23–33, choose the letter of the correct answer.

23. Which set of integers is in order from least to greatest? *(Lesson 6.1)*

   A. $-2, -4, -6, -8$ **B.** $-2, 4, 6, 8$

   C. $-8, -6, 4, -2$ **D.** $4, 6, 8, -12$

24. Which integer is less than -9? *(Lesson 6.1)*

   F. -2 **G.** -5 **H.** -8 **I.** -10

25. Which expression has a value greater than -4? *(Lesson 6.2)*

   A. $6 + (-10)$ **B.** $-7 + (-2)$

   C. $-9 + 4$ **D.** $-13 + 10$

26. The high temperature yesterday was $-8°$F. Today the high temperature was 6 degrees greater. What was the high temperature today? *(Lesson 6.2)*

   F. $-14°$F **G.** $-2°$F **H.** $2°$F **I.** $14°$F

27. Find $118 - (-62)$. *(Lesson 6.3)*

   A. -180 **B.** -56 **C.** 56 **D.** 180

28. What is the value of a^2 when $a = -5$? *(Lesson 6.4)*

   F. -25 **G.** 0 **H.** 1 **I.** 25

29. The table lists Ashley's gains and losses over three days. What is the mean of Ashley's gains and losses over the three days? *(Lesson 6.5)*

Day	Friday	Saturday	Sunday
Gain/Loss	$60	$-45	$15

   A. $10   **B.** $15   **C.** $30   **D.** $40

30. Find $32 \div (-4)$. *(Lesson 6.5)*

   F. -36 **G.** -8 **H.** 8 **I.** 28

31. What is the multiplicative inverse of $2\frac{1}{2}$? *(Lesson 6.6)*

   A. $\frac{1}{2}$ **B.** $\frac{2}{5}$ **C.** $\frac{5}{2}$ **D.** $\frac{2}{1}$

32. What is the value of the expression $-13 + 6(4 - 2)$? *(Lesson 6.7)*

   F. -8 **G.** -1 **H.** 1 **I.** 11

33. In which quadrant is the point represented by $(-2, -3)$ located? *(Lesson 6.8)*

   A. I   **B.** II   **C.** III   **D.** IV

34. Short Response A football team gained 2 yards on one play and lost 9 yards on the next play. Write an expression that represents the situation. Then use a number line to evaluate the expression. *(Lesson 6.2)*

35. Extended Response Use the coordinate plane to answer the questions below. *(Lesson 6.8)*

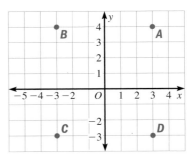

   a. Name a point in Quadrant II.

   b. What is the ordered pair represented by point D?

   c. Find the distance between point C and point D.

   d. What is the area of rectangle $ABCD$?

Algebra, Proportions, and Percents

Chapter **7** Equations, Inequalities, and Functions

- Write and simplify variable expressions.
- Write and solve equations and inequalities.
- Write, evaluate, and graph functions.

Chapter **8** Ratios and Proportions

- Write and compare ratios and rates.
- Find the slope of a line.
- Write and solve proportions.

Chapter **9** Percents

- Convert between percents, fractions, and decimals.
- Use proportions and the percent equation to solve percent problems.
- Use percents to make circle graphs and solve real-world problems.

From Chapter 8, p. 394

How much would you weigh on the moon?

Equations, Inequalities, and Functions

BEFORE

In previous chapters you've...

- Evaluated variable expressions
- Solved equations with mental math

Now

In Chapter 7 you'll study...

- Writing expressions and equations
- Simplifying expressions
- Solving equations and inequalities
- Using equations, tables, and graphs to represent functions

WHY?

So you can solve real-world problems about...

- swimming, p. 320
- space exploration, p. 329
- ski lifts, p. 336
- bicycle repair, p. 343
- scuba diving, p. 353

Internet Preview
CLASSZONE.COM

- eEdition Plus Online
- eWorkbook Plus Online
- eTutorial Plus Online
- State Test Practice
- More Examples

Chapter Warm-Up Games

Review skills you need for this chapter in these quick games.

Deciphering Ancient Numbers

Key Skills:
- Evaluating variable expressions
- Solving equations using mental math

Suppose the equations above are written using an ancient number system. Each symbol represents a number from 1 through 10. Copy and complete the table by matching each symbol with its value.

Value	1	2	3	4	5	6	7	8	9	10
Symbol	?	?	?	?	?	?	?	?	?	?

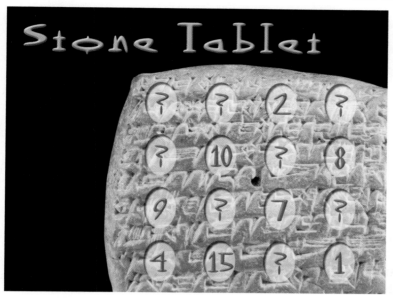

Stone Tablet

BRAIN GAME

Key Skills:
• Evaluating variable expressions
• Solving equations using mental math

Suppose an ancient stone tablet contains numbers that an archeologist suspects are arranged in a magic square. The archeologist has translated most of the numbers on the tablet. Unfortunately, some have been worn away. Copy and complete the magic square using the information below.

• Each integer from 1 through 16 is used exactly once.

• The sum of each row, column, and diagonal is 34.

Stop *and* Think

1. **Critical Thinking** Write expressions that equal 20, 24, 36, and 150 using the symbols in *Deciphering Ancient Numbers*.

2. **Writing** Suppose you multiply each number on the *Stone Tablet* by 2. Show that the resulting square is a magic square. Are there other ways you could use the *Stone Tablet* magic square to generate new magic squares? Explain your reasoning.

Getting Ready to Learn

Review What You Need to Know

Using Vocabulary Copy and complete using a review word.

Word Watch

Review Words

variable, p. 9
variable expression, p. 9
evaluate, p. 9
equation, p. 26
solution, p. 26

1. A mathematical sentence formed by setting two expressions equal is called a(n) _?_ .

2. To _?_ a variable expression, substitute values for the variables and then simplify the resulting numerical expression.

3. A letter used to represent one or more numbers is called a(n) _?_ .

Use mental math to solve the equation. *(p. 26)*

4. $15r = 30$ 5. $w + 4 = 9$ 6. $p - 3 = 12$ 7. $63 = 21t$

Evaluate the expression when x = 4, y = 2, and z = −3.
(pp. 18, 272)

8. $5x^2y$ 9. $zx - 3y$ 10. $7 - yz + x$ 11. $3 - xyz$

Plot the point in a coordinate plane. *(p. 293)*

12. $Q(-3, 4)$ 13. $R(0, 2)$ 14. $S(-2, -1)$ 15. $T(3, -5)$

You should include material that appears on a notebook like this in your own notes.

Know How to Take Notes

Comparing and Contrasting You can compare and contrast related concepts in your notebook. For example, noting similarities and differences between integers and their opposites can help you remember them.

Integers and Their Opposites

Similarity: The integers n and −n are both |n| units from 0 on a number line.

Difference: If n > 0, then n is to the right of 0 on a number line, and −n is to the left of 0 on a number line.

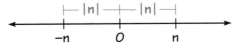

You may find this strategy helpful in Lesson 7.4 where you will be solving multiplication and division equations.

Writing Expressions and Equations

BEFORE	▶ Now	WHY?
You evaluated variable expressions.	You'll write variable expressions and equations.	So you can find the altitude of a hot air balloon, as in Ex. 34.

In the Real World

Word Watch

verbal model, p. 318

Caves You are exploring a cave in which rock formations called *stalagmites* grow up from the cave floor. The tour guide informs you that the tallest stalagmite in the cave is in a pool of water 55 feet deep, and the distance between the tip of the stalagmite and the surface of the water is 41 feet. How tall is the stalagmite? You'll find the answer in Example 3.

Translating Phrases and Sentences To solve real-world problems, you need to translate verbal phrases and sentences into variable expressions and equations. Look for key words that indicate addition, subtraction, multiplication, and division.

Addition	Subtraction	Multiplication	Division
plus the sum of increased by total more than added to	minus the difference of decreased by fewer than less than subtracted from	times the product of multiplied by of	divided by the quotient of

Watch Out!

Order is important in subtraction and division expressions. For example, "2 less than a number" is written as $x - 2$, *not* $2 - x$. Similarly, "a number divided by 5" is written as $x \div 5$, *not* $5 \div x$.

EXAMPLE 1 **Translating Verbal Phrases**

Verbal phrase	Expression
a. A number increased by 5	$x + 5$
b. 7 less than a number	$x - 7$
c. 3 more than twice a number	$2x + 3$
d. 4 decreased by the quotient of a number and 7	$4 - \dfrac{x}{7}$

HELP with **Solving**

When translating verbal sentences into equations, look for the key words "is" and "equals," which can be represented by the symbol =.

EXAMPLE 2 Translating Verbal Sentences

Verbal sentence	Equation
a. 16 increased by a number is 27.	$16 + y = 27$
b. The difference of twice a number and 3 equals -4.	$2y - 3 = -4$
c. The product of $\frac{1}{2}$ and a number is 36.	$\frac{1}{2}y = 36$
d. -3 is equal to twice the sum of a number and 2.	$-3 = 2(y + 2)$

Your turn now Write the verbal phrase or sentence as a variable expression or equation. Let n represent the number.

1. 14 added to a number

2. $\frac{1}{2}$ of a number decreased by 22

3. 42 divided by a number equals 7.

4. 5 minus twice a number is 17.

You can use *verbal models* to solve real-world problems. A **verbal model** uses words to describe ideas and math symbols to relate the words.

EXAMPLE 3 Writing and Solving an Equation

HELP with **Solving**

Assign a meaningful variable to represent what you need to find. In Example 3, *h* is chosen to represent the **height** of the stalagmite.

To find the height of the stalagmite described at the top of page 317, you can write and solve an equation. First write a verbal model.

Let h represent the height of the stalagmite.

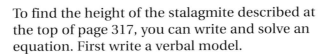

Height of stalagmite	+	Distance between tip of stalagmite and water surface	=	Depth of water
h	+	41	=	55

Use mental math: Because $14 + 41 = 55$, $h = 14$.

ANSWER The height of the stalagmite is 14 feet.

Your turn now Use mental math to solve the following problem.

5. While hiking you descend 2000 feet from the start of a trail to an elevation of 5200 feet. Write and solve an equation to find the elevation at the start of the trail.

Getting Ready to Practice

1. **Vocabulary** Copy and complete: A(n) __?__ uses words to describe ideas and math symbols to relate the words.

Match the verbal phrase with its variable expression.

2. 4 more than a number

3. The quotient of a number and 4

4. The difference of 4 and a number

5. 4 less than a number

A. $4 - x$

B. $x + 4$

C. $x \div 4$

D. $x - 4$

6. **Guided Problem Solving** The Colorado River, which is 1450 miles long, is 450 miles shorter than the Rio Grande River. How long is the Rio Grande River?

  (1) Reread the problem. Decide what you know and what you are asked to find.

  (2) Write a verbal model that represents the situation. Then write an equation.

  (3) Use mental math to solve the equation.

Practice and Problem Solving

HELP with Homework

Example	Exercises
1	7–12, 26–29, 36–40
2	13–17, 36–40
3	31–35, 42

Online Resources
CLASSZONE.COM

· More Examples
· eTutorial Plus

Write the verbal phrase as a variable expression. Let x represent the number.

7. A number added to -7

8. The product of a number and 2

9. $\frac{1}{3}$ of a number

10. A number divided by 16

11. -50 decreased by a number

12. Twice a number

Write the verbal sentence as an equation. Let y represent the number.

13. The sum of a number and -9 equals 24.

14. The product of a number and -5 is 10.

15. 13 is equal to 5 minus a number.

16. $\frac{1}{4}$ of the difference of 6 and a number is 200.

17. The sum of -4 times a number and 3 is 27.

Write a verbal phrase for the variable expression.

18. $3 + a$ **19.** $13b$ **20.** $c - 2$ **21.** $10 \div d$

Write a verbal sentence for the equation.

22. $4p = 16$ **23.** $q + 8 = 34$ **24.** $9 - 2r = 15$ **25.** $90 \div s = 1$

Write the real-world phrase as a variable expression. Be sure to identify what the variable represents.

26. 3 years older than Theo   **27.** Twice a team's score

28. Half of your class   **29.** 5 inches shorter than Ann

30. Writing Describe real-world situations that can be represented by the expressions $n + 3$, $n - 3$, $3n$, and $n \div 3$.

In Exercises 31–35, write an equation to represent the situation described. Then use mental math to solve the equation.

31. Temperature The temperature decreased by 24°F, and it is now 75°F. What was the original temperature?

32. Shopping A sweater is on sale for half off the regular price, and it is now $16. What was the regular price of the sweater?

33. Savings You deposit $30 into your savings account, and your new balance is $100. What was your previous balance?

34. Hot Air Balloon You are in a hot air balloon, and you descend 200 feet to an altitude of 1000 feet. What was your original altitude?

35. Swimming In 1994, Tammy and John Van Wisse became the first brother and sister to swim across the English Channel. Tammy's crossing time, 8 hours 32 minutes, or 512 minutes, was 15 minutes longer than her brother's crossing time. How long, in hours and minutes, did it take John to swim across the English Channel?

Write the verbal phrase or sentence as a variable expression or equation. Let *n* represent the number.

36. The quotient of a number plus 6 and 3

37. 4 added to the square of a number

38. 8 multiplied by the difference of 9 and a number

39. $\frac{1}{3}$ of a number is equal to -8 plus the number.

40. The product of 3 and a number is twice the sum of the number and 5.

41. Critical Thinking Is "three less than a number" equivalent to "the difference of three and a number"? Explain your reasoning.

What do you think?

Sports

■ **Swimming**

By 2001, Tammy Van Wisse had swum enough races to circle Earth 1.5 times. The circumference of Earth is about 25,000 miles. About how many miles had she swum in races by 2001?

42. Braces Amy has an orthodontist's appointment to get her braces checked every 6 weeks. About how many times does she have to go to the orthodontist in 1 year?

43. Geometry Write an expression for the area of a rectangle whose length is 5 inches longer than its width. Evaluate this expression to find the area of such a rectangle whose width is 3 inches.

44. Challenge You walk at 4 miles per hour for $\frac{1}{2}$ hour, and then jog at 6 miles per hour for h hours. The total distance that you cover both walking and jogging is 6 miles. Write an equation that represents this situation.

Mixed Review

Plot the point and describe its location in a coordinate plane.
(Lesson 6.8)

45. $A(-3, 2)$ **46.** $B(9, 2)$ **47.** $C(5, -1)$ **48.** $D(-6, -8)$

Choose a Strategy Use a strategy from the list to solve the following problem. Explain your choice of strategy.

49. There are 60 houses on Independence Road, numbered from 1 to 60. How many houses on Independence Road have at least one 2 as a digit?

> **Problem Solving Strategies**
> ▪ Draw a Diagram
> ▪ Guess, Check, and Revise
> ▪ Make a List

Basic Skills **Find the perimeter.**

50.

51.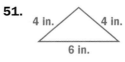

52.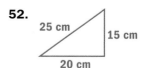

Test-Taking Practice

INTERNET
State Test Practice
CLASSZONE.COM

53. Multiple Choice A vehicle rental company charges $25 to rent a moving van plus $.50 for each mile traveled. Which expression represents the total cost of renting a van and driving d miles?

   A. $25 + d$ **B.** $25 + 0.50d$ **C.** $25 - 0.50d$ **D.** $25d + 0.50$

54. Multiple Choice The perimeter of a square is 20 inches. Which equation can you use to find the length s of a side of the square?

   F. $s^2 = 20$ **G.** $5s = 20$ **H.** $4s = 20$ **I.** $20s = 4$

Simplifying Expressions

BEFORE	▶ Now	WHY?
You wrote variable expressions.	You'll simplify variable expressions.	So you can simplify a soccer field expression, as in Ex. 21.

Word Watch

term, p. 322
like terms, p. 322
equivalent variable
    expressions, p. 322
coefficient, p. 322
constant term, p. 322

The distributive property can be used to simplify a variable expression:

$$2x + 3x = (2 + 3)x = 5x$$

The parts of an expression that are being added together, such as $2x$ and $3x$ in the expression $2x + 3x$, are called **terms**. Terms that have identical variable parts are **like terms**. In the expression $2x + 3x$, $2x$ and $3x$ are like terms. The distributive property allows you to *combine like terms*.

EXAMPLE 1 Combining Like Terms

Simplify the expression $7c + 9 - 3c$.

$$
\begin{aligned}
7c + 9 - 3c &= 7c + 9 + (-3c) && \text{Write expression as a sum.} \\
&= 7c + (-3c) + 9 && \text{Commutative property of addition} \\
&= [7 + (-3)]c + 9 && \text{Distributive property} \\
&= 4c + 9 && \text{Simplify.}
\end{aligned}
$$

HELP with Solving

After Example 1, the step of using the distributive property in order to combine like terms will not be shown.

In Example 1 above, $7c + 9 - 3c$ is *equivalent* to $4c + 9$. **Equivalent variable expressions** are expressions that are equal for every value of each variable they contain.

The **coefficient** of a term that has a variable is the number part of the term. A term that has a number, but no variable, is a **constant term**. In the expression $4a + 1$, 4 is the coefficient of $4a$, and 1 is a constant term.

EXAMPLE 2 Coefficients, Constant Terms, Like Terms

Identify the coefficients, constant terms, and like terms of the expression $x + 4 - 2x - 10$.

First, write the expression as a sum: $x + 4 + (-2x) + (-10)$.

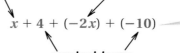

Coefficient is 1. Coefficient is −2.

$x + 4 + (-2x) + (-10)$

constant terms

x and −2*x* are like terms.

4 and −10 are like terms.

EXAMPLE 3 Simplifying an Expression

 **with Solving**

Sometimes you need to use the distributive property to eliminate parentheses or brackets in order to combine like terms in an expression.

Simplify the expression $5(w - 4) + w + 8$.

$$5(w - 4) + w + 8 = 5w - 20 + w + 8 \qquad \text{Distributive property}$$
$$= 5w + (-20) + w + 8 \qquad \text{Write as a sum.}$$
$$= 5w + w + (-20) + 8 \qquad \text{Commutative property}$$
$$= 6w + (-12) \qquad \text{Combine like terms.}$$
$$= 6w - 12 \qquad \text{Rewrite without parentheses.}$$

Your turn now Identify the coefficients, constant term(s), and like terms of the expression. Then simplify the expression.

1. $-3z + 1 + 4z$ **2.** $15 - 9r + 7r - 6$ **3.** $2y + 4 - 2y - 4$

What do you think?
Culture

EXAMPLE 4 Writing and Simplifying an Expression

Tatami Mats A rectangular tatami mat is twice as long as it is wide. Write and simplify an expression for the perimeter of the mat in terms of the width w.

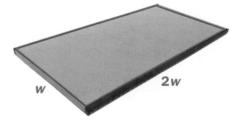

Solution

Because the mat is twice as long as it is wide, its length is $2w$.

$$\text{Perimeter} = 2l + 2w \qquad \text{Formula for perimeter of a rectangle}$$
$$= 2(2w) + 2w \qquad \text{Substitute } 2w \text{ for } l.$$
$$= 4w + 2w \qquad \text{Multiply.}$$
$$= 6w \qquad \text{Combine like terms.}$$

ANSWER An expression for the perimeter of the mat is $6w$.

■ **Tatami Mats**

In Japanese homes, straw tatami mats are used as floor coverings. Room sizes are often measured by the number of 3 foot by 6 foot tatami mats that can fit in the room. What is the area, in square feet, of a room that is "five and a half tatami mats"?

Your turn now Complete the following exercise.

4. A rectangle is 6 inches longer than it is wide. Write and simplify an expression for the perimeter of the rectangle in terms of the width w.

Getting Ready to Practice

1. Vocabulary In the expression $5z - 7 + 2z + 1$, identify the coefficients, constant terms, and like terms.

Simplify the expression.

2. $3a + 9 - a$ **3.** $18 + 4b + 6$ **4.** $-8c + 4 - 5$

5. Geometry A rectangle is three times longer than it is wide. Write and simplify an expression for the perimeter of the rectangle in terms of the width w.

Practice and Problem Solving

with Homework

Example	Exercises
1	9–17, 22–27
2	6–8
3	9–17, 22–27
4	18–21, 29

Online Resources
CLASSZONE.COM

· More Examples
· eTutorial Plus

Identify the coefficients, constant term(s), and like terms of the expression.

6. $3x + 4 - x$ **7.** $10 - 4y + 5y - 8$ **8.** $7z - 9z + 2 + z$

Simplify the expression.

9. $14t + 15 - 2t$ **10.** $4k - 10 + 7 - 7k$ **11.** $6 - 2l - 7 + 3l$

12. $10x + 4 + x - 9$ **13.** $14 - y + y + 5$ **14.** $-p + 3 + 2p - 2p$

15. $6(1 - j) + 2j$ **16.** $5(z + 2) - 8$ **17.** $4b - 2 + 2(b + 1)$

Geometry Write and simplify an expression for the perimeter of the rectangle.

18.

19.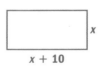

20.

21. Soccer A rectangular soccer field is 30 yards longer than it is wide. Write and simplify an expression for the perimeter of the field in terms of the width w.

Simplify the expression.

22. $m - 2 + 1 - 2m + 1$ **23.** $12v - 3(2 + 4v) + 6$

24. $2(2t + 5 - 2t) + 8t$ **25.** $5 - s(4 - 7) + 3s$

26. $5 + n - p + 2n - 4$ **27.** $5a - 2 + b - 3b + 2a$

Extended Problem Solving **In Exercises 28–30, use the following information.** You have just returned from a 3-day trip. On the first day of your trip, you took 10 photographs. On the third day of the trip, you took twice as many photographs as you did on the second day.

28. Write an expression for the number of photographs you took on each day. Tell what the variable you chose represents.

29. Write and simplify an expression for the total number of photographs you took.

30. **Calculate** If you took 12 photographs on the second day, how many photographs did you take in all? Explain your reasoning.

Critical Thinking **Tell whether the two expressions are equivalent.**

31. $-13 + 7t - 5$;
$9t - 8 - 2t$

32. $10a - 4a + 12$;
$6(a + 2)$

33. $7x + 2x^2$;
$9x^2$

34. **Challenge** Are the expressions "two more than twice a number" and "twice the sum of a number and 1" equivalent? Explain.

Mixed Review

Make a box-and-whisker plot of the data. *(Lesson 3.4)*

35. 26, 55, 14, 25, 35, 40, 28, 43, 44, 25, 18, 21, 42, 38

36. 3, 12, 17, 6, 14, 5, 10, 29, 4, 14, 16

Write a verbal phrase for the variable expression. *(Lesson 7.1)*

37. $p \div 6$

38. $3x - 10$

39. $2(t + 2)$

Basic Skills **Find the sum.**

40. $6.244 + 0.004$

41. $0.9506 + 1.12$

42. $35.008 + 99.99$

Test-Taking Practice

43. **Multiple Choice** Which expression is equivalent to $4x - 5 + 6(1 - x)$?

A. $10x$ **B.** $3x + 1$ **C.** $-2x + 1$ **D.** $5x - 5$

44. **Short Response** Write "6 plus twice the sum of a number and 5" as a variable expression. Then simplify the expression.

Hands-on **Activity**

GOAL
Model and solve addition equations.

MATERIALS
· algebra tiles

Modeling Addition Equations

You can use algebra tiles to model and solve simple addition equations.

x-tile

An *x*-tile represents the variable *x*.

1-tile

A 1-tile represents positive 1.

Explore **Solve $x + 2 = 5$.**

1 Model $x + 2 = 5$ using algebra tiles.

2 Take away two 1-tiles from each side.

3 The *x*-tile is equal to three 1-tiles. So, the solution of the equation $x + 2 = 5$ is 3.

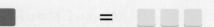

Your turn now **Use algebra tiles to model and solve the equation.**

1. $x + 3 = 8$

2. $x + 4 = 5$

3. $x + 1 = 7$

4. $6 + x = 11$

5. $9 + x = 13$

6. $2 + x = 10$

Stop and Think

7. Writing Explain why, in the example shown above, it is important to take away two 1-tiles from *each* side and not just the left side of the equation.

8. Critical Thinking Describe how you would use algebra tiles to solve the equation $4 + x + 2 = 10$. Then solve.

LESSON 7.3

Solving Addition and Subtraction Equations

BEFORE	Now	WHY?
You wrote equations.	You'll solve addition and subtraction equations.	So you can find the number of neutrons in an atom, as in Ex. 21.

In the Real World

Word Watch

inverse operations, p. 327
equivalent equations, p. 327

Space Exploration You can use equations to help you solve real-world problems. In Example 4, you will see how to write and solve an equation to find the length of time that the Apollo 11 astronauts spent on the moon.

Solving Equations One way to solve an equation is to use *inverse operations*. An **inverse operation** is an operation that "undoes" another operation. Addition and subtraction are inverse operations.

Performing the same operation on each side of an equation results in a new equation that has the same solution as the original equation. Two equations that have the same solution(s) are **equivalent equations**.

Subtraction Property of Equality

Words Subtracting the same number from each side of an equation produces an equivalent equation.

Algebra $x + a = b \longrightarrow x + a - a = b - a$

EXAMPLE 1 Solving an Addition Equation

Solve $x + 7 = -10$.

$x + 7 = -10$	Write original equation.
$\underline{ - 7 \quad -7}$	Subtract 7 from each side.
$x = -17$	Simplify.

✓ **Check** $x + 7 = -10$ Write original equation.

$-17 + 7 \stackrel{?}{=} -10$ Substitute -17 for x.

$-10 = -10$ ✓ Solution checks.

Addition Property of Equality

Words Adding the same number to each side of an equation produces an equivalent equation.

Algebra $x - a = b \longrightarrow x - a + a = b + a$

Watch Out!

You can add or subtract vertically or horizontally to solve equations, but remember to perform the same operation on each side of the equation.

EXAMPLE 2 Solving a Subtraction Equation

Solve $-9 = y - 12$.

$-9 = y - 12$	Write original equation.
$-9 + 12 = y - 12 + 12$	Add 12 to each side.
$3 = y$	Simplify.

✓ **Check**

$-9 = y - 12$	Write original equation.
$-9 \stackrel{?}{=} 3 - 12$	Substitute 3 for y.
$-9 = -9$ ✓	Solution checks.

EXAMPLE 3 Combining Like Terms

Solve $2 = 1.3 + a + 4$.

$2 = 1.3 + a + 4$	Write original equation.
$2 = 1.3 + 4 + a$	Commutative property of addition
$2 = 5.3 + a$	Combine like terms.
$2 - 5.3 = 5.3 - 5.3 + a$	Subtract 5.3 from each side.
$-3.3 = a$	Simplify.

✓ **Check**

$2 = 1.3 + a + 4$	Write original equation.
$2 \stackrel{?}{=} 1.3 + (-3.3) + 4$	Substitute -3.3 for a.
$2 = 2$ ✓	Solution checks.

Your turn now Solve the equation. Check your solution.

1. $t + 8 = 15$ **2.** $n + 10 = 4$ **3.** $8 = m - 6$

4. $r - 10 = 14$ **5.** $p - (-2.2) = 5.6$ **6.** $3.4 + s - 1.3 = 6.8$

Apollo 11 astronaut Buzz Aldrin

EXAMPLE 4 **Writing and Solving an Equation**

Space Exploration The Apollo 11 mission lasted about 195.5 hours. The flight from Earth to the moon lasted about 103 hours, and the flight from the moon back to Earth lasted about 71 hours. About how many hours did the Apollo 11 astronauts spend on the moon?

Solution

Write a verbal model. Let t represent the number of hours the astronauts spent on the moon.

$$\begin{array}{ccc} \text{Length of} \\ \text{mission} \end{array} = \begin{array}{c} \text{Length of} \\ \text{flight to moon} \end{array} + \begin{array}{c} \text{Time spent} \\ \text{on moon} \end{array} + \begin{array}{c} \text{Length of} \\ \text{flight to Earth} \end{array}$$

$195.5 = 103 + t + 71$	Write equation.
$195.5 = 174 + t$	Combine like terms.
$195.5 - 174 = 174 - 174 + t$	Subtract 174 from each side.
$21.5 = t$	Simplify.

ANSWER The Apollo 11 astronauts spent about 21.5 hours on the moon.

7.3 Exercises

More Practice, p. 711

INTERNET
eWorkbook Plus
CLASSZONE.COM

Getting Ready to Practice

1. Vocabulary Name a pair of inverse operations.

Solve the equation. Check your solution.

2. $c + 5 = 8$ **3.** $n + 7 = 10$ **4.** $6 + p = -11$

5. $t - 3 = 2$ **6.** $6 + s - 4 = 8$ **7.** $-16 = 5.5 + x + 3.5$

8. Find the Error Describe and correct the error in solving the equation $x + 5 = 22$.

$$\begin{array}{c} x + 5 = 22 \\ x + 5 - 5 = 22 - 22 \\ x = 0 \end{array}$$

9. Locker Mirrors Locker mirrors are on sale for $5.75. This is $1.50 less than the regular price. Write and solve an equation to find the regular price of the mirrors.

Practice and Problem Solving

Example Exercises

1	10-18
2	10-18
3	24-29
4	21-22

Online Resources
CLASSZONE.COM

· More Examples
· eTutorial Plus

Solve the equation. Check your solution.

10. $n + 9 = 18$ **11.** $y + 13 = -17$ **12.** $14 = c + 10$

13. $13 + w = -7$ **14.** $r + 10 = -10.2$ **15.** $-5.1 = x - 14.2$

16. $h - 9.3 = 28$ **17.** $t - 6.8 = 13.9$ **18.** $-7 = b - (-7)$

Write the verbal sentence as an equation. Then solve the equation.

19. 5 less than a number p is -17. **20.** The sum of 6 and a number x is 3.

21. Atomic Mass For any element, the atomic mass of a single atom is approximated by the sum of the numbers of protons and neutrons it contains. Write and solve an equation to find the number of neutrons in an atom of each element in the table.

Element	Atomic mass	Protons
Gold	197	79
Silver	108	47
Uranium	238	92

22. Cats While holding his cat, Bill steps on a scale. The result is 127 pounds. Alone, Bill weighs 112 pounds. Write and solve an equation to find the weight of Bill's cat.

23. What point on the number line represents the solution of the equation $z - 6.9 = 2.7 - 7.3$?

Solve the equation. Check your solution.

24. $5.7 = 9 + p - 1$ **25.** $2.3 + h - 3.1 = 27$ **26.** $7.2 = 4z + 3 - 3z$

27. $2 + n - \dfrac{3}{7} = \dfrac{6}{7}$ **28.** $\dfrac{3}{8} = \dfrac{5}{16} + x - 1$ **29.** $3y - 2y + \dfrac{3}{5} = \dfrac{4}{7}$

Geometry Write and solve an equation to find the unknown side length.

30. Perimeter: 13 ft **31.** Perimeter: 21.5 in. **32.** Perimeter: 42.5 m

33. Challenge Solve the equation $\dfrac{5}{6} + \dfrac{3}{4} = \dfrac{1}{18} - 6c - \dfrac{2}{3} + 7c + \dfrac{1}{9}$.

34. Costume Party You need to make a costume to wear to your friend's costume party. You have $25 to spend. Write and solve an equation to find how much money you have left after buying 2.5 yards of fabric, a wig, 2 sheets of poster board, and face paints.

Fabric	$3.50 per yard
Wig	$5.39
Poster board	$1.99 per sheet
Face paints	$4.25

Mixed Review

Find the quotient. *(Lesson 6.5)*

35. $8 \div (-2)$ **36.** $-8 \div 2$ **37.** $-8 \div (-2)$

Write a verbal sentence for the equation. *(Lesson 7.1)*

38. $5x = 20$ **39.** $6 + x = 22$ **40.** $14 - 3x = 2$

Basic Skills **Find a low and high estimate for the quotient.**

41. $1780 \div 8$ **42.** $264 \div 23$ **43.** $2919 \div 34$

Test-Taking Practice

44. Multiple Choice Judy is 7 years younger than Lily. Which equation can be used to find Lily's age l if Judy is 14 years old?

     A. $14 = l + 7$ **B.** $14 = l - 7$ **C.** $14 = 7l$ **D.** $14 = 7 - l$

45. Multiple Choice Which equation has 5 as a solution?

     F. $x - 5 = 10$ **G.** $5 + x = 10$ **H.** $10 + x = 5$ **I.** $10 = 5 - x$

BRAIN GAME

Orderly Words

The solution of each equation corresponds to a letter of the alphabet (1 = A, 2 = B, 3 = C, 4 = D, and so on). Solve the equations to answer the following question.

Question: What is the longest word in the English language that has all of its letters in alphabetical order?

Answer:

$x + 9 = 10$ $x - 7 = 5$ $26 - x = 13$ $x - 18 = -3$ $x + 2.4 = 21.4$ $x + 14 = 34$

Hands-on Activity

GOAL
Model and solve multiplication equations.

MATERIALS
• algebra tiles

Modeling Multiplication Equations

You can use algebra tiles to model and solve simple multiplication equations.

Explore Solve $3x = 12$.

1 Model $3x = 12$ using algebra tiles.

2 Divide the x-tiles and 1-tiles into 3 equal groups.

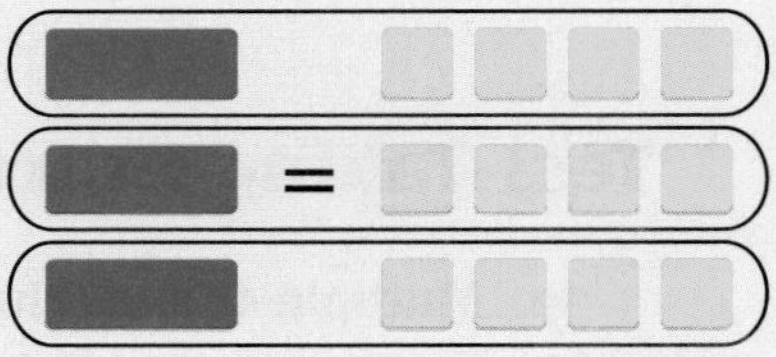

3 One x-tile is equal to four 1-tiles. So, the solution of the equation $3x = 12$ is 4.

Your turn now Use algebra tiles to model and solve the equation.

1. $5x = 15$ **2.** $2x = 4$ **3.** $4x = 8$ **4.** $4x = 20$

5. $3x = 18$ **6.** $7x = 21$ **7.** $2x + 3x = 5$ **8.** $2x + 4x = 12$

Stop and Think

9. Writing The example above uses a property called the *division property of equality*, similar to the addition and subtraction properties of equality in the previous lesson. In your own words, explain what this property allows you to do.

Solving Multiplication and Division Equations

BEFORE	▶ Now	WHY?
You solved addition and subtraction equations.	You'll solve multiplication and division equations.	So you can find the cost of a telephone call, as in Ex. 32.

In the Real World

Review Words
inverse operations, p. 327

Flying Disc You throw a flying disc to your dog. It stays in the air for 2.5 seconds before your dog catches it 30 feet away from you. In Example 4, you'll write and solve a multiplication equation to find the speed of the disc.

Because multiplication and division are inverse operations, you can use division to solve a multiplication equation.

Division Property of Equality

Words Dividing each side of an equation by the same nonzero number produces an equivalent equation.

Algebra $ax = b \ (a \neq 0) \longrightarrow \dfrac{ax}{a} = \dfrac{b}{a}$

EXAMPLE 1 Solving a Multiplication Equation

Solve $-3x = 45$.

$-3x = 45$	Write original equation.
$\dfrac{-3x}{-3} = \dfrac{45}{-3}$	Divide each side by -3.
$x = -15$	Simplify.

✓ **Check**
$-3x = 45$	Write original equation.
$-3(-15) \stackrel{?}{=} 45$	Substitute -15 for x.
$45 = 45$ ✓	Solution checks.

Multiplication Property of Equality

Words Multiplying each side of an equation by the same nonzero number produces an equivalent equation.

Algebra $\dfrac{x}{a} = b \ (a \neq 0)$ ⟶ $a \cdot \dfrac{x}{a} = a \cdot b$

HELP with **Notetaking**

In your notebook, you may want to compare and contrast solving multiplication and division equations. This will help you remember how to solve these types of equations.

EXAMPLE 2 Solving a Division Equation

Solve $\dfrac{x}{2} = 0.75$.

$$\dfrac{x}{2} = 0.75 \qquad \text{Write original equation.}$$

$$2 \cdot \dfrac{x}{2} = 2 \cdot 0.75 \qquad \text{Multiply each side by 2.}$$

$$x = 1.5 \qquad \text{Simplify.}$$

When you are solving an equation containing a fractional coefficient, multiply each side of the equation by the reciprocal of the coefficient.

HELP with **Review**

Need help multiplying by a reciprocal? See p. 222.

EXAMPLE 3 Solving an Equation Using a Reciprocal

Solve $-4 = \dfrac{2}{3}x$.

$$-4 = \dfrac{2}{3}x \qquad \text{Write original equation.}$$

$$\left(\dfrac{3}{2}\right)(-4) = \left(\dfrac{3}{2}\right)\dfrac{2}{3}x \qquad \text{Multiply each side by } \dfrac{3}{2}.$$

$$-6 = x \qquad \text{Simplify.}$$

Your turn now Solve the equation. Check your solution.

1. $6a = 54$ **2.** $-13b = 65$ **3.** $-3.4 = \dfrac{d}{5}$ **4.** $\dfrac{c}{2} = 13$

5. $5p - 3p = 4$ **6.** $16 = -s$ **7.** $\dfrac{4}{5}r = 1$ **8.** $-2 = \dfrac{2}{5}t$

EXAMPLE 4 **Writing and Solving an Equation**

To find the speed of the flying disc described on page 333, use the formula $d = rt$.

Your dog catches the disc 30 feet from you, so the distance the disc travels is 30 feet. The disc spends 2.5 seconds in the air.

$d = rt$	Write formula for distance.
$30 = r(2.5)$	Substitute 30 for d and 2.5 for t.
$\dfrac{30}{2.5} = \dfrac{2.5r}{2.5}$	Divide each side by 2.5.
$12 = r$	Simplify.

ANSWER The speed of the disc is 12 feet per second.

Your turn now **Solve the following problem.**

9. A DVD contains 7.5 hours of bonus material, which is 3 times longer than the movie itself. Write and solve an equation to find the length of the movie.

7.4 Exercises

More Practice, p. 711

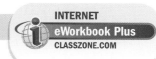

INTERNET
eWorkbook Plus
CLASSZONE.COM

Getting Ready to Practice

1. **Vocabulary** Copy and complete: Multiplication and _?_ are inverse operations.

Solve the equation. Check your solution.

2. $14q = 42$ 3. $20r = 100$ 4. $9s = -27$ 5. $-3t = -9$

6. $\dfrac{w}{2} = 8$ 7. $\dfrac{x}{6} = 12$ 8. $-\dfrac{3}{4}y = 12$ 9. $-\dfrac{3}{10}z = -6$

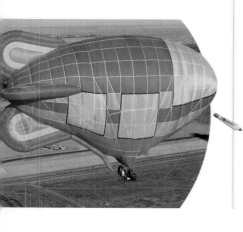

10. **Writing** Write a real-world problem that can be solved using the equation $5t = 20$.

11. **Blimp** A blimp travels 300 miles in 7.5 hours. Assuming that the blimp travels at a constant speed, write and solve an equation to find the speed of the blimp.

Practice and Problem Solving

with Homework

Example	Exercises
1	12–31, 37–44
2	12–31, 37–44
3	12–31, 37–44
4	32–33, 45, 48–49

Online Resources
CLASSZONE.COM

· More Examples
· eTutorial Plus

Describe how to solve each equation without actually solving.

12. $3x = 15$ **13.** $-16x = 4$ **14.** $\frac{x}{9} = -2$ **15.** $\frac{x}{15} = -7$

Solve the equation. Check your solution.

16. $8p = 24$ **17.** $30b = 5$ **18.** $-b = 12.5$ **19.** $-3.5f = 24.5$

20. $-3 = 1.2y$ **21.** $-1.2s = -6$ **22.** $\frac{r}{2} = 10$ **23.** $\frac{a}{3} = -4$

24. $\frac{d}{24} = -0.5$ **25.** $-36 = \frac{r}{5.5}$ **26.** $-0.7 = \frac{z}{3}$ **27.** $\frac{c}{14} = -11$

28. $\frac{4}{3}t = 12$ **29.** $-\frac{5}{7}y = 5$ **30.** $-\frac{1}{2}w = -12$ **31.** $-9 = -\frac{3}{4}e$

32. Telephone Bill Your telephone bill lists a call that lasted 18 minutes and cost \$1.08. Write and solve an equation to find how much you were charged for each minute of the call.

33. Geometry A rectangle has a length of 7.5 meters and an area of 45 square meters. Write and solve an equation to find the rectangle's width.

$A = 45 \text{ m}^2$ w

7.5 m

Write the verbal sentence as an equation. Then solve the equation.

34. The product of 10 and a number is -22.

35. Twice a number is equal to -100.

36. The quotient of a number and 3 is 6.6.

Solve the equation. Round the solution to the nearest hundredth if necessary.

37. $-3a = 4$ **38.** $-14y = -100$ **39.** $22x = -9$ **40.** $1.65t = 9.8$

41. $3.6x = 4.88$ **42.** $-\frac{3}{4} = -2k$ **43.** $3 = m + 3m$ **44.** $6p - 2p = 9$

45. Ski Lift A ski lift can carry 11,200 people in one day. The ski lift operates from 9:00 A.M. to 4:00 P.M. each day. Write and solve an equation to find the number of people the lift can carry in 1 hour.

46. Critical Thinking Is it possible to solve the equation $5x = 29$ by *multiplying* each side of the equation by the same number? If so, what is the number? Explain your reasoning.

47. Geometry The perimeter of a square is 32 inches. What is its area?

Sports

Jump Rope In Exercises 48 and 49, use the following information.
Suppose that in the 3 minute speed event at a jump rope competition, a jumper's right foot strikes the ground 408 times. Assume that the jumper keeps a steady pace.

48. Write and solve an equation to find the number of times the jumper's right foot strikes the ground in 1 minute.

49. How many times does the jumper's right foot strike the ground in 1 second? Round your answer to the nearest tenth.

50. **Challenge** A *mil* is used to measure paper thickness. One mil is equal to 0.001 inch. You have a stack of paper that is about 2.5 inches high. Each sheet of paper is 11.8 mils thick. Write and solve an equation to find the approximate number of sheets of paper in the stack.

 51. **Baseball** The fastest recorded time for circling the 4 bases of a baseball diamond is 13.3 seconds, set by Ernest Swanson in 1932. Consecutive bases are 90 feet apart. Assuming that Swanson ran at a constant speed, write and solve an equation to find Swanson's speed, in feet per second. Round your answer to the nearest tenth.

■ **Jump Rope**

In speed events at jump rope competitions, the number of times a jumper's right foot strikes the ground is counted. The U.S. record for 12–14 year olds in the 2 minute double dutch pairs speed event is 715 right foot strikes. About how many right foot strikes were there in 1 second?

Mixed Review

Write the number in scientific notation. *(Lesson 2.5)*

52. 7000   **53.** 10,200   **54.** 504,060   **55.** 12,050,000

Solve the equation. Check your solution. *(Lesson 7.3)*

56. $x - 12 = 15$ **57.** $x - 2 = -7$ **58.** $5.2 + x = 8.6$ **59.** $x + 5 = \frac{1}{2}$

Basic Skills **Copy and complete.**

60. 3540 sec = _?_ min   **61.** 2.5 h = _?_ min

62. 36 min = _?_ h   **63.** 15,300 sec = _?_ h

64. 12 h = _?_ sec   **65.** 4.25 min = _?_ sec

Test-Taking Practice

66. **Extended Response** The top female runner in the 2001 Boston Marathon completed the 26.2 mile race in about 2 hours 24 minutes. The top female wheelchair racer completed the race in about 1 hour 54 minutes. Convert both times to hours. If you assume that both women traveled at a constant speed, find the speed of each woman, in miles per hour, rounded to the nearest hundredth. About how much faster was the speed of the wheelchair racer?

Notebook Review

Review the vocabulary definitions in your notebook.

Copy the review examples in your notebook. Then complete the exercises.

Check Your Definitions

verbal model, p. 318
term, p. 322
like terms, p. 322

equivalent variable
    expressions, p. 322
coefficient, p. 322
constant term, p. 322

inverse operations, p. 327
equivalent equations,
    p. 327

Use Your Vocabulary

1. Identify the coefficients, constant terms, and like terms of the expression $15y - 6 + 4y + 13$.

7.1 Can you write expressions and equations?

 EXAMPLE Write the phrase or sentence as an expression or equation.

Phrase/Sentence	Expression/Equation
a. A number increased by 7	$n + 7$
b. 6 less than 5 times a number is 9.	$5n - 6 = 9$

☑ **Write the verbal phrase or sentence as a variable expression or equation. Let _w_ represent the number.**

2. 2 plus a number

3. Twice the sum of a number and 4

4. 8 less than a number is -25.

5. 4 times a number divided by 7 is 6.

7.2 Can you simplify expressions?

 EXAMPLE Simplify the expression $4(2z + 1) - 3z$.

$4(2z + 1) - 3z = 8z + 4 - 3z$	Distributive property
$= 8z + 4 + (-3z)$	Write as a sum.
$= 8z + (-3z) + 4$	Commutative property of addition
$= 5z + 4$	Combine like terms.

☑ **Simplify the expression.**

6. $9x + 4 - x - 8$

7. $14 + 2y + 3 - 6y$

8. $8 - 3(g + 2)$

7.3–7.4 Can you solve one-step equations?

EXAMPLE Solve the equation.

a. $n + 31 = 50$

$n + 31 - 31 = 50 - 31$

$n = 19$

b. $6m = -78$

$\dfrac{6m}{6} = \dfrac{-78}{6}$

$m = -13$

☑ **Solve the equation. Check your solution.**

9. $x - 3 = 13$ **10.** $-5 = z - 19$ **11.** $9.6 + g = 11.4$

12. $3.5p = 7$ **13.** $-36 = -2.25t$ **14.** $\dfrac{y}{2.2} = 1.3$

Stop *and* **Think**   about Lessons 7.1–7.4

15. Writing Describe a real-life situation that can be modeled by the equation $x + 12 = 75$.

16. Critical Thinking Write an expression that has four terms and simplifies to $18x + 7$.

Review Quiz 1

Write the real-world phrase as a variable expression. Be sure to identify what the variable represents.

1. Twice the cost of a ticket   **2.** 4 years younger than Sam

3. Museum Admission The cost of admission to a museum is $32 for 4 adults. Write an equation to represent the situation. Then use mental math to find the cost of admission for one adult.

Identify the coefficients, constant terms, and like terms of the expression. Then simplify the expression.

4. $b - 8 - 6b + 10$ **5.** $10a - 15 + a + 7$ **6.** $-6 + 6 - 4c$

Solve the equation. Check your solution.

7. $14 + x = 45$ **8.** $-11 = \dfrac{a}{8}$ **9.** $\dfrac{2}{9}c = -12$

10. $t - 37 = 51$ **11.** $55 = 2.5p$ **12.** $0.2 + y + 6.3 = 5$

Draw a Diagram
Estimate
Make a List
Look for a Pattern
Work Backward
Act It Out
Make a Table

Work Backward

Problem Tickets for a school dance were sold over a three-day period. One third of the tickets were sold on Wednesday, 56 tickets were sold on Thursday, and half of the remaining tickets were sold on Friday. If there are 47 tickets left over, how many tickets were there at the beginning of the ticket sale?

1 Read and Understand

Read the problem carefully.

You know how many tickets are left over and information about the number of tickets sold each day. You need to find how many tickets there were at the beginning of the sale.

2 Make a Plan

Decide on a strategy to use.

Start with the number of tickets left over to find the number sold on Friday, and continue working backward until you find how many tickets there were at the beginning of the sale.

3 Solve the Problem

Reread the problem and work backward.

On Friday, half of the remaining tickets were sold, and 47 tickets were left.
That means that before half were sold, there were $47 \cdot 2 = 94$ tickets.

On Thursday, 56 tickets were sold.
So, before Thursday, there were $94 + 56 = 150$ tickets left.

On Wednesday, one third of the tickets were sold.
If one third of the tickets were sold on Wednesday, then two thirds of the tickets were remaining. So, two thirds of the tickets is equal to 150 tickets.

$$\frac{2}{3}x = 150 \qquad \text{Write equation.}$$

$$\left(\frac{3}{2}\right)\frac{2}{3}x = \left(\frac{3}{2}\right)150 \qquad \text{Multiply each side by } \frac{3}{2}.$$

$$x = 225 \qquad \text{Simplify.}$$

ANSWER At the beginning of the sale, there were 225 tickets.

4 Look Back

Work the problem forward, starting with 225 tickets.

Use the strategy *work backward*.

1. **Fairs** You and a friend go to a fair. You spend one fourth of your money on games. Then you spend two fifths of the remaining money on rides. Next, you spend $3 on cotton candy and $1 on a soda. If you have $5 left over, how much money did you take to the fair?

2. **Arcade Games** You are using tokens to play arcade games. You use half of your tokens on a racing game, and then 4 tokens on a maze game. If you have 2 tokens left after playing the games, how many did you start with?

3. **Wood Shop** Students are making bird houses in wood shop class. Albert spends one third of the class time sawing wood. Then he spends 10 minutes sanding and 5 minutes nailing pieces together. He takes two thirds of the rest of class to paint the bird house. If he finishes 5 minutes early, how long is wood shop class?

4. **Chess Tournament** A school chess tournament works by elimination. In each round, students play each other in pairs. The winners advance to the next round. If Veronica wins the tournament by defeating three opponents, how many students were initially in the competition?

Final Round	Winner
Sarah	
	Veronica
Veronica	

5. **Marbles** Alex, Betty, and Chris are trading marbles. First, Alex gives Betty half of his marbles. Then Betty gives Chris one third of her marbles. Finally, Chris gives Alex 2 marbles. If everyone ends up with 12 marbles, how many marbles did each person start with?

Mixed Problem Solving

Use any strategy to solve the problem.

6. **Basketball** You are planning a basketball tournament for six teams. How many games must you schedule to allow each team to play against each of the other teams just one time? twice?

7. **Lunch Money** The table below lists the amounts of money that you spend on lunch during the week. Did you spend more than $15 on lunch during the week? Explain how you know without adding all of the costs.

Day	Mon.	Tues.	Wed.	Thurs.	Fri.
Cost	$2.50	$3.00	$2.25	$3.15	$3.25

8. **Geometry** What happens to the perimeter of the square shown if you quadruple the side lengths? What happens to its area? Is this true for all squares? Explain your reasoning.

   1 cm, 1 cm

9. **Bricks** Bricks are stacked using the pattern shown below. Each row has 1 more brick than the row above it. How many bricks are in a stack with 10 rows?

Solving Two-Step Equations

BEFORE ▶ **Now** **WHY?**

You solved one-step equations. You'll solve two-step equations. So you can find the width of a basketball court, as in Ex. 25.

Word Watch

Review Words

inverse operations, p. 327

Activity **Work backward to solve the equation** $-3x + 1 = -5$.

(1 Draw a box model to represent the equation $-3x + 1 = -5$.

$$x \xrightarrow{\times (-3)} ? \xrightarrow{+ 1} -5$$

(2 Rewrite the model using inverse operations. Work from right to left. To undo adding 1, subtract 1. To undo multiplying by -3, divide by -3.

$$x \xleftarrow{\div (-3)} ? \xleftarrow{- 1} -5$$

(3 Solve the equation. Because $-5 - 1 = -6$ and $-6 \div (-3) = 2$, you know that $x = 2$. So, the solution of the equation $-3x + 1 = -5$ is 2.

$$2 \xleftarrow{\div (-3)} -6 \xleftarrow{- 1} -5$$

Use a box model to solve the equation.

1. $6x + 1 = 7$ **2.** $2x + 3 = -11$ **3.** $-4x - 5 = 7$

Using Inverse Operations Two-step equations, like $-3x + 1 = -5$ above, involve two operations and require using two inverse operations, in succession, to solve.

EXAMPLE 1 **Solving a Two-Step Equation**

Solve $5x - 6 = -21$.

$5x - 6 = -21$	Write original equation.
$5x - 6 + 6 = -21 + 6$	Add 6 to each side.
$5x = -15$	Simplify.
$\dfrac{5x}{5} = \dfrac{-15}{5}$	Divide each side by 5.
$x = -3$	Simplify.

with Solving

Don't forget to check your solution by substituting back into the original equation.

EXAMPLE 2 **Solving a Two-Step Equation**

Solve $\frac{c}{3} + 13 = 0$.

$$\frac{c}{3} + 13 = 0 \qquad \text{Write original equation.}$$

$$\frac{c}{3} + 13 - 13 = 0 - 13 \qquad \text{Subtract 13 from each side.}$$

$$\frac{c}{3} = -13 \qquad \text{Simplify.}$$

$$3\left(\frac{c}{3}\right) = 3(-13) \qquad \text{Multiply each side by 3.}$$

$$c = -39 \qquad \text{Simplify.}$$

Your turn now **Solve the equation. Check your solution.**

1. $6d - 9 = 15$ **2.** $\frac{x}{2} - 10 = -10$ **3.** $\frac{m}{4} + 7 = -7$

EXAMPLE 3 **Writing and Solving a Two-Step Equation**

Bicycle Repair Your bicycle needs to be fixed. A mechanic charges $40 for each hour of labor, and the new parts cost $35. The total cost of fixing the bicycle is $95. How long did it take the mechanic to fix the bicycle?

Solution

Write a verbal model. Let n represent the number of hours of labor.

Cost of new parts	+	Cost of labor per hour	·	Number of hours of labor	=	Total cost
35	+	40	·	n	=	95

$$35 + 40n = 95 \qquad \text{Write equation.}$$

$$35 - 35 + 40n = 95 - 35 \qquad \text{Subtract 35 from each side.}$$

$$40n = 60 \qquad \text{Simplify.}$$

$$\frac{40n}{40} = \frac{60}{40} \qquad \text{Divide each side by 40.}$$

$$n = 1.5 \qquad \text{Simplify.}$$

ANSWER The mechanic took 1.5 hours to fix the bicycle.

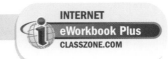
Getting Ready to Practice

1. Vocabulary Which properties would you use to solve the equation $5x - 3 = 12$?

Solve the equation. Check your solution.

2. $3x - 2 = 4$ **3.** $-7x + 5 = -9$ **4.** $\frac{x}{9} + 2 = -7$ **5.** $\frac{x}{5} - 6 = 5$

6. Internet Shopping You have $65 to spend on party favors. On the Internet, you find visors that cost $6 each. The shipping and handling charge is $5 for the entire order. How many visors can you buy?

Practice and Problem Solving

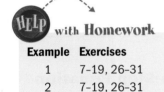
HELP with **Homework**

Example	Exercises
1	7–19, 26–31
2	7–19, 26–31
3	22–23, 25

Online Resources
CLASSZONE.COM
· More Examples
· eTutorial Plus

7. Put the steps for solving the equation $7x - 10 = -3$ in order.

   A. Add 10 to each side.   **B.** Check your answer.

   C. Write original equation.   **D.** Divide each side by 7.

Solve the equation. Check your solution.

8. $9y + 4 = -14$ **9.** $-7b - 7 = -42$ **10.** $13p - 8 = 5$

11. $29 - 2x = 13$ **12.** $\frac{e}{9} - 3 = 3$ **13.** $129 = 12b - 15$

14. $\frac{f}{12} + 20 = 20$ **15.** $\frac{3}{8}w - 14 = 10$ **16.** $-77 = -t + 55$

17. $\frac{d}{5} - 8 = -2$ **18.** $0 = 2.5y + 20$ **19.** $3(x + 1) = 12$

Write the verbal sentence as an equation. Then solve the equation.

20. Twice a number subtracted from 7 is 11.

21. 8 added to 4 times a number equals -4.

22. Souvenirs You are sightseeing in Chicago and have $20 to spend on souvenirs. You buy a baseball cap for $8. You want to buy keychains to bring home to your friends. How many keychains can you buy if each one costs $1.50?

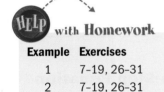
HELP with **Review**

Need help with time conversions? See p. 697.

23. Walking You jog at a speed of 6 miles per hour for 20 minutes, and you walk at a speed of 4 miles per hour for t minutes. If your combined jogging and walking distance is 3 miles, for how long did you walk?

24. Critical Thinking Write a two-step equation whose solution is 2.

25. Basketball The length of a basketball court is 84 feet, and the perimeter is 268 feet. What is the width of the basketball court?

Solve the equation. Check your solution.

26. $\dfrac{f}{6} + 1.2 = -30$ **27.** $6w + \dfrac{11}{2} = 7$ **28.** $\dfrac{5}{13} - 2x = -\dfrac{8}{13}$

29. $\dfrac{z}{0.25} - 5 = -12$ **30.** $3r + 6 - 9r = 24$ **31.** $-\dfrac{2}{3}s - 1 = \dfrac{5}{6}$

32. Challenge Find two solutions of the equation $-3|x| + 10 = -20$.

33. Test Average On the first three 100 point tests of the grading period, your scores were 85, 92, and 76. What score do you need to get on the fourth 100 point test to have a mean score of 85?

Mixed Review

Copy and complete the statement using <, >, or =. *(Lessons 4.5, 4.6)*

34. $\dfrac{3}{5} \ \underline{?} \ \dfrac{2}{3}$ **35.** $\dfrac{1}{8} \ \underline{?} \ \dfrac{1}{9}$ **36.** $\dfrac{5}{2} \ \underline{?} \ \dfrac{3}{4}$ **37.** $3\dfrac{1}{2} \ \underline{?} \ \dfrac{7}{2}$

Solve the equation. Check your solution. *(Lesson 7.4)*

38. $6w = -72$ **39.** $7.5x = 37.5$ **40.** $\dfrac{y}{22} = -9$ **41.** $\dfrac{z}{4.2} = 8.5$

Basic Skills **Use the Venn diagram to tell whether the statement is** *true* **or** *false*.

42. Tina owns a cat.

43. Kevin does not own a dog.

44. Kevin and John both own cats.

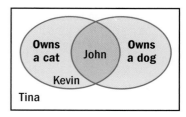

Test-Taking Practice

45. Multiple Choice A shoe store is having a sale, and all shoes are half off the original price. You use a coupon for an additional $5 off the sale price, so that you pay $17 for a pair of shoes. What is the original price?

A. $11 **B.** $24 **C.** $39 **D.** $44

46. Short Response You are using a word processor to create a table. The table will be 5 inches wide. The first column of the table will be 3 inches wide, and the remaining 4 columns will have equal width. How wide should you make each of the 4 columns of equal width?

Solving Inequalities

BEFORE

You wrote and solved equations.

Now

You'll write and solve inequalities.

WHY?

So you can determine the better deal, as in Ex. 38.

In the Real World

Word Watch

inequality, p. 346
solution of an inequality, p. 346
graph of an inequality, p. 346
equivalent inequalities, p. 346

Bumper Cars You must be at least 42 inches tall to ride the bumper cars. This can be represented by the *inequality* $h \geq 42$. An **inequality** is a mathematical sentence formed by placing an inequality symbol between two expressions. The **solution of an inequality** is the set of numbers that you can substitute for the variable to make the inequality true.

The **graph of an inequality** in one variable is the set of points on a number line that represents the solution of the inequality.

HELP with **Reading**

The inequality symbol $\leq$ is read "is less than or equal to." The inequality $\geq$ symbol is read "is greater than or equal to."

EXAMPLE 1 Graphing Inequalities

a. $x < 2$ All numbers less than 2

$$-3\ -2\ -1\ \ 0\ \ 1\ \ 2\ \ 3$$

b. $x \leq -1$ All numbers less than or equal to -1

$$-3\ -2\ -1\ \ 0\ \ 1\ \ 2\ \ 3$$

c. $x > 0$ All numbers greater than 0

$$-3\ -2\ -1\ \ 0\ \ 1\ \ 2\ \ 3$$

d. $x \geq -2$ All numbers greater than or equal to -2

$$-3\ -2\ -1\ \ 0\ \ 1\ \ 2\ \ 3$$

Equivalent inequalities are inequalities that have the same solution. You can produce an equivalent inequality in the following ways.

- Add or subtract the same number on each side.

- Multiply or divide each side by the same *positive* number.

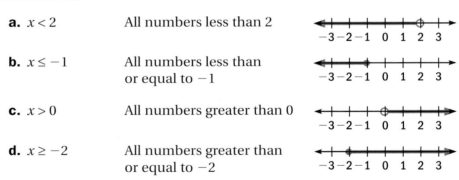

         1 < 3   **Multiply each side by 2.**   **2 < 6**

- Multiply or divide each side by the same *negative* number *and reverse the direction of the inequality.*

         1 < 3   **Multiply each side by −2.**   **−2 > −6**

EXAMPLE 2 Solving an Inequality

Solve $d - 2 \leq 1$. Then graph the solution.

$$d - 2 \leq 1 \qquad \text{Write original inequality.}$$
$$d - 2 + 2 \leq 1 + 2 \qquad \text{Add 2 to each side.}$$
$$d \leq 3 \qquad \text{Simplify.}$$

To graph $d \leq 3$, use a closed dot and draw the arrow pointing to the left.

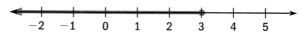

✓ **Check** To check the solution $d \leq 3$, choose any number less than or equal to 3 to substitute for d. The check below uses $d = 0$.

$$d - 2 \leq 1 \qquad \text{Write original inequality.}$$
$$0 - 2 \overset{?}{\leq} 1 \qquad \text{Substitute 0 for } d.$$
$$-2 \leq 1 \checkmark \qquad \text{Solution checks.}$$

Your turn now Solve the inequality. Then graph the solution.

1. $x - 3 \geq -1$ **2.** $6 < t - 5$ **3.** $w + 9 < -4$

EXAMPLE 3 Solving an Inequality

Solve $-4w < 20$. Then graph the solution.

$$-4w < 20 \qquad \text{Write original inequality.}$$
$$\frac{-4w}{-4} > \frac{20}{-4} \qquad \text{Divide each side by } -4. \text{ Reverse inequality.}$$
$$w > -5 \qquad \text{Simplify.}$$

To graph $w > -5$, use an open dot and draw the arrow pointing to the right.

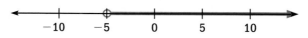

Watch Out!

Don't forget to reverse the inequality when you multiply or divide each side of an inequality by a *negative* number.

Your turn now Solve the inequality. Then graph the solution.

4. $-3n \geq -24$ **5.** $6s < -42$ **6.** $-\frac{1}{2}x \leq 5$

Getting Ready to Practice

1. **Vocabulary** How is the graph of the solution of an inequality, such as $x + 1 > 2$, different than the graph of a solution of an equation, such as $x + 1 = 2$?

Graph the inequality.

2. $a \geq -12$ 3. $x \leq -7$ 4. $w < 5$ 5. $d > 13$

Solve the inequality. Then graph the solution.

6. $r - 17 \leq -21$ 7. $b + 17 \geq 8$ 8. $-5y \geq 35$ 9. $\dfrac{x}{3} < -4$

10. **Writing** When do you use a closed dot in graphing an inequality? When do you use an open dot?

Practice and Problem Solving

Tell whether the value of m is a solution to the inequality $m \leq 5$.

11. 1   12. 5   13. 10   14. 4

Write an inequality represented by the graph.

15.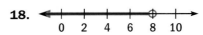

16.

17.

18.

Write an inequality to represent the situation. Then graph the inequality.

19. To vote in the United States, a person must be 18 years old or older.

20. Children under 12 will be admitted to the museum at no charge.

21. In football, you need at least 10 yards for a first down.

Solve the inequality. Then graph the solution.

22. $p + 7 < 13$ 23. $t - 14 \geq -28$ 24. $w - 21 \leq -32$

25. $19 + e > 41$ 26. $-56 + y \geq 113$ 27. $\dfrac{x}{9} \geq \dfrac{1}{3}$

28. $\dfrac{b}{4} > -5$ 29. $\dfrac{c}{-8} < -17$ 30. $3g > -36$

31. $-7s \leq 42$ 32. $-27n < -108$ 33. $z - 8.6 > 16.4$

In Exercises 34–37, solve the inequality and graph the solution. Then check your answer.

EXAMPLE **Solving a Two-Step Inequality**

$2x + 1 \le 4$	**Original inequality**
$2x + 1 - 1 \le 4 - 1$	**Subtract 1 from each side.**
$2x \le 3$	**Simplify.**
$\dfrac{2x}{2} \le \dfrac{3}{2}$	**Divide each side by 2.**
$x \le \dfrac{3}{2}$	**Simplify.**

34. $3 + 6x \le 21$ **35.** $2b - 13 > 9$ **36.** $-2y - 5 > 15$ **37.** $-7 - 4x \le 9$

38. Subway Pass A one-way subway trip costs $.75. A monthly subway pass costs $27. Write and solve an inequality to find the least number of one-way rides you must take for the subway pass to be a better deal than paying by the ride.

39. Writing Write a real-world problem that can be modeled by $3 + x \le 10$.

Challenge **Describe all of the numbers that satisfy both inequalities.**

40. $4x > 2$ and $2.5x + 4 \le 9$ **41.** $2y - 7 < 21$ and $25y + 2 > -23$

Mixed Review

42. Find the greatest common factor of 15, 20, and 30. *(Lesson 4.2)*

43. Solve the equation $-8 - 9x = 73$. *(Lesson 7.5)*

Basic Skills **Find the sum or difference.**

44. $9 + (-15)$ **45.** $-22 + (-13)$ **46.** $-7 - (-3)$ **47.** $-8 - (-9)$

Test-Taking Practice

48. Multiple Choice Which is the solution of the inequality represented by "3 more than twice a number is greater than -20"?

   A. $n < 11.5$ **B.** $n > -11.5$ **C.** $n > -13$ **D.** $n < -7$

49. Short Response A boat lift can lift up to 3600 pounds. An empty boat on the lift weighs 2300 pounds. Write and solve an inequality to find the number of additional pounds allowed in the boat without exceeding the lift's capacity.

Functions and Equations

BEFORE	▶ Now	WHY?
You wrote and evaluated expressions.	You'll write and evaluate function rules.	So you can find the pressure on a scuba diver, as in Ex. 22.

Word Watch

function, p. 350
input, p. 350
output, p. 350
domain, p. 350
range, p. 350

A **function** is a pairing of each number in a given set with exactly one number in another set. Starting with a number called an **input**, the function associates it with exactly one number called an **output**. A function can be represented by a rule, a table, or a graph.

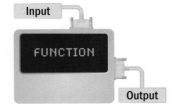

EXAMPLE 1 Evaluating a Function

Evaluate the function $y = 5x$ when $x = 7$.

$y = 5x$ Write rule for function.

$\quad = 5(7)$ Substitute 7 for x.

$\quad = 35$ Multiply.

Domain and Range The set of all input values is called the **domain** of a function. The set of all output values is called the **range** of a function.

EXAMPLE 2 Making an Input-Output Table

Make an input-output table for the function $y = x - 1.3$ using the domain 0, 1, 2, and 3. Then state the range of the function.

Solution

Input x	0	1	2	3
Substitution	$y = 0 - 1.3$	$y = 1 - 1.3$	$y = 2 - 1.3$	$y = 3 - 1.3$
Output y	-1.3	-0.3	0.7	1.7

The range of the function is the set of outputs: -1.3, -0.3, 0.7, and 1.7.

Your turn now Complete the following exercise.

1. Make an input-output table for the function $y = 2x + 2$ using the domain -2, -1, 0, 1, and 2. Then state the range of the function.

EXAMPLE 3 **Writing a Function Rule**

Write a function rule for the input-output table.

Input x	−2	−1	0	1	2	3	4
Output y	0.5	1.5	2.5	3.5	4.5	5.5	6.5

Solution

You can see that you obtain each output by adding 2.5 to the input.

ANSWER The function rule given by the table is $y = x + 2.5$.

EXAMPLE 4 **Writing a Function Rule From a Pattern**

Cakes In the diagrams of the cakes, the input c is the number of cuts made across the cake, and the output p is the number of pieces of cake. Write a rule for the function. Then use the rule to find the number of pieces made from 9 cuts.

Solution

① Begin by making an input-output table.

Input c	1	2	3	4
Output p	2	4	6	8

② Notice that each output value is twice the input value. So, a rule for the function is $p = 2c$.

③ To find the number of pieces made from 9 cuts, evaluate the function when $c = 9$. Because $p = 2(9) = 18$, there are 18 pieces made by 9 cuts.

Your turn now **Write a function rule for the input-output table.**

2.

Input x	−1	0	1	2
Output y	−4	−3	−2	−1

3.

Input x	2	4	6	8
Output y	−1	−2	−3	−4

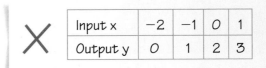
Getting Ready to Practice

1. **Vocabulary** In your own words, explain what a function is.

2. Copy and complete the input-output table for the function $y = 2x - 5$.

Input x	−4	−2	0	2	4	6	8	10
Output y	?	?	?	?	?	?	?	?

3. **Find the Error** Describe and correct the error in making an input-output table for the function $y = x - 2$.

✗

Input x	−2	−1	0	1
Output y	0	1	2	3

4. **Ages** You are 3 years older than your cousin. Write a function rule that represents your age y in terms of your cousin's age x. Then create an input-output table using the domain 10, 15, 20, and 25.

Practice and Problem Solving

HELP with Homework

Example	Exercises
1	5–8
2	9–14, 22
3	15–18
4	20–21

Online Resources
CLASSZONE.COM

· More Examples
· eTutorial Plus

Evaluate the function $y = 3x - 2$ for the given value of x.

5. 4   6. 0   7. 1   8. −3

Make an input-output table for the function using the domain −2, −1, 0, 1, and 2. Then state the range of the function.

9. $y = x + 11$ 10. $y = -20x$ 11. $y = 3.7x$

12. $y = x - 4.56$ 13. $y = 0.8x - 1$ 14. $y = 15 - 2x$

Write a function rule for the input-output table.

15.

Input x	1	2	3	4
Output y	5	10	15	20

16.

Input x	−2	−1	0	1
Output y	13	14	15	16

17.

Input x	2	3	4	5
Output y	0.8	1.8	2.8	3.8

18.

Input x	−3	0	3	6
Output y	1	0	−1	−2

19. Write a function rule that converts y years to m months. Use the function to calculate the number of months in 20 years.

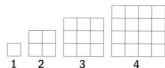

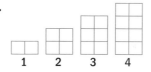

Scuba Diving

A scuba diver can reach −475 feet, relative to sea level. The lowest point in the ocean is −35,802 feet, relative to sea level. What is the difference between the depth a scuba diver can reach and the lowest point in the ocean?

Write a function rule for the pattern. Each figure in the pattern is made using unit squares. The input x is the number below each figure, and the output y is the number of unit squares in the figure.

20.

```
        ┌─┐
    ┌─┬─┤ │
┌─┐ │ │ ├─┤
└─┘ └─┴─┴─┘
 1   2  3  4
```

21.

```
              ┌─┬─┐
        ┌─┬─┐ │ │ │
    ┌─┐ │ │ │ ├─┼─┤
┌─┐ │ │ ├─┼─┤ │ │ │
└─┘ └─┘ └─┴─┘ └─┴─┘
 1   2   3     4
```

22. Scuba Diving The pressure on a scuba diver is given by the function $p = 64d + 2112$, where p is pressure, in pounds per square foot, and d is depth, in feet. Make an input-output table for depths of 0, 20, 40, 60, 80, and 100 feet. As the depth increases, what happens to the pressure?

Decide **Tell whether the table represents a function. If so, write the function rule. If not, explain why not.**

23.

Input p	−1	0	1	2
Output q	1	0	1	4

24.

Input s	1	1	4	4
Output t	−1	1	−2	2

25.

Input m	−2	0	2	4
Output n	−3	1	5	9

26.

Input a	−3	−1	1	3
Output b	13	3	−7	−17

27. Challenge Write three different functions for which an input of −3 gives an output of 15.

Mixed Review

28. Write the prime factorization of 84. *(Lesson 4.1)*

29. Solve $-10z < 20$. Then graph the solution. *(Lesson 7.6)*

Basic Skills **Plot the points in a coordinate plane.**

30. $A(9, -2)$ **31.** $B(0, 2)$ **32.** $C(-3, -4)$ **33.** $D(-4, 0)$

Test-Taking Practice

34. Multiple Choice Which function rule represents the table?

A. $y = x + 2$ **B.** $y = x$

C. $y = -x$ **D.** $y = x - 4$

Input x	−1	0	1	2
Output y	1	0	−1	−2

35. Multiple Choice What is the value of $y = 7x - 2$ when $x = -0.5$?

F. −5.5 **G.** −4.5 **H.** 1.5 **I.** 33

Graphing Functions

BEFORE

Now

WHY?

You graphed ordered pairs in a coordinate plane.

You'll graph functions in a coordinate plane.

So you can write a function for the cost of papayas, as in Ex. 15.

In the Real World

Word Watch

linear function, p. 355

Fabric You are in a craft shop, choosing fabric for a sewing project. The fabric you choose costs $2.50 for each yard. How can you use a graph to represent this situation? You'll find the answer in Example 2.

You can graph a function by creating an input-output table, forming ordered pairs, and plotting the ordered pairs.

EXAMPLE 1 Graphing a Function

Graph the function $y = 2x + 1$.

HELP with Solving

When the domain of a function is not given, assume that it includes every x-value for which the function can produce a corresponding y-value.

① Make an input-output table by choosing several input values and finding the output values.

② Use the table to write a list of ordered pairs:

$(-2, -3)$, $(-1, -1)$, $(0, 1)$, $(1, 3)$, $(2, 5)$

x	Substitution	y
-2	$y = 2(-2) + 1$	-3
-1	$y = 2(-1) + 1$	-1
0	$y = 2(0) + 1$	1
1	$y = 2(1) + 1$	3
2	$y = 2(2) + 1$	5

③ Plot the ordered pairs in a coordinate plane.

④ Notice that all of the points lie on a line. Any other ordered pairs satisfying $y = 2x + 1$ would also lie on the line when graphed. The line represents the complete graph of the function $y = 2x + 1$.

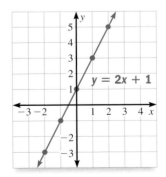

Your turn now Graph the function.

1. $y = x - 3$

2. $y = 3x$

3. $y = 2x - 3$

EXAMPLE 2 **Writing and Graphing a Function**

The situation described on page 354 can be represented by the function $y = 2.50x$, where y is the total cost of the fabric and x is the number of yards of fabric.

Follow these steps to graph the function.

Watch Out!

In Example 2, note that you cannot have less than 0 yards of fabric, so you cannot use any numbers less than 0 in the domain.

(1) Make an input-output table.

Input x	Output y
0	0
1	2.5
2	5
3	7.5
4	10

(2) Plot the ordered pairs and connect them as shown.

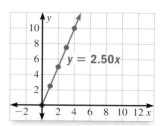

Linear Functions The functions in Examples 1 and 2 are *linear functions*. A **linear function** is a function whose graph is a line or part of a line. Not all graphs are lines, nor do all graphs represent functions.

EXAMPLE 3 **Identifying Linear Functions**

HELP with **Solving**

Recall that a function pairs each input value with *exactly* one output value.

Tell whether each graph represents a function of x. If it does, tell whether the function is *linear* or *nonlinear*.

a.
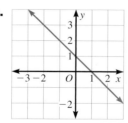

b.
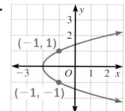

c.
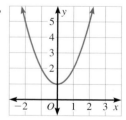

Solution

a. This graph represents a function of x. The function is linear because the graph is a line.

b. This graph does *not* represent a function of x. For each value of x in the domain, excluding -2, there is more than one value of y.

c. This graph represents a function of x. The function is nonlinear because the graph is not a line or part of a line.

Getting Ready to Practice

1. Vocabulary What is the difference between a linear function and a nonlinear function?

Match the function with its graph.

2. $y = 3x$

3. $y = \frac{1}{2}x$

4. $y = 2x + 3$

A.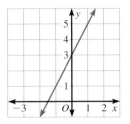

B.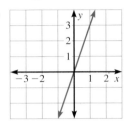

C.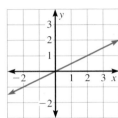

5. Walking When you walk slowly, your body burns about 2 Calories every minute. This situation can be represented by the function $y = 2x$, where y is the number of calories burned and x is the number of minutes you walk. Graph the function.

Practice and Problem Solving

HELP with Homework

Example	Exercises
1	6–14
2	15–16, 18–21
3	22–24, 28

Online Resources
CLASSZONE.COM

· More Examples
· eTutorial Plus

Graph the function.

6. $y = x$

7. $y = 10 - x$

8. $y = \frac{1}{3}x$

9. $y = x + 3$

10. $y = 3x - 5$

11. $y = -4x + 1$

12. $y = \frac{1}{4}x + 2$

13. $y = 0.5x - 2$

14. $y = -x - 4$

15. Papayas Papayas cost $1.50 per pound. Write and graph a function that models the cost y of x pounds of papayas.

16. Bicycles The front wheel of a bicycle travels $6\frac{1}{2}$ feet for every rotation it makes. Write and graph a function that models the distance y the front wheel travels in x rotations.

17. Writing Describe a situation that can be represented by a linear function.

Write and graph a function that converts the units.

18. x yards to y feet

19. x days to y weeks

20. x pints to y cups

21. x millimeters to y centimeters

Tell whether the graph represents a function of x. If it does, tell whether the function is *linear* or *nonlinear*.

22.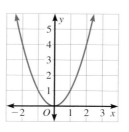

23.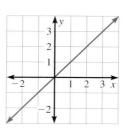

24.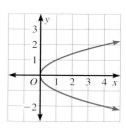

In Exercises 25–27, write y as a function of x. Then graph the function.

> **EXAMPLE** **Writing y as a Function of x**
>
> | | |
> |---|---|
> | $8x + 4y = 1200$ | Original equation |
> | $8x - 8x + 4y = 1200 - 8x$ | Subtract $8x$ from each side. |
> | $4y = 1200 - 8x$ | Simplify. |
> | $\dfrac{4y}{4} = \dfrac{1200 - 8x}{4}$ | Divide each side by 4. |
> | $y = 300 - 2x$ | Simplify. |
>
> **ANSWER** You can write $8x + 4y = 1200$ as $y = 300 - 2x$.

25. $-3x + y = 2$ **26.** $2x + y = 8$ **27.** $15x + 5y = 30$

28. Hot Chocolate The table below shows the temperature y of a cup of hot chocolate after cooling for x minutes. Use the table to write a list of ordered pairs. Plot the ordered pairs and draw a line or curve through the points. Then tell whether the graph represents a function. If so, is it a linear function?

Time (min)	0	2	5	10	20	30	40	50	60
Temperature (°C)	90	85	79	68	58	49	43.5	39.5	37

Graph the functions in the same coordinate plane. Then tell where they intersect.

29. $y = x$ and $y = 3x - 4$ **30.** $y = 5 - x$ and $y = -2x + 11$

31. $y = -x - 3$ and $y = -2x - 8$ **32.** $y = x + 1$ and $y = 3x - 1$

33. Challenge A rectangle has a length of 4 inches and a width of x inches. Write and graph a function that gives the perimeter y of the rectangle.

Write the fraction in simplest form. *(Lesson 4.3)*

34. $\dfrac{63}{81}$ **35.** $\dfrac{77}{343}$ **36.** $\dfrac{120}{360}$ **37.** $\dfrac{65}{78}$

38. Evaluate the function $y = 6x - 7$ when $x = 12$. *(Lesson 7.7)*

Test-Taking Practice

39. Multiple Choice The graph of which function is shown?

    A. $y = -x$ **B.** $y = -6x$

    C. $y = -x - 6$ **D.** $y = x - 6$

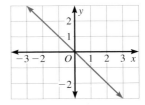

40. Multiple Choice Which ordered pair is a point on the graph of the function $y = 2x - 5$?

    F. $(0, 0)$ **G.** $(5, 5)$ **H.** $(-1, 2)$ **I.** $(-3, 1)$

BRAIN GAME

Fun with Functions

Each player puts a marker on the **START** space. Players alternate turns. On your turn, roll a number cube and evaluate the function using the number rolled as the value of x. If the result is positive, move *forward* that number of spaces. If the result is negative, move *backward* that number of spaces. The first player to land on or pass the **END** space wins.

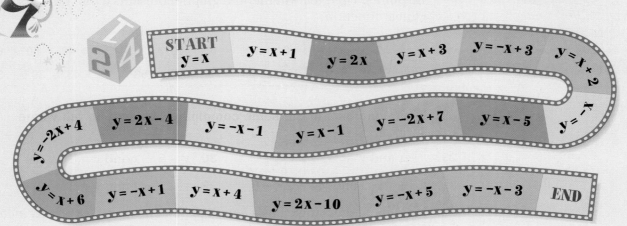

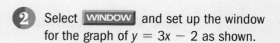

Technology *Activity*

Graphing Functions

GOAL Graph functions using a graphing calculator.

Example Graph $y = 3x - 2$ and find ordered pairs using the *trace* feature on your graphing calculator.

Solution

1 Select 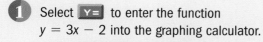 to enter the function $y = 3x - 2$ into the graphing calculator.

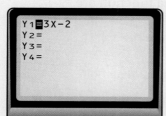

```
Y₁■3X-2
Y₂=
Y₃=
Y₄=
```

2 Select **WINDOW** and set up the window for the graph of $y = 3x - 2$ as shown.

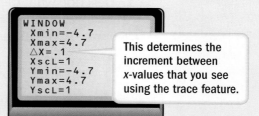

```
WINDOW
Xmin=-4.7
Xmax=4.7
△X=.1
XscL=1
Ymin=-4.7
Ymax=4.7
YscL=1
```

> This determines the increment between *x*-values that you see using the trace feature.

3 Select **GRAPH** to view the graph of the function. Then select **TRACE** to see the coordinates of points on the graph. Use the left and right arrows to move the cursor along the graph.

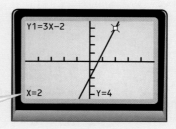

```
Y1=3X-2




X=2        Y=4
```

> Notice that X = 2 and Y = 4 correspond to the ordered pair (2, 4).

Your turn now Use a graphing calculator to graph the function and find the unknown value in the given ordered pairs.

1. $y = 2x$, (_?_ , 1.6) and (2.1, _?_)

2. $y = -x$, (-4.3, _?_) and (_?_ , 0)

3. $y = -3x + 1$, (_?_ , -2) and (-2, _?_)

4. $y = 5x - \frac{1}{2}$, (4.5, _?_) and (_?_ , 1.5)

5. $y = -3x - 1$, (_?_ , 0.8) and (0.2, _?_)

6. $y = 2x + 2.3$, (0, _?_) and (_?_ , 5.5)

7. Critical Thinking Use a graphing calculator to graph $y = 2x + 5$ and $y = -x + 2$ in the same coordinate plane. Tell where they intersect. Check your answer by substituting the values into each equation.

Notebook Review

Review the vocabulary definitions in your notebook.

Copy the review examples in your notebook. Then complete the exercises.

Check Your Definitions

inequality, p. 346
solution of an inequality, p. 346
graph of an inequality, p. 346
equivalent inequalities, p. 346

function, p. 350
input, p. 350
output, p. 350

domain, p. 350
range, p. 350
linear function, p. 355

Use Your Vocabulary

1. Describe what the domain and range of a function are.

7.5 Can you solve a two-step equation?

EXAMPLE

$4x + 6 = 22$	Original equation
$4x + 6 - 6 = 22 - 6$	Subtract 6 from each side.
$4x = 16$	Simplify.
$\dfrac{4x}{4} = \dfrac{16}{4}$	Divide each side by 4.
$x = 4$	Simplify.

✓ **Solve the equation. Check your solution.**

2. $12r - 8 = -32$ **3.** $2s + 6 = 64$ **4.** $-2 = \dfrac{t}{20} + 8$

7.6 Can you solve and graph an inequality?

EXAMPLE

$-3x \leq 48$	Original inequality
$\dfrac{-3x}{-3} \geq \dfrac{48}{-3}$	Divide each side by -3. Reverse inequality.
$x \geq -16$	Simplify.

```
  +--+--+--+--+--+--+--+--+--+--+-->
-20 -18 -16 -14 -12 -10 -8  -6  -4  -2   0
```

✓ **Solve the inequality. Then graph the solution.**

5. $\dfrac{y}{5} \leq -3$ **6.** $x - 8 > 3$ **7.** $-7w > -84$

7.7–7.8 Can you graph a function?

EXAMPLE Make an input-output table for the function $y = -2x - 3$. Then graph the function.

x	Substitution	y
−2	$y = -2(-2) - 3$	1
−1	$y = -2(-1) - 3$	−1
0	$y = -2(0) - 3$	−3
1	$y = -2(1) - 3$	−5

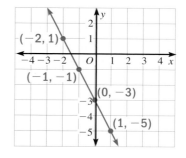

☑ **Make an input-output table for the function. Then graph the function.**

8. $y = x - 5$ **9.** $y = -3x + 3$ **10.** $y = \frac{2}{3}x$

Stop *and* **Think** about Lessons 7.5–7.8

11. Critical Thinking Write two different functions for which an input of 6 gives an output of −12.

Review Quiz 2

Solve the equation. Check your solution.

1. $10 + 5u = -25$ **2.** $40 = 6t - 14$ **3.** $\frac{w}{28} + 6.5 = 11$

4. Musical Each student ticket to a school musical costs $5, and each adult ticket costs $6. The music department collected $1400 in ticket sales. If they sold 150 adult tickets, how many student tickets were sold?

Solve the inequality. Then graph the solution.

5. $-3w > 51$ **6.** $x - 15 \leq -17$ **7.** $34 + y \geq 47$ **8.** $16 - 3z < 28$

Make an input-output table for the function. Then graph the function.

9. $y = -x + 2$ **10.** $y = 7 + 2x$ **11.** $y = -\frac{1}{3}x$ **12.** $y = \frac{1}{2}x - 4$

Chapter Review

 **Vocabulary**

verbal model, p. 318
term, p. 322
like terms, p. 322
equivalent variable
  expressions, p. 322
coefficient, p. 322
constant term, p. 322

inverse operations, p. 327
equivalent equations,
  p. 327
inequality, p. 346
solution of an inequality,
  p. 346
graph of an inequality,
  p. 346

equivalent inequalities,
  p. 346
function, p. 350
input, p. 350
output, p. 350
domain, p. 350
range, p. 350
linear function, p. 355

Vocabulary Review

Copy and complete the statement.

1. Two equations that have the same solution(s) are ?.

2. ? are operations that "undo" each other.

3. The set of all input values is called the ? of a function.

4. Identify the coefficients, constant terms, and like terms of the expression $4x - 2 - 8x + 7$.

5. Give an example of an inequality and graph the solution of the inequality.

6. Explain what a linear function is.

Review Questions

Write the verbal phrase or sentence as a variable expression or equation. Let *m* represent the number. *(Lesson 7.1)*

7. 9 less than a number

8. The sum of a number and 7

9. The quotient of a number and -5

10. 9 more than twice a number

11. 16 multiplied by a number is 48.

12. The product of a number and 1 is -17.

13. -16 added to a number is equal to 11.

14. Twice the sum of a number and 2 is 10.

15. Students There are 24 students in your class, which is 5 more students than are in your friend's class. Write and solve an equation to find the number of students in your friend's class. *(Lesson 7.1)*

Simplify the expression. *(Lesson 7.2)*

16. $2d - 8 + 3d$

17. $-4e - 1 - 2e + 3$

18. $10 + 2(f - 3)$

Review Questions

Solve the equation. Check your solution. *(Lessons 7.3, 7.4, 7.5)*

19. $x - 5 = 16$ **20.** $y + 12 = -25$ **21.** $p + 7 = -10$ **22.** $r - (-6) = 10$

23. $-132 = 4w$ **24.** $-16 = 2.5k$ **25.** $\frac{z}{6} = -10$ **26.** $16 = \frac{q}{3}$

27. $2x + 5 = 11$ **28.** $-3y - 7 = 8$ **29.** $10.4 = 3a + 2.9$ **30.** $\frac{x}{2} - 12 = 0$

31. Hawaiian Islands The island of Kauai is 55.4 square miles less in area than the island of Oahu. Kauai has an area of 552.3 square miles. Write and solve an equation to find the area of Oahu. *(Lesson 7.3)*

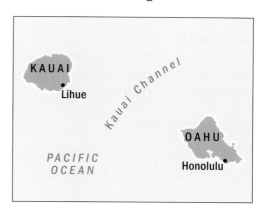

32. Raking Leaves You have a job raking leaves. You make $6.50 each hour plus tips. You made $12.50 in tips last week and made a total of $110. How many hours did you work? *(Lesson 7.5)*

33. Write the inequality represented by the graph. *(Lesson 7.6)*

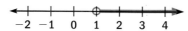

Solve the inequality. Then graph its solution. *(Lesson 7.6)*

34. $-5w \le 20$ **35.** $x - 12 > 0$ **36.** $\frac{y}{4} > -7$ **37.** $z + 1.5 \ge -2.1$

38. Carry on Luggage Most airlines have a carry on luggage weight limit of 40 pounds. Your carry on bag weighs 3.6 pounds when it is empty. How much can the contents of the bag weigh and still comply with the weight limit? *(Lesson 7.6)*

Make an input-output table for the function using the domain −4, −2, 0, 2, and 4. Then state the range of the function. *(Lesson 7.7)*

39. $y = x + 3$ **40.** $y = -3x$ **41.** $y = \frac{1}{2}x + 2$ **42.** $y = 2x + 10$

Write a function rule for the input-output table. *(Lesson 7.7)*

43.

Input x	0	1	2	3
Output y	4	5	6	7

44.

Input x	−2	0	2	4
Output y	0.5	0	−0.5	−1

Graph the function. *(Lesson 7.8)*

45. $y = 9 - 2x$ **46.** $y = -2 + 4x$ **47.** $y = 0.2x + 5$ **48.** $y = 15 - 3x$

Chapter Test

Write the verbal phrase or sentence as a variable expression or equation. Let *x* represent the number.

1. 5 more than twice a number

2. 12 less than a number is -19.

3. Basketball In 1993, Bobby Hurley broke the NCAA all-time assist record for Division I men's basketball. Hurley made 1076 assists, which was 38 more than the previous record. Write and solve an equation to find the previous assist record.

Simplify the expression.

4. $3b - 2 + 4b$

5. $10h + 9 + h - 10$

6. $7x - 4(3 - x)$

7. $3 - 6s - 5 + 2s$

8. Write and simplify an expression for the perimeter of the rectangle.

$$x + 1$$
$$3x$$

Solve the equation. Check your solution.

9. $-3 = x + 4$

10. $12 = n + 7$

11. $c - 10.7 = 14.3$

12. $20k = -320$

13. $\dfrac{m}{6} = -13$

14. $\dfrac{2}{7}y = -10$

15. $8 = -5r + 18$

16. $4 - \dfrac{s}{12} = -6$

17. Potholders It takes you 0.5 hour to make one potholder. Write and solve an equation to find how many potholders you can make in 6 hours.

Solve the inequality. Then graph the solution.

18. $5n \le -10$

19. $z - 3 > 5$

20. $-2p \ge 6$

Write a function rule for the input-output table.

21.

Input *x*	−2	0	2	4
Output *y*	−20	0	20	40

22.

Input *x*	−2	−1	0	1
Output *y*	10	11	12	13

Graph the function.

23. $y = 5x + 2$

24. $y = x - 7$

25. $y = 2x - 2$

26. $y = \dfrac{1}{3}x + 1$

Chapter Standardized Test

Test-Taking Strategy Most standardized tests are based on concepts and skills taught in school. The best way to prepare is to keep up with your regular studies.

Multiple Choice

1. Which equation represents the following sentence?

The difference of a number and 1 is -13.

A. $x - 1 = 13$ **B.** $x - 1 = -13$

C. $1 - x = -13$ **D.** $x + 1 = -13$

2. Which expression is *not* equivalent to $3w + 3$?

F. $3(w + 1)$ **G.** $w(3 + 3)$

H. $3(w - 2) + 9$ **I.** $w(3 + 1) - w + 3$

3. Which expression is equivalent to $-16 - 8(c - 2)$?

A. $-8c$ **B.** $-32 - 8c$

C. $-18 - 8c$ **D.** $-14 - 8c$

4. What is the solution of the equation $x + 3 = -5$?

F. -8 **G.** -2 **H.** 2 **I.** 8

5. Which of the following equations has -8 as a solution?

A. $-4x = 2$ **B.** $\dfrac{x}{4} = -\dfrac{1}{2}$

C. $-16x = 2$ **D.** $3x = -24$

6. When solving the equation $9x + 2 = 7$, what should you do first?

F. Add 2 to each side.

G. Add 7 to each side.

H. Subtract 9 from each side.

I. Subtract 2 from each side.

7. The solution of which inequality is represented by the graph?

$-2 \quad -1 \quad 0 \quad 1 \quad 2 \quad 3 \quad 4$

A. $-12x > -24$ **B.** $\dfrac{3}{4}x \le \dfrac{3}{8}$

C. $x + 14 < -12$ **D.** $x - 23 \ge -21$

8. Which function has an output value of 7 for an input value of 4?

F. $y = 5x - 3$ **G.** $y = -4x + 9$

H. $y = 3x - 5$ **I.** $y = 7x$

9. Which function rule produces the table?

Input x	-2	0	3	5
Output y	-8	-4	2	6

A. $y = 2x - 4$ **B.** $y = x^2 - 4$

C. $y = -6x - 4$ **D.** $y = 3x - 7$

Short Response

10. Graph the function $y = 2x - 1$. Tell whether it is a linear function.

Extended Response

11. You earn $5 an hour for baby-sitting, plus you always get a $5 tip. Write and graph a function that models the money earned y after baby-sitting for x hours. How many hours would you have to baby-sit to earn $20? How can you tell just by looking at the graph?

8

Ratios and Proportions

BEFORE

In previous chapters you've...

- Found equivalent fractions
- Solved multiplication equations

Now

In Chapter 8 you'll study...

- Ratios
- Rates and unit rates
- Slope
- Solving proportions
- Scale drawings

WHY?

So you can solve real-world problems about...

Internet Preview
CLASSZONE.COM

- eEdition Plus Online
- eWorkbook Plus Online
- eTutorial Plus Online
- State Test Practice
- More Examples

Chapter Warm-Up Game

Review skills you need for this chapter in this game. Work with a partner.

Key Skill:
Finding equivalent fractions

FRACTION ACTION

MATERIALS

- colored chips
- number cubes
- game board

PREPARE Each player rolls a number cube. The player with the highest roll goes first and chooses one color of chips to use. Players take turns. On your turn, follow the steps on the next page.

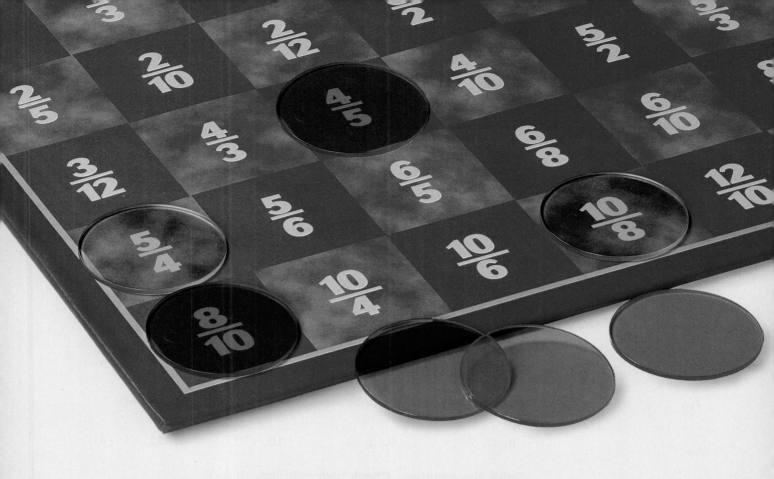

 **ROLL** both of the number cubes.

HOW TO WIN Be the first player to cover three spaces in a row (either horizontally, vertically, or diagonally), or be the first player to use all of your chips.

 FORM a fraction from the numbers rolled. One number is the numerator and the other is the denominator.

 **COVER** the fractions on the board (that are not already covered) that are equivalent to the fraction formed.

Stop *and* Think

1. **Writing** How did you decide which of the numbers you rolled would be the numerator and which would be the denominator?

2. **Critical Thinking** How many spaces can you cover if you roll the same number on both number cubes?

Getting Ready to Learn

Review What You Need to Know ⟲

Using Vocabulary **Copy and complete using a review word.**

1. A(n) _?_ of an equation is a number that you can substitute for the variable to make the equation true.

2. A(n) _?_ is formed by the intersection of a horizontal number line, called the x-axis, and a vertical number line, called the y-axis.

3. Points in a coordinate plane are represented by _?_.

Write the fraction or mixed number as a decimal. *(p. 190)*

4. $\dfrac{7}{10}$ **5.** $\dfrac{15}{150}$ **6.** $2\dfrac{3}{4}$ **7.** $6\dfrac{3}{8}$

Plot the point and describe its location in a coordinate plane. *(p. 293)*

8. $(2, 5)$ **9.** $(0, 6)$ **10.** $(-1, 1)$ **11.** $(3, -4)$

Solve the equation. Check your solution. *(p. 333)*

12. $1.2k = 6$ **13.** $6.3y = 25.2$ **14.** $\dfrac{z}{8} = 36$ **15.** $\dfrac{m}{9.9} = 2$

You should include material that appears on a notebook like this in your own notes.

Know How to Take Notes

Using Multiple Methods As you learn multiple methods for solving a problem, write the methods in your notebook. Each method should solve the same problem. An example is shown below.

Methods for Finding the GCF

List common factors.

12: 1, 2, 3, 4, 6, 12
18: 1, 2, 3, 6, 9, 18

GCF: 6

Use prime factorization.

12: 2 × 2 × 3
18: 2 × 3 × 3

GCF: 2 × 3 = 6

In Lesson 8.4, you will learn two methods for solving a proportion. Include examples of each method in your notebook. Refer to your notes when you work on the exercises.

Ratios

BEFORE	Now	WHY?
You wrote and compared fractions.	You'll write and compare ratios.	So you can write a ratio about reptiles, as in Ex. 23.

In the Real World

Word Watch

ratio, p. 369
equivalent ratios, p. 369

Baseball How can you compare a baseball team's wins to its losses during spring training?

A **ratio** uses division to compare two numbers. There are three ways to write a ratio of two numbers.

2001 Spring Training		
Team	Wins	Losses
San Diego Padres	16	11
L.A. Dodgers	18	13
Chicago Cubs	17	14

Writing a Ratio

Words	Numbers	Algebra
wins to losses	18 to 13	a to b, where b is nonzero.
$\dfrac{\text{wins}}{\text{losses}}$	$\dfrac{18}{13}$	$\dfrac{a}{b}$, where b is nonzero.
wins : losses	18 : 13	$a : b$, where b is nonzero.

All three ways of writing the ratio of two numbers are read "the ratio of a to b," so $18 : 13$ is read "the ratio of eighteen to thirteen." Two ratios are **equivalent ratios** when they have the same value.

EXAMPLE 1 Writing a Ratio

You can make comparisons about games played by the Cubs.

a. Wins to losses

wins = 17, losses = 14

ANSWER $17 : 14$, or $\dfrac{17}{14}$

b. Wins to games played

wins = 17, games = 17 + 14 = 31

ANSWER $17 : 31$, or $\dfrac{17}{31}$

Your turn now Use the table above to write the ratio for the Padres.

1. Wins to losses   **2.** Wins to games played   **3.** Losses to wins

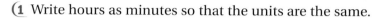

EXAMPLE 2 **Writing Ratios in Simplest Form**

Amusement Parks A ride on a roller coaster lasts 2 minutes. Suppose you wait in line for $1\frac{1}{2}$ hours to ride the roller coaster. Follow the steps below to find the ratio of time spent in line to time spent on the ride.

1 Write hours as minutes so that the units are the same.

$$1\text{ h} + \frac{1}{2}\text{ h} = 60\text{ min} + 30\text{ min}$$ Write hours as minutes.

$$= 90\text{ min}$$ Add.

2 Write the ratio of time spent in line to time spent on the ride.

$$\frac{\text{Time in line}}{\text{Time on ride}} = \frac{90}{2}$$ Write ratio.

$$= \frac{45}{1}$$ Simplify fraction.

ANSWER The ratio of time spent in line to time spent on the ride is $45 : 1$.

Comparing Ratios To compare ratios, you can write the ratios as fractions and compare the fractions. However, sometimes it is easier to write the ratios as decimals and compare the decimals.

EXAMPLE 3 **Comparing Ratios**

Music Luis and Amber compared their CD collections. To determine who has a greater ratio of rock CDs to pop CDs, write the ratios.

	Rock	Pop	Hip-hop
Luis	9	24	16
Amber	42	70	25

 **with Review**

Need help with writing
fractions as decimals?
See p. 190.

Luis: $\frac{\text{Rock}}{\text{Pop}} = \frac{9}{24}$ **Amber:** $\frac{\text{Rock}}{\text{Pop}} = \frac{42}{70}$ Write ratios as fractions.

$$= 0.375 \qquad\qquad = 0.6$$ Write fractions as decimals.

ANSWER Since $0.6 > 0.375$, Amber has a greater ratio of rock to pop CDs.

Your turn now Refer to Example 3.

4. Does Luis or Amber have a greater ratio of pop CDs to hip-hop CDs?

5. Does Luis or Amber have a greater ratio of hip-hop CDs to rock CDs?

Getting Ready to Practice

1. **Vocabulary** Give an example of a ratio in real life.

In Exercises 2–5, write the ratio of the first number to the second number in three ways.

2. 1, 7   3. 1, 1   4. 3, 10   5. 15, 2

6. Write the following ratios in order from least to greatest: 5 to 8, 3 to 6, and 15 to 5.

7. **Raffle Tickets** For a school fundraiser, you sold 33 raffle tickets and your friend sold 15 raffle tickets. Write the ratio of tickets you sold to tickets your friend sold as a fraction in simplest form.

Practice and Problem Solving

HELP with Homework

Example	Exercises
1	8–11, 13
2	14–29, 33–34
3	30–32, 35–36

Online Resources
CLASSZONE.COM
· More Examples
· eTutorial Plus

School The table shows the numbers of boys and girls in the seventh and eighth grades at a school. Use the table to write the specified ratio.

8. Seventh grade boys to eighth grade boys

9. Eighth grade girls to eighth grade boys

10. Seventh grade girls to all seventh graders

11. Eighth grade boys to all eighth graders

	Boys	Girls
Seventh	47	42
Eighth	39	41

12. **Find the Error** Zach was asked to find the ratio of his T-shirts to his jeans. Zach has 14 T-shirts and 9 pairs of jeans. Describe and correct his error.

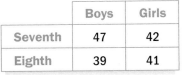
$$\frac{\text{T-shirts}}{\text{Jeans}} = \frac{9}{14}$$

13. **Muscles** Your face uses about 13 muscles to smile and about 43 muscles to frown. Write the ratio of muscles used for frowning to muscles used for smiling in three different ways.

Write the ratio as a fraction in simplest form.

14. $\frac{7}{14}$ 15. $\frac{12}{15}$ 16. $8 : 14$

17. 9 to 5   18. 20 to 35   19. $32 : 48$

20. $30 : 75$ 21. 65 to 130   22. 54 to 72

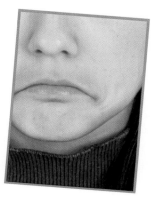

23. Reptiles There are about 4000 known kinds of lizards and 1600 known kinds of snakes. Write the ratio of known kinds of lizards to known kinds of snakes.

Write the ratio of the first measurement to the second measurement. Write both measurements in the same unit.

24. 3 qts, 2 gal   **25.** 5 ft, 10 in.   **26.** 2 lb, 18 oz

27. 2 ft, 4 yd   **28.** 600 m, 5 km   **29.** 7 min, 25 sec

Copy and complete the statement using <, >, or =.

30. $9 : 15 \underline{\ ?\ } 8 : 20$ **31.** $18 : 12 \underline{\ ?\ } 54 : 36$ **32.** $72 : 96 \underline{\ ?\ } 56 : 80$

33. Restaurants You spend a total of $1\frac{3}{4}$ hours at a restaurant with your family. You spend 20 minutes eating your dinner. What is the ratio of your time spent at the restaurant to your time spent eating?

34. Papier-Mâché A recipe for papier-mâché paste uses 2 quarts of white glue and 2 pints of water. What is the ratio of pints of glue to pints of water?

Education The table shows the number of men and women who earned master's degrees in the United States in 1970 and in 1998.

35. Write the ratio of degrees earned by men to degrees earned by women for each year. Express the ratios as decimals rounded to the nearest hundredth.

Master's Degrees Earned		
Year	1970	1998
Men	126,000	184,000
Women	83,000	246,000

36. Which of the ratios in Exercise 35 is less than the other?

37. Estimate In 15 seconds, your dog ran a distance of 97 yards, and you ran a distance of 152 feet. Choose the most reasonable estimate of the ratio of the distance you ran to the distance your dog ran.

    A. $1 : 1.5$ **B.** $1 : 2$ **C.** $1.5 : 1$ **D.** $2 : 1$

 Algebra Find a value for x that makes the first ratio equivalent to the second ratio.

38. x to 6, 20 to 24   **39.** x to 72, 5 to 8   **40.** x to 12, 6 to 9

41. Challenge The ratio of the length of a rectangle to the width of the rectangle is $5 : 4$. If the perimeter of the rectangle is 108 inches, what are the length and the width of the rectangle?

Mixed Review

Solve the equation using mental math. *(Lesson 1.5)*

42. $x + 3 = 10$ **43.** $18 - z = 9$ **44.** $4y = 44$ **45.** $\frac{x}{8} = 6$

Choose a Strategy Use a strategy from the list to solve the following problem. Explain your choice of strategy.

> **Problem Solving Strategies**
> - Find a Pattern
> - Make a Table
> - Work Backward

46. On a trip to the mall, you spent $8 at the first store, then half of your remaining money at a second store. You spent the rest of your money, $16, at a third store. How much money did you start with?

Basic Skills Find the product or quotient.

47. 62×14 **48.** 437×1000 **49.** $405 \div 9$ **50.** $588 \div 12$

Test-Taking Practice

INTERNET
State Test Practice
CLASSZONE.COM

51. Multiple Choice Which ratio is *not* equivalent to 6 to 10?

A. $6 : 10$ **B.** $3 : 5$ **C.** $\frac{3}{5}$ **D.** $\frac{5}{3}$

52. Multiple Choice You used 3 yards of fleece to make a blanket and 2 feet of fleece to make a vest. What is the ratio of fleece used for the blanket to fleece used for the vest?

F. $\frac{2}{9}$ **G.** $\frac{2}{3}$ **H.** $\frac{3}{2}$ **I.** $\frac{9}{2}$

BrAIN GAME

Something to Celebrate

Replace each ratio with the letter of an equivalent ratio to find the name of a famous American born on January 1, 1752. Some letters may be used more than once.

| $\frac{6}{24}$ | $\frac{6}{18}$ | $\frac{12}{16}$ | $\frac{4}{6}$ | $\frac{7}{7}$ | $\frac{12}{20}$ | $\frac{15}{30}$ | $\frac{10}{15}$ | $\frac{12}{18}$ |

B. $\frac{1}{4}$ **E.** $\frac{1}{3}$ **O.** $\frac{1}{2}$ **R.** $\frac{3}{5}$ **S.** $\frac{2}{3}$ **T.** $\frac{3}{4}$ **Y.** $\frac{1}{1}$

Rates

You used ratios to compare two quantities. | You'll use rates to compare two quantities with different units. | So you can find the average speed of a bullet train, as in Ex. 18.

Word Watch

rate, p. 374
unit rate, p. 374

 You can rewrite fractions to compare two rates.

(1) Use a watch to count the number of times your heart beats in 10 seconds. Record your result as a fraction.

$\dfrac{n \text{ heartbeats}}{10 \text{ seconds}}$

(2) Ask your partner to count his or her pulse for 15 seconds. Record the result as a fraction.

(3) Whose pulse is greater? Explain how you decided.

A **rate** is a ratio of two quantities measured in different units.

A **unit rate** is a rate that has a denominator of 1 unit. The three unit rates below are equivalent. In the third rate, "per" means "for every."

$$\dfrac{15 \text{ mi}}{1 \text{ h}} \qquad 15 \text{ mi/h} \qquad 15 \text{ miles per hour}$$

EXAMPLE 1 Finding a Unit Rate

Kudzu During peak growing season, the kudzu vine can grow 6 inches in 12 hours. What is the growth rate of kudzu in inches per hour?

Solution

First, write a rate comparing the inches grown to the hours it took to grow. Then rewrite the fraction so that the denominator is 1.

$$\dfrac{6 \text{ in.}}{12 \text{ h}} = \dfrac{6 \text{ in.} \div 12}{12 \text{ h} \div 12} \qquad \text{Divide numerator and denominator by 12.}$$

$$= \dfrac{0.5 \text{ in.}}{1 \text{ h}} \qquad \text{Simplify.}$$

ANSWER The growth rate of kudzu is about 0.5 inch per hour.

Spring

Fall

 **Find the unit rate.**

1. $54 in 6 hours   **2.** 68 miles in 4 days   **3.** 2 cups in 8 servings

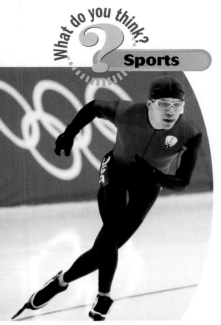
Average Speed If you know the distance traveled and the travel time for a moving object, you can find the average rate, or average speed, by dividing the distance by the time.

$$\text{average rate} = \frac{\text{distance}}{\text{time}}$$

> Average rate is usually written as a unit rate.

EXAMPLE 2 **Finding an Average Speed**

Speed Skating A skater took 2 minutes 30 seconds to complete a 1500 meter race. What was the skater's average speed?

Solution

1 Rewrite the time so that the units are the same.

2 min + 30 sec = 120 sec + 30 sec = 150 sec

2 Find the average speed.

$$\frac{1500 \text{ m}}{150 \text{ sec}} = \frac{1500 \text{ m} \div 150}{150 \text{ sec} \div 150} \qquad \text{Divide numerator and denominator by 150.}$$

$$= \frac{10 \text{ m}}{1 \text{ sec}} \qquad \text{Simplify.}$$

ANSWER The skater's average speed was 10 meters per second.

■ **Olympic Speed Skating**

In the 2002 Winter Olympics, Derek Parra won the gold medal in the 1500 meter speed skating event. His winning time was 1 minute 43.95 seconds. What was his average speed in meters per second? Round your answer to the nearest hundredth.

EXAMPLE 3 **Comparing Unit Rates**

Pasta A store sells the same pasta the following two ways: 10 pounds of bulk pasta for $15.00 and 2 pounds of packaged pasta for $3.98. To determine which is the better buy, find the unit price for both types.

Bulk pasta: $\dfrac{\$15.00}{10 \text{ lb}} = \dfrac{\$1.50}{1 \text{ lb}}$ Write as a unit rate.

Packaged pasta: $\dfrac{\$3.98}{2 \text{ lb}} = \dfrac{\$1.99}{1 \text{ lb}}$ Write as a unit rate.

ANSWER The bulk pasta is the better buy because it costs less per pound.

with Solving

A unit price is a type of unit rate.

Your turn now **Solve the following problems.**

4. It takes you 1 minute 40 seconds to walk 550 feet. What is your average speed?

5. Which of the following is the better buy: 2 AA batteries for $1.50 or 6 AA batteries for $4.80?

Getting Ready to Practice

1. **Vocabulary** Copy and complete: A(n) __?__ is a ratio of two measures with different units.

Match the rate with the equivalent unit rate.

2. $\dfrac{27 \text{ ft}}{6 \text{ sec}}$

3. $\dfrac{18 \text{ ft}}{3 \text{ sec}}$

4. $\dfrac{11 \text{ ft}}{5 \text{ sec}}$

A. 2.2 ft/sec

B. 4.5 ft/sec

C. 6 ft/sec

5. **Guided Problem Solving** To be considered a "fast talker," you should be able to clearly speak 350 words in 60 seconds. Sean can speak 60 words in 15 seconds. At this rate, is Sean a "fast talker"?

(1 Write the "fast talker's" rate as a unit rate. Round your answer to the nearest tenth.

(2 Write Sean's rate as a unit rate.

(3 Compare the unit rates.

Practice and Problem Solving

HELP with Homework

Example	Exercises
1	7–12, 16
2	13–15, 17–18, 21
3	19–20

Online Resources
CLASSZONE.COM
· More Examples
· eTutorial Plus

6. **Writing** Describe the difference between a rate and a ratio.

Find the unit rate.

7. $\dfrac{12 \text{ L}}{2 \text{ days}}$

8. $\dfrac{\$56}{8 \text{ lb}}$

9. $\dfrac{\$16}{5 \text{ people}}$

10. $15 for 2 plants

11. 9 cups in 5 pies

12. 14 cups for 8 servings

In Exercises 13–15, find the average speed.

13. 27 meters in 18 seconds

14. 51 meters in 4 minutes 15 seconds

15. 160 feet in 5 minutes 20 seconds

16. **Socks** You buy a package of 6 pairs of athletic socks for $8.94. Write this rate as a unit rate.

17. **Butterfly Speed** Find the average speed of a butterfly that flies 24.4 miles in 4 hours.

18. **Trains** A bullet train in Japan can travel 93 miles in 30 minutes. Find its average speed in miles per hour.

In Exercises 19 and 20, determine which is the better buy.

19. Juice: 2 quarts for $2.78 or 1.5 quarts for $2.25

20. Cereal: 17 ounces for $3.40 or 14 ounces for $3.08

21. Sea Water The *density* of a substance is the ratio of its mass to its volume. A 500 milliliter sample of sea water has a mass of 514 grams. Write the density of sea water as a unit rate.

22. Hovercraft A hovercraft scooter is traveling at 12 miles per hour. At this rate, how many minutes will it take the hovercraft to travel 1 mile?

Critical Thinking Solve the equation.

23. $\dfrac{d}{3 \text{ hours}} = 80$ miles per hour

24. $\dfrac{d}{2.5 \text{ hours}} = 60$ miles per hour

25. Challenge Emma and Trevor start walking in opposite directions from the same point. Emma walks 0.8 kilometer every 10 minutes, and Trevor walks 2.8 kilometers every 30 minutes. How far apart are Emma and Trevor after 1 hour? after 2 hours?

Mixed Review

Plot the point and describe its location in a coordinate plane. *(Lesson 6.8)*

26. $A(-3, 8)$ **27.** $B(5, 0)$ **28.** $C(6, -10)$ **29.** $D(-7, -7)$

Write the ratio as a fraction in simplest form. *(Lesson 8.1)*

30. 15 to 20   **31.** 16 to 48   **32.** 3 to 39   **33.** 9 to 105

Basic Skills **Copy and complete the statement using <, >, or =.**

34. $\dfrac{2}{3}$? $\dfrac{4}{9}$ **35.** $\dfrac{3}{7}$? $\dfrac{9}{21}$ **36.** $\dfrac{1}{2}$? $\dfrac{1}{3}$ **37.** $\dfrac{15}{26}$? $\dfrac{7}{12}$

Test-Taking Practice

INTERNET
State Test Practice
CLASSZONE.COM

38. Multiple Choice An average 125 pound person can burn 75 Calories in 10 minutes while playing racquetball. At this rate, how many calories are burned per second?

    A. 0.125 Cal/sec   **B.** $\dfrac{2}{5}$ Cal/sec   **C.** 7.5 Cal/sec   **D.** 750 Cal/sec

39. Short Response It takes you 2 hours 30 minutes to travel 155 miles by car. Describe how to find the car's average speed in miles per hour.

Slope

BEFORE   ▶ **Now**   **WHY?**

You used a table to graph a linear function.

You'll find the slope of a line.

So you can compare pay rates for baby-sitting, as in Ex. 16.

Word Watch

slope, p. 378

Activity   **You can use ratios to describe the slope of a line.**

① Draw an *x*-axis and a *y*-axis on graph paper.

② Start at the origin. Move 2 units to the right and 3 units up. Plot this point and label it *A*.

③ Start at *A*. Move 4 units to the right and 6 units up. Plot this point and label it *B*.

④ Draw a line through *A*, *B*, and the origin.

⑤ Find the ratio of rise to run for each of the movements described in Steps 2 and 3. What do you notice?

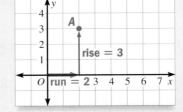

HELP with **Solving**

Run is positive when moving to the right and negative when moving to the left.

Rise is positive when moving up and negative when moving down.

The **slope** of a nonvertical line is the ratio of the rise (vertical change) to the run (horizontal change) between any two points on the line, as shown below. A line has a constant slope.

$$\text{slope} = \frac{\text{rise}}{\text{run}} = \frac{-2}{5} = -\frac{2}{5}$$

Examples of lines with positive, negative, and zero slopes are shown below. The slope of a vertical line is undefined.

A line that rises from left to right has a **positive** slope.

A line that falls from left to right has a **negative** slope.

A horizontal line has a **slope of 0**.

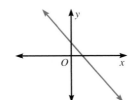

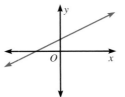

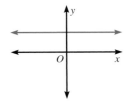

EXAMPLE 1 Finding the Slope of a Line

To find the slope of a line, find the ratio of the rise to the run between two points on the line.

a.

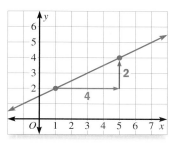

$$\text{slope} = \frac{\text{rise}}{\text{run}} = \frac{2}{4}$$

$$= \frac{1}{2}$$

b.

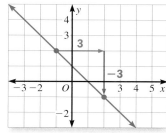

$$\text{slope} = \frac{\text{rise}}{\text{run}} = \frac{-3}{3}$$

$$= -1$$

Slope as a Rate When the graph of a line represents a real-world situation, the slope of the line can often be interpreted as a rate.

EXAMPLE 2 Interpreting Slope as a Rate

Volcanoes The graph represents the distance traveled by a lava flow over time. To find the speed of the lava flow, find the slope of the line.

$$\text{slope} = \frac{\text{rise}}{\text{run}} = \frac{6 \text{ mi}}{4 \text{ h}} \qquad \text{Write rise over run.}$$

$$= \frac{1.5 \text{ mi}}{1 \text{ h}} \qquad \text{Find unit rate.}$$

ANSWER The speed of the lava flow is 1.5 miles per hour.

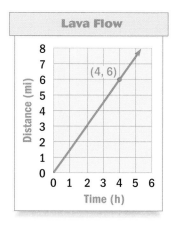

Your turn now Complete the following exercises.

1. Plot the points (3, 4) and (6, 3). Then find the slope of the line that passes through the points.

2. In Example 2, suppose the line starts at the origin and passes through the point (3, 6). Find the speed of the lava flow.

◾ Volcanoes

The molten lava that erupts from volcanoes can be as hot as 1200°C. Find this temperature in degrees Fahrenheit using the equation $F = \frac{9}{5}C + 32$.

EXAMPLE **3** **Using Slope to Draw a Line**

Draw the line that has a slope of −3 and passes through (2, 5).

1 Plot (2, 5).

2 Write the slope as a fraction.

$$\text{slope} = \frac{\text{rise}}{\text{run}} = \frac{-3}{1}$$

3 Move 1 unit to the right and 3 units down to plot the second point.

4 Draw a line through the two points.

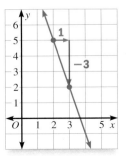

Your turn now **Refer to Example 3.**

3. Draw the line that has a slope of $\frac{1}{3}$ and passes through (2, 5).

8.3 Exercises

More Practice, p. 712

Getting Ready to Practice

1. **Vocabulary** Copy and complete: The slope of a nonvertical line is the ratio of the _?_ to the _?_ between any two points on the line.

Find the slope of the line.

2.

3.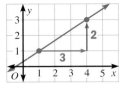

4.

Canoe Trip The graph represents the distance that you traveled in a canoe over time.

5. How far did you travel in 2 hours?

6. What was your speed?

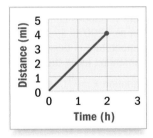

Practice and Problem Solving

 with **Homework**

Example	Exercises
1	7–12, 18–23
2	14–16, 27–28
3	24–26

Online Resources
CLASSZONE.COM

· More Examples
· eTutorial Plus

Without finding the slope of the line, tell whether the slope is positive, negative, or zero.

7.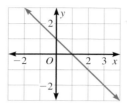

8.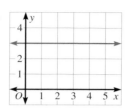

9.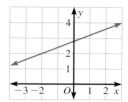

Find the slope of the line.

10.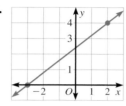

11.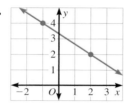

12.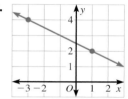

13. **Describe** You are given a graph that shows the distance you travel over time while walking at a steady rate. Describe how to use the graph to find the rate at which you are walking.

Baby-Sitting In Exercises 14–16, use the graph, which shows two pay rates for baby-sitting.

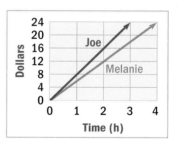

14. Find Joe's pay rate for baby-sitting.

15. Find Melanie's pay rate for baby-sitting.

16. Who has a greater pay rate?

17. **Critical Thinking** Give an example of a rate that can be represented as a line in a coordinate plane. Explain your choice.

Draw the graph of the line that passes through the points. Then find the slope of the line.

18. (3, 4), (5, 6) 19. (0, 0), (8, 7) 20. (2, 5), (5, −2)

21. (7, 2), (−1, −2) 22. (−1, −3), (3, −4) 23. (−1, 5), (1, −1)

 with **Review**

Need help with plotting points in a coordinate plane? See p. 293.

Draw the line that has the given slope and passes through the given point.

24. slope = 3; (3, −1) 25. slope = $\frac{3}{4}$; (−2, −1) 26. slope = $-\frac{5}{6}$; (5, 5)

Green sea turtle

Extended Problem Solving In Exercises 27 and 28, use the graph showing the distance covered by two sea turtles.

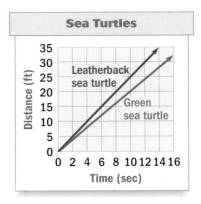

Sea Turtles

27. **Identify** Just by looking at the graphs, tell which turtle swam at a greater speed. Explain your choice.

28. **Compare** A third turtle swims 18 feet in 8 seconds. How does the swimming rate of the third turtle compare with the rates of the other two turtles? Explain your reasoning.

Geometry In Exercises 29–31, use the table which lists the side lengths of four squares.

29. Copy and complete the table.

30. Graph your results as points whose x-coordinates are the side lengths and y-coordinates are the perimeters. Draw a line through the points.

Side length	1	2	3	4
Perimeter	?	?	?	?

31. **Challenge** Explain what the slope of the line in Exercise 30 tells about the relationship between the side length of a square and its perimeter.

Mixed Review

Solve the equation. Check your solution. *(Lesson 7.4)*

32. $4x = 20$ 33. $-36x = 6$ 34. $\dfrac{x}{12} = -3.2$ 35. $\dfrac{x}{11.1} = 7$

36. Write $\dfrac{\$5.60}{7 \text{ lb}}$ as a unit rate. *(Lesson 8.2)*

Basic Skills **Write the decimal as a fraction in simplest form.**

37. 0.4   38. 0.75   39. 0.05   40. 0.32

Test-Taking Practice

41. **Multiple Choice** What is the slope of the blue line?

    A. $-\dfrac{3}{2}$ **B.** $-\dfrac{2}{3}$ **C.** $\dfrac{2}{3}$ **D.** $\dfrac{3}{2}$

42. **Multiple Choice** What is the slope of the red line?

    F. $-\dfrac{3}{2}$ **G.** $-\dfrac{2}{3}$ **H.** $\dfrac{2}{3}$ **I.** $\dfrac{3}{2}$

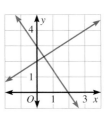

GRAPHING
CALCULATOR

Finding Slope

GOAL Use a graphing calculator to graph a line and find its slope.

Example **Find the slope of the line $y = \frac{2}{3}x$.**

Solution

1 Press [Y=] [(] 2 [÷] 3 [)] [x].

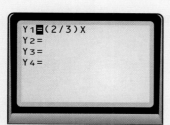

2 Press [2nd] [FORMAT] and make sure that the grid is on.

3 Press [ZOOM] 4 to graph the line.

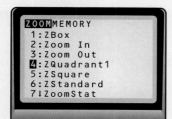

4 Use the grid to find the slope of the line.

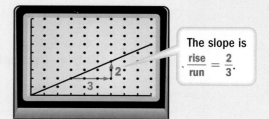

The slope is $\frac{\text{rise}}{\text{run}} = \frac{2}{3}$.

Your turn now **Graph the line. Then find the slope of the line.**

1. $y = 4x$ **2.** $y = \frac{3}{4}x$ **3.** $y = -3x + 8$ **4.** $y = -\frac{1}{3}x + 5$

5. Writing What is the relationship between the slope of the line and the coefficient of x in each of Exercises 1–4?

6. Critical Thinking What do you think is the slope of the line $y = \frac{2}{5}x$? Graph the line and find its slope to check your answer.

Notebook Review

LESSONS **8.1** TO **8.3**

Review the vocabulary definitions in your notebook.

Copy the review examples in your notebook. Then complete the exercises.

Check Your Definitions

ratio, p. 369   rate, p. 374   slope, p. 378

equivalent ratios, p. 369   unit rate, p. 374

Use Your Vocabulary

1. Copy and complete: A(n) _?_ is a rate that has a denominator of 1 unit.

8.1 Can you write and compare ratios?

EXAMPLE On which day did the boarding kennel have a greater ratio of cats to dogs?

	Friday	Saturday
Cats	3	10
Dogs	15	25

Solution

Friday: $\dfrac{\text{cats}}{\text{dogs}} = \dfrac{3}{15}$ **Saturday:** $\dfrac{\text{cats}}{\text{dogs}} = \dfrac{10}{25}$

$= 0.2$ $= 0.4$

Since $0.4 > 0.2$, there was a greater ratio of cats to dogs on Saturday.

☑ **Copy and complete the statement using <, >, or =.**

2. $5 : 10 \underline{\ ?\ } 1 : 5$ **3.** $6 : 14 \underline{\ ?\ } 6 : 10$ **4.** $1 : 4 \underline{\ ?\ } 13 : 52$

8.2 Can you find and compare unit rates?

EXAMPLE A stationery store sells the same mechanical pencils in the following two quantities: 2 pencils for $1.98 and 10 pencils for $8.00. To determine which is the better buy, find the unit price for each.

2 pencils: $\dfrac{\$1.98}{2} = \dfrac{\$.99}{1}$ Write as a unit rate.

10 pencils: $\dfrac{\$8.00}{10} = \dfrac{\$.80}{1}$ Write as a unit rate.

ANSWER The 10 pencils are the better buy.

5. Determine which of the following bags of popcorn is the better buy: a 1.4 ounce bag for $2.10 or a 2.2 ounce bag for $2.64.

8.3 Can you find the slope of a line?

Review **EXAMPLE** To find the slope of a line, find the ratio of the rise to the run between two points on the line.

$$\text{slope} = \frac{\text{rise}}{\text{run}} = \frac{-3}{4} = -\frac{3}{4}$$

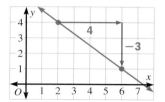

 6. Draw the graph of the line that passes through $(-3, -2)$ and $(5, -5)$. Then find the slope of the line.

Stop *and* **Think** about Lessons 8.1–8.3

7. Critical Thinking A car travels 10 miles in 15 minutes. Find the car's average speed in miles per hour.

Review Quiz 1

In Exercises 1–4, write the ratio as a fraction in simplest form.

1. $\frac{12}{16}$ **2.** 5 to 6   **3.** 18 to 4   **4.** 20 : 5

5. The number of teeth in the upper and lower jaws for each of two animals is shown in the table. Which animal has the greater ratio of teeth in the upper jaw to teeth in the lower jaw?

Animal	Upper teeth	Lower teeth
Elk	14	20
Bear	20	22

Find the unit rate.

6. $2.25 for 5 pounds   **7.** $6 for 5 pens   **8.** 4 laps in 10 minutes

Draw the graph of the line that passes through the points. Then find the slope of the line.

9. $(3, 4)$, $(0, -2)$ **10.** $(1, 1)$, $(-3, -3)$ **11.** $(-5, 5)$, $(-1, 3)$

GOAL

Use a model to find a missing term in a proportion.

MATERIALS

· chips of two different colors (or pennies and dimes)

Modeling Proportions

An equation stating that two ratios are equivalent, such as $\frac{2}{4} = \frac{1}{2}$, is called a *proportion.* You can use a chip model to find a missing term in a proportion.

Explore Use a chip model to find the missing term in the proportion $\frac{2}{3} = \frac{n}{6}$.

1 Model the proportion using red and yellow chips.

> The ratio tells you there should be 2 red chips for every 3 yellow chips.

2 Because the first ratio has a denominator of 3, separate the 6 yellow chips in the second ratio into groups of 3.

3 Place 2 red chips in the numerator of the second ratio for every 3 yellow chips in the denominator. Four red chips are placed, so $n = 4$.

Your turn now Use a chip model to find the missing term.

1. $\frac{1}{3} = \frac{x}{15}$ **2.** $\frac{n}{6} = \frac{5}{2}$ **3.** $\frac{z}{8} = \frac{3}{2}$ **4.** $\frac{3}{4} = \frac{s}{16}$

Stop and Think

5. Writing In Step 2, how many times more yellow chips are in the second ratio than in the first? How could you use this relationship to find n?

LESSON 8.4

Writing and Solving Proportions

BEFORE	▶ Now	WHY?
You learned how to write ratios.	You'll solve proportions using equivalent ratios and algebra.	So you can find the width of a Viking ship, as in Ex. 24.

In the Real World

Word Watch

proportion, p. 387

Sports A person burned about 150 calories while skateboarding for 30 minutes. About how many calories would the person burn while skateboarding for 60 minutes? In Example 1, you will use a *proportion* to answer this question.

Proportions

Words A **proportion** is an equation that states that two ratios are equivalent.

Numbers $\dfrac{3}{5} = \dfrac{6}{10}$ The proportion is read "3 is to 5 as 6 is to 10."

Algebra $\dfrac{a}{b} = \dfrac{c}{d}$, where b and d are nonzero numbers.

Using Equivalent Ratios When one of the numbers in a proportion is unknown, you can find the number by *solving the proportion*. One way to solve a proportion is to use mental math to find an equivalent ratio.

EXAMPLE 1 Using Equivalent Ratios

To find the number C of calories the person would burn while skateboarding for 60 minutes, solve the proportion $\dfrac{150}{30} = \dfrac{C}{60}$.

1 Ask yourself: What number can you multiply 30 by to get 60?

$$\dfrac{150}{30} = \dfrac{C}{60}$$
$\times\,?$

2 Because $30 \times 2 = 60$, multiply the numerator by 2 to find C.

$$\overset{\times\,2}{\dfrac{150}{30} = \dfrac{C}{60}}$$
$\times\,2$

ANSWER Because $150 \times 2 = 300$, $C = 300$. So, the person would burn about 300 Calories while skateboarding for 60 minutes.

Using Algebra The same method you used to solve division equations in Lesson 7.4 can also be used to solve proportions that have the variable in the numerator.

HELP with Notetaking

As you learn different methods for solving a proportion, remember to write an example of each method in your notebook.

EXAMPLE 2 **Solving Proportions Using Algebra**

xy Solve the proportion $\dfrac{6}{10} = \dfrac{x}{25}$.

$$\dfrac{6}{10} = \dfrac{x}{25} \qquad \text{Write original proportion.}$$

$$25 \cdot \dfrac{6}{10} = 25 \cdot \dfrac{x}{25} \qquad \text{Multiply each side by 25.}$$

$$\dfrac{150}{10} = x \qquad \text{Simplify.}$$

$$15 = x \qquad \text{Simplify fraction.}$$

ANSWER The solution is 15.

Your turn now Use equivalent ratios to solve the proportion.

1. $\dfrac{1}{5} = \dfrac{z}{20}$ **2.** $\dfrac{8}{3} = \dfrac{k}{18}$ **3.** $\dfrac{27}{c} = \dfrac{9}{12}$ **4.** $\dfrac{9}{n} = \dfrac{99}{22}$

Use algebra to solve the proportion.

5. $\dfrac{4}{14} = \dfrac{m}{49}$ **6.** $\dfrac{25}{30} = \dfrac{x}{12}$ **7.** $\dfrac{h}{33} = \dfrac{2}{6}$ **8.** $\dfrac{b}{8} = \dfrac{7}{28}$

Setting Up a Proportion There are different ways to set up a proportion. Consider the following problem.

> **Yesterday you bought 8 bagels for $4. Today you want only 5 bagels. How much will 5 bagels cost?**

The information is arranged in the two tables below, in which x represents the cost of 5 bagels. The proportions that follow from the tables appear below the tables.

Watch Out!

You cannot write a proportion that compares bagels to dollars and dollars to bagels.

$$\dfrac{\text{bagels}}{\text{dollars}} \ne \dfrac{\text{dollars}}{\text{bagels}}$$

	Yesterday	Today
Cost	4	x
Bagels	8	5

	Bagels	Cost
Today	5	x
Yesterday	8	4

Proportion: $\dfrac{4}{8} = \dfrac{x}{5}$

Proportion: $\dfrac{5}{8} = \dfrac{x}{4}$

EXAMPLE 3 **Writing and Solving a Proportion**

Empire State Building At maximum speed, the elevators in the Empire State Building can pass 80 floors in 45 seconds. Follow the steps below to find the number of floors that the elevators can pass in 9 seconds.

① Write a proportion. Let x represent the floors passed in 9 seconds.

$$\frac{80}{45} = \frac{x}{9} \xleftarrow{\quad} \text{floors}$$
$$\xleftarrow{\quad} \text{seconds}$$

② Solve the proportion.

$$\frac{80}{45} = \frac{x}{9}$$ **Write original proportion.**

$$9 \cdot \frac{80}{45} = 9 \cdot \frac{x}{9}$$ **Multiply each side by 9.**

$$\frac{720}{45} = x$$ **Simplify.**

$$16 = x$$ **Simplify fraction.**

ANSWER The elevators can pass 16 floors in 9 seconds.

8.4 Exercises

More Practice, p. 712

INTERNET
eWorkbook Plus
CLASSZONE.COM

Getting Ready to Practice

1. **Vocabulary** Copy and complete: A(n) _?_ is an equation that states that two ratios are equivalent.

2. **Writing** Describe two different methods for solving a proportion.

In Exercises 3–6, match the proportion with its solution.

3. $\dfrac{5}{6} = \dfrac{x}{18}$ 4. $\dfrac{15}{20} = \dfrac{x}{4}$ 5. $\dfrac{x}{6} = \dfrac{4}{2}$ 6. $\dfrac{x}{5} = \dfrac{5}{25}$

A. 3   **B.** 15   **C.** 1   **D.** 12

7. **Recipes** A recipe that makes 12 pints of salsa uses 35 tomatoes. Choose the proportion that you can use to determine the number t of tomatoes needed to make 2 pints of salsa.

A. $\dfrac{12}{35} = \dfrac{t}{2}$ **B.** $\dfrac{t}{35} = \dfrac{12}{2}$ **C.** $\dfrac{35}{12} = \dfrac{t}{2}$

Practice and Problem Solving

with Homework

Example	Exercises
1	8–11, 22–23
2	12–15, 22–23
3	17–19, 21–25

Online Resources
CLASSZONE.COM

· More Examples
· eTutorial Plus

Use equivalent ratios to solve the proportion.

8. $\dfrac{3}{7} = \dfrac{a}{21}$ **9.** $\dfrac{4}{36} = \dfrac{w}{9}$ **10.** $\dfrac{2}{s} = \dfrac{18}{45}$ **11.** $\dfrac{4}{c} = \dfrac{2}{10}$

Algebra **Use algebra to solve the proportion.**

12. $\dfrac{h}{8} = \dfrac{3}{12}$ **13.** $\dfrac{k}{27} = \dfrac{4}{6}$ **14.** $\dfrac{6}{14} = \dfrac{m}{21}$ **15.** $\dfrac{20}{16} = \dfrac{n}{12}$

16. Find the Error To make orange food coloring, 2 drops of red are mixed with 3 drops of yellow. Describe and correct the error in the proportion used to find the number of drops r of red to add to 12 drops of yellow.

$$\times \quad \dfrac{3}{2} = \dfrac{r}{12}$$

17. Reading Phoebe can read about 1250 words in 5 minutes. About how many words can she read in 15 minutes?

18. Painting It takes 4 quarts of paint to cover 560 square feet. How many quarts of the same paint are needed to cover 140 square feet?

19. Apples The average American eats 57 pounds of apples over 3 years. At this rate, how many pounds of apples does a person eat in 15 years?

20. Critical Thinking Is it possible to write a proportion using $\dfrac{11}{13}$ and $\dfrac{55}{65}$? Explain your reasoning.

21. Dog Biscuits The table lists the flour needed to make dough for a given number of dog biscuits. Copy and complete the table.

Biscuits	32	48	?
Flour (cups)	2	?	5

In Exercises 22 and 23, write and then solve the proportion.

22. 8 is to 3 as w is to 12.

23. 6 is to 16 as z is to 40.

24. History The remains of the Viking ship *Ladby* were discovered in 1935. The ratio of the width to the length of the ship was 3 to 20. If the ship had a length of 70 feet, what was its width?

25. Population In the United States, 21 out of every 100 people are under the age of 15. In a town of 20,000 people, how many people would you expect to be under the age of 15?

Challenge Solve the proportion.

26. $\dfrac{30}{v} = \dfrac{12}{16}$ **27.** $\dfrac{8}{x} = \dfrac{6}{15}$ **28.** $\dfrac{22}{33} = \dfrac{16}{y}$ **29.** $\dfrac{4}{24} = \dfrac{6}{z}$

30. Cruise Liner A cruise liner moves 6 inches for every gallon of fuel that it burns. How many gallons of fuel will it burn if it travels 100 miles?

Mixed Review

Order the numbers from least to greatest. *(Lesson 4.7)*

31. $0.6, \dfrac{12}{5}, 0.\overline{6}, \dfrac{6}{7}, 0.1$ **32.** $0.5, \dfrac{5}{9}, \dfrac{9}{5}, 0.\overline{9}, 0.8$ **33.** $1.1, \dfrac{2}{5}, 0.15, 0.\overline{1}$

Draw the line that has the given slope and passes through the given point. *(Lesson 8.3)*

34. slope $= 4$; $(1, -4)$ **35.** slope $= \dfrac{1}{2}$; $(-1, 2)$ **36.** slope $= -2$; $(0, 3)$

Basic Skills **Copy and complete the statement using $<$, $>$, or $=$.**

37. 2.22×10^{11} ? 1.89×10^{11} **38.** $623{,}000{,}000$? 6.23×10^{9}

Test-Taking Practice

39. Extended Response The ratio of teachers to students at a school is 2 to 23. The ratio of female students to the total number of students is 4 to 9. If there are 621 total students, find the number of teachers and the number of female students at the school. Explain your reasoning.

Shape Association

Use the two true statements below to copy and complete the proportions at the right.

1. $\dfrac{\blacktriangle}{\blacksquare} = \dfrac{?}{?}$ 2. $\dfrac{\blacksquare}{\bullet} = \dfrac{\blacktriangle}{?}$

3. $\dfrac{\blacktriangle}{\bullet} = \dfrac{?}{\blacksquare}$ 4. $\dfrac{?}{\bullet} = \dfrac{\blacktriangle}{?}$

Problem Solving Strategies

Act it Out

Look for a Pattern

Estimate

Make a Table

Make a List

Act it Out

Draw a Diagram

Solve a Related Problem

Problem Jeremy and Sarah mow lawns on the weekends. Jeremy owns and maintains the lawn mowers and tools, so the ratio of Jeremy's share of the money earned to Sarah's share is 3 : 2. Together they make a total of $65 over a weekend. How should Jeremy and Sarah split the $65?

1 Read and Understand

Read the problem carefully.

You need to use the ratio 3 : 2 to determine how to split the money between Jeremy and Sarah.

2 Make a Plan

Decide on a strategy to use.

You can use pieces of paper to represent one dollar bills. Then use the pieces of paper to act out dividing the money.

3 Solve the Problem

Reread the problem and act it out.

Use 65 pieces of paper to represent 65 one dollar bills.

Divide the pieces of paper into piles for Jeremy and Sarah. For every 3 pieces of paper you put in Jeremy's pile, put 2 pieces in Sarah's pile. Continue doing this until all of the pieces of paper have been used.

Jeremy

Sarah

ANSWER Because Jeremy has 39 pieces of paper and Sarah has 26 pieces, Jeremy should get $39 and Sarah should get $26.

4 Look Back

Make sure that 39 : 26 is equivalent to 3 : 2.

$$\frac{39}{26} = \frac{\overset{1}{\cancel{13}} \times 3}{\underset{1}{\cancel{13}} \times 2} = \frac{3}{2} \checkmark$$

Practice the Strategy

Use the strategy *act it out*.

1. **Kites** A kite has five vertical stripes of different colors. The red, yellow, and blue stripes are not next to each other. The red stripe is at one end. Two stripes separate the blue and orange stripes. Between which two stripes is the green stripe?

2. **Transportation** The number of people who get on and off a city bus at each stop are listed below. How many passengers are on the bus after the fourth stop?

Stop	People who get on the bus	People who get off the bus
1	25	0
2	7	12
3	3	3
4	13	9

3. **Party** You are having a holiday party. Twelve people show up and then one quarter of them leave an hour later to go to another party. Twice the number of people who left to go to the other party show up during that hour. If 9 people leave the party later on that night, how many people remain at your party?

4. **Pennies** Six pennies are arranged on the left. Describe how to get the arrangement on the right by moving only two pennies.

5. **Photos** The ratio of black-and-white photos to color photos in an album is 1 : 4. If there are 40 photos in the album, how many are color photos?

Mixed Problem Solving

Use any strategy to solve the problem.

6. **Clothing** You buy a pair of jeans and two T-shirts for $48. If the cost of a pair of jeans is the same as the cost of four T-shirts, how much do the jeans cost?

7. **Time** A clock that runs fast is set to the correct time at 12 P.M. For every 15 minutes of real time that passes, the clock shows that 20 minutes have passed. What time does the clock show when it is really 5 P.M.?

8. **Money** The cost of a juice drink in a vending machine is $.75. You have 3 quarters, 5 dimes, and 3 nickels. How many different ways can you pay for the juice drink if the machine only accepts exact change?

9. **Jewelry** Jasmine is arranging green, blue, and purple beads on a string using the pattern below. If she continues this pattern, what will the color of the 20th bead be?

10. **Guitar Lesson** You have a guitar lesson at 5:30 P.M. You want to get there 15 minutes early. It takes you 20 minutes to get to your guitar instructor's house from your house. What time should you leave your house?

Solving Proportions Using Cross Products

BEFORE	▶ Now	WHY?
You solved proportions using equivalent ratios and algebra.	You'll solve proportions using cross products.	So you can find the grams of protein in peanut butter, as in Ex. 23.

In the Real World

cross products, p. 394

Science At space camp, you can sit in a chair that simulates the force of gravity on the moon. A person who weighs 105 pounds on Earth would weigh 17.5 pounds on the moon. How much would a 60 pound dog weigh on the moon? You'll find the answer in Example 2.

In the proportion $\frac{2}{3} = \frac{4}{6}$, the products $2 \cdot 6$ and $3 \cdot 4$ are called **cross products**. Notice that the cross products are equal. This suggests the following property.

Cross Products Property

Words The cross products of a proportion are equal.

Numbers $\frac{3}{4} = \frac{15}{20}$ $4 \cdot 15 = 60$
                $3 \cdot 20 = 60$

Algebra If $\frac{a}{b} = \frac{c}{d}$ where b and d are nonzero numbers, then $ad = bc$.

HELP with **Vocabulary**

The phrase *cross products* comes from the "X" shape formed by the diagonal numbers in a proportion.

EXAMPLE 1   Solving a Proportion Using Cross Products

Use the cross products property to solve $\frac{2}{9} = \frac{3}{d}$.

$\frac{2}{9} = \frac{3}{d}$	Write original proportion.
$2d = 9 \cdot 3$	Cross products property
$\frac{2d}{2} = \frac{9 \cdot 3}{2}$	Divide each side by 2.
$d = 13.5$	Simplify.

EXAMPLE 2 **Writing and Solving a Proportion**

Science To find the weight w of a 60 pound dog on the moon, as described on page 394, write and solve a proportion using the weight of the person.

Person Dog

$$\frac{105}{17.5} = \frac{60}{w} \quad \begin{array}{l}\longleftarrow \text{ weight on Earth}\\ \longleftarrow \text{ weight on moon}\end{array}$$

$105w = 17.5 \cdot 60$ **Cross products property**

$\dfrac{105w}{105} = \dfrac{17.5 \cdot 60}{105}$ **Divide each side by 105.**

$w = 10$ **Simplify.**

ANSWER A 60 pound dog would weigh 10 pounds on the moon.

EXAMPLE 3 **Writing and Solving a Proportion**

Penguins At an aquarium, the ratio of rockhopper penguins to African penguins is 3 to 7. If there are 50 penguins, how many are rockhoppers?

Solution

First, determine the ratio of rockhoppers to total penguins.

$$\frac{3}{3 + 7} = \frac{3}{10} \quad \text{For every 10 penguins, 3 are rockhoppers.}$$

To find the number r of rockhoppers, set up a proportion and solve it.

$$\frac{3}{10} = \frac{r}{50} \quad \begin{array}{l}\longleftarrow \text{ rockhoppers}\\ \longleftarrow \text{ total penguins}\end{array}$$

$3 \cdot 50 = 10r$ **Cross products property**

$\dfrac{3 \cdot 50}{10} = \dfrac{10r}{10}$ **Divide each side by 10.**

$15 = r$ **Simplify.**

ANSWER There are 15 rockhoppers at the aquarium.

Rockhopper penguins

Your turn now **Solve the following problems.**

1. In Example 2, how much would a 150 pound person weigh on the moon?

2. In John's class, the ratio of boys to girls is 5 to 8. If there are 39 students in his class, how many are girls?

Getting Ready to Practice

1. **Vocabulary** What are the cross products of $\frac{2}{7} = \frac{10}{35}$?

Use the cross products property to solve the proportion.

2. $\frac{5}{2} = \frac{y}{10}$ 3. $\frac{n}{8} = \frac{3}{12}$ 4. $\frac{5}{20} = \frac{3}{d}$ 5. $\frac{8}{6} = \frac{12}{s}$

6. **Find the Error** Describe and correct the error in solving the proportion $\frac{4}{9} = \frac{x}{18}$.

$$\frac{4}{9} = \frac{x}{18}$$
$$4 \cdot x = 9 \cdot 18$$
$$x = 40.5$$

7. **Hair Growth** Hair grows an average of 0.5 inch in 1 month. Choose the proportion that you can use to determine the number m of months it will take for hair to grow 6 inches. Then solve the proportion.

A. $\frac{0.5}{1} = \frac{6}{m}$ **B.** $\frac{0.5}{1} = \frac{m}{6}$ **C.** $\frac{0.5}{m} = \frac{6}{1}$

Practice and Problem Solving

with Homework

Example	Exercises
1	9–20
2	21–23, 26, 34
3	24–25

Online Resources
CLASSZONE.COM
· More Examples
· eTutorial Plus

8. **Writing** Describe three ways to solve the proportion $\frac{9}{5} = \frac{x}{15}$.

Use the cross products property to solve the proportion.

9. $\frac{9}{2} = \frac{36}{n}$ 10. $\frac{a}{24} = \frac{7}{8}$ 11. $\frac{30}{6} = \frac{b}{7}$ 12. $\frac{3}{x} = \frac{4}{28}$

13. $\frac{4}{p} = \frac{14}{28}$ 14. $\frac{6.8}{z} = \frac{2}{5}$ 15. $\frac{a}{4} = \frac{3.5}{2}$ 16. $\frac{7}{10} = \frac{k}{8}$

17. $\frac{20}{m} = \frac{16}{5}$ 18. $\frac{6}{9.6} = \frac{9}{d}$ 19. $\frac{2.2}{c} = \frac{5.5}{11}$ 20. $\frac{3.6}{3} = \frac{y}{14.4}$

21. **Blinking** The average person blinks about 360 times in 30 minutes. About how many times does a person blink in 9 minutes?

22. **Internet Connections** A digital subscriber line (DSL) connection to the Internet can transfer 42 megabits of information in 5 minutes. How long would it take this connection to transfer 75.6 megabits of information?

23. **Nutrition** There are 5 grams of protein in 3 teaspoons of peanut butter. How many grams of protein are in 4.5 teaspoons of peanut butter?

24. **Music** The ratio of Taylor's CDs to Dave's CDs is 7 to 8. If they have a total of 150 CDs, how many CDs does Taylor have?

25. **Sports** At a typical National Football League game, the ratio of males to females in attendance is 3 : 2. There are 75,000 spectators at an NFL game. How many of the spectators would you expect to be females?

26. **Gold Rush** In 1849, during the Gold Rush, one pioneer attempted to travel west in a wagon with a sail, called a *wind wagon*. An advertisement for the wind wagon claimed that it could travel 15 miles per hour. How far could it travel in 30 minutes?

In Exercises 27–30, tell whether the ratios form a proportion.

EXAMPLE **Deciding Whether Ratios Form a Proportion**

$$\frac{2}{9} \overset{?}{=} \frac{5}{16}$$ Write the possible proportion.

$$2 \cdot 16 \overset{?}{=} 9 \cdot 5$$ Take cross products.

$$32 \neq 45$$ Multiply.

ANSWER The cross products are not equal, so the ratios do not form a proportion.

27. $\dfrac{24}{104}, \dfrac{3}{13}$

28. $\dfrac{6}{7}, \dfrac{21}{18}$

29. $\dfrac{3.4}{4.3}, \dfrac{5.6}{6.5}$

30. $\dfrac{9}{4.3}, \dfrac{54}{25.8}$

■ **Gold Rush**

Between 1848 and 1849, prospectors rushed to California in hopes of finding gold. During this time, the population of California increased from about 15,000 to about 100,000. By what factor did the population increase? Round your answer to the nearest tenth.

Extended Problem Solving
In Exercises 31 and 32, use the dimensions of two ocean waves given in the table at the right.

31. **Compare** Do the heights and wavelengths of the waves in the table form a proportion? Explain.

32. **Interpret** The ratio of the height to the wavelength of a wave when it breaks is 1 to 7. Were the measures of the waves in the table taken just as the waves broke? Explain.

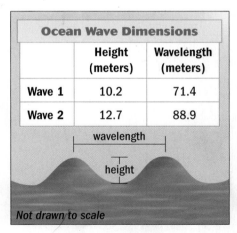

Ocean Wave Dimensions		
	Height (meters)	Wavelength (meters)
Wave 1	10.2	71.4
Wave 2	12.7	88.9

Not drawn to scale

33. **Act it Out** On a sunny day, go outside and have a classmate measure your height and the length of your shadow. The two of you should also measure the length of the shadow of a tall object, such as a tree or flagpole. Given that the shadow lengths of objects and the heights of objects are in proportion, find the height of the tall object.

34. Giant Feet Matthew McGrory has the title of human being with the largest feet. The average man has a foot length of 30 centimeters and a big toe length of 85 millimeters. Each of McGrory's big toes are 12.7 centimeters long. If the ratio of McGrory's big toe length to foot length is the same as the average man's, about how long are his feet?

Critical Thinking Tell whether the statement is *true* or *false*. Give an example that supports your answer.

35. If $\frac{f}{g} = \frac{h}{k}$, then $\frac{f}{k} = \frac{h}{g}$.

36. If $\frac{a}{b} = \frac{c}{d}$, then $\frac{a}{c} = \frac{b}{d}$.

Challenge Solve the proportion.

37. $\frac{15}{4} = \frac{9}{2n}$

38. $\frac{b-3}{16} = \frac{5}{8}$

39. $\frac{3}{4} = \frac{x}{x+3}$

40. $\frac{2}{t} = \frac{5}{t-6}$

Mixed Review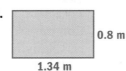

Write the sentence as an equation. Then solve the equation. *(Lesson 7.4)*

41. The product of 9 and a number is -54.

42. The quotient of a number and 2.5 is 7.2.

Use equivalent ratios to solve the proportion. *(Lesson 8.4)*

43. $\frac{2}{9} = \frac{c}{27}$

44. $\frac{49}{w} = \frac{7}{4}$

45. $\frac{s}{11} = \frac{30}{110}$

46. $\frac{21}{56} = \frac{z}{8}$

Basic Skills Find the area of the rectangle.

47.

3.1 ft

2.8 ft

48.

0.8 m

1.34 m

49.

11.2 in.

6.99 in.

Test-Taking Practice

50. Multiple Choice What is the value of b in the proportion $\frac{5}{4} = \frac{b}{2.4}$?

A. 3   **B.** 3.4   **C.** 6.6   **D.** 30

51. Short Response A survey at a school found that the ratio of students who use a pen to do their math homework to the students who use a pencil is 2 to 7. How many of the 45 students surveyed use a pen to do their math homework?

GOAL

Make a scale drawing of an object.

MATERIALS

• ruler
• scissors

Making a Scale Drawing

Explore Make a *scale drawing* of a rectangular bedroom that is 16 feet long and 12 feet wide. In your drawing, let 1 inch represent 8 feet.

1 Write and solve a proportion to find the length l of the bedroom in the drawing.

$$\frac{1}{8} = \frac{l}{16} \quad \leftarrow \text{inches} \\ \leftarrow \text{feet}$$

$$1 \cdot 16 = 8 \cdot l$$

$$2 = l$$

2 Write and solve a proportion to find the width w of the bedroom in the drawing.

$$\frac{1}{8} = \frac{w}{12} \quad \leftarrow \text{inches} \\ \leftarrow \text{feet}$$

$$1 \cdot 12 = 8 \cdot w$$

$$1.5 = w$$

3 Use a ruler to draw a rectangle with a length of 2 inches and a width of 1.5 inches.

Include the *scale* on your drawing.

1 inch : 8 feet

Your turn now Make a scale drawing of the rectangular or square top of the object. In your drawing, let 1 inch represent 8 feet.

1. Dresser:
$l = 4$ ft, $w = 2$ ft

2. Bed:
$l = 6$ ft, $w = 4$ ft

3. Nightstand:
$s = 2$ ft

Stop *and* **Think**

4. Writing Cut out the scale drawings from Exercises 1–3. Arrange the pieces on the scale drawing of the bedroom. Explain why this method might be used to decide the arrangement of the furniture.

LESSON
8.6

Scale Drawings and Models

BEFORE   ▶ **Now**   **WHY?**

You learned how to solve proportions.   You'll use proportions with scale drawings.   So you can find wingspans of airplanes, as in Exs. 12–15.

The floor plan at the right is an example of a *scale drawing*. A **scale drawing** is a diagram of an object in which the dimensions are in proportion to the actual dimensions of the object.

The **scale** on a scale drawing tells how the drawing's dimensions and the actual dimensions are related. The scale "1 in. : 12 ft" means that 1 inch in the floor plan represents an actual distance of 12 feet.

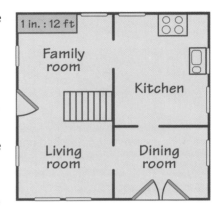

EXAMPLE 1 Using the Scale of a Map

Maps Use the map of Maine to estimate the distance between the towns of China and New Sweden.

Solution

From the map's scale, 1 centimeter represents 65 kilometers. On the map, the distance between China and New Sweden is 4.5 centimeters.

Write and solve a proportion to find the distance d between the towns.

$$\frac{1}{65} = \frac{4.5}{d} \longleftarrow \text{centimeters} \\ \longleftarrow \text{kilometers}$$

$$1 \cdot d = 65 \cdot 4.5$$

$$d = 292.5$$

ANSWER The actual distance between China and New Sweden is about 293 kilometers.

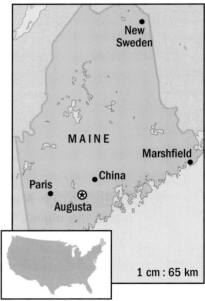

Your turn now Use a metric ruler and the map in Example 1.

1. Estimate the distance, in kilometers, between the towns of Paris and Marshfield.

Scale Models A **scale model** is a model of an object in which the dimensions are in proportion to the actual dimensions of the object. The scale of a scale model is often given as a ratio. The two scales listed below are equivalent.

Scale with units	**Scale without units**
1 in. : 4 ft	1 : 48 ⟵ **Express 4 ft as 48 in.**

EXAMPLE 2 **Finding a Dimension on a Scale Model**

White House A scale model of the White House appears in Tobu World Square in Japan. The scale used is 1 : 25. The height of the main building of the White House is 85 feet. Find this height on the model.

Solution

Write and solve a proportion to find the height h of the main building of the model of the White House.

$$\frac{1}{25} = \frac{h}{85} \quad \begin{array}{l}\longleftarrow \text{ scale model} \\ \longleftarrow \text{ building}\end{array}$$

$$1 \cdot 85 = 25 \cdot h \qquad \text{Cross products property}$$

$$3.4 = h \qquad \text{Divide each side by 25.}$$

ANSWER The height of the main building of the model is 3.4 feet.

Tyrannosaurus rex

EXAMPLE 3 **Finding the Scale**

Dinosaurs A museum is creating a full-size Tyrannosaurus rex from a model. The model is 40 inches in length, from the nose to the tail. The resulting dinosaur will be 40 feet in length. What is the model's scale?

Solution

Write a ratio. Make sure that both measures are in inches. Then simplify the fraction.

$$\frac{40 \text{ in.}}{40 \text{ ft}} = \frac{40 \text{ in.}}{480 \text{ in.}} = \frac{1}{12} \quad \begin{array}{l}\longleftarrow \text{ scale model} \\ \longleftarrow \text{ full size}\end{array}$$

ANSWER The model's scale is 1 : 12.

Your turn now Use the scale in Example 2.

2. The model of the Eiffel Tower in Tobu World Square is 12 meters high. Estimate the height of the actual Eiffel Tower.

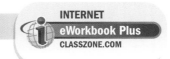
8.6 Exercises

More Practice, p. 712

Getting Ready to Practice

Vocabulary Tell whether the statement is *true* or *false*. Explain.

1. The scale on a scale drawing tells how the drawing's dimensions and the actual dimensions are related.

2. An object and a scale model of the object are the same size, but have different shapes.

In Exercises 3–6, the scale on a floor plan is 1 in. : 15 ft. Match the distance on the floor plan with the actual distance.

3. 2 in.   **4.** 3.5 in.   **5.** 2.2 in.   **6.** 1.6 in.

A. 33 ft   **B.** 30 ft   **C.** 24 ft   **D.** 52.5 ft

7. Miniature Furniture A craftsman makes miniature replicas of Victorian furniture. The scale model of a table that he made is 3 inches long. The full-size table is 36 inches long. What is the model's scale?

Practice and Problem Solving

with Homework

Example	Exercises
1	8–11
2	12–15, 17, 21
3	16

Online Resources
CLASSZONE.COM

· More Examples
· eTutorial Plus

Maps The scale on a map is 1 cm : 25 mi. Find the actual distance in miles for the given length on the map.

8. 3 cm   **9.** 10 cm   **10.** 5.2 cm   **11.** 8.7 cm

Model Airplanes The scale used to build the scale models of four airplanes is 1 : 72. Estimate the actual wingspan of the airplane given the wingspan of the model.

12. Kitty Hawk: 17.1 cm   **13.** Spirit of St. Louis: 19.4 cm

14. Boeing 747: 82.8 cm   **15.** Boeing B-17: 43.9 cm

Mural In Exercises 16 and 17, an artist is painting a mural from a scale drawing of the mural. The scale drawing is 8 inches wide. When the mural is complete, it will be 4 feet wide.

16. What is the drawing's scale?

17. The length of the scale drawing is 10 inches. How long will the mural be when it is complete?

18. Explain A basketball court is 84 feet long and 50 feet wide. You want to make a scale drawing of the court on a piece of paper that is 11 inches long and 8.5 inches wide. What scale should you use? Explain your choice.

Flying Pins
by Claes Oldenburg and
Coosje van Bruggen

19. Writing What does it mean if a drawing is "not to scale"?

20. Critical Thinking A model's scale is 1 : 0.2. Is the scale model larger or smaller than the original object? Explain.

21. Art Each bowling pin in the sculpture at the left is a scale model of a normal bowling pin. The model's scale is 1 : 0.05. If the height of a normal bowling pin is 38 centimeters, estimate the height of a bowling pin in the model.

22. Timeline The table lists six recent U.S. Presidents and their years in office. Make a timeline showing the length of each President's term. Use the scale 1 centimeter : 2 years.

President	Years in Office
Richard Nixon	1969–1974
Gerald Ford	1974–1977
Jimmy Carter	1977–1981
Ronald Reagan	1981–1989
George H. W. Bush	1989–1993
Bill Clinton	1993–2001

23. Challenge A scale drawing of a rectangular garden has a length of 5 inches and a width of 3.5 inches. If the scale is 1 in. : 3 ft, what is the area of the actual garden?

Mixed Review

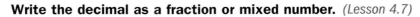

Write the decimal as a fraction or mixed number. *(Lesson 4.7)*

24. 0.6   **25.** 0.28   **26.** 1.75   **27.** 5.025

28. Use the cross products property to solve the proportion $\frac{5}{4} = \frac{c}{28}$. *(Lesson 8.5)*

Basic Skills   **Round the decimal as specified.**

29. 0.008 (nearest hundredth)   **30.** 17.55 (nearest tenth)

Test-Taking Practice

31. Multiple Choice You decide to use a scale of 1 in. : 8 ft to make a scale drawing of your classroom. If the actual length of your classroom is 36 feet, what should the length of the classroom in the drawing be?

   A. 1 in.   **B.** 4.5 in.   **C.** 36 in.   **D.** 288 in.

32. Multiple Choice A child's picnic table is a scale model of an adult picnic table. The child's picnic table is 22 inches tall, and the adult picnic table is 33 inches tall. What is the model's scale?

   F. 1 : 22   **G.** 1 : 15   **H.** 1 : 1.5   **I.** 1 : 1

Notebook Review

NoTe book

Review the vocabulary definitions in your notebook.

Copy the review examples in your notebook. Then complete the exercises.

Check Your Definitions

proportion, p. 387   scale drawing, p. 400   scale model, p. 401
cross products, p. 394   scale, p. 400

Use Your Vocabulary

1. Copy and complete: A(n) _?_ is an equation that states that two ratios are equivalent.

8.4–8.5 Can you write and solve a proportion?

 EXAMPLE During a car wash fundraiser, a group of students washes 2 cars in 10 minutes. How many cars can the students wash in 30 minutes?

Solution

To find the number c of cars washed in 30 minutes, write and solve a proportion.

$$\frac{2}{10} = \frac{c}{30} \quad \leftarrow \text{cars} \\ \phantom{\frac{2}{10} = \frac{c}{30}} \leftarrow \text{minutes}$$

Equivalent Ratios

$$\frac{2}{10} = \frac{c}{30} \quad \substack{\times 3 \\ \times 3}$$

$$c = 2 \times 3 = 6$$

Algebra

$$\frac{2}{10} = \frac{c}{30}$$

$$30 \cdot \frac{2}{10} = 30 \cdot \frac{c}{30}$$

$$6 = c$$

Cross Products Property

$$\frac{2}{10} = \frac{c}{30}$$

$$2 \cdot 30 = 10 \cdot c$$

$$6 = c$$

☑ **Solve the proportion. Tell what method you used.**

2. $\dfrac{5}{4} = \dfrac{a}{20}$ **3.** $\dfrac{10}{25} = \dfrac{m}{5}$ **4.** $\dfrac{k}{16} = \dfrac{5}{10}$ **5.** $\dfrac{7}{21} = \dfrac{x}{6}$

6. $\dfrac{6}{w} = \dfrac{8}{12}$ **7.** $\dfrac{8}{10} = \dfrac{20}{s}$ **8.** $\dfrac{8}{18} = \dfrac{6}{n}$ **9.** $\dfrac{7.5}{b} = \dfrac{9}{24}$

10. You are saving money to buy a new bicycle. If you save $100 every 4 months, how long will it take you to save $250?

8.6 Can you find a dimension on a scale model?

EXAMPLE The scale used to make a scale model of a submarine is 1 : 35. If the length of the actual submarine is 105 meters, what is the length of the model?

Solution

Write and solve a proportion to find the length l of the model.

$$\frac{1}{35} = \frac{l}{105} \quad \longleftarrow \text{ scale model} \atop \longleftarrow \text{ submarine}$$

$$1 \cdot 105 = 35 \cdot l \qquad \textbf{Cross products property}$$

$$3 = l \qquad \textbf{Divide each side by 35.}$$

ANSWER The length of the model is 3 meters.

☑ **11.** Use the scale in the example above to find the length of a scale model of a submarine that has an actual length of 315 feet.

Stop *and* **Think** about Lessons 8.4–8.6

12. Writing Decide whether the ratios $\frac{36}{104}$ and $\frac{9}{26}$ form a proportion. Explain your reasoning.

Review Quiz 2

In Exercises 1–4, solve the proportion. Tell what method you used.

1. $\dfrac{a}{15} = \dfrac{2}{6}$ **2.** $\dfrac{9}{b} = \dfrac{2}{8}$ **3.** $\dfrac{2}{3} = \dfrac{7}{y}$ **4.** $\dfrac{10}{8} = \dfrac{x}{5.6}$

5. The CDs in the discount bin at a CD store cost $12 for 2 CDs. How much will 5 CDs from the discount bin cost?

6. In a magazine, the ratio of pages with advertisements to pages without advertisements is 6 : 5. If the magazine has 143 pages, how many pages have advertisements?

7. The scale on a map is 1 cm : 65 km. If the distance between two cities on the map is 5.5 centimeters, estimate the actual distance between the two cities.

Chapter Review

 **Vocabulary**

ratio, p. 369	slope, p. 378	scale, p. 400
equivalent ratios, p. 369	proportion, p. 387	scale model, p. 401
rate, p. 374	cross products, p. 394	
unit rate, p. 374	scale drawing, p. 400	

Vocabulary Review

Match the definition with the corresponding word.

1. Uses division to compare two numbers

2. A ratio of two quantities measured in different units

3. The ratio of the rise to the run between two points on a line

4. An equation stating that two ratios are equivalent

5. The relationship between a drawing's dimensions and the actual dimensions

A. Proportion

B. Slope

C. Rate

D. Scale

E. Ratio

Review Questions

Write the ratio as a fraction in simplest form. *(Lesson 8.1)*

6. 9 to 81   **7.** 63 to 7   **8.** 11 : 88   **9.** 20 : 35

10. Gardening A rhododendron has a height of 10 feet and a width of 4 feet. Write the ratio of the height to the width. *(Lesson 8.1)*

Write the ratio of the first measurement to the second measurement. Write both measurements in the same unit. *(Lesson 8.1)*

11. 400 m, 2 km   **12.** 14 ft, 4 yd   **13.** 3 min, 15 sec   **14.** 12 oz, 3 lb

Find the unit rate. *(Lesson 8.2)*

15. $20 for 4 people   **16.** 22 ounces for 4 servings   **17.** $17.50 for 10 sodas

18. Sports Salary A football player signs a contract that pays him $28 million over 7 years. What is his average annual salary? *(Lesson 8.2)*

19. Art Supplies Determine which of the following packages of artist's brushes is the better buy: 5 brushes for $2.75 or 8 brushes for $5.20. *(Lesson 8.2)*

Find the slope of the line. *(Lesson 8.3)*

20.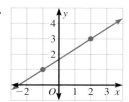

21.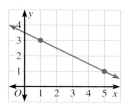

22.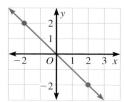

Solve the proportion. Tell what method you used. *(Lessons 8.4, 8.5)*

23. $\dfrac{3}{15} = \dfrac{9}{w}$

24. $\dfrac{66}{x} = \dfrac{11}{4}$

25. $\dfrac{5}{6} = \dfrac{z}{9}$

26. $\dfrac{5}{8} = \dfrac{w}{36}$

27. $\dfrac{n}{12} = \dfrac{4}{16}$

28. $\dfrac{2}{7} = \dfrac{13}{c}$

29. $\dfrac{29}{5} = \dfrac{11.6}{s}$

30. $\dfrac{h}{24} = \dfrac{0.4}{9.6}$

31. Iced Tea Mix If you use 3 tablespoons of iced tea mix for every 8 ounces of water, how many tablespoons of iced tea mix should you add to 32 ounces of water? *(Lessons 8.4, 8.5)*

32. Write 4 is to 11 as 10 is to p as a proportion. Then solve the proportion. *(Lesson 8.5)*

33. Running Stacey can run 2 miles in 11 minutes. How long would it take her to run 3 miles at the same pace? *(Lesson 8.5)*

34. Books The ratio of hardcover books that you own to paperback books is 2 : 5. If you own 56 books, how many are hardcover? *(Lesson 8.5)*

The scale on a floor plan is 1 in. : 12 ft. Find the actual distance, in feet, for the given length on the floor plan. *(Lesson 8.6)*

35. 2 in.

36. 10 in.

37. 5.5 in.

38. Louisville Slugger Museum The bat at the right is a scale model of Babe Ruth's bat displayed at the Louisville Slugger Museum in Louisville, Kentucky. The model's scale is 1 : 0.024. If the model of the bat is 121 feet long, about how long is the actual bat? *(Lesson 8.6)*

8

Chapter Test

Write the ratio as a fraction in simplest form.

1. $\dfrac{168}{28}$

2. 76 to 19

3. 23 : 184

4. 46 : 1012

Copy and complete the statement using <, >, or =.

5. 9 : 2 _?_ 25 : 2

6. 20 : 8 _?_ 50 : 20

7. 11 : 12 _?_ 96 : 144

8. 440 : 5 _?_ 510 : 6

9. Land Sailing Land yachts are used to sail on land. If a land yacht travels 456 feet in 6 seconds, what is the land yacht's average speed?

10. Flowers Determine which of the following is the better buy: 6 cut flowers for $5.94 or 12 cut flowers for $10.68.

Graph the line that passes through the points. Then find the slope of the line.

11. (1, −2), (2, 1)

12. (−3, −4), (0, 0)

13. (5, 0), (1, 1)

14. Draw the line that has a slope of $-\dfrac{3}{4}$ and passes through (6, 3).

15. Staining Three gallons of oil-based stain cover about 1050 square feet of a flat surface. How many gallons of stain are needed to cover 3150 square feet?

Solve the proportion. Tell what method you used.

16. $\dfrac{5}{8} = \dfrac{75}{a}$

17. $\dfrac{8}{b} = \dfrac{2}{3}$

18. $\dfrac{c}{9} = \dfrac{4}{16}$

19. $\dfrac{12}{5} = \dfrac{d}{8}$

20. $\dfrac{1.25}{5} = \dfrac{x}{18}$

21. $\dfrac{y}{3} = \dfrac{24.8}{8}$

22. $\dfrac{9}{10} = \dfrac{3.6}{z}$

23. $\dfrac{5}{r} = \dfrac{6}{8.4}$

Floor Plans **In Exercises 24–26, use the following information.**
The floor plan of the first floor of a house was drawn using the scale 1 cm : 1.5 m. Find the actual length and width of the room given its length and width on the drawing.

24. Living room
length: 5 cm
width: 4 cm

25. Kitchen
length: 4 cm
width: 3.5 cm

26. Family room
length: 5.25 cm
width: 4.5 cm

Chapter Standardized Test

Test-Taking Strategy Be careful about choosing an answer that seems obvious. Read the problem and all of the choices carefully before answering.

Multiple Choice

1. Which ratio is *not* equivalent to the other three?

   A. $2 : 5$ **B.** 6 to 15

   C. 5 to 2   **D.** $\dfrac{10}{25}$

2. Your soccer team finished the season with a record of 16 wins and 6 losses. What is the team's ratio of wins to losses?

   F. 2 to 8   **G.** 3 to 8

   H. 3 to 2   **I.** 8 to 3

3. A car travels 190 miles in 5 hours. What is the average speed of the car?

   A. 3.8 miles per hour

   B. 38 miles per hour

   C. 40 miles per hour

   D. 950 miles per hour

4. Which rate is less than 0.5 meter per second?

   F. $\dfrac{7000 \text{ m}}{4 \text{ h}}$ **G.** $\dfrac{210 \text{ m}}{6 \text{ min}}$

   H. $\dfrac{165 \text{ cm}}{3 \text{ sec}}$ **I.** $\dfrac{105 \text{ m}}{175 \text{ sec}}$

5. What is the slope of the line shown below?

   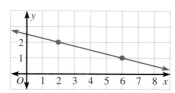

   A. -4 **B.** $-\dfrac{1}{4}$ **C.** $\dfrac{1}{4}$ **D.** 4

6. What is the solution of $\dfrac{x}{9} = \dfrac{42}{54}$?

   F. 5   **G.** 6   **H.** 7   **I.** 8

7. What is the solution of $\dfrac{4}{7} = \dfrac{18}{m}$?

   A. 7   **B.** 28   **C.** 31.5   **D.** 72

8. You can type 330 words in 6 minutes. What proportion can you use to find the number w of words that you can type in 15 minutes?

   F. $\dfrac{w}{6} = \dfrac{15}{330}$ **G.** $\dfrac{w}{15} = \dfrac{330}{6}$

   H. $\dfrac{15}{w} = \dfrac{330}{6}$ **I.** $\dfrac{330}{w} = \dfrac{15}{6}$

9. A scale model of a car is made using the scale $1 : 24$. The height of a wheel on the model is 2.4 centimeters. What is the height of a wheel on the actual car?

   A. 5.76 cm   **B.** 24 cm

   C. 57.6 cm   **D.** 576 cm

Short Response

10. The female Angonoka tortoise lays eggs in groups called clutches. One female tortoise lays 5 clutches and a total of 30 eggs. What is her average rate of eggs per clutch?

Extended Response

11. The ratio of counselors to campers at a camp is $1 : 9$. The ratio of campers who know how to swim to campers who don't know how is $7 : 2$. There are 117 campers. Find the number of counselors and the number of campers who know how to swim. Explain how you found your answers.

Counting Animals in the *Wild*

Capture-Recapture

Scientists often need to use special methods to study animals in the wild. Some animals live in places where it would be impossible to count every animal in a population. So scientists sometimes use a method called *capture-recapture* to estimate the number of animals in a population.

1 Suppose this diagram shows all the animals in a population.

2 Scientists catch a group of animals and mark them. Then they release them.

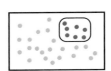

3 Later, the scientists catch a second group of animals and count how many are marked.

4 Now they can use a proportion to estimate the total population.

$$\frac{\text{Marked animals in second group}}{\text{Total animals in second group}} = \frac{\text{Total marked animals}}{\text{Total population of animals}}$$

$$\frac{2}{8} = \frac{7}{x} \qquad 2x = 8 \cdot 7 \qquad x = \frac{8 \cdot 7}{2} = 28$$

1. Is 28 a reasonable estimate for the total number of animals in the population? Explain.

2. **Critical Thinking** Discuss why scientists might not be able to count every animal in a population.

3. **Applying the Method** Scientists trying to estimate the number of fish in a pond caught 61 fish and marked them. They then caught a second group of 68 fish and 36 of them were marked. Write and solve a proportion to estimate the total number of fish in the pond.

Estimating a Shark Population

In a recent year, about 2000 mako sharks were tagged and released in an area off the coast of California. A group of local fishermen volunteered to keep track of how many of the mako sharks that they caught and released had been tagged.

4. That year the fishermen caught 537 mako sharks. Fourteen of the mako sharks they caught had been tagged. Write a proportion that you can use to estimate the population of mako sharks. Solve the proportion to estimate the population.

5. Critical Thinking Choose one of the following points and use it to explain why your solution to Exercise 4 is an *estimate* of the mako shark population.

- Only one sample is used.

- Sharks might leave the area.

- Other fishermen were working in the area.

Project IDEAS

- **Experiment** Design a capture-recapture experiment. Use a small container of beans for the population. You can mark them using a pencil or marker. Describe your experiment and present your results.

- **Report** Find information about other capture-recapture studies involving other animals. Present your information to the class using a poster or an oral report.

- **Research** Scientists who study human populations use a form of capture-recapture to estimate the number of people in a group. Find information about the use of capture-recapture in studying diseases or in making census estimates.

- **Career** A scientist who studies living things is called a *biologist*. Find out what types of work biologists do. What kind of education is required to become a biologist? Present your findings to your class.

INTERNET
Project Support
CLASSZONE.COM

Percents

BEFORE

In previous chapters you've...

- Written fractions as decimals and decimals as fractions
- Used ratios and proportions

Now

In Chapter 9 you'll study...

- Writing fractions and decimals as percents
- Solving percent problems
- Circle graphs
- Discounts, markups, sales tax, tips, and simple interest

WHY?

So you can solve real-world problems about...

- the Martian atmosphere, p. 418
- orangutans, p. 423
- tacos, p. 447
- jeans, p. 450

ⓘ Internet Preview
CLASSZONE.COM

- eEdition Plus Online
- eWorkbook Plus Online
- eTutorial Plus Online
- State Test Practice
- More Examples

Chapter Warm-Up Games

Review skills you need for this chapter in these quick games.

Sunny Days

Upland: There are 5 sunny days for every 2 cloudy days.

Zellwood: There are 6 sunny days per week.

Ashton: There are 11 sunny days every 2 weeks.

Arlington: 17 out of 21 days are sunny.

Yellowfield: For every 3 days, 2 are sunny.

Milltown: 5 out of 21 days are cloudy.

BrAIN GAME

Key Skill:
Writing ratios

You have asked some friends to report how sunny their towns are. Unfortunately, their reports give data in different ways.

- Write each report as a ratio of sunny days to cloudy days. Write the ratios as fractions. Order the fractions from least to greatest.

- Copy the spaces below. In the spaces, write the first letters of the towns in the order you determined. The answer will spell the name and state of the sunniest city in the United States.

? ? ? ? , ? ?

Lightning Math

Clouds: 3, 20, 18, 24, 6, 25, 30, 12

Lightning bolts: $\frac{1}{2}$, $\frac{3}{5}$, $\frac{5}{6}$, $\frac{3}{4}$

BRAIN GAME

Key Skill:
Writing proportions

Use the numbers on the clouds above to form ratios with the same values as the ratios on the lightning bolts. Use each cloud one time.

Stop and Think

1. **Writing** Explain the procedure you used to order the fractions you wrote in *Sunny Days*.

2. **Extension** Use the cloud numbers in *Lightning Math* to write 4 ratios that are different from the ratios shown above.

Getting Ready to Learn

Review What You Need to Know ♻

Using Vocabulary **Copy and complete using a review word.**

1. A(n) _?_ is an equation that states that two ratios are equivalent.

2. A(n) _?_ uses division to compare two numbers.

Write the fraction as a decimal. *(p. 190)*

3. $\frac{1}{2}$ 4. $\frac{3}{4}$ 5. $\frac{4}{5}$ 6. $\frac{7}{10}$

Write the decimal as a fraction. *(p. 190)*

7. 0.6   8. 0.1   9. 0.95   10. 0.45

Find the product or quotient. *(pp. 63, 67)*

11. 82×0.64 12. 0.78×105 13. $15 \div 0.12$ 14. $58 \div 0.29$

Use the cross products property to solve the proportion. *(p. 394)*

15. $\frac{11}{4} = \frac{33}{n}$ 16. $\frac{a}{28} = \frac{6}{7}$ 17. $\frac{25}{5} = \frac{b}{6}$ 18. $\frac{3}{x} = \frac{5}{45}$

You should include material that appears on a notebook like this in your own notes.

Know How to Take Notes

Highlighting the Key Step *Leave space in your notebook to take notes from your textbook. As you use your textbook to review a lesson covered in class, take additional notes. You may want to highlight the key step in an example.*

$$\frac{3}{x} = \frac{5}{15}$$ Write proportion.

$$3 \cdot 15 = x \cdot 5$$ Cross products property

$$\frac{3 \cdot 15}{5} = \frac{x \cdot 5}{5}$$ Divide each side by 5.

$$9 = x$$ Simplify.

The strategy above will be useful in Lesson 9.2, where you will use proportions to solve percent problems.

Percents and Fractions

BEFORE	▶ Now	WHY?
You multiplied fractions and whole numbers.	You'll use a fraction to find the percent of a number.	So you can write a percent for a movie category, as in Ex. 40.

Word Watch

percent, p. 415

In the Real World

Tennis In October of 2001, 16 of the top 100 women's tennis players were from the United States. What percent of the players were *not* from the United States? You'll find the answer in Example 4.

The word *percent* means "per hundred." A **percent** is a ratio whose denominator is 100. The symbol for percent is %.

Understanding Percent

The model at the right has 16 out of 100 squares shaded. You can say that 16 percent of the squares are shaded.

16 percent

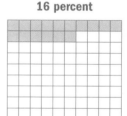

Numbers You can write 16 percent as $\frac{16}{100}$ or as 16%.

Algebra You can write p percent as $\frac{p}{100}$ or as $p\%$.

EXAMPLE 1 **Writing Percents as Fractions**

Write the percent as a fraction.

a. 37% **b.** 50%

Solution

a. $37\% = \frac{37}{100}$ **b.** $50\% = \frac{50}{100} = \frac{1}{2}$

Your turn now Write the percent as a fraction in simplest form.

1. 24% **2.** 55% **3.** 87% **4.** 12%

EXAMPLE 2 Writing Fractions as Percents

To write a fraction as a percent, rewrite the fraction with a denominator of 100.

a. $\dfrac{4}{5} = \dfrac{4 \times 20}{5 \times 20} = \dfrac{80}{100} = 80\%$

b. $\dfrac{3}{4} = \dfrac{3 \times 25}{4 \times 25} = \dfrac{75}{100} = 75\%$

Here are some common percents that you should remember.

Common Percents					
$10\% = \dfrac{1}{10}$	$20\% = \dfrac{1}{5}$	$25\% = \dfrac{1}{4}$	$30\% = \dfrac{3}{10}$	$40\% = \dfrac{2}{5}$	$50\% = \dfrac{1}{2}$
$60\% = \dfrac{3}{5}$	$70\% = \dfrac{7}{10}$	$75\% = \dfrac{3}{4}$	$80\% = \dfrac{4}{5}$	$90\% = \dfrac{9}{10}$	$100\% = 1$

EXAMPLE 3 Finding a Percent of a Number

To find 60% of 75, use the fact that $60\% = \dfrac{3}{5}$ and multiply.

60% of $75 = \dfrac{3}{5} \cdot 75$ Write percent as a fraction.

$= \dfrac{3 \cdot \overset{15}{\cancel{75}}}{\underset{1}{\cancel{5}} \cdot 1}$ Use rule for multiplying fractions. Divide out common factor.

$= 45$ Multiply.

Your turn now In Exercises 5–8, write the fraction as a percent.

5. $\dfrac{10}{25}$ **6.** $\dfrac{3}{20}$ **7.** $\dfrac{7}{10}$ **8.** $\dfrac{1}{50}$

9. Find 70% of 900.   **10.** Find 25% of 200.

EXAMPLE 4 Using Percents

For the tennis players described on page 415, you know that $\dfrac{16}{100} = 16\%$ of the players were from the United States. To find the percent of tennis players who were *not* from the United States, use the fact that the entire group of players represents 100%.

$$100\% - 16\% = 84\%$$

ANSWER In October of 2001, 84% of the top 100 women's tennis players were not from the United States.

Getting Ready to Practice

1. Vocabulary What does percent mean?

Write the percent as a fraction in simplest form.

2. 11%   **3.** 23%   **4.** 82%   **5.** 20%

Write the fraction as a percent.

6. $\frac{3}{10}$ **7.** $\frac{13}{25}$ **8.** $\frac{77}{100}$ **9.** $\frac{2}{5}$

Find the percent of the number.

10. 80% of 55   **11.** 30% of 90   **12.** 50% of 250   **13.** 60% of 85

14. Recycling In the United States, refunding money for the return of bottles is accepted statewide in 10 of the 50 states. What percent of states do *not* refund money for the return of bottles?

Practice and Problem Solving

with Homework

Example	Exercises
1	15–22
2	23–30, 39
3	31–38
4	40

Online Resources
CLASSZONE.COM

· More Examples
· eTutorial Plus

Write the percent as a fraction.

15. 67%   **16.** 34%   **17.** 92%   **18.** 14%

19. 8%   **20.** 25%   **21.** 76%   **22.** 45%

Write the fraction as a percent.

23. $\frac{11}{25}$ **24.** $\frac{13}{50}$ **25.** $\frac{8}{25}$ **26.** $\frac{1}{10}$

27. $\frac{3}{20}$ **28.** $\frac{7}{20}$ **29.** $\frac{9}{10}$ **30.** $\frac{17}{25}$

Find the percent of the number.

31. 20% of 75   **32.** 50% of 32   **33.** 10% of 60   **34.** 90% of 20

35. 40% of 95   **36.** 75% of 52   **37.** 25% of 400   **38.** 60% of 200

39. Houses On your street, 18 out of 20 houses have attached garages. What percent of houses on your street have attached garages?

40. Movies The American Film Institute compiled a list of the top 100 movies of all time. Of the 100 movies, 64 were dramas. What percent of movies were *not* dramas?

Algebra Write the percent as a fraction. Then solve the proportion.

41. $\dfrac{13}{20} = x\%$ **42.** $\dfrac{9}{25} = y\%$ **43.** $\dfrac{1}{10} = z\%$ **44.** $\dfrac{3}{50} = w\%$

Extended Problem Solving In Exercises 45–47, use the following information. The atmosphere of Mars is made up of about 95% carbon dioxide and about 3% nitrogen.

45. Write each percent as a fraction.

46. Interpret About what percent of the atmosphere of Mars consists of gases other than carbon dioxide and nitrogen? What fraction is this?

47. Analyze A probe on Mars took a 500 milliliter sample of the atmosphere. How many milliliters of the sample would you expect to be gases other than carbon dioxide and nitrogen?

Order the given ratios from least to greatest.

48. 6 to 25, 23%, $\dfrac{1}{4}$ **49.** 81%, $\dfrac{41}{50}$, 4 to 5

50. Challenge A tiling pattern is composed of 68 blue tiles and 132 white tiles. What percent of the tiles are blue?

Mixed Review

Use algebra to solve the proportion. *(Lesson 8.4)*

51. $\dfrac{10}{11} = \dfrac{30}{n}$ **52.** $\dfrac{a}{32} = \dfrac{7}{8}$ **53.** $\dfrac{48}{33} = \dfrac{b}{11}$ **54.** $\dfrac{25}{c} = \dfrac{5}{12}$

55. You build a scale model of your house. The model is 8 inches long, and your house is 40 feet long. What is the model's scale? *(Lesson 8.6)*

Basic Skills Find the product.

56. 4.8×6.7 **57.** 0.006×0.06 **58.** 7.52×0.2 **59.** 9.78×12.234

Test-Taking Practice

60. Multiple Choice A bake sale raised $300 for a school trip. If 20% of the money covered bake sale expenses, how much went toward the trip?

A. $20   **B.** $60   **C.** $240   **D.** $280

61. Multiple Choice On opening day of trout season, 8 out of every 10 fishermen caught a trout. What percent did *not* catch a trout?

F. 2%   **G.** 8%   **H.** 20%   **I.** 80%

Hands-on Activity

GOAL
Use a percent bar model to find a percent.

MATERIALS
• paper
• pencil

Using Percent Bar Models

You can find a percent using a percent bar model.

Explore **Find what percent 4 is of 9.**

1 Draw a percent bar model and label it as shown.

Label the left side of the bar from 0 to the whole amount, 9. Then shade the bar to the part of the whole, 4.

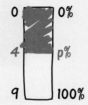

Label the right side of the bar from 0% to 100%. Use $p\%$ to represent the unknown percent.

2 Use the percent bar model to write and solve a proportion.

The arrangement of the numbers in the percent bar model tells you how to set up the proportion.

$$\frac{4}{9} = \frac{p}{100}$$ **Write proportion.**

$$100 \cdot \frac{4}{9} = 100 \cdot \frac{p}{100}$$ **Multiply each side by 100.**

$$\frac{400}{9}, \text{ or } 44\frac{4}{9} = p$$ **Simplify.**

ANSWER The number 4 is $44\frac{4}{9}\%$ of 9.

Your turn now **Use a percent bar model to find the percent.**

1. What percent of 48 is 6? **2.** What percent of 135 is 90?

Stop *and* **Think**

3. Critical Thinking Describe how to use a percent bar model to find what number is 72% of 200. Then find the number.

Percents and Proportions

BEFORE	▶ Now	WHY?
You used a fraction to find a percent of a number.	You will use proportions to solve percent problems.	So you can find the total distance of an auto race, as in Ex. 9.

In the Real World

Water Sports In a survey, 525 teenagers were asked to name the water sport that they would most like to try, and 20% said "surfing." How many teenagers said "surfing"? You'll find the answer in Example 2.

You can use a proportion to solve percent problems.

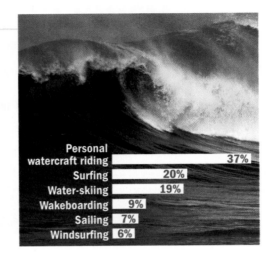

Personal watercraft riding	37%
Surfing	20%
Water-skiing	19%
Wakeboarding	9%
Sailing	7%
Windsurfing	6%

Solving Percent Problems

You can represent "*a* is *p* percent of *b*" with the proportion

$$\frac{a}{b} = \frac{p}{100}$$

where *a* is part of the base *b* and *p*%, or $\frac{p}{100}$, is the percent.

EXAMPLE 1 Finding a Percent

HELP with Reading

In a percent problem, the word that follows "of" is usually the base *b*.

What percent of 3 is 1?

$\dfrac{a}{b} = \dfrac{p}{100}$ Write proportion.

$\dfrac{1}{3} = \dfrac{p}{100}$ Substitute 1 for *a* and 3 for *b*.

$100 \cdot \dfrac{1}{3} = 100 \cdot \dfrac{p}{100}$ Multiply each side by 100.

$33\dfrac{1}{3} = p$ Simplify.

ANSWER 1 is $33\dfrac{1}{3}$% of 3.

1. What percent of 40 is 16? 2. What percent of 400 is 34?

3. In a classroom of 25 students, 16 students were wearing sandals. What percent of the students were wearing sandals?

Writing Fractions as Percents By using a proportion, you can write any fraction as a percent. Example 1 showed that $\frac{1}{3} = 33\frac{1}{3}\%$. Here are some other common percents that you should remember.

Common Percents					
$12\frac{1}{2}\% = \frac{1}{8}$	$33\frac{1}{3}\% = \frac{1}{3}$	$37\frac{1}{2}\% = \frac{3}{8}$	$62\frac{1}{2}\% = \frac{5}{8}$	$66\frac{2}{3}\% = \frac{2}{3}$	$87\frac{1}{2}\% = \frac{7}{8}$

In Lesson 9.1, you found a common percent of a number using a fraction. Now you can use a proportion to find any percent of a number.

What do you think?

Sports

EXAMPLE 2 **Finding a Part of a Base**

Surfing To find the number of teenagers who said "surfing," as discussed on page 420, use a proportion.

$$\frac{a}{b} = \frac{p}{100}$$ Write proportion.

$$\frac{a}{525} = \frac{20}{100}$$ Substitute 525 for b and 20 for p.

$$525 \cdot \frac{a}{525} = 525 \cdot \frac{20}{100}$$ Multiply each side by 525.

$$a = \frac{\overset{105}{\cancel{525}} \cdot \overset{1}{\cancel{20}}}{\underset{20}{\cancel{100}} \, \underset{1}{}}$$ Use rule for multiplying fractions. Divide out common factors.

$$a = 105$$ Multiply.

ANSWER In the survey, 105 of the teenagers said "surfing."

■ **Surfing**

It is recommended that a beginning surfer use a board that is 18-24 inches taller than he or she is. What is this range in feet?

Your turn now Use a proportion to answer the question.

4. What number is 76% of 25? 5. What number is 5% of 400?

6. What number is 12% of 50? 7. What number is 37% of 200?

Cross Products Property When you are asked to find the base in a percent problem, you solve for b in the proportion $\frac{a}{b} = \frac{p}{100}$. In this case, you should use the cross products property, as shown in Example 3.

HELP with Notetaking

To help you remember the process of solving a percent problem, you may want to highlight the key step in the process.

EXAMPLE 3 Finding a Base

42 is 30% of what number?

$\dfrac{a}{b} = \dfrac{p}{100}$	Write proportion.
$\dfrac{42}{b} = \dfrac{30}{100}$	Substitute 42 for a and 30 for p.
$42 \cdot 100 = b \cdot 30$	Cross products property
$\dfrac{42 \cdot 100}{30} = \dfrac{b \cdot 30}{30}$	Divide each side by 30.
$140 = b$	Simplify.

ANSWER 42 is 30% of 140.

9.2 Exercises

More Practice, p. 713

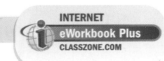

INTERNET
eWorkbook Plus
CLASSZONE.COM

Getting Ready to Practice

1. Vocabulary What do a, b, and p represent in the proportion $\frac{a}{b} = \frac{p}{100}$?

For the given question, identify the values of a, b, and p in the proportion $\frac{a}{b} = \frac{p}{100}$. Then use the proportion to answer the question.

2. What percent of 20 is 5?

3. What percent of 30 is 18?

4. What is 14% of 50?

5. 30 is 75% of what number?

6. 70 is 35% of what number?

7. What is 32% of 200?

8. Theater Students are auditioning for a school play. Only 18 out of the 45 students auditioning will get a part in the play. What percent of the students who audition will be in the play?

9. Auto Racing The first lap of an auto race is 2500 meters. This is 10% of the total race distance. What is the total race distance?

Practice and Problem Solving

with Homework

Example	Exercises
1	10–26, 29
2	10–26, 28
3	12–26

 Online Resources
CLASSZONE.COM

· More Examples
· eTutorial Plus

Copy and complete the proportion. Then answer the question.

10. What percent of 20 is 8?

$$\frac{?}{20} = \frac{p}{100}$$

11. What number is 30% of 50?

$$\frac{a}{?} = \frac{?}{100}$$

Match the question with the correct proportion.

12. 60 is 25% of what number?

A. $\frac{a}{60} = \frac{25}{100}$

13. What percent of 60 is 25?

B. $\frac{25}{60} = \frac{p}{100}$

14. What is 25% of 60?

C. $\frac{60}{b} = \frac{25}{100}$

Use a proportion to answer the question.

15. What percent of 30 is 3?

16. What percent of 50 is 47?

17. 51 is 17% of what number?

18. 16 is 80% of what number?

19. What number is 14% of 350?

20. 12 is 8% of what number?

21. What percent of 600 is 180?

22. What number is 75% of 44?

23. 18 is 45% of what number?

24. What percent of 20 is 6?

25. What number is $12\frac{1}{2}$% of 64?

26. What number is $66\frac{2}{3}$% of 81?

27. Writing Describe in words the proportion you use to solve percent problems.

28. Orangutans Orangutans make up $33\frac{1}{3}$% of a zoo's primate exhibit. If there are 18 primates in the exhibit, how many are orangutans?

29. Women's Soccer A season record for the Boston Breakers, a women's professional soccer team, is shown in the table. What percent of the games did the Breakers lose? Round your answer to the nearest whole percent.

Boston Breakers		
Wins	**Losses**	**Ties**
8	10	3

Write the fraction as a percent. Round your answer to the nearest whole percent.

30. $\frac{1}{7}$

31. $\frac{2}{9}$

32. $\frac{3}{11}$

33. $\frac{4}{13}$

34. Mental Math If 1% of a number is 6, what is the number? Explain.

35. Challenge If 5% of a number is y, then what is 100% of the number?

36. Volcanoes There are about 65 active volcanoes in the United States. This is about $4\frac{1}{3}\%$ of the total number of volcanoes on Earth. About how many volcanoes are there on Earth?

Mixed Review

Make a stem-and-leaf plot of the data. *(Lesson 3.3)*

37. 16, 22, 51, 31, 19, 31, 30   **38.** 62, 104, 87, 62, 75, 109, 78

Write the percent as a fraction. *(Lesson 9.1)*

39. 72%   **40.** 4%   **41.** 35%   **42.** 59%

Basic Skills **Order the numbers from least to greatest.**

43. 17, 25, 1, 102, 9   **44.** 60.01, 60.11, 60.1, 6.1, 60.001

Test-Taking Practice

45. Multiple Choice What percent of 155 is 62?

   A. $2\frac{1}{2}\%$ **B.** 25%   **C.** 40%   **D.** 96%

46. Multiple Choice A business made a $5650 profit this month. Last month the business made about 92% of this month's profit. About how much was last month's profit?

   F. $1628   **G.** $5198   **H.** $5558   **I.** $6141

BrAIN GAME

Running Around in Circles

Copy the puzzle. Then find the number that makes each horizontal and vertical statement true.

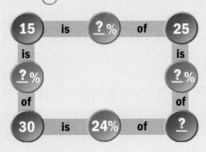

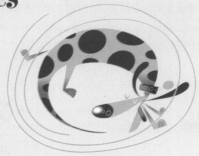

Percents and Decimals

BEFORE	Now	WHY?
You wrote percents as fractions and fractions as percents.	You'll write percents as decimals and decimals as percents.	So you can find the price of a vintage toy, as in Ex. 18.

Word Watch

Review Words

decimal, p. 52
percent, p. 415

In the Real World

Geography The surface area of Lake Tarpon is 0.5% of the surface area of Lake Okeechobee. The surface area of Lake Weohyakapka is 300% of the surface area of Lake Tarpon. How can you write these percents as decimals? You'll find the answer in Example 4.

FLORIDA

Lake Weohyakapka

Lake Tarpon

Lake Okeechobee

You can write a percent as a decimal and a decimal as a percent by using a fraction as an intermediate step. For example:

$$37\% = \frac{37}{100} = 37 \div 100 = 0.37$$

So, 37% = 0.37. Notice that 37% can be written as a decimal by dropping the percent sign and moving the decimal point two places to the left. Similarly, a decimal can be written as a percent by moving the decimal point two places to the right and adding a percent sign.

EXAMPLE 1 Writing Percents as Decimals

a. 48% = 48%

= 0.48

b. 9% = 09%

= 0.09

c. 75.5% = 75.5%

= 0.755

EXAMPLE 2 Writing Decimals as Percents

a. 0.13 = .13

= 13%

b. 0.04 = .04

= 4%

c. 0.027 = .027

= 2.7%

Your turn now Write the percent as a decimal or the decimal as a percent.

1. 25%
2. 1%
3. 5.2%
4. 0.082
5. 0.06
6. 0.578

You can write a fraction as a percent by writing the fraction as a decimal and then moving the decimal point two places to the right.

with Reading

The symbol ≈ is read "is approximately equal to." It indicates that a result has been rounded and is not exact.

EXAMPLE 3 **Writing Fractions as Percents**

a. $\frac{5}{6} \approx 0.833$ Write as a decimal rounded
to the nearest thousandth.

    $= 83.3\%$ Write as a percent.

b. $\frac{3}{7} \approx 0.429$ Write as a decimal rounded
to the nearest thousandth.

    $= 42.9\%$ Write as a percent.

Small and Large Percents Percents less than 1% represent numbers that are less than 0.01, or $\frac{1}{100}$. Percents greater than 100% represent numbers that are greater than 1. For example, the models below represent **0.5%** and **150%**, respectively.

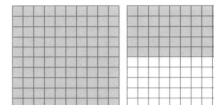

EXAMPLE 4 **Rewriting Small and Large Percents**

To write the percents discussed on page 425 as decimals, follow the same rules as for percents between 1% and 100%.

Lake Tarpon: $0.5\% = 00.5\%$ **Lake Weohyakapka:** $300\% = 300\%$

                    $= 0.005$ $= 3$

Your turn now Write the fraction as a percent. Round to the nearest tenth of a percent.

7. $\frac{6}{7}$ **8.** $\frac{9}{14}$ **9.** $\frac{1}{9}$ **10.** $\frac{5}{11}$

Write the percent as a decimal.

11. 0.25%   **12.** 250%   **13.** 0.0014%   **14.** 0.05%

EXAMPLE 5 **Using a Percent Less Than 1%**

Water The total amount of water on Earth, including salt water and fresh water, is about 326,000,000 cubic miles. Of this amount, 0.009% is in fresh water lakes. What is the amount of water in fresh water lakes?

Solution

$$0.009\% \text{ of } 326,000,000 = 0.00009 \times 326,000,000 \qquad \text{Write percent as a decimal.}$$

$$= 29,340 \qquad \text{Multiply.}$$

ANSWER The amount of water in fresh water lakes is 29,340 cubic miles.

Your turn now **Solve the following problem.**

15. Evan's resting heart rate is 72 beats per minute. During intense exercise, his heart rate is 250% of his resting heart rate. What is Evan's heart rate during intense exercise?

9.3 **Exercises**
More Practice, p. 713

INTERNET
eWorkbook Plus
CLASSZONE.COM

Getting Ready to Practice

1. Vocabulary Write a decimal that is greater than 100%. Write a decimal that is less than 1%.

Write the percent as a decimal or the decimal as a percent.

2. 47%	**3.** 3%	**4.** 0.7%	**5.** 0.02%
6. 324%	**7.** 208%	**8.** 0.29	**9.** 0.642
10. 0.0083	**11.** 0.00105	**12.** 2.03	**13.** 15.5

Write the fraction as a percent. Round to the nearest tenth of a percent.

14. $\frac{1}{6}$ **15.** $\frac{7}{9}$ **16.** $\frac{5}{12}$ **17.** $\frac{9}{16}$

18. Toy Cars The price of a miniature toy car in 1968 was 0.295% of its current price. Today the car is a collector's item and is priced at $200. What was the price of the toy car in 1968?

Practice and Problem Solving

HELP with Homework

Example	Exercises
1	19–26
2	27–34
3	35–42
4	19–26, 48
5	49

Online Resources
CLASSZONE.COM
· More Examples
· eTutorial Plus

Write the percent as a decimal.

19. 11%   **20.** 8%   **21.** 210%   **22.** 0.3%

23. 0.15%   **24.** 42.5%   **25.** 3.01%   **26.** 125%

Write the decimal as a percent.

27. 0.26   **28.** 0.07   **29.** 0.049   **30.** 0.205

31. 0.005   **32.** 1.184   **33.** 2.14   **34.** 0.0085

Write the fraction as a percent.

35. $\frac{11}{15}$ **36.** $\frac{13}{21}$ **37.** $\frac{17}{18}$ **38.** $\frac{23}{30}$

39. $\frac{14}{39}$ **40.** $\frac{5}{26}$ **41.** $\frac{20}{49}$ **42.** $\frac{74}{95}$

43. Mental Math What is 200% of 8? What is 300% of 8? What is 400% of 8? Describe how you can find these answers without performing any written calculations.

44. Number Sense The money you earned this summer is 120% of the money you earned last summer. Did you earn more money or less money this summer than you did last summer? Explain your reasoning.

Explain In Exercises 45–47, tell whether the statement seems reasonable. Explain why or why not.

45. "Work" was listed as an after school activity by 110% of your classmates.

46. Of the 100 people surveyed, 0.05% said that they drive mopeds.

47. Your math test score is 125% of your last test score.

48. Hamsters The mass of a newborn black-bellied hamster is 0.934% of the mass of an adult hamster. Write the percent as a decimal.

49. Population In 2001, Argentina's population was about 0.61% of the world population. The world population was about 6,137,000,000 people. Approximately how many people lived in Argentina in 2001?

Write the percent as a decimal and as a fraction or mixed number.

50. 14%   **51.** 92.3%   **52.** 0.001%   **53.** 252%

Write the decimal as a fraction or mixed number and as a percent.

54. 0.8   **55.** 0.0877   **56.** 0.0021   **57.** 3.13

What do you think?
Science

■ **Hamsters**

The mass of an adult hamster is typically between 112 grams and 908 grams. What is the range of a hamster's mass?

58. Writing Describe a situation in real life where a percent less than 1% or greater than 100% can be used.

Copy and complete the statement using <, >, or =.

59. 0.14% $\underline{?}$ 0.014   **60.** 3.4 $\underline{?}$ 34%   **61.** 0.59 $\underline{?}$ 59%

62. $\frac{4}{9}$ $\underline{?}$ 49%   **63.** 84% $\underline{?}$ $\frac{13}{15}$ **64.** 0.99 $\underline{?}$ $\frac{1}{11}$

65. Consumer Spending In 1998, the average consumer spending per person on books was about 460% as much as on video games. The average consumer spending per person on video games was $18.45. What was the average consumer spending per person on books?

66. Movie Sequels A movie made $1,582,000 at the box office. The sequel to the movie made 104% of the original movie. How much money did the sequel make?

Challenge Order the values from least to greatest.

67. 0.33%, 0.00311, $\frac{1}{300}$, 0.0031   **68.** $\frac{461}{50}$, 920%, 9.02, 9.202

Mixed Review

Use equivalent ratios to solve the proportion. *(Lesson.8.4)*

69. $\frac{1}{5} = \frac{x}{20}$ **70.** $\frac{5}{8} = \frac{x}{24}$ **71.** $\frac{x}{36} = \frac{9}{12}$ **72.** $\frac{x}{11} = \frac{98}{22}$

Use a proportion to find the percent of the number. *(Lesson 9.2)*

73. 70% of 280   **74.** 30% of 210   **75.** 21% of 400   **76.** 32% of 500

Basic Skills Estimate the product.

77. 5.43 × 20.9   **78.** 0.23 × 8.2   **79.** 7.32 × 49.9   **80.** 18.73 × 4.2

Test-Taking Practice

81. Multiple Choice Which list of values is in order from least to greatest?

A. 1018%, 10.2, 102, 1016   **B.** 10.2, 1018%, 102, 1016

C. 10.2, 102, 1018%, 1016   **D.** 10.2, 102, 1016, 1018%

82. Multiple Choice Pager sales represented 0.728% of the total sales of electronics products in 1998. Which value is *not* equal to 0.728%?

F. 0.00728   **G.** $\frac{728}{1000}$ **H.** $\frac{728}{100,000}$ **I.** $\frac{91}{12,500}$

Look for a Pattern
Make a Table
Make a List
Draw a Diagram
Write an Equation
Solve a Related Problem
Work Backward

Write an Equation

Problem A portable CD player goes on sale for 20% off the regular price. If the sale price is $120, what is the regular price?

❶ Read and Understand

Read the problem carefully.

The problem asks you to find the regular price of the CD player. You are given the percent off the regular price and the sale price of the CD player.

❷ Make a Plan

Decide on a strategy to use.

Because you are trying to find an unknown quantity, you can let x represent the regular price of the CD player. Then you can write an equation and solve for x.

❸ Solve the Problem

Reread the problem and write an equation.

Write a verbal model. Let x represent the regular price of the portable CD player.

$$\text{Regular price of CD player} - \text{Percent off} \cdot \text{Regular price of CD player} = \text{Sale price of CD player}$$

$x - 0.2x = 120$	Write equation.
$0.8x = 120$	Combine like terms.
$\dfrac{0.8x}{0.8} = \dfrac{120}{0.8}$	Divide each side by 0.8.
$x = 150$	Simplify.

ANSWER The regular price of the portable CD player is $150.

❹ Look Back

Check your answer in the original equation.

$$x - 0.2x = 150 - 0.2(150)$$
$$= 150 - 30 = 120 \checkmark$$

Use the strategy *write an equation*.

1. **Art Class** There are 24 students in Maria's art class. There are 3 times as many boys as girls. How many girls are in the class?

2. **CD Club** You belong to a CD club run by a local music store. By showing your membership card, you get 10% off the price of any CD. If you pay $18 for a double CD (before sales tax), how much does a person who doesn't belong to the club pay for the same double CD?

3. **Nail Polish** Your sister asks you to pick up a bottle of nail polish for her at the store. While there, you buy a bottle of nail polish for yourself as well as a bottle of nail polish remover. When you get home, you can't find the sales receipt, but you remember that you paid $5.50 for the items and the nail polish remover cost $1.50. How much does your sister owe you for her bottle of nail polish?

4. **Newspaper** A school's newspaper is 19 pages long. The editorial work is divided among three people. Jack edits 5 more pages than Al. Joan edits twice as many pages as Jack. How many pages does Al edit?

5. **Breakfast** You go to the bakery to pick up breakfast treats for a club meeting before school. You have $20 to spend, and you need a treat for each of the 16 people who will be at the meeting including yourself. If you intend to spend all the money you have, how many doughnuts and how many bagels should you buy? Assume no sales tax.

Doughnuts	$1.00 each
Bagels	$1.50 each

Mixed Problem Solving

Use any strategy to solve the problem.

6. **Sports** In a survey asking students how many organized sports they play, $\frac{1}{2}$ of the students said four. Of the remaining students, $\frac{1}{2}$ said three, and 3 said zero. The 2 who were left said one. How many students were surveyed?

7. **Walking** The results of a survey that asked students how many hours a week they spend walking are recorded below. What was the most common number of hours a student spent walking?

> 7, 0, 5, 5, 7, 4, 5, 0, 3, 2, 5, 7, 7, 5, 4, 5, 7, 0, 5, 5, 7, 5, 4, 7, 7

8. **Chairs** You help set up chairs in a row 11 feet long for a graduation ceremony. Each chair has a width of 18 inches, and the chairs will be placed 1 inch apart. How many chairs can you put in the row? (*Hint:* There will be 1 less space between chairs than the number of chairs.)

9. **Family Reunion** Christine, Kelly, Eric, and Gretchen are the only participants in a potato sack race at their family reunion. How many different ways can they finish in the potato sack race if Gretchen or Kelly finishes first?

The Percent Equation

BEFORE	Now	WHY?
You used proportions to solve percent problems.	You'll use equations to solve percent problems.	So you can find an art gallery's commission, as in Ex. 23.

Word Watch

Review Words
percent, p. 415

In the Real World

Fundraising Your class has raised 80% of its goal of $8000 for a trip to Washington, D.C. How much money has your class raised?

In Lesson 9.2, you solved percent problems using the proportion $\frac{a}{b} = \frac{p}{100}$, where a is part of the base b and p is the percent. If you solve this proportion for a, you obtain the percent equation described below.

The Percent Equation

You can represent "a is p percent of b" with the equation

$$a = p\% \cdot b$$

where a is part of the base b and $p\%$ is the percent.

EXAMPLE 1 Finding a Part of a Base

To find how much money your class has raised, as described above, use the percent equation.

$a = p\% \cdot b$	Write percent equation.
$= 80\% \cdot 8000$	Substitute 80 for p and 8000 for b.
$= 0.8 \cdot 8000$	Write percent as a decimal.
$= 6400$	Multiply.

ANSWER Your class has raised $6400.

Your turn now Use the percent equation to answer the question.

1. What number is 20% of 110?   **2.** What number is 29% of 88?

with Solving

In Example 2, you can use common percents to check the reasonableness of the answer. You know that 50%, or $\frac{1}{2}$, of 150 is 75. Because 90 is more than 50% of 150, 60% seems reasonable.

EXAMPLE 2 **Finding a Percent**

What percent of 150 is 90?

$a = p\% \cdot b$	Write percent equation.
$90 = p\% \cdot 150$	Substitute 90 for a and 150 for b.
$\dfrac{90}{150} = \dfrac{p\% \cdot 150}{150}$	Divide each side by 150.
$\dfrac{3}{5} = 60\% = p\%$	Simplify fraction. Then write as a percent.

ANSWER The number 90 is 60% of 150.

EXAMPLE 3 **Finding a Base**

The number 117 is 45% of what number?

$a = p\% \cdot b$	Write percent equation.
$117 = 45\% \cdot b$	Substitute 117 for a and 45 for p.
$\dfrac{117}{0.45} = \dfrac{0.45 \cdot b}{0.45}$	Write percent as a decimal. Then divide each side by 0.45.
$260 = b$	Simplify.

ANSWER The number 117 is 45% of 260.

Your turn now **Use the percent equation to answer the question.**

3. 50 is what percent of 250?   **4.** 130 is 65% of what number?

EXAMPLE 4 **Finding a Commission**

Shoes A shoe salesperson sells a pair of shoes for $125. The salesperson receives a 9% commission on the sale. How much is the commission?

Solution

$a = p\% \cdot b$	Write percent equation.
$= 9\% \cdot 125$	Substitute 9 for p and 125 for b.
$= 0.09 \cdot 125$	Write percent as a decimal.
$= 11.25$	Multiply.

ANSWER The commission is $11.25.

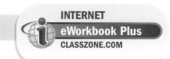

Getting Ready to Practice

1. **Vocabulary** State the percent equation in words.

Use the percent equation to answer the question.

2. What number is 20% of 200?   **3.** What number is 40% of 500?

4. 35 is what percent of 50?   **5.** 54 is what percent of 60?

6. 45 is 25% of what number?   **7.** 91 is 65% of what number?

8. **Find the Error** Describe and correct the error in finding 40% of 70.

9. **Basketball** The Los Angeles Sparks won 87.5% of 32 regular season games on the team's way to winning the WNBA championship in 2001. How many games did the team win?

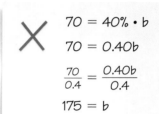

$$70 = 40\% \cdot b$$
$$70 = 0.40b$$
$$\frac{70}{0.4} = \frac{0.40b}{0.4}$$
$$175 = b$$

Practice and Problem Solving

HELP with **Homework**

Example	Exercises
1	10–21, 28, 30
2	10–21, 24, 27, 29
3	10–21
4	23

Online Resources
CLASSZONE.COM
· More Examples
· eTutorial Plus

Use the percent equation to answer the question.

10. What number is 35% of 300?   **11.** What number is 15% of 200?

12. What percent of 25 is 22?   **13.** What percent of 75 is 36?

14. 65 is 65% of what number?   **15.** 8 is 32% of what number?

16. What percent of 125 is 35?   **17.** What percent of 300 is 51?

18. What number is 48% of 400?   **19.** 45 is 90% of what number?

20. 180 is 150% of what number?   **21.** What number is 0.8% of 250?

22. **Writing** Tell whether you would use a proportion or the percent equation to answer the question "What number is 50% of 210?" Explain.

23. **Art Gallery** An art gallery receives a 15% commission on paintings sold in the gallery. If the gallery sells $575 worth of art in one day, what commission is given to the art gallery?

24. **Precipitation** In 2001, it rained 184 days out of the year in Seattle, Washington. What percent of the days in 2001 did it rain in Seattle? Round your answer to the nearest percent.

25. **Compare** Which is greater, 20% of 50 or 25% of 44?

26. Write an Equation Tammy's weekly salary is 120% of the weekly salary of her sister Wanda. The total of their weekly salaries is $165. What is Wanda's weekly salary?

Transportation In Exercises 27–31, use the following information. In a survey asking 2100 students how they get to school, the following results were found: 1365 take the school bus, 7% get a ride from their parents, 9% walk to school, and 294 ride their bikes. The remainder of the students take public transportation to school.

27. What percent of students take the school bus to school?

28. How many students walk to school?

29. What percent of students ride their bikes to school?

30. How many students get a ride from their parents to school?

31. Find what percent of students and how many students take public transportation to school.

32. Challenge Explain how you could use mental math to find a 15% tip for a $26 restaurant bill.

Mixed Review

Find the product or quotient. *(Lessons 2.3, 2.4)*

33. 12.4×0.08 **34.** 1.247×1.6 **35.** $6.3 \div 0.5$ **36.** $0.423 \div 9$

Write the percent as a fraction. *(Lesson 9.1)*

37. 94%   **38.** 73%   **39.** 40%   **40.** 23.5%

Basic Skills   **Use a compass to draw a circle with the given radius.**

41. 4.5 cm   **42.** 2.25 cm   **43.** 7.1 cm   **44.** 0.5 cm

Test-Taking Practice

45. Multiple Choice In Phoenix, Arizona, the average temperature is 85°F or higher during 25% of the months of the year. During how many months of the year is the average temperature below 85°F?

A. 2   **B.** 3   **C.** 9   **D.** 10

46. Short Response The Lions won 72% of the 25 games they played this year. How many games did the team lose? Write and evaluate an expression to find how many games they lost. Explain your reasoning.

Notebook Review

Check Your Definitions

percent, p. 415

Use Your Vocabulary

1. Explain in your own words how to write a decimal as a percent.

9.1 Can you convert between percents and fractions?

 EXAMPLE You can write percents as fractions and fractions as percents.

a. $52\% = \dfrac{52}{100} = \dfrac{13}{25}$
b. $\dfrac{18}{25} = \dfrac{18 \times 4}{25 \times 4} = \dfrac{72}{100} = 72\%$

☑ **Write the percent as a fraction or the fraction as a percent.**

2. 36% **3.** 65% **4.** $\dfrac{2}{25}$ **5.** $\dfrac{23}{50}$

9.2 Can you use proportions to solve percent problems?

 EXAMPLE What percent of 120 is 72?

$$\dfrac{a}{b} = \dfrac{p}{100}$$ Write proportion.

$$\dfrac{72}{120} = \dfrac{p}{100}$$ Substitute 72 for a and 120 for b.

$$100 \cdot \dfrac{72}{120} = 100 \cdot \dfrac{p}{100}$$ Multiply each side by 100.

$$\dfrac{\overset{5}{\cancel{100}} \cdot \overset{12}{\cancel{72}}}{\underset{\underset{1}{\cancel{6}}}{\cancel{120}}} = p$$ Use rule for multiplying fractions. Divide out common factors.

$$60 = p$$ Multiply.

ANSWER 72 is 60% of 120.

☑ **Use a proportion to answer the question.**

6. What number is 16% of 75? **7.** 42 is 60% of what number?

9.3–9.4 Can you use the percent equation?

EXAMPLE What number is 250% of 70?

$a = p\% \cdot b$ Write percent equation.

$\quad = 250\% \cdot 70$ Substitute 250 for p and 70 for b.

$\quad = 2.5 \cdot 70$ Write percent as a decimal.

$\quad = 175$ Multiply.

☑ **Use the percent equation to answer the question.**

8. What number is 125% of 60?   **9.** What percent is 2 of 500?

10. What percent is 252 of 400?   **11.** 24 is 32% of what number?

Stop *and* **Think**   about Lessons 9.1–9.4

12. **Writing** Write and solve a real-life problem that uses a percent greater than 100%.

13. **Critical Thinking** You want to find 55% of 120. Will your answer be *greater than* 60 or *less than* 60? Explain your reasoning.

Review Quiz 1

Write the percent as a fraction or the fraction as a percent.

1. 18%   **2.** 74%   **3.** $\dfrac{17}{20}$ **4.** $\dfrac{12}{25}$

Use a proportion to answer the question.

5. What number is 82% of 50?   **6.** 11 is 22% of what number?

Use the percent equation to answer the question.

7. 82 is 205% of what number?   **8.** What percent is 28 of 50?

9. **Class President** Kathy and Joshua are the only candidates running for class president. Joshua got 45% of the votes. If all 40 students in the class voted, how many votes did Joshua receive? How many votes did Kathy receive?

GOAL

Measure and draw angles using a protractor.

MATERIALS

• protractor
• compass
• tracing paper

Measuring Angles

You can use a protractor to measure and draw angles.

Explore 1 **Measure the angle.**

An *angle* is formed by connecting two *rays*, as shown at the right. An angle is measured in units called *degrees* (°). The measure of an angle can be found by using a *protractor*.

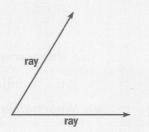

ray

ray

1 Place the protractor on the angle so the protractor's center point is on the point where the two rays meet. Line up one ray with the 0° line.

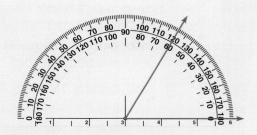

2 The measure of the angle is determined by reading where the other ray crosses the curved portion of the protractor. The measure of the angle is 60°.

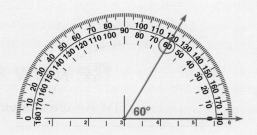

60°

Your turn now Use tracing paper to copy the angle. Then extend the rays and measure the angle using a protractor.

1.

2.

3.

4.

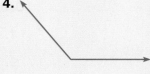

Explore 2 **Draw an angle that measures 115°.**

1 Draw a ray using the straight edge of the protractor.

2 Place your protractor on the ray so that the endpoint lies on the center point of the protractor and the ray coincides with the 0° line.

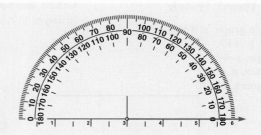

3 Make a mark on your paper where the protractor reads 115°. To draw the angle, use the straight edge of the protractor to draw a ray from the endpoint of the ray through the mark.

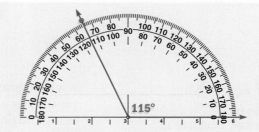

115°

Your turn now **Draw an angle with the given measure.**

5. 120°   **6.** 80°   **7.** 55°   **8.** 105°

9. Using each of the angles from Exercises 5–8, place the point of a compass where each of the angle's two rays meet. Draw an *arc* across the two rays so the figure looks like a pie wedge. Use the same compass setting for each angle. Cut out each figure and put them together so that the corner points of the figures coincide and there are no gaps or overlaps between the edges. How many degrees are in the resulting figure?

Stop *and* **Think**

10. Critical Thinking If 360° represent 100%, what percent does the measure of each angle in Exercises 5–8 represent?

11. Critical Thinking If 360° represent 100%, how many degrees correspond to 25%?

Circle Graphs

LESSON 9.5

BEFORE	▶ Now	WHY?
You found the percent of a number.	You'll use percents to interpret and make circle graphs.	So you can show the results of a movie survey, as in Ex. 17.

In the Real World

Word Watch

circle graph, p. 440
ray, p. 440
angle, p. 440
vertex, p. 440
degrees, p. 440

Class Survey The results of a survey are displayed in the *circle graph* shown. What conclusions can you make about the data?

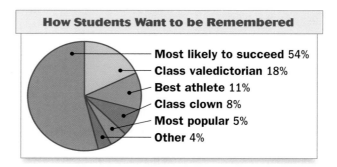

How Students Want to be Remembered

Most likely to succeed 54%
Class valedictorian 18%
Best athlete 11%
Class clown 8%
Most popular 5%
Other 4%

A **circle graph** displays data as sections of a circle. The entire circle represents all the data. Each section is labeled using the actual data or using the data expressed as fractions, decimals, or percents of the sum of the data.

HELP with Solving

When the data in a circle graph are expressed as fractions, decimals, or percents, the sum of the data must equal 1, or 100%.

EXAMPLE 1 Interpreting a Circle Graph

You can make conclusions about the data in the circle graph above.

- The largest section in the circle graph is labeled "most likely to succeed." So, this is how most students want to be remembered.

- More students want to be remembered as "class valedictorian" than as "class clown."

- Together, "class clown" and "best athlete" are more popular than "class valedictorian."

Using Angles The sections of a circle graph can be described mathematically using angles. A **ray** is part of a line. It begins at a point and extends in one direction without end. An **angle** consists of two rays that begin at a common point, called the **vertex** . The plural of vertex is *vertices*.

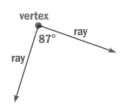

You can use a protractor to find the measure of an angle. Angles are measured in units called **degrees** (°) .

Making Circle Graphs To make a circle graph, you need to find the appropriate angle measure for each section. The sum of all the angle measures must equal 360°.

HELP with **Review**

Need help using a compass? See p. 700.

What do you think?

? **Science**

■ **Siblings**

About 33% of twins born in the United States are identical twins. Given that 57,153 sets of twins were born in the United States in 1999, about how many sets of twins were identical?

EXAMPLE 2 **Making a Circle Graph Given Percents**

Siblings The table shows the results of a survey that asked students how many siblings (brothers and sisters) they have. Display the data in a circle graph.

Siblings	Percent
None	10%
One	40%
Two	25%
Three or more	25%

Solution

(1 Find the angle measure for each section.

None	**One sibling**
10% of 360° = 0.10 × 360°	40% of 360° = 0.40 × 360°
= 36°	= 144°

Two siblings	**Three or more siblings**
25% of 360° = 0.25 × 360°	25% of 360° = 0.25 × 360°
= 90°	= 90°

(2 Draw a circle using a compass.

(3 Use a protractor to draw the angle measuring 36°. Then label the section "None 10%."

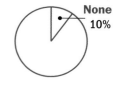

(4 Draw and label the remaining sections.

(5 Write a title for the graph.

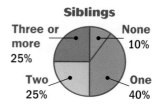

Your turn now **In Exercise 1, refer to the circle graph on page 440.**

1. Can you determine from the circle graph the number of people who chose "best athlete"? Explain your reasoning.

2. The table shows the results of a survey that asked students what they wear to school. Display the data in a circle graph.

Clothing	Percent
Jeans	30%
Skirts	15%
Dress pants	55%

EXAMPLE 3 Making a Circle Graph Given Data

Exercising The table shows the results of a survey that asked people their favorite type of exercise. Display the data in a circle graph.

Favorite Exercise	People
Aerobics	8
Jogging	22
Cycling	6
Weightlifting	12

Solution

(1 Find the total number of people surveyed.

$$8 + 22 + 6 + 12 = 48$$

(2 To find the angle measure of each section, write each group of people as a fraction of all the people and multiply by 360°.

Aerobics

$$\frac{8}{48} \times 360° = \frac{1}{6} \times 360° = 60°$$

Jogging

$$\frac{22}{48} \times 360° = \frac{11}{24} \times 360° = 165°$$

Cycling

$$\frac{6}{48} \times 360° = \frac{1}{8} \times 360° = 45°$$

Weightlifting

$$\frac{12}{48} \times 360° = \frac{1}{4} \times 360° = 90°$$

(3 Draw and label the circle graph.

Favorite Type of Exercise

- Jogging 22
- Weightlifting 12
- Cycling 6
- Aerobics 8

9.5 Exercises

More Practice, p. 713

Getting Ready to Practice

1. **Vocabulary** Describe the steps you would take to make a circle graph if the data is given in percents.

Find the angle measure that corresponds to the percent of a circle.

2. 5%   3. 70%   4. 45%   5. 20%

6. **Music** The table shows the results of a survey that asked students where they most often buy their CDs. Display the data in a circle graph.

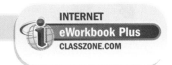

Buying CDs	Percent
Online	30%
Retail store	45%
CD club	25%

Practice and Problem Solving

HELP with Homework

Example	Exercises
1	7–12
2	14–17
3	14–17

Online Resources
CLASSZONE.COM

· More Examples
· eTutorial Plus

In Exercises 7–12, use the circle graphs.

7. Find the percent of people who travel by walking in the Netherlands.

8. What percent of people do not travel by car in the United States?

9. What is the most common form of transportation in the Netherlands?

10. Do more people walk or use public transit in the United States?

11. Find the angle measure of the section that represents people who travel by car in the Netherlands.

12. Find the angle measure of the section that represents people who travel by bicycle in the Netherlands.

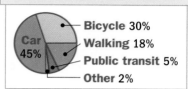

Travel in the Netherlands

Car 45%
Bicycle 30%
Walking 18%
Public transit 5%
Other 2%

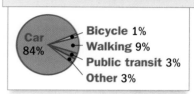

Travel in the United States

Car 84%
Bicycle 1%
Walking 9%
Public transit 3%
Other 3%

13. Compare and Contrast Describe the similarities and the differences between a circle graph and a bar graph.

Display the data in a circle graph.

14.

School Involvement	Students
Very involved	30%
Somewhat involved	50%
Not that involved	15%
Not involved at all	5%

15.

Favorite Fruit	Students
Apples	45%
Grapes	25%
Bananas	10%
Oranges	20%

16.

Favorite Drink	People
Milk	18
Soda	8
Water	16
Juice	36
Other	2

17.

Favorite Movie Type	People
Comedy	10
Horror	4
Science fiction	1
Adventure	9
Suspense	12

18. Writing Explain how the display shown could be potentially misleading.

Challenge Find the percent of a circle that corresponds to the angle measure.

19. 234°   **20.** 99°

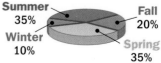

Favorite Season

Summer 35%
Fall 20%
Winter 10%
Spring 35%

21. Geology The chemical composition of the layers of Earth by mass is shown below. Display the data in a circle graph.

Chemical	Iron	Oxygen	Silicon	Magnesium	Other
Percent	34.6%	29.5%	15.2%	12.7%	8%

Mixed Review

Find the mean, median, mode(s), and range of the data. *(Lesson 3.1)*

22. 0, 8, 4.1, 5, 13.3, 5

23. 28, 26.5, 27, 86.4, 27, 29, 56.8

Use the percent equation to answer the question. *(Lesson 9.4)*

24. What percent of 90 is 27?

25. What number is 120% of 36?

Basic Skills **Write the percent as a decimal and as a fraction.**

26. 10%   **27.** 62%   **28.** 48%   **29.** 23%

Test-Taking Practice

30. Extended Response Make a bar graph and a circle graph using the data on students' favorite vegetables. Determine which graph more clearly shows that more than half of the students prefer carrots or corn. Explain.

Favorite Vegetable	Students
Carrots	30
Potatoes	15
Corn	25
Broccoli	5

Who should take the kick?

Your soccer team gets to take a penalty kick for a chance to score a goal and win the game. Data from past games are given for the 5 best players on the team. Based on the data, who should take the kick?

Name	Past Kicks
Brad	Has made 5 goals out of 15 attempts
Tommy	Has made 32% of goals attempted
Aaron	Has made $\frac{3}{10}$ of goals attempted
Sean	Has made 9 goals out of 24 attempts
John	Has made 0.35 of goals attempted

Making Circle Graphs

GOAL Use spreadsheet software to display data in a circle graph.

Example The results of a survey in which students were asked their favorite subject in school are shown below. Use spreadsheet software to make a circle graph.

Solution

1 Enter the data in the first two columns of a spreadsheet as shown.

2 Highlight the data in cells A2:B6. The expression A2:B6 refers to the rectangular array of cells that has A2 and B6 at the corners.

3 Use the Insert menu to insert a chart. Select a pie graph. Then choose the options for your graph, such as the title and labels.

4 To change other features of your graph after it has been created, double click on the part of the graph that you want to change and adjust the formatting.

	A	B
1	Subject	Students
2	Math	42
3	English	30
4	History	24
5	Science	18
6	Art	6

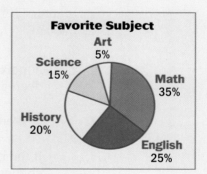

Favorite Subject

Your turn now Use spreadsheet software to complete the following exercises.

1. Cars The table shows the results of a survey that asked people in the United States what type of car they buy. Make a circle graph of the data.

2. Sports Ask a group of your classmates to name their favorite sport. Make a circle graph of the data.

Car Type	People
Luxury	86
Large	35
Midsize	242
Small	142

Percent of Increase and Decrease

BEFORE	▶ Now	WHY?
You found a percent of a number.	You'll find a percent of change in a quantity.	So you can find a soap shop's total sales, as in Ex. 5.

Word Watch

percent of change, p. 446
percent of increase, p. 446
percent of decrease, p. 446

Activity You can use graph paper to find a percent of change.

In the following diagram, the area of the red square is being added to the area of the blue squares. Each square has an area of 1 square unit.

Original ▭▭▭▭ ⟶ New ▭▭▭▭▭

1. Find the change in area by subtracting the original area from the new area.

2. Write the ratio of the change in area to the original area.

3. Express the ratio in Step 2 as a percent, called the *percent of change*.

Solve the following problem.

1. Suppose 2 red squares instead of just 1 red square are added to the 4 blue squares. What is the percent of change?

A **percent of change** shows how much a quantity has increased or decreased in comparison with the original amount:

$$\text{Percent of change, } p\% = \frac{\text{Amount of increase or decrease}}{\text{Original amount}}$$

If the new amount is greater than the original amount, the percent of change is called a **percent of increase**. If the new amount is less than the original amount, the percent of change is called a **percent of decrease**.

EXAMPLE 1 Finding a Percent of Increase

What is the percent of increase from 8 to 13?

$p\% = \dfrac{\text{Amount of increase}}{\text{Original amount}}$ Write percent of increase formula.

$ = \dfrac{13 - 8}{8}$ Substitute amount of increase and original amount.

$ = \dfrac{5}{8} = 62.5\%$ Subtract. Then express fraction as a percent.

ANSWER The percent of increase is 62.5%.

HELP with **Review**

Need help with common percents? See pp. 416 and 421.

HELP with Solving

In Example 2, note that decreasing from 49 to 35 is about the same as decreasing from 50 to 35. Because

$\dfrac{50 - 35}{50} = \dfrac{3}{10} = 30\%$,

the answer is reasonable.

EXAMPLE 2 **Finding a Percent of Decrease**

What is the percent of decrease from 49 to 35?

$p\% = \dfrac{\text{Amount of decrease}}{\text{Original amount}}$ Write percent of decrease formula.

$= \dfrac{49 - 35}{49}$ Substitute amount of decrease and original amount.

$= \dfrac{14}{49}$ Subtract.

$= \dfrac{2}{7}$ Simplify.

$\approx 0.286 = 28.6\%$ Express the fraction as a rounded decimal and as a percent.

ANSWER The percent of decrease is about 28.6%.

Your turn now **Identify the percent of change as an _increase_ or a _decrease_. Then find the percent of change. Use estimation to check your answer.**

1. Original: 16
New: 28

2. Original: 35
New: 91

3. Original: 60
New: 12

EXAMPLE 3 **Using a Percent of Change**

Tacos A taco company puts 24 taco shells in every box. Recently the company expanded the box and put 25% more shells in each box. How many shells are in every box now?

Solution

(**1** Find the amount of increase, 25% of 24.

Increase = **25% of 24**

$= 0.25 \times 24$ Write percent as a decimal.

$= 6$ Multiply.

(**2** Add the increase to the original amount.

New amount = Original amount + Increase

$= 24 + 6 = 30$

ANSWER There are now 30 taco shells in every box.

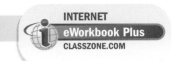

Getting Ready to Practice

1. **Vocabulary** How can you tell whether a percent of change is a percent of increase or a percent of decrease?

Identify the percent of change as an *increase* or a *decrease*. Then find the percent of change. Use estimation to check your answer.

2. Original: 30
New: 51

3. Original: 87
New: 116

4. Original: 124
New: 62

5. **Soap Shop** During the first week a soap shop was open it had $2000 in total sales. During the second week the soap shop had a 100% increase in total sales. Find the soap shop's total sales during the second week.

Practice and Problem Solving

Identify the percent of change as an *increase* or a *decrease*. Then find the percent of change. Use estimation to check your answer.

6. Original: $1953
New: $1085

7. Original: 150
New: 63

8. Original: 10
New: 12

9. Original: $900
New: $250

10. Original: 110
New: 200

11. Original: 20
New: 26

12. **Fundraisers** Last year, your class held a fundraiser and donated $850 to a local charity. This year, your class's donation increased by 24%. How much did your class donate this year?

13. **Soccer** In your first year as the soccer team's goalie, 25 goals were scored against you. In your second year only 15 goals were scored against you. What was the percent of decrease?

14. **Hot Dogs** In 2001, the 12 minute record for eating hot dogs increased by about 100% to 50 hot dogs. Approximately what was the previous record?

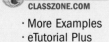
with Homework

Example	Exercises
1	6–11, 17
2	6–11, 13
3	12, 14–15, 18

15. **Land Area** In 1800, the area of the United States was 891,364 square miles. After the Louisiana Purchase in 1803, the area increased by about 93%. What was the area of the United States after the Louisiana Purchase?

United States

Louisiana Purchase (1803)

16. **Critical Thinking** Is the percent of increase from 50 to 70 the same as the percent of decrease from 70 to 50? Why or why not?

Extended Problem Solving In Exercises 17–19, use the table below, which gives the number of people 7–17 years of age who participated more than once in various sports in 1990 and 2000.

Year	Golf	Ice Skating	Snowboarding
1990	22,959	6475	1455
2000	26,401	6724	4347

17. Calculate Find the percent of increase for each sport. Round to the nearest whole percent.

18. Predict Use your answers from Exercise 17 to predict the number of people who will participate more than once in these three sports in 2010. Round to the nearest whole number.

19. Interpret Based on your predictions in Exercise 18, will the sport with the greatest percent of increase become the most popular sport in 2010? Explain your reasoning.

20. Challenge A new car lost 20% of its original value the first year it was owned and lost another 15% the second year. If the car had an original value of $15,000, how much is the car worth after 2 years?

Mixed Review

21. Make a double bar graph of the data for Exercises 17–19 above. *(Lesson 3.2)*

22. On your last 2 report cards, you earned a total of 6 A's, 4 B's, and 2 C's. Display the data in a circle graph. *(Lesson 9.5)*

Basic Skills Write the fraction as a decimal.

23. $\frac{5}{12}$　　　**24.** $\frac{1}{9}$　　　**25.** $\frac{4}{5}$　　　**26.** $\frac{7}{12}$

Test-Taking Practice

27. Multiple Choice A school's population increased from 1250 to 2000 students. What is the percent of increase?

A. 0.375%　　　**B.** 0.6%　　　**C.** 37.5%　　　**D.** 60%

28. Short Response Two brands of potato chips reduced the fat content of their chips. Brand A, which had 8 grams of fat per serving, reduced fat by 30%. Brand B, which had 10 grams of fat per serving, reduced fat by 40%. Which brand now has less fat per serving? Explain.

9.7

Discounts, Markups, Sales Tax, and Tips

BEFORE	▶ Now	WHY?
You solved percent problems.	You'll find discounts, markups, sales tax, and tips.	So you can find the price of a scooter, as in Ex. 13.

In the Real World

📓 Word Watch

Review Words

percent, p. 415

Clothing You buy a pair of jeans that is 33% off the original price of $29. What is the sale price?

A decrease in the price of an item is a discount. To find the sale price of an item, do the following:

(**1** Find the amount of the discount.

(**2** Subtract the discount from the original price.

EXAMPLE 1 **Finding a Sale Price**

Use the following steps to find the sale price of the jeans described above.

(**1** Find the amount of the discount.

$$\text{Discount} = \textbf{33\% of \$29}$$

$$= \textbf{0.33} \times 29 \qquad \text{Write 33\% as a decimal.}$$

$$= 9.57 \qquad \text{Multiply.}$$

(**2** Subtract the discount from the original price.

$$\text{Sale price} = \text{Original price} - \text{Discount}$$

$$= 29 - 9.57 = 19.43$$

ANSWER The sale price is $19.43.

Markup A retail store buys items from manufacturers at *wholesale prices*. The store then sells the items to customers at higher *retail prices*. The increase from the wholesale price to the retail price is the markup. To find the retail price of an item, do the following:

(**1** Find the amount of the markup.

(**2** Add the markup to the wholesale price.

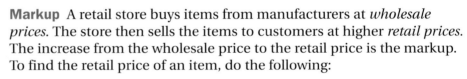

450   Chapter 9   Percents

EXAMPLE 2   **Finding a Retail Price**

Skateboards A store that sells skateboards buys them from a manufacturer at a wholesale price of $57. The store's markup is 150%. What is the retail price?

Solution

1 Find the amount of the markup.

$$\text{Markup} = \textbf{150\%} \text{ of } \$57$$

$$= \textbf{1.5} \times 57 \qquad \textbf{Write 150\% as a decimal.}$$

$$= 85.50 \qquad \textbf{Multiply.}$$

2 Add the markup to the wholesale price.

$$\text{Retail price} = \text{Wholesale price} + \text{Markup}$$

$$= 57.00 + 85.50 = 142.50$$

ANSWER The retail price is $142.50.

Your turn now   **Solve the following problems.**

1. A store is selling all flip-flops at 20% off their original price. What is the sale price of a pair of flip-flops originally priced at $20?

2. A store buys guitars from a manufacturer at a wholesale price of $38. The store's markup is 85%. What is the retail price?

Sales Tax and Tips Sales tax and tips are amounts that are added to the price of a purchase. Sales tax and tips are usually calculated using a percent of the purchase price.

EXAMPLE 3   **Finding Sales Tax and Tip**

Restaurants At a restaurant, you order a meal that costs $12. You leave a 20% tip. The sales tax is 5%. What is the total cost of the meal?

Solution

1 Find the tip. 20% of $\$12 = \textbf{0.20} \times 12 = 2.40$

2 Find the sales tax. 5% of $\$12 = \textbf{0.05} \times 12 = 0.60$

3 Add the food bill, tip, and $12 + 2.40 + 0.60 = 15.00$
   sales tax.

ANSWER The total cost of the meal is $15.00.

Watch Out!

The tip at a restaurant is based on the food bill only. Do not include the sales tax when finding a tip.

Getting Ready to Practice

Vocabulary Based on the calculations shown, identify the dollar value or percent that matches the description.

$0.05 \times 15 = 0.75$

$15 + 0.75 = 15.75$

1. Original price

2. Amount of sales tax

3. Total cost

4. Sales tax percent

5. **Guided Problem Solving** A video game is on sale for 25% off the original price. The original price is $48. What is the sale price?

(**1** What is 25% of the original price?

(**2** Is the amount from Step 1 a discount or a markup? What must you do with this amount?

(**3** Find the sale price.

Practice and Problem Solving

with Homework

Example	Exercises
1	6–11
2	6–11, 13
3	6–11

Online Resources
CLASSZONE.COM

· More Examples
· eTutorial Plus

In Exercises 6–11, use the given information to find the new price.

6. Original price: $36
Discount: 30%

7. Wholesale price: $55
Markup: 50%

8. Food bill before tax: $25
Sales tax: 6%

9. Food bill before tax: $45
Tip: 15%

10. Wholesale price: $70
Markup: 125%

11. Original price: $24
Discount: 20%

12. **Estimate** A baseball hat with an original price of $19 is on sale for 10% off the original price. Estimate the sale price.

13. **Sporting Goods** A sporting goods store purchases in-line skates, skateboards, and scooters for the wholesale prices listed in the table. Find the retail price of each item.

Item	Wholesale Price	Markup
In-line skates	$80	105%
Skateboard	$100	125%
Scooter	$60	110%

14. **Compare** Your dinner bill for Monday evening is $22.79. You leave a 20% tip and are charged 7% sales tax. Your dinner bill for Tuesday evening is $23.84. You leave a 15% tip and are charged 6% sales tax. For which meal do you pay more?

15. **Critical Thinking** A $140 car stereo is marked up 50% and then discounted 50%. Will the final price of the car stereo be $140? Explain.

16. Explain If you know the sales tax amount and the total cost of an item, explain how you can find the original price of the item.

17. Books You have a $20 gift card from a bookstore that you use to buy two books for $18.49. The sales tax is 5.75%. Will your gift card cover the cost? Explain.

18. Jackets You have $50 to spend at a clothing store. You find a jacket that is on sale for 15% off the original price. If the original price of the jacket is $60 and there is no sales tax, do you have enough money to buy the jacket? Explain.

19. Watercolor Kit You have a coupon for an additional 25% off the price of any sale item at a store. The store has put a watercolor kit on sale for 15% off the original price of $40. What is the price of the watercolor kit after both discounts?

20. Challenge A sign says that the price marked on all music equipment is 30% off the original price. You buy a drum set for the sale price of $315. What is the original price?

Mixed Review

Find the product. (Lesson 2.3)

21. 0.24×8 **22.** 1.74×0.65 **23.** 0.03×6.34 **24.** 9.01×4.7

25. A year ago you were 56 inches tall. Now you are 63 inches tall. Find the percent of increase in your height. (Lesson 9.6)

 **Solve the following problem.**

26. A flight leaves Orlando, Florida, at 7:35 A.M. and arrives in San Francisco, California, at 10:15 A.M. Orlando is 3 hours ahead of San Francisco. How long did the flight last?

Test-Taking Practice

27. Multiple Choice You and 5 friends go to lunch. You plan to split the bill evenly, and you plan to leave a 20% tip. The bill comes to $55.50. The sales tax is 7%. How much will each person pay for the meal?

    A. $18.87   **B.** $13.99   **C.** $11.75   **D.** $11.66

28. Multiple Choice A pair of sneakers costs $46.99. You have a coupon for 15% off any purchase. What is the total cost of the sneakers after 5% sales tax is included?

    F. $37.59   **G.** $41.94   **H.** $42.29   **I.** $56.74

LESSON

9.8

Simple Interest

BEFORE

You calculated discounts, markups, sales tax, and tips.

▶ **Now**

You'll calculate simple interest.

WHY?

So you can find the amount of a security deposit, as in Ex. 19.

In the Real World

interest, p. 454
principal, p. 454
simple interest, p. 454
annual interest rate, p. 454
balance, p. 454

Family Loan Tim's parents lend Tim $100 so he can buy a radio-controlled airplane. They charge Tim 5% simple annual interest. What will be the total amount that Tim will owe his parents in 1 year?

The amount earned or paid for the use of money is called **interest** . The amount of money deposited or borrowed is the **principal** . When interest is earned or paid only on the principal, it is **simple interest** . The **annual interest rate** is the percent of the principal earned or paid per year. The sum of the interest and the principal is called the **balance** .

Simple Interest

Words Simple interest I is the product of the principal P, the annual interest rate r written as a decimal, and the time t in years.

Algebra $I = Prt$

Numbers A $500 deposit earns 6% simple annual interest for 4 years. $I = (\$500)(0.06)(4) = \$120$

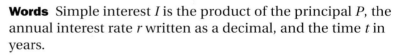

EXAMPLE 1 **Finding a Balance**

To find the total amount that Tim will owe, as described above, first find the interest using the simple interest formula.

$I = Prt$	Write simple interest formula.
$= (100)(0.05)(1)$	Substitute 100 for P, 0.05 for r, and 1 for t.
$= 5$	Multiply.

To find the balance, add the interest to the principal.

ANSWER Tim will owe a balance of $100 + $5, or $105.

EXAMPLE 2 **Finding an Interest Rate**

You deposit $600 into a 6 month certificate of deposit. After 6 months the balance is $618. Find the simple annual interest rate.

1 To find the interest, subtract the principal from the balance.

$$\$618 - \$600 = \$18$$

2 Use the simple interest formula and solve for r.

$I = Prt$	Write simple interest formula.
$18 = (600)(r)\left(\frac{6}{12}\right)$	Substitute 18 for I, 600 for P, and $\frac{6}{12}$ for t.
$18 = 300r$	Multiply.
$\frac{18}{300} = \frac{300r}{300}$	Divide each side by 300.
$0.06 = r$	Simplify.
$6\% = r$	Write decimal as a percent.

ANSWER The simple annual interest rate is 6%.

Your turn now Solve the following problems.

1. If you deposit $500 into an account that earns 6% simple annual interest, what will the account's balance be after 10 months?

2. You deposit $1000 into a 3 month certificate of deposit. After 3 months the balance is $1005. Find the simple annual interest rate.

EXAMPLE 3 **Finding an Amount of Time**

You put $750 into a certificate of deposit. Your simple annual interest rate is 4%. You receive a check for the interest at the end of each year. How long will it take to earn $150 in interest?

$I = Prt$	Write simple interest formula.
$150 = (750)(0.04)t$	Substitute 150 for I, 750 for P, and 0.04 for r.
$150 = 30t$	Multiply.
$\frac{150}{30} = \frac{30t}{30}$	Divide each side by 30.
$5 = t$	Simplify.

ANSWER It will take 5 years to earn $150 in interest.

9.8 Exercises

More Practice, p. 713

Getting Ready to Practice

1. **Vocabulary** What is the amount of money deposited or borrowed called?

For an account that earns simple annual interest, find the interest and the balance of the account.

2. $30 at 1% for 10 months

3. $100 at 8% for 3 years

4. $50 at 10% for 4 years

5. $200 at 4.5% for 8 months

6. **Investments** You deposit $250 into a 6 month certificate of deposit. At the end of the 6 months your balance is $255. What is the simple annual interest rate?

7. **Savings** Suppose you put $750 into a savings account that earns 2% simple annual interest. How long will it take to have $45 in interest?

Practice and Problem Solving

with Homework

Example	Exercises
1	8–13
2	14–17
3	14–17, 21

Online Resources
CLASSZONE.COM

· More Examples
· eTutorial Plus

For an account that earns simple annual interest, find the interest and the balance of the account.

8. $252 at 8% for 2 months

9. $450 at 4% for 6 months

10. $6240 at 10% for 9 months

11. $2000 at 9.6% for 8 months

12. $5000 at 4.5% for 1 year

13. $400 at 3% for 1 month

Use the simple interest formula to find the unknown quantity.

14. $I = \underline{?}$
$P = \$2000$
$r = 9.8\%$
$t = 5$ years

15. $I = \$84$
$P = \underline{?}$
$r = 7\%$
$t = 2$ years

16. $I = \$468$
$P = \$6240$
$r = \underline{?}$
$t = 9$ months

17. $I = \$9$
$P = \$450$
$r = 4\%$
$t = \underline{?}$

18. **Writing** If you borrow money, would you want a higher or lower interest rate? If you open a savings account, would you want a higher or a lower interest rate? Explain.

19. **Security Deposit** When signing a lease for an apartment, your sister pays a security deposit that earns 3.5% simple annual interest. At the end of a year, the interest earned on the security deposit is $17.50. How much was the security deposit?

20. **Critical Thinking** Three months ago you deposited $250 into a savings account, and now your balance is $253. Eight months ago your friend deposited $250 into a different savings account, and her balance is now $257.50. Which account has the greater simple annual interest rate?

21. Savings Suppose Ann has $300 in a savings account that earns 1.75% simple annual interest. In how many years will she have $21 in interest?

22. Credit Cards A credit card charges 9.6% annual interest on any unpaid balance each month. During the past month your older brother had an unpaid balance of $375 from the purchase of a computer desk. What is the interest charge for that month?

23. Challenge Suppose you put $500 in a savings account that earns 4.5% simple annual interest, and your friend puts $400 in a savings account that earns 6% simple annual interest. Which of you will earn $600 first?

Mixed Review

Solve the equation. *(Lesson 7.5)*

24. $5x + 4 = -21$ **25.** $-6 - 12y = -54$ **26.** $\frac{z}{7} - 8 = 3$

27. $\frac{x}{5} + 2 = 12$ **28.** $5 = 3n - 4$ **29.** $-2y - 8 = -10$

Choose a Strategy Use a strategy from the list to solve the following problem. Explain your choice of strategy.

> **Problem Solving Strategies**
> ■ Work Backward
> ■ Make a List
> ■ Act it Out

30. Your friends Tom, Ryan, Jen, Matt, and Al line up in a row. Tom, Jen, and Ryan are not next to each other. Tom is at one end. Two people separate Jen and Matt. Between which two people is Al?

Basic Skills Copy and complete the statement using $<$, $>$, or $=$.

31. 2 h 24 min _?_ 148 min **32.** 13 wk 4 d _?_ 95 d

33. 9 d 17 h _?_ 220 h **34.** 4782 sec _?_ 48 min 16 sec

Test-Taking Practice

35. Multiple Choice Joe put $350 into a 6 month certificate of deposit. After 6 months, the certificate earned 4.2% simple annual interest. How much interest did the certificate earn?

   A. $7.35 **B.** $14.70 **C.** $29.40 **D.** $88.20

36. Short Response Rick wants to borrow $4500 to buy a used car. His sister will lend him the money at a simple annual interest rate of 9% for 6 years. Rick's uncle will lend him the money at a simple annual interest rate of 11.5% for 4 years. From which relative should Rick borrow the money? Explain.

Notebook Review

Review the vocabulary definitions in your notebook.

Copy the review examples in your notebook. Then complete the exercises.

Check Your Definitions

circle graph, p. 440
ray, p. 440
angle, p. 440
vertex, p. 440
degrees, p. 440

percent of change, p. 446
percent of increase, p. 446
percent of decrease, p. 446

interest, p. 454
principal, p. 454
simple interest, p. 454
annual interest rate, p. 454
balance, p. 454

Use Your Vocabulary

1. Copy and complete: Simple interest is the product of the principal, the ? , and the time (in years).

9.5 Can you make a circle graph?

 EXAMPLE In a survey that asked 120 teens their favorite color, 40 said red, 55 said green, and 25 said blue. Display the data in a circle graph.

Red $\quad \frac{40}{120} \times 360° = \frac{1}{3} \times 360° = 120°$

Green $\quad \frac{55}{120} \times 360° = \frac{11}{24} \times 360° = 165°$

Blue $\quad \frac{25}{120} \times 360° = \frac{5}{24} \times 360° = 75°$

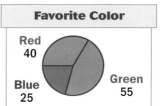

Favorite Color

Red 40
Blue 25
Green 55

✓ **2.** In a survey that asked 150 adults their favorite color, 30 said red, 75 said green, and 45 said blue. Display the data in a circle graph.

9.6 Can you find a percent of change?

 EXAMPLE Yesterday you sold 8 ice cream cones. Today you sold 15 ice cream cones. Find the percent of increase in sales.

$$p = \frac{15 - 8}{8} = \frac{7}{8} = 87.5\%$$

✓ **3.** Find the percent of decrease from an original amount of 420 to 399.

9.7 Can you find a sale price?

 EXAMPLE A $750 sofa is now 30% off. To find the sale price of the sofa, find the amount of the discount and subtract it from the regular price.

Discount: **30%** of $750 = **0.30** × $750 = $225

Sale price: $750 − $225 = $525

☑ **4.** A $40 jacket is on sale for 30% off. What is the sale price of the jacket?

9.8 Can you calculate simple interest?

 EXAMPLE If you have $180 in an account that earns 5% simple annual interest, how much interest will the account earn in 6 months?

$$I = Prt = (180)(0.05)\left(\frac{6}{12}\right) = \$4.50$$

☑ **5.** Suppose you put $200 into a savings account that earns 3% simple annual interest. How long will it take to earn $30 in interest?

Stop *and* **Think** about Lessons 9.5–9.8

6. Writing Explain how you would make a circle graph from a data set.

7. Critical Thinking If you know the price of a book before sales tax and the amount of sales tax charged, how can you find the sales tax rate?

Review Quiz 2

1. Pets The table shows the results of a survey that asked people to name their favorite pet. Display the data in a circle graph.

Pet	People
Dog	35%
Cat	30%
Bird	20%
Other	15%

2. Find the percent of increase from an original amount of 240 to 300.

3. Concert At a concert, you buy a souvenir T-shirt for $25 and a hat for $16. The sales tax on the items is 5%. Find the total cost.

4. Savings Suppose you put $800 into a savings account that earns 2.5% simple annual interest. How long will it take to earn $60 in interest?

Chapter Review

Vocabulary

percent, p. 415
circle graph, p. 440
ray, p. 440
angle, p. 440
vertex, p. 440
degrees, p. 440

percent of change, p. 446
percent of increase,
  p. 446
percent of decrease,
  p. 446
interest, p. 454

principal, p. 454
simple interest, p. 454
annual interest rate,
  p. 454
balance, p. 454

Vocabulary Review

Copy and complete the statement.

1. A(n) ? shows how much a quantity has increased or decreased relative to the original amount.

2. A(n) ? is a ratio whose denominator is 100.

3. A(n) ? displays data as sections of a circle.

4. The amount of money deposited or borrowed is called the ? .

Review Questions

Write the percent as a fraction or the fraction as a percent. *(Lesson 9.1)*

5. $\frac{3}{5}$ **6.** $\frac{1}{4}$ **7.** 55%   **8.** 42%

9. Critical Thinking Would 45% of 160 be greater than or less than 80? Explain. *(Lesson 9.1)*

Use a proportion to answer the question. *(Lesson 9.2)*

10. What number is 43% of 60?   **11.** What percent of 400 is 360?

12. What percent of 45 is 18?   **13.** 63 is 45% of what number?

14. Marbles There are 40 marbles in a bag. If 14 of the marbles are red, what percent of the marbles in the bag are red? *(Lesson 9.2)*

Write the percent as a decimal or the decimal as a percent. *(Lesson 9.3)*

15. 14%   **16.** 6.25%   **17.** 0.25%   **18.** 210%

19. 0.705   **20.** 1.39   **21.** 0.0041   **22.** 0.40

Use the percent equation to answer the question. *(Lesson 9.4)*

23. What number is 18% of 150?

24. What percent of 140 is 105?

25. 54 is 36% of what number?

26. What number is 30% of 50?

27. Test Scores On a recent test, John answered 80% of the questions correctly. If there were 30 questions on the test, how many questions did John answer correctly? *(Lesson 9.4)*

28. Watches The table at the right shows the results of a survey that asked what kind of watch students wear. Display the data in a circle graph. *(Lesson 9.5)*

Watch Type	Students
Digital	65
Analog	35
No watch	50

29. Breakfast Food The table below shows the results of a survey that asked 200 students what they normally eat for breakfast. Display the data in a circle graph. *(Lesson 9.5)*

Food	Eggs	Cold cereal	Pancakes	French toast	Other
Students	27.5%	45%	15%	7.5%	5%

Find the percent of change. *(Lesson 9.6)*

30. Original: 25
New: 10

31. Original: $80
New: $190

32. Original: 25
New: 45

33. Original: $299
New: $179.40

34. Talent Show On the first night of a talent show, 80 tickets were sold. On the second night, 150 tickets were sold. What was the percent of increase? *(Lesson 9.6)*

Use the given information to find the new price. *(Lesson 9.7)*

35. Regular price: $72
Discount: 75%

36. Wholesale price: $67
Markup: 115%

37. Dining You and your family are eating at a restaurant. The food bill is $40. Your family chooses to leave a 20% tip. The sales tax is 6%. What is the total cost of the meal? *(Lesson 9.7)*

Use the simple interest formula to find the unknown quantity.
(Lesson 9.8)

38. $I = \$590$
$P = \underline{\ ?\ }$
$r = 2.5\%$
$t = 10$ years

39. $I = \underline{\ ?\ }$
$P = \$550$
$r = 14.5\%$
$t = 4$ years

40. $I = \$7$
$P = \$175$
$r = 16\%$
$t = \underline{\ ?\ }$

41. $I = \$1210$
$P = \$15,000$
$r = \underline{\ ?\ }$
$t = 11$ months

9

Chapter Test

Write the percent as a fraction.

1. 65%   **2.** 40%   **3.** 48%   **4.** 80%

5. Advertising An advertisement says that 4 out of 5 doctors prefer a certain product. What percent of doctors do *not* prefer the product?

Use a proportion to answer the question.

6. What number is 15% of 30?   **7.** What number is 30% of 210?

8. 12 is 60% of what number?   **9.** What percent of 40 is 18?

10. Savings You have decided to put 12% of your weekly paycheck into a savings account. You made $85.50 last week. How much did you put into the savings account?

Write the percent as a decimal or the decimal as a percent.

11. 0.037   **12.** 208%   **13.** 0.45%   **14.** 1.35

Use the percent equation to answer the question.

15. What number is 134% of 20,000?   **16.** 32 is 40% of what number?

17. What percent of 25 is 24?   **18.** What percent of 60 is 3?

19. United States Symbol The table shows the results of a survey that asked people to name the item that symbolizes the United States the most. Display the data in a circle graph. Round your degree measures to the nearest whole degree.

Item	Percent
American flag	67%
Statue of Liberty	17%
Bald eagle	8%
White House	5%
Liberty Bell	2%
Mount Rushmore	1%

20. Enrollment In the fall of 2002, 500 students were enrolled in a middle school. The enrollment at the same school was 580 students in the fall of 2003. Find the percent of increase from 2002 to 2003.

21. Backpacks A backpack is on sale for 20% off the original price of $40. Another backpack is on sale for 40% off the original price of $50. Which backpack costs less after the discounts are taken?

22. Loan You borrow $240 from your friend. One year later you pay her back $270 to show your appreciation for the loan. How much interest did you pay your friend? What was the simple annual interest rate?

Chapter Standardized Test

Test-Taking Strategy Make notes, sketches, or graphs in your test booklet to help you solve problems, but be sure to keep your answer sheet clean.

Multiple Choice

1. Which proportion can you use to find what percent 60 is of 40?

   A. $\dfrac{60}{40} = \dfrac{p}{100}$ **B.** $\dfrac{60}{100} = \dfrac{p}{40}$

   C. $\dfrac{40}{60} = \dfrac{p}{100}$ **D.** $\dfrac{p}{60} = \dfrac{40}{100}$

2. Which value is *not* equal to the other three?

   F. 75%   **G.** $\dfrac{75}{100}$ **H.** 75   **I.** 0.75

3. Which value is less than all the others?

   A. 91%   **B.** 91.3   **C.** 0.913   **D.** $\dfrac{21}{23}$

4. In a survey of seventh graders, 24 students said that their favorite lunch food was pizza. This was 40% of the students surveyed. How many students were surveyed?

   F. 25   **G.** 34   **H.** 40   **I.** 60

5. What percent of 3000 is 6?

   A. 0.002% **B.** 0.02% **C.** 0.2%   **D.** 2%

6. What number is 350% of 84?

   F. 252   **G.** 294   **H.** 2940   **I.** 29,400

7. The angle measure of a section in a circle graph is 288°. What percent of the circle graph does the section represent?

   A. 0.8%   **B.** 20%   **C.** 80%   **D.** 180%

8. The size of a team increased from 12 to 15 players. What is the percent of increase?

   F. 0.20% **G.** 0.25% **H.** 20%   **I.** 25%

9. The wholesale price of a watch is $12, and the markup is 150%. What is the retail price?

   A. $6   **B.** $18   **C.** $30   **D.** $1800

10. A store is selling sweaters at 60% off the regular price of $49. For final clearance, the store takes $5 off the sale price. What is the final clearance price of a sweater?

   F. $14.60 **G.** $16.60 **H.** $17.60   **I.** $19.60

11. You deposit $1500 into a 6 month certificate of deposit. At the end of the 6 months your balance is $1530. What is the simple annual interest rate?

   A. 0.04% **B.** 0.83% **C.** 2.04% **D.** 4%

Short Response

12. Michael was earning $120 per week when he had to take a 10% decrease in pay. Six months later he received a 10% increase in pay. Now how much does he earn for a week of work? Write and evaluate expressions to describe the situation.

Extended Response

13. The table below shows the results of a survey that asked what students read most often. Display the data in a bar graph and in a circle graph. Which graph more clearly shows that about half of the students read books for fun most often? Explain.

Reading Material	Students
Newspapers	5
Schoolbooks	10
Magazines	35
Books for fun	40

Strategies for Answering
Context-Based Multiple Choice Questions

Some of the information you need to solve a context-based multiple choice question may appear in a table, a diagram, or a graph.

Problem 1

An engraver charges by the letter. How much would it cost to have the name *Margaret* engraved on a bracelet?

Letters	Cost
1	$.35
2	$.70
3	$1.05
4	$1.40

A. $2.45   **B.** $2.80

C. $3.15   **D.** $7.00

Solution

Read the problem carefully. Decide what information you are given and how you can use it to solve the problem.

1) Look for a pattern in the table. You can use the pattern to write a function that models the cost of engraving.

Compare the cost of engraving to the number of letters for each row of the table.

$$\frac{\$.35}{1 \text{ letter}} \qquad \frac{\$.35}{\$.70 \atop 2 \text{ letters}} \qquad \frac{\$.35}{\$1.05 \atop 3 \text{ letters}} \qquad \frac{\$.35}{\$1.40 \atop 4 \text{ letters}}$$

In each case, you get the same unit rate, $.35 per letter.

Write the function.

2) The cost y of engraving x letters is given by the function $y = 0.35x$.

There are 8 letters in *Margaret*.

3) The cost of engraving the name Margaret is the value of the function when $x = 8$. Substitute 8 for x in the function rule.

$$y = 0.35x = 0.35(8) = 2.80$$

The cost is $2.80. The correct answer is B.

Check to see that your answer is reasonable.

4) As a check, extend the table. For each additional letter, the cost increases by $.35. The cost of 8 letters is $2.80. The correct answer is B.

Letters	Cost
5	$1.75
6	$2.10
7	$2.45
8	$2.80

Problem 2

In a survey, 150 English-speaking students who speak a second language were asked to identify that language. For how many of the students surveyed is Spanish not the second language?

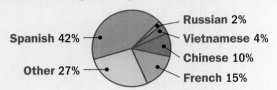

Spanish 42%

Russian 2%
Vietnamese 4%
Chinese 10%
French 15%

Other 27%

F. 42   G. 58   H. 63   I. 87

Solution

Read the problem carefully. Don't overlook the word *not*.

1) You can use the graph to find the percent of students surveyed whose second language is Spanish. Subtract that percent from 100%. Use the result along with the total number of students surveyed to answer the question.

Find the percent.

2) Because 42% of the students surveyed said "Spanish," $100\% - 42\% = 58\%$ did not say "Spanish."

Use the percent equation.

3) $a = p\% \cdot b$ Write percent equation.

$\quad = 58\% \cdot 150$ Substitute 58 for p and 150 for b.

$\quad = 0.58 \cdot 150$ Write percent as a decimal.

$\quad = 87$ Multiply.

The number of students surveyed for whom Spanish is not the second language is 87. The correct answer is I.

Watch Out!

Be sure that you know what question you are asked to answer. Some choices given may be intended to distract you.

Your turn now

1. In Problem 2, what is the angle measure for the "French" section?

   A. 15°   B. 27°   C. 36°   D. 54°

2. The ship in the scale drawing is 5.2 centimeters long. How long is the actual ship?

   F. 17.2 m   G. 60 m

   H. 62.4 m   I. 1200 m

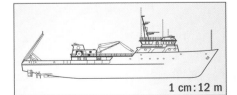

1 cm : 12 m

GO ON

Multiple Choice

1. A video rental store sells previously viewed movies for $10 each. Discounts for buying more than one video are listed in the table. How many videos can you buy with $60?

Buy	2	3	4	5
Save	$4	$8	$12	$16

A. 7   **B.** 8   **C.** 9   **D.** 10

2. The graph of which function is shown?

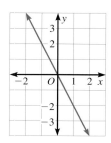

F. $y = x + 2$ **G.** $y = 2x$

H. $y = x - 2$ **I.** $y = -2x$

3. What is the slope of the line in Exercise 2?

A. -2 **B.** $\frac{1}{2}$ **C.** 1   **D.** 2

4. A scale drawing of a stained glass panel is shown below. The actual panel is 56 centimeters long. How wide is the panel?

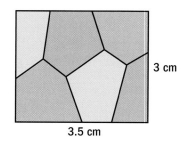

3 cm

3.5 cm

F. 6 cm   **G.** 48 cm

H. 50 cm   **I.** 65 cm

5. Your bill for dinner at a Chinese restaurant is shown. With a 20% tip and no sales tax, how much does the dinner cost?

Chicken with garlic sauce	$7.95
Vegetable fried rice	$5.95
Duck in orange sauce	$9.95

A. $4.77   **B.** $23.85   **C.** $28.62   **D.** $29.82

6. The graph shows the numbers of pitches and strikes thrown by a team's pitchers in a baseball game. Which pitcher has the highest percent of pitches that are strikes?

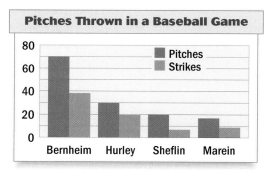

F. Bernheim   **G.** Hurley

H. Sheflin   **I.** Marein

7. The table shows how the $4000 budget for the school newspaper is spent. How much more money is spent on photography than on computer supplies?

Newspaper Budget	
Printing	50%
Photography	25%
Computer supplies	20%
Other	5%

A. $50   **B.** $200   **C.** $300   **D.** $800

Short Response

8. One U.S. dollar is equivalent to 1.79 Aruban guilders. If you purchase something for 190 Aruban guilders, what is the equivalent price, to the nearest cent, in U.S. dollars?

9. Write a function rule from the table.

Input x	1	2	3	4
Output y	5.25	10.5	15.75	21

10. Three tablespoons of lemonade mix makes 8 fluid ounces of lemonade. How much mix should you use to make 1 gallon of lemonade? Explain.

11. Three students work on one project. Sarah completes $\frac{2}{5}$ of the work, and Tim completes 35% of the work. What fraction of the work is left for Carl to finish?

12. The table below shows students' favorite types of television programs. Make a circle graph of the data.

Type of Program	Students
Comedy	18
Drama	12
Cartoon	10
News program	5

Extended Response

13. Your sister is ordering almonds for wedding favors. There are about 110 almonds in 1 pound, and your sister wants the 140 guests to get 11 almonds each. Write and solve an equation to find about how many pounds of almonds she must buy. The almonds cost $4.95 per pound at a store. On an Internet Web site, the almonds cost $4.00 per pound, but there is an additional $10.00 shipping charge. Which is the better deal: buying the almonds at the store or over the Internet?

14. The seventh grade class sold ice cream cones to raise money for a class trip. The ratio of small to medium cones sold was 3 to 1, and the ratio of medium to large cones sold was 9 to 25. If the class sold 27 medium cones, how many small cones were sold? How many large cones were sold? If the class sold small cones for $1.50, medium cones for $2.00, and large cones for $2.50, how much money did the class raise?

15. Students at a middle school made 5000 paper roses for a parade float. The color distribution of the roses is shown in the circle graph. Explain how to use the information in the circle graph to find the combined number of blue and purple roses. If you know that the students made three times as many blue roses as purple roses, how many purple roses did they make? How many blue roses did they make?

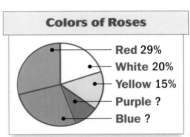

Colors of Roses

Red 29%
White 20%
Yellow 15%
Purple ?
Blue ?

GO ON

Cumulative Practice for Chapters 7–9

Chapter 7

Multiple Choice In Exercises 1–9, choose the letter of the correct answer.

1. A bus company charges $55 and an additional $4.50 for each student attending a field trip. Which expression represents the cost for n students? *(Lesson 7.1)*

    A. $55 \div 4.5n$ **B.** $55(4.5n)$

    C. $55 - 4.5n$ **D.** $55 + 4.5n$

2. Which expression is equivalent to $4b - 2$? *(Lesson 7.2)*

    F. $b + 3b + 2$ **G.** $5b + 7 - 5 + b$

    H. $6b - 1 - 2b - 1$ **I.** $2b - 2 - 6b$

3. What is the solution of the equation $6 + p = 18$? *(Lesson 7.3)*

    A. -12 **B.** 3 **C.** 12 **D.** 24

4. For which equation is 5 the solution? *(Lesson 7.3)*

    F. $c + 12 = 7$ **G.** $14 - c = 19$

    H. $c - 4 = -1$ **I.** $16 + c = 21$

5. You walk at a speed of 4 miles per hour. Which equation can be used to find how long it takes you to walk 3 miles? *(Lesson 7.4)*

    A. $x - 3 = 4$ **B.** $\dfrac{x}{4} = 3$

    C. $4x = 3$ **D.** $3x = 4$

6. What is the solution of the equation $4y + 2 = 10$? *(Lesson 7.5)*

    F. -8 **G.** -2 **H.** 2 **I.** 8

7. What is the solution of the inequality $x - 2 < 3$? *(Lesson 7.6)*

    A. $x > 5$ **B.** $x < 5$ **C.** $x = 5$ **D.** $x < -5$

8. Which function can be represented by the input-output table shown? *(Lesson 7.7)*

Input x	-4	-2	0	2	4
Output y	12	6	0	-6	-12

    F. $y = -3x$ **G.** $y = x + 16$

    H. $y = 3x$ **I.** $y = -2x + 4$

9. The graph of which function is shown? *(Lesson 7.8)*

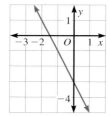

    A. $y = -2x - 3$

    B. $y = -2x$

    C. $y = \dfrac{1}{3}x$

    D. $y = 2x - 3$

10. **Short Response** Make an input-output table for the equation $y = -x - 2$ using the domain 0, 1, 2, and 3. Tell whether the table represents a function. Explain. *(Lesson 7.7)*

11. **Extended Response** John charges a flat rate of $15 for every lawn he mows plus $5.50 for each hour he spends mowing and trimming. *(Lessons 7.1, 7.5)*

    a. Write an expression that represents the total amount John charges for h hours of mowing and trimming.

    b. If he charges a customer $31.50, how long did John spend mowing and trimming the lawn?

Chapter 8

Multiple Choice In Exercises 12–20, choose the letter of the correct answer.

12. A jar contains 15 red marbles, 3 green marbles, 2 white marbles, and 10 blue marbles. What is the ratio of red marbles to all marbles? *(Lesson 8.1)*

A. $\frac{1}{2}$ **B.** $\frac{1}{1}$ **C.** $\frac{2}{1}$ **D.** $\frac{5}{1}$

13. A car travels 120 miles and uses 4 gallons of gasoline. Which unit rate gives the car's fuel efficiency? *(Lesson 8.2)*

F. 30 miles per gallon

G. 60 miles per gallon

H. 120 miles per gallon

I. 480 miles per gallon

14. Trisha runs 26.2 miles in 3 hours and 30 minutes. To the nearest tenth, what is Trisha's average speed in miles per hour? *(Lesson 8.2)*

A. 7.1 **B.** 7.5 **C.** 7.9 **D.** 122.5

15. What is the slope of the blue line? *(Lesson 8.3)*

F. -2

G. $-\frac{1}{2}$

H. $\frac{1}{2}$

I. 2

16. What is the slope of the red line in Exercise 15? *(Lesson 8.3)*

A. $-\frac{4}{3}$ **B.** $-\frac{3}{4}$ **C.** $\frac{3}{4}$ **D.** $\frac{4}{3}$

17. For which proportion is 2 the solution? *(Lessons 8.4, 8.5)*

F. $\frac{2}{5} = \frac{x}{10}$ **G.** $\frac{5}{8} = \frac{x}{4}$

H. $\frac{1}{3} = \frac{x}{6}$ **I.** $\frac{1}{7} = \frac{x}{21}$

18. You buy 6 pairs of socks for \$4.50. Which proportion can be used to find the cost of 9 pairs of socks? *(Lessons 8.4, 8.5)*

A. $\frac{6}{4.5} = \frac{x}{9}$ **B.** $\frac{4.5}{6} = \frac{x}{9}$

C. $\frac{9}{6} = \frac{4.5}{x}$ **D.** $\frac{4.5}{9} = \frac{6}{x}$

19. You make 3 quarts of tomato sauce from 2 baskets of tomatoes. How much tomato sauce can you make from 5 baskets of tomatoes? *(Lessons 8.4, 8.5)*

F. $3\frac{1}{3}$ qt **G.** 4 qt **H.** 6 qt **I.** $7\frac{1}{2}$ qt

20. The scale on an amusement park map is 1 inch : 300 feet. On the map, the distance from the roller coaster to the log flume is 3.25 inches. What is the actual distance? *(Lesson 8.6)*

A. 92.3 ft **B.** 325 ft **C.** 975 ft **D.** 1020 ft

21. Short Response Mindy can type 248 words in 4 minutes. Find the unit rate. Then find how long it would take Mindy to type 558 words. Explain your reasoning. *(Lessons 8.2, 8.5)*

22. Extended Response The scale on a map is 1 inch : 40 miles. The distance that you plan to drive measures 4.75 inches on the map. If you drive at an average speed of 50 miles per hour, how long will it take you to drive this distance? Explain your reasoning. *(Lesson 8.6)*

 GO ON

Chapter 9

Multiple Choice In Exercises 23–31, choose the letter of the correct answer.

23. Which fraction is *not* equivalent to 44%? *(Lesson 9.1)*

A. $\frac{11}{25}$ **B.** $\frac{4}{11}$ **C.** $\frac{22}{50}$ **D.** $\frac{44}{100}$

24. What percent of 72 is 24? *(Lesson 9.2)*

F. 25%   **G.** 33%   **H.** $33\frac{1}{3}\%$ **I.** 300%

25. Which proportion can you use to find 29% of 67? *(Lesson 9.2)*

A. $\frac{29}{a} = \frac{67}{100}$ **B.** $\frac{a}{67} = \frac{29}{100}$

C. $\frac{a}{100} = \frac{67}{100}$ **D.** $\frac{a}{67} = \frac{100}{29}$

26. Which percent is equivalent to 0.425? *(Lesson 9.3)*

F. 0.425% **G.** 4.25%   **H.** 42.5%   **I.** 425%

27. What percent of the Jackson family budget is spent on rent? *(Lesson 9.4)*

Jackson Family Monthly Budget	
Clothing	$150
Entertainment	$200
Food	$400
Rent	$750

A. 47%   **B.** 50%   **C.** 54%   **D.** 100%

28. The number of members in the math club increased from 15 to 18. What was the percent of increase? *(Lesson 9.6)*

F. 16.5% **G.** 20%   **H.** $33\frac{1}{3}\%$ **I.** 83%

29. A coat costs $84.00. What is the total cost of the coat after 7% sales tax is included? *(Lesson 9.7)*

A. $5.88   **B.** $86.08 **C.** $89.88 **D.** $142.80

30. A radio is on sale for 60% off the original price. What is the sale price of the radio if the original price of the radio is $87.95? *(Lesson 9.7)*

F. $27.95 **G.** $35.18 **H.** $52.77   **I.** $140.72

31. You deposit $300 into a 6 month certificate of deposit. At the end of six months your balance is $309.75. What is the simple annual interest rate? *(Lesson 9.8)*

A. 6.5%   **B.** 7%   **C.** 9.75% **D.** 54%

32. **Short Response** On the first three tests of the term, you earned scores of 82%, 95%, and 86%. On the fourth test, you correctly answered 17 out of 20 questions. Assuming that all questions on the test are of equal value, what is the mean of your test scores? Explain. *(Lessons 9.1, 9.2, 9.3)*

33. **Extended Response** The table shows the results of a survey that asked 240 high school students how many hours they work in a typical week. *(Lessons 9.4, 9.5)*

Hours	Students
0	55%
1–10	10%
11–20	20%
More than 20	15%

a. Display the data in a circle graph.

b. How many of the students work more than 20 hours in a typical week?

c. How many of the students work 10 hours or fewer in a typical week?

Geometry and Measurement

Chapter **10** Geometric Figures

- Classify angles, triangles, and other polygons.
- Use properties of congruent and similar polygons to solve problems.
- Describe transformations and symmetry of geometric figures.

Chapter **11** Measurement and Area

- Use square roots and the Pythagorean theorem to solve problems.
- Find areas of parallelograms, triangles, and trapezoids.
- Find circumferences and areas of circles.

Chapter **12** Surface Area and Volume

- Classify and sketch solids.
- Find surface areas of rectangular prisms and cylinders.
- Find volumes of rectangular prisms and cylinders.

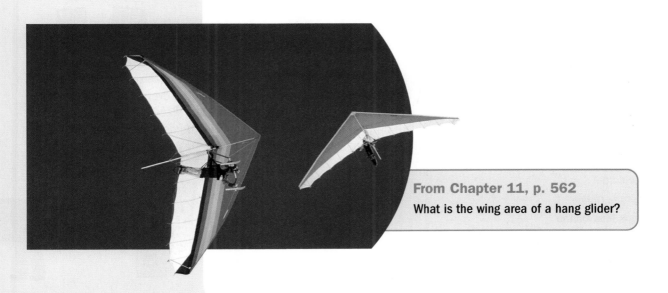

From Chapter 11, p. 562

What is the wing area of a hang glider?

10

Geometric Figures

BEFORE

In previous chapters you've...

- Solved equations
- Multiplied and divided decimals
- Performed operations on fractions
- Used ratios and proportions

Now

In Chapter 10 you'll study...

- Angles, triangles, and other polygons
- Congruent and similar polygons
- Transformations

WHY?

So you can solve real-world problems about...

- hockey, p. 477
- drawbridges, p. 488
- paintings, p. 503
- computer graphics, p. 518

Internet Preview
CLASSZONE.COM

- eEdition Plus Online
- eWorkbook Plus Online
- eTutorial Plus Online
- State Test Practice
- More Examples

Chapter Warm-Up Game

Review skills you need for this chapter in this game. Work with a partner.

Key Skill:
Finding equivalent ratios

RAPID RATIOS

MATERIALS

- 1 deck of number cards
- 1 deck of ratio cards

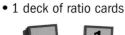

PREPARE Deal three number cards to each player and place the rest face down to form a draw pile. Turn over one number card from the draw pile to form a discard pile. Place five ratio cards face up between you and your partner. Take turns following the directions on the next page.

1. DRAW a number card so that you have four cards in your hand. You may take the card from the top of the draw pile or from the top of the discard pile.

2. DECIDE whether you can use two of your cards to form a ratio that is equivalent to one of the displayed ratios. If you can, then take the displayed ratio and place it and your pair of cards in front of you.

3. FINISH your turn by drawing one card to replenish your hand, or by discarding one card if you were unable to form an equivalent ratio. You should have three cards at the end of your turn.

HOW TO WIN Be the first player to form three equivalent ratios.

Stop and Think

1. **Critical Thinking** Based on the number cards you saw as you played *Rapid Ratios*, which ratio do you think is easier to form, $\frac{8}{9}$ or $\frac{1}{2}$? Explain your reasoning.

2. **Writing** Explain how you decided which cards to discard in *Rapid Ratios*.

Getting Ready to Learn

Review What You Need to Know

Using Vocabulary **Copy and complete using a review word.**

1. A coordinate plane is formed by the intersection of a horizontal number line, called the __?__, and a vertical number line, called the __?__.

2. A(n) __?__ consists of two rays that begin at a common point, called the __?__.

Plot the point and describe its location in a coordinate plane. *(p. 293)*

3. $A(7, 0)$ **4.** $B(-3, -4)$ **5.** $C(9, -5)$ **6.** $D(-1, 2)$

Use the cross products property to solve the proportion. *(p. 394)*

7. $\dfrac{3}{a} = \dfrac{5}{15}$ **8.** $\dfrac{2}{3} = \dfrac{12}{m}$ **9.** $\dfrac{2}{5} = \dfrac{p}{40}$ **10.** $\dfrac{b}{4} = \dfrac{5}{2}$

Use a protractor to draw an angle with the given measure. *(p. 438)*

11. $45°$ **12.** $135°$ **13.** $155°$ **14.** $75°$

You should include material that appears on a notebook like this in your own notes.

Know How to Take Notes

Connecting Try to connect the new ideas and procedures you learn to concepts you have studied previously. You can include diagrams in your notebook to show how new concepts are related to those you already know.

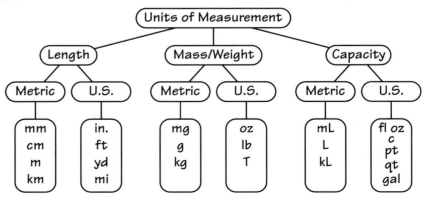

In Lesson 10.4, you can use diagrams like the one above to help you connect new geometry concepts to those you already know.

Angles

BEFORE	▶ Now	WHY?
You used angles to make circle graphs.	You'll classify angles by their measures.	So you can find the angle of a hockey stick, as in Ex. 24.

In the Real World

📓 Word Watch

acute angle, p. 475
right angle, p. 475
obtuse angle, p. 475
straight angle, p. 475
complementary, p. 476
supplementary, p. 476

Gymnastics This gymnast's arm makes a *right angle* with his body as he performs on the rings. A right angle has a measure of 90°.

Angles are classified by their measures. The notation ∠A is read "angle A," and the notation m∠A is read "the measure of angle A."

Classifying Angles

An **acute angle** is an angle whose measure is less than 90°.

A **right angle** is an angle whose measure is exactly 90°.

Indicates a right angle

An **obtuse angle** is an angle whose measure is between 90° and 180°.

A **straight angle** is an angle whose measure is exactly 180°.

🆘 with Solving

A quick way to check the size of an angle is to use the corner of a piece of paper. Since the corner forms a right angle, it is easy to determine whether the angle's measure is less than 90°, exactly 90°, or greater than 90°.

EXAMPLE 1 Classifying an Angle

Estimate to classify the angle as *acute*, *right*, *obtuse*, or *straight*.

Because m∠A is between 90° and 180°, ∠A is obtuse.

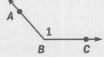

The angle above can be named in several ways: ∠ABC, ∠CBA, ∠B, and ∠1. Notice that the vertex label must be the middle or only letter used in the name of an angle.

Angle Relationships Two angles are **complementary** if the sum of their measures is 90°. Two angles are **supplementary** if the sum of their measures is 180°.

EXAMPLE 2 **Complementary and Supplementary Angles**

Tell whether the angles are *complementary*, *supplementary*, or *neither*.

a.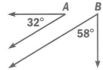

b.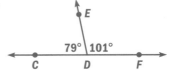

Solution

a. $32° + 58° = 90°$ So, ∠A and ∠B are complementary.

b. $79° + 101° = 180°$ So, ∠CDE and ∠EDF are supplementary.

Your turn now Classify the angle as *acute*, *obtuse*, *right*, or *straight*.

1. $m∠A = 90°$ **2.** $m∠B = 118°$ **3.** $m∠C = 180°$ **4.** $m∠D = 55°$

5. Give the measures of two angles that are supplementary.

EXAMPLE 3 **Using Supplementary Angles**

For the lounge chair at the right, ∠1 and ∠2 are supplementary. If $m∠1 = 130°$, find $m∠2$.

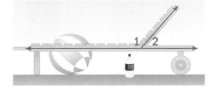

$m∠1 + m∠2 = 180°$ Definition of supplementary angles

$130° + m∠2 = 180°$ Substitute 130° for $m∠1$.

$m∠2 = 50°$ Subtract 130° from each side.

Your turn now Use the definitions of complementary and supplementary angles to find the measure of the angle.

6. ∠D and ∠E are supplementary. If $m∠D = 84°$, find $m∠E$.

7. ∠R and ∠S are complementary. If $m∠S = 9°$, find $m∠R$.

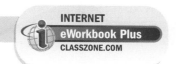
Getting Ready to Practice

Vocabulary Match the angle measure with its classification.

1. 78°   **2.** 90°   **3.** 168°   **4.** 180°

A. Right   **B.** Straight   **C.** Obtuse   **D.** Acute

5. Give the measures of two angles that are complementary.

6. Folding Fan A folding fan forms a straight angle when fully opened. If the fan is opened to a 138° angle, how many more degrees does it need to be opened to be fully opened?

Practice and Problem Solving

Estimate to classify the angle as *acute*, *right*, *obtuse*, or *straight*.

7.   **8.**   **9.**   **10.**

Tell whether the angles are *complementary*, *supplementary*, or *neither*. Explain your reasoning.

11.   **12.**   **13.**

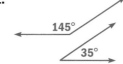
145°
35°

40°   40°

47°
41°

For the given angle measure, find the measure of a supplementary angle and the measure of a complementary angle, if possible.

14. 19°   **15.** 73°   **16.** 118°   **17.** 90°

18. 22°   **19.** 162°   **20.** 180°   **21.** 3°

Find the measure of the angle.

22. $\angle F$ and $\angle G$ are supplementary. If $m\angle G = 57°$, what is $m\angle F$?

23. $\angle X$ and $\angle Y$ are complementary. If $m\angle X = 43°$, what is $m\angle Y$?

24. Hockey Stick The *lie* is the angle the blade of a hockey stick makes with the shaft. The diagram shows a stick with a lie of 135°. What is the value of x?

135° $x°$

25. Critical Thinking Which has a greater measure, an angle complementary to an angle measuring 15° or an angle supplementary to an angle measuring 125°? Explain.

26. Kites The line of a kite is tied to the ground as shown. Name the two supplementary angles. Then find $m\angle LMK$.

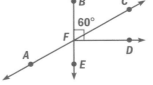

Critical Thinking Copy and complete the statement using *always*, *sometimes*, or *never*.

27. If an angle is acute, an angle supplementary to it is ___?___ acute.

28. An angle supplementary to a right angle is ___?___ a right angle.

In Exercises 29–33, refer to the diagram.

29. Find $m\angle CFD$. **30.** Find $m\angle AFB$.

31. Find $m\angle AFE$. **32.** Find $m\angle AFD$.

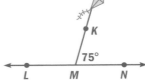

33. Writing Why is it important to name each angle in the diagram with three letters?

34. Challenge Suppose $\angle DCG$ is a straight angle made up of $\angle DCE$, $\angle ECF$, and $\angle FCG$. If $\angle ECF$ is a right angle and $m\angle DCE = 40.7°$, what is $m\angle FCG$?

Mixed Review

Write the percent as a fraction in simplest form. *(Lesson 9.1)*

35. 28% **36.** 38% **37.** 66% **38.** 72%

39. You deposit $200 into a savings account that earns 4.2% simple annual interest. What will the balance be after 10 months? *(Lesson 9.8)*

Basic Skills **Find the quotient. Then check your answer.**

40. $0.085 \div 5$ **41.** $6.75 \div 0.15$ **42.** $12 \div 3.75$ **43.** $1.125 \div 4.5$

Test-Taking Practice

44. Multiple Choice What type of angle is $\angle RST$ if $m\angle RST = 56°$?

A. Acute **B.** Obtuse **C.** Right **D.** Straight

45. Multiple Choice An angle measuring 16° and an angle measuring $x°$ are complementary. What is the value of x?

F. 16 **G.** 74 **H.** 106 **I.** 164

Special Pairs of Angles

BEFORE	▶ Now	WHY?
You classified angles according to their measures.	You'll identify special pairs of angles and types of lines.	So you can find the measure of an angle in Jamaica's flag, as in Ex. 2.

📓 Word Watch

adjacent angles, p. 479
vertical angles, p. 479
congruent angles, p. 479
plane, p. 480
parallel lines, p. 480
intersecting lines, p. 480
perpendicular lines, p. 480
corresponding angles,
    p. 480

Activity You can find angle relationships when lines meet.

① Draw and label $\overleftrightarrow{AB}$, the line containing points A and B. Then draw $\overleftrightarrow{CD}$ so that it meets $\overleftrightarrow{AB}$ as shown.

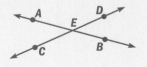

② Copy the table. Then measure each angle to the nearest degree and record the results.

③ Make a conclusion about the angles that are opposite each other.

④ Repeat Steps 1 and 2 using another pair of lines. Is your conclusion from Step 3 still true?

Angle	Measure
∠AEC	?
∠CEB	?
∠BED	?
∠AED	?

Adjacent Angles Two angles that share a common side and a vertex and do not overlap are called **adjacent angles**. When two lines meet at a point, as in the activity, adjacent angles are supplementary.

EXAMPLE 1 Identifying Adjacent Angles

Name all pairs of adjacent, supplementary angles.

Adjacent, supplementary angles:

∠1 and ∠2   ∠2 and ∠3

∠3 and ∠4   ∠1 and ∠4

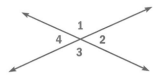

Vertical Angles When two lines meet at a point, as in the activity, the angles that are opposite each other are called **vertical angles**. Vertical angles are **congruent angles** because they have the same measure. The symbol ≅ indicates congruence and is read "is congruent to."

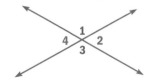

Vertical angles: ∠1 ≅ ∠3

Vertical angles: ∠2 ≅ ∠4

EXAMPLE 2 **Using Vertical Angles**

Given that $m\angle 1 = 75°$, find $m\angle 3$.

Because $\angle 1$ and $\angle 3$ are vertical angles,
they are congruent. So, $m\angle 3 = m\angle 1 = 75°$.

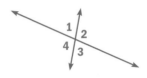

Your turn now **Refer to the diagram in Example 2.**

1. Name all pairs of adjacent, supplementary angles.

2. Given that $m\angle 1 = 75°$, find $m\angle 2$.

3. Use your answer from Exercise 2 to find $m\angle 4$.

Lines in a Plane You can think of a **plane** as a flat surface that extends without end. Two lines in the same plane that do not intersect are called **parallel lines** . Two lines that meet at a point are called **intersecting lines** . **Perpendicular lines** intersect to form four right angles. The symbol ∥ is used to indicate parallel lines, and the symbol ⊥ is used to indicate perpendicular lines.

HELP with **Reading**

Arrowheads are used to
indicate that lines are
parallel.

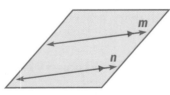

**Parallel lines in
a plane ($m \parallel n$)**

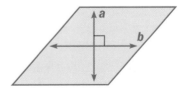

**Perpendicular lines
in a plane ($a \perp b$)**

Angles that occupy corresponding positions when a line intersects two other lines are called **corresponding angles** . When a line intersects two parallel lines, corresponding angles are congruent.

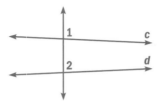

**Lines c and d are not parallel,
so corresponding angles, such
as $\angle 1$ and $\angle 2$, are not congruent.**

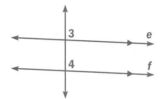

**Lines e and f are parallel, so
corresponding angles, such as
$\angle 3$ and $\angle 4$, are congruent.**

EXAMPLE 3 **Using Corresponding Angles**

Maps The map shows a section of New York City. Streets shown on maps often appear to form parallel or intersecting lines.

a. Name two streets that are parallel and two streets that intersect.

b. Given that $m\angle 7 = 68°$, find $m\angle 1$.

Solution

a. There are several possible answers. For example, 34th St. is parallel to 23rd St., and 34th St. intersects Broadway.

b. Because $\angle 7$ and $\angle 5$ are vertical angles, $m\angle 5 = m\angle 7 = 68°$. Because 34th St. and 23rd St. are parallel lines, $\angle 5$ and $\angle 1$ are congruent corresponding angles. So, $m\angle 1 = m\angle 5 = 68°$.

Your turn now Refer to the map in Example 3.

4. Find $m\angle 6$ and $m\angle 2$. Explain your reasoning.

10.2 **Exercises**
More Practice, p. 714

Getting Ready to Practice

1. **Vocabulary** Copy and complete: When two lines intersect, _?_ angles are supplementary and _?_ angles are congruent.

2. **Jamaican Flag** Name two pairs of adjacent angles and two pairs of vertical angles in the Jamaican flag. Then find $m\angle 2$, given that $m\angle 1 = 127°$.

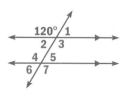

In Exercises 3–6, refer to the diagram.

3. Name two pairs of vertical angles.

4. Name two pairs of corresponding angles.

5. Find $m\angle 3$. **6.** Find $m\angle 7$.

Practice and Problem Solving

HELP with **Homework**

Example	Exercises
1	7–10, 24–29
2	7–10, 15–20
3	15–20, 24–29

Online Resources
CLASSZONE.COM

· More Examples
· eTutorial Plus

In Exercises 7–10, refer to the diagram.

7. Name all pairs of adjacent, supplementary angles.

8. Name all pairs of vertical angles.

9. Given that $m\angle 3 = 147°$, find $m\angle 1$.

10. Given that $m\angle 3 = 147°$, find $m\angle 2$.

11. **Explain** Two lines intersect to form an angle that measures 72°. Draw a diagram and find the measures of the three other angles that are not straight. Explain your reasoning.

Tell whether the objects appear to be *parallel*, *perpendicular*, or *neither*.

12.

Chopsticks

13.

Soccer goal bars

14.

Road lines

Road Map In Exercises 15–20, refer to the road map.

15. Find $m\angle 1$. 16. Find $m\angle 2$.

17. Find $m\angle 3$. 18. Find $m\angle 4$.

19. Find $m\angle 5$. 20. Find $m\angle 6$.

Critical Thinking Copy and complete the statement using *always*, *sometimes*, or *never*.

21. Vertical angles are __?__ congruent.

22. Intersecting lines are __?__ perpendicular.

23. When a line intersects two parallel lines, corresponding angles are __?__ congruent.

Construction In Exercises 24–29, refer to the photograph.

24. Find $m\angle 1$. 25. Find $m\angle 2$.

26. Find $m\angle 3$. 27. Find $m\angle 4$.

28. Find $m\angle 5$. 29. Find $m\angle 6$.

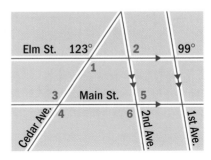

30. Challenge Write and solve an equation to find the values of x and $3x$. Then find $m\angle 1$ and $m\angle 2$.

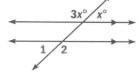

Mixed Review

Copy and complete the statement using <, >, or =. *(Lesson 8.1)*

31. $\dfrac{2}{3}$ $\underline{?}$ $\dfrac{5}{9}$ **32.** $12:6$ $\underline{?}$ $6:3$ **33.** $4:7$ $\underline{?}$ $8:13$ **34.** $\dfrac{6}{10}$ $\underline{?}$ $\dfrac{9}{15}$

Classify the angle as *acute*, *right*, *obtuse*, or *straight*. *(Lesson 10.1)*

35. $m\angle W = 112°$ **36.** $m\angle X = 29°$ **37.** $m\angle Y = 180°$ **38.** $m\angle Z = 90°$

Basic Skills **Find the perimeter and area of the rectangle or square with the given dimensions.**

39. $l = 5$ meters, $w = 2$ meters   **40.** $s = 5$ inches

Test-Taking Practice

41. Multiple Choice Name a pair of congruent angles in the diagram.

A. $\angle 1$ and $\angle 4$ **B.** $\angle 3$ and $\angle 4$

C. $\angle 4$ and $\angle 8$ **D.** $\angle 6$ and $\angle 8$

42. Multiple Choice In the diagram, $m\angle 2 = 100°$. What is $m\angle 8$?

F. $10°$ **G.** $80°$ **H.** $100°$ **I.** $180°$

Acorn-y Riddle

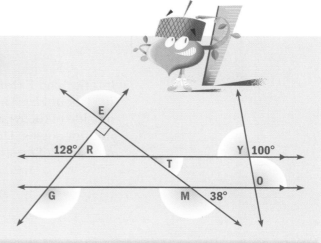

To find the answer to the riddle, replace the angle measure with the letter of the angle having that measure in the diagram.

Riddle: What did the acorn say when it grew up?

Answer: $\underline{128°}$ $\underline{90°}$ $\underline{100°}$ $\underline{142°}$ $\underline{90°}$ $\underline{38°}$ $\underline{52°}$ $\underline{80°}$

Triangles

BEFORE	▶ Now	WHY?
You classified angles.	You'll classify triangles.	So you can classify Research Triangle Park, as in Ex. 26.

Word Watch

acute triangle, p. 485
right triangle, p. 485
obtuse triangle, p. 485
congruent sides, p. 486
equilateral triangle, p. 486
isosceles triangle, p. 486
scalene triangle, p. 486

Activity **You can find the sum of the angle measures in a triangle.**

1. Cut a triangle from the corner of a piece of paper. Label the corners ∠A, ∠B, and ∠C.

2. Tear the corners off the triangle.

3. Rearrange ∠A, ∠B, and ∠C so that they are adjacent. Then make a conclusion about the angles of the triangle.

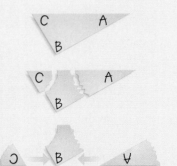

In the activity, you found that the sum of the angle measures in △ABC is 180°. The sum of the angle measures in any triangle is 180°.

**with Reading**

Triangles are named by their *vertices*. The vertices of the triangle in the activity are A, B, and C, so the triangle can be named with the notation △ABC. This notation is read "triangle ABC."

EXAMPLE 1 Finding an Angle Measure in a Triangle

 Find the value of x in the triangle shown.

$x° + 83° + 26° = 180°$	Sum of angle measures in a triangle is 180°.
$x + 109 = 180$	Add 83 and 26.
$x = 71$	Subtract 109 from each side.

ANSWER The value of x is 71.

Interior and Exterior Angles The three angles of any triangle are called *interior angles*. The sides of a triangle can be extended to form angles outside of the triangle that are adjacent and supplementary to the interior angles. These angles are called *exterior angles*. You can use the measures of interior angles to find the measures of exterior angles.

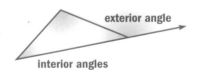
exterior angle
interior angles

EXAMPLE 2 Finding the Measure of an Exterior Angle

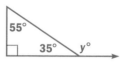

Find the value of *y* in the figure.

To find the value of *y*, use the fact that
adjacent interior and exterior angles
of a triangle are supplementary.

$y° + 35° = 180°$ **Definition of supplementary angles**

$y = 145$ **Subtract 35 from each side.**

ANSWER The value of *y* is 145.

Your turn now Find the value of *x* or *y.*

1.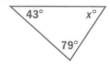

2.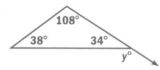

You can classify any triangle by the measures of its interior angles.

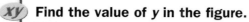

Classifying Triangles by Angle Measures

Acute Triangle

An **acute triangle**
has three acute angles.

Right Triangle

A **right triangle** has
one right angle.

Obtuse Triangle

An **obtuse triangle**
has one obtuse angle.

EXAMPLE 3 Classifying a Triangle by Angle Measures

Classify the triangle formed by the plant
hanger by its angle measures.

The triangle has one right angle, so it is
a right triangle.

The notation $\overline{AB}$ is read "line segment *AB*" and represents a line segment with endpoints *A* and *B*. The notation *AB* represents the *length* of $\overline{AB}$.

Congruent Sides Just as congruent angles have the same measure, **congruent sides** of a triangle have the same length. You can use special marks to indicate that two sides or two angles of a triangle are congruent. In the triangle at the right, the marks show that $\overline{XY} \cong \overline{XZ}$ and that $\angle Y \cong \angle Z$. You can classify any triangle by the lengths of its sides.

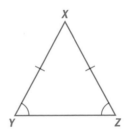

Classifying Triangles by Side Lengths

Equilateral Triangle

An **equilateral triangle** has 3 congruent sides.

9 in.
9 in.
9 in.

Isosceles Triangle

An **isosceles triangle** has at least 2 congruent sides.

8 m
5 m
8 m

Scalene Triangle

A **scalene triangle** has no congruent sides.

5 ft
14 ft
11 ft

EXAMPLE 4 **Classifying a Triangle by Side Lengths**

Classify the triangle by the lengths of its sides.

All three sides of the triangle are congruent, so the triangle is both isosceles and equilateral.

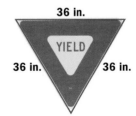
36 in.
36 in.
36 in.

Your turn now **Classify the triangle by its angle measures.**

3.

80°
60° 40°

4.
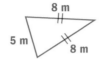
45° 35°
100°

5.
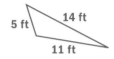
53°
37°

Classify the triangle by the lengths of its sides.

6.
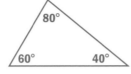
3 ft
2 ft
2 ft

7.
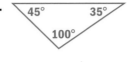
18 cm
15 cm 6 cm

8.
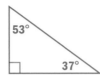
7 m
7 m
7 m

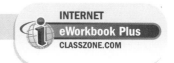

10.3 Exercises

More Practice, p. 714

Getting Ready to Practice

Vocabulary In Exercises 1 and 2, tell whether the statement is *true* or *false*. Explain your reasoning.

1. A triangle that has one angle whose measure is greater than 90° is called an acute triangle.

2. An equilateral triangle can also be classified as an isosceles triangle.

3. The measures of two of the angles in a triangle are 90° and 57°. Find the measure of the third angle.

4. **Camera Tripod** A tripod is used to keep a camera steady while taking pictures. A tripod has three legs that are each connected to a vertical shaft by a support bar. Find the value of *y*.

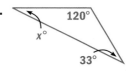

Classify the triangle by its angle measures.

5. 68°, 22°, 90°   6. 53°, 57°, 70°

Classify the triangle by the lengths of its sides.

7. 10 m, 12 m, 16 m   8. 12 in., 30 in., 30 in.

Practice and Problem Solving

with Homework

Example	Exercises
1	9–11, 13–15
2	16–19
3	20–22
4	23–26

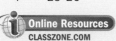

Online Resources
CLASSZONE.COM

· More Examples
· eTutorial Plus

xy Algebra Find the value of *x*.

9.   10.   11.

  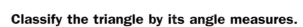

12. **Find the Error** Describe and correct the error in finding the value of *x*.

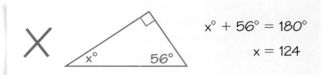

$x° + 56° = 180°$

$x = 124$

 The measures of two of the angles in a triangle are given. Find the measure of the third angle.

13. 112° and 34.8°   14. 55.5° and 90.2°   15. 128.7° and 30.4°

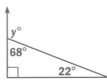

xy Algebra **Find the value of y.**

16.

17.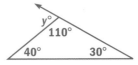

18.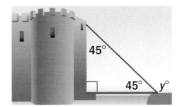

19. Drawbridge A castle has a drawbridge that can be raised or lowered. When the drawbridge is lowered, what angle does the chain form with the road leading up to the castle?

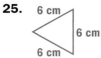

What do you think?

Design

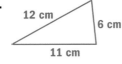

■ **Drawbridge**

The Lasalle Street Bridge in Chicago is a drawbridge on the Chicago River. The drawbridge can be raised 70°. When fully opened, what angle does the drawbridge form with the road leading up to the bridge?

Classify the triangle by its angle measures.

20. 68°, 22°, 90°   **21.** 82°, 64°, 34°   **22.** 135°, 24°, 21°

Classify the triangle by the lengths of its sides.

23.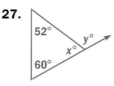

24.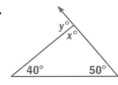

25.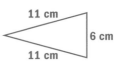

26. Research Triangle Park Duke University, the University of North Carolina, and North Carolina State University make up the three vertices of Research Triangle Park in North Carolina. The distances between the three universities are 9 miles, 21 miles, and 23 miles. Classify Research Triangle Park by the lengths of its sides.

xy Algebra **Find the values of x and y.**

27.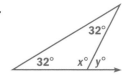

28.

29.

30. Post and Beam In some houses, wall posts and ceiling beams are connected by support braces. Find the unknown angle measures in the post-and-beam design shown.

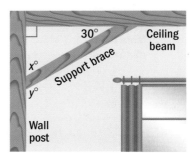

31. Challenge The measure of one angle in a triangle is 36°. The other two angles are congruent. What are their measures? Explain your reasoning.

Order the numbers from least to greatest. *(Lesson 4.7)*

32. $\frac{3}{7}$, 0.42, $\frac{7}{2}$, 0.4

33. 6.64, $6\frac{3}{5}$, $6\frac{2}{3}$, $\frac{27}{4}$

34. 3.25, $3\frac{2}{3}$, 3.1, $3\frac{5}{7}$

35. Choose a Strategy Use a strategy from the list to solve the following problem. **Explain your choice of strategy.**

You buy a prepaid phone card with a fixed number of minutes on it. You use one half of your minutes during the weekend and 6 minutes on Monday. If 24 minutes are left on your phone card, how many minutes did you start with?

> **Problem Solving Strategies**
> ▪ Draw a Diagram
> ▪ Write an Equation
> ▪ Work Backward

Basic Skills Use a straightedge and a compass to draw a segment whose length is the sum of the lengths of the two given segments.

36. ━━━━━

37. ━━━━━━

Test-Taking Practice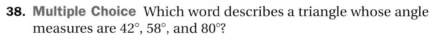

INTERNET
State Test Practice
CLASSZONE.COM

38. Multiple Choice Which word describes a triangle whose angle measures are 42°, 58°, and 80°?

A. Right   **B.** Obtuse   **C.** Equilateral   **D.** Acute

39. Short Response A triangle has two angles that measure 53° and 65°. Find the measure of the third angle. Explain your reasoning.

BRAIN GAME

The Shape of Things

Draw a square with a side length of 4 inches on a piece of paper. Divide the square into 16 smaller squares with side length 1 inch. Then mark off the lines shown in blue on the diagram. Cut carefully along these lines to produce the seven pieces of a tangram.

Arrange all seven tangram pieces to form each figure.

Constructions

GOAL Construct geometric figures.

Word Watch

arc, p. 490

You can use a straightedge and a compass to construct geometric figures. To draw an **arc**, or part of a circle, with a given center, first place the point of a compass on the center. Then rotate the compass to draw the arc.

EXAMPLE 1 Copying an Angle

HELP with **Review**

Need help using a compass? See p. 700.

You can use a straightedge and a compass to copy an angle.

1 Draw any ∠A. Use a straightedge to draw a ray with endpoint P. Use a compass to draw an arc with center A. Label B and C as shown. Then, with the same compass setting, draw an arc with center P. Label Q as shown.

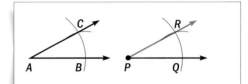

2 Put the compass point at B and adjust the compass so you can draw an arc through C. Then, with the same compass setting, draw an arc with center Q. Label R as shown.

3 Use a straightedge to draw $\overrightarrow{PR}$, the ray from P through R. ∠P is congruent to ∠A.

EXAMPLE 2 Bisecting an Angle

You can use a straightedge and a compass to bisect an angle.

1 Draw any ∠J. Then use a compass to draw an arc with center J that intersects both sides of ∠J. Label K and L as shown.

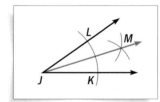

2 Use a compass to draw an arc with center K. Then, with the same compass setting, draw an arc with center L. Label the intersection M.

3 Use a straightedge to draw $\overrightarrow{JM}$. This ray bisects ∠J.

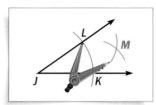

EXAMPLE 3 **Constructing an Isosceles Triangle**

You can use a straightedge and a compass to construct an isosceles triangle.

① Draw $\overline{AB}$. With the compass opened more than half the length of $\overline{AB}$, draw an arc with center A as shown.

② Use the same compass setting to draw an arc with center B. Label the point of intersection C.

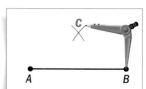

③ Use a straightedge to draw $\overline{AC}$ and $\overline{BC}$. $\triangle ABC$ is an isosceles triangle.

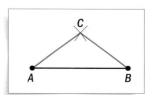

Exercises

In Exercises 1 and 2, use a straightedge to draw the specified type of angle. Then copy the angle.

1. An acute angle

2. An obtuse angle

3. Bisect the angle in Exercise 1.

4. Bisect the angle in Exercise 2.

5. Construct perpendicular lines by bisecting a straight angle. Explain how you know that the lines are perpendicular.

6. Construct an equilateral triangle using the steps in Example 3. In Step 1, first measure the line segment with your compass. Then use this setting to draw the two arcs.

7. Follow the steps below to construct parallel lines.

① Draw a line m.

② Choose a point on m and draw a line l perpendicular to m at that point. (*Hint:* See Exercise 5.)

③ Choose another point on m and draw a line p perpendicular to m at that point. Lines l and p are parallel.

- Draw a Diagram
- Write an Equation
- Guess, Check, and Revise
- Act it Out
- Break into Parts
- Work Backward
- Estimate

Break into Parts

Problem What is the sum of the angle measures in any four-sided figure?

❶ Read and Understand

Read the problem carefully.

You need to find the sum of the angle measures in any four-sided figure.

❷ Make a Plan

Decide on a strategy to use.

One way to approach this problem is to break a four-sided figure into smaller parts. Because you know that the sum of the angle measures in any triangle is 180°, break the figure into triangles.

❸ Solve the Problem

Reread the problem and break into parts.

First, draw and label a four-sided figure. Then draw a line segment that breaks the figure into two triangles.

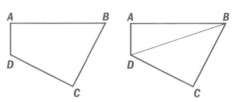

The sum of the angle measures in any triangle is 180°. From the figure at the far right, you can see that the sum of the angle measures in the four-sided figure is equal to the sum of the angle measures in the two triangles.

ANSWER The sum of the angle measures in the four-sided figure $ABCD$ is $180° + 180° = 360°$.

❹ Look Back

You can see that your answer is reasonable by considering the sum of the angle measures in a four-sided figure you are already familiar with, a rectangle. Because a rectangle has four right angles, the sum of the angle measures in a rectangle is $90° + 90° + 90° + 90° = 360°$.

Practice the Strategy

Use the strategy *break into parts*.

1. **Cafeteria** The floor plan of a cafeteria is shown below. Find the total area of the floor of the cafeteria.

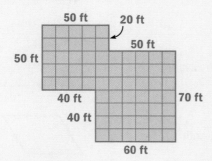

50 ft   20 ft
            50 ft
50 ft
    40 ft   70 ft
    40 ft
        60 ft

2. **Angle Measures** Use the fact that the sum of the angle measures in any four-sided figure is 360° to find the sum of the angle measures in the figure below.

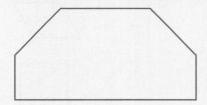

3. **Cards** You are making a card for your friend's birthday. You want to make a frame out of construction paper for the front of the card. The front of the card is 10 inches long and 8 inches wide. You want the frame to have a width of 2 inches. What is the area of the frame?

4. **Long Distance Calls** A calling plan charges $2.99 for the first 30 minutes of a long distance phone call and another rate for each additional minute. If a 45 minute call costs $5.24, how much does each additional minute cost?

Mixed Problem Solving

Use any strategy to solve the problem.

5. **Movie Seats** Four friends go to the movies. There are four seats in a row. Patrick wants to sit next to Nicole but not next to Richard. If Richard will not sit next to Julie, who sits next to Julie?

6. **Digit Sum** The sum of the digits in a two digit number is 12. If the tens' digit is 3 times the ones' digit, what is the number?

7. **Reading Record** Trey records the number of pages he reads each week in a table. About how many pages did he read in 7 weeks?

Week	Pages Read
1	81
2	131
3	79
4	189
5	127
6	148
7	103

8. **Apartment Floors** Monica climbed the stairs in her building from the floor she lives on to the eleventh floor. She climbed 80 steps altogether. If there are 16 steps between each floor, on which floor does Monica live?

Polygons

BEFORE	Now	WHY?
You classified triangles.	You'll classify quadrilaterals and other polygons.	So you can classify the polygons in a stained glass window, as in Ex. 15.

Word Watch

quadrilateral, p. 494
trapezoid, p. 494
parallelogram, p. 494
rhombus, p. 494
polygon, p. 495
pentagon, p. 495
hexagon, p. 495
heptagon, p. 495
octagon, p. 495
regular polygon, p. 496

A **quadrilateral** is a geometric figure that is made up of four line segments, called sides, that intersect only at their endpoints. Some quadrilaterals have special names.

Special Quadrilaterals	Diagram
Trapezoid A **trapezoid** is a quadrilateral with exactly 1 pair of parallel sides.	
Parallelogram A **parallelogram** is a quadrilateral with 2 pairs of parallel sides.	
Rectangle A *rectangle* is a parallelogram with 4 right angles.	
Rhombus A **rhombus** is a parallelogram with 4 congruent sides.	
Square A *square* is a parallelogram with 4 right angles and 4 congruent sides.	

EXAMPLE 1 Classifying a Quadrilateral

Sketch and classify a quadrilateral with opposite sides parallel, one side of length 3 cm, and another side of length 1 cm.

(1 Draw two sides, one of length 3 cm and one of length 1 cm. The angle between the two sides does not matter.

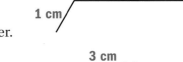

(2 Draw sides parallel to the first two sides to complete the figure.

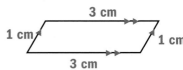

ANSWER The figure is a parallelogram.

HELP with Notetaking

To help you classify quadrilaterals, you could draw a diagram that shows how the special quadrilaterals are related to each other.

Your turn now Sketch and classify the quadrilateral described.

1. A quadrilateral with 4 right angles, 4 congruent sides of length 2.5 centimeters, and both pairs of opposite sides parallel

Polygons A **polygon** is a geometric figure that is made up of three or more line segments that intersect only at their endpoints. The number of sides determines the name of the polygon.

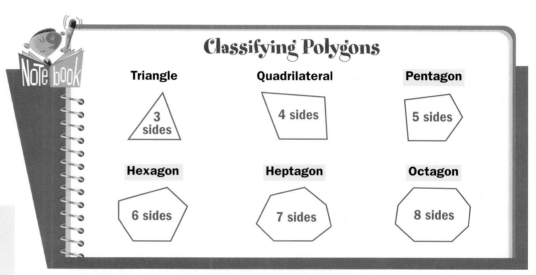

Classifying Polygons

Triangle	Quadrilateral	Pentagon
3 sides	4 sides	5 sides
Hexagon	Heptagon	Octagon
6 sides	7 sides	8 sides

HELP with Reading

The prefixes used in the names of polygons tell you the number of sides the figure has.

Prefix	Meaning
tri-	three
quad-	four
penta-	five
hexa-	six
hepta-	seven
octa-	eight

EXAMPLE 2 Classifying Polygons

Tell whether the figure is a polygon. If it is, classify it. If it is not, explain why not.

a.

b.

Solution

a. This figure is a polygon with 5 sides. So, it is a pentagon.

b. This figure is not a polygon because it is not made up entirely of line segments.

Your turn now Tell whether the figure is a polygon. If it is, classify it. If it is not, explain why not.

2.   **3.**   **4.**

Regular Polygons A **regular polygon** is a polygon with all sides equal in length and all angles equal in measure. The pentagon shown is an example of a regular polygon.

Watch Out!

Just because a polygon has sides that are all congruent does not necessarily mean that it is a regular polygon. All angles must also be congruent.

EXAMPLE 3 **Using a Regular Polygon**

The polygon shown is a regular pentagon. Find the perimeter of the pentagon. Then find the sum of the angle measures in the pentagon.

3 ft

1 A regular pentagon has 5 sides of equal length, so the perimeter of the pentagon is 5(3) = 15 feet.

2 A pentagon can be divided into three triangles. The sum of the angle measures in a triangle is 180°, so the sum of the angle measures in any pentagon is 180° + 180° + 180° = 540°.

10.4 Exercises
More Practice, p. 714

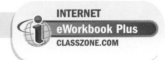

INTERNET
eWorkbook Plus
CLASSZONE.COM

Getting Ready to Practice

1. **Vocabulary** Copy and complete: Two types of quadrilaterals that have four right angles are ? and ? .

Tell whether the figure is a polygon. If it is a polygon, classify it. If it is not, explain why not.

2.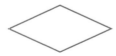

3.

4.

5. **Guided Problem Solving** The quilt design shown repeatedly uses regular hexagons and other polygons. What is the sum of the angle measures in a hexagon?

1 Sketch a hexagon on a piece of paper.

2 Draw three line segments to divide the hexagon into triangles.

3 Use the triangles to find the sum of the angle measures in a hexagon.

Practice and Problem Solving

HELP with **Homework**

Example	Exercises
1	6–8
2	9–16
3	21–22

Online Resources
CLASSZONE.COM

· More Examples
· eTutorial Plus

Use the clues to sketch and classify the quadrilateral described.

6. This figure has four right angles. Not all of the sides are the same length.

7. This figure's opposite sides are parallel and congruent. Not all of the angles are congruent.

8. This figure has exactly one pair of opposite sides that are parallel.

Classify the polygon and tell if it is regular. If it is not regular, explain why not.

9. 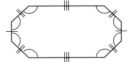   **10.**   **11.**

12. 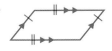   **13.**   **14.**

15. Stained Glass Window Sketch and classify four different polygons contained in the stained glass window. Do any of the polygons appear to be regular? Explain your reasoning.

16. Geometry Graph and connect the ordered pairs (0, 5), (3, 2), (2, −2), (−2, −1), (−3, 2), and (0, 5) in the order they are given. Is the figure that results a polygon? If it is, classify it and tell if it is regular. If it is not a polygon, explain why not.

Critical Thinking Tell whether the statement is *true* or *false*. Explain your reasoning.

17. All squares are rectangles.

18. A scalene triangle is regular.

19. A trapezoid is a parallelogram.

20. Every rhombus is a square.

 Find the measure of each side of the polygon described.

21. A regular octagon with a perimeter of 46 centimeters

22. A regular heptagon with a perimeter of 52.5 inches

Extended Problem Solving In Exercises 23–26, you will examine the angle measures of polygons.

23. Break into Parts Copy and complete the table below. Use the problem solving strategy of breaking into parts.

Polygon	Triangle	Quadrilateral	Pentagon	Hexagon
Sum of angle measures	?	?	?	?
Measure of each angle in a regular polygon	?	?	?	?

24. Look for a Pattern What pattern do you notice in the sum of the angle measures in the table?

25. Predict Use the pattern you identified to predict the sum of the angle measures in a heptagon. What do you predict is the measure of each angle in a regular heptagon?

26. Challenge Write an expression for the sum of the angle measures in a regular polygon with n sides. Then write an expression for the measure of each angle in a regular polygon with n sides.

27. Critical Thinking Name a quadrilateral that is always a regular polygon. Explain your reasoning.

Mixed Review

28. Your average monthly checking account balance was $580 in January and $957 in March. What was the percent of increase in your account balance from January to March? *(Lesson 9.6)*

29. Classify a triangle that has angle measures of 25°, 105°, and 50°. *(Lesson 10.3)*

Basic Skills Evaluate the power.

30. 2^3 **31.** 3^2 **32.** 1^8 **33.** 5^4

Test-Taking Practice

34. Multiple Choice What is the sum of the angle measures in a parallelogram?

A. 360° **B.** 270° **C.** 180° **D.** 90°

35. Multiple Choice What is the perimeter of a regular octagon with a side length of 4 centimeters?

F. 12 cm **G.** 16 cm **H.** 32 cm **I.** 64 cm

Notebook Review

Review the vocabulary definitions in your notebook.

Copy the review examples in your notebook. Then complete the exercises.

Check Your Definitions

angles: acute, right, obtuse, straight, p. 475

complementary, p. 476

supplementary, p. 476

adjacent angles, p. 479

vertical angles, p. 479

congruent angles, p. 479

plane, p. 480

lines: parallel, intersecting, perpendicular, p. 480

corresponding angles, p. 480

triangles: acute, right, obtuse, p. 485

congruent sides, p. 486

triangles: equilateral, isosceles, scalene, p. 486

quadrilateral, p. 494

trapezoid, parallelogram, rhombus, p. 494

polygon, p. 495

pentagon, hexagon, heptagon, octagon, p. 495

regular polygon, p. 496

Use Your Vocabulary

1. Writing Explain why an equilateral triangle is also an isosceles triangle.

10.1–10.2 Can you use angle relationships?

 EXAMPLE Find (a) $m\angle ADC$ and (b) $m\angle DGF$.

a. $\angle ADC$ and $\angle ADB$ are supplementary angles.

$$m\angle ADC + m\angle ADB = 180°$$ **Supplementary angles**

$$m\angle ADC + 105° = 180°$$ **Substitute 105° for $m\angle ADB$.**

$$m\angle ADC = 75°$$ **Subtract 105° from each side.**

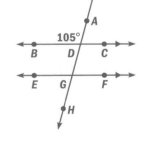

b. Congruent corresponding angles are formed when a line intersects two parallel lines. $\angle DGF$ and $\angle ADC$ are corresponding angles, so $m\angle DGF = m\angle ADC = 75°$.

 Refer to the diagram above.

2. Find $m\angle DGE$.

3. Find $m\angle CDG$.

10.3–10.4 Can you classify polygons?

 EXAMPLE Classify the polygon shown.

Because the polygon is a triangle with three acute angles and two congruent sides, it is an acute, isosceles triangle.

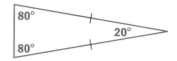

 Tell whether the figure is a polygon. If it is, classify it. If it is not, explain why not.

4. 　　　　5.

Stop and Think about Lessons 10.1–10.4

6. **Writing** Explain why the acute angles of a right triangle are always complementary.

7. **Critical Thinking** If one of the angles formed by two intersecting lines is acute, what can you conclude about the classification of each of the other three angles? Explain your reasoning.

Review Quiz 1

In Exercises 1–4, use the diagram shown.

1. Name all pairs of adjacent, supplementary angles.

2. Name all pairs of vertical angles.

3. Given that $m\angle 2 = 125°$, find $m\angle 3$.

4. Given that $m\angle 2 = 125°$, find $m\angle 4$.

5. Find the value of y.

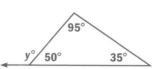

6. Classify a triangle that has side lengths 7 cm, 12 cm, and 7 cm.

7. **Stop Sign** The shape of a stop sign is an octagon. Find the sum of the angle measures in a stop sign.

Investigating Similar Rectangles

Similar rectangles have the same shape but not necessarily the same size. You can draw rectangles on graph paper to identify properties of similar rectangles.

Explore **Find the ratio relating the lengths and widths of two similar rectangles.**

1 On a piece of graph paper, draw a rectangle. Use a ruler to draw a diagonal line segment from the lower left corner of the rectangle through the upper right corner.

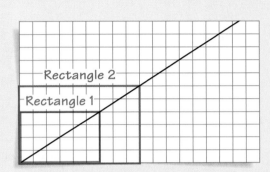

2 Draw a second rectangle that shares the lower left corner and diagonal line segment with the first rectangle. The two rectangles are similar.

3 Copy and complete the table by recording the length and width of each rectangle.

	Rectangle 1	Rectangle 2
Length	?	?
Width	?	?

4 Use the table to find each of the following ratios. What do you notice?

$$\frac{\text{Length of rectangle 1}}{\text{Length of rectangle 2}} \qquad \frac{\text{Width of rectangle 1}}{\text{Width of rectangle 2}}$$

Stop and Think

1. Look for a Pattern Draw a third rectangle that shares the lower left corner and diagonal line with the first rectangle you drew. Then repeat Steps 3 and 4, comparing rectangle 1 and rectangle 3.

2. Critical Thinking Rectangle A is similar to rectangle B, which is 21 units long and 7 units wide. If rectangle A has a width of 6 units, how long is rectangle A? Explain your reasoning.

Similar and Congruent Polygons

BEFORE	▶ Now	WHY?
You classified polygons.	You'll use properties of similar and congruent polygons.	So you can compare two sails, as in Exs. 2–3.

Word Watch

similar polygons, p. 502
congruent polygons, p. 502

Two polygons are **similar** if they have the same shape but not necessarily the same size. The symbol ~ is used to indicate that two polygons are similar. **Congruent polygons** are similar polygons that have the same shape *and* the same size.

Similar Polygons	**Congruent Polygons**
△**LMN** ~ △**PQR**	△**ABC** ≅ △**DEF**

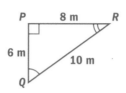 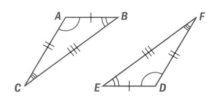

Angles Corresponding angles are congruent:

$\angle L \cong \angle P$, $\angle M \cong \angle Q$, and $\angle N \cong \angle R$

Angles Corresponding angles are congruent:

$\angle A \cong \angle D$, $\angle B \cong \angle E$, and $\angle C \cong \angle F$

Sides Ratios of lengths of corresponding sides are equal:

$\dfrac{LM}{PQ} = \dfrac{MN}{QR} = \dfrac{LN}{PR}$

Sides Corresponding sides are congruent:

$\overline{AB} \cong \overline{DE}$, $\overline{AC} \cong \overline{DF}$, and $\overline{BC} \cong \overline{EF}$

HELP with **Reading**

If two polygons are similar, then the ratio of the lengths of corresponding sides is called the *scale factor*.

EXAMPLE 1 **Finding Measures of Congruent Polygons**

Watch Out!

When naming congruent or similar polygons, list the letters for the corresponding vertices in the same order. For instance, in Example 1 you cannot write "△RST ≅ △YXZ" because ∠R and ∠Y are not corresponding angles.

Given that △**RST** ≅ △**XYZ**, name the corresponding sides and corresponding angles. Then find **XY**.

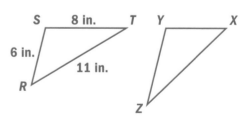

Corresponding sides: $\overline{RS}$ and $\overline{XY}$, $\overline{RT}$ and $\overline{XZ}$, $\overline{ST}$ and $\overline{YZ}$

Corresponding angles: $\angle R$ and $\angle X$, $\angle S$ and $\angle Y$, $\angle T$ and $\angle Z$

Because $\overline{XY}$ and $\overline{RS}$ are corresponding sides, they are equal in length.

$XY = RS = 6$ inches

1. Name the corresponding sides and corresponding angles.

2. Find the unknown angle measures.

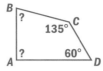
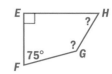

What do you think?

Art

■ **Painting**

Alexandra Nechita's first art exhibit was held when she was 8 years old. Her painting "My Future Rainbow" is a 36 in. by 24 in. rectangle. Her painting "Sharing Moments" is a 28 in. by 22 in. rectangle. Are the two paintings similar figures?

EXAMPLE 2 **Finding the Ratio of Lengths**

Given that △*ABC* ~ △*DEF*, find the ratio of the lengths of the corresponding sides of △*ABC* to △*DEF*.

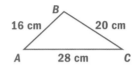
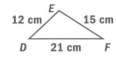

Write a ratio for each pair of corresponding sides. Then substitute the lengths of the sides and simplify each ratio.

$$\frac{AB}{DE} = \frac{16}{12} = \frac{4}{3} \qquad \frac{BC}{EF} = \frac{20}{15} = \frac{4}{3} \qquad \frac{AC}{DF} = \frac{28}{21} = \frac{4}{3}$$

ANSWER The ratio of the lengths of the corresponding sides is $\frac{4}{3}$.

EXAMPLE 3 **Checking for Similarity**

Painting A rectangular painting has a length of 48 inches and a width of 36 inches. A rectangular print of the painting has a length of 32 inches and a width of 24 inches. Are the original and the print similar figures?

Solution

Because both figures are rectangles, all angles are right angles, so corresponding angles are congruent. To determine whether the figures are similar, see if the ratios of the lengths of the corresponding sides are equal.

$$\frac{\text{Length of original}}{\text{Length of print}} \overset{?}{=} \frac{\text{Width of original}}{\text{Width of print}}$$ Write ratios for lengths of corresponding sides.

$$\frac{48}{32} \overset{?}{=} \frac{36}{24}$$ Substitute values.

$$\frac{3}{2} = \frac{3}{2}$$ Simplify.

ANSWER The corresponding angles are congruent and the ratios of the lengths of the corresponding sides are equal, so the figures are similar.

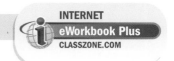
Getting Ready to Practice

1. **Vocabulary** Copy and complete: Two polygons that have the same shape but not necessarily the same size are _?_ polygons.

Sails **Use the diagram of the two sailboat sails and the fact that** △**ABC** ~ △**DEF.**

2. Name the corresponding sides and the corresponding angles.

3. Find the ratio of the lengths of the corresponding sides of △ABC to △DEF.

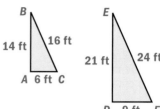

Practice and Problem Solving

Name the corresponding sides and the corresponding angles of the congruent polygons. Then find the unknown measures.

4. *KLMN* ≅ *QRST*

5. △*FGH* ≅ △*JKL*

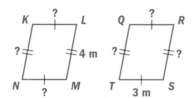

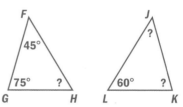

Tell whether the two polygons are similar. If they are similar, find the ratio of the lengths of the corresponding sides of figure A to figure B.

6.

7.

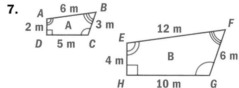

8.

9.

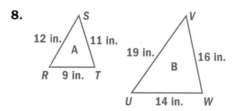

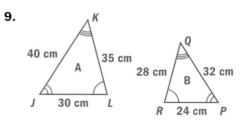

10. Photo Sticker A standard photograph is a rectangle with a length of 6 inches and a width of 4 inches. You have a camera that makes photo stickers. Each sticker is a rectangle with a length of 1.4 inches and a width of 0.9 inch. Are the photograph and sticker similar figures? Explain your reasoning.

Critical Thinking **Tell whether the statement is *true* or *false*. If it is false, give an example to show why.**

11. Two rectangles are congruent if they have the same perimeter.

12. Two squares are congruent if they have the same perimeter.

13. Critical Thinking Draw a rectangle similar to rectangle *DEFG* shown. Then draw a rectangle congruent to *DEFG*. Explain why each rectangle is similar or congruent to *DEFG*.

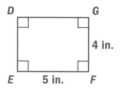

14. Athletic Fields An NCAA football field has a width of 160 feet and a length of 360 feet. An NCAA soccer field can vary from 195 feet to 240 feet in width and from 330 feet to 360 feet in length. Can NCAA football and soccer fields ever be similar rectangles? Explain.

15. Challenge Two rectangles are similar. The ratio of the lengths of their corresponding sides is 1 : 2. Find the ratio of the perimeters of the two rectangles. Then find the ratio of the areas. Explain your answers.

Mixed Review

16. Use equivalent ratios to solve the proportion $\frac{15}{18} = \frac{x}{6}$. *(Lesson 8.4)*

17. Find the perimeter of a regular quadrilateral with a side length of 16 meters. *(Lesson 10.4)*

Basic Skills **Test the number for divisibility by 2, 3, 5, 6, 9, and 10.**

18. 136　　　　**19.** 942　　　　**20.** 1675　　　　**21.** 2458

Test-Taking Practice

22. Multiple Choice If $\triangle ABC \cong \triangle DEF$ and both triangles are scalene, which of the following is *not* true?

  A. $\overline{AC} \cong \overline{DF}$　　　**B.** $\overline{AB} \cong \overline{EF}$　　　**C.** $\angle B \cong \angle E$　　　**D.** $\angle C \cong \angle F$

23. Short Response Rectangle *JKLM* has a length of 30 feet and a width of 9 feet. Rectangle *NPQR* has a length of 50 feet and a width of 15 feet. Tell whether the two rectangles are similar. Explain your reasoning.

Using Proportions with Similar Polygons

BEFORE	▶ Now	WHY?
You identified corresponding parts of similar polygons.	You'll use similar triangles to find lengths indirectly.	So you can find the height of the Gateway Arch, as in Ex. 10.

In the Real World

Groundhog Day A 16 inch tall groundhog emerges on Groundhog Day near a tree and sees its shadow. The length of the groundhog's shadow is 5 inches, and the length of the tree's shadow is 35 inches. What is the height of the tree?

This problem can be solved using similar triangles, as you will see in Example 2. Because the ratios of the lengths of corresponding sides are equal in similar polygons, you can write and solve proportions to find unknown lengths.

EXAMPLE 1 **Finding an Unknown Length**

Quadrilaterals *ABCD* and *EFGH* are similar. Find *FG*.

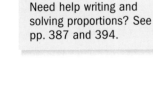

with Review

Need help writing and solving proportions? See pp. 387 and 394.

Solution

Use the ratios of the lengths of corresponding sides to write a proportion involving the unknown length.

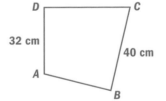

$$\frac{AD}{EH} = \frac{BC}{FG}$$ Write proportion involving *FG*.

$$\frac{32}{20} = \frac{40}{x}$$ Substitute known values.

$$32x = 20 \cdot 40$$ Cross products property

$$\frac{32x}{32} = \frac{20 \cdot 40}{32}$$ Divide each side by 32.

$$x = 25$$ Simplify.

ANSWER The length of $\overline{FG}$ is 25 centimeters.

Your turn now Find the unknown length *x* given that the polygons are similar.

1.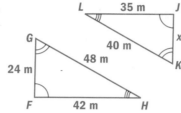

2.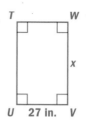

Indirect Measurement Because the sun's rays hit objects that are perpendicular to the ground at the same angle, similar triangles are formed by objects and their shadows. You can use these similar triangles to find lengths that are difficult to measure directly.

EXAMPLE 2 Making an Indirect Measurement

Groundhog Day You can use indirect measurement to find the height of the tree described at the top of page 506.

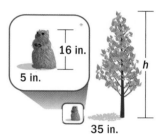

Solution

Use the ratios of the lengths of corresponding parts to write a proportion involving the unknown height *h*.

$$\frac{\text{Height of tree}}{\text{Height of groundhog}} = \frac{\text{Length of tree's shadow}}{\text{Length of groundhog's shadow}}$$

$$\frac{h}{16} = \frac{35}{5} \qquad \text{Substitute known values.}$$

$$16 \cdot \frac{h}{16} = 16 \cdot \frac{35}{5} \qquad \text{Multiply each side by 16.}$$

$$h = 16 \cdot 7 \qquad \text{Simplify fraction.}$$

$$h = 112 \qquad \text{Multiply.}$$

ANSWER The tree has a height of 112 inches, or 9 feet 4 inches.

Your turn now Use indirect measurement to solve the problem.

3. The shadow cast by a lighthouse is 30 feet long. At the same time, the shadow cast by a 4 foot tall sign is 3 feet long. How tall is the lighthouse?

10.6 Exercises

More Practice, p. 714

Getting Ready to Practice

1. **Vocabulary** Copy and complete: An equation that states that two ratios are equivalent is called a(n) _?_.

Find the unknown length *x* given that the polygons are similar.

2.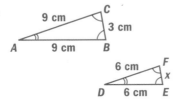

3.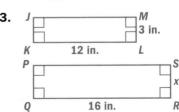

4. **Guided Problem Solving** A tourist who is 5 feet tall stands next to a Saguaro cactus. The length of the tourist's shadow is 2 feet, and the length of the cactus's shadow is 13 feet. How tall is the cactus?

   (1 Draw a diagram to represent the situation.

   (2 Write a proportion involving the unknown height of the cactus.

   (3 Solve the proportion.

Practice and Problem Solving

with Homework

Example	Exercises
1	5–8, 11–12
2	9–10

Online Resources
CLASSZONE.COM

· More Examples
· eTutorial Plus

Find the unknown length *x* given that the polygons are similar.

5.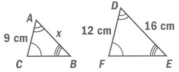

6.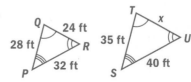

7.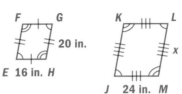

8.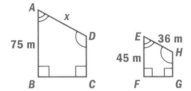

9. **Dinosaurs** A person who is 6 feet tall stands next to a life-size model of a dinosaur. The shadow cast by the person is 4 feet long. At the same time, the shadow cast by the dinosaur model is 12 feet long. How tall is the dinosaur model?

Tourism

10. **Gateway Arch** A boy who is 5 feet tall stands under the Gateway Arch in St. Louis and casts a shadow that is 1 foot long. At the same time, the shadow of the arch is 126 feet long. How tall is the arch?

Find the unknown lengths given that the polygons are similar.

11.
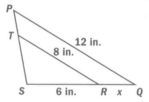

12.

13. **Writing** Suppose you want to find the height of your school building. Describe a method for finding the height that involves indirect measurement.

14. **Challenge** Find the unknown length given that $\triangle RST \sim \triangle QSP$.

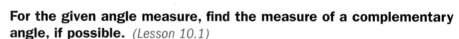

Mixed Review

For the given angle measure, find the measure of a complementary angle, if possible. *(Lesson 10.1)*

15. $39°$ 16. $63°$ 17. $75°$ 18. $100°$

19. Given that $\triangle RST \cong \triangle CDE$, name the corresponding sides and corresponding angles. *(Lesson 10.5)*

Basic Skills Use a compass to draw a circle with the given radius.

20. 3 in.   21. 6 cm   22. 4.5 cm   23. $2\frac{1}{4}$ in.

Test-Taking Practice

24. **Multiple Choice** Rectangles *RSTU* and *LMNP* are similar. Rectangle *RSTU* has a length of 7 cm and a width of 4 cm. Rectangle *LMNP* has a length of 21 cm. What is the width of rectangle *LMNP*?

   A. $1.\overline{3}$ cm   B. 3 cm   C. 9 cm   D. 12 cm

25. **Short Response** A man who is 6 feet tall stands next to a street sign. The man's shadow is 4 feet long. At the same time, the sign's shadow is 6 feet long. Write and solve a proportion to find the height of the sign.

GOAL

Investigate line and rotational symmetry.

MATERIALS

· tape
· paper

Investigating Symmetry

A figure has *line symmetry* if you can fold it into two halves that are mirror images. A figure has *rotational symmetry* if you can turn it 180° or less about a fixed point so that it matches up with itself again. You can fold and turn paper to investigate symmetry in a rectangle.

Explore 1 **Determine whether a rectangle has line symmetry.**

1 Fold a rectangular piece of paper horizontally.

2 Open the paper and fold it vertically. Notice that both the horizontal and vertical folds produce two mirror images.

3 Now fold the paper along its diagonals. Notice that for each of these folds the two halves are not mirror images. Experiment with other folds. You will find that a rectangle has only 2 lines of symmetry.

Explore 2 **Determine whether a rectangle has rotational symmetry.**

1 Tape a rectangular piece of paper down on your desk. Place a second piece of paper over the first so that they match up.

2 Place the tip of your pencil on the center of the top piece of paper. Slowly turn the top piece of paper clockwise. Notice that the pieces of paper match up again after a turn of 180°, so the rectangle has 180° rotational symmetry.

Stop and Think

1. Determine the line symmetry and rotational symmetry of a square. Explain your reasoning.

2. **Critical Thinking** Draw a triangle that has three lines of symmetry.

Transformations and Symmetry

BEFORE

You identified congruent figures.

▶ **Now**

You'll identify transformations and symmetry in figures.

WHY?

So you can find the symmetry in an insect, as in Ex. 20.

Word Watch

transformation, p. 511
image, p. 511
translation, p. 511
reflection, p. 511
line of reflection, p. 511
rotation, p. 511
center of rotation, p. 511
angle of rotation, p. 512
line symmetry, p. 513
line of symmetry, p. 513
rotational symmetry, p. 513

A **transformation** is a movement of a figure in a plane. The new figure formed by a transformation is the **image** . In this book, the original figure will always be blue and the image will always be red. Each of the three transformations illustrated below results in an image that is congruent to the original figure.

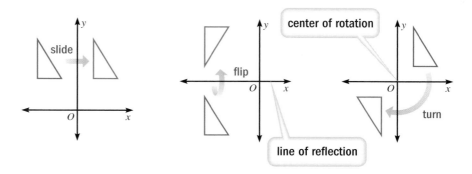

In a **translation** , or *slide*, each point of a figure is moved the same distance in the same direction. In the translation above, the triangle is translated to the right.

In a **reflection** , or *flip*, a figure is reflected in a line called the **line of reflection** , creating a mirror image of the figure. In the reflection above, the triangle is reflected in the *x*-axis.

In a **rotation** , or *turn*, a figure is rotated through a given angle and in a given direction about a fixed point called the **center of rotation** . In the rotation above, the triangle is rotated 180° about the origin.

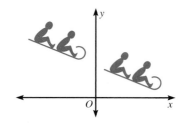

EXAMPLE 1 Identifying a Translation

Tell whether the image is a translation of the original figure. Explain your reasoning.

Each point on the original figure is moved the same number of units in a "downhill" direction. The image is a translation of the original figure.

EXAMPLE 2 Identifying a Reflection

Tell whether the image is a reflection of the original figure. If it is, identify the line of reflection.

The two figures are mirror images of each other, so the image is a reflection of the original figure. The line of reflection is the *x*-axis.

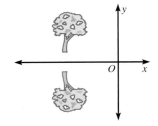

HELP with **Reading**

Clockwise means to go in the direction of the hands on a clock. Counterclockwise means to go in the opposite direction.

Rotations The center of rotation for all rotations in this book will be the origin. Rays drawn from the center of rotation through corresponding points on an original figure and its image form an angle called the **angle of rotation** . Rotations are described by the angle and direction of rotation. The direction of rotation can be either *clockwise* or *counterclockwise*. The figure at the right is rotated 45° clockwise about the origin.

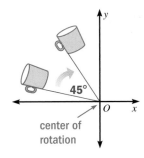

EXAMPLE 3 Identifying a Rotation

Tell whether the image is a rotation of the original figure. If it is, give the angle and direction of rotation.

The image is a rotation of the original figure about the origin. The original figure is rotated 90° counterclockwise.

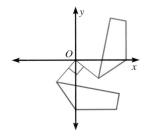

Your turn now Identify the transformation. If it is a reflection, identify the line of reflection. If it is a rotation, give the angle and direction of rotation.

1.

2.

3.

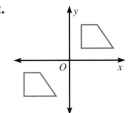
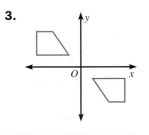

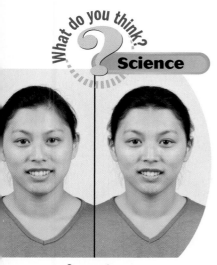

■ **Symmetry**

A person's face appears to have line symmetry, but the two parts are not exact mirror images. One of the pictures above is a normal photograph of a woman. The other is the right side of the woman's face and its exact mirror image. Explain how you can tell which picture is which.

Symmetry A figure has **line symmetry** if it can be divided by a line, called a **line of symmetry**, into two parts that are mirror images of each other. A figure has **rotational symmetry** if a turn of 180° or less produces an image that fits exactly on the original figure. The center of rotation for checking rotational symmetry in this book will always be the center of the figure.

EXAMPLE 4 **Identifying Symmetry**

Tell whether the mirror shown below has (a) line symmetry and (b) rotational symmetry.

a. The mirror has line symmetry. There are 4 lines of symmetry.

b. The mirror has rotational symmetry. A turn of 90° or 180° clockwise (or counterclockwise) produces an image that fits exactly on the original figure.

10.7 Exercises
More Practice, p. 714

INTERNET
eWorkbook Plus
CLASSZONE.COM

Getting Ready to Practice

1. **Vocabulary** Copy and complete: A transformation that results in a mirror image of the original figure is a(n) ? .

Identify the transformation. If it is a reflection, identify the line of reflection. If it is a rotation, give the angle and direction of rotation.

2.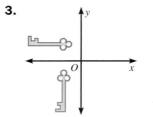

3.

4.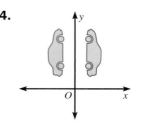

Practice and Problem Solving

with Homework

Example	Exercises
1	5-7
2	5-7
3	5-10
4	12-17, 19-20

Online Resources
CLASSZONE.COM
· More Examples
· eTutorial Plus

Identify the transformation. If it is a reflection, identify the line of reflection. If it is a rotation, give the angle and direction of rotation.

5.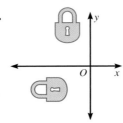

6.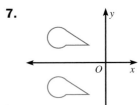

7.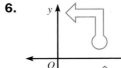

Match the figure with the correct rotation description.

8.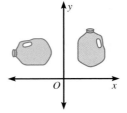

9.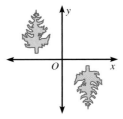

10.

A. 90° counterclockwise **B.** 180° counterclockwise **C.** 90° clockwise

11. Writing Explain why the words *clockwise* and *counterclockwise* do not need to be used to describe a 180° rotation.

Sketch the figure and draw any line(s) of symmetry. Then tell whether the figure has rotational symmetry. If it does, give the angle(s) and direction of rotation.

12.

13.

14.

15.

16.

17.

18. Compare and Contrast Explain how a line of reflection and a line of symmetry are alike and how they are different.

19. Geometry Draw two polygons that have rotational symmetry. Then give the angle(s) and direction of rotation.

20. Biology The bodies of most animals show some kind of symmetry. Many animals have *bilateral symmetry*, meaning that their bodies can be divided into roughly identical halves along a single plane. Where would a plane divide this stag beetle into two identical halves? How are bilateral symmetry and line symmetry alike? How are they different?

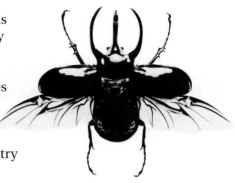

21. Challenge A figure has line symmetry. Does the number of lines of symmetry in the figure change when the figure is translated? rotated? reflected? Explain your reasoning.

Mixed Review

Draw the graph of the line that passes through the points. Then find the slope of the line. *(Lesson 8.3)*

22. (3, 3), (7, 6) **23.** (0, 0), (−3, −9) **24.** (6, −1), (4, 3)

Find the unknown length *x* given that the polygons are similar. *(Lesson 10.6)*

25. 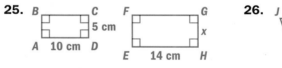 **26.**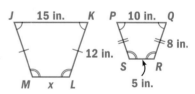

Basic Skills **Find the mean, median, mode(s), and range of the data.**

27. 20, 54, 21, 81, 64, 19, 22, 20 **28.** 4.2, 0, 5, 2.8, 4.6

Test-Taking Practice

29. Multiple Choice Which describes the transformation shown?

A. Translation **B.** Reflection in the *x*-axis

C. Rotation **D.** Reflection in the *y*-axis

30. Multiple Choice Which letter has both a vertical line of symmetry and a horizontal line of symmetry?

F. T **G.** S **H.** H **I.** E

Tessellations

GOAL Recognize and design tessellations.

A **tessellation** is a covering of a plane with congruent copies of the same pattern so that there are no gaps or overlaps. A **regular tessellation** is made from only one type of regular polygon. The figure below is a regular tessellation made from regular triangles.

EXAMPLE 1 **Identifying Polygons that Tessellate**

Tell whether each type of polygon can form a regular tessellation.

a. Square

b. Regular pentagon

Solution

a. Start with a square. Make copies of the square and fit them together so that they cover the plane without gaps or overlaps. One possible arrangement is shown. So, a square forms a regular tessellation.

b. Start with a regular pentagon. Make copies of the pentagon. When you try to fit them together, you find that three pentagons can share a common vertex, but there is a gap that is too small to fit a fourth pentagon. So, a regular pentagon does not form a regular tessellation.

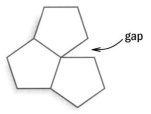

gap

Other Tessellations You can also make tessellations using one or more nonregular polygons by translating, reflecting, or rotating the figures to cover a plane. An isosceles triangle is reflected and translated to form the tessellation at the right.

EXAMPLE **2** **Making a Tessellation**

**Make a tessellation of the quadrilateral shown.
Describe the transformation(s) you use.**

(1 Mark the point at the middle of one of the sides of the quadrilateral. Then rotate the quadrilateral 180° about that point.

(2 Translate the new figure as shown. The pattern that results covers the plane without gaps or overlaps. So, the quadrilateral forms a tessellation.

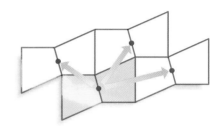

Exercises

Tell whether the polygon can form a regular tessellation. If it can, draw the tessellation.

1. Regular hexagon

2. Regular heptagon

Make a tessellation of the indicated polygon. Describe the transformation(s) you use.

3. Parallelogram

4. Right triangle

5. Can you make a tessellation of the quadrilateral shown in Example 2 using *only* rotations? *only* translations? *only* reflections? Explain your reasoning.

Tell whether the two polygons can be used to make a tessellation. If they can, draw the tessellation.

6. A regular octagon and a square with all sides from both figures equal in length

7. A regular triangle and a rhombus with all sides from both figures equal in length

8. Critical Thinking In the tessellation shown at the top of page 516, notice that six triangles fit around a common vertex because each angle at the vertex measures 60°, for a total of 360°. Explain how this observation applies to the square and pentagon in Example 1.

Transformations in the Coordinate Plane

BEFORE	▶ Now	WHY?
You identified translations, reflections, and rotations.	You'll graph transformations in a coordinate plane.	So you can describe movement in a cartoon, as in Ex. 17.

In the Real World

Computer Graphics Computer and video game programmers use transformations to create patterns and animations. How can you use coordinates to describe the transformation shown?

The transformation is a translation. You can use *coordinate notation* to describe a translation. An arrow is used in coordinate notation to signify "goes to."

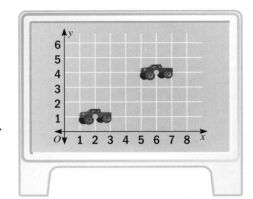

Coordinates of   Coordinates
original point   of image

$$(x, y) \rightarrow (x + a, y + b)$$

The number *a* tells how many units to shift the figure to the **left or right**.

The number *b* tells how many units to shift the figure **up or down**.

EXAMPLE 1 Describing a Translation

You can use coordinate notation to describe the translation shown above. Each point on the original figure is moved 4 units to the left and 3 units down.

ANSWER In coordinate notation you write this translation as:

$(x, y) \rightarrow (x + (-4), y + (-3))$ or $(x, y) \rightarrow (x - 4, y - 3)$

Your turn now Describe the translation using coordinate notation.

1. A figure is moved 5 units to the right and 4 units up.

2. A figure is moved 7 units to the left and 2 units up.

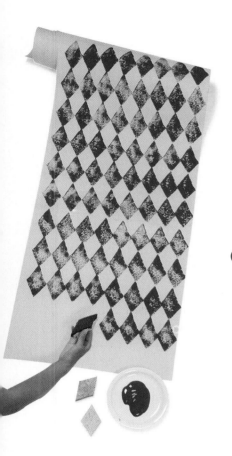

EXAMPLE 2 **Translating a Figure**

Draw quadrilateral *JKLM* with vertices $J(-5, 3)$, $K(-4, 5)$, $L(-3, 3)$, and $M(-4, 1)$. Then find the coordinates of the vertices of the image after the translation $(x, y) \rightarrow (x + 6, y - 2)$, and draw the image.

For each vertex of the original figure, add 6 to the *x*-coordinate and subtract 2 from the *y*-coordinate.

Original   **Image**

$J(-5, 3) \rightarrow J'(1, 1)$

$K(-4, 5) \rightarrow K'(2, 3)$

$L(-3, 3) \rightarrow L'(3, 1)$

$M(-4, 1) \rightarrow M'(2, -1)$

Each point on the original figure is translated 6 units to the right and 2 units down. The graph shows both figures.

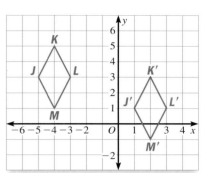

Your turn now **Complete the following exercise.**

3. Draw $\triangle ABC$ with vertices $A(-4, 0)$, $B(0, -4)$, and $C(0, 0)$. Then find the coordinates of the vertices of the image after the translation $(x, y) \rightarrow (x + 4, y + 6)$, and draw the image.

Reflections You can also use coordinate notation to describe reflections.

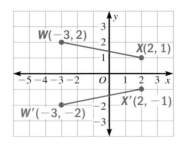 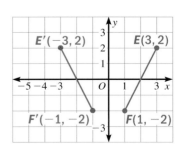

Reflection in the *x*-axis:

Multiply *y*-coordinate by -1.
   $(x, y) \rightarrow (x, -1 \cdot y)$ or
   $(x, y) \rightarrow (x, -y)$

Reflection in the *y*-axis:

Multiply *x*-coordinate by -1.
   $(x, y) \rightarrow (-1 \cdot x, y)$ or
   $(x, y) \rightarrow (-x, y)$

EXAMPLE 3 **Reflecting a Figure**

Draw parallelogram *ABCD* with vertices *A*(−3, 3), *B*(2, 3), *C*(4, 1), and *D*(−1, 1). Then find the coordinates of the vertices of the image after a reflection in the *x*-axis, and draw the image.

For each vertex of the original figure, multiply the *y*-coordinate by −1.

Original   Image

$A(-3, 3) \rightarrow A'(-3, -3)$

$B(2, 3)\ \ \rightarrow B'(2, -3)$

$C(4, 1)\ \ \rightarrow C'(4, -1)$

$D(-1, 1) \rightarrow D'(-1, -1)$

The graph shows both figures.

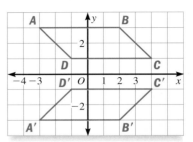

10.8 Exercises

More Practice, p. 714

INTERNET
eWorkbook Plus
CLASSZONE.COM

Getting Ready to Practice

1. **Vocabulary** Copy and complete: The figure that results from performing a transformation on an original figure is called the __?__.

Describe the translation using coordinate notation.

2.
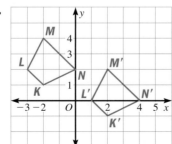

3.
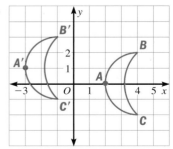

Draw △*GHJ* with vertices *G*(−4, 1), *H*(−2, 4), and *J*(0, 1). Then find the coordinates of the vertices of the image after the specified transformation, and draw the image.

4. $(x, y) \rightarrow (x - 4, y + 4)$

5. $(x, y) \rightarrow (x + 2, y - 3)$

6. Reflect △*GHJ* in the *x*-axis.

7. Reflect △*GHJ* in the *y*-axis.

Practice and Problem Solving

with Homework

Example	Exercises
1	8–9, 17
2	10–16, 18
3	13–16

Online Resources
CLASSZONE.COM

· More Examples
· eTutorial Plus

Describe the transformation using coordinate notation.

8.
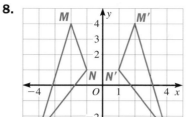

9.
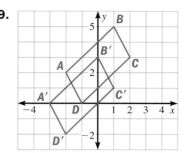

Draw the triangle with the given vertices. Then find the coordinates of the vertices of the image after the specified translation, and draw the image.

10. $P(1, 1)$, $Q(3, 5)$, $R(5, 4)$; $(x, y) \rightarrow (x - 2, y - 4)$

11. $F(-2, 3)$, $G(3, 3)$, $H(3, -1)$; $(x, y) \rightarrow (x - 3, y - 6)$

12. $L(-6, 0)$, $M(-6, -4)$, $N(-3, -4)$; $(x, y) \rightarrow (x, y + 5)$

Draw rectangle *FGHJ* with vertices *F*(−2, 3), *G*(3, 3), *H*(3, −1), and *J*(−2, −1). Then find the coordinates of the vertices of the image after the specified transformation, and draw the image.

13. $(x, y) \rightarrow (x + 3, y + 6)$ **14.** $(x, y) \rightarrow (x - 7, y)$

15. Reflect *FGHJ* in the *x*-axis. **16.** Reflect *FGHJ* in the *y*-axis.

17. Motion Transformations can be used to show motion. Use coordinate notation to describe the transformation of the drummer from one picture to the next picture.

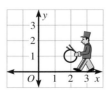 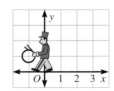 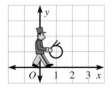 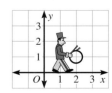

18. Explain Draw a rectangle with vertices $K(0, 0)$, $L(-3, 0)$, $M(-3, 4)$, and $N(0, 4)$. Find the length, width, and area of the rectangle. Then translate the rectangle 2 units to the right. Find the length, width, and area of the image. Explain your results.

19. Critical Thinking Draw one triangle with vertices (2, 1), (3, 4), and (4, 1) and a second triangle with vertices (−4, 1), (−3, 4), and (−2, 1). Describe two different transformations that could move the first triangle onto the second.

What do you think?

Art

■ **Motion**

Photography can show motion by using repeated flashes to record overlapping images. Capturing a drum stroke may require 200 flashes in 4 seconds. What is this rate as a unit rate?

Rotations In Exercises 20–23, the vertices of a triangle are given. Find the coordinates of the vertices of the image after a rotation of 90° clockwise about the origin. The coordinate notation $(x, y) \rightarrow (y, -x)$ describes such a rotation.

20. $F(0, 2), G(-3, 1), H(-1, 1)$ **21.** $L(2, 2), M(4, -1), N(2, -2)$

22. $R(-3, 3), S(-3, 0), T(-1, 0)$ **23.** $W(0, 0), X(5, -3), Y(3, 4)$

24. Critical Thinking The vertices of quadrilateral $ABCD$ are $A(-3, 4)$, $B(2, 4), C(3, 2)$, and $D(-4, -1)$. After a translation, the coordinates of A' are $(-5, 1)$. Describe the translation using coordinate notation. Then find the coordinates of B', C', and D'.

25. Challenge Line segment EF has endpoints $E(4, 3)$ and $F(4, -3)$. Its image after a 180° rotation has endpoints $E'(-4, -3)$ and $F'(-4, 3)$. Describe a 180° rotation using coordinate notation.

Mixed Review

Solve the equation. Check your solution. *(Lesson 7.5)*

26. $3x + 5 = 23$ **27.** $8 - 4x = -20$ **28.** $35 = 3 - 16x$

29. Choose a Strategy Use a strategy from the list to solve the following problem. Explain your choice of strategy.

You paid three times as much for lunch as you paid for a snack. Altogether, you spent $5. How much did you pay for the snack? for lunch?

> *Problem Solving Strategies*
> - *Guess, Check, and Revise*
> - *Write an Equation*
> - *Look for a Pattern*

Basic Skills Copy and complete the statement.

30. $0.53 \text{ kg} = \underline{?} \text{ g}$ **31.** $8.9 \text{ m} = \underline{?} \text{ cm}$ **32.** $62 \text{ mL} = \underline{?} \text{ L}$

Test-Taking Practice

33. Extended Response Describe a combination of two transformations that would move figure A to figure B. Then describe a combination of two transformations that would move figure B to figure A.

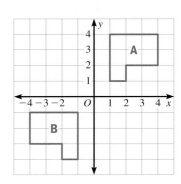

Translating Points

GOAL Use a spreadsheet to graph translations in the coordinate plane.

Example **Translate the point (3, 4) left 1 unit and up 2 units.**

1 In rows 1 and 2, enter the labels for and the coordinates of the original point.

2 In rows 3 and 4, enter the labels and the numbers for the translation.

	A	B
1	Original *x*	3
2	Original *y*	4
3	Translate left/right	−1
4	Translate up/down	2
5	Image *x*	=B1+B3
6	Image *y*	=B2+B4

3 In rows 5 and 6, enter the labels and the formulas for the coordinates of the image.

4 Draw the graph by selecting Insert, then Chart. Choose XY (Scatter) as the chart type, and click Next. Under the Series tab, click Add and enter "=Sheet1!$B$1" for X values and "=Sheet1!$B$2" for Y values. Then click Add, and enter "=Sheet1!$B$5" for X values and "=Sheet1!$B$6" for Y values. Click Next, and make sure that the Major Gridlines boxes are checked under the Gridlines tab. Click Next, then Finish.

5 You can change the numbers in cells B3 and B4 to produce other translations of the original point.

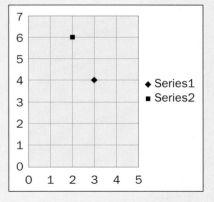

Your turn now **Use the spreadsheet to translate the point (3, 4) as specified.**

1. 3 units to the right and 6 units down

2. 2 units to the left and 7 units up

3. $(x, y) \rightarrow (x - 5, y - 2)$

4. $(x, y) \rightarrow (x + 1, y + 3)$

Notebook Review

Review the vocabulary definitions in your notebook.

Copy the review examples in your notebook. Then complete the exercises.

Check Your Definitions

similar polygons, p. 502	translation, p. 511	angle of rotation, p. 512
congruent polygons, p. 502	reflection, p. 511	line symmetry, p. 513
	line of reflection, p. 511	line of symmetry, p. 513
transformation, p. 511	rotation, p. 511	rotational symmetry,
image, p. 511	center of rotation, p. 511	p. 513

Use Your Vocabulary

1. Writing Are two congruent polygons always similar? Are two similar polygons always congruent? Explain.

10.5–10.6 Can you use properties of similar polygons?

 EXAMPLE Given that $\triangle BCD \sim \triangle FGH$, (a) name the corresponding sides and corresponding angles, and (b) find *FG*.

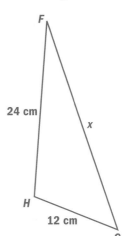

a. Corresponding sides: $\overline{BC}$ and $\overline{FG}$, $\overline{CD}$ and $\overline{GH}$, $\overline{DB}$ and $\overline{HF}$

Corresponding angles: $\angle B$ and $\angle F$, $\angle C$ and $\angle G$, $\angle D$ and $\angle H$

b.

$\dfrac{BC}{FG} = \dfrac{DB}{HF}$	Write proportion involving **FG**.
$\dfrac{10}{x} = \dfrac{8}{24}$	Substitute known values.
$10 \cdot 24 = x \cdot 8$	Cross products property
$\dfrac{10 \cdot 24}{8} = \dfrac{x \cdot 8}{8}$	Divide each side by 8.
$30 = x$	Simplify.

ANSWER The length of $\overline{FG}$ is 30 centimeters.

☑ **2.** Find *CD* in the example above.

10.7–10.8 Can you describe transformations?

 Review

EXAMPLE Describe the translation using coordinate notation.

Each point on the original
figure is moved 7 units to
the left and 3 units down.
In coordinate notation
you write this translation
as $(x, y) \rightarrow (x - 7, y - 3)$.

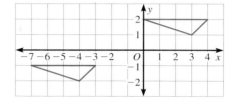

 3. Draw $\triangle FGH$ with vertices $F(-2, 1)$, $G(-3, 3)$, and $H(-6, 3)$. Then
find the coordinates of the vertices of the image after a reflection
in the y-axis, and draw the image.

Stop *and* **Think** about Lessons 10.5–10.8

4. Writing If you translate a figure and then translate it again, is the
image that results a translation of the original figure? Explain your
reasoning.

5. Critical Thinking Copy and complete using *always*, *sometimes*, or
never: A right triangle and a regular triangle are _?_ similar.

Review Quiz 2

**In Exercises 1 and 2, use the diagram and the fact that
$\triangle JKL \sim \triangle FGH$.**

1. Name the corresponding sides
and corresponding angles.

2. Find $m\angle G$.

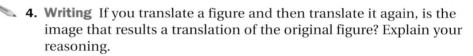

3. Geometry Sketch a regular pentagon and draw any lines of symmetry.
Then tell whether the figure has rotational symmetry. If it does, give the
angle(s) and direction of rotation.

**Draw quadrilateral *QRST* with vertices *Q*(3, 2), *R*(4, 5), *S*(−2, 4),
and *T*(−1, 1). Then find the coordinates of the vertices of the
image after the specified transformation, and draw the image.**

4. $(x, y) \rightarrow (x - 4, y - 8)$ **5.** Reflect *QRST* in the *x*-axis.

Chapter Review

 **Vocabulary**

angles: acute, right,
  obtuse, straight, p. 475
complementary, p. 476
supplementary, p. 476
adjacent angles, p. 479
vertical angles, p. 479
congruent angles, p. 479
plane, p. 480
lines: parallel,
  intersecting,
  perpendicular, p. 480
corresponding angles,
  p. 480

triangles: acute, right,
  obtuse, p. 485
congruent sides, p. 486
triangles: equilateral,
  isosceles, scalene,
  p. 486
quadrilaterals: trapezoid,
  parallelogram,
  rhombus, p. 494
polygons: pentagon,
  hexagon, heptagon,
  octagon, p. 495
regular polygon, p. 496

similar polygons, p. 502
congruent polygons,
  p. 502
transformations:
  translation, reflection,
  rotation, p. 511
image, p. 511
line of reflection, p. 511
center of rotation, p. 511
angle of rotation, p. 512
line symmetry, p. 513
line of symmetry, p. 513
rotational symmetry,
  p. 513

Vocabulary Review

1. What is the measure of a straight angle?

2. How are parallel lines different from perpendicular lines?

3. How many congruent sides does a scalene triangle have?

4. Which type of quadrilateral is not a parallelogram? Explain why it is not.

5. In your own words, describe a line of symmetry.

6. Draw a figure that has rotational symmetry.

Review Questions

Classify the angle as *acute*, *right*, *obtuse*, or *straight*. Then, find the measure of a supplementary angle and the measure of a complementary angle, if possible. *(Lesson 10.1)*

7. $m\angle A = 25°$ **8.** $m\angle B = 140°$ **9.** $m\angle C = 5°$ **10.** $m\angle D = 90°$

In Exercises 11–15, refer to the diagram. *(Lesson 10.2)*

11. Name two parallel lines.

12. Name two intersecting lines.

13. Name two adjacent, supplementary angles.

14. Find $m\angle 2$.   **15.** Find $m\angle 4$.

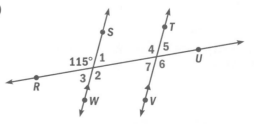

Find the value of *x* or *y*. Then classify the triangle by its angle measures. *(Lesson 10.3)*

16.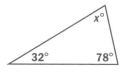

17.

18.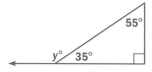

Tell whether the figure is a polygon. If it is a polygon, classify it and tell if it is regular. If it is not a polygon, explain why not. *(Lesson 10.4)*

19.

20.

21.

22. Given that $\triangle ABC \cong \triangle XYZ$, name the corresponding sides and corresponding angles. Then find the unknown measures. *(Lesson 10.5)*

23. Tell whether the two polygons are similar. If they are similar, find the ratio of the lengths of the corresponding sides of figure A to figure B. *(Lesson 10.5)*

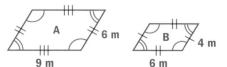

24. Movie Posters A rectangular movie poster has a length of 28 inches and a width of 22 inches. A print of the poster is similar to the original and has a length of 14 inches. What is the width of the print? *(Lesson 10.6)*

25. How many lines of symmetry does a regular triangle have? Explain your reasoning. *(Lesson 10.7)*

26. Tell whether the image is a *translation, reflection,* or *rotation* of the original figure. If it is a translation, describe it using coordinate notation. If it is a reflection, identify the line of reflection. If it is a rotation, give the angle and direction of rotation. *(Lessons 10.7, 10.8)*

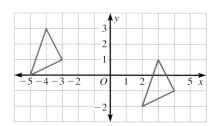

Draw quadrilateral *ABCD* with vertices *A*(−2, −1), *B*(−5, −2), *C*(−3, −5), and *D*(2, −2). Then find the coordinates of the vertices of the image after the specified transformation, and draw the image. *(Lesson 10.8)*

27. $(x, y) \rightarrow (x + 6, y - 2)$

28. $(x, y) \rightarrow (x - 7, y - 4)$

29. Reflect *ABCD* in the *x*-axis.

Chapter Test

Tell whether ∠A and ∠B are *complementary*, *supplementary*, or *neither*. Explain your reasoning.

1. $m\angle A = 21°$, $m\angle B = 79°$
2. $m\angle A = 45°$, $m\angle B = 135°$
3. $m\angle A = 48°$, $m\angle B = 42°$

Find the unknown angle measures.

4.

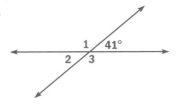

5.

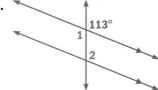

6.

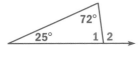

7. The measures of two of the angles in a triangle are 63° and 26°. Find the measure of the third angle. Then classify the triangle by its angle measures.

Classify the polygon and tell if it is regular. If it is not regular, explain why not.

8.

9.

10.

11. Given that $\triangle QRS \cong \triangle XYZ$, name the corresponding sides and the corresponding angles. Then find XZ and YZ.

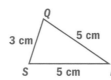

12. Building Height A building casts a 50 foot shadow at the same time that a 5 foot sign casts a 2 foot shadow. What is the height of the building?

13. Draw a polygon that has exactly 4 lines of symmetry.

14. Draw rectangle $CDEF$ with vertices $C(0, 0)$, $D(0, -4)$, $E(-4, -4)$, and $F(-4, 0)$. Then find the coordinates of the vertices of the image after the translation $(x, y) \rightarrow (x - 5, y + 2)$, and draw the image.

15. Draw $\triangle FGH$ with vertices $F(-8, 6)$, $G(-4, 7)$, and $H(-2, 4)$. Then find the coordinates of the vertices of the image after a reflection in the y-axis, and draw the image.

Chapter Standardized Test

Test-Taking Strategy Do not worry about how fast others are working. Work at the pace that is right for you.

Multiple Choice

1. What is the measure of an angle that is complementary to an angle measuring 73°?

    A. 17°   **B.** 73°   **C.** 107°   **D.** 163°

2. Find the value of x.

    F. 28   **G.** 62   **H.** 118   **I.** 124

3. Find the value of y.

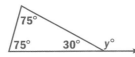

    A. 30   **B.** 60   **C.** 75   **D.** 150

4. Which of the following statements *cannot* be true about a triangle?

    F. It is obtuse and right.

    G. It is acute and equilateral.

    H. It is obtuse and isosceles.

    I. It is right and isosceles.

5. What is the the perimeter a regular octagon with a side length of 8 meters?

    A. 16 m   **B.** 48 m   **C.** 64 m   **D.** 80 m

6. Quadrilateral *ABCD* is congruent to quadrilateral *EFGH*. Which side of quadrilateral *EFGH* corresponds to $\overline{AD}$?

    F. $\overline{EF}$ **G.** $\overline{FG}$ **H.** $\overline{GH}$ **I.** $\overline{EH}$

7. Rectangle A has a length of 10 inches and a width of 6 inches and is similar to rectangle B. Rectangle B has a width of 9 inches. What is the length of rectangle B?

    A. 5 inches   **B.** 5.4 inches

    C. 13 inches   **D.** 15 inches

8. Identify the transformation.

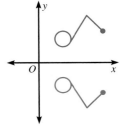

    F. Translation

    G. Reflection in x-axis

    H. Reflection in y-axis

    I. Rotation

9. The point $(2, 7)$ is reflected in the x-axis. What are the coordinates of the image?

    A. $(2, 7)$ **B.** $(2, -7)$ **C.** $(-2, 7)$ **D.** $(-2, -7)$

Short Response

10. A 7 foot tall welcome sign in a city park casts a shadow that is 2 feet long. At the same time, a monument in the park casts a shadow that is 16 feet long. Draw a diagram to represent the situation. Then find the height of the monument.

Extended Response

11. Sketch each figure and draw any line(s) of symmetry. Then tell whether each figure has rotational symmetry. If a figure does have rotational symmetry, give the angle(s) and direction of rotation.

Measurement and Area

Chapter Warm-Up Games

Review skills you need for this chapter in these quick games.

In previous chapters you've...

- Evaluated powers
- Classified polygons
- Explored congruent and similar polygons

Now

In Chapter 11 you'll study...

- Square roots
- The Pythagorean theorem
- Areas of parallelograms, triangles, trapezoids, and circles

WHY?

So you can solve real-world problems about...

- pole vaulting, p. 533
- television screens, p. 546
- geometric art, p. 555
- giant sequoias, p. 564
- circus rings, p. 568

 Internet Preview
CLASSZONE.COM

- eEdition Plus Online
- eWorkbook Plus Online
- eTutorial Plus Online
- State Test Practice
- More Examples

Key Skill:
Evaluating powers

- Evaluate the powers. Order the answers from least to greatest. Then write the letters associated with these answers in the same order to spell out the name of the world's longest suspension bridge. The name consists of two six-letter words.

- Now cross off the answers that are divisible by 3. Cross off the answers that are greater than 100 but less than 200. Add the three remaining numbers to find the length, in feet, of the main span of the bridge. The main span lies between the two towers of the bridge.

Key Skill:
Classifying polygons

The bridge above is drawn on graph paper. All line segments
that appear to be equal in length are equal in length. All
yellow segments intersect at right angles, and yellow
segments that have the same slope are parallel.

• Find at least 20 triangles in the bridge.

• Find at least 3 rectangles in the bridge.

• Find at least 9 parallelograms in the bridge.

• Find at least 13 trapezoids in the bridge.

Stop *and* Think

1. **Writing** In *Exponent Suspension*, how can you tell by looking at the
   base of a power whether the power is divisible by 3?

2. **Critical Thinking** In *Building Bridges*, all the triangles are isosceles
   right triangles. Each triangle has two congruent angles. What is the
   measure of each of these angles? Explain how you know.

Getting Ready to Learn

Review What You Need to Know

Using Vocabulary **Copy and complete using a review word.**

Word Watch

Review Words

perimeter, p. 32
area, p. 32
trapezoid, p. 494
parallelogram, p. 494

1. A(n) ? is a quadrilateral with exactly one pair of parallel sides.

2. The ? of a figure is measured in units such as square inches (in.²) and square meters (m²).

Evaluate the expression when $p = 3$ and $q = 6$. *(pp. 18, 272)*

3. p^3 **4.** $p^3 + q$ **5.** $q^2 - 4p$

6. $-6q + q^3$ **7.** $-3p^2 + pq$ **8.** pq^2

Find the perimeter and the area of the rectangle. *(pp. 32, 63, 216)*

9.
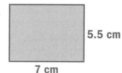
5.5 cm
7 cm

10.

5.2 mm
5 mm

11.

$1\frac{1}{2}$ ft
$\frac{3}{4}$ ft

Know How to Take Notes

Illustrating with Examples In your notebook, include examples that illustrate how a math concept is applied or how a formula is used. You may want to divide your notebook page in half lengthwise, with concepts or formulas on the left and examples on the right.

You should include material that appears on a notebook like this in your own notes.

Formula	Example
distance = rate × time	You drive for 3.5 hours at 60 miles per hour. How far do you travel?
d = rt	d = rt
	= 60(3.5)
	= 210 miles

In Chapter 11, you will use formulas to find areas of different geometric figures. You can use the strategy above to organize these formulas.

Square Roots

BEFORE	▶ Now	WHY?
You evaluated expressions involving squares.	You'll evaluate expressions involving square roots.	So you can find the dimensions of a crater, as in Ex. 45.

Word Watch

square root, p. 533
perfect square, p. 533
radical expression, p. 534

In the Real World

Pole Vaulting How fast should a pole vaulter run to vault over a height of 16 feet? You'll find the answer in Example 3.

Square Roots The minimum speed that a pole vaulter needs to run in order to vault over a given height can be found using an equation involving a *square root*. A **square root** of a number n is a number m which, when multiplied by itself, equals n.

If $m^2 = n$, then m is a square root of n.

Numbers that are squares of integers, such as $1 = 1^2$ and $4 = 2^2$, are called **perfect squares**. In this lesson, you will find square roots of perfect squares.

EXAMPLE 1 Finding Square Roots

a. You know that $9^2 = 81$ and $(-9)^2 = 81$. Therefore, the square roots of 81 are 9 and −9.

b. You know that $7^2 = 49$ and $(-7)^2 = 49$. Therefore, the square roots of 49 are 7 and −7.

HELP with Reading

The expression $\sqrt{4}$ is read "the positive square root of 4."

Radical Signs The symbol $\sqrt{}$, called a *radical sign*, represents a nonnegative square root. For example, $\sqrt{4} = 2$ is the positive square root of 4, and $-\sqrt{4} = -2$ is the negative square root of 4.

EXAMPLE 2 Evaluating Square Roots

a. $\sqrt{36} = 6$ because $6^2 = 36$.

b. You know that $\sqrt{16} = 4$ because $4^2 = 16$. So, $-\sqrt{16} = -4$.

c. $\sqrt{0} = 0$ because $0^2 = 0$.

EXAMPLE 3 **Solving a Square Root Equation**

To find the minimum speed of the pole vaulter described on page 533, you can use the equation $s = 8\sqrt{h}$, where s is the pole vaulter's speed, in feet per second, and h is the height vaulted, in feet. If the pole vaulter vaults over a height of 16 feet, find the pole vaulter's minimum speed.

$s = 8\sqrt{h}$ Write equation for speed of a pole vaulter.

$ = 8\sqrt{16}$ Substitute 16 for h.

$ = 8(4) = 32$ Evaluate square root. Then multiply.

ANSWER The pole vaulter's minimum speed is 32 feet per second.

Your turn now Find the two square roots of the number.

1. 9   **2.** 64   **3.** 100   **4.** 169

Evaluate the square root.

5. $\sqrt{25}$ **6.** $-\sqrt{1}$ **7.** $-\sqrt{144}$ **8.** $\sqrt{121}$

Radical Expressions An expression involving a radical sign is called a **radical expression**. The horizontal bar on a radical sign acts as a grouping symbol, so you evaluate the expression under a radical sign before evaluating the square root.

EXAMPLE 4 **Evaluating Radical Expressions**

HELP with **Review**

Need help with order of operations? See p. 18.

Evaluate the expression when $z = 7$ and $m = -2$.

a. $\sqrt{29 + z}$ **b.** $\sqrt{z^2 + m^2 + 11}$

Solution

a. $\sqrt{29 + z} = \sqrt{29 + 7}$ Substitute 7 for z.

$\phantom{\sqrt{29 + z}} = \sqrt{36}$ Add.

$\phantom{\sqrt{29 + z}} = 6$ Evaluate square root.

b. $\sqrt{z^2 + m^2 + 11} = \sqrt{(7)^2 + (-2)^2 + 11}$ Substitute 7 for z and -2 for m.

$\phantom{\sqrt{z^2 + m^2 + 11}} = \sqrt{49 + 4 + 11}$ Evaluate powers.

$\phantom{\sqrt{z^2 + m^2 + 11}} = \sqrt{64}$ Add.

$\phantom{\sqrt{z^2 + m^2 + 11}} = 8$ Evaluate square root.

EXAMPLE 5 **Solving Equations Using Square Roots**

Solve the equation.

a. $x^2 = 25$ **b.** $h^2 + 5 = 54$

HELP with **Reading**

The symbol $\pm$ is read "plus or minus." The statement $x = \pm 5$ means that 5 and -5 are solutions of $x^2 = 25$.

Solution

a. $x^2 = 25$ Write original equation.

     $x = \pm\sqrt{25}$ Use definition of square root.

     $x = \pm 5$ Evaluate square root.

b. $h^2 + 5 = 54$ Write original equation.

     $h^2 + 5 - 5 = 54 - 5$ Subtract 5 from each side.

     $h^2 = 49$ Simplify.

     $h = \pm\sqrt{49}$ Use definition of square root.

     $h = \pm 7$ Evaluate square root.

Your turn now **Solve the equation.**

9. $x^2 = 1$ **10.** $x^2 + 7 = 88$ **11.** $12x^2 = 108$ **12.** $x^2 - 5 = -1$

11.1 **Exercises**

More Practice, p. 715

INTERNET
eWorkbook Plus
CLASSZONE.COM

Getting Ready to Practice

1. Vocabulary Copy and complete: A(n) _?_ is an expression involving a radical sign.

2. Find the Error Describe and correct the error in evaluating $\sqrt{16}$.

$$\sqrt{16} = 8$$
Check: $8 \times 2 = 16$

Evaluate the expression when $h = 11$ and $m = 6$.

3. $\sqrt{4h - 8}$ **4.** $-\sqrt{h^2}$ **5.** $-\sqrt{24m}$ **6.** $\sqrt{10m + 21}$

Solve the equation.

7. $b^2 = 4$ **8.** $a^2 = 16$ **9.** $c^2 + 9 = 34$ **10.** $8 + t^2 = 89$

11. Dance Floor The area of a square dance floor is 256 square feet. What is the side length of the dance floor?

Practice and Problem Solving

Find the two square roots of the number.

12. 625   **13.** 900   **14.** 289   **15.** 729

16. 484   **17.** 10,000   **18.** 441   **19.** 529

Example	Exercises
1	12–19, 46–49
2	20–27
3	28, 55
4	32–37
5	38–43

Online Resources
CLASSZONE.COM
· More Examples
· eTutorial Plus

Evaluate the square root.

20. $\sqrt{81}$ **21.** $\sqrt{225}$ **22.** $-\sqrt{169}$ **23.** $-\sqrt{324}$

24. $-\sqrt{1225}$ **25.** $-\sqrt{676}$ **26.** $\sqrt{361}$ **27.** $\sqrt{1024}$

28. Distance to the Horizon When you look at the horizon, the approximate distance to the horizon can be found using the equation $d = 112.88\sqrt{h}$, where d is the distance to the horizon, in kilometers, and h is your height above the ground, in kilometers. Find the approximate distance to the horizon if you are on top of a mountain that is 4 kilometers high.

Geometry **Find the side length of a square having the given area.**

29. $A = 49 \text{ cm}^2$ **30.** $A = 64 \text{ yd}^2$ **31.** $A = 196 \text{ m}^2$

Evaluate the expression when $x = 3$, $y = 4$, and $z = -1$.

32. $-\sqrt{7x + 100}$ **33.** $\sqrt{-4z}$ **34.** $\sqrt{60 - xy + 1}$

35. $\sqrt{z^2 - yz + 11}$ **36.** $\sqrt{3(x + y) + y}$ **37.** $-\sqrt{x^2 + y^2}$

Solve the equation.

38. $3w^2 = 675$ **39.** $d^2 - 12 = 132$ **40.** $5 + 14c^2 = 229$

41. $11x^2 = 891$ **42.** $13r^2 - 5 = 203$ **43.** $-w^2 = -576$

44. Critical Thinking The area of a square is 144 square meters. What is the perimeter of the square?

45. Craters The Barringer Meteor Crater in Winslow, Arizona, is approximately square in shape. The crater covers an area of about 1,690,000 square meters. What is the approximate side length of the crater?

Find the two square roots of the number. Check your answers by squaring.

46. 0.16   **47.** 2.25   **48.** 0.0256   **49.** 0.0025

50. Critical Thinking What is $\frac{1}{3} \times \frac{1}{3}$? What are the square roots of $\frac{1}{9}$? What are the square roots of $\frac{16}{25}$?

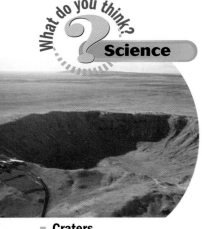

What do you think?

Science

■ **Craters**

The Barringer Meteor Crater is an impact crater. An impact crater is created when a meteoroid hits the surface of a planet or moon. There are 158 known impact craters on Earth, and 34.2% of these are in North America. About how many impact craters are in North America?

Critical Thinking Evaluate the expression.

51. $\sqrt{2^2}$ **52.** $(\sqrt{4})^2$ **53.** $(\sqrt{4})^3$ **54.** $\sqrt{2^4}$

Extended Problem Solving In Exercises 55 and 56, use the following information. The maximum speed s, in knots or nautical miles per hour, for some boats can be found using the equation $s = \frac{4}{3}\sqrt{x}$ where x is the waterline length of a boat, in feet.

55. Calculate A boat has a waterline length of 16 feet. Another boat has a waterline length of 64 feet. Find the maximum speed for each boat.

56. Analyze The waterline length of the larger boat is 4 times the waterline length of the smaller boat. Does the same relationship hold for the maximum speeds of the boats? Explain.

57. The figure is made up of squares of the same size. The area of the figure is 324 square meters. Find the side length of the squares.

58. Challenge Make an input-output table for the function $y = \sqrt{x}$ using the domain 0, 1, 4, 9, and 16. Then graph the ordered pairs from the table. Tell whether the function is linear. Explain your reasoning.

Mixed Review

Round 146.5547 to the specified place value. *(Lesson 2.1)*

59. ones   **60.** tenths   **61.** hundredths   **62.** thousandths

63. Draw $\triangle ABC$ with vertices $A(1, 3)$, $B(-1, -1)$, and $C(3, 0)$. Then find the coordinates of the vertices of the image after the translation $(x, y) \rightarrow (x + 3, y - 2)$, and draw the image. *(Lesson 10.8)*

Basic Skills Find a low and high estimate for the product or quotient.

64. 15×27 **65.** 1124×460 **66.** $687 \div 23$ **67.** $6520 \div 9$

Test-Taking Practice

68. Multiple Choice The area of a square is 242 square meters. The area of a second square is half the area of the first square What is the side length of the second square?

A. 11 m   **B.** 22 m   **C.** 60.5 m   **D.** 121 m

69. Short Response The figure shown is composed of two squares. The area of the shaded region is 48 square centimeters. What is the side length of the larger square? Explain your reasoning.

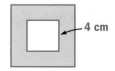

4 cm

Break into Parts

Look for a Pattern

Estimate

Make a List

Guess, Check, and Revise

Solve a Related Problem

Write an Equation

Guess, Check, and Revise

Problem A playground at a park has an area of 2116 square feet. If the playground is square, what is the side length of the playground?

❶ Read and Understand

Read the problem carefully.

You know that the area of a square is equal to the square of its side length.

You want to find the side length of a square with an area of 2116 square feet.

❷ Make a Plan

Decide on a strategy to use.

One way to find the side length of the playground is to guess the square root of 2116. Then you can use the formula for the area of a square to check if your guess is correct. If it isn't correct, you can revise your guess.

❸ Solve the Problem

Reread the problem. Then guess, check, and revise your guess.

Guess a number that is easy to square. Try 50 as your first guess.

$$50^2 = 2500$$

Because 2500 is greater than 2116, try a number that is less than 50. This time, try 40.

$$40^2 = 1600$$

Because 1600 is less than 2116, try a number between 40 and 50.

$$45^2 = 2025$$

Because 2025 is slightly less than 2116, try a number that is slightly greater than 45, like 46.

$$46^2 = 2116$$

So, $\sqrt{2116} = 46$.

ANSWER The side length of the playground is 46 feet.

❹ Look Back

After the initial guess of 50, you might have tried counting down from 50: $49^2 = 2401$, $48^2 = 2304$, $47^2 = 2209$, $46^2 = 2116$.

Practice the Strategy

Use the strategy *guess, check, and revise.*

1. **Bowling** A bowler's scores are 149, 183, and 151 in the first three of four games. If the bowler wants to bowl a mean score of 164 per game, what must the bowler score in the fourth game?

2. **Cubing a Number** The cube of what number is 2197?

3. **Concert Tickets** Tickets to a concert just went on sale. Balcony seats cost $17.50 per ticket, and floor seats cost $20. So far, the ticket sales total $155. How many of each type of ticket has been sold?

4. **Gift Card** You have a $20 gift card for a used book and CD store. You're interested in 3 different books and 3 different CDs. Which combination of books and CDs can you buy to have the least amount of money left on the gift card?

Books	$2.48, $4.90, $3.37
CDs	$10.75, $8.20, $5.99

5. **Baseball Game** You and your friends are going to a baseball game together. You pay $27.50 for 2 tickets and a hot dog. Your friend pays $43 for 3 tickets and 2 hot dogs. If the tickets are the same price, how much does one ticket cost? How much does one hot dog cost?

6. **Student Committees** Students are being arranged into 2 committees of 3 students. Jane and Sarah have to be on the same committee. Sarah and Tom cannot be on the same committee. Juan and Tom can be on the same committee only if Lynn is on the committee. If Will and Tom are not on the same committee, list the members on each committee.

Mixed Problem Solving

Use any strategy to solve the problem.

7. **Angle Measures** Find the sum of the angle measures of a hexagon.

8. **Coins** Your friend Mike has $.78 in his pocket. He says that he has at least one quarter, at least one dime, at least one nickel, and exactly 3 pennies. What are all the possible combinations of coins that Mike could have?

9. **Guitar** You are saving for a guitar that costs $200. Your allowance is $20 a week, and your weekly babysitting job pays between $10 and $20. What is the minimum number of weeks that you have to wait before you can buy the guitar? What is the maximum number of weeks that you have to wait?

10. **Magic Square** Complete the magic square using each of the numbers 1, 3, 5, 7, 9, 11, 13, 15, and 17 only once. Place the numbers so that all the vertical, horizontal, and diagonal sums are 27.

?	?	?
?	?	?
?	?	?

Approximating Square Roots

BEFORE | ▶ **Now** | **WHY?**

You found square roots of perfect squares.

You'll approximate square roots of numbers.

So you can find the falling speed of a skydiver, as in Ex. 22.

In the Real World

Word Watch

irrational number, p. 541
real number, p. 541

Animals Dr. R. McNeill Alexander studies the motion of animals. From his studies, he determined that the maximum speed s, in feet per second, that an animal can walk is

$$s = 5.66\sqrt{l}$$

where l is the animal's leg length, in feet. What is the maximum walking speed for a giraffe with a leg length of 11 feet? You'll find the answer in Example 3.

Evaluating Square Roots
You know how to evaluate square roots like $\sqrt{1}$, $\sqrt{4}$, and $\sqrt{9}$ because 1, 4, and 9 are perfect squares. But what about square roots like $\sqrt{2}$, $\sqrt{3}$, and $\sqrt{5}$? The values of these square roots fall between whole numbers, as shown on the number line below.

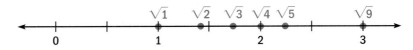

EXAMPLE 1 Approximating to a Whole Number

Approximate $\sqrt{11}$ to the nearest whole number.

Make a list of whole numbers that are perfect squares: 0, 1, 4, 9, 16, ...

$9 < 11 < 16$ **Identify perfect squares closest to 11.**

$\sqrt{9} < \sqrt{11} < \sqrt{16}$ **Take positive square root of each number.**

$3 < \sqrt{11} < 4$ **Evaluate square roots.**

ANSWER Because 11 is closer to 9 than to 16, $\sqrt{11}$ is closer to $\sqrt{9} = 3$. So, to the nearest whole number, $\sqrt{11} \approx 3$.

with Solving

Once you find the approximation of a square root to the tenths' place, you can use the same method to find the approximation to the hundredths' place, thousandths' place, and so on.

EXAMPLE 2 **Approximating to the Nearest Tenth**

Approximate $\sqrt{11}$ to the nearest tenth.

$3.1^2 =$	9.61
$3.2^2 =$	10.24
$3.3^2 =$	10.89
$3.4^2 =$	11.56
$3.5^2 =$	12.25

You know from Example 1 that $\sqrt{11}$ is between 3 and 4. Make a list of squares of 3.1, 3.2, . . . , 3.9. From the list, you can see that 11 is between 3.3^2 and 3.4^2. So, $\sqrt{11}$ is between 3.3 and 3.4.

ANSWER Because 11 is closer to 10.89 than to 11.56, $\sqrt{11}$ is closer to $\sqrt{10.89} = 3.3$. So, to the nearest tenth, $\sqrt{11} \approx 3.3$.

Your turn now Approximate the square root to the nearest whole number and then to the nearest tenth.

1. $\sqrt{10}$ **2.** $\sqrt{22}$ **3.** $\sqrt{45}$ **4.** $\sqrt{115}$

EXAMPLE 3 **Using Square Roots**

You can use the approximation of $\sqrt{11}$ from Example 2 to estimate the maximum walking speed of the giraffe described on the previous page.

$$s = 5.66\sqrt{l} \qquad \text{Write maximum walking speed formula.}$$
$$= 5.66\sqrt{11} \qquad \text{Substitute 11 for } l.$$
$$\approx 5.66(3.3) \qquad \text{Use approximation of } \sqrt{11} \text{ to the nearest tenth.}$$
$$\approx 19 \qquad \text{Multiply.}$$

ANSWER The maximum walking speed is about 19 feet per second.

Irrational Numbers The number $\sqrt{11}$ is an example of an *irrational number.* An **irrational number** cannot be written as a quotient of two integers, and the decimal form of an irrational number neither terminates nor repeats. If n is a positive integer which is not a perfect square, then $\sqrt{n}$ is an irrational number.

The set of **real numbers** consists of all rational and irrational numbers. The Venn diagram shows the relationships among numbers in the real number system.

Real Numbers

Irrational numbers

Rational numbers

Integers

Whole numbers

EXAMPLE **4** Identifying Rational and Irrational Numbers

Tell whether the number is *rational* or *irrational*. Explain.

  a. $\sqrt{2}$ **b.** $-\dfrac{1}{9}$ **c.** $-\sqrt{169}$ **d.** 1.21121112. . .

Solution

  a. $\sqrt{2}$ is irrational because 2 is a positive integer but not a perfect square.

  b. $-\dfrac{1}{9}$ is rational because $-\dfrac{1}{9} = \dfrac{-1}{9}$, which is a quotient of integers.

  c. $-\sqrt{169}$ is rational because $-\sqrt{169} = -13$, which is an integer.

  d. 1.21121112. . . is irrational because it neither terminates nor repeats.

HELP with **Review**

Need help with rational numbers? See p. 283.

11.2 Exercises

More Practice, p. 715

INTERNET
eWorkbook Plus
CLASSZONE.COM

Getting Ready to Practice

1. Vocabulary Copy and complete: A number that cannot be represented as a quotient of two integers is called a(n) _?_ number.

Approximate the square root to the nearest whole number and then to the nearest tenth.

  2. $\sqrt{15}$ **3.** $\sqrt{23}$ **4.** $\sqrt{42}$ **5.** $\sqrt{131}$

Tell whether the number is *rational* or *irrational*. Explain your reasoning.

  6. -2.6 **7.** $\sqrt{1600}$ **8.** $\sqrt{45}$ **9.** $-\sqrt{115}$

10. Guided Problem Solving You buy 140 square feet of carpet to cover the floor in a square bedroom. There are 12 square feet of carpet left over. Approximate the side length of the bedroom floor to the nearest foot.

  (1 How many square feet of carpet did you use to cover the bedroom floor?

  (2 The amount of carpet used falls between which two whole numbers that are perfect squares?

  (3 The square root of which whole number is the better approximation for the side length of the bedroom floor? What is the approximate side length of the bedroom floor to the nearest foot?

with Homework

Example	Exercises
1	11–18
2	11–18, 21
3	22
4	23–30

Online Resources
CLASSZONE.COM

· More Examples
· eTutorial Plus

Recreation

■ **Skydiving**

In 2000, there were 3.5 million skydives, but only 317,741 people who skydived. What is the mean number of skydives per person?

Practice and Problem Solving

Approximate the square root to the nearest whole number and then to the nearest tenth.

11. $\sqrt{35}$ **12.** $\sqrt{89}$ **13.** $\sqrt{57}$ **14.** $\sqrt{63}$

15. $\sqrt{125}$ **16.** $\sqrt{188}$ **17.** $\sqrt{200}$ **18.** $\sqrt{253}$

19. Find the Error Describe and correct the error in approximating $\sqrt{29}$ to the nearest whole number.

 29 falls between 25 and 36. Because 29 is closer to 25, $\sqrt{29} \approx 25$.

20. Guess, Check, and Revise Guess a value of x that solves the equation $x^2 = 24$. Square the value and compare it with 24. Revise your guess. Repeat the process to approximate solutions to the nearest tenth.

21. Mural You use one gallon of white paint to apply a base coat of paint on a square wall mural. The paint covers 350 square feet per gallon. Approximate the side length of the mural to the nearest tenth of a foot.

22. Skydiving A skydiver falls at a rate given by $s = 1.05\sqrt{w}$ where s is the falling speed, in feet per second, and w is the total weight of the skydiver with gear, in pounds. To the nearest tenth, what is the approximate falling speed of a 150 pound man with 35 pounds of gear?

Tell whether the number is *rational* or *irrational*. Explain your reasoning.

23. $5.6537891\ldots$ **24.** $\sqrt{64}$ **25.** $\dfrac{1}{11}$ **26.** $\dfrac{7}{9}$

27. $\sqrt{21}$ **28.** $5\dfrac{3}{8}$ **29.** $1.\overline{375}$ **30.** $30.23233\ldots$

Approximate the square root to the nearest hundredth.

31. $\sqrt{87}$ **32.** $\sqrt{91}$ **33.** $\sqrt{140}$ **34.** $\sqrt{210}$

35. Critical Thinking Consider the square roots of the whole numbers from 1 to 10. Are there more rational numbers or irrational numbers? Explain your reasoning.

Use a number line to order the numbers from least to greatest.

36. $\sqrt{5}, 5, \sqrt{9}, 1.5$ **37.** $4.3, 4.\overline{3}, \sqrt{17}, \dfrac{17}{3}$ **38.** $\sqrt{21}, \sqrt{27}, 5, \dfrac{27}{5}, 4.8$

Algebra **Solve the equation. Round solutions to the nearest hundredth.**

39. $5x^2 = 65$ **40.** $14x^2 = 123.2$ **41.** $9x^2 + 3 = 48$

42. Challenge If $a = 2b$, then does $\sqrt{a} = 2\sqrt{b}$? Explain your reasoning.

Mixed Review

Simplify the expression. *(Lesson 7.2)*

43. $8(3 - j) + 4j$ **44.** $7h - 11 - 4h$ **45.** $3(2t - 3u)$ **46.** $5r(r + 6) - 9$

Solve the equation. *(Lesson 11.1)*

47. $a^2 = 144$ **48.** $c^2 + 9 = 45$ **49.** $y^2 - 20 = -4$ **50.** $5z^2 + 5 = 25$

Basic Skills **Find the greatest common factor of the numbers.**

51. 64, 80 **52.** 28, 42 **53.** 18, 36, 66 **54.** 80, 96, 112

Test-Taking Practice

55. Multiple Choice A square kitchen floor has an area of 260 square feet. To the nearest foot, what is the side length of the kitchen floor?

A. 13 ft **B.** 14 ft **C.** 16 ft **D.** 17 ft

56. Multiple Choice To find the time it takes for a dropped object to hit the ground, you can use the equation $h = 16t^2$, where h is height, in feet, and t is time, in seconds. If an object is dropped from a height of 48 feet, how long (to the nearest tenth of a second) does the object fall?

F. 1.7 sec **G.** 1.8 sec **H.** 2.4 sec **I.** 5.7 sec

BRAIN GAME

Who nose?

Evaluate the square roots. Then decipher the code to find the answer to the riddle: Why can't your nose be 12 inches long?

| 3 | 2 | 10 | 9 | 11 | 12 | 2 | | 8 | 5 |

| 4 | 7 | 11 | 13 | 6 | | 5 | 15 | 2 | 14 |

| 3 | 2 | | 9 | | 16 | 7 | 7 | 5 |

$A = \sqrt{81}$	$B = \sqrt{9}$
$C = \sqrt{100}$	$D = \sqrt{36}$
$E = \sqrt{4}$	$F = \sqrt{256}$
$H = \sqrt{225}$	$I = \sqrt{64}$
$L = \sqrt{169}$	$N = \sqrt{196}$
$O = \sqrt{49}$	$S = \sqrt{144}$
$T = \sqrt{25}$	$U = \sqrt{121}$
$W = \sqrt{16}$	

GOAL
Use graph paper to relate the side lengths of a right triangle.

MATERIALS
· graph paper
· scissors

Modeling the Pythagorean Theorem

You can use graph paper to find the length of a right triangle's *hypotenuse*, which is the side opposite the right angle.

Explore **Find the length of the hypotenuse of a right triangle if the other side lengths are 3 units and 4 units.**

① Draw the right triangle on graph paper. For each of the triangle's known side lengths, draw a square that has the same side length and shares a side with the triangle.

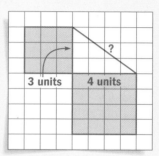

② Find the sum of the areas of the two squares:

$3^2 + 4^2 = 9 + 16 = 25$ square units

Use scissors to cut out a third square whose area is equal to the sum of the areas of the two drawn squares.

③ Place the cut-out square against the hypotenuse. You can see that the length of the hypotenuse is 5 units.

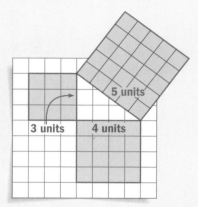

Your turn now

1. Repeat Steps 1–3 to find the length of the hypotenuse of the right triangle shown.

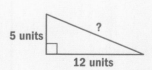

Stop *and* **Think**

2. **Critical Thinking** For the right triangle shown, suppose the lengths *a* and *b* are known. Show how to find the unknown length *c* by relating it to *a* and *b*.

The Pythagorean Theorem

BEFORE	▶ Now	WHY?
You classified triangles.	You'll find the length of a side of a right triangle.	So you can find the lengths of exit ramps, as in Exs. 16–17.

In the Real World

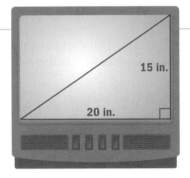

15 in.

20 in.

Televisions A television screen is rectangular and is measured by the length of a diagonal. The screen at the right is 15 inches by 20 inches. What is the length of the diagonal?

In a right triangle, the side opposite the right angle is the **hypotenuse** . The hypotenuse is the longest side of a right triangle. The two sides that form the right angle in a right triangle are **legs** . The lengths of the legs and the hypotenuse of any right triangle are related by the *Pythagorean theorem*.

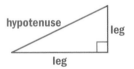

hypotenuse

leg

leg

Pythagorean Theorem

Words For any right triangle, the sum of the squares of the lengths of the legs equals the square of the length of the hypotenuse.

Algebra $a^2 + b^2 = c^2$

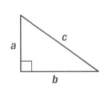

a

c

b

EXAMPLE 1 **Finding the Length of a Hypotenuse**

HELP with **Solving**

Take the positive square root in Example 1 because length is never negative.

To find c, the length of the television's diagonal, as described above, use the Pythagorean theorem. Let $a = 15$ and $b = 20$.

$a^2 + b^2 = c^2$	Write Pythagorean theorem.
$15^2 + 20^2 = c^2$	Substitute 15 for a and 20 for b.
$625 = c^2$	Simplify.
$\sqrt{625} = c$	Take positive square root of each side.
$25 = c$	Evaluate square root.

ANSWER The length of the television's diagonal is 25 inches.

EXAMPLE 2 **Approximating the Length of a Hypotenuse**

For the right triangle shown, find the length of the hypotenuse to the nearest tenth.

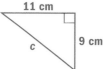

$a^2 + b^2 = c^2$ Write Pythagorean theorem.

$8^2 + 8^2 = c^2$ Substitute 8 for *a* and 8 for *b*.

$128 = c^2$ Simplify.

$\sqrt{128} = c$ Take positive square root of each side.

$11.3 \approx c$ Approximate square root.

ANSWER The length of the hypotenuse is about 11.3 millimeters.

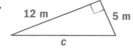

HELP with **Review**

Need help with approximating square roots? See p. 540.

Your turn now **Find the length of the hypotenuse. Round to the nearest tenth if necessary.**

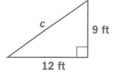

1. *c*, 9 ft, 12 ft   **2.** 12 m, 5 m, *c*   **3.** 11 cm, 9 cm, *c*

EXAMPLE 3 **Finding the Length of a Leg**

Camping You are setting up a tent. The ropes that are used to hold the tent down are 5 feet long, and the roof of the tent ends 3 feet above the ground. What is the farthest distance from the base of the tent that the rope can be staked down?

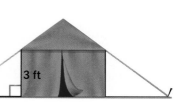

Solution

$a^2 + b^2 = c^2$ Write Pythagorean theorem.

$3^2 + b^2 = 5^2$ Substitute 3 for *a* and 5 for *c*.

$9 + b^2 = 25$ Evaluate powers.

$b^2 = 16$ Subtract 9 from each side.

$b = \sqrt{16}$ Take positive square root of each side.

$b = 4$ Evaluate square root.

ANSWER The farthest distance that the rope can be staked down is 4 feet from the base of the tent.

Getting Ready to Practice

1. **Vocabulary** Copy and complete: The ? is the side opposite the right angle in a right triangle.

Find the unknown length. Round to the nearest tenth if necessary.

2.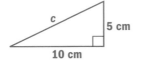

3.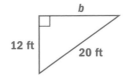

4.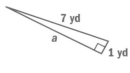

5. **Kite** Find the wingspan of the kite shown if the height is perpendicular to the wingspan. Round to the nearest tenth.

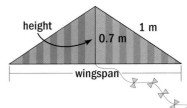

Practice and Problem Solving

HELP with Homework

Example	Exercises
1	6–12
2	6–17
3	6–12

Online Resources
CLASSZONE.COM

· More Examples
· eTutorial Plus

Find the unknown length. Round to the nearest tenth if necessary.

6.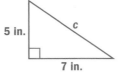

7.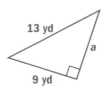

8.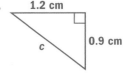

A right triangle has legs of length a and b and hypotenuse of length c. Find the unknown length. Round to the nearest tenth if necessary.

9. $b = 1.5$ mm, $c = 2.5$ mm

10. $b = 11$ in., $c = 13$ in.

11. $a = 10$ ft, $b = 24$ ft

12. $a = 7$ cm, $c = 11.2$ cm

13. **Compare** Measure the length and width of a rectangular room. Use the Pythagorean theorem to calculate the length of a diagonal. Then measure the length of the diagonal and compare with your calculation.

Tiling In Exercises 14 and 15, use the following information. You are tiling a floor. You cut several 1 foot by 1 foot tiles along a diagonal as shown.

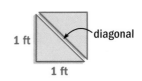

14. Find the length of a diagonal of a tile to the nearest tenth of a foot.

15. How many whole diagonal edges will fit along a wall that is 6 feet in length? along a wall that is 8 feet in length?

Handicap Exit Ramps **In Exercises 16 and 17, use the following information.** According to federal construction codes, exit ramps should decrease 1 foot in height every 12 feet in horizontal length.

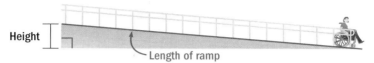

Height

Length of ramp

16. Find the length of the ramp to the nearest tenth if the ramp has a height of 1 foot.

17. Find the length of the ramp to the nearest tenth if the ramp has a height of 1.5 feet.

18. Describe What happens to the length of the hypotenuse when you double the lengths of the legs of a right triangle? Give an example to support your conclusion.

19. Challenge The length of the hypotenuse of an isosceles right triangle is 32 m. Find the length of the legs. Round to the nearest tenth.

Mixed Review

Find the measure of an angle complementary to ∠A. *(Lesson 10.1)*

20. $m\angle A = 18°$ **21.** $m\angle A = 59.2°$ **22.** $m\angle A = 78.4°$

Order the numbers from least to greatest. *(Lesson 11.2)*

23. $\sqrt{81}, \sqrt{72}, 9.2, 8.6$ **24.** $\sqrt{1}, \frac{1}{3}, 2.5, \sqrt{2}$ **25.** $1\frac{2}{5}, \sqrt{3}, 0.3, 1.\overline{3}$

Basic Skills **Find the perimeter and the area of the rectangle with the given dimensions.**

26. $l = 14$ in., $w = 8$ in.   **27.** $l = 25$ m, $w = 10$ m   **28.** $l = 12$ ft, $w = 15$ ft

Test-Taking Practice

29. Multiple Choice The length of a leg of a right triangle is 12 meters, and the hypotenuse is 20 meters. What is the length of the other leg?

A. 8 m   **B.** 12 m   **C.** 16 m   **D.** 23.3 m

30. Multiple Choice An airplane leaves a runway and travels 1105 feet through the air. It travels a ground distance of 1100 feet. What is the altitude of the airplane at this moment?

F. 5 ft   **G.** 25 ft

H. 105 ft   **I.** 1559 ft

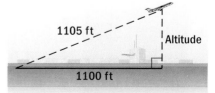

1105 ft

Altitude

1100 ft

Not drawn to scale

Notebook Review

Review the vocabulary definitions in your notebook.

Copy the review examples in your notebook. Then complete the exercises.

Check Your Definitions

square root, p. 533

perfect square, p. 533

radical expression, p. 534

irrational number, p. 541

real number, p. 541

hypotenuse, p. 546

leg, p. 546

Pythagorean theorem, p. 546

Use Your Vocabulary

1. Copy and complete: The numbers 0, 1, 4, 9, 16, 25, 36, and 49 are all __?__.

11.1 Can you solve equations using square roots?

 EXAMPLE Solve the equation $y^2 + 9 = 45$.

$y^2 + 9 = 45$	Write original equation.
$y^2 = 36$	Subtract 9 from each side.
$y = \pm\sqrt{36}$	Use definition of square root.
$y = \pm 6$	Evaluate square root.

☑ **Solve the equation.**

2. $a^2 = 289$ **3.** $b^2 - 15 = 106$ **4.** $6c^2 = 96$

11.2 Can you approximate square roots?

 EXAMPLE Approximate $\sqrt{86}$ to the nearest whole number.

List several perfect squares: 0, 1, 4, 9, 16, 25, 36, 49, 64, 81, 100, ...

$81 < 86 < 100$	Identify perfect squares closest to 86.
$\sqrt{81} < \sqrt{86} < \sqrt{100}$	Take positive square root of each number.
$9 < \sqrt{86} < 10$	Evaluate square roots.

ANSWER Because 86 is closer to 81 than to 100, $\sqrt{86} \approx 9$.

☑ **Approximate the square root to the nearest whole number.**

5. $\sqrt{29}$ **6.** $\sqrt{52}$ **7.** $\sqrt{230}$

11.3 Can you use the Pythagorean theorem?

 Review **EXAMPLE** Find the unknown length.

$a^2 + b^2 = c^2$ Write Pythagorean theorem.

$9^2 + b^2 = 15^2$ Substitute 9 for *a* and 15 for *c*.

$b^2 = 144$ Simplify.

$b = \sqrt{144}$ Take positive square root of each side.

$b = 12$ ft   Evaluate square root.

☑ **A right triangle has legs of length *a* and *b* and hypotenuse of length *c*. Find the unknown length. Round to the nearest tenth if necessary.**

8. $a = 6$ in., $c = 10$ in.   **9.** $a = 2.9$ cm, $b = 1.2$ cm

Stop and Think about Lessons 11.1–11.3

10. Critical Thinking Explain how to find the perimeter of a square when you know its area. Give an example to support your answer.

Review Quiz 1

Evaluate the expression when $h = -3$ and $x = 2$.

1. $\sqrt{3h + 73}$ **2.** $\sqrt{8x}$ **3.** $\sqrt{24x + 4h}$ **4.** $\sqrt{3h^2 - 2}$

Solve the equation.

5. $3r^2 = 363$ **6.** $t^2 + 33 = 114$ **7.** $\frac{1}{5}s^2 = 45$ **8.** $z^2 - 4 = -3.91$

Tell whether the number is *rational* or *irrational*. Explain your reasoning.

9. $-\sqrt{256}$ **10.** -18.45 **11.** $\frac{2}{9}$ **12.** $3.34353\ldots$

13. Rugs A square rug has an area of 60 square feet. Find the side length of the rug to the nearest tenth of a foot.

Find the unknown length. Round to the nearest tenth if necessary.

14.   **15.**   **16.**

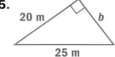
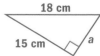

Area of a Parallelogram

BEFORE	▶ Now	WHY?
You found the areas of rectangles and squares.	You'll find the areas of parallelograms.	So you can estimate the area of Missouri, as in Exs. 14–15.

Activity You can find the area of a parallelogram.

① On graph paper, draw the parallelogram shown.

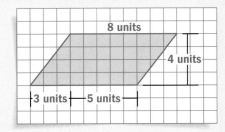

8 units
4 units
3 units — 5 units

② Cut a right triangle from one side of the parallelogram and move it to the other side to form a rectangle.

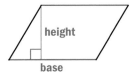 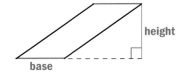

Cut the parallelogram.   Form a rectangle.

③ Find the area of the rectangle. How does the area of the rectangle compare with the area of the parallelogram?

The **base of a parallelogram** is the length of any one of the sides.
The **height of a parallelogram** is the perpendicular distance between the side whose length is the base and the opposite side.

height   height
base   base

Area of a Parallelogram

Words The area A of a parallelogram is the product of a base and the corresponding height.

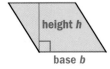

height h
base b

Algebra $A = bh$

EXAMPLE 1 Finding the Area of a Parallelogram

Find the area of the parallelogram.

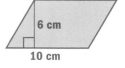

6 cm

10 cm

$A = bh$ Write formula for area.

$= 10(6)$ Substitute 10 for b and 6 for h.

$= 60$ Multiply.

ANSWER The area of the parallelogram is 60 square centimeters.

Your turn now Find the area of the parallelogram with the given base and height.

1. $b = 8$ in., $h = 11$ in. **2.** $b = 9.3$ m, $h = 7$ m **3.** $b = 3.25$ ft, $h = 12$ ft

EXAMPLE 2 Finding the Base of a Parallelogram

Exercising A treadmill's belt is in the shape of a parallelogram before its ends are joined to form a loop. The belt's area is 2052 square inches. The belt's width, which is the height of the parallelogram, is 18 inches. Find the length of the belt, which is the base of the parallelogram.

Not drawn to scale

Solution

$A = bh$ Write formula for area of a parallelogram.

$2052 = b(18)$ Substitute 2052 for A and 18 for h.

$\dfrac{2052}{18} = \dfrac{b(18)}{18}$ Divide each side by 18.

$114 = b$ Simplify.

ANSWER The length of the treadmill's belt is 114 inches.

Your turn now Find the unknown base or height of the parallelogram.

4. $A = 56$ in.^{2}

8 in.

b

5. $A = 36$ mm^2

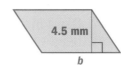

4.5 mm

b

6. $A = 54$ cm^2

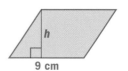

h

9 cm

Getting Ready to Practice

1. Vocabulary Draw a parallelogram. Label a base and the height.

Find the area of the parallelogram.

2.
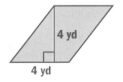
4 yd

4 yd

3.
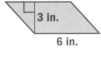
3 in.

6 in.

4.
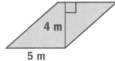
4 m

5 m

5. Find the Error Describe and correct the error in finding the area of the parallelogram.

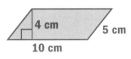
4 cm   5 cm
10 cm

$A = bh$
$= 10 \times 5$
$= 50 \text{ cm}^2$

6. Stained Glass The area of a parallelogram in a stained glass window is 71.5 square inches, and the height is 6.5 inches. What is the base?

Practice and Problem Solving

HELP with Homework

Example	Exercises
1	7–9
2	10–13

 Online Resources
CLASSZONE.COM
· More Examples
· eTutorial Plus

Find the perimeter and the area of the parallelogram.

7.
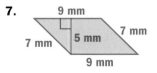
9 mm

7 mm   5 mm   7 mm

9 mm

8.
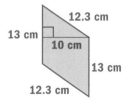
12.3 cm

13 cm   10 cm

13 cm

12.3 cm

9.
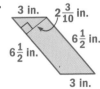
3 in. $2\frac{3}{10}$ in.

$6\frac{1}{2}$ in. $6\frac{1}{2}$ in.

3 in.

Find the unknown base or height of the parallelogram.

10. $A = 48 \text{ cm}^2$, $b = 12 \text{ cm}$, $h = \underline{?}$

11. $A = 117 \text{ ft}^2$, $b = \underline{?}$, $h = 9 \text{ ft}$

12. $A = 80 \text{ m}^2$, $b = \underline{?}$, $h = 15 \text{ m}$

13. $A = 15 \text{ in.}^2$, $b = \frac{5}{6} \text{ in.}$, $h = \underline{?}$

Estimation In Exercises 14 and 15, use the following information. The state of Missouri has approximately the shape of a parallelogram.

14. Use a metric ruler to find the base and height of the parallelogram.

15. Use the scale 1 cm : 120 miles to estimate the area of Missouri.

MISSOURI

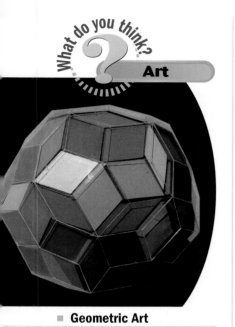
16. Critical Thinking Two parallelograms have the same area. Do they necessarily have the same base and height? Explain your reasoning.

17. The area of a parallelogram is 216 square feet, and the base is 6 times the height. Find the parallelogram's height.

Geometric Art Approximate the height of the rhombus, from the sculpture at the left. Then estimate the area to the nearest square inch.

18.

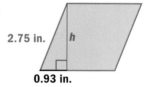

2.75 in. *h*

2.06 in.

19.

2.75 in. *h*

0.93 in.

Challenge Plot and connect the points to form a parallelogram. Then find the area.

20. $R(2, -2)$, $S(-1, -2)$, $T(1, 2)$, $U(4, 2)$

21. $K(-3, 2)$, $L(-3, -2)$, $M(3, -4)$, $N(3, 0)$

22. $A(-3, 3)$, $B(-1, 3)$, $C(2, 0)$, $D(0, 0)$

Mixed Review

Use the distributive property to evaluate the expression. *(Lesson 6.7)*

23. $6\left(\dfrac{5}{7}\right) + 6\left(\dfrac{2}{7}\right)$　　　**24.** $3(5.9) + 3(0.1)$　　　**25.** $8(2.6) + 8(4.4)$

The lengths of the legs of a right triangle are given. Find the length of the hypotenuse. Round to the nearest tenth if necessary. *(Lesson 11.3)*

26. 15 m, 20 m　　　**27.** 90 m, 120 m　　　**28.** 30 in., 50 in.

Basic Skills **Tell whether the number is *prime* or *composite*.**

29. 29　　　**30.** 111　　　**31.** 78

Test-Taking Practice

32. Multiple Choice What is the area of the parallelogram shown?

A. 208 cm²　　　**B.** 192 cm²

C. 143 cm²　　　**D.** 132 cm²

13 cm

16 cm

33. Short Response The base of a parallelogram is 24.5 feet, and the height is 10 feet. If you divide the base and the height in half, what happens to the area of the parallelogram?

GOAL
Use graph paper to find the areas of triangles and trapezoids.

MATERIALS
• graph paper
• scissors

Modeling Areas of Triangles and Trapezoids

You can use the area of a parallelogram to find the area of a triangle and of a trapezoid.

Explore 1 **Find the area of the triangle shown.**

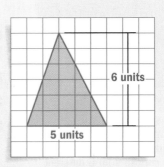

1 Use graph paper to draw two triangles that are congruent to the one shown. Cut out both triangles.

2 Fit the triangles together to form a parallelogram by flipping one of the triangles over. Then find the area of the parallelogram.

The area of the parallelogram is 5 • 6 = 30 square units.

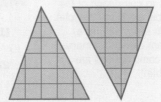

3 Use the area of the parallelogram to find the area of one triangle. Because two congruent triangles make up the parallelogram, the area of the triangle is $\frac{1}{2}$ • 30 = 15 square units.

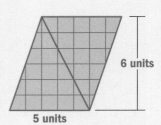

Your turn now

1. Repeat Steps 1–3 to find the area of the triangle shown.

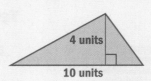

2. **Critical Thinking** For the triangle shown, suppose the lengths b and h are known. Show how to find the area of the triangle in terms of b and h.

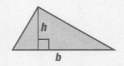

EXAMPLE 2 **Finding the Base of a Triangle**

A triangle has a height of 10 centimeters and an area of 35 square centimeters. Find the base of the triangle.

$$A = \frac{1}{2}bh \qquad \text{Write formula for area of a triangle.}$$

$$35 = \frac{1}{2}b(10) \qquad \text{Substitute 35 for } A \text{ and 10 for } h.$$

$$35 = 5b \qquad \text{Simplify.}$$

$$7 = b \qquad \text{Divide each side by 5.}$$

ANSWER The base of the triangle is 7 centimeters.

Your turn now **Find the unknown area or height of the triangle.**

1. $A = \underline{\ ?\ }$, $b = 9$ ft, $h = 6$ ft   **2.** $A = 61.6$ m^2, $b = 11$ m, $h = \underline{\ ?\ }$

HELP with Reading

Because a trapezoid has more than one base, the bases of a trapezoid are usually labeled b_1 and b_2. b_1 is read "*b* sub one."

Trapezoids You can use the *bases* and the *height* of a trapezoid to find the area of the trapezoid. The lengths of the parallel sides of a trapezoid are the **bases of a trapezoid** . The **height of a trapezoid** is the perpendicular distance between the bases.

Notebook

Area of a Trapezoid

Words The area A of a trapezoid is half the product of the sum of the bases and the height.

Algebra $A = \frac{1}{2}(b_1 + b_2)h$

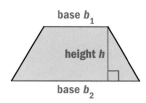

base b_1

height h

base b_2

EXAMPLE 3 **Finding the Area of a Trapezoid**

Find the area of the trapezoid shown.

$$A = \frac{1}{2}(b_1 + b_2)h \qquad \text{Write formula for area of a trapezoid.}$$

$$= \frac{1}{2}(5 + 10)(8) \qquad \text{Substitute 5 for } b_1, \text{ 10 for } b_2, \text{ and 8 for } h.$$

$$= 60 \qquad \text{Simplify.}$$

ANSWER The area of the trapezoid is 60 square feet.

5 ft

8 ft

10 ft

EXAMPLE 4 **Finding the Height of a Trapezoid**

A trapezoid has an area of 66 square meters. The bases are 8 meters and 14 meters. Find the height.

$$A = \frac{1}{2}(b_1 + b_2)h$$ 　　Write formula for area of a trapezoid.

$$66 = \frac{1}{2}(8 + 14)h$$ 　　Substitute 66 for A, 8 for b_1, and 14 for b_2.

$$66 = \frac{1}{2}(22)h$$ 　　Add.

$$66 = 11h$$ 　　Multiply.

$$6 = h$$ 　　Divide each side by 11.

ANSWER The height of the trapezoid is 6 meters.

Your turn now Find the unknown area, base, or height of the trapezoid.

3. $A = 180 \text{ cm}^2$, $b_1 = \underline{?}$, $b_2 = 12 \text{ cm}$, $h = 5 \text{ cm}$

4. $A = \underline{?}$, $b_1 = 13 \text{ in.}$, $b_2 = 15 \text{ in.}$, $h = 6 \text{ in.}$

5. $A = 216 \text{ m}^2$, $b_1 = 11 \text{ m}$, $b_2 = 13 \text{ m}$, $h = \underline{?}$

11.5 Exercises

More Practice, p. 715

Getting Ready to Practice

1. Vocabulary Draw a triangle and trapezoid. Label the bases and heights.

Find the area of the triangle or trapezoid.

2.
7 in.
7 in.
9 in.

3.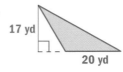
17 yd
20 yd

4.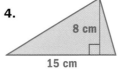
8 cm
15 cm

5. Backpacks You are making a reflective patch for your backpack. The patch is a triangle with a base of 12 centimeters and a height of 6 centimeters. What is the area of the patch?

Practice and Problem Solving

HELP with Homework

Example	Exercises
1	6–8, 22–24
2	9–12
3	13–15, 22–24
4	16–20

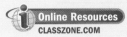

Online Resources
CLASSZONE.COM

· More Examples
· eTutorial Plus

Find the area of the triangle.

6.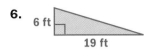
6 ft
19 ft

7.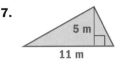
5 m
11 m

8.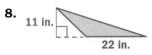
11 in.
22 in.

Find the unknown base or height of the triangle.

9. $A = 45 \text{ km}^2$, $b = \underline{?}$, $h = 15$ km

10. $A = 71.5 \text{ mm}^2$, $b = 11$ mm, $h = \underline{?}$

11. $A = 98 \text{ mi}^2$, $b = 21$ mi, $h = \underline{?}$

12. $A = 13 \text{ cm}^2$, $b = \underline{?}$, $h = 2.5$ cm

Find the area of the trapezoid.

13.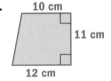
10 cm
11 cm
12 cm

14.
7 in.
6 in.
9 in.

15.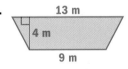
13 m
4 m
9 m

Find the unknown base or height of the trapezoid.

16. $A = 180 \text{ ft}^2$, $b_1 = \underline{?}$, $b_2 = 26$ ft, $h = 9$ ft

17. $A = 114 \text{ cm}^2$, $b_1 = 13$ cm, $b_2 = \underline{?}$, $h = 6$ cm

18. $A = 444.5 \text{ m}^2$, $b_1 = 18$ m, $b_2 = 17$ m, $h = \underline{?}$

19. $A = 33 \text{ in.}^2$, $b_1 = 3\frac{3}{4}$ in., $b_2 = \underline{?}$, $h = 6$ in.

20. A trapezoid has an area of 311.2 square feet. The bases are 25.2 feet and 13.7 feet. Find the height of the trapezoid.

21. Writing If the base of a triangle is doubled and the height is doubled, how does the area change? Give an example to support your conclusion.

Find the area of the triangle or trapezoid.

22.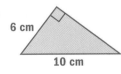
6 cm
10 cm

23.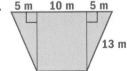
5 m   10 m   5 m
13 m

24.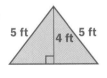
5 ft   5 ft
4 ft

25. Space Shuttle Find the area of a wing of the space shuttle shown. The wing is composed of a triangle, a rectangle, and a trapezoid.

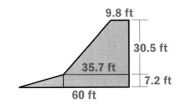
9.8 ft
30.5 ft
35.7 ft
7.2 ft
60 ft

26. Hang Glider The wings of a hang glider are composed of two congruent obtuse triangles as shown. Find the wing area. Round to the nearest square foot.

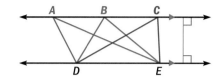

9 ft

8 ft

16 ft

Not drawn to scale

27. Challenge Explain why triangles *ADE, BDE,* and *CDE* have the same area.

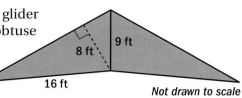

Mixed Review

Classify the triangle by its angle measures. *(Lesson 10.3)*

28. 27°, 90°, 63°   **29.** 84°, 54°, 42°   **30.** 38°, 62°, 80°   **31.** 33°, 43°, 104°

32. A parallelogram has an area of 234 square inches. The base is 13 inches. What is the height? *(Lesson 11.4)*

Basic Skills   **Find the product.**

33. 5.2×12.8 **34.** 20.6×8.54 **35.** 34×9.88 **36.** 5.678×3.2

Test-Taking Practice

37. Extended Response A trapezoid's bases are 10 inches and 15 inches, and the height is 5 inches. What happens to the area of the trapezoid if you double only the bases? What happens to the area of the trapezoid if you double only the height? What happens to the area of the trapezoid if you double the bases and the height?

BrAIN GAME

Getting Bigger

Order the polygons from least area to greatest area to spell out the secret message.

E   10

10

S   9

15

8   R

12

12

A

14

11

10   A

14

Circumference of a Circle

LESSON 11.6

BEFORE	**Now**	**WHY?**
You found the perimeters of polygons.	You'll find the circumferences of circles.	So you can find the distance around a Ferris wheel, as in Ex. 20.

Word Watch

circle, p. 563
center, p. 563
radius, p. 563
diameter, p. 563
circumference, p. 563

A **circle** is the set of all points in a plane that are the same distance from a fixed point called the **center**. The distance from the center to any point on the circle is the **radius**. The distance across the circle through the center is the **diameter**.

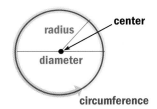

The **circumference** of a circle is the distance around the circle. The ratio of a circle's circumference to its diameter is represented by the Greek letter π (*pi*). From the figure, you can see that π is slightly greater than 3. The values 3.14 and $\frac{22}{7}$ are often used as approximations of the number π, which is a nonterminating, nonrepeating decimal: 3.14159. . . .

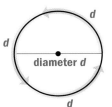

Circumference of a Circle

Words The circumference C of a circle is the product of π and the diameter, or twice the product of π and the radius.

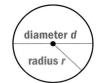

Algebra $\quad C = \pi d \qquad\qquad C = 2\pi r$

EXAMPLE 1 **Finding the Circumference of a Circle**

Find the circumference of the clock. Use 3.14 for π.

$$C = \pi d \qquad \text{Write formula for circumference.}$$
$$\approx 3.14(25) \qquad \text{Substitute 3.14 for } \pi \text{ and 25 for } d.$$
$$= 78.5 \qquad \text{Multiply.}$$

ANSWER The circumference of the circle is about 78.5 centimeters.

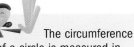

Watch Out!

The circumference of a circle is measured in linear units, not square units.

EXAMPLE 2 **Finding the Circumference of a Circle**

Find the circumference of the circle. Use $\frac{22}{7}$ for π.

21 in.

$$C = 2\pi r \qquad \text{Write formula for circumference.}$$

$$\approx 2\left(\frac{22}{7}\right)(21) \qquad \text{Substitute } \frac{22}{7} \text{ for } \pi \text{ and 21 for } r.$$

$$= 132 \qquad \text{Multiply.}$$

ANSWER The circumference of the circle is about 132 inches.

Your turn now **Find the circumference of the circle. Use $\frac{22}{7}$ or 3.14 for π.**

1.

9 mm

2.
100 cm

3.

49 in.

■ **Giant Sequoias**

The largest tree in the United States is 275 feet tall. About how many times taller is the tree than a person who is 5 foot 9 inches tall?

EXAMPLE 3 **Finding the Diameter of a Circle**

Giant Sequoias The largest tree in the United States is growing in Sequoia National Park in California. The tree is a giant sequoia whose trunk is roughly circular and has a circumference of 998 inches. What is the tree's diameter?

Solution

$$C = \pi d \qquad \text{Write formula for circumference.}$$

$$998 \approx 3.14d \qquad \text{Substitute 998 for } C \text{ and 3.14 for } \pi.$$

$$\frac{998}{3.14} \approx \frac{3.14d}{3.14} \qquad \text{Divide each side by 3.14.}$$

$$318 \approx d \qquad \text{Simplify.}$$

ANSWER The tree's diameter is about 318 inches.

Your turn now **Solve the following problem.**

4. The circumference of a circle is 22 inches. Find the circle's diameter. Round your answer to the nearest whole number.

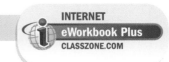
Getting Ready to Practice

1. Vocabulary Label a circle's diameter, center, radius, and circumference.

Match the radius or diameter of a circle with the circle's circumference.

2. $r = 4$ cm

3. $d = 2$ cm

4. $r = 2$ cm

A. $C = 2\pi$ cm

B. $C = 4\pi$ cm

C. $C = 8\pi$ cm

5. Find the Error Describe and correct the error in finding the circumference of a circle with a radius of 5 meters.

$$C = \pi d$$
$$\approx 3.14(5)$$
$$= 15.7 \text{ m}$$

6. Monocycle A giant monocycle wheel has a diameter of 7 feet. What is the circumference of the wheel? Use $\frac{22}{7}$ for π.

Practice and Problem Solving

Find the circumference of the circle. Use $\frac{22}{7}$ or 3.14 for π.

7. $d = 9$ in.

8. $d = 30$ in.

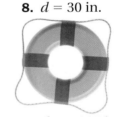

9. $d = 6.5$ cm

10. $r = 3.4$ in.

11. $d = 1.205$ in.

12. $r = 14$ cm

HELP with **Homework**

Example	Exercises
1	7–12
2	7–12
3	13–18

Online Resources
CLASSZONE.COM

· More Examples
· eTutorial Plus

Find the diameter and the radius of the circle with the given circumference. Use $\frac{22}{7}$ or 3.14 for π.

13. $C = 28.26$ in.

14. $C = 119.32$ m

15. $C = 81.64$ mm

16. $C = 42.39$ km

17. $C = 39\frac{3}{5}$ cm

18. $C = 19.468$ ft

19. Writing If you triple the diameter of a circle, what happens to the circle's circumference? Give an example to support your conclusion.

20. Ferris Wheel The original Ferris wheel, designed by George Ferris in 1892 for the World's Columbian Exposition in Chicago, had a radius of 125 feet. What was the circumference of the original Ferris wheel?

21. Critical Thinking What is the circumference of the largest circle that can fit inside a square with a side length of 5 inches?

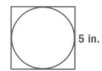

22. Compare To 9 decimal places, the number π is 3.141592654. To how many decimal places is $\frac{22}{7}$ an accurate approximation of π?

23. Challenge How fast does the tip of a 5 inch minute hand on a clock travel? How fast does the tip of a 6 inch second hand on a clock travel? Express your answers in inches per hour.

Mixed Review

Use a proportion to answer the question. *(Lesson 9.2)*

24. What percent of 180 is 81?   **25.** What percent of 90 is 36?

Choose a Strategy Use a strategy from the list at the right to solve the following problem. Explain your choice of strategy.

> **Problem Solving Strategies**
> ▪ Make a List
> ▪ Break into Parts
> ▪ Write an Equation

26. You joined a summer reading group. You've read 2 books: 194 pages and 212 pages. Your goal is to read 1000 pages by the end of August. If there are 45 days until the end of August, what is the mean number of pages you must read each day in order to reach your goal?

Basic Skills **Copy and complete the statement.**

27. 45 mi = _?_ ft   **28.** 54 oz = _?_ lb _?_ oz

Test-Taking Practice

29. Multiple Choice The Astrodome in Houston, Texas, is circular and has a diameter of 710 feet. What is the approximate circumference of the Astrodome?

A. 1110 ft   **B.** 2230 ft   **C.** 4460 ft   **D.** 15,600 ft

30. Multiple Choice A circular wading pool has a diameter of 4 feet. A circular swimming pool has a radius of 16 feet. How many times larger is the circumference of the swimming pool than the wading pool?

F. 2 times   **G.** 4 times   **H.** 8 times   **I.** 12 times

Area of a Circle

BEFORE	▶ Now	WHY?
You found the areas of polygons.	You'll find the areas of circles.	So you can find the area of a circus ring, as in Example 2.

Word Watch

Review Words

radius, p. 563
diameter, p. 563

The circle shown has a radius of 3 units. To estimate the area of the circle, you can count the number of squares entirely inside the circle, almost entirely inside the circle, and about halfway inside the circle.

- **16** of the squares are *entirely* inside the circle.

- **8** of the squares are *almost entirely* in the circle.

- **8** of the squares are about *halfway* inside the circle.

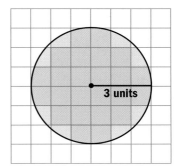

You can then estimate the area of the circle.

$$\text{Area} \approx 16 + 8 + \frac{1}{2}(8) = 16 + 8 + 4 = 28 \text{ square units}$$

The following formula gives the exact area of a circle.

Area of a Circle

Words The area A of a circle is the product of π and the square of the radius.

Algebra $A = \pi r^2$

radius *r*

EXAMPLE 1 Finding the Area of a Circle

To find the area of the circle at the top of the page, use 3.14 for π and 3 for r in the area formula.

$A = \pi r^2$	Write formula for area of a circle.
$\approx (3.14)(3)^2$	Substitute 3.14 for π and 3 for *r*.
$= 28.26$	Simplify.

ANSWER The area of the circle is about 28.26 square units.

EXAMPLE **2**   **Finding the Area of a Circle**

Circus The central performance area at a circus is a circular ring having a diameter of 42 feet. Find the area of the ring.

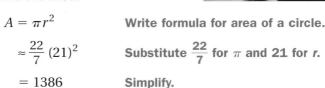

Solution

1 Find the radius.

$$r = \frac{42}{2} = 21 \text{ ft}$$

2 Find the area.

$A = \pi r^2$	Write formula for area of a circle.
$\approx \frac{22}{7}(21)^2$	Substitute $\frac{22}{7}$ for π and 21 for r.
$= 1386$	Simplify.

ANSWER The area of the ring is about 1386 square feet.

Your turn now   Find the area of the circle. Use $\frac{22}{7}$ or 3.14 for π.

1.
8 mm

2.
14 in.

3.
11 ft

EXAMPLE **3**   **Finding the Radius of a Circle**

Find the radius of a circle that has an area of 615.44 square yards. Use 3.14 for π.

$A = \pi r^2$	Write formula for area of a circle.
$615.44 \approx (3.14)r^2$	Substitute 615.44 for A and 3.14 for π.
$\frac{615.44}{3.14} \approx \frac{(3.14)r^2}{3.14}$	Divide each side by 3.14.
$196 \approx r^2$	Simplify.
$\sqrt{196} \approx r$	Take positive square root of each side.
$14 \approx r$	Evaluate square root.

ANSWER The radius of the circle is about 14 yards.

Getting Ready to Practice

Vocabulary Match the measurement with the value for the circle.

1. Radius, in ft   **A.** 28.26

2. Area, in ft²   **B.** 18.84

3. Diameter, in ft   **C.** 6

4. Circumference, in ft   **D.** 3

3 ft

Find the radius of the circle. Then find the area. Use 3.14 for π.

5. $d = 8$ m   **6.** $d = 16$ ft   **7.** $d = 9$ mi

8. Find the Error Describe and correct the error in finding the area of a circle with a diameter of 4 inches.

$$A = \pi r^2$$
$$\approx (3.14)(4)^2$$
$$= 50.24 \text{ in.}^2$$

9. Calendars The surface of the Aztec calendar stone is a circle 12 feet in diameter. What is the area of the surface of the stone? Use 3.14 for π.

Practice and Problem Solving

with Homework

Example	Exercises
1	10–15
2	10–15
3	16–18

Online Resources
CLASSZONE.COM

· More Examples
· eTutorial Plus

Find the area of the circle. Use 3.14 for π.

10. $d = 13$ in.   **11.** $d = 24.2$ cm   **12.** $r = 5$ in.

13. $d = 34$ mm   **14.** $r = 9.525$ mm   **15.** $r = 1.3$ in.

Find the radius and the diameter of the circle with the given area. Use 3.14 for π.

16. $A = 200.96$ cm²   **17.** $A = 254.34$ ft²   **18.** $A = 2122.64$ m²

19. Writing Given the circumference of a circle, how can you find the area?

Find the area of the circle with the given circumference. Use 3.14 for π.

20. $C = 15.7$ mm   **21.** $C = 18.84$ m   **22.** $C = 62.8$ ft

23. $C = 9.42$ in.   **24.** $C = 37.68$ cm   **25.** $C = 21.98$ yd

26. Look for a Pattern Copy and complete the table. Describe how changing the radius of a circle affects the circumference and the area.

Radius (m)	Circumference (m)	Area (m²)
2	$2\pi(2) = 4\pi$	$\pi(2)^2 = 4\pi$
4	?	?
6	?	?
8	?	?

 Challenge Each figure is composed of a circle and a parallelogram, a square, or a triangle. Find the area of the shaded part. Use 3.14 for π.

27.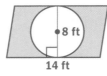
8 ft
14 ft

28.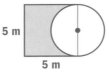
5 m
5 m

29.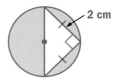
2 cm

Mixed Review

30. A radio is on sale for 15% off the original price. The original price is $89. What is the sale price? *(Lesson 9.7)*

Find the circumference of the circle with the given radius or diameter. Use $\frac{22}{7}$ or 3.14 for π. *(Lesson 11.6)*

31. $r = 45$ km   **32.** $d = 105$ in.   **33.** $d = 21.4$ yd   **34.** $r = 10\frac{1}{2}$ cm

Basic Skills Write the decimal as a fraction.

35. 0.6   **36.** 0.32   **37.** 0.48   **38.** 0.012

Test-Taking Practice

39. Multiple Choice The coin pictured has a diameter of 26.5 millimeters. What is the approximate area of one side of the coin?

A. 83 mm²   **B.** 166 mm²   **C.** 551 mm²   **D.** 2205 mm²

40. Multiple Choice The circumference of a circle is 25 centimeters. What is the approximate area of the circle?

F. 7.96 cm²   **G.** 15.8 cm²   **H.** 49.8 cm²   **I.** 156 cm²

Using Square Roots and Pi

GOAL Use a calculator to evaluate expressions involving square roots and π.

You can use the keystrokes **2nd** $[\sqrt{}]$ and the $\boxed{\pi}$ key to evaluate expressions.

Example 1 **A square field has an area of 4840 square yards, or 1 acre. Between what two whole-number lengths does the length of a side of the field fall? Use a calculator to check your answer.**

Solution

Because 4840 falls between the perfect squares $4761 = 69^2$ and $4900 = 70^2$, you know that $\sqrt{4840}$ falls between 69 and 70.

Check your answer by evaluating $\sqrt{4840}$.

Keystrokes	Display
2nd $[\sqrt{}]$ **4840** $\boxed{)}$ $\boxed{=}$	**69.57010852**

ANSWER The length falls between 69 yards and 70 yards.

Example 2 **Evaluate 16π. Round to the nearest hundredth.**

Solution

Keystrokes	Display
16 $\boxed{\pi}$ $\boxed{=}$	**50.26548246**

ANSWER $16\pi \approx 50.27$

Your turn now Approximate the square root to the nearest hundredth. Then use a calculator to check your answer.

1. $\sqrt{467}$　　　**2.** $\sqrt{1056}$　　　**3.** $\sqrt{4356}$　　　**4.** $\sqrt{37,888}$

Use a calculator to evaluate the expression. Round to the nearest hundredth.

5. 41π　　　**6.** 36π　　　**7.** π^3　　　**8.** $14\pi^2$

Notebook Review

Review the vocabulary definitions in your notebook.

Copy the review examples in your notebook. Then complete the exercises.

Check Your Definitions

base of a parallelogram, p. 552

height of a parallelogram, p. 552

base of a triangle, p. 558

height of a triangle, p. 558

bases of a trapezoid, p. 559

height of a trapezoid, p. 559

circle, p. 563

center, p. 563

radius, p. 563

diameter, p. 563

circumference, p. 563

Use Your Vocabulary

1. Copy and complete: The diameter of a circle is twice the _?_.

11.4 Can you find the area of a parallelogram?

Review

EXAMPLE Find the area of the parallelogram shown below.

$A = bh$

$= 12(7) = 84 \text{ cm}^2$

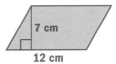

7 cm

12 cm

 2. Find the area of a parallelogram with a base of 6 inches and a height of 10.5 inches.

11.5 Can you find the areas of triangles and trapezoids?

Review

EXAMPLE Find the area of the triangle or trapezoid.

a.

17 m 4 m

b.

8 ft

3 ft

5 ft

$A = \frac{1}{2}bh$

$= \frac{1}{2}(17)(4)$

$= 34 \text{ m}^2$

$A = \frac{1}{2}(b_1 + b_2)h$

$= \frac{1}{2}(5 + 8)(3)$

$= 19.5 \text{ ft}^2$

 3. Find the area of a trapezoid with bases of 21 yards and 16 yards and a height of 9 yards.

11.6–11.7 Can you find circumference, area of circles?

 EXAMPLE Find (a) the circumference and
(b) the area of the circle. Use 3.14 for π.

1.5 ft

a. $C = 2\pi r$
   $\approx 2(3.14)(1.5)$
   $= 9.42$ ft

b. $A = \pi r^2$
   $\approx (3.14)(1.5)^2$
   $= 7.065$ ft^2

☑ **4.** Find the circumference and the area of a circle with a diameter of 34 inches. Use 3.14 for π.

Stop *and* **Think** about Lessons 11.4–11.7

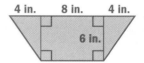
4 in. 8 in. 4 in.

6 in.

5. Critical Thinking Describe how you could find the area of the trapezoid shown without using the area formula for a trapezoid.

Review Quiz 2

Find the area of the triangle, trapezoid, or circle. Use 3.14 for π.

1.
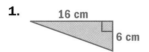
16 cm

6 cm

2.
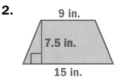
9 in.

7.5 in.

15 in.

3.
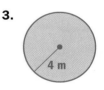
4 m

4. Wristwatch The face of a wristwatch is a parallelogram. The base is 2.75 centimeters, and the height is 2 centimeters. Find the area.

Find the unknown height, diameter, or base of the parallelogram, circle, or trapezoid. Use 3.14 for π.

5. $A = 11.7$ m^2

h

7.8 m

6. $C = 396$ cm

d

7. $A = 10.72$ mm^2

1.9 mm

4 mm

b_2

8. The area of a triangle is 14.6 square inches. The height of the triangle is 4 inches. Find the base of the triangle.

Chapter Review

Vocabulary

square root, p. 533
perfect square, p. 533
radical expression, p. 534
irrational number, p. 541
real number, p. 541
hypotenuse, p. 546
leg, p. 546
Pythagorean theorem,
  p. 546

base of a parallelogram,
  p. 552
height of a parallelogram,
  p. 552
base of a triangle, p. 558
height of a triangle,
  p. 558
bases of a trapezoid,
  p. 559

height of a trapezoid,
  p. 559
circle, p. 563
center, p. 563
radius, p. 563
diameter, p. 563
circumference, p. 563

Vocabulary Review

Copy and complete the statement.

1. The expression $\sqrt{5(3 + 4)}$ is called a(n) _?_.

2. The side opposite the right angle in a right triangle is the _?_.

3. The _?_ of a circle is the distance across the circle through the center.

4. The lengths of the legs and the hypotenuse of any right triangle are related by the _?_.

5. The number π is a(n) _?_ number.

6. The _?_ of a circle is the distance around the circle.

Review Questions

Evaluate the expression when $t = 4$ and $d = 6$. *(Lesson 11.1)*

7. $\sqrt{9t}$

8. $-\sqrt{3t^3 + 4}$

9. $\sqrt{d^2 + dt - 11}$

10. $\sqrt{6dt}$

11. Fire Hoses The flow rate for a particular fire hose can be modeled by $f = 120\sqrt{p}$, where f is the flow rate, in gallons per minute, and p is the nozzle pressure, in pounds per square inch. When water flows through the hose, the nozzle pressure is 144 pounds per square inch. What is the flow rate? *(Lesson 11.1)*

Solve the equation. *(Lesson 11.1)*

12. $m^2 + 8 = 33$

13. $n^2 - 20 = 29$

14. $10p^2 = 1000$

15. $-12q^2 = -12$

Approximate the square root to the nearest whole number and then to the nearest tenth. *(Lesson 11.2)*

16. $\sqrt{14}$

17. $\sqrt{31}$

18. $\sqrt{47}$

19. $\sqrt{288}$

Tell whether the number is *rational* **or** *irrational*. **Explain your reasoning.**
(Lesson 11.2)

20. $-\sqrt{9}$ **21.** $\sqrt{65}$ **22.** $-\sqrt{33}$ **23.** 3.34

Find the unknown length. Round to the nearest tenth if necessary.
(Lesson 11.3)

24.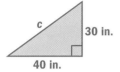

25.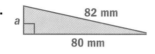

26.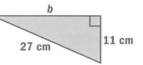

Find the unknown base or height of the parallelogram. *(Lesson 11.4)*

27. $A = 92 \text{ cm}^2$ **28.** $A = 24.15 \text{ ft}^2$ **29.** $A = 384 \text{ in.}^2$

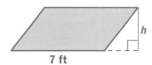
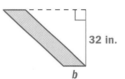

Aircraft Wings **The aircraft wings below are triangles or trapezoids.**
Find the area of the aircraft's wing. *(Lesson 11.5)*

30. Concorde wing   **31.** F-18 wing   **32.** Boeing 747 wing

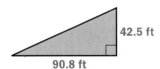
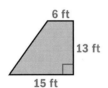
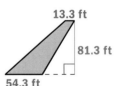

Find the circumference and the area of the circle.
Use $\dfrac{22}{7}$ **or 3.14 for** π. *(Lessons 11.6, 11.7)*

33.   **34.**

35. Basketball Hoop The circumference of the rim of a
basketball hoop is about 56.52 inches. What is the
approximate diameter of the rim? *(Lesson 11.6)*

Chapter Test

Find the two square roots of the number.

1. 225   **2.** 1   **3.** 16   **4.** 324

Evaluate the expression when $a = 25$ and $b = 7$.

5. $\sqrt{a^2 + 104}$ **6.** $\sqrt{10b + 11}$ **7.** $\sqrt{3b + 15}$ **8.** $\sqrt{a^2 + 150b - 75}$

Approximate the square root to the nearest tenth.

9. $\sqrt{18}$ **10.** $\sqrt{43}$ **11.** $-\sqrt{105}$ **12.** $-\sqrt{135}$

Tell whether the number is *rational* or *irrational*. Explain your reasoning.

13. $\sqrt{5}$ **14.** $\sqrt{121}$ **15.** $\sqrt{54}$ **16.** 2.67

Find the unknown length. Round to the nearest tenth if necessary.

17.

18.

19.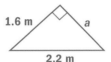

Find the area of the parallelogram, triangle, or trapezoid.

20.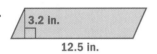

21.

22.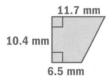

Find the unknown base or height of the parallelogram, triangle, or trapezoid.

23. $A = 289 \text{ m}^2$ **24.** $A = 126.1 \text{ yd}^2$ **25.** $A = 202.5 \text{ in.}^2$

Find the circumference and the area of the circle. Use $\dfrac{22}{7}$ or 3.14 for π.

26. $r = 20 \text{ ft}$ **27.** $r = 0.4 \text{ mm}$ **28.** $d = 28 \text{ in.}$

29. Eyeglasses The diameter of a circular eyeglass lens is $\dfrac{3}{4}$ inch. What is the approximate circumference?

Chapter Standardized Test

Test-Taking Strategy When checking your work, try to use a method different from the one you originally used. You may make the same mistake twice if you use the same method.

Multiple Choice

1. What is the value of $\sqrt{7w - 41}$ when $w = 15$?

    A. 4   **B.** 8   **C.** 32   **D.** 64

2. What are the solutions of $8x^2 = 72$?

    F. ± 81 **G.** ± 24 **H.** ± 9 **I.** ± 3

3. A square has an area of 78 square inches. What is the approximate length of a side of the square?

    A. 7.8 in. **B.** 8.8 in. **C.** 8.9 in. **D.** 19.5 in.

4. Which number is irrational?

    F. $-\sqrt{36}$ **G.** $\sqrt{15}$ **H.** 6.778 **I.** $\sqrt{144}$

5. What is the length of the hypotenuse of the right triangle shown?

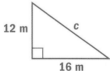

    A. 13 m   **B.** 20 m

    C. 28 m   **D.** 192 m

6. The length of the hypotenuse of a right triangle is 15 cm, and the length of one leg is 12 cm. What is the length of the other leg?

    F. 81 cm **G.** 19 cm **H.** 9 cm **I.** 3 cm

7. What is the area of a parallelogram that has a height of $1\frac{1}{5}$ miles and a base of 2 miles?

    A. $\frac{3}{10}$ mi^2 **B.** $1\frac{2}{3}$ mi^2 **C.** $2\frac{2}{5}$ mi^2 **D.** $3\frac{3}{5}$ mi^2

8. A triangle has an area of 23.4 square inches. The base is 1.2 inches. What is the height of the triangle?

    F. 9.75 in. **G.** 19.5 in. **H.** 28 in. **I.** 39 in.

9. The top of a table in your classroom is shaped like a trapezoid. The area of the trapezoid is 1131 square inches. What is the height h of the trapezoid?

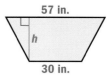

    A. 6.5 in. **B.** 15.7 in. **C.** 26 in. **D.** 83.8 in.

10. The circumference of a circle is 163.28 meters. What is the approximate radius of the circle?

    F. 13 m   **G.** 26 m   **H.** 52 m   **I.** 78 m

11. A circle has an area of 78.5 square inches. What is the approximate radius of the circle?

    A. 5 in. **B.** 8.7 in. **C.** 13 in. **D.** 25 in.

Short Response

12. A parallelogram's area is 75 square meters. The base of the parallelogram is three times as long as its height. What are the base and height of the parallelogram? Explain how you found your answer.

Extended Response

13. A rotating sprinkler sprays a circular garden with a radius of 24 meters. A second rotating sprinkler sprays another circular garden with a radius of 8 meters. How many times greater is the area sprayed by the first sprinkler than the area sprayed by the second sprinkler?

Modeling the Motion of a Pendulum

Relating a Pendulum's Length and Period

A *pendulum* is a weight suspended from a fixed support by a string or a rod. The pendulum must be able to swing freely under the influence of gravity. The *period T* is the time it takes for the pendulum to complete one back-and-forth motion.

If the pendulum's starting angle (∠1 in the diagram) is small, then the period depends only on the length of the pendulum. The equation

$$T = 0.2\sqrt{l}$$

gives the period T, in seconds, for a pendulum of length l centimeters.

T = time required for one back-and-forth swing

 1. Copy and complete the table. Round to the nearest hundredth of a second.

Length (cm)	0	10	20	30	40	50	60	70
Period (sec)	?	?	?	?	?	?	?	?

2. Make a scatter plot of the data pairs in the table. Show length on the x-axis and period on the y-axis. Draw a smooth curve that passes through the plotted points.

3. Decide Is period a *linear* or *nonlinear* function of length? Explain.

4. A more general equation for the period of a pendulum is $T = \dfrac{2\pi}{\sqrt{g}} \cdot \sqrt{l}$, where g is the acceleration due to gravity. On Earth, $g \approx 981$ cm/sec². Find the approximate value of $\dfrac{2\pi}{\sqrt{g}}$ when $g = 981$. What do you notice?

Pendulums and Clocks

Because the swings of a pendulum measure out equal time intervals, some clocks use pendulums to keep time. The equation

$$l = 25T^2$$

gives the length l, in centimeters, that a pendulum should have in order to swing with a period of T seconds. The desired period for many wall-mounted pendulum clocks is 1 second, so the length of the pendulum should be:

$$l = 25(1)^2 = 25 \text{ cm}$$

5. **Applying the Method** For many grandfather clocks, the period of the pendulum is 2 seconds. Find the pendulum's length. Compare this length with the length found above for a pendulum with a 1 second period.

6. **Critical Thinking** Explain why a pendulum with a 4 second period is not practical for most clocks.

7. Use the equation $l = 25T^2$ to find the period of a pendulum with a length of 50 centimeters. (*Hint:* Substitute 50 for l and solve the resulting equation for T.) Compare your answer with the period you found for a 50 centimeter pendulum in your table from Exercise 1.

Project IDEAS

- **Experiment** Use the equation $T = 0.2\sqrt{l}$ to predict the period of a pendulum with a length of 35 centimeters. Check your prediction by using a string and washer to make a pendulum 35 centimeters long, timing how long it takes for the pendulum to complete 10 back-and-forth swings, and dividing this time by 10 to obtain the period. Compare the predicted and actual periods.

- **Report** Write a report on the history of pendulum clocks. Discuss the contributions of Galileo Galilei, Christiaan Huygens, and other scientists who helped develop pendulum clocks.

- **Research** Find out about *Foucault pendulums*. Describe the history and purpose of this type of pendulum.

- **Career** The study of pendulums and their motion is part of a broader branch of science called *physics*. A physicist investigates motion, matter, energy, and force. Find out about the kinds of jobs physicists do and the type of education they need. Present your findings to your class.

INTERNET
Project Support
CLASSZONE.COM

CHAPTER 12

Surface Area and Volume

BEFORE

In previous chapters you've...

- Evaluated expressions
- Used area formulas

Now

In Chapter 12 you'll study...

- Classifying solids
- Sketching solids
- Finding the surface area and volume of rectangular prisms and cylinders

WHY?

So you can solve real-world problems about...

- stadium cushions, p. 595
- balance boards, p. 603
- watermelons, p. 609
- coins, p. 614

Internet Preview
CLASSZONE.COM

- eEdition Plus Online
- eWorkbook Plus Online
- eTutorial Plus Online
- State Test Practice
- More Examples

Chapter Warm-Up Game

Review skills you need for this chapter in this quick game.

Key Skill: Using area formulas

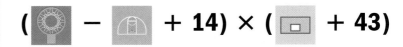

Did you know that basketball is the most popular indoor sport in the world? In this chapter warm-up game, you'll find the areas of different parts of a basketball court in order to find the year in which basketball was invented.

HOW TO PLAY

1 **FIND** the areas of the different parts of a basketball court, as described on the next page.

2 **USE** the numbers from your answers to evaluate the expression below. The value of the expression is the year in which basketball was invented.

6 ft

19 ft

4 ft

12 ft

The blue rectangle and half circle are called the key. Find the area of the key to the nearest square foot.

18 in.

The rim of the basket is a circle. Find the area enclosed by the rim to the nearest square inch. Use 3.14 for π.

2 ft

1.5 ft

3.5 ft

6 ft

The diagram above shows a rectangular backboard. Find the area of the red region.

Stop *and* Think

1. **Critical Thinking** A player stands on the edge of the key as far from the basket as possible. How far is the player from the basket?

2. **Writing** In the diagram of the backboard, are the large and small rectangles similar? Explain your reasoning.

Getting Ready to Learn

Review What You Need to Know

Using Vocabulary Copy and complete using a review word.

Word Watch

Review Words

perimeter, p. 32
area, p. 32
circle, p. 563
radius, p. 563
diameter, p. 563
circumference, p. 563
rectangle, p. 701

1. A(n) _?_ is the set of all points in a plane that are the same distance from a fixed point.

2. The distance around a circle is called its _?_.

3. The _?_ of a rectangle is the sum of the lengths of the sides.

Find the perimeter and the area of the rectangle. *(p. 32)*

4.
4 cm
3 cm

5.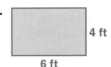
4 ft
6 ft

6.
6 in.
7 in.

Evaluate the expression. *(pp. 18, 58, 63)*

7. $4^2 + 3 \times 4 - 10$

8. $3.14(5^2)(6)$

9. $2(3.14)(7^2) + 9.5$

Find the radius and the diameter of the circle with the given area. Use 3.14 for π. *(p. 567)*

10. $A = 78.5 \text{ in.}^2$

11. $A = 530.66 \text{ ft}^2$

12. $A = 314 \text{ cm}^2$

You should include material that appears on a notebook like this in your own notes.

Know How to Take Notes

Summarizing When you finish a lesson or group of lessons, write a summary of the main ideas in your notebook. Later, when you prepare for a test, you can use your summary as a starting point for checking your knowledge of the material.

A circle has a radius r and a diameter d.

Area $= \pi r^2$

Circumference $= \pi d = 2\pi r$

π is an irrational number approximately equal to 3.14 or $\frac{22}{7}$.

$A = \pi r^2$

$C = \pi d$

By the end of the chapter you will have learned many properties and formulas related to solids. Summarizing what you learned will help you prepare for a test.

Classifying Solids

BEFORE	▶ Now	WHY?
You classified polygons.	You'll classify solids and identify their parts.	So you can classify real-world objects, as in Exs. 6–11.

A **solid** is a three-dimensional figure that encloses a part of space.

📓 **Word Watch**

solid, p. 583
prism, p. 583
pyramid, p. 583
cylinder, p. 583
cone, p. 583
sphere, p. 583
face, p. 584
edge, p. 584
vertex, p. 584

Classifying Solids

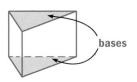
bases

A **prism** is a solid formed by polygons. Prisms have two congruent bases that lie in parallel planes.

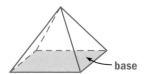
base

A **pyramid** is a solid formed by polygons. The base can be any polygon, and the other polygons are triangles.

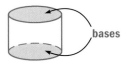
bases

A **cylinder** is a solid with two congruent circular bases that lie in parallel planes.

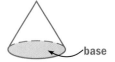
base

A **cone** is a solid with one circular base.

center

A **sphere** is a solid formed by all points in space that are the same distance from a fixed point called the center.

EXAMPLE 1 Classifying Solids

Classify the solid as a *prism*, *pyramid*, *cylinder*, *cone*, or *sphere*.

a.

b.

c.

Solution

a. The ice cream treat is a cone.

b. The building is a pyramid.

c. The ceramic box is a cylinder.

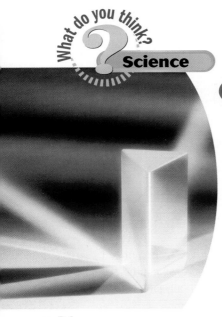
Prisms and Pyramids Prisms and pyramids can be more specifically classified by the shapes of their bases. For example, a prism whose bases are triangles is a *triangular prism*.

EXAMPLE 2 **Types of Prisms and Pyramids**

Classify the solid. Be as specific as possible.

a. 　　　　　　b.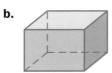

Solution

a. The base is a pentagon, so the solid is a pentagonal pyramid.

b. The bases are rectangles, so the solid is a rectangular prism.

■ **Prism**

When white light enters a glass prism, it is separated into colors because different colors bend at different angles. The angle of bending is 42° for red light and 40° for violet light. Are these angles acute or obtuse?

Faces, Edges, and Vertices When polygons form the sides of a solid, they are called **faces**. The line segments where the faces meet are **edges**. Each point where the edges meet is a **vertex**.

EXAMPLE 3 **Counting Faces, Edges, and Vertices**

A *cube* is a rectangular prism whose faces are all congruent squares. Count the number of faces, edges, and vertices in a cube.

　6 faces　　　　　**12 edges**　　　　**8 vertices**

 **with Solving**

Dashed lines are used to show the hidden edges of a solid.

ANSWER A cube has 6 faces, 12 edges, and 8 vertices.

Your turn now **Classify the solid. Be as specific as possible.**

1. 　　**2.** 　　**3.**

4. Count the number of faces, edges, and vertices in the solid in Exercise 1.

Getting Ready to Practice

1. **Vocabulary** Copy and complete: The polygons that form the sides of a prism or pyramid are called _?_ .

Match the diagram with the name of the solid.

2. Prism   3. Pyramid   4. Cylinder   5. Cone

A.   B.   C. 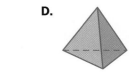   D.

Practice and Problem Solving

HELP with Homework

Example	Exercises
1	6–11
2	6–11
3	17–20

Online Resources
CLASSZONE.COM
· More Examples
· eTutorial Plus

Classify the solid represented by the object. Be as specific as possible.

6.    7.    8.

9.    10.    11.

12. **Compare and Contrast** Describe the similarities and differences between pyramids and prisms.

Tell whether the statement is *true* or *false*. If it is false, explain why.

13. A prism can have a single base.

14. A cylinder has two congruent circular bases.

15. A cube has 12 congruent edges.

16. Any pair of opposite faces of a rectangular prism can be the bases.

17. Architecture Classify the solid represented by the house shown at the right. Be as specific as possible. Then count the number of faces, edges, and vertices in the solid.

Classify the solid. Be as specific as possible. Then count the number of faces, edges, and vertices in the solid.

18. 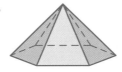   **19.** 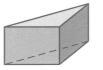   **20.**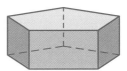

21. Writing The diagram at the right shows a *hemisphere*. What do you think the prefix "hemi-" means? Explain your reasoning.

22. Critical Thinking What type of pyramid has 9 vertices? Explain your reasoning.

In Exercises 23–25, use the definition of *skew* in the following example and the lines that contain the edges of the triangular prism shown.

EXAMPLE **Parallel, Perpendicular, and Skew Lines**

Two lines are *skew* if they do not intersect and are not parallel. Identify a pair of parallel lines, perpendicular lines, and skew lines that contain the edges of the rectangular prism shown.

Lines *e* and *f* are parallel.

Lines *g* and *f* are perpendicular.

Lines *e* and *g* are skew because they do not intersect and are not parallel.

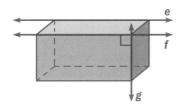

23. Name a pair of parallel lines.

24. Name a pair of perpendicular lines.

25. Name a pair of skew lines.

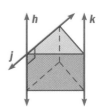

26. **Challenge** Copy and complete the table for each solid shown. Then use your results to describe the relationship between the number of edges and the sum of the number of faces and number of vertices.

Solid				
Faces *F*	?	?	?	?
Vertices *V*	?	?	?	?
Edges *E*	?	?	?	?
F + *V*	?	?	?	?

Mixed Review

Use the simple interest formula to find the unknown quantity.
(Lesson 9.8)

27. $I = \underline{\ ?\ }$
$P = \$2500$
$r = 6.7\%$
$t = 3$ years

28. $I = \$478.80$
$P = \underline{\ ?\ }$
$r = 5.7\%$
$t = 7$ years

29. $I = \$130$
$P = \$6500$
$r = \underline{\ ?\ }$
$t = 6$ months

30. $I = \$36$
$P = \$600$
$r = 8\%$
$t = \underline{\ ?\ }$

Find the radius and the diameter of the circle with the given area. Use 3.14 for π. *(Lesson 11.7)*

31. $A = 254.34$ in.^{2}
32. $A = 200.96$ m^2
33. $A = 1384.74$ ft^2

34. $A = 12.56$ cm^2
35. $A = 113.04$ mm^2
36. $A = 153.86$ yd^2

Basic Skills Write the improper fraction as a mixed number.

37. $\frac{5}{3}$
38. $\frac{13}{2}$
39. $\frac{25}{7}$
40. $\frac{41}{6}$

Test-Taking Practice

41. Multiple Choice What is the name of the solid shown?

A. Triangular pyramid
B. Rectangular prism
C. Triangular prism
D. Rectangular pyramid

42. Multiple Choice How many faces does the solid in Exercise 41 have?

F. 3
G. 4
H. 5
I. 8

Sketching Solids

BEFORE | ▶ **Now** | **WHY?**

You classified solids. | You'll sketch solids. | So you can sketch three views of a gift box, as in Ex. 16.

📓 **Word Watch**

Review Words

solid, p. 583
prism, p. 583
pyramid, p. 583
cylinder, p. 583
cone, p. 583
sphere, p. 583
edge, p. 584
vertex, p. 584

In the Real World

City Buildings The building shown in the photograph at the right is shaped like a rectangular prism. Artists use various methods to draw solids so that they appear to be three-dimensional.

In Example 1, you will learn a method to sketch a rectangular prism. You can use this method to sketch other solids.

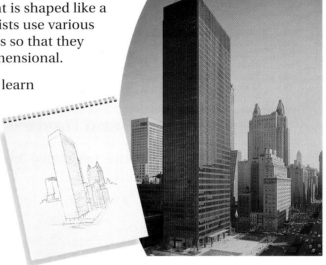

EXAMPLE 1 **Sketching a Prism**

Sketch a rectangular prism.

(1 Sketch two congruent rectangles.

(2 Connect the corresponding vertices using line segments.

(3 Make any "hidden" lines dashed.

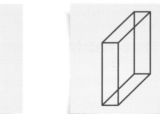

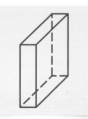

HELP with **Solving**

In Example 1, notice that four of the faces appear to be parallelograms even though they are actually rectangles. The parallelograms give the illusion of depth.

Your turn now **Sketch the solid.**

1. Triangular prism

2. Prism with square bases

EXAMPLE 2 **Sketching a Pyramid**

Sketch a pentagonal pyramid.

(1 Sketch a pentagon for the base and draw a dot directly above the pentagon.

(2 Connect the vertices of the pentagon to the dot.

(3 Make any "hidden" lines dashed.

Three Views Another way to represent a three-dimensional figure using a two-dimensional drawing is to sketch three different views of the figure: a *top* view, a *side* view, and a *front* view.

EXAMPLE 3 **Sketching Three Views of a Solid**

Sketch the top, side, and front views of the cone.

Solution

The top view of a cone is a circle.

The side view of a cone is a triangle.

The front view of a cone is also a triangle.

Your turn now **Complete the following exercises.**

3. Sketch a rectangular pyramid.

4. Sketch the top, side, and front views of the rectangular pyramid you sketched in Exercise 3.

Getting Ready to Practice

1. **Vocabulary** Copy and complete: Three two-dimensional views of a solid are the ? view, the ? view, and the ? view.

2. Copy the partial sketch of a pyramid with a square base. Then complete the drawing.

Cars **Tell whether the view shown is the *top*, *side*, or *front* view of a car.**

3.

4.

5.

Practice and Problem Solving

with Homework

Example	Exercises
1	6–11
2	6–11
3	13–16

Online Resources
CLASSZONE.COM

· More Examples
· eTutorial Plus

Sketch the solid.

6. Triangular pyramid 7. Pentagonal prism 8. Hexagonal prism

9. Cone 10. Cylinder 11. Hexagonal pyramid

12. **Writing** Describe how to sketch a sphere.

Sketch the top, side, and front views of the solid.

13.

14.

15.

16. **Gift Box** Sketch the top, side, and front views of the gift box shown.

17. Critical Thinking A student sketches a solid that has five faces. Four of the faces are triangles, and one of the faces is a rectangle. What type of solid did the student sketch? Be as specific as possible.

18. For which solid(s) is at least one of its three views a rectangle? a triangle? a circle?

A.

B.

C.

Challenge Sketch a solid with the given numbers of faces, edges, and vertices.

19. 5 faces, 8 edges, 5 vertices

20. 4 faces, 6 edges, 4 vertices

Mixed Review

Write the percent as a decimal. *(Lesson 9.3)*

21. 76%

22. 209%

23. 0.1%

Classify the solid. Be as specific as possible. *(Lesson 12.1)*

24.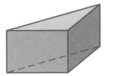

25.

26.

Basic Skills Copy and complete the statement.

27. 1.2 cm = _?_ m

28. 20 kL = _?_ L

29. 0.27 g = _?_ mg

Test-Taking Practice

30. Multiple Choice Which solid has the three views shown?

Top	Side	Front

A. Triangular prism

B. Triangular pyramid

C. Rectangular prism

D. Rectangular pyramid

31. Short Response Sketch a triangular pyramid. Then count the number of faces, edges, and vertices in the pyramid.

Viewing and Building Solids

GOAL Use top, side, and front views to build or draw a solid.

The solid shown below can be built using unit cubes. There are 9 unit cubes on the bottom layer and 3 unit cubes on the top layer. Modeling with unit cubes can help you identify the top, side, and front views of a solid.

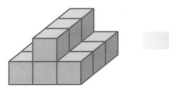
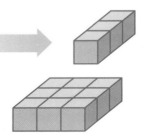

with Solving

For the solids shown here, assume that there are no missing blocks in views that are not shown.

EXAMPLE 1 **Drawing Top, Side, and Front Views**

Draw the top, side, and front views of the solid shown above.

① To draw the top view, imagine what you would see if you were looking at the solid from directly above.

Top

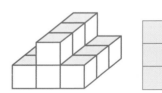

② To draw the side view, imagine what you would see if you were looking directly at one of the sides.

Side

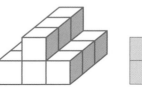

③ To draw the front view, imagine what you would see if you were looking directly at the front.

Front

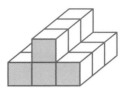

Drawing a Solid Given the top, side, and front views of a solid, you can build or draw the solid. You need to use the information about the solid that each view gives to piece together the shape of the entire solid. It is necessary to look at more than one view at the same time to get a complete picture of the solid.

EXAMPLE 2 **Using Top, Side, and Front Views**

Use the three views of a solid to build and draw the solid.

Top   **Side**   **Front**

Solution

(**1** The top view gives you information about the bottom layer of the solid.

Top

(**2** The side view gives you information about the number of layers and how to form them.

Side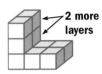

2 more layers

(**3** The front view also gives you information about the number of layers and how to form them.

Front

Exercises

Use unit cubes to build the solid. Then draw the top, side, and front views.

1.   **2.**

Use the three views of a solid to build the solid using unit cubes. Then draw the solid.

3. Top Side Front 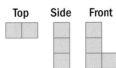   **4.** Top Side Front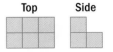

5. Critical Thinking It is possible for two different solids to have the same front and side views. Draw two solids and their corresponding front and side views to show that this statement is true.

12.3 Surface Area of Rectangular Prisms

BEFORE	Now	WHY?
You found the areas of rectangles and squares.	You'll find the surface area of rectangular prisms.	So you can find how much wrapping paper is needed, as in Ex. 14.

Word Watch

surface area, p. 594
net, p. 594

The **surface area** of a solid is the sum of the areas of its outside surfaces. The two-dimensional representation of a solid is called a **net** . The surface area of a rectangular prism is equal to the area of its net.

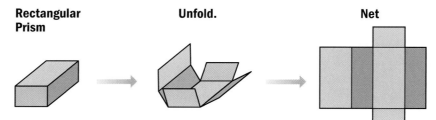

Rectangular Prism   Unfold.   Net

EXAMPLE 1   **Finding Surface Area Using a Net**

Find the surface area of the rectangular prism.

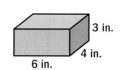

3 in.
4 in.
6 in.

(1   Find the area of each face.

Area of top or bottom: $6 \times 4 = 24$

Area of front or back: $6 \times 3 = 18$

Area of either side: $4 \times 3 = 12$

(2   Add the areas of all six faces.

$24 + 24 + 18 + 18 + 12 + 12 = 108$

ANSWER The surface area of the prism is 108 square inches.

6 in.
4 in.
3 in.
6 in.
3 in.

HELP with Solving

In this book, every rectangular prism is also a *right prism*, which means that the edges connecting the bases are perpendicular to the bases.

Surface Area of a Rectangular Prism

Words The surface area S of a rectangular prism is the sum of the areas of its faces.

Algebra $S = 2lw + 2lh + 2wh$

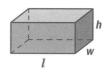

h
w
l

EXAMPLE 2 **Finding Surface Area Using a Formula**

Find the surface area of the rectangular prism.

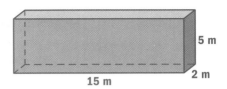
5 m
15 m
2 m

$S = 2lw + 2lh + 2wh$ Write formula for surface area.

$= 2(15)(2) + 2(15)(5) + 2(2)(5)$ Substitute 15 for l, 2 for w, and 5 for h.

$= 60 + 150 + 20$ Multiply.

$= 230$ Add.

ANSWER The surface area of the prism is 230 square meters.

Your turn now **Find the surface area of the rectangular prism. Check your answer by finding the area of the prism's net.**

1.
5 cm
5 cm
10 cm

2.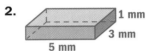
1 mm
3 mm
5 mm

3.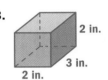
2 in.
3 in.
2 in.

EXAMPLE 3 **Using Surface Area**

Stadium Cushion You are making the stadium cushion shown. The foam for the cushion costs $1.50, and the fabric costs $.50 per square foot. How much does it cost to make the cushion?

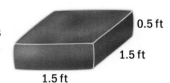
0.5 ft
1.5 ft
1.5 ft

Solution

(1 Find the surface area of the cushion.

$S = 2lw + 2lh + 2wh$ Write formula.

$= 2(1.5)(1.5) + 2(1.5)(0.5) + 2(1.5)(0.5)$ Substitute values.

$= 7.5 \text{ ft}^2$ Simplify.

(2 Find the cost of the fabric: $7.5 \text{ ft}^2 \times \$.50/\text{ft}^2 = \$3.75$

(3 Find the total cost of fabric and foam: $\$3.75 + \$1.50 = \$5.25$

ANSWER It costs $5.25 to make the stadium cushion.

Getting Ready to Practice

1. **Vocabulary** Copy and complete: The _?_ of a rectangular prism is the sum of the areas of its faces.

2. Find the surface area of the rectangular prism whose net is shown.

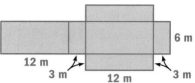

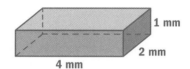

3. Find the area of each face of the rectangular prism. Then find the surface area of the prism.

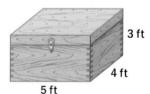

4. **Storage Box** You are building a storage box out of plywood using the dimensions shown. Plywood costs $1.50 per square foot. Find the total cost of the plywood.

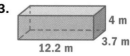

Practice and Problem Solving

Draw a net for the rectangular prism. Then use the net to find the surface area of the prism.

5.
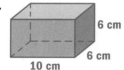

6.

7.

Find the surface area of the rectangular prism.

8.

9.
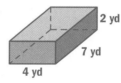

10.
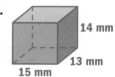

11.
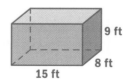

12.
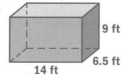

13.
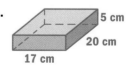

14. Wrapping Paper You are wrapping a gift box that is 18 inches by 12 inches by 3 inches. What is the least amount of wrapping paper you need in order to wrap the box?

Find the surface area of a rectangular prism with the given dimensions.

15. 2 m by 15 cm by 1.2 m

16. 3.5 ft by 10 in. by 6 in.

 17. Algebra Find the width of a rectangular prism that is 12 inches high, 27 inches long, and has a surface area of 1194 square inches.

18. Photo Cube The length of each edge of a photo cube is 3 inches. Does the photo cube have more or less viewing surface than a flat photograph that is 8 inches wide and 10 inches long? Explain.

19. Unit Cubes The solid shown is made of unit cubes where each edge is 1 unit. None of the hidden cubes are missing. What is the surface area of the solid?

20. Challenge A room is 13 feet long, 11 feet wide, and 10 feet high. In the room, there are three windows that are each 4 feet wide and 5 feet tall. If one gallon of paint covers 350 square feet, how many gallons of paint do you need to paint the walls and door of the room? Explain.

Mixed Review

Find the diameter and the radius of the circle with the given circumference. Use 3.14 for π. *(Lesson 11.6)*

21. $C = 69.08$ mm
22. $C = 116.18$ ft
23. $C = 142.87$ cm

24. Sketch a cube. *(Lesson 12.2)*

Basic Skills **Evaluate the expression when $s = 5$ and $t = 7$.**

25. $7s + 3t$
26. $4(3.14)s$
27. $2(3.14)st$
28. $6.28s(2 + t)$

Test-Taking Practice

29. Multiple Choice What is the surface area of a rectangular prism that is 8 inches long, 4 inches wide, and 12 inches high?

A. 176 in.^{2}
B. 332 in.^{2}
C. 352 in.^{2}
D. 384 in.^{2}

30. Multiple Choice If the length, width, and height of a rectangular prism are all doubled, by how much does the surface area increase?

F. 2 times
G. 4 times
H. 8 times
I. 16 times

Notebook Review

Review the vocabulary definitions in your notebook.

Copy the review examples in your notebook. Then complete the exercises.

Check Your Definitions

solid, p. 583	cone, p. 583	vertex, p. 584
prism, p. 583	sphere, p. 583	surface area, p. 594
pyramid, p. 583	face, p. 584	net, p. 594
cylinder, p. 583	edge, p. 584	

Use Your Vocabulary

1. Copy and complete: A triangular prism has 6 _?_, 5 _?_, and 9 _?_.

12.1–12.2 Can you classify and sketch solids?

 EXAMPLE Sketch a hexagonal prism. Then count the number of faces, edges, and vertices.

A hexagonal prism has 8 faces, 18 edges, and 12 vertices.

☑ **Sketch the solid. Then count the number of faces, edges, and vertices.**

    2. Pentagonal prism   **3.** Triangular pyramid

12.3 Can you find the surface area of rectangular prisms?

 EXAMPLE Find the surface area of the rectangular prism.

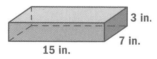

3 in.
7 in.
15 in.

$S = 2lw + 2lh + 2wh$ **Write formula for surface area.**

$= 2(15)(7) + 2(15)(3) + 2(7)(3)$ **Substitute values.**

$= 210 + 90 + 42$ **Multiply.**

$= 342$ in.^{2} **Add.**

☑ **Find the surface area of the rectangular prism.**

4.
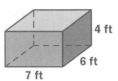
4 ft
6 ft
7 ft

5.
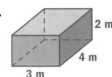
2 m
4 m
3 m

6.

8 in.
8 in.
8 in.

Stop *and* **Think** about Lessons 12.1–12.3

7. Estimation Choose the best estimate for the surface area of a standard door. Explain your reasoning in words and numbers.

A. 9 ft² **B.** 44 ft² **C.** 105 ft²

Review Quiz 1

Classify the solid. Be as specific as possible.

1.

2.

3.

Sketch the solid. Then count the number of faces, edges, and vertices.

4. Triangular prism **5.** Cube **6.** Pentagonal pyramid

7. School Play You are making sets for a school play. One of the set pieces is the rectangular prism shown, to be used as a stand for a statue. If you paint all of the faces except the bottom, what surface area must you paint?

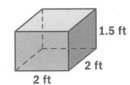
1.5 ft
2 ft
2 ft

Face Painting

You have a cube made out of 27 smaller cubes of the same size. If you paint the six faces of the large cube, how many of the 27 smaller cubes have three faces painted? two faces painted? one face painted? no faces painted?

12.4 Problem Solving Strategies

Make a Model

Break into Parts
Work Backward
Write an Equation
Make a List
Make a Model
Draw a Diagram
Guess, Check, and Revise

Problem A solid is formed by joining the base of a square pyramid to a face of a cube. The base of the pyramid is congruent to the faces of the cube. Count the number of faces, edges, and vertices in the solid.

① Read and Understand

Read the problem carefully.

The solid is made up of a square pyramid and a cube. You need to figure out how many faces, edges, and vertices are in the solid. Because the pyramid and the cube are attached, you cannot simply count the faces, edges, and vertices of the pyramid and cube separately.

② Make a Plan

Decide on a strategy to use.

You need to know what the solid looks like to be able to count its faces, edges, and vertices. You can make a model of the solid using a net for a cube and a net for a square pyramid. You'll need paper, scissors, tape, and a ruler to make the model.

③ Solve the Problem

Reread the problem and make a model.

Draw a net for a cube and a net for a square pyramid. Make the base of the square pyramid congruent to a face of the cube. For convenience, make each triangular face of the pyramid an equilateral triangle.

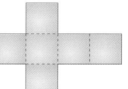

For each figure, cut out the net, fold along the dashed lines, and use tape to join the faces together. Then tape the square base of the pyramid to a face of the cube to form the solid.

ANSWER Now you can see that the solid has 9 faces, 16 edges, and 9 vertices.

④ Look Back

When separated, the cube and the square pyramid have a total of 11 faces, 20 edges, and 13 vertices. When joined together, the resulting solid should have 2 fewer faces, 4 fewer edges, and 4 fewer vertices than the separated cube and pyramid. So, it makes sense that the solid has 9 faces, 16 edges, and 9 vertices.

Use the strategy *make a model*.

1. **Science Fair** You are building a cone-shaped volcano for a science fair. You want the base of the cone to have a diameter of 18 in. and the distance from the top of the cone to the edge of the base to be 15 in. What will the height be?

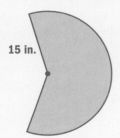

15 in.   15 in.

18 in.

2. **Properties of a Solid** A solid is formed by joining the bases of two identical triangular pyramids. Count the number of faces, edges, and vertices in the solid.

3. **Art** For art class you build a solid by attaching six identical square pyramids to the faces of a cube. The bases of the pyramids are congruent to the faces of the cube. Now you want to cover the solid with construction paper. How many triangular pieces of paper will you need? How many square pieces?

4. **Rectangular Prisms** A rectangular prism is built using 20 unit cubes. How many different prisms can be built?

5. **Unit Cube Pyramid** A pyramid-like structure is made from unit cubes. Each layer of the structure is a square arrangement of cubes. The bottom layer is 5×5, the middle layer is 3×3, and the top layer is a singe cube. How many cubes form the structure? How many faces of the cubes are visible (assuming that you can pick up the structure to view the bottom)?

Mixed Problem Solving

Use any strategy to solve the problem.

6. **Guitars** You are buying an electric guitar. The body of the guitar can be either hollow or solid. You can choose from two types of necks, rosewood or maple. The guitar's color can be black, red metallic, blue metallic, or white. How many different guitars can you choose from?

7. **Running Track** The running track at your school has the dimensions given below. The ends of the track are half circles. If you make one complete lap around the track, how far have you run? Use 3.14 for π. Round your answer to the nearest meter.

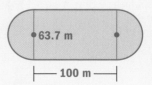

63.7 m

100 m

8. **Sibling Ages** In 10 years your sister will be twice the age of your brother. If the sum of their ages now is 25, how old is your brother and how old is your sister?

9. **Driving** Matt, Jeff, and Sam take turns driving on a road trip. Matt drives half of the way to their destination. Then Jeff drives two thirds of the remaining distance. That leaves 50 miles for Sam to drive. How far will they drive altogether?

Surface Area of Cylinders

BEFORE	**Now**	**WHY?**
You found the surface area of rectangular prisms.	You'll find the surface area of cylinders.	So you can find the area of a circular cake to frost, as in Ex. 18.

Word Watch

Review Words

cylinder, p. 583
surface area, p. 594
net, p. 594

Activity **You can make a model to find the surface area of a cylinder.**

(1) Cut out pieces of paper to cover a cylindrical can. What shape are the pieces of paper that cover the top and bottom of the can? What shape is the piece of paper that covers the side of the can?

(2) Describe the relationship between the length of the paper used to cover the side of the can and the circumference of the paper used to cover the top of the can.

(3) Use your pieces of paper to find the surface area of the can.

In the activity, you saw that the net of a cylinder consists of two circles that form the bases and a rectangle that forms the curved surface of the cylinder. The circumference of a base, $2\pi r$, is equal to the length of the rectangle, and the height of the cylinder is the width of the rectangle.

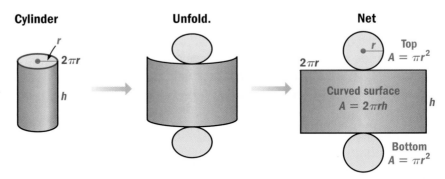

HELP with Solving

In this book, all cylinders are *right cylinders*, which means that the line connecting the centers of the bases is perpendicular to the bases.

Surface Area of a Cylinder

Words The surface area S of a cylinder is the sum of the area of the curved surface and the areas of the circular bases.

Algebra $S = 2\pi rh + 2\pi r^2$

EXAMPLE 1 **Finding the Surface Area of a Cylinder**

Find the surface area of the cylinder. Use 3.14 for π.

3 cm
8 cm

$$S = 2\pi rh + 2\pi r^2 \qquad\qquad \text{Write formula.}$$

$$\approx 2(3.14)(3)(8) + 2(3.14)(3)^2 \qquad \text{Substitute values.}$$

$$= 150.72 + 56.52 \qquad\qquad \text{Multiply.}$$

$$\approx 207 \qquad\qquad\qquad\qquad \text{Add.}$$

ANSWER The surface area is about 207 square centimeters.

EXAMPLE 2 **Finding the Height of a Cylinder**

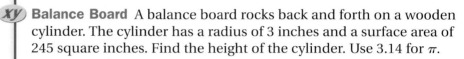

Balance Board A balance board rocks back and forth on a wooden cylinder. The cylinder has a radius of 3 inches and a surface area of 245 square inches. Find the height of the cylinder. Use 3.14 for π.

Solution

$$S = 2\pi rh + 2\pi r^2 \qquad\qquad \text{Write formula for surface area.}$$

$$245 \approx 2(3.14)(3)h + 2(3.14)(3)^2 \qquad \text{Substitute values.}$$

$$245 \approx 18.84h + 56.52 \qquad\qquad \text{Multiply.}$$

$$245 - 56.52 \approx 18.84h + 56.52 - 56.52 \qquad \text{Subtract 56.52 from each side.}$$

$$188.48 \approx 18.84h \qquad\qquad \text{Simplify.}$$

$$\frac{188.48}{18.84} \approx \frac{18.84h}{18.84} \qquad\qquad \text{Divide each side by 18.84.}$$

$$10 \approx h \qquad\qquad\qquad \text{Simplify.}$$

ANSWER The height of the wooden cylinder is about 10 inches.

Your turn now **Find the surface area of the cylinder. Use 3.14 for π.**

1.
5 mm
3 mm

2.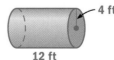
4 ft
12 ft

3.
11 m
11 m

4. Find the height of a cylinder that has a radius of 20 feet and a surface area of 9700 square feet. Use 3.14 for π. Round your answer to the nearest foot.

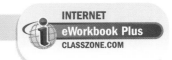

Getting Ready to Practice

What do you think?

Food

1. **Vocabulary** Copy and complete: The net for a cylinder consists of two _?_ and a(n) _?_.

Match the cylinder with its approximate surface area.

2. 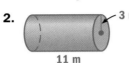 3 m, 11 m

3. 6 m, 7 m

4. 4 m, 10 m

A. 264 m² **B.** 352 m² **C.** 490 m²

5. **Cheese Wheel** A cylindrical cheese wheel has a diameter of 8 inches and a height of 5 inches. A wax coating covers the cheese wheel to keep the cheese fresh. How much surface area must the wax coating cover? Use 3.14 for π.

■ **Cheese Wheel**

The cheese wheel pictured above weighs 567 kilograms. About how many pounds does the cheese wheel weigh? Use 1 kg ≈ 2.2 lb.

Practice and Problem Solving

Draw a net for the cylinder and label the dimensions. Then use the net to find the surface area of the cylinder. Use 3.14 for π.

6.  9 in., 6 in.

7. 2 cm, 7 cm

8. 5 ft, 6 ft

Find the surface area of the cylindrical object. Use 3.14 for π.

9.  8 cm, 19 cm

10.  0.25 in., 2 in.

11.  20 in., 24 in.

HELP with Homework

Example	Exercises
1	6–11, 15–17
2	12–14

Online Resources
CLASSZONE.COM
· More Examples
· eTutorial Plus

Algebra Find the height of a cylinder with the given radius and surface area. Use 3.14 for π.

12. $r = 25$ cm
$S = 4867$ cm²

13. $r = 10$ in.
$S = 1570$ in.²

14. $r = 4.5$ ft
$S = 141.3$ ft²

Find the surface area of a cylinder with the given dimensions. Use 3.14 for π. Write your answer using the smaller unit.

15. Radius: 1 cm
Height: 3 mm

16. Radius: 6 in.
Height: 2 ft

17. Diameter: 17 cm
Height: 0.5 m

18. Cake You are frosting a circular cake that has three layers. Each layer has a 5 inch diameter and is 2 inches tall. You frost in between each layer and the exposed surface of the cake, excluding the bottom. To the nearest square inch, what is the total area that you frost? Use 3.14 for π.

19. Critical Thinking The surface area of a cylinder is 408.2 square feet. The area of one of the bases is 78.5 square feet. Find the height of the cylinder. Use 3.14 for π.

20. Challenge The height and the radius of a cylinder are equal. The cylinder has a surface area of 113.04 square feet. Find the height of the cylinder. Use 3.14 for π.

Mixed Review

Find the area of the parallelogram. *(Lesson 11.4)*

21.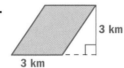
3 km
3 km

22.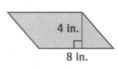
4 in.
8 in.

23.
7 m   6 m

Find the surface area of a rectangular prism with the given dimensions. *(Lesson 12.3)*

24. 6 m by 1 m by 8 m   **25.** 7 ft by 2.5 ft by 3 ft   **26.** 15 cm by 3 cm by 5 cm

Basic Skills **Find the product.**

27. 6.4×3.5 **28.** 11.7×8.2 **29.** 0.09×0.9

Test-Taking Practice

30. Multiple Choice Which of the following is the net for a cylinder?

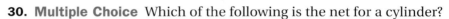

A.   B.   C.   D.

31. Short Response Cylinder A has a radius of 2 meters and a height of 4 meters. Cylinder B has a radius of 4 meters and a height of 2 meters. Which cylinder has the greater surface area? Explain.

Hands-on Activity

Investigating Volume

You can use unit cubes to build rectangular prisms and find their volumes.

Explore   Find the volume of a rectangular prism that is 4 units long, 2 units wide, and 1 unit high.

1 Use unit cubes to build a rectangular prism that is 4 units long, 2 units wide, and 1 unit high.

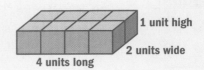

1 unit high

2 units wide

4 units long

2 Count the number of unit cubes used to build the prism. The rectangular prism is made up of 8 unit cubes. This means that the rectangular prism has a *volume* of 8 cubic units.

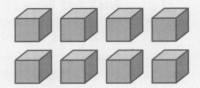

Your turn now   Complete the following exercises.

1. Copy the table. Build all of the rectangular prisms whose dimensions are given in the table. Then find the volume of each rectangular prism by counting the number of unit cubes you used to build the prism. Record your results in the table.

Length *l*	Width *w*	Height *h*	Volume *V*
4	2	1	8
2	1	5	?
1	1	7	?
2	2	3	?
3	3	1	?
5	1	3	?

2. Use 16 unit cubes to build three different rectangular prisms. What are the length, width, height, and volume of each prism? Include your results in the table.

Stop and Think

3. Critical Thinking Look for a pattern in the table. Then write an equation that relates the volume *V* of a rectangular prism to its length *l*, width *w*, and height *h*.

Volume of Rectangular Prisms

BEFORE	▶ **Now**	**WHY?**
You found the surface area of rectangular prisms.	You'll find the volume of rectangular prisms.	So you can find the cost to fill a window box, as in Ex. 19.

In the Real World

Word Watch

volume, p. 607

Aquarium An aquarium shaped like a rectangular prism has a length of 120 centimeters, a width of 60 centimeters, and a height of 100 centimeters. How much water is needed to fill the aquarium?

The **volume** of a solid is the amount of space it contains. Volume is measured in cubic units, such as cubic feet (ft^3) and cubic meters (m^3).

Volume of a Rectangular Prism

Words The volume V of a rectangular prism is the product of the length, width, and height.

Algebra $V = lwh$

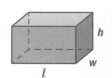

EXAMPLE 1 **Volume of a Rectangular Prism**

To find the amount of water needed to fill the aquarium described above, find the volume of the aquarium.

$V = lwh$ Write formula for volume of a rectangular prism.

$\quad = (120)(60)(100)$ Substitute 120 for l, 60 for w, and 100 for h.

$\quad = 720,000$ Multiply.

ANSWER You need 720,000 cubic centimeters of water to fill the aquarium.

Your turn now **Find the volume of the rectangular prism.**

1. 10 in.   6 in.   16 in.

2. 6 ft   5 ft   4 ft

3. 2 m   3.5 m   1 m

EXAMPLE 2 Finding the Height of a Rectangular Prism

xy The rectangular prism shown has a volume of 1440 cubic millimeters. Find the prism's height.

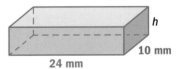

24 mm, 10 mm, h

$$V = lwh$$ Write formula for volume of a rectangular prism.

$$1440 = (24)(10)h$$ Substitute 1440 for *V*, 24 for *l*, and 10 for *w*.

$$1440 = 240h$$ Multiply.

$$\frac{1440}{240} = \frac{240h}{240}$$ Divide each side by 240.

$$6 = h$$ Simplify.

ANSWER The height of the prism is 6 millimeters.

Your turn now Find the unknown length, width, or height of the rectangular prism.

4. $V = 24$ in.^{3}, $l = 6$ in., $w = 2$ in., $h = \underline{\ ?\ }$

5. $V = 360$ ft^3, $l = 10$ ft, $w = \underline{\ ?\ }$, $h = 9$ ft

6. $V = 125$ cm^3, $l = \underline{\ ?\ }$, $w = 2$ cm, $h = 12.5$ cm

What do you think?

Recreation

■ **Sand Sculpture**

The tallest hand-built sand sculpture was 24 feet tall and used 200 tons of sand. How many pounds of sand is that?

EXAMPLE 3 Using the Volume of a Rectangular Prism

Sand Sculpture A truck whose bed is 8 feet long, 5 feet wide, and 3 feet high is delivering sand for a sand sculpture competition. How many trips must the truck make to deliver 300 cubic feet of sand?

Solution

(1 Find the volume of the bed of the truck.

$$V = lwh$$

$$= 8(5)(3) = 120 \text{ ft}^3$$

(2 To find the number of truckloads of sand needed, divide 300 ft^3 by 120 ft^3.

$$300 \text{ ft}^3 \div 120 \text{ ft}^3 = 2.5$$

ANSWER Because it doesn't make sense to make 2.5 trips, the truck must make 3 trips to deliver 300 cubic feet of sand for the competition.

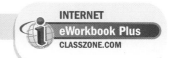
Getting Ready to Practice

1. Vocabulary Explain the difference between volume and surface area.

Find the volume of the rectangular prism.

2.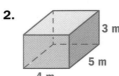
3 m
5 m
4 m

3.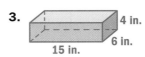
4 in.
6 in.
15 in.

4.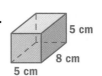
5 cm
8 cm
5 cm

5. Watermelons In Japan, farmers have developed watermelons that are shaped like cubes and therefore fit better in refrigerators. What is the volume of a cubic watermelon whose edge length is 18 centimeters?

Practice and Problem Solving

Find the volume of the rectangular prism.

6.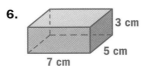
3 cm
5 cm
7 cm

7.
12 m
18 m
3 m

8.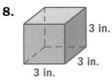
3 in.
3 in.
3 in.

9.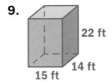
22 ft
14 ft
15 ft

10.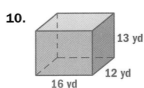
13 yd
12 yd
16 yd

11.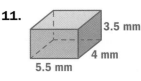
3.5 mm
4 mm
5.5 mm

(xy) Algebra Find the unknown length, width, or height of the rectangular prism.

12. $V = 160 \text{ cm}^3$, $l = 10$ cm, $w = \underline{\ ?\ }$, $h = 8$ cm

13. $V = 400 \text{ ft}^3$, $l = 10$ ft, $w = 5$ ft, $h = \underline{\ ?\ }$

14. $V = 28 \text{ yd}^3$, $l = \underline{\ ?\ }$, $w = 1$ yd, $h = 7$ yd

15. Estimation Which of the following items would likely have a volume of 300 cubic inches? Explain your reasoning.

A. Sugar cube   **B.** Cereal box   **C.** Refrigerator

16. Aquarium The dimensions of an aquarium are half as long as those of the aquarium on page 607. If the aquarium is filled with water, what is the mass of the water? Use the fact that for water $1 \text{ cm}^3 = 1$ g.

HELP with **Homework**

Example	Exercises
1	6–11
2	12–14
3	16–19

Online Resources
CLASSZONE.COM
· More Examples
· eTutorial plus

Extended Problem Solving In Exercises 17–19, use the following information. A window box shaped like a rectangular prism has a length of 12 feet, a width of 9 inches, and a height of 9 inches.

17. Measurement Convert the dimensions of the window box to feet. Then find the volume of the window box.

18. Calculate One bag contains 2 cubic feet of soil. How many bags of soil must you buy to fill the window box? You must buy full bags of soil.

19. Estimation Each bag of soil costs $4.97, including tax. Estimate the cost of filling the window box with soil.

Favorite Books In Exercises 20 and 21, use the bar graph.

20. Writing Explain how the bar graph shown could be potentially misleading.

21. Critical Thinking How could the bar graph be redrawn using 3-D bars so it is not potentially misleading?

22. Challenge Find the volume and surface area of the solid.

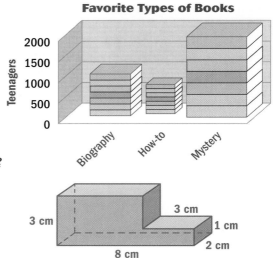

Favorite Types of Books

Mixed Review

Solve the equation. Check your solution. *(Lesson 7.4)*

23. $11a = 44$ **24.** $9b = 180$ **25.** $450 = 5c$ **26.** $36 = 4.5d$

27. Find the surface area of a cylinder that has a radius of 9 centimeters and a height of 5 centimeters. Use 3.14 for π. *(Lesson 12.4)*

Basic Skills **Find the mean, median, mode(s), and range of the data.**

28. 45, 56, 35, 45, 57, 51, 52, 43   **29.** 2.2, 2.6, 3.3, 2, 7, 4.5, 3.3, 2, 1.1, 2

Test-Taking Practice

30. Extended Response Make an input-output table for a cube's edge length x and its volume y for edge lengths of 1 unit, 2 units, 3 units, and 4 units. Plot the ordered pairs in a coordinate plane. Then use the graph to decide whether the volume of a cube is a linear function of the cube's edge length. Explain your reasoning.

Volume of Cylinders

LESSON 12.6

BEFORE	Now	WHY?
You found the volume of rectangular prisms.	You'll find the volume of cylinders.	So you can find the volumes of stacks of coins, as in Ex. 16.

In the Real World

Word Watch

Review Words
cylinder, p. 583
volume, p. 607

Candles You buy two cylindrical candles with different dimensions. How can you determine which candle took more wax to make? In Example 2, you'll find out by finding their volumes.

In the previous lesson, you learned that the volume of a rectangular prism is the product of the area of a base (length × width) and the height. The volume of a cylinder can be found the same way.

The area of the base is the number of unit squares that cover the base.

The height is the number of layers of unit cubes that fit in the solid.

Volume of a Cylinder

Words The volume V of a cylinder is the product of the area of a base and the height.

Algebra $V = \pi r^2 h$

EXAMPLE 1 Finding the Volume of a Cylinder

HELP with Notetaking

You have learned many properties and formulas related to solids. Writing a summary of what you have learned may help you prepare for the chapter test.

Find the volume of the cylinder. Use 3.14 for π.

2 m

3 m

$$V = \pi r^2 h \qquad \text{Write formula for volume of a cylinder.}$$

$$\approx (3.14)(2)^2(3) \qquad \text{Substitute 3.14 for } \pi, \text{ 2 for } r, \text{ and 3 for } h.$$

$$\approx 37.7 \qquad \text{Multiply.}$$

ANSWER The volume of the cylinder is about 37.7 cubic meters.

Lesson 12.6   Volume of Cylinders   **611**

Watch Out!

Make sure to use the radius, not the diameter, in the formula for the volume of a cylinder.

EXAMPLE 2 **Comparing Volumes of Cylinders**

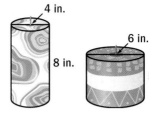

To find which of the candles from page 611 took more wax to make, find their volumes.

① Find the radius of each candle, which is half of the diameter.

Tall candle: $r = \dfrac{4}{2} = 2$ in.   **Short candle:** $r = \dfrac{6}{2} = 3$ in.

② Find the volume of each candle. Use 3.14 for π.

Tall candle: $V = \pi r^2 h$ **Short candle:** $V = \pi r^2 h$

$\approx (3.14)(2)^2(8)$ $\approx (3.14)(3)^2(5)$

≈ 100 in.^{3} ≈ 141 in.^{3}

ANSWER The short candle took more wax to make than the tall candle.

EXAMPLE 3 **Finding the Radius of a Cylinder**

xy **A cylinder has a height of 9 feet and a volume of 706.5 cubic feet. Find the radius of the cylinder. Use 3.14 for π.**

$V = \pi r^2 h$	Write formula for volume of a cylinder.
$706.5 \approx (3.14) r^2 (9)$	Substitute 706.5 for V, 3.14 for π, and 9 for h.
$706.5 \approx 28.26 r^2$	Multiply.
$25 \approx r^2$	Divide each side by 28.26.
$\sqrt{25} \approx r$	Take positive square root of each side.
$5 \approx r$	Evaluate square root.

ANSWER The radius of the cylinder is about 5 feet.

HELP with **Review**

Need help with solving equations using square roots? See p. 533.

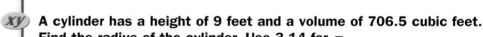

Your turn now **Find the volume of the cylinder. Use 3.14 for π.**

1.   **2.**   **3.**

 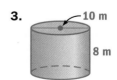

4. Find the radius of a cylinder that has a height of 5 inches and a volume of 251.2 cubic inches. Use 3.14 for π.

Getting Ready to Practice

1. Vocabulary Copy and complete: To find the volume of a cylinder, multiply the area of a(n) ? and the ? .

Find the volume of the cylinder. Use 3.14 for π.

2. 1 in.
3 in.

3.  5 m
4 m

4.  7 mm
11 mm

xy **5. Algebra** Find the height of a cylinder that has a radius of 3 feet and a volume of 56.52 cubic feet. Use 3.14 for π.

6. Guided Problem Solving A cheese filled pretzel snack is a cylinder that has a radius of 1.4 centimeters and a height of 2.2 centimeters. The cheese center has a radius of 0.6 centimeter and height of 2.2 centimeters. What percent of the snack is cheese?

(1 Find the volume of the snack. Use 3.14 for π.

(2 Find the volume of the cheese. Use 3.14 for π.

(3 What percent of the snack is cheese? Round to the nearest percent.

Practice and Problem Solving

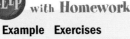
with **Homework**

Example	Exercises
1	7–9
2	10–11
3	12–14

Online Resources
CLASSZONE.COM
· More Examples
· eTutorial Plus

Find the volume of the cylinder. Use 3.14 for π.

7.  8 ft
8 ft

8.  3 in.
4 in.

9. 8 cm
9 cm

Tell which cylinder has the greater volume.

10. Cylinder A: $r = 6$ m, $h = 13$ m; Cylinder B: $r = 8$ m, $h = 7.5$ m

11. Cylinder C: $r = 3$ yd, $h = 9$ yd; Cylinder D: $r = 10$ ft, $h = 25$ ft

xy **Algebra** **Find the unknown radius, diameter, or height of the cylinder. Use 3.14 for π.**

12. $V = 5024$ in.^{3}
$d = 16$ in.
$h = $?

13. $V = 25.12$ cm^3
$r = $?
$h = 8$ cm

14. $V = 5338$ ft^3
$d = $?
$h = 17$ ft

15. **Swimming Pools** A cylindrical above-ground swimming pool has a diameter of 16 feet and a height of 4 feet. A cylindrical kiddie pool has a diameter of 8 feet and a height of 2 feet. Find the volume of each pool. Use 3.14 for π. The larger pool can hold 25 tons of water. Write and solve a proportion to find how much water the smaller pool can hold.

16. **Coins** The dimensions of different coins are given in the table. To the nearest hundred cubic millimeters, find the volume of a $1.00 stack of each coin. Use estimation to check the reasonableness of your answers.

Coin	Penny	Nickel	Dime	Quarter
Diameter (mm)	19.05	21.21	17.91	24.26
Thickness (mm)	1.55	1.95	1.35	1.75

17. **Challenge** Each tennis ball is a sphere with a radius of 3.25 centimeters. Find the volume of the can of tennis balls. Round to the nearest cubic centimeter.

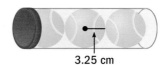

3.25 cm

Mixed Review

18. Find the height of a rectangular prism that has a length of 9 inches, a width of 7 inches, and a volume of 31.5 cubic inches. *(Lesson 12.5)*

Choose a Strategy Use a strategy from the list to solve the following exercise. Explain your choice of strategy.

Problem Solving Strategies
- Write an Equation
- Guess, Check, and Revise
- Estimate

19. What number raised to the fourth power is equal to 1296?

Basic Skills Find the LCM and the GCF of the numbers.

20. 12, 42   21. 15, 70   22. 96, 120

Test-Taking Practice

23. **Multiple Choice** Which of the following are possible dimensions of a cylinder that has a volume of about 250 cubic units?

   A. $r = 8, h = 10$ **B.** $r = 1, h = 4$ **C.** $r = 2, h = 6$ **D.** $r = 3, h = 9$

24. **Multiple Choice** What is the approximate height of a cylinder that has a diameter of 8 feet and a volume of 502.4 cubic feet?

   F. 2.5 ft   **G.** 5 ft   **H.** 10 ft   **I.** 20 ft

Surface Area and Volume

GOAL Use spreadsheet software to calculate the surface area and volume of a solid.

Example Find the volume and surface area of the rectangular prism shown. Then double all the dimensions and compare the surface area and volume of the new prism with those of the original.

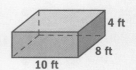

Solution

1 Label five columns for length, width, height, surface area, and volume in the first row. Then enter the dimensions of the first prism and the formulas for surface area and volume as shown. Use * for multiplication.

	A	B	C	D	E
1	Length	Width	Height	Surface area	Volume
2	10	8	4	=2*A2*B2+2*A2*C2+2*B2*C2	=A2*B2*C2

2 Enter the doubled dimensions into row 3. Then use the *Fill down* feature to have the spreadsheet calculate the surface area and volume of the new prism.

	A	B	C	D	E
1	Length	Width	Height	Surface area	Volume
2	10	8	4	304	320
3	20	16	8	1216	2560

ANSWER The surface area of the new prism is 4 times as great as the surface area of the original prism. Its volume is 8 times as great.

Your turn now Use the spreadsheet to find the surface area and volume of a rectangular prism with the given dimensions.

1. $l = 4$ in., $w = 3$ in., $h = 2.3$ in.   **2.** $l = 6.5$ cm, $w = 2.5$ cm, $h = 1.5$ cm

3. Critical Thinking Make a conjecture about the effect that tripling all three dimensions of a rectangular prism has on the surface area and volume of the prism. Use the spreadsheet program to check your conjecture.

4. Create a spreadsheet that calculates the surface area and volume of a cylinder, given its radius and height. Use PI() for π and ^2 for squaring.

Notebook Review

LESSONS 12.4 TO 12.6

Review the vocabulary definitions in your notebook.

Copy the review examples in your notebook. Then complete the exercises.

Check Your Definitions

volume, p. 607

Use Your Vocabulary

1. Write the formulas for the surface area and volume of a cylinder.

12.4 Can you find the surface area of cylinders?

Review

EXAMPLE Find the surface area of the cylinder. Use 3.14 for π.

Because the diameter is 4 feet, the radius is 2 feet.

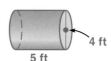

$$S = 2\pi rh + 2\pi r^2 \qquad \text{Write formula for surface area.}$$
$$\approx 2(3.14)(2)(5) + 2(3.14)(2)^2 \qquad \text{Substitute values.}$$
$$= 62.8 + 25.12 \qquad \text{Multiply.}$$
$$= 87.92 \text{ ft}^2 \qquad \text{Add.}$$

☑ **Find the surface area of the cylinder. Use 3.14 for π.**

2. 11 in.
6 in.

3. 2 m
5.7 m

4. 6 ft
6 ft

12.5–12.6 Can you find the volume of solids?

Review

EXAMPLE Find the volumes of the rectangular prism and cylinder. Use 3.14 for π.

a. 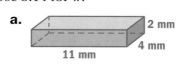 2 mm
4 mm
11 mm

b.  10 cm
5 cm

$$V = lwh \qquad\qquad V = \pi r^2 h$$
$$= (11)(4)(2) \qquad\qquad \approx (3.14)(10)^2(5)$$
$$= 88 \text{ mm}^3 \qquad\qquad = 1570 \text{ cm}^3$$

Find the volume of the solid. Use 3.14 for π.

5. Rectangular prism that has a length of 5.5 feet, a width of 2 feet, and a height of 3 feet

6. Cylinder that has a diameter of 6 inches and a height of 6.5 inches

Stop *and* **Think** about Lessons 12.4–12.6

7. Writing The volume of a rectangular prism is 240 cubic meters. What additional information do you need to find its height?

Review Quiz 2

Find the volume of the rectangular prism.

1.
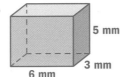
5 mm
3 mm
6 mm

2.

7 cm
4 cm
4 cm

3.
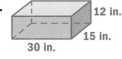
12 in.
15 in.
30 in.

Find the surface area and volume of the cylinder. Use 3.14 for π.

4.

9 yd
13 yd

5.

5 m
2.4 m

6.

32 ft
10 ft

7. Bricks A brick has a width of 3.75 inches, a height of 2.25 inches, and a volume of 67.5 cubic inches. Find the length of the brick.

Chapter Review

Vocabulary

solid, p. 583	cone, p. 583	vertex, p. 584
prism, p. 583	sphere, p. 583	surface area, p. 594
pyramid, p. 583	face, p. 584	net, p. 594
cylinder, p. 583	edge, p. 584	volume, p. 607

Vocabulary Review

Copy and complete the statement.

1. A(n) _?_ is a three-dimensional figure that encloses a part of space.

2. The _?_ of a rectangular prism is the sum of the areas of its faces.

3. The _?_ of a solid is the amount of space it contains.

4. Polygons that form the sides of a prism or pyramid are called _?_.

5. The two-dimensional representation of a solid is called a(n) _?_.

6. A(n) _?_ is a solid with two congruent circular bases that lie in parallel planes.

Review Questions

Classify the solid. Be as specific as possible. *(Lesson 12.1)*

7.

8.

9.
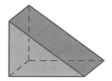

10. A pyramid has 5 faces. What type of a pyramid is it? *(Lesson 12.1)*

Sketch the solid. *(Lesson 12.2)*

11. Triangular pyramid   **12.** Rectangular prism   **13.** Cone

Find the surface area of the rectangular prism. *(Lesson 12.3)*

14.

7 ft
6 ft
4 ft

15.
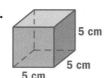
5 cm
5 cm
5 cm

16.
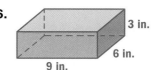
3 in.
6 in.
9 in.

17. Write and simplify an expression for the surface area of a cube with edge length x. *(Lesson 12.3)*

Find the surface area of the cylinder. Use 3.14 for π. *(Lesson 12.4)*

18.

19.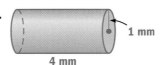

20.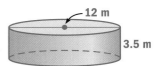

Find the volume of the rectangular prism. *(Lesson 12.5)*

21.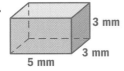

22.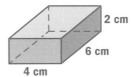

23.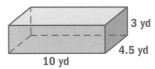

Find the unknown length, width, height, or volume of the rectangular prism. *(Lesson 12.5)*

24. $V = \underline{\ ?\ }$
$l = 20$ in.
$w = 4$ in.
$h = 5$ in.

25. $V = 100 \text{ m}^3$
$l = 5$ m
$w = \underline{\ ?\ }$
$h = 20$ m

26. $V = 47 \text{ ft}^3$
$l = \underline{\ ?\ }$
$w = 2$ ft
$h = 1$ ft

27. $V = 81 \text{ cm}^3$
$l = 9$ cm
$w = 4.5$ cm
$h = \underline{\ ?\ }$

In Exercises 28 and 29, use the cylinders below. *(Lessons 12.4, 12.6)*

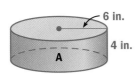

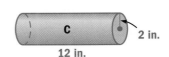

28. Order the cylinders from greatest to least surface area.

29. Order the cylinders from greatest to least volume.

30. **Pencils** An unsharpened wooden pencil is a cylinder that has a radius of 3.5 millimeters and a height of 175 millimeters. The pencil's lead is a cylinder that has a radius of 2 millimeters. Find the volume of the wood in the pencil. Use 3.14 for π. *(Lesson 12.6)*

31. Find the height of a cylinder that has a volume of 923.16 cubic feet and a radius of 7 feet. *(Lesson 12.6)*

Chapter Test

In Exercises 1 and 2, use the diagram of the solid.

1. Classify the solid. Be as specific as possible.

2. Count the number of faces, edges, and vertices in the solid.

3. Sketch a rectangular pyramid.

4. Find the surface area of a rectangular prism that has a length of 15 meters, a width of 7 meters, and a height of 2 meters.

5. Order the rectangular prisms from least to greatest surface area.

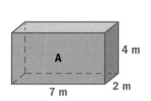

6. Find the surface area of a cylinder that has a radius of 1 millimeter and a height of 3.5 millimeters. Use 3.14 for π.

7. Find the height of a cylinder that has a radius of 3 centimeters and a surface area of 108.33 square centimeters. Use 3.14 for π.

Find the volume of the rectangular prism or cylinder. Use 3.14 for π.

8.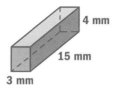

9.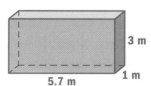

10.

11. **DVD Case** A standard DVD case is a rectangular prism that is 19 centimeters long, 13.5 centimeters wide, and 1.4 centimeters high. Find the surface area and volume of the DVD case.

12. Find the length of a rectangular prism that has a width of 4.5 inches, a height of 5 inches, and a volume of 135 cubic inches.

13. Find the radius of a cylinder that has a height of 3 centimeters and a volume of 942 cubic centimeters. Use 3.14 for π.

Chapter Standardized Test

Test-Taking Strategy After you finish the test, use the remaining time to go back and check as many of your answers as you can.

Multiple Choice

1. Which solid is a triangular prism?

A.

B.

C.

D.

2. What is the surface area of a cube that has edges that are 2 inches long?

F. 4 in.^{2} **G.** 8 in.^{2} **H.** 24 in.^{2} **I.** 64 in.^{2}

3. What are possible dimensions of a rectangular prism with a surface area of 372 square meters?

A. 12 m by 10 m by 3 m

B. 93 m by 1 m by 4 m

C. 9 m by 9 m by 7 m

D. 14 m by 6 m by 2 m

4. What is the approximate surface area of the cylinder whose net is shown?

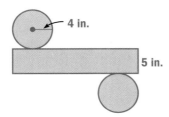

F. 100 in.^{2} **G.** 176 in.^{2}

H. 226 in.^{2} **I.** 251 in.^{2}

5. What is the height of a rectangular prism that has a length of 5 feet, a width of 2 feet, and a volume of 60 cubic feet?

A. 6 feet **B.** 7 feet

C. 10 feet **D.** 600 feet

6. What is the approximate volume of the cylinder shown?

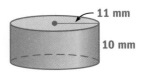

F. 345 mm^3 **G.** 1210 mm^3

H. 1450 mm^3 **I.** 3800 mm^3

Short Response

7. Which solid has the greater surface area: the rectangular prism or the cylinder? Which has the greater volume? Explain your reasoning.

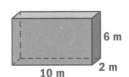

Extended Response

8. You are pouring water from a cylindrical can into a cylindrical pan. The can has a radius of 3.5 inches and a height of 10 inches. The pan has a radius of 10 inches and a height of 4 inches. How many full cans of water can you pour into the pan? Explain your reasoning.

Strategies for Answering
Extended Response Questions

Problem 1

A company prints labels for soup cans. The labels are printed on sheets of 36 inch by 48 inch paper. Find the dimensions of the label to the nearest inch. Then determine the greatest number of labels that can be printed on a sheet of paper. Explain your reasoning.

Can   Can label

> **Full credit solution**

The label length is correctly calculated by finding the circumference of the can.

- Label length $= 2\pi(2.5) \approx 2(3.14)(2.5) \approx 16$ in.
  Label width $= 5$ in.

There are two directions that the labels can be printed onto a sheet of paper. I found the number of labels by dividing each of the dimensions of a sheet of paper by each of the dimensions of a label.

The diagrams support the answer.

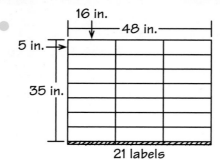

21 labels

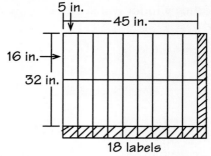

18 labels

The answer is correct. The explanation is clear, complete, and reflects correct mathematical thinking.

- The greatest number of labels can be printed when the length of the label is placed along the length of the sheet of paper, creating 21 labels per sheet of paper.

Partial credit solution

The label length is incorrect because an approximation of π is not substituted. ------ Label dimensions:

length $= 2\pi(2.5) = 5$ in.

width $= 5$ in.

The reasoning is correct. ------ Label placement: 9 labels fit along the 48 in. side of the sheet of paper because $48 \div 5 \approx 9$, and 7 labels fit along the 36 in. side because $36 \div 5 \approx 7$.

The diagram is incorrect because the label length was calculated incorrectly. ------

5 in.
45 in.
5 in.→
35 in.

63 labels

The answer is incorrect. ------ The greatest number of labels that can be printed on a sheet of paper is 63.

Watch Out!

Scoring is often based on how clearly you explain your reasoning.

Your turn now

1. A student's answer to the problem on page 622 is given below. Score the solution as *full credit, partial credit,* or *no credit.* Explain your choice. If you choose *partial credit* or *no credit,* explain how you would change the answer to earn a score of *full credit.*

The can's label is 16 in. long and 5 in. wide.

Because $48 \div 5 = 9.6$, 9 label widths fit along the length of the sheet of paper. Because $36 \div 16 = 2.25$, 2 label lengths fit along the width of the sheet.

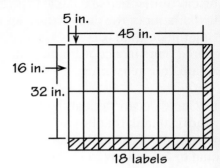

5 in.
45 in.
16 in.→
32 in.

18 labels

The greatest number of labels that you can fit on each sheet of paper is 18.

Extended Response

1. In the regular hexagon *ABCDEF*, $\overline{AF}$, $\overline{BE}$, and $\overline{CD}$ are parallel, and $\overline{BC}$, $\overline{AD}$, and $\overline{FE}$ are also parallel. Find the measures of all the numbered angles. Explain your reasoning.

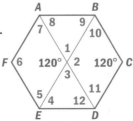

2. Sarah has a make-your-own candle set that includes a block of wax in the shape of a rectangular prism. The length of the prism is 8 inches, the width is 6 inches, and the height is 3 inches. She wants to make 4 cylindrical candles, which are called pillar candles. The pillar candle mold has a diameter of 3 inches and a height of 6 inches. Does she have enough wax to make the pillar candles? Explain your reasoning.

3. The vertices of $\triangle RST$ are $R(0, 4)$, $S(0, 0)$, and $T(-4, 0)$. Draw $\triangle RST$ in a coordinate plane. Find the area of $\triangle RST$. Reflect $\triangle RST$ in the *y*-axis. Then reflect the image of $\triangle RST$ in the *x*-axis. Reflect the second image of $\triangle RST$ in the *y*-axis. Describe the figure formed by $\triangle RST$ and its 3 images. Then find the area of the figure.

4. Two faces of a hexagonal pyramid with a regular base are shown. Use the faces to sketch the pyramid. Then use the sketch of the pyramid to draw a net. Then use the net to find the surface area of the pyramid.

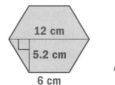

5. The circumference of a circle is given by the function $y = \pi x$ where *x* is the diameter of the circle. Make an input-output table for the function using the domain 0, 0.5, 1, 1.5, 2, 2.5, and 3. Use 3.14 for π. Plot the ordered pairs in a coordinate plane. Tell whether the function is linear. Explain your reasoning.

6. The Giant Ocean Tank at the New England Aquarium in Boston is a cylindrical tank that has a radius of 20 feet and a height of 43 feet. Find the volume of the tank. Use the fact that 1 cubic foot is approximately equal to 7.5 gallons to find the capacity of the tank in gallons. Then use the fact that a gallon of water weighs approximately 8.33 pounds to find the total weight of the water in the tank when filled.

Multiple Choice

7. Which of the following best describes the triangle shown?

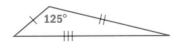

A. Acute scalene   **B.** Right isosceles

C. Obtuse scalene   **D.** Equilateral

8. How many edges and vertices does a triangular prism have?

F. 9 edges, 6 vertices

G. 8 edges, 4 vertices

H. 12 edges, 8 vertices

I. 6 edges, 6 vertices

9. What is the height of a parallelogram if the area is 98 square feet and the base is 7 feet?

A. 7 ft   **B.** 14 ft   **C.** 91 ft   **D.** 686 ft

10. What is the value of x?

F. 236   **G.** 124

H. 76   **I.** 56

11. A trapezoid has an area of 18.75 square meters. One of the bases is twice as long as the other base. The height is 2 meters. What are the bases of the trapezoid?

A. 2.2 m, 4.4 m   **B.** 2.5 m, 5 m

C. 5 m, 10 m   **D.** 6.25 m, 12.5 m

12. Which angles are complementary?

F. 79°, 11°   **G.** 67°, 113°

H. 39°, 151°   **I.** 37°, 88°

13. The diameter of a circle is 35 centimeters. What is the circumference? Use $\frac{22}{7}$ for π.

A. $\frac{245}{22}$ cm   **B.** 55 cm

C. 110 cm   **D.** 220 cm

Short Response

14. Find the sum of the measures of the interior angles of a 9-sided polygon. Explain your reasoning.

15. Two angles are supplementary and the measure of one angle is three times the measure of the other angle. What are the measures of the two angles?

16. Zack is building a model of a prism. He uses balls of clay for the vertices and straws for the edges. How many straws does he use if he uses 8 balls of clay for the model? Explain your reasoning.

17. Parallelogram *ABCD* has a base of 18 inches and a height of 15 inches. Parallelogram *FGHI* has a base of 6 inches and a height of 5 inches. Can you conclude that the two parallelograms are similar? Why or why not?

18. The figure shown is composed of a half circle and a trapezoid. Find the area of the figure. Then find the perimeter.

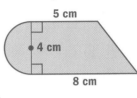

19. A cylinder has a radius of 2.5 meters and a height of 7 meters. Sketch the cylinder. Find the surface area of the cylinder. Then find the volume of the cylinder.

GO ON   **625**

Cumulative Practice for Chapters 10–12

Chapter 10

Multiple Choice In Exercises 1–9, choose the letter of the correct answer.

1. At which of the following times would the hands of a clock form a right angle? *(Lesson 10.1)*

   A. 1:00   **B.** 6:00   **C.** 9:00   **D.** 12:00

2. Which angle is supplementary to an angle measuring 54°? *(Lesson 10.1)*

   F. 26°   **G.** 36°   **H.** 126°   **I.** 136°

3. What kind of lines always intersect to form 90° angles? *(Lesson 10.2)*

   A. Intersecting   **B.** Parallel

   C. Perpendicular   **D.** Skew

4. Which angles are corresponding angles? *(Lesson 10.2)*

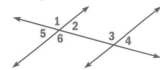

   F. ∠1 and ∠6   **G.** ∠1 and ∠4

   H. ∠2 and ∠4   **I.** ∠3 and ∠6

5. What is $m\angle 1$? *(Lesson 10.3)*

   A. 67°   **B.** 58°

   C. 44°   **D.** 4°

6. What quadrilateral is a parallelogram and has 4 congruent sides? *(Lesson 10.4)*

   F. Trapezoid   **G.** Parallelogram

   H. Rhombus   **I.** Rectangle

7. △*ABC* and △*DEF* are similar. What is the value of *x*? *(Lesson 10.5)*

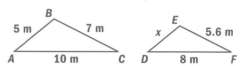

   A. 2 m   **B.** 4 m   **C.** 6 m   **D.** 12 m

8. At the same time that a maple tree's shadow is 9 feet long, a nearby redwood tree's shadow is 22.5 feet long. If the maple tree is 30 feet tall, how tall is the redwood? *(Lesson 10.6)*

   F. 60 ft   **G.** 75 ft   **H.** 100 ft   **I.** 125 ft

9. How many lines of symmetry does an equilateral triangle have? *(Lesson 10.7)*

   A. 0   **B.** 1   **C.** 2   **D.** 3

10. Short Response Sketch the figure below and draw any line(s) of symmetry. Tell whether the figure has rotational symmetry. Then draw a reflection of the figure in the *y*-axis. *(Lessons 10.7, 10.8)*

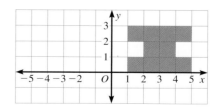

11. Extended Response The vertices of △*HJK* are *H*(−4, 0), *J*(2, 4), and *K*(4, 1). Draw △*HJK* in a coordinate plane. Write a rule that will translate point *J* to the origin. Graph the image of △*HJK* using the rule. *(Lesson 10.8)*

Chapter 11

Multiple Choice In Exercises 12–22, choose the letter of the correct answer.

12. Evaluate $\sqrt{49} - 2 + 5$. *(Lesson 11.1)*

    A. 5   **B.** 10   **C.** 25   **D.** 34

13. What are the solutions of the equation $16w^2 = 144$? *(Lesson 11.1)*

    F. ± 12 **G.** ± 4 **H.** ± 3 **I.** ± 2

14. What is $\sqrt{40}$ to the nearest whole number? *(Lesson 11.2)*

    A. 5   **B.** 6   **C.** 12   **D.** 16

15. Which number is irrational? *(Lesson 11.2)*

    F. 2.1223334444. . .   **G.** 3.56842

    H. $10.\overline{157}$ **I.** $15\frac{7}{9}$

16. What is the approximate length of the hypotenuse of a right triangle if the lengths of the legs are 10 meters and 25 meters? *(Lesson 11.3)*

    A. 14 m   **B.** 20 m   **C.** 27 m   **D.** 35 m

17. What is the area of the parallelogram? *(Lesson 11.4)*

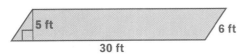

    F. 75 ft^2 **G.** 124 ft^2 **H.** 150 ft^2 **I.** 180 ft^2

18. What is the area of a triangle with a height of 28 centimeters and a base of 34 centimeters? *(Lesson 11.5)*

    A. 238 cm^2 **B.** 386 cm^2

    C. 476 cm^2 **D.** 952 cm^2

19. What is the area of the trapezoid? *(Lesson 11.5)*

    F. 55.296 m^2

    G. 16.32 m^2

    H. 14.4 m^2

    I. 13.44 m^2

In Exercises 20 and 21, use $\frac{22}{7}$ for π.

20. What is the circumference of a circle with a diameter of 7 centimeters? *(Lesson 11.6)*

    A. 11 cm **B.** 14 cm **C.** 22 cm **D.** $38\frac{1}{2}$ cm

21. What is the area of a circle with a diameter of 7 centimeters? *(Lesson 11.7)*

    F. 11 cm^2 **G.** 14 cm^2

    H. 22 cm^2 **I.** $38\frac{1}{2}$ cm^2

22. The large circle has a radius of 4 feet. The small circle has a radius of 2 feet. What is the approximate area of the shaded region? *(Lesson 11.7)*

    A. 6.28 ft^2 **B.** 9.42 ft^2 **C.** 37.7 ft^2 **D.** 62.8 ft^2

23. **Short Response** The length of a right triangle's hypotenuse is 15 meters. The length of one leg is twice the length of the other leg. What are the approximate lengths of the two legs? *(Lesson 11.3)*

24. **Extended Response** Plot the points $A(2, 4)$ and $B(7, 16)$ in a coordinate plane. Draw a line connecting the two points. Using the horizontal and vertical grid lines, form a right triangle. Then find the lengths of the legs. What is the distance between points A and B? *(Lesson 11.3)*

GO ON

Chapter 12

Multiple Choice In Exercises 25–32, choose the letter of the correct answer.

25. Which solid has 4 faces, 4 vertices, and 6 edges? *(Lesson 12.1)*

   A. Pentagonal prism

   B. Rectangular prism

   C. Triangular pyramid

   D. Triangular prism

26. Name the solid shown. *(Lesson 12.1)*

   F. Square pyramid

   G. Triangular pyramid

   H. Cone

   I. Cube

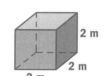

27. What is the surface area of the rectangular prism? *(Lesson 12.3)*

   A. 48 in.^{2}

   B. 52 in.^{2}

   C. 64 in.^{2}

   D. 88 in.^{2}

28. Which solid has a net composed of two circles and a rectangle? *(Lesson 12.4)*

   F. Cylinder   **G.** Square prism

   H. Cube   **I.** Cone

29. What is the approximate surface area of the cylinder? *(Lesson 12.4)*

   A. 17.3 ft^2 **B.** 18.4 ft^2

   C. 19.6 ft^2 **D.** 21.2 ft^2

30. A rectangular prism is 7 centimeters long, 5 centimeters wide, and 8 centimeters high. What is the volume of the prism? *(Lesson 12.5)*

   F. 280 cm^3 **G.** 262 cm^3

   H. 140 cm^3 **I.** 70 cm^3

31. The volume of a rectangular prism is 64 cubic meters. Its length is 10 meters, and its height is 2 meters. What is the width of the prism? *(Lesson 12.5)*

   A. 32 m   **B.** 6.4 m   **C.** 3.2 m   **D.** 1.6 m

32. What is the approximate volume of a cylinder with a diameter of 8 centimeters and a height of 8 centimeters? *(Lesson 12.6)*

   F. 25.1 cm^3 **G.** 50.2 cm^3

   H. 301 cm^3 **I.** 402 cm^3

33. **Short Response** Sketch a pentagonal pyramid. Then count the number of faces, edges, and vertices in the pyramid. *(Lessons 12.1, 12.2)*

34. **Extended Response** A rectangular prism is placed inside a hollow cylinder as shown. The prism and the cylinder both have a height of 9 inches. What is the volume of the rectangular prism? What is the approximate volume of the cylinder? What is the volume of the space between the rectangular prism and the cylinder? *(Lessons 12.5, 12.6)*

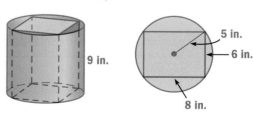

Chapter **13** **Probability**

- Find theoretical and experimental probabilities.
- Use tree diagrams, the counting principle, permutations, and combinations to solve problems.
- Find probabilities of disjoint, independent, and dependent events.

From Chapter 13, p. 650

How many ways can you line up to buy ride tickets?

Probability

BEFORE

In previous chapters you've...

- Used Venn diagrams
- Worked with fractions, decimals, and percents

Now

In Chapter 13 you'll study...

- Tree diagrams
- The counting principle
- Permutations and combinations
- Probabilities of events

WHY?

So you can solve real-world problems about...

- basketball, p. 637
- inflatable chairs, p. 641
- lockers, p. 646
- sunglasses, p. 652
- sign language, p. 659

Internet Preview
CLASSZONE.COM

- eEdition Plus Online
- eWorkbook Plus Online
- eTutorial Plus Online
- State Test Practice
- More Examples

Chapter Warm-Up Games

Review skills you need for this chapter in these quick games.

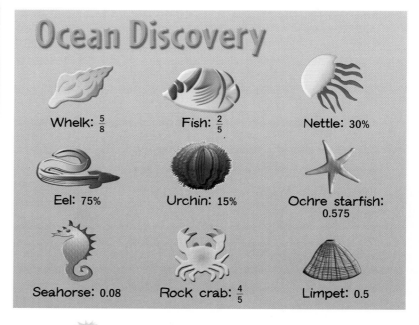

Ocean Discovery

Whelk: $\frac{5}{8}$ Fish: $\frac{2}{5}$ Nettle: 30%

Eel: 75%   Urchin: 15%   Ochre starfish: 0.575

Seahorse: 0.08   Rock crab: $\frac{4}{5}$ Limpet: 0.5

Key Skill:
Working with fractions, decimals, and percents

- Order the numbers from least to greatest. Write the names associated with the numbers in the same order. The first letters of the names will spell out the largest and fastest-moving type of starfish.

- Write all the numbers as decimals. Add the decimals and round to the nearest whole number to find how quickly, in feet per minute, this starfish can move.

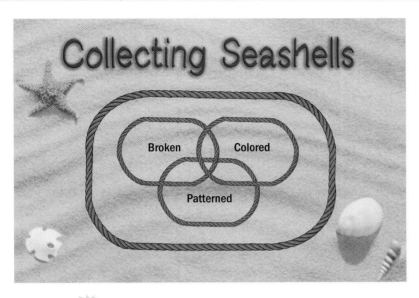

Collecting Seashells

Broken Colored

Patterned

BrAIN GAME

Key Skills:
• Using Venn diagrams
• Using logical reasoning

Suppose you find 76 seashells. You want to sort them into the categories shown in the Venn diagram above. Copy the diagram and use the information below to complete it.

- You have 8 seashells that are broken and are neither colored nor patterned.

- You have 51 unbroken seashells and 25 broken ones.

- You have 17 colored seashells and 16 patterned seashells.

- One of the 3 colored and patterned seashells is broken.

- You have 7 colored seashells that are broken.

Stop *and* Think

1. **Critical Thinking** In *Ocean Discovery*, you had to add decimals. Suppose you had to find the sum of the repeating decimals $0.\overline{3}$ and $0.\overline{6}$. Use fractions to show that the sum of these numbers is 1.

2. **Writing** In *Collecting Seashells*, suppose you find 5 additional unbroken seashells. These seashells are colored and patterned. Explain how you would change your Venn diagram.

CHAPTER 13 Getting Ready to Learn

Review What You Need to Know

Using Vocabulary Copy and complete using a review word.

Word Watch

Review Words
decimal, p. 52
frequency table, p. 130
fraction, p. 169
percent, p. 415
Venn diagram, p. 702
data, p. 703

1. A(n) ? uses shapes to show how sets are related.

2. A(n) ? is a number written in the form $\frac{a}{b}$ ($b \neq 0$).

3. A(n) ? is a ratio whose denominator is 100.

Use the Venn diagram to tell whether the statement is *true* or *false*. (p. 702)

4. Lisa plays basketball.

5. Two students play soccer but not basketball.

6. More students play basketball than play soccer.

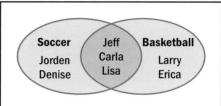

Write the fraction as a decimal and as a percent. (pp. 190, 425)

7. $\frac{7}{10}$ 8. $\frac{14}{16}$ 9. $\frac{9}{15}$ 10. $\frac{15}{24}$

Know How to Take Notes

Concept Grid You can use a concept grid to take notes on new concepts you learn. A concept grid includes a definition and a list of characteristics, as well as examples and nonexamples.

You should include material that appears on a notebook like this in your own notes.

Definition: A proportion is an equation that states that two ratios are equivalent.	**Characteristics:** The cross-products of a proportion are equal.
Examples: $\frac{8}{10} = \frac{20}{25}$ and $\frac{4}{12} = \frac{20}{x}$	**Nonexamples:** The ratios $\frac{3}{7}$ and $\frac{6}{15}$ do not form a proportion because 3×15 is not equal to 7×6.

proportion

You can make concept grids for new concepts you learn in Chapter 13, such as disjoint and overlapping events in Lesson 13.5.

Hands-on Activity

GOAL
Use an experiment to find the probability of an event.

MATERIALS
· two number cubes

Investigating Probability

The *probability* of an event is a measure of the likelihood that the event will occur. You can conduct an experiment to find the probability of an event.

Explore **Two number cubes are rolled. Find the probability that the sum of the resulting numbers is 7.**

1 Roll two number cubes 50 times. Record the sums of the resulting numbers and the corresponding frequencies in a frequency table like the one shown below.

Sum	2	3	4	5	6	7	8	9	10	11	12
Frequency	?	?	?	?	?	?	?	?	?	?	?

2 Find the probability of a sum of 7 by dividing the number of rolls that have a sum of 7 by the total number of rolls.

$$\text{Probability of a sum of 7} = \frac{\text{Number of rolls that have a sum of 7}}{\text{Total number of rolls}}$$

Your turn now

1. To find the sums of the numbers that can result when two number cubes are rolled, copy and complete the table at the right.

2. Use your completed table to find the fraction of the outcomes that have a sum of 7. How does your answer compare with the probability that you found in Step 2?

Stop and Think

3. Writing Suppose that two number cubes are rolled 90 times. For each roll, the product of the resulting numbers is found. How many rolls would you expect to have a product of 6?

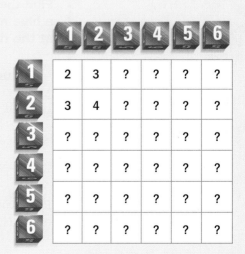

	1	2	3	4	5	6
1	2	3	?	?	?	?
2	3	4	?	?	?	?
3	?	?	?	?	?	?
4	?	?	?	?	?	?
5	?	?	?	?	?	?
6	?	?	?	?	?	?

Introduction to Probability

LESSON **13.1**

BEFORE	▶ Now	WHY?
You wrote ratios.	You'll find probabilities.	So you can find the probability of making a free throw, as in Ex. 16.

In the Real World

Word Watch

outcomes, p. 634
event, p. 634
favorable outcomes, p. 634
probability, p. 634
theoretical probability,
  p. 635
experimental probability,
  p. 635

Cat Tricks A cat that knows the shake command offers either of its front paws to shake. The table shows the number of times the cat offered each of its paws when asked to shake. What is the likelihood that the cat will offer its right paw when asked to shake? You'll find out in Example 2.

Paw Offered to Shake	
Left paw	38
Right paw	12

When you perform an experiment, the possible results are called **outcomes**. An **event** is a collection of outcomes. Once you specify an event, the outcomes for that event are called **favorable outcomes**.

The **probability** of an event is a measure of the likelihood that the event will occur. Use the formula below to find the probability P of an event when all of the outcomes are equally likely.

$$P(\text{event}) = \frac{\text{Number of favorable outcomes}}{\text{Total number of outcomes}}$$

HELP with Solving

You can write probabilities as fractions, decimals, or percents.

EXAMPLE 1   Finding a Probability

Find the probability of randomly choosing a blue marble from the marbles shown at the right.

$P(\text{blue}) = \dfrac{3}{10}$ ◀—— There are 3 blue marbles.
               ◀—— There are 10 marbles in all.

ANSWER The probability of choosing a blue marble is $\dfrac{3}{10}$, 0.3, or 30%.

Probabilities can range from 0 to 1. The closer the probability of an event is to 1, the more likely the event will occur.

P = 0	**P = 0.25**	**P = 0.5**	**P = 0.75**	**P = 1**
Impossible	Unlikely	Likely to occur half the time	Likely	Certain

Your turn now **Find the probability of the event.**

1. From the marbles in Example 1, you randomly choose a green marble.

2. You get tails when you flip a coin.

3. You get a 5 when you roll a number cube.

with Solving

Experimental probabilities can be based on scientific experiments, surveys, historical data, or simple activities.

Types of Probability The probability found in Example 1 is a **theoretical probability** because it is based on knowing all of the equally likely outcomes. Probability that is based on repeated *trials* of an experiment is called an **experimental probability**. Each trial in which the event occurs is a *success*.

Use the formula below to find the experimental probability of an event.

$$\text{Experimental probability of an event} = \frac{\text{Number of successes}}{\text{Number of trials}}$$

EXAMPLE 2 **Finding an Experimental Probability**

To find the probability that the cat will offer its right paw when asked to shake, use the information in the table on page 634.

(1 Determine the number of successes and the number of trials.

Because a success is offering a right paw, there are **12** successes.

There are 38 + 12 = **50** trials.

(2 Find the probability.

$$P(\text{right paw}) = \frac{12}{50} \quad \longleftarrow \quad \text{There are 12 successes.}$$
$$\phantom{P(\text{right paw})} \quad \longleftarrow \quad \text{There are 50 trials.}$$
$$= \frac{6}{25} \qquad \text{Simplify.}$$

ANSWER The probability that the cat will offer its right paw when asked to shake is $\frac{6}{25}$, 0.24, or 24%.

Your turn now **Solve the following problems.**

4. In Example 2, what is the probability that the cat will offer its left paw when asked to shake?

5. Of the 20 voters polled after an election for class president, 14 of the voters voted for Sean. What is the probability that a randomly chosen voter voted for Sean?

13.1 Exercises

More Practice, p. 717

Getting Ready to Practice

1. **Vocabulary** Copy and complete: The _?_ of an event is a measure of the likelihood that the event will occur.

Suppose you spin the spinner below, which is divided into equal parts. Match the event with the letter on the number line that indicates the probability of the event.

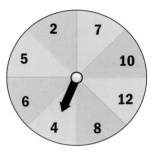

2. Pointer lands on green.

3. Pointer lands on 7.

4. Pointer lands on an even number.

5. Pointer lands on a prime number.

Practice and Problem Solving

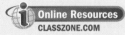

Example Exercises
1   6–14, 21
2   15–18, 21

Online Resources
CLASSZONE.COM
· More Examples
· eTutorial Plus

Each letter in MISSISSIPPI is written on a separate piece of paper and put into a bag. You randomly choose a piece of paper from the bag. Find the probability of the event. Write the probability as a fraction.

6. You choose an M.   7. You choose an I.

8. You choose an S.   9. You choose a P.

You randomly choose a marble from the marbles below. Find the probability of choosing a marble of the given color. Write the probability as a fraction, a decimal, and a percent.

10. Blue   11. Red   12. Green   13. Yellow

14. **Cereal** Each box of your favorite cereal contains one of two action figures from a movie. A supermarket has 50 boxes of the cereal. In 30 of the boxes there is an action figure of the hero, and in 20 of the boxes there is an action figure of the villain. What is the probability that you randomly choose a box of cereal that has the action figure of the hero?

■ **Tongue Rolling**

The ability to roll your tongue into a U-shape is a genetic trait inherited from your parents. The results of a survey state that 78% of people can roll their tongues. If 500 people were surveyed, then how many of the people surveyed can roll their tongues?

15. Tongue Rolling You asked 80 students at your school whether they can roll their tongues. Of the students surveyed, 64 said yes. Find the probability that a randomly selected student can roll his or her tongue. Write the probability as a fraction, a decimal, and a percent.

Basketball The table below shows the shots attempted and made by Kobe Bryant in basketball games during a season. Find the probability that Bryant makes the given shot. Write the probability as a decimal rounded to the nearest hundredth.

16. Free throw

17. Two point

18. Three point

	Free throw	Two point	Three point
Attempted	589	1597	132
Made	488	749	33

19. Critical Thinking Suppose Abby tosses a baseball hat. Abby reasons that because the hat will land in one of two positions (right side up, or upside down), the probability of the hat landing upside down is 50%. What is wrong with Abby's reasoning?

20. Writing Describe the difference between theoretical and experimental probability.

21. Collect Data What is the theoretical probability of getting tails when flipping a coin? Flip a coin 20 times and record the outcomes. Find the experimental probability and compare it with the theoretical probability.

Finding Odds In Exercises 22–24, you are playing a game which uses the spinner in the following example. The spinner is divided into equal parts. Find the odds in favor and the odds against the event.

EXAMPLE **Finding Odds**

The odds in favor and the odds against the pointer landing on orange are shown below.

$$\text{Odds in favor} = \frac{\text{Favorable outcomes}}{\text{Unfavorable outcomes}} = \frac{3}{7}$$

The odds in favor of landing on orange are 3 to 7.

$$\text{Odds against} = \frac{\text{Unfavorable outcomes}}{\text{Favorable outcomes}} = \frac{7}{3}$$

The odds against landing on orange are 7 to 3.

22. Lands on blue   **23.** Lands on green   **24.** Lands on yellow

Automobiles In Exercises 25 and 26, use the circle graph, which shows the popularity of colors for new automobiles among Americans.

25. Of the 200 new automobiles in a parking lot, how many would you expect to be blue?

26. If a parking lot has 30 new automobiles that are red, how many of the automobiles in the lot would you expect to be new?

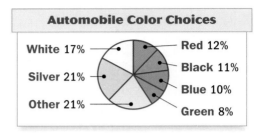

Automobile Color Choices

White 17%
Silver 21%
Other 21%
Red 12%
Black 11%
Blue 10%
Green 8%

27. **Marbles** A bag contains red and blue marbles. The probability of randomly choosing a red marble is 25%, and the probability of randomly choosing a blue marble is 75%. Determine the number of red marbles and blue marbles in the bag if there is a total of 16 marbles in the bag.

28. **Challenge** Find the theoretical probability of flipping a coin three times and getting tails each time.

Mixed Review

29. Sketch a quadrilateral that has four right angles and four congruent sides. Then classify the quadrilateral. *(Lesson 10.4)*

30. Find the height of a cylinder with a radius of 4 feet and a volume of 502.4 cubic feet. Use 3.14 for π. *(Lesson 12.6)*

Basic Skills **Find the product.**

31. $3\frac{1}{2} \times 3$

32. $\frac{1}{3} \times 1\frac{4}{5}$

33. $2\frac{2}{7} \times 2\frac{1}{4}$

34. $4\frac{1}{6} \times 6\frac{3}{5}$

Test-Taking Practice

INTERNET
State Test Practice
CLASSZONE.COM

35. **Multiple Choice** Tanya decides to listen to a CD with 12 songs, 3 of which are her favorite songs. If Tanya listens to the CD in random play, what is the probability that the first song played is one of her favorites?

   A. $\frac{1}{4}$ **B.** $\frac{1}{3}$ **C.** $\frac{1}{2}$ **D.** $\frac{3}{4}$

36. **Short Response** At a blood drive held at a school, 2 students out of the 40 students who gave blood have type AB blood. Find the probability that a randomly selected student has type AB blood. Write the probability as a fraction, a decimal, and a percent.

Tree Diagrams

BEFORE	▶ Now	WHY?
You used outcomes to find a probability.	You'll use a tree diagram to find all possible outcomes.	So you can find the number of school lunch combinations, as in Ex. 7.

In the Real World

Word Watch

tree diagram, p. 639

Fruit Smoothies You are ordering a fruit smoothie. You have your choice of a small, medium, or large smoothie, and you can include one of the following fruits: strawberries, bananas, or oranges. How many different choices of smoothies do you have?

A **tree diagram** can help you find the possible outcomes of an event by using branching (as seen on trees) to list choices.

EXAMPLE 1 Making a Tree Diagram

Make a tree diagram to find all of the possible choices for smoothies.

List the sizes.	List the fruit choices for each size.	List the outcomes.
small	strawberry	small strawberry
	banana	small banana
	orange	small orange
medium	strawberry	medium strawberry
	banana	medium banana
	orange	medium orange
large	strawberry	large strawberry
	banana	large banana
	orange	large orange

ANSWER There are 9 different choices of smoothies.

Your turn now Make a tree diagram to solve the problem.

1. You decide to get popcorn at a movie theater. The popcorn comes in regular, large, and jumbo sizes, and you have your choice of plain or buttered popcorn. How many choices of popcorn do you have?

EXAMPLE 2 Making a Tree Diagram

Science Camp You will be attending two sessions at a science camp. At each session, you will be assigned to one of the following groups: red, green, blue, or yellow. If you will not be assigned to the same group for both sessions, how many group assignments are possible?

Solution

Because you cannot be in the same group for both sessions, do not include the same group in both sessions in the tree diagram.

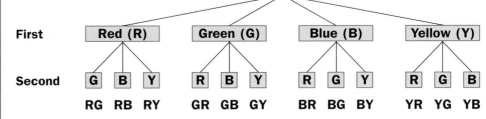

First   Red (R)   Green (G)   Blue (B)   Yellow (Y)

Second   G   B   Y   R   B   Y   R   G   Y   R   G   B

          RG RB RY   GR GB GY   BR BG BY   YR YG YB

ANSWER There are 12 possible group assignments.

EXAMPLE 3 Using a Tree Diagram

To find the probability of getting at least 2 heads when tossing a coin 3 times, make a tree diagram to find the outcomes.

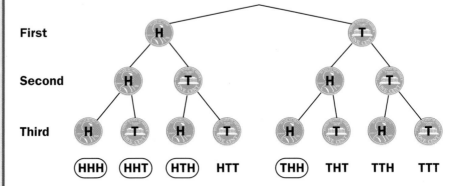

First

Second

Third

(HHH) (HHT) (HTH) HTT (THH) THT TTH TTT

ANSWER Because 4 of the 8 outcomes have at least 2 heads, the probability is $\frac{4}{8}$, or $\frac{1}{2}$.

Your turn now Use a tree diagram to find the probability.

2. You roll a number cube and flip a coin. What is the probability that you get a 3 and tails?

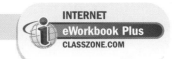
Getting Ready to Practice

1. **Vocabulary** Explain how to draw a tree diagram that shows the possible outcomes of rolling a number cube two times.

2. **Guided Problem Solving** Your wallet contains the following three bills: $10, $5, and $1. Suppose that you randomly choose a bill from your wallet. Then you randomly choose a second bill. What is the probability that the two bills that you take out of your wallet total $15?

   ① Make a tree diagram to find the possible outcomes. The part of your tree diagram that represents the second bill being chosen should show only the two remaining bills.

   ② List the possible outcomes. Then circle the outcomes that total $15.

   ③ Use the list of outcomes to find the probability that the two bills that you take out of your wallet total $15.

Practice and Problem Solving

with Homework

Example	Exercises
1	3–8
2	10–11
3	9, 12–13

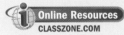
Online Resources
CLASSZONE.COM

· More Examples
· eTutorial Plus

Make a tree diagram to find the number of possible outcomes involving the spinner(s). Each spinner is divided into equal parts.

3. Spin spinner A two times.

4. Spin spinner A and spinner B.

5. Spin spinner B two times.

6. Spin spinner B three times.

Spinner A   **Spinner B**

7. **School Lunch** Students buying school lunch are offered one of the following entrées: chicken fajita, turkey sandwich, or yogurt with fresh fruit. Students are also offered one of the following side dishes: broccoli, potato wedges, or pretzels. Make a tree diagram to find all of the possible lunch combinations.

Inflatable Chairs In Exercises 8 and 9, use the following information.
A store that sells inflatable chairs offers the two following styles: a low-back chair and a high-back chair with arms. The chairs come in the following colors: black, clear, orange, lime, and purple.

8. Make a tree diagram to find all the different kinds of inflatable chairs at the store.

9. The store receives a shipment of inflatable chairs. Each box contains one of every kind of chair. If you randomly choose a chair from a box, what is the probability that the chair is black?

10. **Cheerleading** In cheerleading, a flyer is a person who performs a stunt. A cheerleading coach has to select the right outside flyer and the left outside flyer that are needed for a stunt from the five flyers on the squad: Anne, Mandy, Zoe, Laura, and Janie. Make a tree diagram to find the number of ways that the two flyers can be selected.

11. **Muffins** A bag contains one of each of the following muffins: blueberry, cranberry, bran, corn, carrot, and chocolate chip. A muffin is randomly chosen from the bag, then a second muffin is randomly chosen. Make a tree diagram to find the number of ways two muffins can be chosen.

In Exercises 12 and 13, suppose that you roll two number cubes. Use a tree diagram to find the probability of the event.

12. Both numbers are the same.   13. You roll a 5 and a 3.

14. **Explain** Is it more likely for exactly one of the numbers to be 2 or for both of the numbers to be odd when rolling two number cubes? Explain.

15. **Challenge** A bag contains 2 green marbles, 2 red marbles, and 1 blue marble. What is the probability of randomly choosing a green marble and then a blue marble, without replacing the first marble chosen?

Mixed Review

Use a proportion to answer the question. *(Lesson 9.2)*

16. What percent of 150 is 90?   17. 81 is 30% of what number?

18. A jar has 4 red, 2 blue, and 2 white marbles. What is the probability of randomly choosing a white marble from the jar? *(Lesson 13.1)*

Basic Skills   **Write the product as a power.**

19. $10 \cdot 10 \cdot 10 \cdot 10$ 20. $6 \cdot 6 \cdot 6 \cdot 6 \cdot 6 \cdot 6$ 21. $x \cdot x \cdot x$

Test-Taking Practice

22. **Multiple Choice** A store sells general, outdoor, and waterproof disposable cameras. Each type comes with 15 and 27 exposures. How many different disposable cameras does the store sell?

    A. 2   **B.** 3   **C.** 6   **D.** 8

23. **Multiple Choice** In Exercise 22, suppose that the store has only one camera for each combination of type and number of exposures. What is the probability of randomly choosing a waterproof camera with 27 exposures?

    F. $\frac{1}{8}$ **G.** $\frac{1}{6}$ **H.** $\frac{1}{3}$ **I.** $\frac{2}{3}$

GOAL
Determine the number of possible outcomes.

MATERIALS
· paper
· pencil

Determining Outcomes

Explore **Find the number of outcomes of spinning each spinner once. Each spinner is divided into equal parts.**

Spinner 1

Spinner 2

Spinner 3

1 Make a tree diagram to determine the number of outcomes of spinning spinner 1, followed by spinner 2, followed by spinner 3.

2 In your tree diagram, how many different letters are listed for spinner 1? spinner 2? spinner 3?

3 Find the product of the three numbers from Step 2. What do you notice?

Your turn now

1. Suppose that spinner 3 is divided into 3 equal parts, and the choices for the letters are T, G, and Y as shown. Repeat Steps 1–3.

2. If you know the number of ways that event A can occur and the number of ways that event B can occur, how can you find the number of ways that event A followed by event B can occur?

Stop and Think

3. **Critical Thinking** Suppose that each of the three spinners is divided into 26 equal parts so that each spinner can include all of the letters of the alphabet. Find the number of outcomes of spinning spinner 1, followed by spinner 2, followed by spinner 3, without using a tree diagram.

LESSON 13.3 The Counting Principle

BEFORE	Now	WHY?
You used a tree diagram to find outcomes.	You'll use the counting principle to find outcomes.	So you can find the number of election results, as in Ex. 8.

In the Real World

Word Watch

Review Words

outcomes, p. 634
event, p. 634
probability, p. 634

Track Events At a track meet there are 6 running events, 3 throwing events, and 2 relay events. If you want to compete in one running event, one throwing event, and one relay event, how many different choices do you have?

In the activity on page 643, you may have noticed a way to use multiplication to find the number of possible outcomes of an experiment. This method, called the *counting principle*, is stated below.

The Counting Principle

If one event can occur in *m* ways, and for each of these a second event can occur in *n* ways, then the number of ways that the two events can occur together is *m* • *n*.

The counting principle can be extended to three or more events.

EXAMPLE 1 Using the Counting Principle

To find the number of different choices of track events at the track meet described above, use the counting principle.

Find the product of the number of choices for each track event.

Number of running events	×	Number of throwing events	×	Number of relay events	=	Number of choices
6	×	3	×	2	=	36

ANSWER There are 36 different choices for your track events.

EXAMPLE 2 Using the Counting Principle

License Plates The standard New York state license plate has 3 letters followed by 4 digits. How many different license plates are possible if the digits and letters can be repeated?

Solution

Use the counting principle to find the number of different license plates.

> There are 26 choices for each letter.

> There are 10 choices for each digit.

$$26 \times 26 \times 26 \times 10 \times 10 \times 10 \times 10 = 175,760,000$$

ANSWER There are 175,760,000 different license plates possible.

License plate sculpture by Michael Kalish

EXAMPLE 3 Finding a Probability

Passwords You are assigned a computer-generated 4 digit password to access your new voice mail account. If the digits can be repeated, what is the probability that your assigned password is 1234?

Solution

(1 Find the number of different passwords.

$$10 \times 10 \times 10 \times 10 = 10,000 \qquad \text{Use the counting principle.}$$

(2 Find the probability that your password is 1234.

$$P(1234) = \frac{1}{10,000} \qquad \text{Only one of the outcomes is 1234.}$$

ANSWER The probability that your password is 1234 is $\frac{1}{10,000}$.

Watch Out!

In both Example 2 and Example 3, notice that the digits 0 through 9 represent 10 digits, not 9 digits.

Your turn now Use the counting principle to solve the problem.

1. You have 35 rock CDs and 12 pop CDs. How many outcomes are possible if you randomly choose 1 rock CD and 1 pop CD?

2. You roll a green number cube, a red number cube, and a blue number cube. How many different outcomes are possible?

3. In Exercise 2, what is the probability that the green number cube is a 2, the red number cube is a 6, and the blue number cube is a 3?

Getting Ready to Practice

1. Vocabulary If one event has 5 outcomes and another event has 12 outcomes, then what does 5 • 12 represent?

Sandwiches In Exercises 2 and 3, use the following information.
You want to order a ham-and-cheese sandwich at a sandwich shop that has 5 kinds of bread, 4 kinds of cheese, and 2 kinds of ham.

2. How many ham-and-cheese sandwiches are possible if you are limited to one kind of bread, one kind of cheese, and one kind of ham?

3. The sandwich shop has a pre-made ham-and-cheese sandwich. What is the probability that the sandwich has the kinds of bread, cheese, and ham that you want?

Practice and Problem Solving

with Homework

Example	Exercises
1	4–8
2	9–10
3	14–15

Online Resources
CLASSZONE.COM
· More Examples
· eTutorial Plus

In Exercises 4–7, use the number of outcomes of the events to find the number of ways that the events can occur together.

4. Event A: 6 outcomes
Event B: 15 outcomes

5. Event J: 12 outcomes
Event K: 13 outcomes

6. Event F: 10 outcomes
Event G: 26 outcomes
Event H: 10 outcomes

7. Event P: 19 outcomes
Event Q: 15 outcomes
Event R: 4 outcomes

8. Class Election Your class is having an election. There are 3 candidates for president, 5 for vice president, 2 for secretary, and 6 for treasurer. How many election results are possible?

9. Lockers The combinations for the lockers at your school consist of 3 numbers. Each number in the combination can be a number from 0 through 49. How many locker combinations are possible?

10. Digital Clocks On a digital clock, the numbers 1 through 12 are used for the hour display and the numbers 00 through 59 are used for the minute display. How many time displays are possible?

11. Find the Error Find and correct the error in finding the number of outcomes of rolling a number cube three times.

$$\times \quad 6 + 6 + 6 = 18$$

12. Writing What are the advantages of using the counting principle instead of making a tree diagram when counting possibilities?

13. **Decide** The number of ways that both events A and B can occur is 36. If event B can occur in 3 ways, in how many ways can event A occur?

14. **Clothing** A T-shirt at a clothing store is available in 2 sleeve lengths, 8 colors, and 5 sizes. If your friend randomly chooses one of these T-shirts to give you as a gift, what is the probability that the T-shirt is the sleeve length, color, and size that you want?

15. **Bicycle Locks** A bicycle lock has a 4 digit combination. Each of the digits is a number from 1 through 9. Find the probability that the lock has a combination in which all of the digits are the same number.

16. **Challenge** In a competition, 5 figure skaters will skate in a randomly assigned order. Why can't you evaluate the product $5 \times 5 \times 5 \times 5 \times 5$ to find the number of possible orders in which the skaters can skate?

Mixed Review

17. A right triangle has legs of length 9 inches and 12 inches. Find the length of the hypotenuse. *(Lesson 11.3)*

Choose a Strategy Use a strategy from the list to solve the following problem. Explain your choice of strategy.

> **Problem Solving Strategies**
> - Look for a Pattern
> - Make a Model
> - Guess, Check, and Revise

18. A cylinder is formed by first taping together the opposite edges of a rectangular piece of paper that is 11 inches long and 8.5 inches wide. If the height of the completed cylinder is 8.5 inches, what is its volume? Use 3.14 for π.

Basic Skills Make a stem-and-leaf plot of the data.

19. 97, 101, 52, 75, 85, 95, 105, 78, 97, 116, 104, 88, 85, 97

20. 30, 47, 67, 42, 66, 27, 67, 23, 36, 23, 40, 41, 59, 75, 56, 54

Test-Taking Practice

21. **Multiple Choice** You have 8 kinds of wrapping paper and 5 colors of ribbons. How many combinations of one kind of wrapping paper and one color of ribbon are possible?

 A. 8   **B.** 13   **C.** 40   **D.** 80

22. **Multiple Choice** A license plate has 2 letters followed by 4 digits. How many license plates are possible if the digits and letters can be repeated?

 F. 8   **G.** 92   **H.** 676,000   **I.** 6,760,000

Notebook Review

Review the vocabulary definitions in your notebook.

Copy the review examples in your notebook. Then complete the exercises.

Check Your Definitions

outcomes, p. 634
event, p. 634

favorable outcomes, p. 634

probability, p. 634

theoretical, experimental probability, p. 635

tree diagram, p. 639

Use Your Vocabulary

1. Copy and complete: A(n) _?_ is a collection of outcomes.

13.1 Can you find probabilities?

EXAMPLE Each letter in PENNSYLVANIA is written on a separate piece of paper and put into a bag. You randomly choose a piece of paper from the bag. Find the probability of choosing an N.

$$P(\text{N}) = \frac{\text{Number of favorable outcomes}}{\text{Total number of outcomes}} = \frac{3}{12} = \frac{1}{4}$$

ANSWER The probability of choosing an N is $\frac{1}{4}$, 0.25, or 25%.

2. In the Example above, what is the probability of randomly choosing an A?

13.2 Can you make tree diagrams?

EXAMPLE In a community service project, you can volunteer as a crew leader or crew worker in the areas of street repair, litter cleanup, or painting. Find the number of options you have.

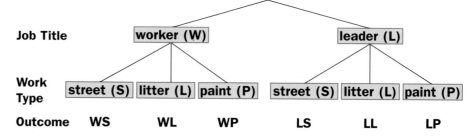

ANSWER You have 6 different options.

3. A restaurant offers choices of a chicken, beef, or pork entrée, soup or salad, and baked potato, mashed potatoes, or home fries. Make a tree diagram to find the number of meal options.

13.3 Can you use the counting principle?

EXAMPLE A pizza comes with a choice of crust (thin or thick), one meat topping (sausage, pepperoni, or ham), and one vegetable topping (peppers, mushrooms, or onions). Your friend orders the pizza for you. What is the probability that she orders a thin crust pizza with pepperoni and onions?

Solution

Use the counting principle to find the number of different pizzas.

Number of crust choices	×	Number of meat toppings	×	Number of vegetable toppings	=	Number of pizzas
2	×	3	×	3	=	18

ANSWER Because only 1 pizza can have the combination of thin crust, pepperoni, and onions, the probability is $\frac{1}{18}$.

4. What is the probability that your friend orders the same pizza above if there were 2 meat toppings to choose from instead of 3?

Stop *and* **Think** about Lessons 13.1–13.3

5. Critical Thinking You have 4 shirts and 3 pairs of pants. Explain how the number of outfit choices changes if you buy a new shirt.

Review Quiz 1

1. What is the probability of getting an odd number when rolling a number cube?

2. Vacation You are planning a family vacation. You have the choice of 2 modes of transportation: bus or plane. You have the choice of 4 destinations: Las Vegas, San Francisco, Miami, or Denver. Make a tree diagram to find the number of possible vacations.

3. Web Page Design You are designing a Web page. You have a choice of 6 different borders, 12 different fonts, and 40 different background colors. How many possible combinations are there for the Web page?

Permutations and Combinations

BEFORE	▶ Now	WHY?
You used tree diagrams and the counting principle.	You'll use permutations and combinations.	So you can find the number of batting orders, as in Ex. 22.

Word Watch

permutation, p. 650
combination, p. 651

Activity **You can investigate numbers of arrangements.**

(1 Line up 3 chairs and choose 3 students.

(2 How many ways can 1 of the 3 students be chosen to sit in the first chair? Have one of the students sit in the first chair.

(3 Repeat Step 2 for the second and third chairs.

(4 Apply the counting principle to your answers from Steps 2 and 3 to find the number of arrangements of 3 students in 3 chairs.

In the activity, you found the number of *permutations* of 3 students. A **permutation** is an arrangement of a group of objects in a particular order. For example, the 6 permutations of 3 letters in the word CAT are shown below.

CAT	ACT	TCA
CTA	ATC	TAC

EXAMPLE 1 **Counting Permutations**

Amusement Parks You and 3 of your friends go to an amusement park. How many ways can you stand in line to buy tickets for the rides?

Solution

Use the counting principle.

Choices for first in line	×	Choices for second in line	×	Choices for third in line	×	Choices for fourth in line	=	Ways to stand in line
4	×	3	×	2	×	1	=	24

ANSWER There are 24 ways that you and your 3 friends can stand in line.

2000–2001 Federal Duck Stamp winner

EXAMPLE 2 **Counting Permutations**

Stamp Competition There were 52 entries in the 2002–2003 Federal Junior Duck Stamp contest. In how many ways could the first, second, and third places be awarded?

Solution

Choices for first place	×	Choices for second place	×	Choices for third place	=	Ways to award first, second, and third
52	×	51	×	50	=	132,600

ANSWER There were 132,600 ways to award first, second, and third places.

Your turn now **Find the number of permutations.**

1. In how many ways can you arrange the letters in the word COMPUTER?

2. There are 8 volleyball teams in a tournament. In how many ways can teams place first, second, third, and fourth?

Combinations In a permutation, the order of the objects is important. A **combination** is a grouping of objects in which the order is not important.

EXAMPLE 3 **Listing Combinations**

School Electives You need to choose 2 different electives from the following 4 electives: Spanish (S), consumer and family studies (C), industrial technology (I), and art (A). How many different choices do you have, if the order in which you choose the classes does not matter?

Solution

Start by listing all of the permutations of 2 electives. Because the order in which you choose the electives does not matter, cross out one of any pair of permutations that lists the same two electives.

SC   SI   SA
C̶S̶   CI   CA
I̶S̶   I̶C̶   ⟨IA⟩
A̶S̶   A̶C̶   ⟨A̶I̶⟩

Because IA and AI list the same electives, cross one of them out.

ANSWER You have 6 different choices for choosing 2 electives.

HELP with **Solving**

In Example 3, you can use a tree diagram to find the permutations of 2 electives. Then cross out one of any pair of permutations that lists the same two electives.

Relating Permutations and Combinations In Example 3, another way to find the number of combinations is to divide the number of permutations when choosing 2 electives from 4 by the number of permutations when arranging 2 electives, as shown below.

$$\frac{\text{Permutations when choosing 2 objects from 4}}{\text{Permutations when arranging 2 objects}} = \frac{4 \times 3}{2 \times 1} = 6 \text{ combinations}$$

This method is useful when there are too many arrangements to list.

EXAMPLE 4 Relating Combinations and Permutations

Sunglasses You win a door prize at the grand opening of a department store. For your prize, you get to choose 5 different pairs of sunglasses from the 20 styles that the store carries. How many choices do you have?

Solution

Because the order in which the sunglasses are chosen does not matter, you need to find the number of combinations.

1 Find the number of permutations when choosing 5 pairs from 20 styles.

$$20 \times 19 \times 18 \times 17 \times 16 = \mathbf{1,860,480}$$

2 Find the number of permutations when arranging 5 objects.

$$5 \times 4 \times 3 \times 2 \times 1 = \mathbf{120}$$

3 Divide the number of permutations when choosing 5 pairs from 20 styles by the number of permutations when arranging 5 objects.

$$\frac{1,860,480}{120} = 15,504$$

ANSWER There are 15,504 ways for you to choose the sunglasses.

Your turn now Find the number of combinations.

3. You want to buy 5 CDs at a music store. If you have enough money for only 2 CDs, how many choices do you have?

4. As part of a summer reading program, you need to read 4 books. Your school gives you a list of 15 books from which to choose. How many ways can you choose the 4 books if the order in which you choose them is not important?

Getting Ready to Practice

Vocabulary Copy and complete the statement.

1. A(n) ? is a grouping of objects in which the order is not important.

2. A(n) ? is an arrangement of a group of objects in a particular order.

3. **Relay Race** There are 12 members of a track team who want to run one of the legs in a 4 person relay race. Choose the calculation that you can use to find the number of ways that runners can be chosen for each of the legs of the relay race.

   A. $12 \times 11 \times 10 \times 9$ **B.** $4 \times 3 \times 2 \times 1$ **C.** $\dfrac{12 \times 11 \times 10 \times 9}{4 \times 3 \times 2 \times 1}$

4. **Guided Problem Solving** You need to choose 3 different colors of balloons to be used as decorations at a school graduation. The balloons are available in 24 colors. How many ways can you choose 3 different colors of balloons?

   1. Decide whether the situation describes a permutation or a combination.

   2. Find the number of permutations or combinations.

Practice and Problem Solving

with Homework

Example	Exercises
1	8–11, 17–22
2	8–11, 17–22
3	13–16, 17–22
4	13–16, 17–22

Online Resources
CLASSZONE.COM
· More Examples
· eTutorial Plus

Simplify the expression.

5. $5 \times 4 \times 3 \times 2 \times 1$ 6. $\dfrac{11 \times 10 \times 9}{3 \times 2 \times 1}$ 7. $\dfrac{20 \times 19 \times 18 \times 17}{4 \times 3 \times 2 \times 1}$

Find the number of permutations.

8. Ways to arrange the letters in the word GUITAR

9. Ways to arrange 7 DVDs on a shelf

10. Ways to choose a president, vice-president, treasurer, and secretary from the 18 members of a club

11. Ways to choose first, second, and third prize from 27 posters in a contest.

12. **Critical Thinking** Decide whether the list below contains all of the permutations of the 3 symbols. If the list is incomplete, determine which permutations are missing.

Find the number of combinations.

13. Ways to choose 3 different kinds of apples from the following kinds: Red Delicious, Granny Smith, Empire, McIntosh, and Fuji

14. Ways to choose 4 different colors from the following colors: red, blue, purple, yellow, green, and orange

15. Ways to choose 8 students to be extras in a play from 14 students

16. Ways to choose 4 different fish from 26 kinds of fish

Cards **In Exercises 17 and 18, use the following information.** As part of a magic trick, you are asked to choose a number of cards from a deck of 52 cards.

17. How many ways can you choose 4 cards from the deck, if the order in which the cards are chosen is not important?

18. How many ways can you choose 6 cards from the deck, if the order in which the cards are chosen is important?

Tell whether the situation describes a *permutation* or a *combination*. Then answer the question.

19. How many ways can a disc jockey choose 4 different songs from 10?

20. How many ways can you choose 3 different pizza toppings from 15?

21. How many ways can a judge award first, second, and third places at a science fair with 23 entries?

22. How many ways can the coach arrange the batting order of the 9 starting players of a baseball team?

23. **Writing** Describe a real-world situation that involves a permutation and a real-world situation that involves a combination.

In Exercises 24 and 25, answer the questions about the word ALASKA.

24. Why can't you use the expression $6 \times 5 \times 4 \times 3 \times 2 \times 1$ to find the number of *different* arrangements of the letters in the word?

25. How many different ways can the letters in the word be arranged?

26. **Computers** A group of 40 computers contains exactly 2 defective computers. Suppose 2 computers are randomly selected from the group. What is the probability that the 2 computers are defective? Write the probability as a decimal rounded to the nearest thousandth.

27. **Challenge** How many different 3 digit numbers can you make using the digits 1, 4, 5, 6, 8, and 9, if no digit appears more than once in the number?

Mixed Review

You randomly choose a marble from the marbles below. Find the probability of choosing a marble of the given color. Write the probability as a fraction, a decimal, and a percent. *(Lesson 13.1)*

28. Red **29.** Blue **30.** Purple **31.** Green

32. At a restaurant, you can have your eggs cooked 4 different ways, and you can choose from 3 kinds of bread for your toast. How many eggs and toast combinations are possible? *(Lesson 13.3)*

Basic Skills **Find the sum or difference.**

33. $\dfrac{1}{8} + \dfrac{3}{8}$ **34.** $\dfrac{2}{7} + \dfrac{4}{9}$ **35.** $\dfrac{8}{13} - \dfrac{6}{13}$ **36.** $\dfrac{1}{5} - \dfrac{1}{6}$

Test-Taking Practice

37. Multiple Choice There are 8 students participating in a car wash. How many ways can 2 of the students be chosen to hold signs advertising the car wash?

A. 8 **B.** 16 **C.** 28 **D.** 56

38. Short Response A bag contains 1 green marble, 1 blue marble, 1 red marble, and 1 white marble. How many ways can 3 marbles be randomly chosen from the bag, if the order in which the marbles are chosen is important?

Creating Quadrilaterals

Ten pegs are arranged in a circle on a board. A rubber band is stretched to create a quadrilateral as shown. How many quadrilaterals can be created? (If two quadrilaterals have the same shape but are made using different pegs, then the quadrilaterals are different.)

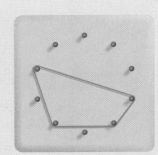

Finding Permutations and Combinations

GOAL Use a calculator to find permutations and combinations.

Example **There are 14 school bands participating in a competition.**

    a. How many ways can first, second, and third places be awarded?

    b. After the top 3 places have been awarded, how many ways can 2 honorable mentions be awarded?

Solution

a. The situation describes a permutation. Use the following keystrokes to find the number of permutations of 3 bands chosen from 14 bands.

> *n*P*r* represents the number of permutations of *r* objects chosen from *n* objects.

Keystrokes
14 [PRB] [=] 3 [=]

Display
| 14 nPr 3 |
| 2184 |

ANSWER There are 2184 ways for first, second, and third places to be awarded.

b. The situation describes a combination. Use the following keystrokes to find the number of combinations of 2 bands chosen from the remaining 11 bands.

> *n*C*r* represents the number of combinations of *r* objects chosen from *n* objects.

Keystrokes
11 [PRB] [▶] [=] 2 [=]

Display
| 11 nCr 2 |
| 55 |

ANSWER There are 55 ways for 2 honorable mentions to be awarded.

Your turn now **Use a calculator to answer the question.**

    1. A bowling league has 19 teams. How many ways can teams place first, second, third, and fourth?

    2. How many ways can 6 people be chosen from 25 people?

Disjoint Events

BEFORE	▶ **Now**	**WHY?**
You found the probability of a single event.	You'll find the probability that either of two events occurs.	So you can analyze results of a survey, as in Exs. 17–20.

Disjoint events are events that have no outcomes in common. **Overlapping events** are events that have one or more outcomes in common. The Venn diagrams below show how the events that involve rolling a number cube are related.

Disjoint events

Event A: Get an odd number.

Event B: Get a 4.

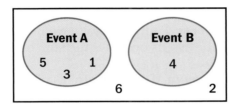

Overlapping events

Event A: Get a number less than 3.

Event B: Get an even number.

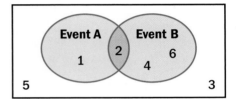

EXAMPLE 1 **Disjoint and Overlapping Events**

Tell whether the events involving the spinner are *disjoint* or *overlapping*.

Event P: Get an odd number.

Event Q: Get a prime number.

Solution

Make a list of the outcomes for each event. Then determine whether the events have any outcomes in common.

Event P: 3, 7, 9, 15   List the odd numbers.

Event Q: 2, 3, 7   List the prime numbers.

ANSWER There are outcomes in common, so the events are overlapping.

 **with Notetaking**

To help you understand the difference between disjoint and overlapping events, you can make a concept grid for each term.

Your turn now Tell whether the events involving the spinner in Example 1 are *disjoint* or *overlapping*.

1. **Event J:** Get an even number.
   Event K: Get a number greater than 9.

Probability of Disjoint Events The Venn diagram at the right shows two disjoint events that involve rolling a number cube.

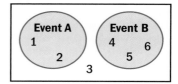

Event A: Get a number less than 3.

Event B: Get a number greater than 3.

The probability of event A *or* event B is $\frac{5}{6}$ because there are 5 favorable outcomes out of 6 possible outcomes. Another way to find the probability of event A or event B is to add the probabilities of each event: $\frac{2}{6} + \frac{3}{6} = \frac{5}{6}$.

Probability of Disjoint Events

Words For two disjoint events, the probability that either of the events occurs is the sum of the probabilities of the events.

Algebra If A and B are disjoint events, then
$P(\text{A or B}) = P(\text{A}) + P(\text{B})$.

What do you think?

Sports

■ **Arena Events**

To prepare for an ice hockey game, the arena staff needs to remove the 264 pieces of the wooden floor used for a basketball game. If each piece of the floor weighs 180 pounds, how much does the entire floor weigh?

EXAMPLE 2 **Probability of Disjoint Events**

Arena Events The table shows the events at an arena during one year. What is the probability that a randomly chosen event is an ice hockey game or an ice show?

Event	Percent
Basketball	24%
Ice hockey	23%
Concert	16%
Ice show	11%
Trade show	8%
Other	18%

Solution

The events are disjoint because two arena events cannot occur at the same time.

$$P(\text{ice hockey}) + P(\text{ice show}) = 23\% + 11\%$$
$$= 34\%$$

ANSWER The probability that an arena event is either an ice hockey game or an ice show is 34%.

Your turn now **Refer to Example 2.**

2. What is the probability that a randomly chosen event is a concert or a trade show?

Complementary Events Two disjoint events in which one or the other must occur are called **complementary events**. If event A and event B are complementary events and you know the probability of one event, you can use the following rule to find the probability of the other event.

$$P(B) = 1 - P(A)$$

> This rule comes from the fact that the sum of the probabilities of two complementary events is 1.

EXAMPLE 3 **Probability of Complementary Events**

Sign Language At your school, 3% of the students know sign language. What is the probability that a randomly chosen student at your school does *not* know sign language?

Solution

$P(\text{does not know}) = 1 - P(\text{knows})$	Write verbal model.
$= 1 - 0.03$	Substitute 3%, or 0.03, for $P(\text{knows})$.
$= 0.97$	Subtract.

ANSWER The probability that a randomly chosen student does not know sign language is 0.97, or 97%.

13.5 Exercises
More Practice, p. 717

Getting Ready to Practice

1. **Vocabulary** Describe the difference between disjoint events and overlapping events.

Events A and B are disjoint events. Find $P(A \text{ or } B)$.

2. $P(A) = 0.3$
$P(B) = 0.2$

3. $P(A) = 0.25$
$P(B) = 0.35$

4. $P(A) = 0.12$
$P(B) = 0.3$

Events A and B are complementary events. Find $P(A)$.

5. $P(B) = 0.4$

6. $P(B) = 0.75$

7. $P(B) = 0.23$

8. **Pets** Are the events "dog owner" and "cat owner" disjoint or overlapping? Explain.

Practice and Problem Solving

HELP with Homework

Example	Exercises
1	9-10
2	11-13, 17-20, 24-27
3	14-20

Online Resources
CLASSZONE.COM

· More Examples
· eTutorial Plus

Tell whether the events are _disjoint_ or _overlapping_.

9. **Event A:** A student knows how to play a musical instrument.
   Event B: A student doesn't know how to play a musical instrument.

10. **Event A:** A student knows how to play the clarinet.
    Event B: A student knows how to play the guitar.

Events A and B are disjoint events. Find _P_(A or B).

11. $P(A) = 0.24$
    $P(B) = 0.37$

12. $P(A) = 33\%$
    $P(B) = 8\%$

13. $P(A) = 16.1\%$
    $P(B) = 28.2\%$

Events A and B are complementary events. Find _P_(A).

14. $P(B) = 0.51$

15. $P(B) = \frac{2}{5}$

16. $P(B) = 64\%$

History The circle graph shows the results of a survey. Find the probability that a randomly chosen student who participated in the survey responded as indicated.

17. Chose Ancient Egypt or the Aztecs

18. Chose Ancient Greece or the Incas

19. Didn't choose Ancient Egypt

20. Didn't choose the Aztecs

Which ancient civilization would you visit?

Ancient Greece 29%
Aztecs 11%
Incas 8%
Ancient Egypt 52%

Machu Picchu is an ancient Incan fortress in Peru.

Extended Problem Solving In Exercises 21–23, use the following information. You and 19 other students volunteer to clean up the outside of a community center. The table shows the number of volunteers who will be randomly assigned to work in specific areas.

21. **Calculate** Find the probability that you will be assigned to work in the front yard, the back yard, or the side yard by dividing the sum of the numbers of volunteers assigned to these areas by the total number of volunteers.

Area	Volunteers
Front yard	6
Back yard	8
Playground	4
Side yard	2

22. **Calculate** Find the probability of the events in Exercise 21 by adding the probabilities of being assigned to the front yard, of being assigned to the back yard, and of being assigned to the side yard.

23. **Conjecture** Can you find the probability that one of three disjoint events will occur by adding the probabilities of each event? Explain.

You randomly choose a letter from the word PINEAPPLE. Find the probability of choosing either of the given letters.

24. P or N **25.** E or A **26.** I or P **27.** N or E

Critical Thinking In Exercises 28–30, tell whether the statement is *always*, *sometimes*, or *never* true.

28. Two disjoint events are complementary.

29. Two overlapping events are disjoint.

30. Two complementary events are overlapping.

31. Writing Events A and B involve rolling two number cubes. If the probability of event A is 0.75 and the probability of event B is 0.5, are events A and B disjoint events? Explain.

32. Challenge There are red, blue, and green marbles in a bag. The probability of randomly choosing a blue marble is 0.3, and the probability of randomly choosing a blue or red marble is 0.7. If there are a total of 20 marbles in the bag, how many marbles of each color are in the bag?

Mixed Review

Solve the equation. *(Lesson 11.1)*

33. $x^2 + 3 = 39$ **34.** $20 + y^2 = 24$ **35.** $55 = z^2 - 9$

36. Find the number of ways to arrange the letters in the word EQUATION. *(Lesson 13.4)*

Basic Skills **Find the mean, median, mode, and range of the data.**

37. 8, 10, 10, 13, 9, 7, 12, 11, 10 **38.** 23, 15, 23, 27, 28, 25, 26, 17

39. 3.6, 2.7, 3.8, 3.6, 2.9, 3.3, 2.5 **40.** 8.4, 8.5, 7.3, 7.5, 7.9, 8.9, 8.5, 6.2

Test-Taking Practice

41. Multiple Choice The spinner shown is divided into equal parts. What is the probability that the spinner lands on green or an odd number?

A. $\frac{1}{6}$ **B.** $\frac{1}{3}$ **C.** $\frac{1}{2}$ **D.** $\frac{5}{6}$

42. Multiple Choice What is the probability that the spinner shown does *not* land on green?

F. $\frac{1}{3}$ **G.** $\frac{1}{2}$ **H.** $\frac{2}{3}$ **I.** $\frac{5}{6}$

Perform an Experiment

Estimate

Make a List

Draw a Diagram

Act it Out

Perform an Experiment

Guess, Check, and Revise

Make a Model

Problem Your older sister wants to flip a bottle cap to decide who does the chores this week. If the cap lands top side up, then you do the chores. If the cap lands top side down, then she does the chores. Should you agree to your sister's plan? Explain your reasoning.

❶ Read and Understand

Read the problem carefully.

You want to know whether it is more likely for the bottle cap to land top side up or top side down. So, this is a problem about probability.

❷ Make a Plan

Decide on a strategy to use.

Because a bottle cap is heavier on top, the two outcomes are not equally likely, so you can't use theoretical probability. You need to perform an experiment to calculate an experimental probability.

❸ Solve the Problem

Reread the problem and perform an experiment.

To calculate an experimental probability, you need to flip a bottle cap several times and count how many times it lands top side up and how many times it lands top side down. For example, you can flip a bottle cap 10 times and record your results in a table like the one below.

| Cap lands top side up | III |
| Cap lands top side down | ℍ II |

From the table, it seems that it is more likely that the cap will land top side down. So, you should agree to your sister's plan if you don't like doing chores.

❹ Look Back

To make sure that the bottle cap is really more likely to land top side down, you can repeat the experiment several times to see if the probability of landing top side down remains greater than 50%.

Use the strategy *perform an experiment*.

1. **Favorite Games** Ask 15 of your classmates to name their favorite board game (such as chess). Record your results in a table. Use your results to find the probability that a randomly selected student would respond with your favorite board game.

2. **Your Last Name** Write each letter of your last name on a small piece of paper and put all of the letters in a bag. Randomly choose a letter, record the results in a table, and put the letter back in the bag. Repeat this process 19 times. Use your results to find the experimental probability of choosing the first letter of your last name.

3. **Game Pieces** With each purchase of a meal at a fast food restaurant, you receive a game piece. If you collect all 6 game pieces, you win a prize. Letting the numbers 1 through 6 represent the 6 different game pieces, roll a number cube to simulate receiving a game piece. Continue to roll the cube until you have one of each game piece, and record your results in a table like the one below. Repeat the experiment several times to estimate the mean number of meals you need to buy to collect all 6 game pieces.

Piece	1	2	3	4	5	6
Meals	?	?	?	?	?	?

4. **Money** Ask someone to put 12 pieces of play money of 3 different denominations in a hat. Randomly choose a bill, record the denomination, and put the bill back in the hat. Repeat this process 24 times. Using your results, guess the number of bills of each denomination that was put in the hat.

Mixed Problem Solving

Use any strategy to solve the problem.

5. **Road Trip** You are taking a road trip with your family. The trip is 250 miles long, and your family's car gets about 24 miles per gallon. The current price of gasoline is $1.40 per gallon. Road tolls will cost $12.75. Estimate the amount of money you need to pay for gas and tolls.

6. **Room Decorating** You want to redecorate your bedroom, and you can choose among 4 comforters, 3 pairs of curtains, and 3 rugs. If you want 1 comforter, 1 pair of curtains, and 1 rug, how many different ways can you redecorate?

7. **Toothpick Puzzle** Nine toothpicks are arranged to form three triangles as shown below. How can the toothpicks be rearranged to form five triangles by moving only three toothpicks?

8. **Standing in Line** Amy, Ben, Chloe, and Dan are standing in line. Ben is standing somewhere behind Chloe. Amy is not first. Dan is not last. Ben and Dan are not standing next to each other. Amy and Chloe are standing next to each other. Chloe and Ben are standing next to each other. In what order are they standing?

Independent and Dependent Events

BEFORE	▶ Now	WHY?
You found the probability of disjoint events.	You'll find the probability of dependent events.	So you can find the probability of choosing socks, as in Example 3.

Activity You can find the probability of two events occurring under different circumstances.

(1) A bag contains 9 pieces of paper, with 5 pieces having an O and 4 pieces having an X. Suppose you randomly choose a piece of paper from the bag, you get an O, and you don't put it back. Then you randomly choose a second piece of paper. What is the probability that the second piece of paper has an X?

(2) Suppose that you repeat Step 1, but this time the first piece of paper has an X. What is the probability that the second piece of paper also has an X?

(3) Why do you think the probabilities in Steps 1 and 2 are different?

Two events are **independent events** if the occurrence of one event does not affect the likelihood that the other event will occur. Two events are **dependent events** if the occurrence of one event does affect the likelihood that the other will occur.

EXAMPLE 1 **Independent and Dependent Events**

In Step 1 of the activity, you chose an O first, then an X. Are these events *independent* or *dependent*?

As Step 2 of the activity showed, whether or not you choose an O first *does* affect the likelihood that you choose an X second. This is because the ratio of X's to O's in the bag changes after the first piece of paper is chosen and not put back.

ANSWER The events are dependent.

HELP with Solving

When you consider the outcomes of two events, the events are called *compound events*. Independent, dependent, and disjoint events are compound events.

Your turn now A jar contains 5 red and 7 blue marbles.

1. You randomly choose a marble, put it back, then randomly choose another marble. Are the events "choose a red marble first" and "choose a blue marble second" *independent* or *dependent*?

HELP with **Vocabulary**

In common usage, being independent means being free from the control of others. This may help you remember the meaning of independent events.

Independent Events A coin is flipped and a number cube is rolled. The table of outcomes helps you see the relationship between the probability of two events together and the probabilities of the individual events.

$$P(\text{H and odd}) = \frac{1 \cdot 3}{2 \cdot 6}$$

$$= \frac{1}{2} \cdot \frac{3}{6}$$

$$= P(\text{H}) \cdot P(\text{odd})$$

This result suggests the following rule.

	H	T
1	H, 1	T, 1
2	H, 2	T, 2
3	H, 3	T, 3
4	H, 4	T, 4
5	H, 5	T, 5
6	H, 6	T, 6

Probability of Independent Events

Words For two independent events, the probability that both events occur is the product of the probabilities of the events.

Algebra If A and B are independent events, then
$P(\text{A and B}) = P(\text{A}) \cdot P(\text{B})$.

EXAMPLE 2 **Probability of Independent Events**

Game Show As a contestant on a game show, you need to spin the money wheel at the right, which is divided into equal sections. Find the probability that you get $200 on your first spin and go bankrupt on your second spin.

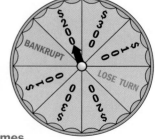

1 Find the probability of each event.

$$P(\$200) = \frac{2}{8} = 0.25 \qquad \text{``\$200'' appears 2 times.}$$

$$P(\text{bankrupt}) = \frac{1}{8} = 0.125 \qquad \text{``Bankrupt'' appears once.}$$

2 Because the events are independent, multiply the probabilities.

$$P(\$200 \text{ and bankrupt}) = P(\$200) \times P(\text{bankrupt})$$

$$= 0.25 \times 0.125$$

$$= 0.03125$$

ANSWER The probability that you get $200 on your first spin and go bankrupt on your second spin is 0.03125, or about 3%.

Dependent Events If A and B are dependent events, the probability that B occurs given A is not the same as the probability of B. So, you should use *P*(B given A) instead of *P*(B) to represent the probability that B will occur given that A has occurred.

Probability of Dependent Events

Words For two dependent events, the probability that both events occur is the product of the probability of the first event and the probability of the second event given the first.

Algebra If A and B are dependent events, then
$P(\text{A and B}) = P(\text{A}) \cdot P(\text{B given A})$.

EXAMPLE 3 Probability of Dependent Events

Socks A drawer has 12 white, 7 black, and 6 striped socks. You randomly choose 1 sock from the drawer, then randomly choose another sock without replacing the first. Find the probability that both are white.

Solution

Find the probability of the first event and the probability of the second event given the first. Then multiply the probabilities.

(1 $P(\text{white}) = \dfrac{12}{25}$ **Of the 25 socks, 12 are white.**

(2 $P(\text{white given white}) = \dfrac{11}{24}$ **Of the remaining 24 socks, 11 are white.**

(3 $P(\text{white and white}) = \dfrac{12}{25} \times \dfrac{11}{24}$ **Multiply probabilities.**

$= \dfrac{\overset{1}{\cancel{12}} \times 11}{25 \times \underset{2}{\cancel{24}}}$ **Divide out common factor.**

$= \dfrac{11}{50}$ **Multiply.**

ANSWER The probability that both socks are white is $\dfrac{11}{50}$, or 22%.

Your turn now Refer to Example 3.

2. Find the probability that both socks are black when the first sock chosen is not replaced.

Getting Ready to Practice

1. **Vocabulary** Explain the difference between independent and dependent events.

Events A and B are independent events. Find *P*(A and B).

2. $P(A) = 0.3$
   $P(B) = 0.7$

3. $P(A) = 0.5$
   $P(B) = 0.5$

4. $P(A) = 0.8$
   $P(B) = 0.2$

Events A and B are dependent events. Find *P*(A and B).

5. $P(A) = 0.9$
   $P(B \text{ given } A) = 0.8$

6. $P(A) = 0.6$
   $P(B \text{ given } A) = 0.25$

7. $P(A) = 0.25$
   $P(B \text{ given } A) = 0.2$

8. **Baseball** You are watching a baseball game. Tell whether the events are *independent* or *dependent*.
   Event A: The third batter in the lineup hits a home run.
   Event B: The fourth batter in the lineup hits a home run.

Practice and Problem Solving

HELP with Homework

Example	Exercises
1	9–10
2	11–13, 18–20
3	14–16, 21–22

Online Resources
CLASSZONE.COM

· More Examples
· eTutorial Plus

Tell whether the events are *independent* or *dependent*.

9. You roll a number cube and get a 5, and you flip a coin and get tails.

10. Your CD player has a random play button that chooses songs at random and plays each song exactly once before repeating. While listening to a CD in random play, you hear track 3 first and track 1 second.

Events A and B are independent events. Find the unknown probability.

11. $P(A) = 0.6$
    $P(B) = 0.3$
    $P(A \text{ and } B) = \underline{?}$

12. $P(A) = 0.2$
    $P(B) = \underline{?}$
    $P(A \text{ and } B) = 0.08$

13. $P(A) = \underline{?}$
    $P(B) = 0.5$
    $P(A \text{ and } B) = 0.35$

Events A and B are dependent events. Find the unknown probability.

14. $P(A) = 0.25$
    $P(B \text{ given } A) = 0.5$
    $P(A \text{ and } B) = \underline{?}$

15. $P(A) = 0.4$
    $P(B \text{ given } A) = \underline{?}$
    $P(A \text{ and } B) = 0.36$

16. $P(A) = \underline{?}$
    $P(B \text{ given } A) = 0.3$
    $P(A \text{ and } B) = 0.09$

17. **Writing** Describe a way to randomly choose one of the 6 lettered tiles, then another, so that the events are independent.

Shoes The tables give data about the shoes manufactured at a factory during a day. Assuming that the events are independent, find the probability that a randomly chosen pair of shoes has the given description.

Gender	Percent
Men's	46%
Women's	54%

Shoe Style	Percent
Athletic	22%
Casual	61%
Dress	17%

18. Men's athletic shoes

19. Women's casual shoes

20. Men's casual shoes

Each whole number from 1 through 10 is written on a separate piece of paper. You randomly choose numbers one at a time, but you do not replace them. Find the probability that both events A and B will occur.

21. Event A: The first number you choose is an odd number.
Event B: The second number you choose is an odd number.

22. Event A: The first number you choose is a 2.
Event B: The second number you choose is an even number.

In Exercises 23 and 24, tell whether the situation describes *independent events* **or** *dependent events.* **Then answer the question.**

23. Gumballs A bag contains 24 blue, 20 green, and 16 yellow gumballs. You randomly choose a gumball from the bag, and you do not replace it. Then you randomly choose another gumball. What is the probability that both gumballs are green?

24. Shopping The table shows the T-shirts on a clearance rack at a clothing store. Suppose that you randomly choose one T-shirt and put it back. Then you randomly choose a second T-shirt. What is the probability that the first T-shirt is a small and the second T-shirt is a large?

Size	Number
Small	12
Medium	24
Large	14

25. Perform an Experiment First, roll 2 number cubes 25 times. For each roll, record whether you get 2 of a kind. What is the experimental probability of getting 2 of a kind? Now, suppose you roll the 2 number cubes 2 more times. Use your experimental probability from the first 25 rolls to find the probability of getting 2 of a kind for both of the rolls.

26. Challenge The table shows the size and color of paper clips in a box. You randomly choose paper clips one at a time from the box, but you do not replace them. What is the probability that the first three paper clips that you choose are small and yellow?

	Small	Large
Red	10	10
Blue	10	10
Yellow	15	15

■ **Gumballs**

The elephant shown above is part of a gumball mural by Franz Spohn. He used 14,300 gumballs to create the rectangular mural, which is 8 feet long and 6 feet wide. How many gumballs are in 1 square foot of the mural? Round your answer to the nearest whole number.

Mixed Review

Write the decimal as a percent. *(Lesson 9.3)*

27. 0.364 **28.** 0.0048 **29.** 2.35 **30.** 0.10006

In Exercises 31 and 32, use the table at the right, which shows the results of a survey that asked students their favorite type of pet. *(Lesson 13.5)*

Pet	Percent
Dog	36%
Cat	31%
Bird	12%
Other	21%

31. What is the probability that a randomly selected student voted for a cat or a bird?

32. What is the probability that a randomly selected student voted for a dog or a cat?

Basic Skills **Find the product.**

33. 5×1.7 **34.** 6.8×4.1 **35.** 8.44×2.5 **36.** 9.9×3.33

Test-Taking Practice

INTERNET
State Test Practice
CLASSZONE.COM

37. Extended Response Each of the letters in the word PROBABILITY is written on a separate piece of paper and put in a bag. Which of the methods of selecting two letters will have a greater probability of getting two B's? Explain your reasoning.

Method 1: You randomly choose a letter from the bag, but you don't replace it. Then you randomly choose another letter.

Method 2: You randomly choose a letter from the bag and replace it. Then you randomly choose another letter.

What's in the bag?

A bag contains blue, red, orange, and green cubes, and there are 50 cubes in the bag. The probability of randomly choosing each cube is listed below. How many cubes of each color are in the bag?

 = 14%   = 42%

 = 26%   = 18%

Notebook Review

Review the vocabulary definitions in your notebook.

Copy the review examples in your notebook. Then complete the exercises.

Check Your Definitions

permutation, p. 650
combination, p. 651
disjoint events, p. 657

overlapping events, p. 657
complementary events, p. 659

independent events, p. 664
dependent events, p. 664

Use Your Vocabulary

1. Copy and complete: A(n) __?__ is an arrangement of a group of objects in a particular order.

13.4 Can you find permutations and combinations?

 EXAMPLE You are given a random 4 digit personal identification number (PIN) for your bank card. How many 4 digit PINs are there?

$$
\begin{array}{ccccccccc}
\text{Choices for} & & \text{Choices for} & & \text{Choices for} & & \text{Choices for} & & \text{Number} \\
\text{first digit} & \times & \text{second digit} & \times & \text{third digit} & \times & \text{fourth digit} & = & \text{of PINs} \\
10 & \times & 10 & \times & 10 & \times & 10 & = & 10{,}000
\end{array}
$$

ANSWER There are 10,000 different 4 digit PINs.

☑ **2.** Suppose that a 4 digit PIN cannot have any digits that repeat. Then how many different 4 digit PINs are there?

13.5 Can you find the probability of disjoint events?

 EXAMPLE The table shows the blood types of donors during a week at a hospital. What is the probability that a randomly selected donor has type O+ or type A− blood?

Type	O	A	B	AB
+	38%	34%	9%	3%
−	7%	6%	2%	1%

The events are disjoint because a person can have only one blood type.

$$P(\text{O+ or A−}) = P(\text{O+}) + P(\text{A−}) = 38\% + 6\% = 44\%$$

The probability that a donor has type O+ or type A− blood is 44%.

☑ **3.** Use the table to find $P(\text{B+ or O−})$.

13.6 Can you find the probability of independent events?

EXAMPLE A cookie jar has 3 oatmeal and 5 sugar cookies, and a second jar has 2 oatmeal and 4 sugar cookies. You randomly choose 1 cookie from the first jar and 1 cookie from the second jar. What is the probability that both cookies are oatmeal?

Solution

The choice you make from the first jar does *not* affect the choice you make from the second jar. So, the events are independent.

$$P(\text{oatmeal from each jar}) = \frac{3}{8} \times \frac{2}{6} = \frac{\overset{1}{\cancel{3}} \times \overset{1}{\cancel{2}}}{\underset{4}{\cancel{8}} \times \underset{2}{\cancel{6}}} = \frac{1}{8}$$

ANSWER The probability that both cookies are oatmeal is $\frac{1}{8}$, or 12.5%.

 4. You randomly choose a cookie from the first jar described above, do not replace it, and randomly choose a second cookie. What is the probability that both cookies are sugar cookies?

Stop and Think about Lessons 13.4–13.6

 5. Writing Are disjoint events necessarily independent? Explain.

Review Quiz 2

1. **Computer Password** A 5 letter computer password is randomly assigned to you. How many different passwords are possible?

2. **Flowers** You are making floral arrangements. You choose to use only 3 different types of flowers from the 6 types of flowers available. How many ways can you choose 3 different types of flowers?

3. **Age Distribution** The estimated distribution of the U.S. population in 2005 is shown in the table. Find the probability that a randomly chosen person is in the age group 15–19 or 60 and over.

Age Group	14 and under	15–19	20–24	25–39	40–59	60 and over
Percent	20.5%	7.3%	7.0%	19.9%	28.3%	17.0%

Events A and B are dependent events. Find $P(A \text{ and } B)$.

4. $P(A) = 0.6$, $P(B \text{ given } A) = 0.3$ 5. $P(A) = 0.11$, $P(B \text{ given } A) = 0.45$

Chapter Review

 **Vocabulary**

outcomes, p. 634	tree diagram, p. 639	complementary events,
event, p. 634	permutation, p. 650	p. 659
favorable outcomes,	combination, p. 651	independent events,
p. 634	disjoint events, p. 657	p. 664
probability, p. 634	overlapping events,	dependent events, p. 664
theoretical, experimental	p. 657	
probability, p. 635		

Vocabulary Review

Match the phrase with the word(s) it describes.

1. The possible results of an experiment

2. A collection of outcomes

3. A measure of the likelihood that an event will occur

4. A probability based on repeated trials of an experiment

5. An arrangement of a group of objects in a particular order

6. A grouping of objects in which order is not important

A. Event

B. Experimental probability

C. Permutation

D. Outcomes

E. Combination

F. Probability

Review Questions

Suppose you spin the spinner shown, which is divided into equal parts. Find the probability of the given event. Write the probability as a fraction, a decimal, and a percent. *(Lesson 13.1)*

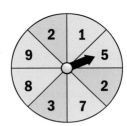

7. Pointer lands on green.

8. Pointer lands on 5.

9. Pointer lands on an odd number.

10. Pointer lands on yellow.

As you wait for the bus, you keep track of the color of each passing car. The results are given at the right. Find the probability that the next car that passes is the given color. *(Lesson 13.1)*

White	5		Silver	8
Blue	14		Red	7
Green	6		Black	10

11. White

12. Black

13. Silver

14. Blue

15. Green

16. Red

17. Sweatshirts You are ordering sweatshirts for the football team. You can get the sweatshirts in one of the two school colors: blue or gray. The sweatshirts can be hooded or crewneck, and the team name can be either on the front, on the back, or on both the front and the back of the sweatshirt. Make a tree diagram to find the number of ways the sweatshirts can be ordered. *(Lesson 13.2)*

18. What is the probability of getting at least one head when you toss a coin 3 times? *(Lesson 13.2)*

In Exercises 19–21, use the counting principle to find the number of ways that the events can occur together. *(Lesson 13.3)*

19. Event A: 5 outcomes
Event B: 11 outcomes

20. Event F: 10 outcomes
Event G: 17 outcomes
Event H: 9 outcomes

21. Event L: 14 outcomes
Event M: 3 outcomes
Event N: 21 outcomes

22. Diary Lock A diary lock has a 3 digit combination. Each of the digits is a whole number from 1 through 5. Find the probability that the lock has a combination in which all of the digits are the same number. *(Lesson 13.3)*

Tell whether the situation describes a *permutation* or a *combination*. Then answer the question. *(Lesson 13.4)*

23. How many ways can you arrange 8 books on a bookshelf?

24. If 4 friends sit in a row together at a movie theater, how many different seating arrangements are possible?

Events A and B are disjoint events. Find *P*(A or B). *(Lesson 13.5)*

25. $P(A) = 0.2$
$P(B) = 0.7$

26. $P(A) = 0.13$
$P(B) = 0.27$

27. $P(A) = 0.25$
$P(B) = 0.42$

28. Weather The probability that it will rain on Tuesday is 48%. What is the probability that it will not rain on Tuesday? *(Lesson 13.5)*

Events A and B are independent events. Find *P*(A and B). *(Lesson 13.6)*

29. $P(A) = 0.4$
$P(B) = 0.6$

30. $P(A) = 0.1$
$P(B) = 0.7$

31. $P(A) = 0.5$
$P(B) = 0.3$

32. Shoes You have 8 pairs of shoes (16 individual shoes) in the back of your closet. Because your closet is dark, you randomly choose one shoe, and without replacing it, you randomly choose another shoe. What is the probability that you choose a matching pair? *(Lesson 13.6)*

Chapter Test

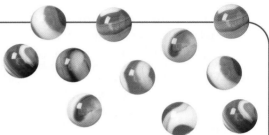

You randomly choose a marble from the marbles at the right. Find the probability of choosing a marble of the given color. Write the probability as a fraction, a decimal, and a percent.

1. Red   **2.** Blue   **3.** Green

4. Juice Survey You asked 60 students at your school to name their favorite type of juice. Of the students surveyed, 42 said orange juice. Find the probability that a randomly selected student who participated in the survey named orange juice as his favorite juice. Write the probability as a fraction, a decimal, and a percent.

5. Painting You are painting your dog's dog house. You can choose red, green, dark blue, or light blue for the main color, and white or tan for the trim color. Make a tree diagram to find the number of ways you can paint the dog house.

6. Find the number of ways to arrange the letters in the word VIDEO.

7. How many ways can you choose 3 forwards from 7 soccer players?

Relaxation The circle graph shows the results of a survey. Find the probability that a randomly chosen student who participated in the survey responded as indicated.

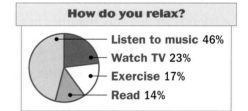

How do you relax?

- Listen to music 46%
- Watch TV 23%
- Exercise 17%
- Read 14%

8. Chose TV or music

9. Chose music or reading

10. Didn't choose exercise

In Exercises 11–13, events A and B are independent events. Find the unknown probability.

11. $P(A) = 0.2$
$P(B) = 0.4$
$P(A \text{ and } B) = \underline{?}$

12. $P(A) = 0.5$
$P(B) = \underline{?}$
$P(A \text{ and } B) = 0.2$

13. $P(A) = \underline{?}$
$P(B) = 0.7$
$P(A \text{ and } B) = 0.21$

14. Pillowcases There are 18 pillowcases stacked in your linen closet. Four of the pillowcases are blue. You randomly choose one pillowcase, then randomly choose another pillowcase without replacing the first. Find the probability that both pillowcases chosen are blue.

Chapter Standardized Test

Test-Taking Strategy Some questions may involve more than one step. Read each question carefully to avoid missing preliminary steps.

Multiple Choice

1. You spin the spinner below, which is divided into equal parts. What is the probability of the pointer landing on yellow?

    A. $\frac{1}{8}$ **B.** $\frac{1}{3}$

    C. $\frac{3}{8}$ **D.** $\frac{3}{5}$

2. You can have a grilled cheese sandwich on white, whole wheat, or rye bread. You can choose from American, provolone, Swiss, or cheddar cheese. How many sandwiches are possible?

    F. 3   **G.** 4   **H.** 7   **I.** 12

3. There are 30 runners participating in a marathon. How may ways can runners place first, second, and third?

    A. 30   **B.** 4060   **C.** 24,360   **D.** 27,000

4. How many ways can you choose 3 students from a group of 15 students?

    F. 6   **G.** 455   **H.** 910   **I.** 2730

5. You roll a number cube. Which events are disjoint?

    A. Event J: Get an odd number.
    Event K: Get a number greater than 3.

    B. Event J: Get a prime number.
    Event K: Get an even number.

    C. Event J: Get a prime number.
    Event K: Get a 4.

    D. Event J: Get a number less than 3.
    Event K: Get an even number.

6. A school consists of 36% sixth graders, 31% seventh graders, and 33% eighth graders. What is the probability that a randomly chosen student is a seventh grader or an eighth grader?

    F. 22%   **G.** 45%   **H.** 55%   **I.** 64%

7. One jar has 3 red and 6 green marbles. Another jar has 2 red and 3 blue marbles. You randomly choose a marble from each jar. What is the probability that both marbles are red?

    A. $\frac{1}{45}$ **B.** $\frac{2}{15}$ **C.** $\frac{2}{5}$ **D.** $\frac{11}{15}$

8. Events A and B are dependent events. If $P(A \text{ and } B) = 0.4$ and $P(B \text{ given } A) = 0.5$, what is $P(A)$?

    F. 0.1   **G.** 0.2   **H.** 0.8   **I.** 0.9

Short Response

9. The combination for a locker consists of 3 one-digit numbers. If the digits can repeat, what is the probability that a randomly chosen combination will have all the same digits?

Extended Response

10. A bucket contains 16 yellow, 6 orange, and 3 white tennis balls. You randomly choose 1 ball, put it back in the bucket, then randomly choose another ball. Are events A and B below independent or dependent? Explain. What is $P(A \text{ and } B)$?

    Event A: Choose an orange ball first.
    Event B: Choose a yellow ball second.

End-of-Course Test

Number Sense, Decimals, and Data

Evaluate the expression for the given value(s) of the variable(s).

1. $n - 4$ when $n = 9$　**2.** p^6 when $p = 2$　　**3.** $(50 + x) \div y$ when $x = 10$ and $y = 5$

4. You walk at approximately the same speed for 2 hours. If you walk 8 miles, what is your speed?

5. Find the perimeter and the area of a rectangle that has a length of 15 inches and a width of 8 inches.

6. Describe the following pattern: 2, 3, 4, 3, 6, 3, ... Then write the next three numbers.

Find the sum, difference, product, or quotient.

7. $5.29 + 4.99$　　　**8.** $35.88 - 4.4$　　　**9.** 34×0.063　　　**10.** $49.68 \div 21.6$

Order the numbers from least to greatest.

11. 7×10^4, 7.07×10^5, 8.1×10^5, 7.62×10^4　**12.** 5.23×10^4, 6×10^2, 5.6×10^3, 6.36×10^2

Copy and complete the statement.

13. 0.85 g = __?__ mg　　**14.** 4639 cm = __?__ m　　**15.** 8.53 kL = __?__ L　　**16.** $115{,}000$ mm = __?__ km

17. In a survey that asked students for the source of their spending money, 58 asked their parents, 100 got a weekly allowance, 92 did chores, and 40 had a job. Make a bar graph of the data.

18. The points scored per game by a basketball team are 67, 78, 92, 84, 83, 94, 71, 55, and 75. Make an ordered stem-and-leaf plot of the data.

19. The numbers of stories in 12 tall buildings are 110, 80, 100, 64, 65, 60, 66, 74, 63, 58, 70, and 61. Make a box-and-whisker plot of the data.

20. The daily low temperatures, in degrees Fahrenheit, for two weeks are 44, 33, 44, 48, 49, 32, 24, 26, 18, 45, 38, 19, 26, and 30. Make a histogram of the data using the intervals 10–19, 20–29, 30–39, 40–49.

Fractions and Integers

Use a factor tree to write the prime factorization of the numbers. Then find the GCF and the LCM of the numbers.

21. 25, 30　　　　**22.** 12, 15　　　　**23.** 64, 32　　　　**24.** 35, 10

Write the fraction in simplest form.

25. $\dfrac{12}{16}$ **26.** $\dfrac{15}{18}$ **27.** $\dfrac{25}{100}$ **28.** $\dfrac{24}{40}$

Order the numbers from least to greatest.

29. $\dfrac{1}{2}, \dfrac{5}{6}, \dfrac{2}{3}, \dfrac{3}{5}$ **30.** $3\dfrac{2}{5}, \dfrac{10}{3}, \dfrac{16}{5}, 3$ **31.** $\dfrac{11}{8}, 1.4, 1.3\overline{7}, 1\dfrac{4}{7}$ **32.** $2.\overline{20}, 2\dfrac{4}{9}, \dfrac{9}{4}, 2.22$

Find the sum, difference, product, or quotient.

33. $\dfrac{5}{8} + \dfrac{1}{4}$ **34.** $15\dfrac{1}{6} - 3\dfrac{2}{3}$ **35.** $\dfrac{8}{9} \times 5\dfrac{1}{2}$ **36.** $4\dfrac{1}{5} \div \dfrac{7}{10}$

Copy and complete the statement.

37. $9 \text{ lb} = \underline{\ ?\ } \text{ oz}$ **38.** $21{,}120 \text{ ft} = \underline{\ ?\ } \text{ mi}$ **39.** $240 \text{ fl oz} = \underline{\ ?\ } \text{ pt}$ **40.** $38 \text{ in.} = \underline{\ ?\ } \text{ ft } \underline{\ ?\ } \text{ in.}$

Order the integers from least to greatest.

41. $-12, -17, 27, -27, -8, 4$ **42.** $-38, -39, 42, -29, 43, 32$

Find the sum, difference, product, or quotient.

43. $-17 + 18$ **44.** $21 - 34$ **45.** $6(-5)$ **46.** $-72 \div (-9)$

Evaluate the expression. Justify each step you take.

47. $(-50)(-18)(2)$ **48.** $\dfrac{2}{3} + \dfrac{5}{8} + \left(-\dfrac{2}{3}\right)$ **49.** $16(5)\left(\dfrac{1}{5}\right)$ **50.** $4(8.2) + 4(2.3)$

Algebra, Proportions, and Percents

Simplify the expression.

51. $15r - 16 + 3r$ **52.** $5m - 2 + 8 - m$ **53.** $3(4 + n) - 5$ **54.** $3x - 7 + 2(4 - x)$

Solve the equation or inequality.

55. $8 = d - 3$ **56.** $\dfrac{3}{5}y = -4$ **57.** $3h + 4 = 5$ **58.** $-2x \le 16$

Make an input-output table for the function using the domain -2, -1, 0, 1, and 2. Then state the range of the function.

59. $y = x + 3$ **60.** $y = -4.2x$ **61.** $y = \dfrac{1}{2}x$ **62.** $y = 2x - 6$

63. Write the ratios $\frac{16}{24}$, 23 to 35, and 66 : 100 in order from least to greatest.

64. It cost $32 for 4 movie tickets. Write this rate as a unit rate.

65. Plot the points (2, 2) and (6, −1). Then find the slope of the line that passes through the points.

Solve the proportion.

66. $\dfrac{d}{5} = \dfrac{24}{40}$ **67.** $\dfrac{6}{9} = \dfrac{r}{72}$ **68.** $\dfrac{7}{12} = \dfrac{42}{h}$ **69.** $\dfrac{4}{x} = \dfrac{5}{25}$

70. What number is 35% of 40?   **71.** 18 is 360% of what number?

72. In your class, 2 out of every 20 students are left-handed. What percent of students in your class are left-handed?

73. Last year you earned $3500. This year you will earn 4% more. How much will you earn this year?

74. At a restaurant, your bill is $24. You leave a 15% tip. What is the total amount of money that you left?

75. If you deposit $2100 into an account that earns 5% simple annual interest, what will the account's balance be after 8 months?

Geometry and Measurement

In Exercises 76–78, use the diagram.

76. Find $m\angle 1$.   **77.** Find $m\angle 2$.   **78.** Find $m\angle 3$.

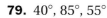

Classify the triangle by its angle measures.

79. 40°, 85°, 55°   **80.** 90°, 59°, 31°   **81.** 100°, 27°, 53°

82. Sketch and classify a quadrilateral that has 4 right angles and 4 congruent sides.

83. $\triangle LMN \cong \triangle PQR$. Name the corresponding sides and the corresponding angles.

84. Rectangles *ABCD* and *WXYZ* are similar. Rectangle *ABCD* has a length of 3 inches and a width of 2 inches. Rectangle *WXYZ* has a width of 3 inches. What is the length of rectangle *WXYZ*?

85. Draw $\triangle TUV$ with vertices $T(1, 2)$, $U(1, −1)$, and $V(3, −1)$. Find the coordinates of the vertices of the image after the translation $(x, y) \rightarrow (x − 5, y + 3)$, and draw the image.

Approximate the square root to the nearest whole number and then to the nearest tenth.

86. $\sqrt{38}$ **87.** $\sqrt{87}$ **88.** $\sqrt{126}$ **89.** $\sqrt{300}$

A right triangle has legs of length a and b, and hypotenuse c. Find the unknown length. Round to the nearest tenth if necessary.

90. $a = 7$ m, $b = 24$ m   **91.** $b = 18$ ft, $c = 30$ ft

Find the area of the parallelogram or trapezoid with the given base(s) and height.

92. Parallelogram: $b = 14$ in., $h = 11$ in.   **93.** Trapezoid: $b_1 = 8$ yd, $b_2 = 10$ yd, $h = 5$ yd

Find the circumference and the area of the circle with the given radius or diameter. Use 3.14 or $\frac{22}{7}$ for π.

94. $r = 17$ mm   **95.** $r = 63$ in.   **96.** $d = 28$ cm   **97.** $d = 11$ ft

98. Classify the solid. Be as specific as possible. Then count the number of faces, edges, and vertices in the solid.

99. Sketch a hexagonal pyramid.

Find the surface area and volume of the rectangular prism or cylinder with the given dimensions. Use 3.14 for π.

100. Cylinder: $r = 2.5$ in., $h = 5$ in.   **101.** Rectangular prism: $l = 9$ cm, $w = 5$ cm, $h = 2$ cm

Counting and Probability

102. Find the probability that you get an odd number when you roll a number cube.

103. A coat comes in 3 colors, 4 sizes, and 2 lengths. How many coats are possible?

104. How many ways can you choose 3 different movies from a list of 10?

105. You randomly choose a letter from the word MATHEMATICS. What is the probability that you choose either an M or an S?

106. A bag has 5 red and 8 blue marbles. You randomly choose a marble, and you do not replace it. Then you randomly choose another marble. What is the probability that both marbles are red?

Contents of Student Resources

Skills Review Handbook

Whole Number Place Value

The **whole numbers** are the numbers 0, 1, 2, 3, ... A **digit** is any of the numbers 0, 1, 2, 3, 4, 5, 6, 7, 8, or 9. For example, the whole number 16 has the digits 1 and 6. The value of each digit in a whole number depends on its position within the number. For example, in the number 146,783 the 8 has a value of $8 \times 10 = 80$ because it is in the tens' place.

millions | hundred thousands | ten thousands | thousands | hundreds | tens | ones

| , | 1 | 4 | 6 , | 7 | 8 | 3 |

EXAMPLE Write the number 65,309 in expanded form.

$$65,309 = 60,000 + 5000 + 300 + 9$$

The zero in the tens' place is a placeholder.

$$= 6 \times 10,000 + 5 \times 1000 + 3 \times 100 + 9 \times 1$$

EXAMPLE Write the number in standard form.

a. $8 \times 10,000 + 2 \times 1000 + 4 \times 100 + 1 \times 1$

b. Three million, six hundred ten thousand, fifty

Solution

a. $8 \times 10,000 + 2 \times 1000 + 4 \times 100 + 1 \times 1 = 80,000 + 2000 + 400 + 1$

$$= 82,401$$

b. Write 3 in the millions' place, 6 in the hundred thousands' place, 1 in the ten thousands' place, and 5 in the tens' place. Use zeros as placeholders for the other places. The answer is 3,610,050.

● Practice

Write the number in expanded form.

1. 3802   **2.** 10,649   **3.** 901,003   **4.** 4,003,506

Write the number in standard form.

5. $4 \times 10,000 + 5 \times 1000 + 9 \times 10 + 7 \times 1$ **6.** $7 \times 100,000 + 6 \times 1000 + 4 \times 100 + 5 \times 10$

7. Two thousand, three hundred sixty-one   **8.** Eight million, forty-five thousand, ten

Skills Review

Comparing and Ordering Whole Numbers

A **number line** is a line whose points are associated with numbers. You can use a number line to compare and order whole numbers. First graph the numbers on a number line. The numbers from left to right are in order from least to greatest. Remember that the symbol < means *is less than* and the symbol > means *is greater than*.

EXAMPLE Use a number line to order 11, 3, 5, 10, 8, and 15 from least to greatest.

Graph all six numbers on the same number line.

ANSWER From the positions of the graphed numbers, you can see that the order from least to greatest is 3, 5, 8, 10, 11, 15.

EXAMPLE Use a number line to compare the numbers.

    a. 14 and 2   **b.** 25 and 42

Solution

    a.

        ANSWER 14 is to the right of 2, so 14 is greater than 2. Write 14 > 2.

    b.

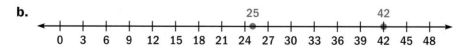

        ANSWER 25 is to the left of 42, so 25 is less than 42. Write 25 < 42.

● Practice

Use a number line to order the numbers from least to greatest.

1. 4, 10, 0, 2, 1, 8   **2.** 12, 5, 6, 7, 2, 16   **3.** 29, 9, 0, 19, 11, 6   **4.** 26, 20, 18, 13, 31, 15

Use a number line to compare the numbers.

5. 5 and 12   **6.** 6 and 16   **7.** 15 and 11   **8.** 43 and 34

Rounding Whole Numbers

To **round** a whole number means to approximate the number to a given place value. When rounding, look at the digit to the right of the given place value. If the digit to the right is less than 5 (0, 1, 2, 3, or 4), round down. If the digit to the right is 5 or greater (5, 6, 7, 8, or 9), round up.

EXAMPLE **Round the number to the place value of the red digit.**

a. 7839   **b.** 19,712

Solution

a. Because the 8 is in the hundreds' place, round 7839 to the nearest hundred. Notice that 7839 is between 7800 and 7900, so it will round to one of these two numbers.

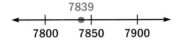

7839 is closer to 7800 than to 7900.

The digit to the right of the 8 in the hundreds' place is the 3 in the tens' place. Because 3 is less than 5, round down.

ANSWER 7839 rounded to the nearest hundred is 7800.

b. Because the 9 is in the thousands' place, round 19,712 to the nearest thousand. Notice that 19,712 is between 19,000 and 20,000, so it will round to one of these two numbers.

19,712 is closer to 20,000 than to 19,000.

The digit to the right of the 9 in the thousands' place is the 7 in the hundreds' place. Because 7 is 5 or greater, round up.

ANSWER 19,712 rounded to the nearest thousand is 20,000.

● Practice

Round the number to the place value of the red digit.

1. 342   **2.** 8351   **3.** 27,945   **4.** 184,920   **5.** 9395

6. 652   **7.** 298,725   **8.** 644,087   **9.** 58,920   **10.** 349,657

11. 5205   **12.** 24,618   **13.** 27,830,643   **14.** 156,970   **15.** 1,463,562

Number Fact Families

Inverse operations are operations that "undo" each other, such as addition and subtraction or multiplication and division. A **number fact family** consists of three whole numbers related by inverse operations. For example, the facts $8 + 2 = 10$, $2 + 8 = 10$, $10 - 2 = 8$, and $10 - 8 = 2$ are in the same number fact family.

EXAMPLE Copy and complete the number fact family.

$$6 + 3 = 9 \qquad 3 + \underline{?} = 9 \qquad 9 - \underline{?} = 3 \qquad 9 - \underline{?} = 6$$

Solution

The numbers in this fact family are 6, 3, and 9. Identify which of the three numbers is missing in each of the last three equations.

The 6 is missing in $3 + \underline{?} = 9$ and in $9 - \underline{?} = 3$.
The 3 is missing in $9 - \underline{?} = 6$.

ANSWER $6 + 3 = 9 \qquad 3 + 6 = 9 \qquad 9 - 6 = 3 \qquad 9 - 3 = 6$

EXAMPLE Copy and complete the equation $\underline{?} \div 3 = 4$.

Use the multiplication and division number fact family that contains 3 and 4 to find the missing number. The equation $4 \times 3 = 12$ is in this family. This means that 12 is missing in the equation $\underline{?} \div 3 = 4$.

ANSWER $12 \div 3 = 4$

Practice

Copy and complete the number fact family.

1. $7 + 9 = 16$ $\qquad \underline{?} + 7 = 16$ $\qquad 16 - \underline{?} = 7$ $\qquad \underline{?} - 7 = 9$

2. $9 \times 3 = 27$ $\qquad \underline{?} \times 9 = 27$ $\qquad \underline{?} \div 3 = 9$ $\qquad 27 \div \underline{?} = 3$

3. $7 - 4 = 3$ $\qquad 7 - \underline{?} = 4$ $\qquad \underline{?} + 3 = 7$ $\qquad 3 + \underline{?} = 7$

4. $8 \div 2 = 4$ $\qquad 8 \div \underline{?} = 2$ $\qquad 2 \times \underline{?} = 8$ $\qquad 4 \times \underline{?} = 8$

Copy and complete the equation.

5. $\underline{?} \div 8 = 7$ $\qquad$ **6.** $6 + \underline{?} = 14$ $\qquad$ **7.** $\underline{?} - 3 = 8$ $\qquad$ **8.** $72 \div \underline{?} = 9$

9. $\underline{?} \times 5 = 35$ $\qquad$ **10.** $8 + \underline{?} = 16$ $\qquad$ **11.** $\underline{?} - 6 = 4$ $\qquad$ **12.** $9 \times \underline{?} = 63$

Divisibility Tests

When two nonzero whole numbers are multiplied together, each number is a **factor** of the product. A number is **divisible** by another number if the second number is a factor of the first. For example, $3 \times 6 = 18$, so 3 and 6 are factors of 18, and 18 is divisible by both 3 and 6.

You can use the following tests to test a number for divisibility by 2, 3, 5, 6, 9, and 10.

Divisible by 2:	The last digit of the number is 0, 2, 4, 6, or 8.
Divisible by 3:	The sum of the digits of the number is divisible by 3.
Divisible by 5:	The last digit of the number is 0 or 5.
Divisible by 6:	The number is divisible by both 2 and 3.
Divisible by 9:	The sum of the digits of the number is divisible by 9.
Divisible by 10:	The last digit of the number is 0.

EXAMPLE Test the number for divisibility by 2, 3, 5, 6, 9, and 10.

a. 3564   **b.** 20,415

Solution

a. The last digit of 3564 is 4, so it is divisible by 2 but not by 5 or 10.
The sum of the digits is $3 + 5 + 6 + 4 = 18$, so it is divisible by 3 and 9.
Because 3564 is divisible by both 2 and 3, it is divisible by 6.

ANSWER 3564 is divisible by 2, 3, 6, and 9.

b. The last digit of 20,415 is 5, so it is divisible by 5 but not by 2 or 10.
The sum of the digits is $2 + 0 + 4 + 1 + 5 = 12$, so it is divisible by 3 but not by 9.
Because 20,415 is divisible by 3, but not by 2, it is not divisible by 6.

ANSWER 20,415 is divisible by 3 and 5.

Practice

Test the number for divisibility by 2, 3, 5, 6, 9, and 10.

1. 26	**2.** 99	**3.** 183	**4.** 348	**5.** 990
6. 1300	**7.** 1785	**8.** 2340	**9.** 3125	**10.** 4455
11. 17,820	**12.** 25,002	**13.** 47,320	**14.** 79,191	**15.** 93,295

Modeling Fractions

A **fraction** is used to describe one or more parts of a set or a whole. Each part must have the same size. A **mixed number** is a sum of a whole number and a fraction.

EXAMPLE Write a fraction to represent the shaded part of the set.

There are 9 objects in this set, and 5 of the objects are shaded.

ANSWER The fraction that represents the shaded part of the set is $\frac{5}{9}$.

EXAMPLE Write a mixed number to represent the shaded region.

Each region is divided into 4 equal parts. The whole first region is shaded along with 3 parts of the second region.

ANSWER The mixed number that represents the shaded region is $1\frac{3}{4}$.

● Practice

Write a fraction to represent the shaded part of the set or region.

1.

2.

3.

4.

5.

6.

Write a mixed number to represent the shaded region.

7.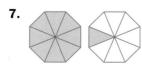

8.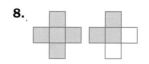

9.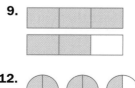

10.

11.

12.

Using a Number Line to Add and Subtract

To **add** two whole numbers on a number line:

(1) Start at 0. Move to the right to locate the first number.

(2) To add the second number, start at the location of the first number and move to the *right* the amount indicated by the second number. The final location is the **sum** of the two numbers.

To **subtract** two whole numbers on a number line:

(1) Start at 0. Move to the right to locate the first number.

(2) To subtract the second number, start at the location of the first number and move to the *left* the amount indicated by the second number. The final location is the **difference** of the two numbers.

EXAMPLE Use a number line to find the sum 8 + 6.

Start at 0. Move 8 units to the right. Then move 6 more units to the right.

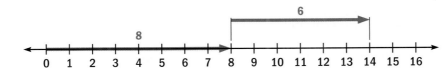

ANSWER $8 + 6 = 14$

EXAMPLE Use a number line to find the difference 18 − 11.

Start at 0. Move 18 units to the right. Then move 11 units to the left.

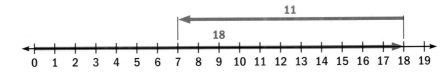

ANSWER $18 - 11 = 7$

● Practice

Use a number line to find the sum or difference.

1. $5 + 8$ **2.** $11 - 4$ **3.** $10 + 5$ **4.** $13 + 7$ **5.** $15 - 7$

6. $25 - 10$ **7.** $16 + 9$ **8.** $12 - 8$ **9.** $20 - 16$ **10.** $14 + 8$

Addition and Subtraction of Whole Numbers

To add and subtract whole numbers, start with the digits in the ones' place. Moving to the left, add or subtract the digits one place value at a time, regrouping as needed.

EXAMPLE **Find the sum 329 + 75.**

1 Add the ones. Regroup 14 ones as 1 ten and 4 ones.

$$
\begin{array}{r}
{\scriptstyle 1} \\
329 \\
+\ 75 \\
\hline
4
\end{array}
$$

2 Add the tens. Regroup 10 tens as 1 hundred and 0 tens.

$$
\begin{array}{r}
{\scriptstyle 11} \\
329 \\
+\ 75 \\
\hline
04
\end{array}
$$

3 Add the hundreds.

$$
\begin{array}{r}
{\scriptstyle 11} \\
329 \\
+\ 75 \\
\hline
404
\end{array}
$$

EXAMPLE **Find the difference 402 − 235.**

1 Start with the ones. There are not enough ones in 402 to subtract 5.

$$
\begin{array}{r}
402 \\
-\ 235 \\
\hline
\end{array}
$$

2 Move to the tens. There are no tens in 402, so regroup 1 hundred as 9 tens and 10 ones.

$$
\begin{array}{r}
{\scriptstyle 9} \\
{\scriptstyle 3\ 10\ 12} \\
\cancel{402} \\
-\ 235 \\
\hline
\end{array}
$$

3 Subtract.

$$
\begin{array}{r}
{\scriptstyle 9} \\
{\scriptstyle 3\ 10\ 12} \\
\cancel{402} \\
-\ 235 \\
\hline
167
\end{array}
$$

✓**Check** Because addition and subtraction are inverse operations, you can check your answer by adding: $167 + 235 = 402$.

Practice

Find the sum or difference.

1. $79 + 23$ **2.** $53 + 38$ **3.** $206 + 84$ **4.** $515 + 196$

5. $62 - 28$ **6.** $97 - 59$ **7.** $312 - 27$ **8.** $283 - 195$

9. $4259 + 57$ **10.** $1207 - 78$ **11.** $2725 - 807$ **12.** $3052 + 958$

13. $12{,}235 + 876$ **14.** $10{,}782 - 927$ **15.** $23{,}008 + 6913$ **16.** $27{,}091 - 3493$

Multiplication of Whole Numbers

To **multiply** two whole numbers, multiply the entire first number by the digit in each place value of the second number to obtain partial products. To find the **product** of the original numbers, add the partial products.

EXAMPLE Find the product 935 × 306.

(1 Multiply 935 by the ones' digit in 306.

$$\begin{array}{r} 23 \\ 935 \\ \times\ 306 \\ \hline 5610 \end{array}$$

(2 Skip the 0 in the tens' place, and multiply by the hundreds' digit. Start the partial product in the hundreds' place.

$$\begin{array}{r} 11 \\ 935 \\ \times\ 306 \\ \hline 5610 \\ 2805 \end{array}$$

(3 Add the partial products.

$$\begin{array}{r} 935 \\ \times\ 306 \\ \hline 5610 \\ 2805 \\ \hline 286{,}110 \end{array}$$

To multiply a whole number by a *power of 10*, such as 10, 100, or 1000, write the number followed by the number of zeros in the power. Because multiplying by such powers of 10 shifts each digit of the number to a higher place value, the zeros are needed as placeholders.

EXAMPLE Find the product.

a. 823 × 100

b. 4200 × 1000

Solution

a. 100 is a power of 10 with 2 zeros, so write 2 zeros after 823.

823 × 100 = 82,3**00**

b. 1000 is a power of 10 with 3 zeros, so write 3 zeros after 4200.

4200 × 1000 = 4,200,**000**

● Practice

Find the product.

1. 89 × 54

2. 326 × 12

3. 452 × 708

4. 6290 × 2050

5. 167 × 100

6. 52 × 10,000

7. 970 × 1000

8. 2000 × 100

Division of Whole Numbers

In a division problem, the number being divided is called the **dividend** and the number it is being divided by is called the **divisor**. The result of the division is called the **quotient**. To **divide** two whole numbers, you start with the leftmost digits of the dividend and move to the right. If the divisor does not divide the dividend evenly, then there is a **remainder**.

EXAMPLE Find the quotient $252 \div 7$.

(**1** Because 7 is between 2 and 25, place the first digit above the 5. Because $7 \times 3 = 21$, estimate that 7 divides 25 about 3 times.

$$\text{divisor} \rightarrow 7\overline{)252} \leftarrow \text{dividend} \quad \begin{array}{c} 3 \\ \end{array}$$

(**2** Multiply 3 and 7. Then subtract 21 from 25. Be sure the difference is less than the divisor: $4 < 7$.

$$\begin{array}{r} 3 \\ 7\overline{)252} \\ \underline{21} \\ 4 \end{array}$$

(**3** Bring down the next digit, 2. Divide 42 by 7 to get 6. Multiply 6 and 7. Subtract 42 from 42. There are no more digits to bring down.

$$\begin{array}{r} 36 \leftarrow \text{quotient} \\ 7\overline{)252} \\ \underline{21} \\ 42 \\ \underline{42} \\ 0 \end{array}$$

EXAMPLE Find the quotient $2533 \div 63$.

(**1** Because 63 is between 25 and 253, place the first digit above the first 3. Because $60 \times 4 = 240$, estimate that 63 divides 253 about 4 times.

$$\begin{array}{r} 4 \\ 63\overline{)2533} \end{array}$$

(**2** Multiply 4 and 63. Then subtract 252 from 253. Be sure the difference is less than the divisor: $1 < 63$.

$$\begin{array}{r} 4 \\ 63\overline{)2533} \\ \underline{252} \\ 1 \end{array}$$

(**3** Bring down the last digit, 3. Because $13 < 63$, write a 0 in the quotient. Then write the remainder next to the quotient.

$$\begin{array}{r} 40 \text{ R13} \\ 63\overline{)2533} \\ \underline{252} \\ 13 \leftarrow \text{remainder} \end{array}$$

Practice

Find the quotient.

1. $225 \div 5$

2. $413 \div 8$

3. $276 \div 12$

4. $430 \div 61$

5. $5286 \div 48$

6. $5776 \div 361$

7. $1048 \div 131$

8. $13,327 \div 665$

Estimating Sums

To **estimate** the solution of a problem means to find an approximate answer. One way to estimate a sum is to use *front-end estimation*: First add the front-end digits. Then estimate the sum of the remaining digits. Finally, add the two sums together.

EXAMPLE Estimate the sum 575 + 220 + 365.

  (1 Add the digits in the hundreds' place.

$$\begin{array}{r} 575 \\ 220 \\ + 365 \\ \end{array} \longrightarrow \begin{array}{r} 500 \\ 200 \\ + 300 \\ \hline 1000 \end{array}$$

  (2 Round the remaining digits to the nearest ten and add.

$$\begin{array}{r} 80 \\ 20 \\ + 70 \\ \hline 170 \end{array}$$

  (3 Add the two sums.

$$1000 + 170 = 1170$$

ANSWER The sum 575 + 220 + 365 is *about* 1170.

When numbers being added have about the same value, you can use *clustering* to estimate their sum.

EXAMPLE Estimate the sum 482 + 529 + 498.

$$\begin{array}{r} 482 \\ 529 \\ + 498 \\ \end{array} \longrightarrow \begin{array}{r} 500 \\ 500 \\ + 500 \\ \hline 1500 \end{array}$$

The numbers all cluster around the value 500.

ANSWER The sum 482 + 529 + 498 is *about* 1500.

● Practice

Estimate the sum.

1. 221 + 389 + 105

2. 524 + 168 + 912

3. 729 + 376 + 857

4. 4568 + 2157 + 1982

5. 5649 + 6125 + 2914

6. 9270 + 7632 + 5718

7. 659 + 719 + 684

8. 734 + 658 + 709

9. 931 + 863 + 874 + 917

Estimating Differences

One way to estimate a difference is to first subtract the digits in the greatest place. Then round the remaining parts of the numbers and subtract the lesser number from the greater number. Finally, combine the two differences using addition or subtraction as shown below.

EXAMPLE Estimate the difference.

a. $46{,}398$
$- 21{,}759$

b. 7276
$- 3814$

Solution

a. First subtract the digits in the ten thousands' place.

$\begin{array}{r} 46{,}398 \\ -\ 21{,}759 \end{array} \longrightarrow \begin{array}{r} 40{,}000 \\ -\ 20{,}000 \\ \hline 20{,}000 \end{array}$

Then round the remaining parts to the nearest thousand. Subtract the lesser number from the greater number.

$\begin{array}{r} 6{,}000 \\ -\ 2{,}000 \\ \hline 4{,}000 \end{array}$

Because the greater remaining number was originally on the *top*, you *add* the differences.

$20{,}000 + 4{,}000 = 24{,}000$

ANSWER The difference $46{,}398 - 21{,}759$ is *about* 24,000.

b. First subtract the digits in the thousands' place.

$\begin{array}{r} 7276 \\ -\ 3814 \end{array} \longrightarrow \begin{array}{r} 7000 \\ -\ 3000 \\ \hline 4000 \end{array}$

Then round the remaining parts to the nearest hundred. Subtract the lesser number from the greater number.

$\begin{array}{r} 800 \\ -\ 300 \\ \hline 500 \end{array}$

Because the greater remaining number was originally on the *bottom*, you *subtract* the differences.

$4000 - 500 = 3500$

ANSWER The difference $7276 - 3814$ is *about* 3500.

● Practice

Estimate the difference.

1. $891 - 252$ **2.** $921 - 542$ **3.** $587 - 175$ **4.** $674 - 328$

5. $3245 - 1097$ **6.** $7658 - 3109$ **7.** $9123 - 2345$ **8.** $55{,}903 - 14{,}872$

Estimating Products

One way to estimate a product is to find a range for the product by finding a low estimate and a high estimate.

EXAMPLE Find a low and high estimate for the product 47 × 34.

For the low estimate, round both factors *down*.

$$\begin{array}{r} 40 \\ \times\ 30 \\ \hline 1200 \end{array}$$

For the high estimate, round both factors *up*.

$$\begin{array}{r} 50 \\ \times\ 40 \\ \hline 2000 \end{array}$$

ANSWER The product 47 × 34 is between 1200 and 2000.

Another way to estimate a product is to use *compatible numbers*, which are numbers that make a calculation easier.

EXAMPLE Use compatible numbers to estimate the product 345 × 18.

$$\begin{array}{r} 345 \\ \times\ 18 \end{array}$$ ⟹ Round 345 to 350. Round 18 to 20. ⟹ $$\begin{array}{r} 350 \\ \times\ 20 \\ \hline 7000 \end{array}$$

ANSWER The product 345 × 18 is *about* 7000.

● Practice

Find a low and high estimate for the product.

1. $\begin{array}{r} 28 \\ \times\ 12 \end{array}$
2. $\begin{array}{r} 46 \\ \times\ 81 \end{array}$
3. $\begin{array}{r} 56 \\ \times\ 29 \end{array}$
4. $\begin{array}{r} 74 \\ \times\ 32 \end{array}$

5. $\begin{array}{r} 387 \\ \times\ 21 \end{array}$
6. $\begin{array}{r} 640 \\ \times\ 74 \end{array}$
7. $\begin{array}{r} 183 \\ \times\ 27 \end{array}$
8. $\begin{array}{r} 819 \\ \times\ 55 \end{array}$

Use compatible numbers to estimate the product.

9. 452 × 153
10. 389 × 173
11. 628 × 921
12. 476 × 293

13. 807 × 504
14. 127 × 836
15. 6509 × 23
16. 7091 × 98

Estimating Quotients

One way to estimate a quotient is to find a low estimate and a high estimate by using numbers that divide with no remainder.

EXAMPLE **Find a low and high estimate for the quotient 14,682 ÷ 63.**

When the divisor has more than one digit, round it as described below.

For a *low* estimate, round the divisor *up* and replace 14,682 with a number that is divisible by 70 and is *less* than 14,682.

$$\frac{200}{70)\overline{14,000}}$$

For a *high* estimate, round the divisor *down* and replace 14,682 with a number that is divisible by 60 and is *greater* than 14,682.

$$\frac{300}{60)\overline{18,000}}$$

ANSWER The quotient 14,682 ÷ 63 is between 200 and 300.

Another way to estimate a quotient is to use compatible numbers.

EXAMPLE **Use compatible numbers to estimate the quotient 147 ÷ 22.**

Look for numbers close to 147 and 22 that divide evenly.

$$22)\overline{147} \longrightarrow \frac{7}{20)\overline{140}}$$

ANSWER The quotient 147 ÷ 22 is *about* 7.

● Practice

Find a low and high estimate for the quotient.

1. 133 ÷ 4   **2.** 2397 ÷ 6   **3.** 1580 ÷ 6   **4.** 1957 ÷ 8

5. 528 ÷ 28   **6.** 8091 ÷ 92   **7.** 1735 ÷ 34   **8.** 3196 ÷ 42

9. 14,453 ÷ 6   **10.** 21,895 ÷ 9   **11.** 55,912 ÷ 59   **12.** 29,021 ÷ 74

Use compatible numbers to estimate the quotient.

13. 238 ÷ 5   **14.** 8319 ÷ 9   **15.** 4175 ÷ 7   **16.** 3214 ÷ 4

17. 633 ÷ 32   **18.** 4332 ÷ 78   **19.** 1462 ÷ 53   **20.** 2581 ÷ 83

21. 36,012 ÷ 8   **22.** 13,906 ÷ 3   **23.** 32,164 ÷ 62   **24.** 67,428 ÷ 76

Solving Problems Using Addition and Subtraction

You can use the following guidelines to tell whether to use addition or subtraction to solve a word problem.

- Use addition when you need to combine, join, or find a total.

- Use subtraction when you need to separate, compare, take away, find how many are left, or find how many more are needed.

EXAMPLE **You paid $14 for a CD and $30 for a DVD. How much did you pay in all?**

You need to find a total, so you need to add.

$14 + $30 = $44

ANSWER You paid $44 in all.

EXAMPLE **You have 25 invitations to your birthday party. You hand out 16 invitations. How many invitations do you have left?**

You need to find how many are left, so you need to subtract.

25 − 16 = 9

ANSWER You have 9 invitations left.

● Practice

1. You have $18 to spend. You buy a book for $6. How much money do you have left?

2. You spend $25 for a shirt and $35 for a pair of jeans. How much more did you spend for the jeans?

3. You invited 18 boys and 26 girls to your party. How many people did you invite in all?

4. You need to study 6 hours for your tests. You have studied for 4 hours. How many more hours do you need to study?

5. You have $35. Your sister gives you $9 more. How much money do you have now?

6. You have 200 sheets of notebook paper. You give your friend 65 sheets. How many sheets do you have left?

Solving Problems Using Multiplication and Division

You can use the following guidelines to tell whether to use multiplication or division to solve a word problem.

- Use multiplication when you need to find the total number of objects that are in groups of equal size.

- Use division when you need to find the number of equal groups or find the number in each equal group.

EXAMPLE **You bought 3 packages of socks. Each package contains 6 pairs of socks. How many pairs of socks did you buy?**

You need to find the total number of objects, so you need to multiply.

$3 \times 6 = 18$

ANSWER You bought 18 pairs of socks.

EXAMPLE **You bake 36 cookies. You put the same number of cookies in 9 bags. How many cookies do you put in each bag?**

You need to find the number in each equal group, so you need to divide.

$36 \div 9 = 4$

ANSWER You put 4 cookies in each bag.

● Practice

1. You order 3 packages of pencils for the school store. Each package contains 12 pencils. How many pencils do you get?

2. You bought 4 bags of apples. Each bag contains 6 apples. How many apples did you buy?

3. You bought 6 packages of muffins and have a total of 24 muffins. How many muffins are in a package?

4. You have 5 boxes of dog biscuits. Each box contains 10 dog biscuits. How many dog biscuits do you have?

5. You split a deck of 52 playing cards evenly among 4 people. How many cards does each person get?

Units of Time

Use the equivalent units of time given below to convert one unit of time to another. Multiply to convert from a larger unit to a smaller unit. Divide to convert from a smaller unit to a larger unit.

$$1 \text{ week (wk)} = 7 \text{ days (d)}$$
$$1 \text{ day (d)} = 24 \text{ hours (h)}$$
$$1 \text{ hour (h)} = 60 \text{ minutes (min)}$$
$$1 \text{ minute (min)} = 60 \text{ seconds (sec)}$$

EXAMPLE Copy and complete.

a. 21 d = ? wk   **b.** 3 h = ? min

Solution

a. You are converting days to weeks, a smaller unit to a larger unit. There are 7 days in one week, so divide by 7.

$$21 \text{ d} = (21 \div 7) \text{ wk}$$
$$= 3 \text{ wk}$$

b. You are converting hours to minutes, a larger unit to a smaller unit. There are 60 minutes in one hour, so multiply by 60.

$$3 \text{ h} = (3 \times 60) \text{ min}$$
$$= 180 \text{ min}$$

EXAMPLE Compare 1 h 20 min and 120 min.

To compare times you must express them in the same units, so convert 1 hour 20 minutes to minutes.

$$1 \text{ h } 20 \text{ min} = 1 \text{ h} + 20 \text{ min}$$
$$= 60 \text{ min} + 20 \text{ min}$$
$$= 80 \text{ min}$$

ANSWER Because 80 min < 120 min, 1 h 20 min < 120 min.

Practice

Copy and complete.

1. 5 h = ? min

2. 120 sec = ? min

3. 3 d = ? h

4. 4 wk = ? d

5. 48 h = ? d

6. 4 min = ? sec

Copy and complete the statement using <, >, or =.

7. 1 min 15 sec ? 65 sec

8. 2 d 12 h ? 62 h

9. 190 min ? 3 h 10 min

10. 75 h ? 5 d 5 h

11. 14 wk 2 d ? 100 d

12. 425 sec ? 7 min 5 sec

Solving Problems Involving Time

When given a start time and an end time, you can find the *elapsed time* by subtracting the end time from the start time.

EXAMPLE **A study session began at 9:40 A.M. and ended at 10:10 A.M. How long did the study session last?**

Subtract to find the elapsed time.
Subtract the minutes first, then the hours.

$$\begin{array}{r} 10{:}10 \\ -\ 9{:}40 \end{array}$$

You cannot subtract 40 from 10. Rename 1 hour as 60 minutes. Then subtract.

$$\begin{array}{r} {}^{9\ \ 70} \\ \cancel{10{:}10} \\ -\ 9{:}40 \\ \hline 30 \end{array}$$

ANSWER The study session lasted 30 minutes.

When you need to estimate solutions of problems involving minutes, round times to the nearest 10 minutes or 15 minutes.

EXAMPLE **Solve the following problem.**

You spent 22 minutes doing your math homework, 1 hour 27 minutes writing a book report, and 44 minutes working on your science project. Estimate how much time you spent doing your homework.

$$\begin{array}{r} 22 \text{ min} \\ 1 \text{ h } 27 \text{ min} \\ +\quad 44 \text{ min} \end{array} \longrightarrow \begin{array}{r} \mathbf{20 \text{ min}} \\ \mathbf{1 \text{ h } 30 \text{ min}} \\ +\quad \mathbf{40 \text{ min}} \\ \hline 2 \text{ h } 30 \text{ min} \end{array}$$

> These rounded times add up to 1 hour.

ANSWER You spent about 2 hours 30 minutes doing your homework.

● Practice

1. How long was a soccer game that started at 1:15 P.M. and ended at 3:30 P.M.?

2. A movie started at 8:40 P.M. and ended at 10:05 P.M. How long did it last?

3. You talked with your grandfather for 18 min, your friend for 25 min, and your lab partner for 22 min. Estimate how long you were on the phone.

4. Some friends are working at a car wash. If it takes them 14 minutes to wash a car, about how many cars can they wash in 3 hours?

Using a Ruler

An **inch ruler** has markings for inches, halves of an inch, fourths of an inch, eighths of an inch, and sixteenths of an inch. As the lengths get shorter, so do the markings.

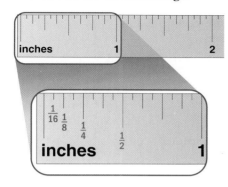

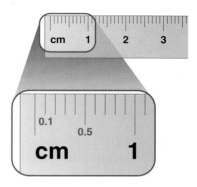

A **centimeter ruler** has markings for centimeters, halves of a centimeter, and tenths of a centimeter (also called *millimeters*). Like an inch ruler, as the lengths get shorter, so do the markings.

EXAMPLE Use a ruler to draw a segment with the given length.

a. $1\frac{3}{4}$ inches

b. 2.9 centimeters

Solution

a. Start at the leftmost mark on the ruler.

Draw a segment so that the other end is at the $1\frac{3}{4}$ in. mark.

b. Start at the leftmost mark on the ruler.

Draw a segment so that the other end is at the 2.9 cm mark.

● Practice

Use a ruler to draw a segment with the given length.

1. $\frac{9}{16}$ inch

2. $4\frac{1}{4}$ inches

3. 1.8 centimeters

4. 6.2 centimeters

5. $3\frac{7}{8}$ inches

6. 2.3 centimeters

7. 5.5 centimeters

8. $1\frac{1}{2}$ inches

Using a Compass

A **compass** is an instrument used to draw circles. A **straightedge** is any object that can be used to draw a segment.

EXAMPLE Use a compass to draw a circle with radius 1 cm.

Recall that the *radius* of a circle is the distance between the center of the circle and any point on the circle.

Use a metric ruler to open the compass so that the distance between the point and the pencil is 1 cm.

Place the point on a piece of paper and rotate the pencil around the point to draw the circle.

1 cm

EXAMPLE Use a straightedge and a compass to draw a segment whose length is the sum of the lengths of $\overline{AB}$ and $\overline{CD}$.

$\overline{}$
A   B   C   D

Solution

Use a straightedge to draw a segment longer than both given segments.

Open your compass to measure segment *AB*. Using this compass setting, place the point at the left end of your segment and make a mark that crosses your segment.

Then open your compass to measure segment *CD*. Using this compass setting, place the point at the first mark you made on your segment and make another mark that crosses your segment.

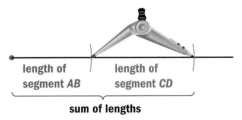

length of segment *AB*   length of segment *CD*

sum of lengths

● Practice

1. Use a compass to draw a circle with radius 5 centimeters.

2. Use a compass to draw a circle with radius 1 inch.

3. Use a straightedge and a compass to draw a segment whose length is the *sum* of the lengths of the two given segments.

$\overline{}$
A   B

$\overline{}$
C   D

4. Use a straightedge and a compass to draw a segment whose length is the *difference* of the lengths of the two given segments in Exercise 3.

Basic Geometric Figures

A **triangle** is a geometric figure having 3 sides and 3 angles.

A **rectangle** has 4 sides and 4 right angles. Opposite sides have the same length.

A **square** is a rectangle with all four sides the same length.

 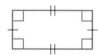

The distance around a figure is called its **perimeter**. If a figure has straight sides, you can find its perimeter by adding the lengths of the sides.

EXAMPLE Find the perimeter.

The perimeter is
5 in. + 4 in. + 4 in. = 13 in.

EXAMPLE Draw and label a rectangle with a length of 3 cm and a width of 2 cm. Then find its perimeter.

Draw a horizontal side 3 cm long. Then draw the two vertical sides 2 cm long. Finally, draw the second horizontal side 3 cm long.

The perimeter is 3 cm + 2 cm + 3 cm + 2 cm = 10 cm.

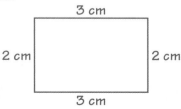

Practice

Find the perimeter.

1.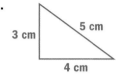

2.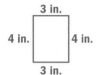

3.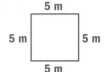

4.

Draw and label the figure described. Then find its perimeter.

5. A square with sides 1 in. long

6. A square with sides 4 cm long

7. A rectangle with a length of 4 cm and a width of 3 cm

8. A rectangle with a length of 2 in. and a width of 1 in.

Venn Diagrams and Logical Reasoning

A **Venn diagram** uses shapes to show how sets are related.

EXAMPLE **Draw and use a Venn diagram.**

a. Draw a Venn diagram of the whole numbers between 10 and 20 where set *A* consists of odd numbers and set *B* consists of multiples of 3.

b. Is the following statement *true* or *false*? Explain.
No odd whole number between 10 and 20 is a multiple of 3.

c. Is the following statement *always, sometimes,* or *never* true? Explain.
A multiple of 3 between 10 and 20 is even.

Solution

a.

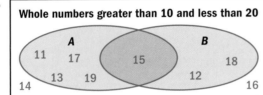

b. False. 15 is an odd whole number that is a multiple of 3.

c. Sometimes. It is true that 12 and 18 are multiples of 3 that are even, but 15 is a multiple of 3 that is odd.

Practice

Draw a Venn diagram of the sets described.

1. Of the whole numbers less than 10, set *A* consists of numbers that are greater than 7 and set *B* consists of even numbers.

2. Of the whole numbers less than 15, set *C* consists of multiples of 4 and set *D* consists of odd numbers.

Use the Venn diagrams from Exercises 1 and 2 to answer the question. Explain your reasoning.

3. Is the following statement *true* or *false*?
There is only one even number greater than 7 and less than 10.

4. Is the following statement *always, sometimes,* or *never* true?
A whole number less than 15 is both a multiple of 4 and odd.

Reading Bar Graphs and Line Graphs

Data are numbers or facts. Two ways to display data are **bar graphs**, which use bars to show how quantities compare, and **line graphs**, which use line segments to show how a quantity changes over time.

EXAMPLE The bar graph shows the results of a survey on favorite pizza toppings. Which topping is favored the most? Which is favored the least?

Solution

The longest bar on the graph represents the 7 students who favor pepperoni, and the shortest bar represents the 2 students who favor mushrooms. So, pepperoni is most favored, and mushrooms are least favored.

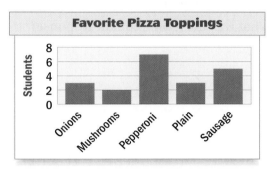

EXAMPLE The line graph shows temperature data collected hourly for 5 times on Monday. Between which two consecutive times was the greatest increase in temperature? What was the increase?

Solution

The steepest segment in the line graph is from 11 A.M. to 12 P.M. The students recorded a temperature of 55°F at 11 A.M. and a temperature of 62°F at 12 P.M., which is an increase of 7°F.

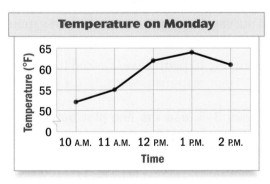

● Practice

Use the graphs shown above.

1. How many students chose sausage as a favorite pizza topping?

2. Which two pizza toppings were chosen by the same number of students?

3. At what time was the temperature 52°F?

4. Between which two consecutive times did the temperature decrease?

Reading and Making Line Plots

A **line plot** uses a number line to show how often data values occur.

EXAMPLE You surveyed 15 of your neighbors and asked them how many brothers and sisters they have. Their responses were: 5, 3, 2, 1, 6, 3, 4, 3, 1, 2, 3, 2, 5, 3, 4.

   a. Make a line plot of the data.

   b. What was the least frequent response?

Solution

   a.

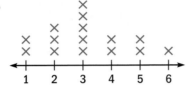

   b. There is only one × above 6, so 6 was the least frequent response.

● Practice

Make a line plot of the data.

   1. In a survey, 12 people were asked how many pets they own. Their responses were: 1, 2, 1, 1, 0, 4, 1, 0, 0, 2, 1, 3.

   2. In a survey, 16 people were asked how many times they exercise during a week. Their responses were: 1, 3, 4, 2, 3, 3, 3, 5, 3, 4, 5, 2, 3, 3, 5, 6.

In Exercises 3–5, use the line plot below, which shows the results of a questionnaire asking people how many hours of television they watch each week.

   3. How many people completed the questionnaire?

   4. How many more people watch 3 hours of television each week than watch 5 hours of television?

   5. How many people watch less than 4 hours of television each week?

Extra Practice

Chapter 1

1.1 **Describe the pattern. Then write the next three numbers.**

1. 57, 49, 41, 33, . . .   **2.** 5, 15, 45, 135, . . .   **3.** 1600, 800, 400, 200, . . .

1.1 **4.** Describe the pattern. Then draw the next figure.

1.2 **Evaluate the expression for the given value of the variable.**

5. $75 \div m$ when $m = 5$ **6.** $k - 26$ when $k = 43$ **7.** $4x$ when $x = 9$

1.2 **8.** The expression $60h$ can be used to find the number of minutes in h hours. Find the number of minutes in 24 hours.

1.3 **Write the product as a power.**

9. $11 \cdot 11 \cdot 11$ **10.** $8 \cdot 8 \cdot 8 \cdot 8 \cdot 8$ **11.** $y \cdot y \cdot y \cdot y$ **12.** $a \cdot a \cdot a \cdot a \cdot a \cdot a$

1.3 **Evaluate the power.**

13. 10^2 **14.** 7^4 **15.** 0^6 **16.** 2^8

1.4 **Evaluate the expression.**

17. $1 + (7 - 3)^3$ **18.** $\dfrac{36 - 8}{2 + 5}$ **19.** $72 \div 4 \div 3$ **20.** $(3^3 - 2)(1 + 2)$

1.5 **Solve the equation using mental math.**

21. $x + 6 = 13$ **22.** $\dfrac{z}{8} = 2$ **23.** $1 = 10 - p$ **24.** $280 = 20t$

1.6 **Find the perimeter and the area of the rectangle or square with the given dimensions.**

25. $l = 11$ feet, $w = 7$ feet   **26.** $l = 8$ yards, $w = 7$ yards   **27.** $s = 16$ centimeters

1.7 **28.** You are ordering pitchers of lemonade for you and 6 of your friends. One pitcher of lemonade can fill 5 glasses. How many pitchers should you order if each person wants 3 glasses of lemonade?

1.7 **29.** There are 5 tennis players in a tournament. If each tennis player plays every other player once, how many games will be played?

1.7 **30.** The items that Frank needs to buy for his cookout are given in the table. If Frank spends $7, how much does each ear of corn cost?

Item	Total Cost
1 package of ground beef	$3
1 bag of rolls	$2
4 ears of corn	?

Chapter 2

2.1 **Order the numbers from least to greatest.**

1. 0.25, 0.5, 0.05, 5.2   **2.** 7.9, 9.7, 0.97, 0.79   **3.** 6.2, 6.08, 6.28, 6.82

2.1 **4.** Round 8.4746 to the nearest thousandth.

2.2 **Find the sum or difference. Use estimation to check your answer.**

5. $8.33 - 7.41$ **6.** $16.7 + 129.413$ **7.** $702.85 + 35.2$ **8.** $42.9 - 26.74$

2.2 **Evaluate the expression when $a = 13.2$ and $b = 7.49$.**

9. $6.4 + a$ **10.** $a + b$ **11.** $8.613 - b$ **12.** $8 + a - b$

2.3 **Find the product. Then check that your answer is reasonable.**

13. 2.7×0.8 **14.** 3.05×0.26 **15.** 1.48×0.037 **16.** 46×2.718

17. 0.89×8.76 **18.** 3.5×6.3 **19.** 6.4×9.05 **20.** 0.006×1.2

2.4 **Find the quotient. Then check that your answer is reasonable.**

21. $84.14 \div 7$ **22.** $19.98 \div 2.7$ **23.** $6.4 \div 0.08$ **24.** $0.115 \div 5.75$

25. $0.126 \div 2.8$ **26.** $0.884 \div 0.26$ **27.** $23.24 \div 1.12$ **28.** $3.91 \div 3.4$

2.4 **29.** Find the quotient $18 \div 3.21$. Round your answer to the nearest hundredth.

2.5 **Write the number in scientific notation.**

30. 5210   **31.** 8,200,000,000   **32.** 900,000   **33.** 431.6

2.5 **Write the number in standard form.**

34. 1.4×10^4 **35.** 4.221×10^8 **36.** 6×10^1 **37.** 5.3761×10^6

2.6 **Copy and complete using the appropriate metric unit.**

38. The mass of a pencil is 6 ? .   **39.** A bottle of mouthwash holds 710 ? .

40. A pair of scissors is 14 ? long.   **41.** The mass of a pair of sneakers is 1 ? .

2.7 **Copy and complete the statement.**

42. 24 cm = ? mm   **43.** 0.4 g = ? mg   **44.** 795 g = ? kg

45. 120 L = ? kL   **46.** 0.07 kL = ? mL   **47.** 36,100 mm = ? km

2.7 **Copy and complete the statement using <, >, or =.**

48. 3 km ? 3200 m   **49.** 9450 g ? 9.45 kg   **50.** 5.4 L ? 540 mL

Chapter 3

3.1   **Find the mean, median, mode(s), and range of the data.**

1. 18, 22, 57, 29, 22, 41

2. 7, 7.5, 7.1, 7.9, 7.5, 7, 7.3, 7.5

3. 8, 7, 2, 9, 11, 7, 10, 3, 12, 2, 6

4. 94, 108, 145, 171, 162, 197, 186, 76, 88, 143

3.1   **5.** The record low temperatures in July in 8 cities are 43°F, 69°F, 35°F, 51°F, 40°F, 35°F, 44°F, and 35°F. Which average best represents the data? Explain.

3.2   **6.** The table below shows the life spans of various U.S. currency bills. Make a bar graph of the data. Make a conclusion about the data.

Denomination (dollars)	1	5	10	20	50
Life Span (years)	1.5	2	3	4	9

3.2   **7.** Describe a real-life data set that could be displayed in a line graph.

3.3   **8.** Make an ordered stem-and-leaf plot of the data in Exercise 5. Then make a conclusion about the data.

In Exercises 9–12, use the prices, in dollars, of several DVD players and VCRs listed below.

DVD players 250, 200, 160, 180, 160, 300, 185, 190, 130, 115, 250, 160, 200, 180

VCRs 130, 100, 80, 200, 100, 100, 100, 90, 90, 120, 200, 230

3.4   **9.** Using the same number line, make a box-and-whisker plot for each data set.

3.4   **10.** Use the box-and-whisker plots from Exercise 9 to make a conclusion about the price of a DVD player as compared with the price of a VCR.

3.5   **11.** Make a frequency table of each data set using the intervals 70–109, 110–149, 150–189, 190–229, 230–269, and 270–309.

3.5   **12.** Use the frequency tables from Exercise 11 to make a histogram for each data set.

3.6   **13.** Explain why the data display at the right could be misleading.

3.6   **14.** You want to display the winning long jump distances for men and women in various years of the summer Olympics. What type of data display should you use? Explain your choice.

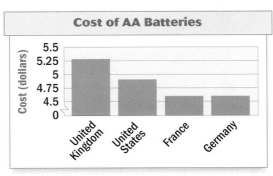

Chapter 4

4.1 **Tell whether the number is *prime* or *composite*. Then write all the factors of the number.**

1. 75   **2.** 71   **3.** 83   **4.** 91

4.1 **Use a factor tree to write the prime factorization of the number.**

5. 84   **6.** 117   **7.** 125   **8.** 225

4.2 **Find the greatest common factor of the numbers using prime factorization. Then tell whether the numbers are relatively prime.**

9. 72, 96   **10.** 35, 105   **11.** 32, 76   **12.** 51, 175

4.3 **Write the fractions in simplest form. Tell whether they are equivalent.**

13. $\dfrac{20}{24}, \dfrac{30}{36}$ **14.** $\dfrac{21}{56}, \dfrac{28}{84}$ **15.** $\dfrac{12}{16}, \dfrac{14}{18}$ **16.** $\dfrac{14}{35}, \dfrac{22}{55}$

4.4 **Find the least common multiple of the numbers by listing multiples.**

17. 12, 16   **18.** 20, 25   **19.** 9, 14   **20.** 32, 160

4.5 **Copy and complete the statement using <, >, or =.**

21. $\dfrac{5}{6}\, \underline{?\,}\, \dfrac{3}{4}$ **22.** $\dfrac{2}{5}\, \underline{?\,}\, \dfrac{1}{4}$ **23.** $\dfrac{35}{42}\, \underline{?\,}\, \dfrac{30}{36}$ **24.** $\dfrac{3}{10}\, \underline{?\,}\, \dfrac{1}{3}$

25. $\dfrac{23}{45}\, \underline{?\,}\, \dfrac{4}{9}$ **26.** $\dfrac{14}{56}\, \underline{?\,}\, \dfrac{18}{72}$ **27.** $\dfrac{7}{18}\, \underline{?\,}\, \dfrac{7}{10}$ **28.** $\dfrac{22}{25}\, \underline{?\,}\, \dfrac{9}{10}$

4.6 **Write the mixed number as an improper fraction.**

29. $7\dfrac{1}{3}$ **30.** $2\dfrac{3}{10}$ **31.** $5\dfrac{4}{9}$ **32.** $10\dfrac{1}{4}$

4.6 **Write the improper fraction as a mixed number.**

33. $\dfrac{25}{7}$ **34.** $\dfrac{52}{11}$ **35.** $\dfrac{33}{8}$ **36.** $\dfrac{47}{6}$

4.7 **Write the fraction or mixed number as a decimal.**

37. $\dfrac{7}{9}$ **38.** $\dfrac{26}{125}$ **39.** $8\dfrac{9}{10}$ **40.** $3\dfrac{7}{12}$

4.7 **Write the decimal as a fraction or mixed number.**

41. 0.68   **42.** 0.5   **43.** 5.625   **44.** 1.925

Chapter 5

Find the sum or difference.

5.1

1. $\dfrac{5}{8} + \dfrac{1}{8}$

2. $\dfrac{1}{6} + \dfrac{5}{12}$

3. $\dfrac{8}{11} - \dfrac{3}{11}$

4. $\dfrac{8}{9} - \dfrac{5}{6}$

5. $\dfrac{7}{18} + \dfrac{1}{3}$

6. $\dfrac{3}{7} + \dfrac{5}{7}$

7. $\dfrac{13}{15} - \dfrac{1}{5}$

8. $\dfrac{11}{12} - \dfrac{7}{12}$

5.2

9. $3\dfrac{1}{4} + 3\dfrac{3}{4}$

10. $8\dfrac{7}{9} + 1\dfrac{8}{9}$

11. $2\dfrac{2}{5} + 4\dfrac{3}{10}$

12. $7\dfrac{3}{4} + 1\dfrac{5}{6}$

13. $11\dfrac{3}{5} - 8\dfrac{4}{5}$

14. $5\dfrac{1}{2} - 3\dfrac{3}{8}$

15. $6 - 5\dfrac{4}{7}$

16. $8\dfrac{3}{8} - 3\dfrac{2}{3}$

5.3 **Find the product.**

17. $\dfrac{7}{9} \cdot \dfrac{3}{4}$

18. $\dfrac{7}{10} \cdot 24$

19. $3\dfrac{1}{5} \cdot 1\dfrac{1}{4}$

20. $\dfrac{5}{8} \cdot 4\dfrac{4}{9}$

21. $12 \times \dfrac{1}{6}$

22. $\dfrac{7}{24} \times \dfrac{8}{14}$

23. $4\dfrac{2}{5} \times \dfrac{2}{11}$

24. $10\dfrac{1}{2} \times 5\dfrac{1}{3}$

5.4 **Write the reciprocal of the number.**

25. $\dfrac{2}{9}$

26. $\dfrac{1}{5}$

27. $3\dfrac{1}{6}$

28. $1\dfrac{9}{10}$

5.4 **Find the quotient.**

29. $\dfrac{3}{4} \div \dfrac{7}{8}$

30. $\dfrac{6}{25} \div 4$

31. $7\dfrac{4}{5} \div \dfrac{13}{15}$

32. $2\dfrac{1}{6} \div 1\dfrac{1}{3}$

5.5 **Copy and complete using the appropriate customary unit.**

33. A hockey rink is 200 _?_ long.

34. A hockey puck weighs 6 _?_.

35. A washing machine holds 24 _?_.

36. A bottle of lotion holds $8\dfrac{1}{2}$ _?_.

37. A watermelon weighs 11 _?_.

38. A computer keyboard is $18\dfrac{1}{2}$ _?_ long.

5.6 **Copy and complete the statement.**

39. 3 yd = _?_ in.

40. 5 pt = _?_ c

41. 4 lb = _?_ oz

42. 8000 lb = _?_ T

43. 19 qt = _?_ gal _?_ qt

44. 13,200 ft = _?_ mi _?_ ft

5.6 **Find the sum or difference.**

45.
$$\begin{array}{r} 7 \text{ qt } 1 \text{ pt} \\ + 2 \text{ qt } 1 \text{ pt} \\ \hline \end{array}$$

46.
$$\begin{array}{r} 3 \text{ ft } 7 \text{ in.} \\ + 1 \text{ ft } 9 \text{ in.} \\ \hline \end{array}$$

47.
$$\begin{array}{r} 3 \text{ T } 100 \text{ lb} \\ - 1 \text{ T } 400 \text{ lb} \\ \hline \end{array}$$

48.
$$\begin{array}{r} 5 \text{ c } 2 \text{ fl oz} \\ - 4 \text{ c } 7 \text{ fl oz} \\ \hline \end{array}$$

Chapter 6

6.1 **Order the integers from least to greatest.**

1. $-3, 0, 6, -10, 3$ **2.** $63, -48, -9, 32, -106$ **3.** $71, -70, 15, 99, -10, -84$

6.1 **4.** Write the integer that represents a depth of 128 feet below sea level. Then write the opposite of that integer.

Find the sum, difference, product, or quotient.

6.2 **5.** $-18 + 14$ **6.** $75 + (-38)$ **7.** $12 + 27 + (-12)$ **8.** $-8 + (-5) + 6$

6.3 **9.** $7 - 11$ **10.** $-25 - 10$ **11.** $64 - (-15)$ **12.** $-8 - (-7)$

6.4 **13.** $-9(-8)$ **14.** $20(-7)$ **15.** $-3(-4)(-1)$ **16.** $6(0)(-100)$

6.5 **17.** $65 \div (-5)$ **18.** $0 \div (-3)$ **19.** $-42 \div (-14)$ **20.** $-60 \div 12$

6.6 **Show that the number is rational by writing it in $\frac{a}{b}$ form. Then give the multiplicative inverse and the additive inverse of the number.**

21. -0.9 **22.** $8\frac{1}{6}$ **23.** -1 **24.** $-\frac{7}{9}$

6.6 **Evaluate the expression. Justify each step you take.**

25. $-6 \cdot 10 \cdot \left(-\frac{1}{6}\right)$ **26.** $-\frac{3}{5} + \frac{7}{11} + \frac{3}{5}$ **27.** $50 \cdot 13 \cdot 2$ **28.** $0.5 + (-9 + 2.5)$

6.7 **Use the distributive property to evaluate the expression.**

29. $8(9.1) + 8(0.9)$ **30.** $11\left(\frac{5}{9}\right) + 11\left(\frac{4}{9}\right)$ **31.** $12\left(\frac{5}{8}\right) - 12\left(\frac{1}{8}\right)$ **32.** $6(4.8)$

6.7 **33.** You buy 4 teddy bears for $24.95 each. Write an expression for the total cost of the teddy bears. Then use the distributive property to evaluate the expression.

6.8 **Plot the point and describe its location in a coordinate plane.**

34. $W(-3, -4)$ **35.** $Z(0, 2)$ **36.** $N(6, -1)$ **37.** $L(-1, 6)$

6.8 **38.** Plot and connect the points $P(-4, 5)$, $Q(-4, 1)$, $R(2, 1)$, and $S(2, 5)$ to form a rectangle. Find the length, width, and area of the rectangle.

6.8 **39.** The table shows the pressures at various depths underwater. Make a scatter plot of the data. Then make a conclusion about the data.

Depth (ft)	5	10	15	20	25	30	35
Pressure (lb/in.^2)	17	19	21	23.5	26	28	30

Chapter 7

7.1 **Write the verbal phrase as a variable expression. Let _x_ represent the number.**

    1. 17 fewer than a number   **2.** The quotient of a number and 7

7.1 **Write the verbal sentence as an equation. Let _y_ represent the number.**

    3. Half of a number is equal to -5.   **4.** 1 more than 6 times a number is 19.

7.2 **Simplify the expression.**

    5. $-r + 4 - 2 + r$ **6.** $6 + z + 3z - 4$ **7.** $6y + 12 - 4y$

    8. $8a - 2(3 + 4a)$ **9.** $2(3 - x) - 12 - 3x$ **10.** $3(2t - 5) + 4t$

Solve the equation. Check your solution.

7.3   **11.** $n + 6 = -4$ **12.** $15 = d - 3$ **13.** $1.4 = 3.8 + w$ **14.** $z - (-7) = 3$

7.4   **15.** $-7y = -49$ **16.** $1.2 = \dfrac{k}{4}$ **17.** $18 = -\dfrac{2}{3}m$ **18.** $10c = -110$

7.5   **19.** $2x - 7 = 6$ **20.** $\dfrac{p}{4} + 1 = -1$ **21.** $8.1 = 5j - 7.4$ **22.** $6 = 6(-x + 1)$

7.6 **Write an inequality represented by the graph.**

    23. 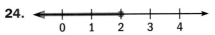   **24.**

7.6 **Solve the inequality. Then graph the solution.**

    25. $-24 + b > -30$ **26.** $\dfrac{t}{-3} \le 1$ **27.** $s - 3.5 \le 1.5$ **28.** $9r < -45$

7.7 **Make an input-output table for the function using the domain $-4, -2, 0, 2,$ and 4. Then state the range of the function.**

    29. $y = x - 1.5$ **30.** $y = -9x$ **31.** $y = 8 - x$ **32.** $y = \dfrac{3}{2}x + 1$

7.7 **Write a function rule for the input-output table.**

33.

Input x	-2	-1	0	1
Output y	-8	-7	-6	-5

34.

Input x	-4	0	4	8
Output y	1	0	-1	-2

7.8 **Graph the function.**

    35. $y = -0.5x$ **36.** $y = 6 - x$ **37.** $y = 2x + 3$ **38.** $y = -2 + \dfrac{1}{2}x$

Chapter 8

8.1 In the 2001–2002 season, the Michigan State men's hockey team had 18 wins, 6 losses, and 4 ties in their conference. Use this information to write the specified ratio.

    1. Wins to losses   **2.** Wins to games played   **3.** Losses to games played

8.1 Write the ratio as a fraction in simplest form.

    4. $30 : 36$ **5.** 12 to 48   **6.** 28 to 70

8.2 Find the unit rate.

    7. \$11.89 for 8.2 gallons   **8.** \$370 for 40 hours   **9.** 432 words in 12 minutes

8.2 **10.** Find the average speed of a runner who completes a 1500 meter race in 4 minutes 10 seconds.

8.2 **11.** Determine which bottle of shampoo is the better buy: 15 fluid ounces for \$2.59 or 20 fluid ounces for \$3.59.

8.3 Draw the graph of the line that passes through the points. Then find the slope of the line.

    12. $(7, 2), (-5, 4)$ **13.** $(-6, 0), (-5, 1)$ **14.** $(3, 4), (5, 9)$ **15.** $(-2, -3), (1, -3)$

8.3 **16.** Draw a line that has a slope of -2 and passes through $(0, -5)$.

8.4 Use equivalent ratios or algebra to solve the proportion.

    17. $\dfrac{x}{30} = \dfrac{5}{6}$ **18.** $\dfrac{28}{24} = \dfrac{r}{6}$ **19.** $\dfrac{t}{36} = \dfrac{3}{4}$ **20.** $\dfrac{12}{15} = \dfrac{c}{10}$

8.5 Use the cross products property to solve the proportion.

    21. $\dfrac{a}{39} = \dfrac{6.5}{13}$ **22.** $\dfrac{30}{12} = \dfrac{6}{z}$ **23.** $\dfrac{9}{x} = \dfrac{5}{14}$ **24.** $\dfrac{2.4}{9} = \dfrac{n}{1.5}$

8.5 **25.** There are 180 calories in a 30 gram serving of walnuts. How many calories are there in a 100 gram serving of walnuts?

8.6 In Exercises 26–28, use the fact that a floor plan of a house is drawn using a scale of 1 in. : 8 ft.

    26. Find the actual dimensions of a rectangular basement that is 2.5 inches long and 2.25 inches wide on the floor plan.

    27. Find the actual dimensions of a rectangular deck that is 3.75 inches long and 1.875 inches wide on the floor plan.

    28. Find the actual dimensions of a rectangular bedroom that is 2.75 inches long and 1.75 inches wide on the floor plan.

Chapter 9

9.1 **Write the percent as a fraction.**

1. 60% **2.** 49% **3.** 84% **4.** 56%

9.1 **Write the fraction as a percent.**

5. $\frac{2}{5}$ **6.** $\frac{9}{10}$ **7.** $\frac{1}{4}$ **8.** $\frac{17}{25}$

9.2 **Use a proportion to answer the question.**

9. What percent of 25 is 16? **10.** 54 is 75% of what number?

11. What number is 27% of 250? **12.** What percent of 32 is 12?

9.3 **Write the percent as a decimal or the decimal as a percent.**

13. 2% **14.** 20.4% **15.** 106% **16.** 0.94%

17. 0.575 **18.** 0.082 **19.** 0.0012 **20.** 4.2

9.4 **Use the percent equation to answer the question.**

21. 57 is 125% of what number? **22.** What number is 3% of 18?

23. What percent of 64 is 20? **24.** 60 is 40% of what number?

9.5 **25.** The table shows Jake's work schedule at a video store during the week. Display the data in a circle graph.

Day	Monday	Tuesday	Wednesday	Thursday	Friday
Hours	3.5	5	6	3	2.5

9.6 **Identify the percent of change as an *increase* or a *decrease*. Then find the percent of change.**

26. Original: 32 New: 28 **27.** Original: 48 New: 45 **28.** Original: $375 New: $400 **29.** Original: $32 New: $35

9.7 **Use the given information to find the new price.**

30. Original price: $58 Discount: 25% **31.** Wholesale price: $96 Markup: 120% **32.** Food bill before tax: $62 Sales tax: 7%

9.8 **For an account that earns simple annual interest, find the interest and the balance of the account.**

33. $250 at 2.5% for 2 years **34.** $1000 at 3% for 8 months **35.** $600 at 4.4% for 1 month

9.8 **36.** Suppose you deposit $500 into an account that earns 4% simple annual interest. How long will it take to earn $10 in interest?

Chapter 10

10.1 **For the given angle measure, find the measure of a supplementary angle and the measure of a complementary angle, if possible.**

1. 86°   **2.** 151°   **3.** 90°   **4.** 7°

10.2 **Find the unknown angle measures.**

5.    **6.**    **7.**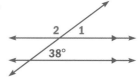

10.3 **8.** The measures of two of the angles in a triangle are 52° and 38°. Find the measure of the third angle. Then classify the triangle by its angle measures.

10.3 **9.** The side lengths of a triangle are 11 feet, 8 feet, and 11 feet. Classify the triangle by the lengths of its sides.

10.4 **10.** Sketch a parallelogram that is both a rectangle and a rhombus. Then classify the parallelogram.

10.4 **11.** Find the sum of the angle measures in an octagon.

10.5 **12.** Given that $\triangle ABC \cong \triangle DEF$, name the corresponding sides and the corresponding angles.

10.5 **13.** One square has a side length of 8 meters, and another square has a side length of 10 meters. Are the squares similar? Explain.

10.6 **14.** Find the unknown lengths given that the triangles are similar.

10.6 **15.** The shadow cast by a tree is 18 feet long. At the same time, a girl who is 5 feet tall casts a 3 foot long shadow. How tall is the tree?

10.7 **16.** Sketch an equilateral triangle and draw any line(s) of symmetry. Then tell whether the triangle has rotational symmetry. If it does, give the angle(s) and direction of rotation.

10.8 **Draw triangle *ABC* with vertices *A*(−2, 1), *B*(−5, 2), and *C*(−1, 4). Then find the coordinates of the vertices of the image after the specified transformation, and draw the image.**

17. $(x, y) \rightarrow (x + 7, y - 4)$ **18.** $(x, y) \rightarrow (x - 3, y + 2)$

19. Reflect $\triangle ABC$ in the *y*-axis.   **20.** Reflect $\triangle ABC$ in the *x*-axis.

Chapter 11

11.1 Evaluate the expression when $x = 5$ and $y = 12$.

1. $\sqrt{3y}$ **2.** $-\sqrt{61 - xy}$ **3.** $\sqrt{x^2 + y^2}$ **4.** $\sqrt{y - x + 2}$

11.1 Solve the equation.

5. $a^2 - 4 = 140$ **6.** $5b^2 = 500$ **7.** $2c^2 + 9 = 81$ **8.** $2 + 3d^2 = 194$

11.2 Approximate the square root to the nearest whole number and then to the nearest tenth.

9. $\sqrt{19}$ **10.** $\sqrt{94}$ **11.** $\sqrt{135}$ **12.** $\sqrt{229}$

11.2 Tell whether the number is *rational* or *irrational*. Explain your reasoning.

13. $1.23456789\ldots$ **14.** $2.\overline{62}$ **15.** $-\sqrt{49}$ **16.** $\sqrt{11}$

11.3 Find the unknown length. Round to the nearest tenth if necessary.

17.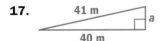

18.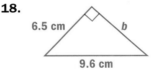

19.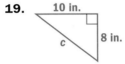

11.4 Find the unknown area, base, or height of the parallelogram.

20. $b = 14$ cm, $h = 9$ cm, $A = \underline{\ ?\ }$ **21.** $A = 96$ ft^2, $b = 12$ ft, $h = \underline{\ ?\ }$

22. $A = 20$ in.^{2}, $b = \underline{\ ?\ }$, $h = 1.6$ in. **23.** $b = 8$ m, $h = 4$ m, $A = \underline{\ ?\ }$

11.5 Find the area of the triangle or trapezoid.

24.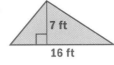

25.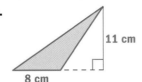

26.

11.6 Find the circumference of the circle with the given radius or diameter. Use $\frac{22}{7}$ or 3.14 for π.

27. $r = 42$ mi **28.** $r = 12$ in. **29.** $d = 50$ cm **30.** $d = 35$ mm

11.7 Find the area of the circle with the given radius or diameter. Use $\frac{22}{7}$ or 3.14 for π.

31. $r = 40$ yd **32.** $r = 84$ m **33.** $d = 14$ ft **34.** $d = 0.2$ km

Chapter 12

12.1 Classify the solid. Be as specific as possible.

1.

2.

3.

4.

12.1 Count the number of faces, edges, and vertices in the solid.

5. Triangular pyramid **6.** Rectangular prism **7.** Hexagonal pyramid

12.2 Sketch the solid.

8. Cube **9.** Triangular prism **10.** Pentagonal prism

12.2 11. Sketch the top, side, and front views of the cylinder shown at the right.

12.3 Find the surface area of the rectangular prism.

12.
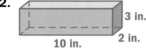
3 in.
10 in.
2 in.

13.
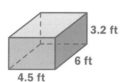
3.2 ft
6 ft
4.5 ft

14.

21 cm
15 cm
12 cm

12.4 Find the surface area of the cylinder. Use 3.14 for π.

15.
2 m
1 m

16.
7 in.
2 in.

17.
3 ft
10 ft

12.5 Find the volume of the rectangular prism with the given dimensions.

18. 3 m by 4 m by 0.5 m **19.** 14 in. by 10 in. by 2 in. **20.** 7 ft by 7 ft by 3.5 ft

21. 5 cm by 2.5 cm by 11 cm **22.** 9 yd by 20 yd by 15 yd **23.** 8 mm by 6 mm by 5.25 mm

12.5 24. Find the width of a rectangular prism that has a length of 15 meters, a height of 9 meters, and a volume of 1080 cubic meters.

12.6 Find the unknown volume, radius, or height of the cylinder. Use 3.14 for π.

25. $V = \underline{?}$
$r = 6$ in.
$h = 10$ in.

26. $V = 25.12$ cm^3
$r = 2$ cm
$h = \underline{?}$

27. $V = 39.25$ ft^3
$r = \underline{?}$
$h = 0.5$ ft

Chapter 13

13.1 Each number from 1 to 20 is written on a separate piece of paper and put in a bag. You randomly choose a piece of paper from the bag. Find the probability of the event. Write the probability as a fraction, a decimal, and a percent.

    1. You choose a multiple of 6.   **2.** You choose a factor of 12.

13.1   **3.** When a bottle cap is tossed, it lands top side down 36 times and top side up 14 times. Find the probability that the next time the bottle cap is tossed, it will land top side down.

13.2   **4.** A store sells sweatshirts in blue, black, and white. The sizes available are small, medium, large, and extra large. Make a tree diagram to find all the possible sweatshirt choices you have to choose from.

13.2   **5.** Suppose a pitcher can throw a fastball, a curve ball, or a slider. If the pitcher chooses any two pitches at random, what is the probability that one pitch is a fastball and one is a slider?

13.3 **A monogram consists of the first letters of a person's first, middle, and last names.**

    6. How many different monograms are possible?

    7. If a monogram is chosen at random, what is the probability that the monogram is ABC? Assume that all monograms are equally likely.

13.4   **8.** How many 4 digit numbers can be formed from the digits 1, 2, 3, 4, 5, and 6 if each digit is used only once?

13.4   **9.** A teacher chooses 3 students from a class of 30 students to present their projects during today's class. If the order in which the students are chosen does not matter, how many different ways are there for the students to be chosen?

13.5 **Two number cubes are rolled. Find the probability of the event(s).**

    10. Either both numbers are odd or both are even.

    11. The sum of the numbers is *not* 11.

13.6 **A bag contains 10 red beads and 6 white beads. You randomly choose one bead, and then randomly choose another bead.**

    12. Find the probability that both beads are red if you replace the first bead before choosing the second bead.

    13. Find the probability that both beads are red if you do not replace the first bead before choosing the second bead.

Table of Symbols

Symbol	Meaning	Page
...	continues on	5
=	equals, is equal to	9, 26
$\frac{14}{2}$	14 divided by 2	10
$3 \cdot x$ $3(x)$ $3x$	3 times x	10
4^3	4 to the third power	14
<	is less than	17, 682
>	is greater than	17, 682
( )	parentheses—a grouping symbol	19
[ ]	brackets—a grouping symbol	19
$\stackrel{?}{=}$	is equal to?	26
≠	is not equal to	26
28.6	decimal point	52
$1.1\overline{6}$	repeating decimal 1.16666. . .	191
−3	negative 3	251
−3	the opposite of 3	251
$\lvert a \rvert$	the absolute value of a number a	259
(x, y)	ordered pair	293
≤	is less than or equal to	346
≥	is greater than or equal to	346
$a : b, \frac{a}{b}$	ratio of a to b	369

Symbol	Meaning	Page
%	percent	415
≈	is approximately equal to	426
°	degree(s)	438, 440
$\angle PQR$	angle PQR	475
$m\angle B$	the measure of angle B	475
∟	right angle	475
≅	is congruent to	479
$\overleftrightarrow{AB}$	line AB	479
⇉	parallel lines	480
∥	is parallel to	480
⊥	is perpendicular to	480
$\triangle ABC$	triangle with vertices A, B, and C	484
$\overline{AB}$	line segment AB	486
AB	the length of line segment AB	486
$\overrightarrow{AB}$	ray AB	490
~	is similar to	502
A'	the image of point A	519
$\sqrt{a}$	the positive square root of a number a where $a > 0$	533
±	plus or minus	535
π	pi—a number approximately equal to 3.14	563

Table of Measures

Time

60 seconds (sec) = 1 minute (min)
60 minutes = 1 hour (h)
24 hours = 1 day (d)
7 days = 1 week (wk)
4 weeks (approx.) = 1 month

365 days ⎤
52 weeks (approx.) ⎬ = 1 year
12 months ⎦
10 years = 1 decade
100 years = 1 century

METRIC

Length

10 millimeters (mm) = 1 centimeter (cm)

100 cm ⎤
1000 mm ⎦ = 1 meter (m)

1000 m = 1 kilometer (km)

Area

100 square millimeters = 1 square centimeter
(mm²)   (cm²)

$10,000 \text{ cm}^2 = 1$ square meter (m²)
$10,000 \text{ m}^2 = 1$ hectare (ha)

Volume

1000 cubic millimeters = 1 cubic centimeter
(mm³)   (cm³)

$1,000,000 \text{ cm}^3 = 1$ cubic meter (m³)

Liquid Capacity

1000 milliliters (mL) ⎤
1000 cubic centimeters (cm³) ⎦ = 1 liter (L)

1000 L = 1 kiloliter (kL)

Mass

1000 milligrams (mg) = 1 gram (g)
1000 g = 1 kilogram (kg)
1000 kg = 1 metric ton (t)

Temperature   Degrees Celsius (°C)

0°C = freezing point of water
37°C = normal body temperature
100°C = boiling point of water

UNITED STATES CUSTOMARY

Length

12 inches (in.) = 1 foot (ft)

36 in. ⎤
3 ft ⎦ = 1 yard (yd)

5280 ft ⎤
1760 yd ⎦ = 1 mile (mi)

Area

144 square inches (in.²) = 1 square foot (ft²)
$9 \text{ ft}^2 = 1$ square yard (yd²)

$43,560 \text{ ft}^2$ ⎤
4840 yd^2 ⎦ = 1 acre (A)

Volume

1728 cubic inches (in.³) = 1 cubic foot (ft³)
$27 \text{ ft}^3 = 1$ cubic yard (yd³)

Liquid Capacity

8 fluid ounces (fl oz) = 1 cup (c)
2 c = 1 pint (pt)
2 pt = 1 quart (qt)
4 qt = 1 gallon (gal)

Weight

16 ounces (oz) = 1 pound (lb)
2000 lb = 1 ton

Temperature   Degrees Fahrenheit (°F)

32°F = freezing point of water
98.6°F = normal body temperature
212°F = boiling point of water

Table of Formulas

Geometric Formulas

Rectangle (p. 32)

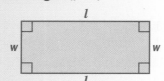

Area
$A = lw$

Perimeter
$P = 2l + 2w$

Square (p. 32)

Area
$A = s^2$

Perimeter
$P = 4s$

Parallelogram (p. 552)

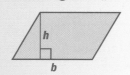

Area
$A = bh$

Triangle (p. 558)

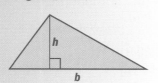

Area
$A = \frac{1}{2}bh$

Trapezoid (p. 559)

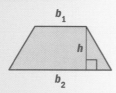

Area
$A = \frac{1}{2}(b_1 + b_2)h$

Circle (pp. 563, 567)

Area
$A = \pi r^2$

Circumference
$C = \pi d$ or
$C = 2\pi r$

Rectangular Prism (pp. 594, 607)

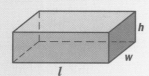

Surface Area
$S = 2lw + 2lh + 2wh$

Volume
$V = lwh$

Cylinder (pp. 602, 611)

Surface Area
$S = 2\pi rh + 2\pi r^2$

Volume
$V = \pi r^2 h$

Other Formulas

Distance traveled (p. 27)	$d = rt$ where d = distance, r = rate, and t = time
Temperature (p. 279)	$F = \frac{9}{5}C + 32$ and $C = \frac{5}{9}(F - 32)$ where F = degrees Fahrenheit and C = degrees Celsius
Simple interest (p. 454)	$I = Prt$ where I = simple interest, P = principal, r = annual interest rate, and t = time in years
Pythagorean theorem (p. 546)	In a right triangle, $a^2 + b^2 = c^2$ where a and b are the lengths of the legs, and c is the length of the hypotenuse.

Table of Formulas

Table of Properties

Number Properties

Commutative Property of Addition (p. 284) In a sum, you can add terms in any order.	**Numbers** **Algebra**	$-2 + 5 = 5 + (-2)$ $a + b = b + a$
Associative Property of Addition (p. 284) Changing the grouping of terms in a sum will not change the sum.	**Numbers** **Algebra**	$(2 + 4) + 6 = 2 + (4 + 6)$ $(a + b) + c = a + (b + c)$
Commutative Property of Multiplication (p. 284) In a product, you can multiply factors in any order.	**Numbers** **Algebra**	$3(-6) = -6(3)$ $ab = ba$
Associative Property of Multiplication (p. 284) Changing the grouping of factors in a product will not change the product.	**Numbers** **Algebra**	$(6 \times 2.5) \times 4 = 6 \times (2.5 \times 4)$ $(ab)c = a(bc)$
Inverse Property of Addition (p. 285) The sum of a number and its additive inverse, or opposite, is 0.	**Numbers** **Algebra**	$4 + (-4) = 0$ $a + (-a) = 0$
Identity Property of Addition (p. 285) The sum of a number and the additive identity, 0, is the number.	**Numbers** **Algebra**	$7 + 0 = 7$ $a + 0 = a$
Inverse Property of Multiplication (p. 285) The product of a nonzero number and its multiplicative inverse, or reciprocal, is 1.	**Numbers** **Algebra**	$\frac{2}{3} \cdot \frac{3}{2} = 1$ For any nonzero integers a and b, $\frac{a}{b} \cdot \frac{b}{a} = 1$.
Identity Property of Multiplication (p. 285) The product of a number and the multiplicative identity, 1, is the number.	**Numbers** **Algebra**	$3 \cdot 1 = 3$ $a \cdot 1 = a$
Distributive Property (p. 288) You can multiply a number and a sum by multiplying each term of the sum by the number and then adding these products. The same property applies to subtraction.	**Numbers** **Algebra**	$3(4 + 6) = 3(4) + 3(6)$ $2(8 - 5) = 2(8) - 2(5)$ $a(b + c) = a(b) + a(c)$ $a(b - c) = a(b) - a(c)$
Cross Products Property (p. 394) The cross products of a proportion are equal.	**Numbers** **Algebra**	If $\frac{3}{4} = \frac{6}{8}$, then $3 \cdot 8 = 4 \cdot 6$. If $\frac{a}{b} = \frac{c}{d}$ and b and d do not equal 0, then $ad = bc$.

Finding Squares and Square Roots

EXAMPLE 1 Finding a Square

Find 54².

Find 54 in the column labeled *No.* (an abbreviation for *Number*). Read across to the column labeled *Square*.

No.	Square	Sq. Root
51	2601	7.141
52	2704	7.211
53	2809	7.280
54	2916	7.348
55	3025	7.416

ANSWER So, $54^2 = 2916$.

EXAMPLE 2 Finding a Square Root

Find a decimal approximation of $\sqrt{54}$.

Find 54 in the column labeled *No.* Read across to the column labeled *Sq. Root*.

No.	Square	Sq. Root
51	2601	7.141
52	2704	7.211
53	2809	7.280
54	2916	7.348
55	3025	7.416

ANSWER So, to the nearest thousandth, $\sqrt{54} \approx 7.348$.

EXAMPLE 3 Finding a Square Root

Find a decimal approximation of $\sqrt{3000}$.

Find the two numbers in the *Square* column that 3000 is between. Read across to the column labeled *No.*; $\sqrt{3000}$ is between 54 and 55, but closer to 55.

No.	Square	Sq. Root
51	2601	7.141
52	2704	7.211
53	2809	7.280
54	2916	7.348
55	3025	7.416

ANSWER So, $\sqrt{3000} \approx 55$. A more accurate approximation can be found using a calculator: 54.772256.

Table of Squares and Square Roots

No.	Square	Sq. Root	No.	Square	Sq. Root	No.	Square	Sq. Root
1	1	1.000	51	2601	7.141	101	10,201	10.050
2	4	1.414	52	2704	7.211	102	10,404	10.100
3	9	1.732	53	2809	7.280	103	10,609	10.149
4	16	2.000	54	2916	7.348	104	10,816	10.198
5	25	2.236	55	3025	7.416	105	11,025	10.247
6	36	2.449	56	3136	7.483	106	11,236	10.296
7	49	2.646	57	3249	7.550	107	11,449	10.344
8	64	2.828	58	3364	7.616	108	11,664	10.392
9	81	3.000	59	3481	7.681	109	11,881	10.440
10	100	3.162	60	3600	7.746	110	12,100	10.488
11	121	3.317	61	3721	7.810	111	12,321	10.536
12	144	3.464	62	3844	7.874	112	12,544	10.583
13	169	3.606	63	3969	7.937	113	12,769	10.630
14	196	3.742	64	4096	8.000	114	12,996	10.677
15	225	3.873	65	4225	8.062	115	13,225	10.724
16	256	4.000	66	4356	8.124	116	13,456	10.770
17	289	4.123	67	4489	8.185	117	13,689	10.817
18	324	4.243	68	4624	8.246	118	13,924	10.863
19	361	4.359	69	4761	8.307	119	14,161	10.909
20	400	4.472	70	4900	8.367	120	14,400	10.954
21	441	4.583	71	5041	8.426	121	14,641	11.000
22	484	4.690	72	5184	8.485	122	14,884	11.045
23	529	4.796	73	5329	8.544	123	15,129	11.091
24	576	4.899	74	5476	8.602	124	15,376	11.136
25	625	5.000	75	5625	8.660	125	15,625	11.180
26	676	5.099	76	5776	8.718	126	15,876	11.225
27	729	5.196	77	5929	8.775	127	16,129	11.269
28	784	5.292	78	6084	8.832	128	16,384	11.314
29	841	5.385	79	6241	8.888	129	16,641	11.358
30	900	5.477	80	6400	8.944	130	16,900	11.402
31	961	5.568	81	6561	9.000	131	17,161	11.446
32	1024	5.657	82	6724	9.055	132	17,424	11.489
33	1089	5.745	83	6889	9.110	133	17,689	11.533
34	1156	5.831	84	7056	9.165	134	17,956	11.576
35	1225	5.916	85	7225	9.220	135	18,225	11.619
36	1296	6.000	86	7396	9.274	136	18,496	11.662
37	1369	6.083	87	7569	9.327	137	18,769	11.705
38	1444	6.164	88	7744	9.381	138	19,044	11.747
39	1521	6.245	89	7921	9.434	139	19,321	11.790
40	1600	6.325	90	8100	9.487	140	19,600	11.832
41	1681	6.403	91	8281	9.539	141	19,881	11.874
42	1764	6.481	92	8464	9.592	142	20,164	11.916
43	1849	6.557	93	8649	9.644	143	20,449	11.958
44	1936	6.633	94	8836	9.695	144	20,736	12.000
45	2025	6.708	95	9025	9.747	145	21,025	12.042
46	2116	6.782	96	9216	9.798	146	21,316	12.083
47	2209	6.856	97	9409	9.849	147	21,609	12.124
48	2304	6.928	98	9604	9.899	148	21,904	12.166
49	2401	7.000	99	9801	9.950	149	22,201	12.207
50	2500	7.071	100	10,000	10.000	150	22,500	12.247

Glossary

	Example
a	
absolute value (p. 259) The absolute value of a number *a* is the distance between *a* and 0 on a number line. The absolute value of *a* is written $\|a\|$.	$\|4\| = 4 \qquad \|-7\| = 7 \qquad \|0\| = 0$
acute angle (p. 475) An angle whose measure is less than 90°.	
acute triangle (p. 485) A triangle with three acute angles.	60° 70° 50°
addition property of equality (p. 328) Adding the same number to each side of an equation produces an equivalent equation.	If $x - 5 = 2$, then $x - 5 + 5 = 2 + 5$, so $x = 7$. If $x - a = b$, then $x - a + a = b + a$.
additive identity (p. 285) The number 0 is the additive identity because the sum of any number and 0 is the original number.	$-7 + 0 = -7$ $a + 0 = a$
additive inverse (p. 285) The additive inverse of a number *a* is the opposite of the number, or $-a$. The sum of a number and its additive inverse is 0.	The additive inverse of 6 is -6, so $6 + (-6) = 0$.
adjacent angles (p. 479) Two angles that share a common side and a vertex and do not overlap.	∠1 and ∠2 are adjacent angles.
angle (p. 440) A figure formed by two rays that begin at a common point, called the vertex.	vertex ray ray
angle of rotation (p. 512) In a rotation, the angle formed by two rays drawn from the center of rotation through corresponding points on the original figure and its image.	*See* rotation.
annual interest rate (p. 454) The percent of the principal earned or paid per year.	*See* simple interest.

Glossary

	Example
arc (p. 490) Part of a circle.	The arc intersects $\angle A$ at points B and C.
area (p. 32) The number of square units needed to cover a figure.	3 units / 7 units / $Area = 21$ square units
associative property of addition (p. 284) Changing the grouping of terms in a sum does not change the sum.	$(9 + 4) + 6 = 9 + (4 + 6)$ $(a + b) + c = a + (b + c)$
associative property of multiplication (p. 284) Changing the grouping of factors in a product does not change the product.	$(2 \cdot 5) \cdot 3 = 2 \cdot (5 \cdot 3)$ $(ab)c = a(bc)$

b

balance (p. 454) The sum of the interest and the principal.	*See* simple interest.
bar graph (p. 108) A type of graph in which the lengths of bars are used to represent and compare data.	**Annual Sales at an Automobile Dealership**
base of a parallelogram (p. 552) The length of any side of the parallelogram can be used as the base.	height h / base b
base of a power (p. 14) The number or expression that is used as a factor in a repeated multiplication.	In the power 5^3, the base is 5.
base of a triangle (p. 558) The length of any side of the triangle can be used as the base.	height h / base b

	Example
bases of a trapezoid (p. 559) The lengths of the parallel sides of the trapezoid.	
biased sample (p. 106) A sample that is not representative of the population from which it is selected.	The members of a football team are a biased sample if you want to determine the average amount of time students spend playing sports each week.
box-and-whisker plot (p. 123) A data display that divides a data set into four parts using the lower extreme, lower quartile, median, upper quartile, and upper extreme.	

C

center of a circle (p. 563) The point inside the circle that is the same distance from all points on the circle.	*See* circle.
center of rotation (p. 511) The point about which a figure is turned when the figure undergoes a rotation.	*See* rotation.
circle (p. 563) The set of all points in a plane that are the same distance, called the radius, from a fixed point, called the center.	
circle graph (p. 440) A circle graph displays data as sections of a circle. The entire circle represents all the data. Each section is labeled using the actual data or using data expressed as fractions, decimals, or percents of the sum of the data.	
circumference (p. 563) The distance around a circle.	*See* circle.
coefficient (p. 322) The number part of a term that includes a variable.	The coefficient of $7x$ is 7.

	Example
combination (p. 651) A grouping of objects in which the order is not important.	There are 6 combinations of 2 letters chosen from the 4 letters in the word VASE: VA VS VE AS AE SE
common factor (p. 164) A whole number that is a factor of two or more nonzero whole numbers.	The common factors of 8 and 12 are 1, 2, and 4.
common multiple (p. 175) A multiple that is shared by two or more numbers.	The common multiples of 4 and 6 are 12, 24, 36, ...
commutative property of addition (p. 284) In a sum, you can add terms in any order.	$4 + 7 = 7 + 4$ $a + b = b + a$
commutative property of multiplication (p. 284) In a product, you can multiply factors in any order.	$5(-8) = -8(5)$ $ab = ba$
compatible numbers (p. 67) Numbers that make a calculation easier.	To estimate the quotient $377.25 \div 21$, use compatible numbers: $377.25 \div 21 \approx 380 \div 20 = 19$
complementary angles (p. 476) Two angles whose measures have a sum of 90°.	32° 58°
complementary events (p. 659) Two disjoint events such that one or the other of the events must occur.	When rolling a number cube, the events "getting an odd number" and "getting an even number" are complementary events.
composite number (p. 157) A whole number greater than 1 that has positive factors other than 1 and itself.	6 is a composite number because its factors are 1, 2, 3, and 6.
cone (p. 583) A solid with one circular base.	base
congruent angles (p. 479) Angles that have the same measure.	*See* congruent polygons.

	Example
congruent polygons (p. 502) Similar polygons that have the same shape and the same size. For congruent polygons, corresponding angles are congruent and corresponding sides are congruent. The symbol $\cong$ indicates congruence and is read "is congruent to."	 $\triangle ABC \cong \triangle DEF$
congruent sides (p. 486) Sides that have the same length.	*See* congruent polygons.
constant term (p. 322) A term that has a number but no variable.	In the expression $5y + 9$, the term 9 is a constant term.
coordinate plane (p. 293) A coordinate system formed by the intersection of a horizontal number line, called the x-axis, and a vertical number line, called the y-axis.	
corresponding angles (p. 480) Angles that occupy corresponding positions when a line intersects two other lines.	$\angle 1$ and $\angle 2$ are corresponding angles.
counting principle (p. 644) If one event can occur in m ways, and for each of these a second event can occur in n ways, then the number of ways that the two events can occur together is $m \cdot n$. The counting principle can be extended to three or more events.	If a T-shirt is made in 5 sizes and in 7 colors, then the number of different T-shirts that are possible is $5 \cdot 7 = 35$.
cross products (p. 394) In a proportion $\dfrac{a}{b} = \dfrac{c}{d}$ where $b \neq 0$ and $d \neq 0$, the cross products are ad and bc.	The cross products of the proportion $\dfrac{2}{3} = \dfrac{4}{6}$ are $2 \cdot 6$ and $3 \cdot 4$.

Glossary

	Example
cross products property (p. 394) The cross products of a proportion are equal.	If $\frac{4}{9} = \frac{x}{27}$, then $4 \cdot 27 = 9x$. If $\frac{a}{b} = \frac{c}{d}$ where $b \neq 0$ and $d \neq 0$, then $ad = bc$.
cylinder (p. 583) A solid with two congruent circular bases that lie in parallel planes.	
d	
decimal (p. 52) A number written using the base-ten place value system where a decimal point separates the ones' and tenths' digits.	2.6 and 7.053 are decimals.
degrees (p. 440) Units of measure for angles. The symbol for degrees is °. There are 360° in a circle.	
denominator (p. 169) The number b in the fraction $\frac{a}{b}$ where $b \neq 0$.	The denominator of $\frac{7}{13}$ is 13.
dependent events (p. 664) Two events such that the occurrence of one affects the likelihood that the other will occur.	A bag contains 5 red and 8 blue marbles. You randomly choose a marble, do not replace it, then randomly choose another marble. The events "first marble is red" and "second marble is red" are dependent events.
diameter of a circle (p. 563) The distance across the circle through the center.	*See* circle.
disjoint events (p. 657) Events that have no outcomes in common.	When rolling a number cube, the events "getting an odd number" and "getting a 4" are disjoint events.
distributive property (p. 288) For all numbers a, b, and c, $a(b + c) = ab + ac$ and $a(b - c) = ab - ac$.	$8(10 + 4) = 8(10) + 8(4)$ $3(4 - 2) = 3(4) - 3(2)$
division property of equality (p. 333) Dividing each side of an equation by the same nonzero number produces an equivalent equation.	If $6x = 54$, then $\frac{6x}{6} = \frac{54}{6}$, so $x = 9$. If $ax = b$ and $a \neq 0$, then $\frac{ax}{a} = \frac{b}{a}$.

	Example

domain of a function (p. 350) The set of all input values for the function.

See function.

e

edge of a solid (p. 584) A line segment where two faces of the solid meet.

equation (p. 26) A mathematical sentence formed by setting two expressions equal.

$3 \cdot 6 = 18$ and $x + 7 = 12$ are equations.

equilateral triangle (p. 486) A triangle with three congruent sides.

equivalent equations (p. 327) Equations that have the same solution(s).

$2x - 6 = 0$ and $2x = 6$ are equivalent equations because the solution of both equations is 3.

equivalent expressions (p. 288) Expressions that have the same value when simplified.

$4(3 + 5)$ and $4(3) + 4(5)$ are equivalent expressions because $4(3 + 5) = 4(8) = 32$ and $4(3) + 4(5) = 12 + 20 = 32$.

equivalent fractions (p. 169) Fractions that represent the same part-to-whole relationship. Equivalent fractions have the same simplest form.

$\frac{6}{8}$ and $\frac{9}{12}$ are equivalent fractions that both represent $\frac{3}{4}$.

equivalent inequalities (p. 346) Inequalities that have the same solution.

$3x \leq 12$ and $x \leq 4$ are equivalent inequalities because the solution of both inequalities is all numbers less than or equal to 4.

equivalent ratios (p. 369) Ratios that have the same value.

$\frac{15}{12}$ and $\frac{25}{20}$ are equivalent ratios because $\frac{15}{12} = 1.25$ and $\frac{25}{20} = 1.25$.

equivalent variable expressions (p. 322) Expressions that are equal for every value of each variable they contain.

$5(x - 3)$ and $5x - 15$ are equivalent variable expressions.

	Example
evaluating a variable expression (p. 9) Substituting a value for each variable in the expression and simplifying the resulting numerical expression.	Evaluating $2x + 3y$ when $x = 1$ and $y = 4$ gives $2(1) + 3(4) = 2 + 12 = 14$.
event (p. 634) A collection of outcomes of an experiment.	An event that involves tossing a coin is "getting heads."
experimental probability (p. 635) A probability based on repeated trials of an experiment. The experimental probability of an event is given by: $$P(\text{event}) = \frac{\text{Number of successes}}{\text{Number of trials}}$$	During one month, your school bus is on time 17 out of 22 school days. The experimental probability that the bus is on time is: $$P(\text{bus is on time}) = \frac{17}{22} \approx 0.773$$
exponent (p. 14) A number that represents how many times a base is used as a factor in a repeated multiplication.	In the power 5^3, the exponent is 3.

f

	Example
face of a solid (p. 584) A polygon that is a side of the solid.	*See* edge of a solid.
factor tree (p. 158) A diagram that can be used to write the prime factorization of a number.	54 6 $\times$ 9 2 $\times$ 3 $\times$ 3 $\times$ 3
favorable outcomes (p. 634) Outcomes corresponding to a specified event.	When rolling a number cube, the favorable outcomes for the event "getting a number greater than 4" are 5 and 6.
fraction (p. 169) A number of the form $\frac{a}{b}$ where $b \neq 0$.	$\frac{5}{7}$ and $\frac{18}{10}$ are fractions.
frequency (p. 130) The number of data values that lie in an interval of a frequency table or histogram.	*See* frequency table *and* histogram.
frequency table (p. 130) A table used to group data values into intervals.	

Interval	Tally	Frequency
0–9	II	2
10–19	IIII	4
20–29	JHHT	5
30–39	III	3
40–49	IIII	4

	Example
front-end estimation (p. 59) A method for estimating the sum of two or more numbers. In this method, you add the front-end digits, estimate the sum of the remaining digits, and then add the results.	To estimate $3.81 + 1.32 + 5.74$, first add the front-end digits: $3 + 1 + 5 = 9$. Then estimate the sum of the remaining digits: $0.81 + (0.32 + 0.74) \approx 1 + 1 = 2$. The sum is about $9 + 2 = 11$.
function (p. 350) A pairing of each number in a given set with exactly one number in another set. Starting with a number called an input, the function associates with it exactly one number called an output.	<table><tr><td>Input x</td><td>1</td><td>2</td><td>3</td><td>4</td></tr><tr><td>Output y</td><td>2</td><td>4</td><td>6</td><td>8</td></tr></table> The input-output table above represents a function.

g

graph of an inequality (p. 346) On a number line, the set of points that represents the solution of the inequality.	The graph of the inequality $x < 2$ is shown below.
greatest common factor (GCF) (p. 164) The greatest whole number that is a factor of two or more nonzero whole numbers.	The GCF of 18 and 27 is 9. The GCF of 48, 24, and 36 is 12.

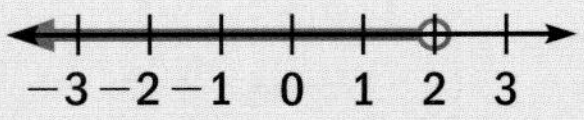

h

height of a parallelogram (p. 552) The perpendicular distance between the side whose length is the base and the opposite side.	*See* base of a parallelogram.
height of a trapezoid (p. 559) The perpendicular distance between the bases of the trapezoid.	*See* bases of a trapezoid.
height of a triangle (p. 558) The perpendicular distance between the side whose length is the base and the vertex opposite that side.	*See* base of a triangle.
heptagon (p. 495) A polygon with seven sides.	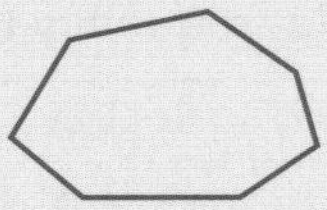
hexagon (p. 495) A polygon with six sides.	

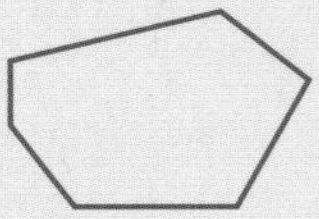

	Example
histogram (p. 131) A graph that displays data from a frequency table. A histogram has one bar for each interval of the table that contains data values. The length of the bar indicates the frequency for the interval.	**Library Visitors on a Saturday** Frequency values: 6, 5, 4, 3, 2, 1, 0 Ages (years): 0–9, 10–19, 20–29, 30–39, 40–49
hypotenuse (p. 546) The side of a right triangle that is opposite the right angle.	hypotenuse leg leg
identity property of addition (p. 285) The sum of a number and the additive identity, 0, is the number.	$8 + 0 = 8$ $a + 0 = a$
identity property of multiplication (p. 285) The product of a number and the multiplicative identity, 1, is the number.	$4 \cdot 1 = 4$ $a \cdot 1 = a$
image (p. 511) The new figure formed by a transformation.	*See* reflection, rotation, *and* translation.
improper fraction (p. 185) A fraction whose numerator is greater than or equal to its denominator.	$\frac{8}{7}$ is an improper fraction.
independent events (p. 664) Two events such that the occurrence of one does not affect the likelihood that the other will occur.	You toss a coin and roll a number cube. The events "getting heads" and "getting a 6" are independent events.
inequality (p. 346) A mathematical sentence formed by placing an inequality symbol between two expressions.	$3 < 5$ and $x + 2 \geq -4$ are inequalities.
input (p. 350) A number on which a function operates. An input value is in the domain of the function.	*See* function.
integers (p. 251) The numbers . . . , $-4, -3, -2, -1, 0, 1, 2, 3, 4, \ldots$ consisting of the negative integers, zero, and the positive integers.	-8 and 14 are integers. $-8\frac{1}{3}$ and 14.5 are *not* integers.

	Example
interest (p. 454) The amount earned or paid for the use of money.	*See* simple interest.
intersecting lines (p. 480) Two lines that meet at a point.	
inverse operations (p. 327) Operations that "undo" each other.	Addition and subtraction are inverse operations. Multiplication and division are also inverse operations.
inverse property of addition (p. 285) The sum of a number and its additive inverse, or opposite, is 0.	$5 + (-5) = 0$ $a + (-a) = 0$
inverse property of multiplication (p. 285) The product of a nonzero number and its multiplicative inverse, or reciprocal, is 1.	$\frac{3}{4} \cdot \frac{4}{3} = 1$ $\frac{a}{b} \cdot \frac{b}{a} = 1 \quad (a, b \neq 0)$
irrational number (p. 541) A real number that cannot be written as a quotient of two integers. The decimal form of an irrational number neither terminates nor repeats.	$\sqrt{2}$ and $0.313113111\ldots$ are irrational numbers.
isosceles triangle (p. 486) A triangle with at least two congruent sides.	

L

	Example
leading digit (p. 63) The first nonzero digit in a number.	The leading digit of 725 is 7. The leading digit of 0.002638 is 2.
least common denominator (LCD) (p. 181) The least common multiple of the denominators of two or more fractions.	The LCD of $\frac{7}{10}$ and $\frac{3}{4}$ is 20, the least common multiple of 10 and 4.
least common multiple (LCM) (p. 175) The least number that is a common multiple of two or more numbers.	The LCM of 4 and 6 is 12. The LCM of 3, 5, and 10 is 30.
legs of a right triangle (p. 546) The two sides of a right triangle that form the right angle.	*See* hypotenuse.
like terms (p. 322) Terms that have identical variable parts. (Two or more constant terms are considered like terms.)	In the expression $x + 4 - 2x + 1$, x and $-2x$ are like terms, and 4 and 1 are like terms.

	Example
line graph (p. 109) A type of graph in which points representing data pairs are connected by line segments.	**Average Price of Gold** A line graph titled "Average Price of Gold" showing Dollars per ounce (y-axis with values 275, 300, 325, 350, 375, 400) versus Year (x-axis: 1996, 1997, 1998, 1999, 2000).
line of reflection (p. 511) The line in which a figure is flipped when the figure undergoes a reflection.	*See* reflection.
line of symmetry (p. 513) A line that divides a figure into two parts that are mirror images of each other.	*See* line symmetry.
line symmetry (p. 513) A figure has line symmetry if it can be divided by a line, called a line of symmetry, into two parts that are mirror images of each other.	A square with its 4 lines of symmetry drawn. A square has 4 lines of symmetry.
linear function (p. 355) A function whose graph is a line or part of a line.	A coordinate graph showing the line $y = -x + 1$.
lower extreme (p. 123) The least value in a data set.	*See* box-and-whisker plot.
lower quartile (p. 123) The median of the lower half of a data set.	*See* box-and-whisker plot.

m

mean (p. 101) The sum of the values in a data set divided by the number of values.	The mean of the data set $$85, 59, 97, 71$$ is $\dfrac{85 + 59 + 97 + 71}{4} = \dfrac{312}{4} = 78.$

	Example
median (p. 101) The middle value in a data set when the values are written in numerical order. If the data set has an even number of values, the median is the mean of the two middle values.	The median of the data set 8, 17, 21, 23, 26, 29, 34, 40, 45 is the middle value, 26.
mixed number (p. 185) A number that has a whole number part and a fraction part.	$3\frac{2}{5}$ is a mixed number.
mode (p. 101) The value in a data set that occurs most often. A data set can have no mode, one mode, or more than one mode.	The mode of the data set 73, 42, 55, 77, 61, 55, 68 is 55 because it occurs most often.
multiple (p. 175) The product of a number and any nonzero whole number.	The multiples of 3 are 3, 6, 9, ...
multiplication property of equality (p. 334) Multiplying each side of an equation by the same nonzero number produces an equivalent equation.	If $\frac{x}{3} = 7$, then $3 \cdot \frac{x}{3} = 3 \cdot 7$, so $x = 21$. If $\frac{x}{a} = b$ and $a \neq 0$, then $a \cdot \frac{x}{a} = a \cdot b$.
multiplicative identity (p. 285) The number 1 is the multiplicative identity because the product of any number and 1 is the original number.	$9 \cdot 1 = 9$ $a \cdot 1 = a$
multiplicative inverse (p. 285) The multiplicative inverse of a number $\frac{a}{b}$ ($a, b \neq 0$) is the reciprocal of the number, or $\frac{b}{a}$. The product of a number and its multiplicative inverse is 1.	The multiplicative inverse of $\frac{3}{2}$ is $\frac{2}{3}$, so $\frac{3}{2} \cdot \frac{2}{3} = 1$.

n

	Example
negative integers (p. 251) The integers that are less than zero.	The negative integers are -1, -2, -3, -4, ...
net (p. 594) A two-dimensional representation of a solid.	
numerator (p. 169) The number a in the fraction $\frac{a}{b}$.	The numerator of $\frac{7}{13}$ is 7.

	Example

O

obtuse angle (p. 475) An angle whose measure is between 90° and 180°.

obtuse triangle (p. 485) A triangle with one obtuse angle.

120°
35°   25°

octagon (p. 495) A polygon with eight sides.

opposites (p. 251) Two numbers that are the same distance from 0 on a number line but are on opposite sides of 0.

−3 and 3 are opposites.

order of operations (p. 18) A set of rules for evaluating an expression involving more than one operation.

To evaluate 3 + 2 • 4, you perform the multiplication before the addition:

$$3 + 2 \cdot 4 = 3 + 8 = 11$$

ordered pair (p. 293) A pair of numbers (x, y) that can be used to represent a point in a coordinate plane. The first number is the x-coordinate, and the second number is the y-coordinate.

$(-2, 1)$

origin (p. 293) The point (0, 0) where the x-axis and the y-axis meet in a coordinate plane.

See coordinate plane.

outcomes (p. 634) The possible results when an experiment is performed.

When tossing a coin, the outcomes are heads and tails.

output (p. 350) A number produced by evaluating a function using a given input. An output value is in the range of the function.

See function.

overlapping events (p. 657) Events that have one or more outcomes in common.

When rolling a number cube, the events "getting a number less than 3" and "getting an even number" are overlapping events because they have the outcome 2 in common.

Glossary

	Example
parallel lines (p. 480) Two lines in the same plane that do not intersect. The symbol ‖ is used to indicate parallel lines.	$a \parallel b$
parallelogram (p. 494) A quadrilateral with two pairs of parallel sides.	
pentagon (p. 495) A polygon with five sides.	
percent (p. 415) A ratio whose denominator is 100. The symbol for percent is %.	$\dfrac{17}{20} = \dfrac{17 \cdot 5}{20 \cdot 5} = \dfrac{85}{100} = 85\%$
percent of change (p. 446) A percent that shows how much a quantity has increased or decreased in comparison with the original amount: Percent of change $p = \dfrac{\text{Amount of increase or decrease}}{\text{Original amount}}$	The percent of change p from 15 to 19 is: $p = \dfrac{19 - 15}{15} = \dfrac{4}{15} \approx 0.267 = 26.7\%$
percent of decrease (p. 446) The percent of change in a quantity when the new amount of the quantity is less than the original amount.	*See* percent of change.
percent of increase (p. 446) The percent of change in a quantity when the new amount of the quantity is greater than the original amount.	*See* percent of change.
perfect square (p. 533) A number that is the square of an integer.	49 is a perfect square because $49 = 7^2$.
perimeter (p. 32) The distance around a figure. For a figure with straight sides, the perimeter is the sum of the lengths of the sides.	7 ft 4 ft 4 ft 7 ft *Perimeter* = 22 ft
permutation (p. 650) An arrangement of a group of objects in a particular order.	There are 6 permutations of the 3 letters in the word CAT: CAT ACT TCA CTA ATC TAC

	Example
perpendicular lines (p. 480) Two lines that intersect to form four right angles. The symbol ⊥ is used to indicate perpendicular lines.	$a \perp b$
plane (p. 480) A plane can be thought of as a flat surface that extends without end.	
polygon (p. 495) A geometric figure made up of three or more line segments that intersect only at their endpoints.	**Polygon** **Not a polygon**
population (p. 106) In statistics, the entire group of people or objects about which you want information.	If a biologist wants to determine the average age of the elephants in a wildlife refuge, the population consists of every elephant in the refuge.
positive integers (p. 251) The integers that are greater than zero.	The positive integers are 1, 2, 3, 4, ...
power (p. 14) A product formed from repeated multiplication by the same number or expression. A power consists of a base and an exponent.	2^4 is a power with base 2 and exponent 4.
prime factorization (p. 158) Expressing a whole number as a product of prime numbers.	The prime factorization of 54 is $54 = 2 \times 3 \times 3 \times 3 = 2 \times 3^3$.
prime number (p. 157) A whole number greater than 1 whose only whole number factors are 1 and itself.	5 is a prime number because its only whole number factors are 1 and 5.
principal (p. 454) An amount of money that is deposited or borrowed.	*See* simple interest.
prism (p. 583) A solid, formed by polygons, that has two congruent bases lying in parallel planes.	bases **Rectangular prism** **Triangular prism**

	Example
probability of an event (p. 634) A number from 0 to 1 that measures the likelihood that the event will occur.	*See* experimental probability *and* theoretical probability.
proper fraction (p. 185) A fraction whose numerator is less than its denominator.	$\frac{7}{8}$ is a proper fraction.
proportion (p. 387) An equation stating that two ratios are equivalent.	$\frac{3}{5} = \frac{6}{10}$ and $\frac{x}{12} = \frac{25}{30}$ are proportions.
pyramid (p. 583) A solid, formed by polygons, that has one base. The base can be any polygon, and the other polygons are triangles.	base
Pythagorean theorem (p. 546) For any right triangle, the sum of the squares of the lengths a and b of the legs equals the square of the length c of the hypotenuse: $a^2 + b^2 = c^2$.	15 c 20 $15^2 + 20^2 = c^2$

q

quadrant (p. 293) One of the four regions that a coordinate plane is divided into by the x-axis and the y-axis.	*See* coordinate plane.
quadrilateral (p. 494) A geometric figure made up of four line segments, called sides, that intersect only at their endpoints; a polygon with four sides.	

r

radical expression (p. 534) An expression involving a radical sign, $\sqrt{\ }$.	$\sqrt{3}(22 + 5)$ is a radical expression.
radius of a circle (p. 563) The distance between the center and any point on the circle.	*See* circle.
random sample (p. 106) A sample selected in such a way that each member of the population has an equally likely chance to be part of the sample.	A random sample of 5 seventh graders can be selected by putting the names of all seventh graders in a hat and drawing 5 names without looking.
range of a data set (p. 102) The difference between the greatest and least values in the data set.	The range of the data set 60, 35, 22, 46, 81, 39 is $81 - 22 = 59$.

Glossary

	Example
range of a function (p. 350) The set of all output values for the function.	*See* function.
rate (p. 374) A ratio of two quantities measured in different units.	An airplane climbs 18,000 feet in 12 minutes. The airplane's rate of climb is $\frac{18,000 \text{ ft}}{12 \text{ min}} = 1500$ ft/min.
ratio (p. 369) A comparison of two numbers using division. The ratio of a to b (where $b \neq 0$) can be written as a to b, as $\frac{a}{b}$, or as $a:b$.	The ratio of 17 to 12 can be written as 17 to 12, as $\frac{17}{12}$, or as $17:12$.
rational number (p. 283) A number that can be written as $\frac{a}{b}$ where a and b are integers and $b \neq 0$.	$6 = \frac{6}{1}$, $-\frac{3}{5} = \frac{-3}{5}$, $0.75 = \frac{3}{4}$, and $2\frac{1}{3} = \frac{7}{3}$ are all rational numbers.
ray (p. 440) A part of a line that begins at a point and extends in one direction without end.	
real numbers (p. 541) The set of all rational numbers and irrational numbers.	0, $-\frac{5}{9}$, 2.75, and $\sqrt{3}$ are all real numbers.
reciprocals (p. 222) Two nonzero numbers whose product is 1.	$\frac{2}{3}$ and $\frac{3}{2}$ are reciprocals.
reflection (p. 511) A transformation that reflects a figure in a line, called the line of reflection, creating a mirror image of the figure; also known as a *flip*.	
regular polygon (p. 496) A polygon with all sides equal in length and all angles equal in measure.	 **Regular pentagon**

	Example
regular tessellation (p. 516) A tessellation made from only one type of regular polygon.	
relatively prime numbers (p. 165) Two or more nonzero whole numbers whose greatest common factor is 1.	9 and 16 are relatively prime because their GCF is 1.
repeating decimal (p. 191) A decimal that has one or more digits that repeat without end.	$0.7777\ldots$ and $1.\overline{29}$ are repeating decimals.
rhombus (p. 494) A parallelogram with four congruent sides.	
right angle (p. 475) An angle whose measure is exactly 90°.	
right triangle (p. 485) A triangle with one right angle.	
rotation (p. 511) A transformation that rotates a figure through a given angle, called the angle of rotation, and in a given direction about a fixed point, called the center of rotation; also known as a *turn*.	
rotational symmetry (p. 513) A figure has rotational symmetry if a turn of 180° or less produces an image that fits exactly on the original figure.	 A square has rotational symmetry.

Glossary

	Example
sample (p. 106) A part of a population.	To predict the results of an election, a survey is given to a sample of voters.
scale (p. 400) In a scale drawing, the scale gives the relationship between the drawing's dimensions and the actual dimensions.	The scale "1 in. : 10 ft" means that 1 inch in the scale drawing represents an actual distance of 10 feet.
scale drawing (p. 400) A diagram of an object in which the dimensions are in proportion to the actual dimensions of the object.	 1 cm : 12 m
scale model (p. 401) A model of an object in which the dimensions are in proportion to the actual dimensions of the object.	A scale model of the White House appears in Tobu World Square in Japan. The scale used is 1 : 25.
scalene triangle (p. 486) A triangle with no congruent sides.	
scatter plot (p. 295) The graph of a set of data pairs (x, y), which is a collection of points in a coordinate plane.	
scientific notation (p. 74) A number is written in scientific notation if it has the form $c \times 10^n$ where c is greater than or equal to 1 and less than 10, and n is an integer.	In scientific notation, 328,000 is written as 3.28×10^5, and 0.00061 is written as 6.1×10^{-4}.

Glossary

	Example
similar polygons (p. 502) Polygons that have the same shape but not necessarily the same size. Corresponding angles of similar polygons are congruent, and the ratios of the lengths of corresponding sides are equal. The symbol ~ is used to indicate that two polygons are similar.	$\triangle LMN \sim \triangle PQR$
simple interest (p. 454) Interest that is earned or paid only on the principal. The simple interest I is the product of the principal P, the annual interest rate r written as a decimal, and the time t in years: $I = Prt$.	Suppose you deposit \$700 into a savings account. The account earns 3% simple annual interest. After 5 years, the interest is $I = Prt = (700)(0.03)(5) = \$105$, and your account balance is \$700 + \$105 = \$805.
simplest form of a fraction (p. 170) A fraction is in simplest form if its numerator and denominator have a greatest common factor of 1.	The simplest form of the fraction $\frac{6}{8}$ is $\frac{3}{4}$.
slope (p. 378) The slope of a nonvertical line is the ratio of the rise (vertical change) to the run (horizontal change) between any two points on the line.	The slope of the line above is: $$\text{slope} = \frac{\text{rise}}{\text{run}} = \frac{-2}{5} = -\frac{2}{5}$$
solid (p. 583) A three-dimensional figure that encloses a part of space.	*See* cone, cylinder, prism, pyramid, *and* sphere.
solution of an equation (p. 26) A number that, when substituted for the variable in the equation, makes the equation true.	The solution of the equation $n - 3 = 4$ is 7.
solution of an inequality (p. 346) The set of all numbers that, when substituted for the variable in the inequality, make the inequality true.	The solution of the inequality $y + 2 > 5$ is $y > 3$.
solving an equation (p. 27) Finding all solutions of the equation by using mental math or the properties of equality.	To solve the equation $4x = 20$, find the number that can be multiplied by 4 to equal 20; $4(5) = 20$, so the solution is 5.

	Example
sphere (p. 583) A solid formed by all points in space that are the same distance from a fixed point called the center.	center
square root (p. 533) A square root of a number n is a number m which, when multiplied by itself, equals n.	The square roots of 81 are 9 and -9 because $9^2 = 81$ and $(-9)^2 = 81$.
stem-and-leaf plot (p. 116) A data display that helps you see how data values are distributed. Each data value is separated into a leaf (the last digit) and a stem (the remaining digits). In an ordered stem-and-leaf plot, the leaves for each stem are listed in order from least to greatest.	**stems** **leaves** 10 │ 8 11 │ 2 2 5 12 │ 1 3 4 7 13 │ 0 6 Key: 10│8 = 108
straight angle (p. 475) An angle whose measure is exactly 180°.	
subtraction property of equality (p. 327) Subtracting the same number from each side of an equation produces an equivalent equation.	If $x + 7 = 9$, then $x + 7 - 7 = 9 - 7$, so $x = 2$. If $x + a = b$, then $x + a - a = b - a$.
supplementary angles (p. 476) Two angles whose measures have a sum of 180°.	79° 101°
surface area of a solid (p. 594) The sum of the areas of the outside surfaces of the solid.	3 in. 4 in. 6 in. *Surface area* = $2(6)(4) + 2(6)(3) + 2(4)(3) = 108$ in.^{2}
t	
terminating decimal (p. 191) A decimal that has a final digit.	0.4 and 3.6125 are terminating decimals.
terms of an expression (p. 322) The parts of an expression that are added together.	The terms of $2x + 3$ are $2x$ and 3.

Glossary

	Example
tessellation (p. 516) A covering of a plane with congruent copies of the same pattern so that there are no gaps or overlaps.	
theoretical probability (p. 635) A probability based on all of the equally likely outcomes of an experiment. The theoretical probability of an event is given by: $$P(\text{event}) = \frac{\text{Number of favorable outcomes}}{\text{Total number of outcomes}}$$	A bag of 20 marbles contains 7 red marbles. The theoretical probability of randomly choosing a red marble is: $$P(\text{red}) = \frac{7}{20} = 0.35$$
transformation (p. 511) A movement of a figure in a plane.	*See* translation, reflection, *and* rotation.
translation (p. 511) A transformation that moves each point of a figure the same distance in the same direction; also known as a *slide*.	
trapezoid (p. 494) A quadrilateral with exactly one pair of parallel sides.	
tree diagram (p. 639) A branching diagram that shows all the possible outcomes of a process carried out in several stages.	
u	
unit rate (p. 374) A rate that has a denominator of 1 unit.	$9 per hour is a unit rate.
upper extreme (p. 123) The greatest value in a data set.	*See* box-and-whisker plot.
upper quartile (p. 123) The median of the upper half of a data set.	*See* box-and-whisker plot.

Glossary

	Example
V	
variable (p. 9) A letter that is used to represent one or more numbers.	In the expression $m + 5$, the letter m is the variable.
variable expression (p. 9) An expression that consists of numbers, variables, and operations.	$n - 3$, $\frac{2s}{t}$, and $x + 4yz + 1$ are variable expressions.
verbal model (p. 318) A word equation that represents a real-world situation.	$\begin{array}{c}\text{Distance}\\\text{traveled}\end{array} = \begin{array}{c}\text{Speed}\\\text{of car}\end{array} \cdot \begin{array}{c}\text{Time}\\\text{traveled}\end{array}$
vertex of an angle (p. 440) The common endpoint of the two rays that form the angle.	*See* angle.
vertex of a solid (p. 584) A point where the edges of the solid meet.	*See* edge of a solid.
vertical angles (p. 479) A pair of opposite angles formed when two lines meet at a point.	$\angle 1$ and $\angle 3$ are vertical angles. $\angle 2$ and $\angle 4$ are also vertical angles.
volume of a solid (p. 607) The amount of space the solid contains.	Volume $= \pi r^2 h \approx (3.14)(2)^2(3) \approx$ 37.7 m^3
X	
x-axis (p. 293) The horizontal axis in a coordinate plane.	*See* coordinate plane.
x-coordinate (p. 293) The first number in an ordered pair representing a point in a coordinate plane.	The x-coordinate of the ordered pair $(-2, 1)$ is -2.
Y	
y-axis (p. 293) The vertical axis in a coordinate plane.	*See* coordinate plane.
y-coordinate (p. 293) The second number in an ordered pair representing a point in a coordinate plane.	The y-coordinate of the ordered pair $(-2, 1)$ is 1.

Glossary

Index

Index

of a parallelogram, 552
of a rectangle, 31
of a trapezoid, 557
of a triangle, 556
to show percent, 415
greater than 100, 426
less than 1, 426
to show surface area, 594

Arrangements
combinations, 651–656
permutations, 650–656

Assessment, *See also* Internet; Review
Chapter Standardized Test, 47, 95,
145, 201, 245, 305, 365, 409,
463, 529, 577, 621, 675
Chapter Test, 46, 94, 144, 200, 244,
304, 364, 408, 462, 528, 576,
620, 674
Cumulative Practice, 150–152,
310–312, 468–470, 626–628
End-of-Course Test, 676–679
Pre-Course Practice, xxviii–xxi
Pre-Course Test, xxvi–xxvii
Review Quiz, 25, 43, 73, 91, 121,
141, 174, 197, 229, 241, 271,
301, 339, 361, 385, 405, 437,
459, 500, 525, 551, 573, 599,
617, 649, 671
Test-Taking Practice, 8, 12, 17, 22,
30, 35, 41, 55, 62, 66, 71, 77,
84, 89, 105, 113, 119, 127, 134,
139, 161, 167, 172, 178, 184,
189, 194, 209, 214, 219, 226,
234, 239, 254, 263, 269, 275,
282, 287, 291, 298, 321, 325,
331, 337, 345, 349, 353, 358,
373, 377, 382, 391, 398, 403,
418, 424, 429, 435, 444, 449,
453, 457, 478, 483, 489, 498,
505, 509, 515, 522, 537, 544,
549, 555, 562, 566, 570, 587,
591, 597, 605, 610, 614, 638,
642, 647, 655, 661, 669
Test-taking skills
building, 146–147, 306–307,
464–465, 622–623
practicing, 148–152, 308–312,
466–470, 624–628
Test-taking strategies, 47, 95, 145,
201, 245, 305, 365, 409, 463,
529, 577, 621, 675

Associative property
of addition, 284
of multiplication, 284

Average, *See also* Mean; Median; Mode
choosing the best average, 102
game, 105
Axis (axes), coordinate, 293

b

Bar graph, *See also* Double bar
graph; Histogram
double, 109, 111–114
examples, 100, 310, 703, 707
legend for, 109
making, 108, 111
using spreadsheet software,
114–115
misleading, 136
multiple, 113, 139
reading and interpreting, 108, 113,
703
scale for, 108, 114
Bar notation, for repeating decimals,
191
Base(s)
of a cone, 583
of a cylinder, 583
of a parallelogram, 552
of a percent equation, 432
of a power, 14
of a prism, 583
of a proportion, 420
of a pyramid, 583
of a trapezoid, 559
of a triangle, 558
Base-ten pieces
for modeling
decimal addition, 58
decimals, 51
Benchmark(s)
for capacity
customary, 232
metric, 82
for fractions and percents, 416, 421
for length
customary, 230
metric, 80
for mass, 81
for weight, 231
Better buy, 375
Biased question, 107
Biased sample, 106
Bilateral symmetry, 515
Bisector, angle, 490

Box-and-whisker plot(s), 123–127
comparing, 125–127
extremes of, 123
interpreting, 124–127
making, 123, 125–127
quartiles of, 123
Box model, 342
Brackets, grouping symbols, 19
Brain Games, *See* Games
Break a problem into parts,
problem solving strategy,
492–493, 498

c

Calculator, *See also* Technology
activities
2nd key, 299, 571
EE key, 78
exercises, 8, 12, 239, 281, 291,
331, 337, 372, 377, 397, 449,
487, 497, 561, 570, 578, 614,
637, 654
parentheses keys, 23
pi key, 571
power key, 23
PRB key, 656
square root key, 571
Capacity
adding and subtracting measures
of, 237
customary units, 232–234
benchmarks for, 232
changing to metric units, 87
choosing appropriate units,
232–234
converting, 236–239
definition of, 232
metric units, 82–84
benchmarks for, 82
choosing appropriate units,
82–84
converting, 85–89
Career
architect, 219
astronomer, 247
bicycle mechanic, 343
biologist, 411
city planner, 305
conductor, 209
oceanographer, 97
physicist, 579
Cartesian plane, *See* Coordinate plane

487, 488, 543, 597, 604, 609, 613

geometry, 65, 70, 308, 321, 323, 324, 330, 336, 341, 382, 497, 514, 536, 624, 625, 627, 628

Connections to other disciplines, *See also* Applications; Math in Science

architecture, 586

art, 219, 503, 521, 555, 668

astronomy, 75

geography, 267

health, 187

history, 35, 160, 178, 238, 254, 397, 660

science, 8, 12, 112, 126, 172, 234, 269, 295, 353, 379, 428, 441, 513, 536, 584, 637

Connections to real-world applications, *See* Applications

Constant term, 322

Constructions

angle bisector, 490

arc, 490

copy an angle, 490

equilateral triangle, 491

isosceles triangle, 491

parallel lines, 491

perpendicular lines, 491

Conversions, *See* Decimal; Fraction; Measurement; Percent

Coordinate notation, 518

Coordinate plane

definition of, 293

finding segment lengths in, 294, 296

naming ordered pairs, 293, 296

parts of, 293

plotting points in, 294–299

slope of lines in, 378–383

transformations in, 518–523

Copy an angle, 490

Corresponding angles, 480–483, 502–509

Corresponding sides, 502–509

Counting principle, 644–647

Critical thinking

describe, 3, 134, 269, 326, 381, 419, 522, 557, 573, 637

exercises, 7, 12, 13, 17, 21, 25, 29, 31, 35, 49, 55, 73, 77, 99, 103, 118, 122, 133, 159, 167, 174, 188, 193, 203, 219, 246, 247, 249, 257, 263, 265, 271, 281, 287, 315, 325, 339, 345, 359,

361, 367, 377, 383, 385, 403, 410, 439, 448, 456, 459, 478, 482, 505, 510, 525, 536, 537, 545, 556, 566, 581, 591, 593, 605, 606, 610, 615, 631, 643, 653, 661

explain, 41, 61, 66, 70, 71, 91, 113, 121, 126, 155, 208, 210, 213, 229, 234, 238, 257, 262, 320, 336, 381, 390, 403, 411, 437, 452, 460, 473, 497, 498, 500, 501, 505, 517, 521, 531, 543, 551, 555, 579, 586, 649

Cross products, 394

Cross products property, 394, 422

Cube, 584

Cup, 232

Customary units

benchmarks for, 230–234

capacity, 232–234

choosing appropriate units, 231–234

converting, 235–239

length, 230, 231, 233–234, 699

measuring with a ruler, 699

table of, 719

temperature, 279

weight, 231, 233–234

Cylinder, 583, 585

bases of, 583

definition of, 583

right, 602

surface area of, 602–605, 615

volume of, 611–614, 615

d

Data

biased question, 107

biased sample, 106, 107

collecting, 633, 637

definition of, 703

displays

bar graph, 108–114, 703

box-and-whisker plot, 123–127

choosing, 135–139

line graph, 109–113, 115, 703

making, 114–115

misleading, 136, 137, 138

scatter plot, 292, 295–297

interpreting, mean, median, and mode, 101–105

lower extreme, 123

lower quartile, 123

organizing

box-and-whisker plots, 123–127

frequency table, 128–134

histogram, 131–134

line plot, 704

stem-and-leaf plots, 116–119

tree diagram, 639–643

population, 106

random sample, 106

range of, 102–104

samples, 106–107

upper extreme, 123

upper quartile, 123

Decimal(s)

adding, 58–62

game, 62

comparing, 51–55

definition of, 52

dividing, 67–71

estimating

differences, 60–61

quotients, 67, 70

sums, 59–62

fractions and, 190–195

mixed numbers and, 190–195

modeling

addition, 58

multiplication, 63

order, 53, 72

place value, 51

multiplying, 63–66

checking, 63, 64

ordering, 53–55

to order fractions, 192

percent and, 425–429

place value, 52–55

probability expressed as, 634

repeating, 191–194

rounding, 53–55

scientific notation and, 74–78

subtracting, 58–62

game, 62

terminating, 191–194

Decimal point, 52

Decision making, *See also* Choose a strategy

checking reasonableness, 63, 67

choosing the best average, 102

choosing a scale, 402

exercises, 60, 65, 70, 112, 177, 578, 647

identifying biased samples, 106

supporting conclusions, 113

Index

with leading digits, 63
low/high estimates, 693, 694
of pi, 563
as a problem solving strategy,
    56–57
using the Pythagorean theorem,
    547–549
using rounding, 56–57, 563–570,
    691–693
using scale, 400, 401, 402
square root, 540–544, 547–549
of time, 698
whole number, 23
    differences, 692
    products, 693
    quotients, 694
    sums, 691
Events, *See also* Outcome
    complementary, 659–661
    compound, 664
    dependent, 664, 666, 667–669
    disjoint, 657–661
    independent, 664–665, 667–669
    overlapping, 657–661
Expanded form
    of decimals, 51
    of whole numbers, 681
Experiment
    conducting, 579, 633, 662, 663,
        664, 668
    designing, 411
Experimental probability, 633, 635,
    662, *See also* Probability
Exponent(s), 13–17
    negative, 255–256
    prime factorization and, 158–161
    scientific notation and, 74–78
    zero, 255–256
Expression(s)
    addition, 9–12
        modeling, 9
    algebraic, 9–12, 317–325, 369,
        534–537
    division, 10–12
    equations and, 26
    equivalent, 288–291
    evaluating, 9–12
        game, 22
        using properties, 284–287
    exponents in, 18–22
    integer, 273, 274–275
    left-to-right rule, 19
    multiplication, 10–12

order of operations and, 18–23
    radical, 534–537
    simplifying, 322–325
    subtraction, 9, 11–12
    two-variable, 10, 12
    variables and, 9–12
    writing, 317–321
Extended response questions,
    See also Problem solving
    strategies for answering, 622–623
Exterior angle, 484–489

f

Faces, of a solid, 584
Fact families, 684
Factor(s)
    common, 164–167, 217
    definition of, 685
    divisibility tests and, 685
    game, 161
    greatest common, 164–167
    of a number, 157
    perfect number and, 163
    prime, 165–167
    relatively prime numbers and, 165
Factor tree, 158, 160, 165, 173, 176
Fahrenheit temperature, 279
Favorable outcome, 634
Fluid ounce, 232
Foot, 230
Formula(s)
    area
        of a circle, 567
        of a parallelogram, 552
        of a rectangle, 32
        of a square, 32
        of a trapezoid, 559
        of a triangle, 558
    circumference, 563
    distance, 27, 335
    Fahrenheit/Celsius temperature,
        279
    percent of change, 446
    perimeter, 32
    probability, 634
        of complementary events, 659
        of dependent events, 666
        of disjoint events, 658
        of independent events, 665
    simple interest, 454
    spreadsheets and, 615

surface area
    of a cylinder, 602
    of a rectangular prism, 594
table of, 721
volume
    of a cylinder, 611
    of a rectangular prism, 607
Fraction(s), *See also* Mixed numbers;
    Proportion; Rate; Ratio
    adding, 205–214
        with common denominators,
            205–209
        with different denominators,
            206–209
        with models, 205
    benchmarks for percents and,
        416, 421
    comparing, 179–184
        using approximation, 182, 183,
            184
        using cross products, 180
        using least common
            denominator, 181–184
        using models, 179–180
    decimals and, 190–195
    definition of, 169
    denominator, 169
    dividing, 222–226
        using models, 222
        using reciprocals, 222–226
    equivalent, 168–172
        identifying, 169
        modeling, 168
        writing, 169
    game, 189
    improper, 185
        mixed numbers and, 185–189
    least common denominator, 181
    modeling, 686
        addition, 205
        to compare, 179–180
        division, 222
        equivalent, 168
        multiplication, 215
        subtraction, 205
    multiplying, 215–219
        dividing out common factors, 217
        with models, 215
    numerator, 169
    operations on a calculator, 227
    ordering
        using decimals, 192
        using LCD, 182–184
    percent and, 415–419, 421

508, 514, 521, 536, 543, 548,
554, 561, 565, 569, 585, 590,
596, 609, 613, 636, 641, 646,
653, 660, 667
eWorkbook Plus, 7, 11, 16, 20, 28,
34, 40, 54, 60, 65, 69, 76, 83,
87, 103, 111, 118, 125, 132,
137, 159, 166, 171, 177, 183,
187, 192, 207, 213, 218, 224,
233, 237, 253, 261, 268, 274,
280, 286, 290, 295, 319, 324,
329, 335, 344, 348, 352, 356,
371, 376, 380, 389, 396, 402,
422, 427, 434, 442, 448, 452,
456, 477, 481, 487, 496, 504,
508, 513, 520, 535, 542, 548,
554, 560, 565, 569, 585, 590,
596, 609, 613, 636, 641, 646,
653, 659, 667
project support, 97, 247, 411, 579
state test practice, 8, 12, 17, 22, 30,
35, 41, 55, 62, 66, 71, 77, 84,
89, 105, 113, 119, 127, 134,
139, 161, 167, 172, 178, 184,
189, 194, 209, 214, 219, 226,
234, 239, 254, 263, 269, 275,
282, 287, 291, 298, 321, 325,
331, 337, 345, 349, 353, 373,
377, 382, 391, 398, 403, 418,
424, 429, 435, 444, 449, 453,
457, 478, 483, 489, 498, 505,
509, 515, 522, 537, 544, 549,
555, 562, 566, 570, 587, 591,
597, 605, 610, 638, 642, 647,
655, 661, 669
Intersecting lines, 480–483
Interval, 130
Inverse operations, 327, 684
Inverse property
of addition, 285
of multiplication, 285
Investigations, *See* Activities;
Technology activities
Irrational number, 541–543
Irregular figure
area of, 35
perimeter of, 35
Irregular polygon, *See* Polygons
Isosceles triangle, 486–489
constructing, 491

j

Journal, *See* Notebook; Notebook
Review; Notetaking; Writing
in mathematics

k

Key, stem-and-leaf plot, 116
Kilogram, 81
Kiloliter, 82
Kilometer, 80

l

Labs, *See* Activities; Technology
activities
Leading digit, estimation and, 63
Leaf, stem-and-leaf plot, 116
Least common denominator (LCD),
181
for adding fractions, 206–209
for comparing fractions, 181–184
for subtracting fractions, 207–209
Least common multiple (LCM),
175–178
prime factorization and, 176
Left-to-right rule, 19
Legend, graph, 109
Legs, of a right triangle, 546
Length
adding and subtracting measures
of, 237–238
customary units, 230, 231,
233–234, 699
benchmarks for, 230
choosing appropriate units,
233–234
converting, 235, 237–239
measuring with a ruler, 699
metric units, 79–80, 83–84, 699
benchmarks for, 80
choosing appropriate units, 80,
83–84
converting, 85–89
game, 89
measuring with a ruler, 79–81,
83, 699
Likelihood, of an event, 633, 634
Like terms, combining, 322
Line(s)
intersecting, 480–483

parallel, 480–483, 586
perpendicular, 480–483, 586
of reflection, 511
skew, 586
of symmetry, 510, 513–515
Linear function
definition of, 355
graphing, 354–359
identifying, 355, 357
Line graph, 109–113, 115
double, 112
drawing, 110, 111, 112, 115
identifying misleading, 136, 137, 141
reading and interpreting, 109,
112, 703
scale for, 110
Line plot
definition of, 704
examples, 104
making, 704
reading, 704
Line of reflection, 511
Line segment, drawing with a
compass, 700
Line symmetry, 510, 513–515
Line of symmetry, 510, 513–515
List, make a, problem solving
strategy, 162–163, 164
Liter, 82
Logical reasoning, *See also*
Classification; Critical
thinking; Error analysis;
Games; Number sense;
Problem solving
concept grid, 474, 632, 657
tree diagram, 639–643
Venn diagram, 632, 702
Look for a pattern, problem solving
strategy, 36–37, 39
Lower extreme, 123
Lower quartile, 123

m

Make a list, problem solving strategy,
162–163, 164
examples, 175, 541, 657
Make a model, problem solving
strategy, 600–601, 602
Make a table, problem solving
strategy, 128–129, 130

Index

Index

n

Index

Output, function, 350
Overlapping events, 657–661
 Venn diagram of, 657

P

Parallel lines, 480–483, 586
 constructing, 491
Parallelogram, 494
 area of, 552–555
 base of, 552
 height of, 552
Parentheses, grouping symbols, 19
Pattern(s)
 exercises, 37, 40, 44, 46, 47, 55, 66,
  71, 163, 208, 292, 498, 501,
  606, 705
 geometric, 36, 570
 integer, 272
 meaning of ending dots, 5
 numeric, 5–8, 68, 163
 tessellation, 516–517
 visual, 6–8
 writing function rules from, 351
Pentagon, 495
 sum of angle measures, 496
Percent
 area model, 415
 benchmarks for fractions and,
  416, 421
 of change, 446–449
  activity, 446
 circle graphs and, 440–445
 commission and, 433–435
 cross products property and,
  422–424
 decimals and, 425–429
 decrease, 446–449
 definition of, 415
 discount, 450, 452–453
 equation, 432–435
 fractions and, 415–419, 420, 421
 greater than 100, 426–429
 increase, 446–449
 less than 1, 426–429
 markup, 450–453
 modeling, 415, 419, 426
 of a number, 416–418
 one number is of another, 420–424
 probability expressed as, 634
 proportion and, 420–424
 sales tax, 451–453

 simple interest and, 454–457
 tip, 451–453
Percent bar model, 419
Perfect number, 163
Perfect square, 533
Perform an experiment, problem
  solving strategy, 662–663, 664
Perimeter
 comparing, 162
 definition of, 32
 of irregular figures, 35
 of a rectangle, 32–36, 162, 701
 of a square, 32–35, 701
 of a triangle, 701
Permutation, 650–656
 definition of, 650
Perpendicular lines, 480–483, 586
 constructing, 491
Pi
 approximation of, 563
 on a calculator, 571
 definition of, 563
Pint, 232
Place value
 decimal, 52–55
  chart, 52
  comparing, 52
  modeling, 51
 in measurement, 85
 rounding and, 53, 683
 whole number, 681
Place-value chart
 decimals on, 52
  comparing, 52
 metric prefixes and, 85
Plane, 480, *See also* Coordinate plane
 definition of
Plane figures, *See* Geometry
Point(s)
 of intersection, 479–483
 locating on a number line, 53, 54,
  252, 283, 682
 plotting in a coordinate plane,
  294–299
Polygon(s), 494–498
 classifying, 494–498
 congruent, 502–505
  naming, 502
 nonregular, 516
 quadrilaterals, 494–498
 regular, 496–498
 similar, 502–509
  naming, 502
 tessellation and, 516–517

Population, 106
Positive integer, 251
Positive slope, 378
Pound, 231
Powers
 base, 14
 cubed, 15
 evaluating, 15–17, 255, 256
 exponents and, 14–17
 metric units and, 85–89
 modeling, 13
 negative, 255–256
 and scientific notation, 74–78
 squared, 15
 of ten, multiplication by, 689
 writing, 14, 16–17
 zero, 255, 256
Precision, in measurement, 234
Precision of measurement tools,
  See Measurement tools
Prediction
 using common multiples, 178
 exercises, 112, 238, 292, 297, 449,
  498, 579, 633
 using a graph, 112, 134
 using a pattern, 46, 194
 using a table, 128, 129
Prime factorization, 157–161
 factor tree, 158, 160, 165
 to find GCF, 165–167
 to find LCM, 176–178
Prime factors, 165
Prime number(s), 157–161
 relatively prime, 165
Principal, interest and, 454–457
Prism
 bases of, 583
 definition of, 583
 right, 594
 sketching, 588, 590–591
 surface area of, 594–597, 615
 types of, 584–587
 volume of, 606–610, 615
Probability
 combinations, 651–656
 counting principle, 644–647
 definition of, 633, 634
 events, 634
  complementary, 659–661
  compound, 664
  dependent, 664, 666, 667–669
  disjoint, 657–661
  independent, 664–665, 667–669
  overlapping, 657–661

experimental, 633, 635, 662, 663, 664

finding, 633–638

formula, 634

odds, 637

outcome, 634

permutations, 650–656

theoretical, 633, 635

tree diagrams and, 639–643

types of, 635

Problem solving, *See also*
  Error analysis

choose an operation
  addition or subtraction, 695
  multiplication or division, 696

choose a strategy, 37, 41, 57, 62, 105, 129, 161, 163, 177, 221, 234, 263, 277, 298, 321, 341, 373, 393, 431, 457, 489, 493, 522, 539, 566, 601, 614, 647, 663

eliminate possibilities, 47, 147

extended problem solving, 21, 71, 119, 138, 178, 238, 262, 297, 325, 382, 397, 418, 498, 537, 610, 660

extended response questions, 41, 47, 89, 95, 139, 149, 150, 151, 152, 178, 201, 226, 245, 282, 305, 309, 310, 311, 312, 337, 365, 391, 409, 444, 463, 467, 468, 469, 470, 522, 529, 562, 577, 610, 621, 624, 626, 627, 628, 669, 675

  strategies for answering, 622–623

guided problem solving, 7, 20, 40, 60, 87, 111, 159, 268, 274, 319, 376, 452, 496, 508, 542, 613, 641, 653

interpret, exercises, 8, 127, 138, 397, 418, 449

multiple choice questions, 8, 12, 17, 22, 30, 35, 47, 55, 62, 66, 71, 77, 84, 95, 105, 113, 119, 127, 134, 145, 161, 167, 172, 178, 184, 189, 194, 201, 209, 214, 219, 234, 239, 245, 254, 263, 269, 275, 287, 291, 298, 305, 309, 310, 311, 312, 321, 325, 331, 345, 349, 353, 358, 365, 373, 377, 382, 398, 403, 409, 418, 424, 429, 435, 449, 453, 457, 463, 466, 468, 469, 470, 478, 483, 489, 498, 505,

509, 515, 529, 537, 544, 549, 555, 562, 566, 570, 577, 587, 591, 597, 605, 614, 621, 625, 626, 627, 628, 638, 642, 647, 655, 661, 675

  context-based, 464–470

  strategies for answering, 146–147

multi-step problems, 18–23

short response questions, 8, 22, 35, 47, 55, 77, 84, 95, 105, 134, 149, 150, 151, 152, 161, 184, 201, 219, 239, 245, 254, 269, 275, 305, 308, 310, 311, 312, 325, 345, 349, 365, 377, 398, 409, 435, 449, 457, 463, 467, 468, 469, 470, 489, 505, 509, 529, 537, 555, 577, 591, 605, 621, 625, 626, 627, 628, 638, 655, 675

  strategies for answering, 306–307

Problem solving plan, 38–41

Problem solving strategies, *See also*
  Test-taking skills; Test-taking strategies

act it out, 392–393, 397

break a problem into parts, 492–493, 498

draw a diagram, 220–221, 223, 225

estimate, 56–57, 59

guess, check, and revise, 538–539, 543

look for a pattern, 36–37, 39

make a list, 21, 162–163, 164, 175, 541, 657

make a model, 600–601, 602

make a table, 128–129, 130

perform an experiment, 662–663, 664

solve a related/simpler problem, 276–277, 278

work backward, 340–341

write an equation, 430–431

Product, 689

Product form, 74–75, 256

Project ideas, 97, 247, 411, 579, *See also* Math in Science

Proper fraction, 185

Properties

associative
  addition, 284
  multiplication, 284

commutative
  addition, 284
  multiplication, 284

cross products, 394, 422

distributive, 288–291

of equality
  addition, 328
  division, 332, 333
  multiplication, 334
  subtraction, 327
  symmetric, 289

identity
  of addition, 285
  of multiplication, 285

inverse
  of addition, 285
  of multiplication, 285

table of, 721

Proportion(s), 386–398

using algebra to solve, 388–391

using cross products to solve, 394–398, 422–424

definition of, 386, 387

using equivalent ratios to solve, 387–391

indirect measurement and, 507–509

modeling, 386

percent and, 420–424

scale drawing and, 399–403

similar figures and, 501–509

writing, 389, 395

Proportional reasoning

bar models for percent, 419

converting metric units, 85–89

cross products and, 180, 394–398

equivalent fractions, 169–172

interpreting slope, 379

multiplying dimensions of a prism, 615

percent of decrease, 446–449

percent of increase, 446–449

percent one number is of another, 420–424

perimeter and area relationships, 36, 162

rate, 374–377

scale drawing, 399–403

similar figures, 501–509

unit rate, 374–377

volume and, 614

Protractor, 438–439, 441–444, 490–491

of negative and zero exponents, 255
of operations with common
  denominators, 205
of percent problems as equations,
  432–435
of percents as decimals, 425–429
of percents as fractions, 415,
  417–418
of percents and proportions,
  420–424
of perimeter and area, 32
of powers and exponents, 14
of problems as equations, 430–431
of ratios, 369
of ratios as percents, 419
using scientific notation, 74
of the subtraction property of
  equality, 327
of surface area using nets, 594, 602
of a three-dimensional figure in
  two dimensions, 594, 602
of transformations using
  coordinate notation, 518–523
using a Venn diagram, 283
verbal phrases as equations,
  318–321
verbal phrases as expressions,
  317–321
Research, project, 97, 247, 411, 579
Retail price, 450–453
Review, *See also* Assessment;
  Internet; Notebook Review;
  Skills Review Handbook
  Basic Skills, 8, 12, 17, 22, 30, 35, 41,
    55, 62, 66, 71, 77, 84, 89, 105,
    113, 119, 127, 134, 139, 161,
    167, 172, 178, 184, 189, 194,
    209, 214, 219, 226, 234, 239,
    254, 263, 269, 275, 282, 287,
    291, 298, 321, 325, 331, 337,
    345, 349, 353, 358, 373, 377,
    382, 391, 398, 403, 418, 424,
    429, 435, 444, 449, 453, 457,
    478, 483, 489, 498, 505, 509,
    515, 522, 537, 544, 549, 555,
    562, 566, 570, 587, 591, 597,
    605, 610, 614, 638, 642, 647,
    655, 661, 669,
  Chapter Review, 44–45, 92–93,
    142–143, 198–199, 242–243,
    302–303, 362–363, 405–407,
    460–461, 526–527, 574–575,
    618–619, 672–673
Extra Practice, 705–717

Mixed Review, 8, 12, 17, 22, 30, 35,
  41, 55, 62, 66, 71, 77, 84, 89,
  105, 113, 119, 127, 134, 139,
  161, 167, 172, 178, 184, 189,
  194, 209, 214, 219, 226, 234,
  239, 254, 263, 269, 275, 282,
  287, 291, 298, 321, 325, 331,
  337, 345, 349, 353, 358, 373,
  377, 382, 391, 398, 403, 418,
  424, 429, 435, 444, 449, 453,
  457, 478, 483, 489, 498, 505,
  509, 515, 522, 537, 544, 549,
  555, 562, 566, 570, 587, 591,
  597, 605, 610, 614, 638, 642,
  647, 655, 661, 669
  student help with, 6, 33, 71, 102,
    104, 158, 190, 191, 206, 256,
    266, 272, 280, 334, 344, 370,
    381, 400, 441, 446, 490, 506,
    534, 542, 547, 586, 612
Rhombus, 494–498
Right angle, 475–478
Right cylinder, 602
Right prism, 594
Right triangle, 485–489
  hypotenuse of, 545, 546
  legs of, 546
  Pythagorean theorem and,
    545–549
Rotation, 511–515
  angle of, 512
  center of, 511
Rotational symmetry, 510, 513–515
Rounding
  compatible numbers and, 67
  decimal quotients, 69
  decimals, 53–55
    leading digit, 63
  definition of, 683
  degree measures, 442
  to estimate, 56–57
    measurements, 563–570
    with money, 56
    whole number differences, 692
    whole number products, 693
    whole number sums, 691
  percents, 426–429, 442
  whole numbers, 683

S

Sale price, 450, 452–453
Sales tax, percent and, 451–453

Sample, 106–107
  biased, 106
  random, 106
Scaffolding, *See* Problem solving
Scale
  for a bar graph, 108
  for a drawing, 399–403
  for a line graph, 110
  for a map, 400, 402
  misleading graphs and, 136, 138
  model, 401–403
Scale drawing, 399–403
  definition of, 400
  making, 399
Scale factor, 502
Scale model, 401–403
  definition of, 401
Scalene triangle, 486–489
Scatter plot
  definition of, 295
  exercises, 578
  making, 292, 295–297
Scientific notation, 74–78
  comparing numbers in, 75–77
  using zero and negative
    integers, 256
Second, 697
Sector, of a circle graph, 440
Segment
  drawing with a compass, 700
  length in the coordinate plane,
    294, 296
Sequences, *See* Patterns
Sets, Venn diagrams and, 702
Short response questions, *See also*
    Problem solving
  strategies for answering, 306–307
Side view
  of a solid, 589–591
    drawing, 592–593
Similar figures, 501–509
  naming, 502
  scale factor, 502
Simple interest, 454–457
  definition of, 454
Simplest form fractions, 170–172
  for percent, 415–418
Simplifying fractions, 170–172
Skew lines, 586
Skills Review Handbook, 681–704
  data displays
    bar graph, 703
    line graph, 703
    line plot, 704

Credits

Cover Photography

Ralph Mercer

Photography

iii *top to bottom* Meridian Creative Group, RMIP/Richard Haynes, Michael Girard, Jerry Head Jr.; **vi** Myrleen Ferguson Cate/PhotoEdit; **vii** Bob Krist/ Corbis; **viii** Stefano Rellandini/Reuters; **ix** Frank Siteman; **x** Michael Heron/Corbis; **xi** Cydney Conger/Corbis; **xii** Stephen Frink/Corbis; **xiii** Ted Spiegel/Corbis; **xiv** Annie Griffiths Belt/Corbis; **xv** Brian Bailey/Getty Images; **xvi** Jim Naughten/Getty Images; **xvii** Dennis McDonald/ PhotoEdit; **xviii** NeoVision/Photonica; **1** Michelle D. Bridwell/PhotoEdit; **2** *center, top to bottom* Corbis, AFP Photo/Anatoly Maltsev/Corbis, Wally McNamee/Corbis, *background* Lawrence Manning/Corbis, *gold medal* AFP Photo/George Frey/Corbis; **3** *top row, left to right* Robert Glusic/Corbis, Dallas and John Heaton/Corbis, *center row, left to right,* Joseph Sohm/ ChromoSohm/Corbis, Rudi Von Briel/ Photorush/Corbis, Harry Spurling/ Corbis, *bottom row, left to right* Robert Glusic/Corbis, Randy Faris/Corbis, AFP Photo/Todd Warshaw/Getty Images/Corbis, *snowboarder* Chris Trotman/Duomo/Corbis; **5** *center left* Monica Stevenson/FoodPix, *top right* Dandy Zipper/Getty Images; **6** Steve Dunwell Photography/Getty Images; **7** Ezio Geneletti/ Getty Images; **8** Andy Williams/Getty Images; **10** *bottom left* Dawn Villella/AP Wide World Photos, *bottom right* School Division/Houghton Mifflin Co.; **11** School Division/Houghton Mifflin Co.; **12** *left* Keren Su/Corbis, *right* Wolfgang Kaehler/Corbis; **14** Lester V. Bergman/Corbis; **17** Frank Siteman; **18** *bottom left* School Division/ Houghton Mifflin Co., *top right* Myrleen Ferguson Cate/PhotoEdit; **20** Naki Rocker Pad © 2002 Naki International. Photograph by Ken O'Donoghue; **21** Pedro Ugarte/AFP/Corbis; **27** Davis Barker/PhotoEdit; **29** Kelly-Mooney Photography/Corbis; **33** Karl DeBlaker/AP Wide World Photos; **34** Michelle D. Bridwell/PhotoEdit; **35** Donald Cooper/Shakespeare's Globe; **36** Frank Siteman; **37** Tony Freeman/PhotoEdit; **38** Myrleen Ferguson Cate/ PhotoEdit; **39** Paul A. Souders/Corbis; **40** Frank Siteman; **41** *background* © 2002 Hiroaki Ohya Design Zoo, Ltd. Photograph courtesy of ikjeld.com, *foreground* © 2002 Hiroaki Design Zoo, Ltd. Photograph by Silvia Mantner. Courtesy of the Fashion Institute of Design and Merchandising (FIDM), Los Angeles, California; **45** Tony Freeman/PhotoEdit; **48–49** Ken O'Donoghue; **52** Gianni Giansanti/Corbis Sygma; **54** Roger Ressmeyer/Corbis; **55** Phil Long/AP Wide World Photos; **56** Frank Siteman; **57** David Young-Wolff/ Getty Images; **60** Wilfredo Lee/AP Wide World Photos; **61** Courtesy of The MAiZE, www.cornfieldmaze.com; **64** Bob Krist/Corbis; **65** Ken O'Donoghue; **66** Bettmann/Corbis; **69** EyeWire Collection/Getty Images; **74** © 2001 Ripley Entertainment, Inc. "Believe It or Not!" is a registered trademark of Ripley Entertainment, Inc.; **75** NASA/Roger Ressmeyer/ Corbis; **77** William Sallaz/Duomo/Corbis; **79** Ken O'Donoghue; **82** Tony Freeman/PhotoEdit; **84** Desmond Boylan/Reuters; **85** Jim Cummins/Getty Images; **87** Rusty Hill/FoodPix; **88** Ken O'Donoghue; **96** Inner Light/Getty Images; **97** *background* Werner Dieterich/Getty Images, *top inset* Corbis, *bottom inset* Tom Walker/Getty Images; **98** Joseph Sohm/ChromoSohm/ Corbis, *inset* Corbis; **99** PhotoDisc; **101** Emanuele Taroni/Getty Images; **102** Tony Anderson/Getty Images; **103** School Division/Houghton Mifflin Co.; **104** Jeff Roberts/AFP/Corbis; **106** PhotoDisc; **107** Mary Kate Denny/ PhotoEdit; **108** Roger Ressmeyer/Corbis; **109** Michael T. Sedan/Corbis; **111** PhotoDisc; **112** Tom Bean/Corbis; **113** Vicky Kasala/Getty Images; **116** Corbis; **117** Todd Gipstein/Corbis; **118** Myrleen Ferguson Cate/ PhotoEdit; **119** Stefano Rellandini/Reuters; **122** Frank Siteman; **123** Andy Burriss/AP Wide World Photos; **124** Plastock/Photonica; **125** Pierre Ducharme/Reuters New Media Inc./Corbis; **126** Lake County Museum/ Corbis; **128** Frank Siteman; **129** Flip Nicklin/Minden Pictures; **130** *center* Spencer Jones/Getty Images, *bottom left* Roger Ressmeyer/Corbis; **131** Robert Llewellyn/Corbis; **132** *left* James A. Sugar/Corbis, *right* PhotoSpin; **133** © 1995 Kindra Clineff; **134** Douglas Peebles/Corbis; **135** Stephen Frink/Corbis; **137** Frank Siteman; **138** Jose Carillo/PhotoEdit; **143** School Division/Houghton Mifflin Co.; **144** PhotoDisc; **153** Yukimasa Hirota/Photonica; **154–155** *spread* Lester Lefkowitz/Corbis; **155** *top* Craig T. Mathew/AP Wide World Photos, *left* Mansfield News Journal/Jason

Molyet/AP Wide World Photos, *right* Rick Norton/AP Wide World Photos; **157** Buddy Mays/Corbis; **159** School Division/Houghton Mifflin Co.; **160** China Photo/Reuters; **162** Frank Siteman; **163** Neil Rabinowitz/Corbis; **164** *bottom left* Artville, *top right* Photograph by Jonathan Wiggs. Republished with permission of Globe Newspaper Company, Inc., from the 7/25/01 issue of *The Boston Globe*, © 2001; **167** Vince Bucci/AFP/ Corbis; **169** *top* Michael Pole/Corbis, *center right goldfish* Michael Pole/ Corbis, *center right blue fish* Frank and Joyce Burek/Getty Images; **170** David Young-Wolff/PhotoEdit; **172** Maxine Hall/Corbis; **175** Daniel Hulshizer/AP Wide World Photos; **176** Alan Schein Photography/Corbis; **177** Frank Siteman; **178** Michael T. Sedan/Corbis; **181** Mike Brinson/Getty Images; **183** Peter Gridley/Getty Images; **184** Arthur Tilley/Getty Images; **187** Jeff Greenberg/PhotoEdit; **188** From *The Unbelievable Bubble Book*, by John Cassidy. Photograph by Peter Fox. Used with permission. © 1987 Klutz ®; **192** Ric Ergenbright/Corbis; **193** *bottom left* Frans Lanting/ Minden Pictures, *bottom right* Al Franklin/Corbis; **199** School Division/ Houghton Mifflin Co.; **200** PhotoDisc; **203** *top* David Madison/Getty Images, *bottom* John Slater/Corbis; **207** Mike Yoder/AP Wide World Photos; **208** Jeffrey L. Rotman/Corbis; **209** Photograph by Dan Rest. Courtesy of the Chicago Symphony Orchestra; **211** David J. Phillip/AP Wide World Photos; **213** Michael Heron/Corbis; **214** Frank Siteman; **216** Frank Siteman; **217** *badges* Ken O'Donoghue, *badge photos* PhotoDisc; **218** Kit Houghton/Corbis; **219** Leaded-glass window (1902–4), Frank Lloyd Wright. Susan Lawrence Dana House (library door), Springfield, Illinois. Photograph © 2002 Julie L. Sloan and Albert L. Lewis; **220** Frank Siteman; **221** Tim O'Hara/Corbis; **223** Gregg Adams/Getty Images; **225** Tony Anderson/Getty Images; **232** Frank Siteman; **233** Plastock/Photonica; **234** Wolfgang Kaehler/Corbis; **235** Tim Page/Corbis; **236** Yukimasa Hirota/ Photonica; **237** Martin Bydalek/Corbis; **238** Epix Photography/Getty Images; **244** Ken O'Donoghue; **246–247** *background* Corbis; **246** *top, bottom* Courtesy of NASA, *center* Getty Images; **247** *top, bottom* Courtesy of NASA; **248–249** Ken O'Donoghue; **251** William Sallas/Duomo/Corbis; **253** *bottom left* Chuck Savage/Corbis Stock Market, *bottom right* Plastock/ Photonica; **254** Charles and Josette Lenars/Corbis; **256** Ho/Reuters; **262** *top left* © 2002 Susan Wilder Crane, *bottom right* Ken O'Donoghue; **267** Alan Puzey/Getty Images; **268** Cydney Conger/Corbis; **269** NASA/JPL/ Caltech/AP Wide World Photos; **273** Michael Freeman; **274** Mitsuaki Iwago/Minden Pictures; **275** Danny Lehman/Corbis; **276** Frank Siteman; **277** Bob Krist/Corbis; **279** James Marshall/Corbis; **280** Darrell Gulin/ Corbis; **281** Michael Freeman/Corbis; **286** William James Warren/Corbis; **287** Ricardo Magalan/AP Wide World Photos; **288** Brigid Davis; **289** Comstock; **290** *left* Mary Jane Cardenas/Getty Images, *right* Siede Preis/Getty Images; **291** Norm Dettlaff/Las Cruces Sun-News/AP Wide World Photos; **295** Tony Wharton/Frank Lane Picture Agency/Corbis; **296** Jonathan Blair/Corbis; **297** Nancy Sheehan/PhotoEdit; **303** Frank Siteman; **304** Ken O'Donoghue; **313** Richard T. Nowitz/Corbis; **314** Staffan Widstrand/Corbis; **315** *left* Christie's Images/Corbis, *right* Archivo Iconografico/Corbis; **317** Michael Nichols/NGS Image Collection; **320** Jeff Christensen/Reuters; **321** Chip Simons/Getty Images; **323** *left* Akira Kaede/Getty Images, *right* © 2002 tatamiroom.com; **325** *background* Getty Images, *foreground* Frank Siteman; **327** Courtesy of NASA; **329** Courtesy of NASA; **333** William James Warren/Corbis; **335** Vince Streano/Corbis; **336** Tony Freeman/PhotoEdit; **337** Michael Geissinger/The Image Works; **340** Frank Siteman; **341** Joe McBride/Getty Images; **343** Walter Hodges/ Getty Images; **344** Ken O'Donoghue; **345, 346** Pictor International/Pictor International, Ltd./Picture Quest; **349** Johner/Photonica; **353** Stephen Frink/Corbis; **354, 357, 364** Ken O'Donoghue; **366–367** Ken O'Donoghue; **369** Sue Ogrocki/Reuters/Corbis; **370** Joe McBride/Getty Images; **371** Frank Siteman; **372** *left* JH Pete Carmichael/Getty Images, *right* Duncan Smith/Getty Images; **374** Jack Anthony, Dahlonega, Georgia; **375** Jerry Lampen/Reuters; **377** www.internationalrobotics.com; **379** G. Brad Lewis/Getty Images; **381** Mary Kate Denny/PhotoEdit; **382** Frans Lanting/Minden Pictures; **387** Patty Segovia, Silver Photo and Talent Agency; **388** PhotoDisc; **389** Johner/Photonica; **390** *left* Ken O'Donoghue, *right* Ted Spiegel/NGS Image Collection; **392** Frank Siteman; **393** Richard Hamilton Smith/Corbis; **394** Richard Nowitz/Corbis; **395** *left*

Credits

Mitsuaki Iwago/Minden Pictures, *right* Frans Lanting/Minden Pictures; **396** Frank Siteman; **397** Courtesy of the California History Room, California State Library, Sacramento, California; **399** Ken O'Donoghue; **401** Ted Spiegel/Corbis; **402** Samuel Chase Side Chair, c. 1755. © Raine and Willitts Design. All rights reserved. "Take a Seat" and "Raine" are trademarks of Raine. Mount Vernon® is a trademark of Mount Vernon, the home of George Washington. Style No. 24025. Photograph by Frank Siteman; **403** "Flying Pins," 2000, Claes Oldenburg and Coosje van Bruggen. Steel, fiber-reinforced plastic, foam, epoxy; painted with polyester gelcoat and polyurethane enamel. Ten pins, including partially buried pins, combined pins, and individual pins; each 24' 7'' (7.5 m) high x 7' 7'' (2.3 m) widest diameter; and ball, 9' 2'' (2.8 m) high x 21' 12'' (6.7 m) diameter, in an area approximately 123' (37.5 m) long x 65' x 7'' (20 m) wide. Intersection of John F. Kennedylaan and Fellenoord Avenues, Eindhoven, the Netherlands; **407** Tony Gutierrez/AP Wide World Photos; **408** Mike King/Corbis; **410** *left background* Bob Gibbons/Photo Researchers, *fish* Patuxent Wildlife Research Center, US Geological Survey; **411** SuperStock; **412** Stocktreck/Corbis; **413** *left* Martin Barraud/Getty Images, *right* Frank Siteman; **415** *top* Bob Child/AP Wide World Photos, *bottom* PhotoDisc; **417** Bob Krist/Corbis; **418** Corbis; **419** Ken O'Donoghue; **420** Corbis; **421** Peter Wilson/AP Wide World Photos; **422** Michael Newman/PhotoEdit; **423** Frans Lanting/Minden Pictures; **425** *top* Amy E. Conn/AP Wide World Photos, *bottom* Alan Diaz/AP Wide World Photos; **427** HOT WHEELS ® trademark owned by and used with permission from Mattel, Inc. © 2002 Mattel, Inc. All Rights Reserved. Cougar trademark used under license to Mattel, Inc. from Ford Motor Company. Photograph courtesy of David Williamson, ToyCarCollector.com; **428** G.K. and Vikki Hart/Getty Images; **430** Frank Siteman; **431** Jeff Greenberg/PhotoEdit; **432** *top* Annie Griffiths Belt/Corbis, *bottom* Robert Giroux/Reuters; **434** Mike Blake/Reuters/Corbis; **441** Frank Siteman; **442** Michael Newman/PhotoEdit; **443** Frank Siteman; **447** Tim Hawley/FoodPix; **448** Ken O'Donoghue; **449** Richard Hamilton Smith/Corbis; **450** *bottom* Frank Siteman, *top* Ken O'Donoghue; **451, 453** Ken O'Donoghue; **454** Air Hogs Intruder™ courtesy of Spin Master Toys. Photograph by Frank Siteman; **462** Reza Estakharian/Getty Images; **471** Johner/Photonica; **475** AFP Photo/Timothy Clary/Corbis; **478** Joaquin Palting/Getty Images; **481** Frank Siteman; **482** *top left* Johner/Photonica, *top center* Corbis, *top right* Ron Watts/Corbis, *bottom* Harris ("Butterfly") House, 1997, designed by Samuel Mockbee and students, Rural Studio, Auburn University, Alabama. Photograph by Timothy Hursley; **486** David Pollack/Corbis; **487** Jeanne Moutoussamy-Ashe; **488** Robert Frerck/Odyssey; **491** Ken O'Donoghue; **492** Frank Siteman; **493** Peter Cosgrove/AP Wide World Photos; **496** "Tumbling Blocks," 1880–1900. Anonymous, Lancaster, Pennsylvania. 97'' x 92'', cotton, hand-pieced and quilted. Gift of the Binney Family, 1991.09. Courtesy of the New England Quilt Museum. Photograph by Ken Burriss; **497** Leaded-glass window (1909), Frank Lloyd Wright. Frederick C. Robie House, Chicago; Frank Lloyd Wright, architect. Photograph by Farrell Grehan/Corbis; **501** Ken O'Donoghue; **503** Power Press/Corbis Sygma; **505** Frank Siteman; **506** Gene J. Puskar/AP Wide World Photos; **508** Dave G. Houser/Corbis; **509** Bettmann/Corbis; **511** Brian Bailey/Getty Images; **513** Frank Siteman; **514** Ken O'Donoghue; **515** Merton Gauster/Photonica; **519** Ken O'Donoghue; **521** Percussionist Gene Krupa, 1941. Gjon Mili/Timepix; **530** Oliver Strewe/Lonely Planet Images; **531** Eric O'Connell/Getty Images; **533** Steven E. Sutton/Corbis; **535** David Turnley/Corbis; **536** Charles O'Rear/Corbis; **537** Rick Rycroft/AP Wide World Photos; **538** Frank Siteman; **539** Charles Gupton/Corbis; **540** Jim Naughten/Getty Images; **543** Jump Run Productions/Getty Images; **547** Martha Granger/EDGE Productions; **549** Toby Talbot/AP Wide World Photos; **553** Roberto Candia/AP Wide World Photos; **555** © 2002 George W. Hart; **558** Rock and Roll Hall of Fame, Cleveland, Ohio (1998), I. M. Pei, architect. Photograph by Bill Ross/Corbis; **560** Ken O'Donoghue; **562** Johner/Photonica; **564** Phil Schermeister/Corbis; **565** *top left* Arthur Dillon in his monocycle. Photograph by Eric Sander, *center, top row from left* PhotoDisc, PhotoDisc, School Division/Houghton Mifflin, *bottom row from left* PhotoDisc, School Division/Houghton Mifflin Co., PhotoDisc; **566** Dallas and Jean

Heaton/Corbis; **568** Dean Conger/Corbis; **569** *top left* Gianni Dagli/Corbis, *center, top row* School Division/Houghton Mifflin Co., *bottom row from left* PhotoDisc, School Division/Houghton Mifflin Co., Artville; **570** Courtesy of the United States Mint; **575** Markus Boesch/Allsport/Getty Images; **576** Ken O'Donoghue; **578, 579** Ken Reid/Getty Images; **580–581** Mike Powell/Allsport/Getty Images; **583** *bottom left* Ken O'Donoghue, *bottom center* Dennis McDonald/PhotoEdit, *bottom right* Ken O'Donoghue; **584** Elizabeth Simpson/Getty Images; **585** *top row from left* PhotoDisc, Michael S. Yamashita, Ken O'Donoghue, *bottom row from left* Ken O'Donoghue, Siede Preis/Getty Images, Comstock; **586** *top left* D. Finnin/AP Wide World Photos, *top right* Lee Snider/Corbis; **588** *left inset* Ken O'Donoghue, *right* Ezra Stoller/© Esto; **590** Ken O'Donoghue; **597** *photocube* Ken O'Donoghue, *photos in cube* PhotoDisc; **600** Frank Siteman; **601** Tony Freeman/PhotoEdit; **603** Courtesy of IndoBoard.com. Rider: Serena Brooke. Photograph by Tom Servais; **604** Michael Porro/Getty Images; **607** *all* Dorling Kindersley; **608** Rich Pedroncelli/AP Wide World Photos; **609** Hironori Miyata/On Location; **611, 613** Ken O'Donoghue; **614** Randall Fung/Corbis; **619** Ken O'Donoghue; **629** Ryuichi Sato/Photonica; **631** *left* Tecmap Corporation/Eric Curry/Corbis, *right* Ken O'Donoghue; **634** *top* Ken O'Donoghue, *bottom* Corbis; **635** Neo Vision/Photonica; **636** Corbis; **637** Frank Siteman; **639** *top* PhotoDisc, *bottom* Ken O'Donoghue; **640** Richard T. Nowitz/National Geographic Collection; **641** Monica Lau/Getty Images; **642** George Shelley/Corbis; **644** *top* Jake Martin/Allsport/Getty Images, *bottom* Caron P./Corbis Sygma; **645** Michael Kalish; **647** Ken O'Donoghue; **650** Ryuichi Sato/Photonica; **651** Hillery Smith Garrison/AP Wide World Photos; **652** Frank Siteman; **653** Jey Inoue/Photonica; **654** Rodney White/AP Wide World Photos; **655** Corbis; **658** Ben Garvin/© 1999 The Christian Science Monitor; **659** Myrleen Ferguson Cate/PhotoEdit; **660** Robert Frerck/Odyssey; **662** Frank Siteman; **663** Jonathan Nourok/PhotoEdit; **666** Frank Siteman; **667** Ken O'Donoghue; **668** Courtesy of Franz Spohn. Photograph by Phillip Spohn; **673** Comstock; **674** Corbis

Illustration

Daniel Guidera

16, 22, 28, 30, 59, 62, 66 *inset*, **70, 89, 105, 110, 127, 139, 161, 166, 171, 189, 239, 241, 252, 282, 285, 319, 330, 331, 358, 373, 376, 391, 398, 424, 435, 444, 483, 507, 544, 595, 599, 605, 610, 617, 636, 646, 655, 665, 669**

Rob Dunlavey

48–49 *bottom*, **248–249** *bottom*, **366–367** *bottom*, **472–473** *bottom*

Steve Cowden

99

Selected Answers

Chapter 1

1.1 Getting Ready to Practice (p. 7)

5. The pattern is to alternate squares and triangles.

7. Step 1: The times are one-half hour apart. Step 2: It is. Step 3: The song will next be played at 4:10.

1.1 Practice and Problem Solving (pp. 7–8)

9. Each number is 9 less than the previous number; 64, 55, 46. **11.** Each number is 7 more than the previous number; 30, 37, 44. **13.** Each number is 3 times the previous number; 324, 972, 2916. **15.** Each number is the previous number divided by 3; 9, 3, 1. **17.** 6, 14, 22, 30 **19.** Each figure is a square array of dots with one more column and row than the previous figure.

 21.

23. Each number is 43 more than the previous number; 217, 260, 303. **25.** Each number is the previous number divided by 3; 18, 6, 2.

27.

29. The pattern alternates the next letter from the beginning of the alphabet with the next letter backwards from the end of the alphabet; C, X, D. **35.** $8 \times 100 + 4 \times 1$ **37.** $3 \times 1000 + 3 \times 100 + 9 \times 10 + 5 \times 1$ **39.** 380 **41.** 9000 **43.** 153 **45.** 24

1.2 Getting Ready to Practice (p. 11)
1. *Sample answer:* $x - 25$; $\frac{13}{n}$ **3.** 1 **5.** 15 **7.** 21 **9.** 2 **11.** $11

1.2 Practice and Problem Solving (pp. 11–12)
13. 4(8); $4 \cdot 8$ **15.** 8 **17.** 2 **19.** 35 **21.** 72 **23.** 48 min **25.** 8 **27.** 34 **29.** 4 **31.** 39 **33.** 22 **35.** 84 in. **41.** 1631 **43.** 765 **45.** Each number is 7 more than the previous number; 29, 36, 43. **47.** Each number is 11 less than the previous number; 55, 44, 33. **49.** *Sample answer:* low: 30; high: 40 **51.** *Sample answer:* low: 1500; high: 1600

1.3 Getting Ready to Practice (p. 16)
1. base = 9; exponent = 4 **3.** 4^4 **5.** a^3 **7.** 25 **9.** 81 **11.** $2^5 = 32$ cells

1.3 Practice and Problem Solving (pp. 16–17)
13. nine to the eighth power **15.** x cubed **17.** 10^2 **19.** 7^5 **21.** t^5 **23.** s^4 **25.** 125 **27.** 1024 **29.** 1 **31.** 729 **33.** $8^2 = 64$ **35.** 18 **37.** 2^4 or 4^2 **39.** 10^2 **41.** > **43.** =

45. $3, 6, 2^3, 9, 6^2, 9^2$

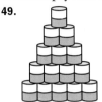

47. Multiply 256 by 2, and you get $2^9 = 512$.

49. **51.** 88 **53.** 8 **55.** 15

1.4 Getting Ready to Practice (p. 20)
1. expressions within grouping symbols; exponents; multiplication and division from left to right; addition and subtraction from left to right **3.** 7 **5.** 5 **7.** 3 **9.** 63 **11.** 4 **13.** 2

1.4 Practice and Problem Solving (pp. 21–22)
15. 32 **17.** 35 **19.** 2 **21.** 3 **23.** 25 **25.** 3 **27.** $(6 + 7) \cdot 5 + 8$ **29.** $15 + 4 \times 25 + 2 \times 15 = 145$ kg **33.** You could buy 6 chattering teeth. **35.** $5 \times 3 + 1 \times 4 = \$19$; $4 \times 3 + 2 \times 4 = \$20$; $3 \times 3 + 3 \times 4 = \$21$; $2 \times 3 + 4 \times 4 = \$22$; $1 \times 3 + 5 \times 4 = \$23$; you could buy either 5 chattering teeth and 1 hand buzzer or 4 chattering teeth and 2 hand buzzers with your $20. **39.** 145 min **41.** 169 **43.** 243 **45.** 73 **47.** 99

1.4 Technology Activity (p. 23) **1.** 23 **3.** 4
5. about 1080 blueberries

1.1–1.4 Notebook Review (pp. 24–25)
1. variable **2.** Each number is 10 more than the previous number; 50, 60, 70. **3.** Each number is twice the previous number; 112, 224, 448. **4.** 11 **5.** 5 **6.** 8^4 **7.** 100,000 **8.** 151 **9.** 17 **10.** 84

11. *Sample answer:* First, you need to discover how each number is related to the previous numbers. Is the difference the same between each term and the previous terms? Or is there some other relationship? After you find the relationship, you can use it to generate the next few terms.
12. $3 + 9 \times (6 - 4)$

1.5 Getting Ready to Practice (p. 28) **1.** *Sample answer:* An expression contains numbers and/or variables with operations, while an equation is a sentence that says two expressions are equal. An example of an expression is $n + 6$; an example of an equation is $n + 6 = 23$. **3.** no **5.** 6 **7.** 21
9. 17 **11.** about 600 ft/min

1.5 Practice and Problem Solving (pp. 29–30)
13. no **15.** 9 **17.** 4 **19.** 7 **21.** 8 **23.** 17 **25.** 48
27. 6 **29.** 9 mi/h **31.** 3 min **33.** yes **35.** 3 sec
41. 54 **43.** 108 **45.** 7 **47.** 35 **49.** 16 in.

1.6 Getting Ready to Practice (p. 34) **1.** perimeter
3. $P = 32$ in.; $A = 48$ in.^{2} **5.** $P = 28$ cm; $A = 49$ cm^2
7. $P = 22$ ft; $A = 28$ ft^2

1.6 Practice and Problem Solving (pp. 34–35)
9. $P = 80$ in.; $A = 400$ in.^{2} **11.** $P = 16$ cm;
$A = 16$ cm^2 **13.** $P = 34$ in.; $A = 66$ in.^{2}
15. $P = 48$ cm; $A = 144$ cm^2 **17.** $P = 26$ m;
$A = 40$ m^2 **19.** The square; the area of the rectangle is $5 \times 7 = 35$ square feet, while the area of the square is $6^2 = 36$ square feet. **21.** The rectangle is about 1 inch wide and 2 inches long; $P = 6$ in.; $A = 2$ in.^{2} **23.** 6 in. **27.** $48 **29.** 5 **31.** 7 **33.** 7

1.7 Problem Solving Strategies (p. 37) **1.** 2000 m
3. The perimeter is three times as large as the original perimeter, and the area is 9 times as large as the original area. The perimeter is four times as large as the original perimeter, and the area is 16 times as large as the original area. **5.** 28 seats
7. 27 **9.** $1.65

1.7 Getting Ready to Practice (p. 40)
1. read and understand, make a plan, solve the problem, look back

1.7 Practice and Problem Solving (pp. 40–41)
3. $6 of the $22 went for snacks rather than movie tickets. You need to subtract the $6 first, then divide by 2: $22 − $6 = $16; $16 ÷ 2 = $8. Each ticket cost $8. **5.** 7:55 P.M. **7.** 24 torches
9. 6 different arrangements **11.** No. *Sample answer:* You are not told how many apples are in a pound, or how many apples are in the bag.
15. 30 ft^2 **17.** $8 < 18$ **19.** $26 > 21$

1.5–1.7 Notebook Review (pp. 42–43) **1.** To find the perimeter, add twice the length to twice the width. To find the area, multiply the length times the width. **2.** 7 **3.** 13 **4.** $P = 46$ in.; $A = 112$ in.^{2}
5. $P = 16$ m; $A = 16$ m^2 **6.** 5 buses **7.** *Sample answer:* If you want to fence a rectangular area, you would need to know the perimeter to determine how much fencing would be needed. If you were going to paint the wall of a room, you would need to know its area in order to decide how much paint to buy.

Chapter Review (pp. 44–45) **1.** solution
3. an equal sign **5.** Each number is 10 more than the previous number; 41, 51, 61. **7.** Each number is twice the previous number; 400, 800, 1600.
9. Each number is 3 less than the previous number; 88, 85, 82. **11.** Each figure is a square divided by a diagonal, with the lower half shaded. The diagonal alternates from top left to bottom right, followed by top right to bottom left.

13. 63 **15.** 5 **17.** 32 **19.** $12
21. 9^2 **23.** 15^3 **25.** 343 **27.** 243
29. 30 **31.** 2 **33.** 22 **35.** 40 **37.** 4
39. 21 **41.** 5 **43.** 28 **45.** 40 mi/h
47. $P = 34$ m; $A = 70$ m^2 **49.** 6 ft, 4 ft
51. 6 different combinations

Chapter 2

2.1 Getting Ready to Practice (p. 54)
5. $A = 5.24$, $B = 5.28$, $C = 5.35$, $D = 5.4$, $E = 5.47$
7. < **9.** 22 **11.** 21.68 **13.** 8.7, 8.8, 9.5

2.1 Practice and Problem Solving (pp. 54-55)
19. > **21.** > **23.** < **25.** < **27.** your friend's **29.** 6.2, 6.5, 6.6, 6.8 **31.** 0.03, 0.2, 0.86, 0.91 **33.** 7.63, 7.65, 8.56, 8.65 **35.** 18 **37.** 5.6 **39.** 2.29 **41.** 0.0 **43.** *Sample answer:* 5.68 and 5.73 **45.** Each number has a 2 followed by a decimal. The decimal has a number of zeros followed by a digit that is the same as the number of zeros, starting with 1 zero and the number 1, and counting on from there; 2.000005, 2.0000006. **47.** 15 **49.** 16 **51.** *Sample answer:* 170 **53.** *Sample answer:* 2000

2.2 Problem Solving Strategies (p. 57) **1.** Yes; the total cost will be about $7 + $7.50 = $14.50, so $15 is enough. **3.** Cheryl is the winner. Her items will total a little over $9, while Jim's are less than $8 total. **5.** 2 pennies, 2 nickels, 1 dime, and 2 quarters **7.** 6:35 P.M.

2.2 Getting Ready to Practice (p. 60) **1.** Add the front-end digits, estimate the sum of the remaining digits, and then add the results. **3.** 3.4 **5.** 53.591

2.2 Practice and Problem Solving (pp. 60-62)
7. 6 + 0.9 + 0.01 + 0.002 **9.** 40 + 3 + 0.07 **11.** Subtract; you want to know the difference in the two temperatures. **13.** 23.4 **15.** 67.263 **17.** 82.7 **19.** 0.834 **21.** 884.3 **23.** Line up the decimal points before adding. Fill in four 0's after the decimal point in the second number so that it is easier to line them up. The correct sum is 628.8504. **25.** 46.4 **27.** 14.02 **29-33.** Estimates may vary. **29.** 15 **31.** 18 **33.** 3 **35.** Yes; 3 + 7 + 5 = 15 and each of the rainfall amounts in April, May, and June were greater than 3, 7, and 5, respectively. So, the sum of 3.57, 7.30, and 5.14 will be greater than 15. **37.** 483.83 **39.** 13.95 **41.** 19.068 **43.** 110.825 **45.** 138.746 **51.** 2.42, 2.46, 2.64, 4.06, 4.26 **53.** 45 tickets; use Look for a Pattern since the problem said the number of tickets sold each day would continue the pattern started on Monday-Wednesday. **55.** 105 **57.** 319

2.3 Getting Ready to Practice (p. 65) **1.** 4 **3.** 0.819 **5.** 0.007 **7.** Yes. *Sample answer:* Each bottle costs less than $3 and 3 × $3 = $9.

2.3 Practice and Problem Solving (pp. 65-66)
9. 22.1 **11.** 0.036 **13.** 343.64 **15.** 0.0126 **17.** 13.188 **19.** 1.3 **21.** 270 **23.** 1000 **25.** 13.5 mm^2 **27.** 52.9104 yd^2 **29.** 17.52766 **31.** 0.07786 **33.** *Sample answer:* The pattern in each of the products is that the decimal point is moved one place to the right each time a move to the right is made on the table. Multiplying by the next greater power of 10 will always move the decimal point one place to the right. **35.** 3.17262 **37.** 866.640042 **39.** 1.4314 **43.** 6 **45.** 8 **47.** 487.6 **49.** 14.73 **51.** 51 **53.** 146

2.4 Getting Ready to Practice (p. 69) **1.** 56 and 7 **3.** 4.9 **5.** 8.6 **7.** 0.064 **9.** 0.053

2.4 Practice and Problem Solving (pp. 70-71)
11. 10.7 **13.** 61.98 **15.** 5 **17.** 100 **19.** 7.3 **21.** 3.4 **23.** 8.06 **25.** 0.08 **27.** 30 ÷ 10 = 3, so the quotient must be 3.2. **29.** *Sample answer:* 40 **31.** about 160 cars **33.** 0.04 **35.** 21.94 **37.** 3.44 **39.** 19.33 **41.** 28.38 **43.** 4.37 **45.** 5.05 cm **47.** about 360,000,000 acres **49.** About $18.12; $12.80; *Sample answer:* Alaska; it was more than $5 less per square mile. **51.** Each number is the previous number divided by 2.5; 1.2, 0.48, 0.192. **53.** 25 **55.** 2401 **57.** 167.99 **59.** 230.88 **61.** 130,716

2.1–2.4 Notebook Review (pp. 72-73) **1.** decimal **2.** 1, 1.008, 1.02, 1.1 **3.** 0.7, 0.77, 7.07, 7.7 **4.** 9.04, 9.3, 9.32, 9.41 **5.** 8.384 **6.** 269.92 **7.** 4.113 **8.** 0.384 **9.** 0.53465 **10.** 39.5 **11.** 63 **12.** *Sample answer:* 19.231, 19.225, 19.228 **13.** A good answer will include: • how each division is related to dividing one whole number by another • how to multiply a decimal divisor by a power of 10 to make it a whole number • multiplying the dividend by the same power of 10 • lining up the decimal points in the dividend and quotient • using place-holder zeros

2.5 Getting Ready to Practice (p. 76) **1.** scientific notation **3.** standard form **5.** 2.845 × 10^8 **7.** 3,410,000 **9.** 50

2.5 Practice and Problem Solving (pp. 76–77)
11. 4.12×10^4 **13.** 2.92×10^7 **15.** 1.54×10^5
17. 1.024×10^2 **19.** 5.35×10^2 **21.** 2000 **23.** 150
25. 5,884,000,000 **27.** 60.7 **29.** < **31.** =
33. 7.98×10^4, 3.25×10^5, 3.5×10^5, 2.61×10^6
35. 1.10×10^7, 1.1×10^8, 1.101×10^8, 1.11×10^8,
1.01×10^9 **37.** 2400 lb **39.** 5; 2 **43.** 21 **45.** 49
47. 4.9 **49.** *Sample answer:* 1800; 2400
51. *Sample answer:* 45,000; 52,000

2.5 Technology Activity (p. 78) 1. 7.3×10^9
3. 9.24×10^{18} **5.** about 3.9 times

2.6 Getting Ready to Practice (p. 83) 1. mass
3. millimeter **5.** grams **7.** liters

2.6 Practice and Problem Solving (pp. 83–84)
9. Answers may vary. **11.** about 26 cm **13.** 3.1 kg
15. 350 mL **17.** kilometers **19.** milligrams
21. grams **23.** liters **27.** 30 **29.** 3 **35.** > **37.** =
39. 3.504×10^5 **41.** 9, 15, 19, 51, 59 **43.** 232, 233,
322, 323

2.7 Getting Ready to Practice (p. 87)
1. millimeters **3.** kilometer **5.** 0.89 **7.** 3750
9. 0.28 **11.** Step 1: 64 fl oz; Step 2: about 1920 mL;
Step 3: 1.92 L

2.7 Practice and Problem Solving (pp. 88–89)
13. divide **15.** multiply **17.** 750 **19.** 45.25
21. 4900 **23.** 1763 **25.** 840 **27.** = **29.** > **31.** <
33. > **35.** 5.448 L **37.** 2,420,000 **39.** 0.0013
41. 900,000 **43.** 3965 mL **45.** 15 cm **47.** 9.5 mg,
69 mg, 0.04 kg, 45 g, 60 g **49.** 2.4 mm, 420 mm,
240 cm, 4.2 m, 24 m, 0.24 km, 42 km **51.** 12.71
53. 3.774 **55.** 480 **57.** 1920 **59.** 5

2.5–2.7 Notebook Review (pp. 90–91)
1. meter, gram, liter **2.** 9.024×10^{11} **3.** 76,200
4. millimeters **5.** grams **6.** 4600 **7.** 8.923
8. 0.095 **9.** No; 35.89 is not between 1 and 10.
10. *Sample answer:* To compare two lengths
written in different units of measure, convert one
of the measurements so that both are written in
the same unit, then order the two numbers just as
you would any decimals.

Chapter Review (pp. 92–93) 1. *Sample answer:*
9.25, 0.018, 205.61 **3.** 3 **5.** capacity **7.** >
9. 0.01, 0.1, 0.11, 1.01, 1.1, 1.11 **11.** 73.45
13. 83.426 **15.** 13.07 **17.** 12.291 **19.** Yes. *Sample
answer:* Your total time was 78.29 seconds, which
is less than 80.63 seconds, your friend's time.
21. 86.5 **23.** 0.018018 **25.** 142 **27.** 0.24 **29.** 0.53
31. 3.356×10^6 **33.** 7.8×10^5 **35.** 406,000,000
37. 125 **39.** 4 **41.** mass **43.** capacity **45.** meters
47. liters **49.** 802,000 **51.** < **53.** < **55.** 6 cm,
0.08 m, 97 mm, 2.5 m, 256 cm, 0.8 km

Chapter 3

3.1 Getting Ready to Practice (p. 103) 1. true
3. 2 **5.** 1 **7.** You must order the data, and then
find the middle value. The data, ordered from
least to greatest, are 10, 11, 15, 24, 24, 41, 45, 45,
50. The median is the fifth value, 24.

3.1 Practice and Problem Solving (pp. 103–105)
9. 11; 11; 4; 18 **11.** 42; 43; no mode; 55
13. 42; 35; 87; 79 **15.** 8.32; 7.6; 7.6; 8.3 **17.** 66; 65.7;
no mode; 27 **19.** *Sample answer:* The median is
most representative of the data. The mean is a little
higher, and does not reflect the smaller values as
well. Since the mean and median are so close, both
represent the data fairly well. **21.** 224.341, 225.573.
Sample answer: The median is the better measure,
because the one value that is quite a bit bigger
than the others also makes the mean too large to
represent the data well. **23.** mean: 1.5 h; mode:
1 h; range: 3 h **25.** *Sample answer:* All three values
are very close together. The mean best represents
the data; the median and the mode are both near
the end of the data. **27.** The mean increases from
83 to 84.7, the median increases from 85 to 85.5,
while the mode stays at 95. **29.** 12 **31.** 5000
33. 0.48 **35.** 1235 **37.** 53

Special Topic Exercises (p. 107) 1. *Sample
answer:* Asking people who are active users of the
library could bias the sample in favor of increased
spending. This sample may not reflect the
opinions of voters or taxpayers on the whole.

3. *Sample answer:* This is a good sampling method. The sample is random, and not likely to be biased. **5.** This could be biased because of the loaded adjectives "exciting" and "crying" that seem to beg for a response in favor of the movie. **7.** The "information" provided by the statement seems to ask respondents to say yes. Rather than make an unsubstantiated claim, surveyors could collect some hard data by introducing a few extra trash cans in one area, keeping another area as is as a control, and see what kind of effect additional trash cans actually has. Then they have real information to present to voters.

3.2 Getting Ready to Practice (p. 111)
1. *Sample answer:* Bar graphs are often used with data that falls in various categories, giving a visual representation of the frequency of each one. It is made by drawing equal-width bars whose heights represent the data. A line graph shows a trend in data over time. It is made by graphing a sequence of points and connecting them by line segments. **3.** canned drinks

3.2 Practice and Problem Solving (pp. 111–113)
5.
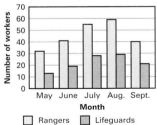
Wingspans of Birds

7.

Workers on Duty at a State Park

9. *Sample answer:* The number of tornadoes recorded each year in the United States fluctuates randomly, with most values between 1100 and 1300.

11.
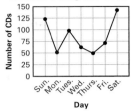
CD Sales During One Week

13. *Sample answer:* Each year from 1994 to 1999, the circulation of evening newspapers has decreased, while that of morning papers has increased, but not enough to make up for the entire decrease, resulting in an overall decrease in newspaper circulation. **15.** It is more appropriate to make a double line graph, since the data will show a trend over time for each country's population. **17.** No; the data are not entirely numerical, and do not show a change in data over time. Type of pet is a category, and only the frequency for each type of pet is numerical. **19.** < **21.** = **23.** 0, 5, 9, 19, 23, 29 **25.** 47, 48, 51, 54, 60

3.3 Getting Ready to Practice (p. 118) **1.** 10; 5
3. *Sample answer:* Half of the recent presidents have been in their 50s at the time of their inauguration.

3.3 Practice and Problem Solving (pp. 118–119)
5.
```
0 | 9
1 | 0 1 1 1 2 3 5
2 | 9
3 | 0 4 5

Key: 2 | 9 = 29
```
7.
```
0 | 8
1 | 1 2 5 5
2 | 4 8
3 |
4 | 1 3
5 | 9

Key: 4 | 3 = 4.3
```

9. 61 years old **11.** *Sample answer:* The great-grandfather's age is an outlier because there is a large difference (37 years) between his age and the age of the next oldest person. **13.** The median is the middle value of the ordered data set. You must order the set in order to determine which value is the median (or which two values it lies between, if there are an even number of data items). **15.** *Sample answer:* Only 4 tenths of a second separated the top finisher from the woman in fifth place. All of the top five finishers completed the course in less than 74 seconds.

17. *Sample answer:* Organic fertilizer: all but 3 data values are over 35, and the most common interval is 40–49. Chemical fertilizer: the data values are fairly evenly distributed, with the most common interval being 20–29. **21.** 6.475 **23.** 350 **25.** 2; 1.9; no mode; 2.1 **27.** 3830 **29.** 72

3.1–3.3 Notebook Review (pp. 120–121)
1. To find the median of a data set, first order the set from smallest value to largest value. Then count how many values are in the set. If the number is odd, the middle value in the ordered set is the median. If the number of values is even, the average of the two middle values is the median. **2.** 19; 17; 5; 34

3.
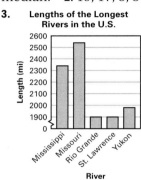
Lengths of the Longest Rivers in the U.S.

4.
```
1 | 0 2 3 3 7 9
2 | 2 5 7
3 | 6 8
4 | 1 8
5 | 5 5
```
Key: 3 | 8 = 38

5. *Sample answer:* The median and mean are close together in value, and they both represent the data set fairly well. The mean seems to represent the data a little better, since the two 5's are quite low and the 39 is very high, whereas the median's value of 17 is a data value and is right in the middle of a whole cluster of data values.

3.4 Getting Ready to Practice (p. 125) **1.** false
3. true **5.**
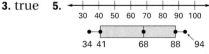
30 40 50 60 70 80 90 100
34 41 68 88 94

3.4 Practice and Problem Solving (pp. 126–127)
9.
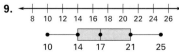
8 10 12 14 16 18 20 22 24 26
10 14 17 21 25

11. They are about equal. **13.** *Sample answer:* About half of the small car models get better gas mileage than all of the sport utility vehicles.

15.
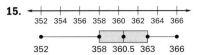
352 354 356 358 360 362 364 366
352 358 360.5 363 366

The values of the median and upper and lower quartiles each decreased by 0.5, and the upper extreme dropped to 366 while the lower extreme dropped to 352.

17.
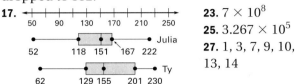
50 90 130 170 210 250
Julia
52 118 151 167 222
Ty
62 129 155 201 230

23. 7×10^8
25. 3.267×10^5
27. 1, 3, 7, 9, 10, 13, 14

3.5 Problem Solving Strategies (p. 129)
1. 6 dolphins **3.** the following Sunday **5.** at least $111.49 **7.** 2 blocks east

3.5 Getting Ready to Practice (p. 132)
1. *Sample answer:* The categories in a bar graph are often things other than numbers, for example, types of pets or music preferences. The categories in a histogram are always intervals of numbers. The bars in a bar graph do not touch one another, while those in a histogram are drawn without gaps in between (unless there is a zero frequency). The heights of bars in a histogram are the frequencies with which each interval is represented. The heights in a bar graph can be any numeric quantity, such as lengths of rivers or median prices of homes.

3.

Interval	Frequency
61–70	2
71–80	7
81–90	8
91–100	7

5. *Sample answer:* The scores in class 1 are heavily concentrated in the range 81–90, while those in class 2 are more spread out over the entire interval 71–100.

3.5 Practice and Problem Solving (pp. 133–134)
7.

Interval	Frequency
5–8	5
9–12	6
13–16	3
17–20	6

11. *Sample answer:* Almost half of the historic walking trails have lengths between 7 and 8.9 miles.

13.

Interval	Frequency
3–6.9	9
7–10.9	19
11–14.9	7

There will be fewer bars in the histogram, and each individual bar will have a height that is the sum of two bars from the previous histogram.

15. *Sample answer:* Almost half the teams scored 14 or fewer points, while the three top teams all scored more than 4 times as much.   **19.** 1.16
21. 4.444   **23.** divisible by 5   **25.** divisible by 2, 3, 6, 9

3.6 Getting Ready to Practice (p. 137) 1. bar graph, stem-and-leaf plot, histogram, line graph, and box-and-whisker plot

3.6 Practice and Problem Solving (pp. 137–139)
5. Histogram; you want to create a visual display of how the data fall into equal intervals.

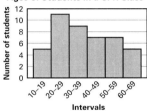

Ages of Students in a CPR Class

7. Bar graph; the categories here are not numerical, but the names of basketball teams.
9. Check work. Possible choices of graphs might be a stem-and-leaf plot or a box-and-whisker plot to show the distribution of data.   **11.** True; fish was chosen by about 48 students, just over half of the 90 who chose chicken.   **13.** False; twice the other is 80 which is more than the 60 students who chose beef.   **15.** about 4 times; no   **19.** 8.483
21.   **23.** 9

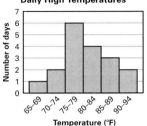

Daily High Temperatures

3.4–3.6 Notebook Review (pp. 140–141) 1. First, find the median of the data set. Next, find the median of all data values below the median. This is the lower quartile. Finally, find the median of all data values above the median. This is the upper quartile.   **2.** *Sample answer:* There are about the same number of data values between 4 and 6 as between 6 and the median, 15.5. This indicates that the first interval, between the lower extreme and the lower quartile, is more crowded than is that between the lower quartile and the median.

3.

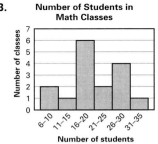

Number of Students in Math Classes

Interval	Frequency
6–10	2
11–15	1
16–20	6
21–25	2
26–30	4
31–35	1

4. *Sample answer:* You would probably use a line graph. Line graphs are used to show variation over time.   **5.** *Sample answer:* One way a data display could be misleading is when an inappropriate scale is used for the vertical axis. A break in scale can make changes in the data appear more dramatic than is really warranted, while too large an increment can make a real trend in the data seem to be insignificant.

Chapter Review (pp. 142–143) 1. bar graph
3. lower extreme, lower quartile, median, upper quartile, upper extreme   **5.** mode   **7.** 6; 5; 4; 13
9. 6; 6.15; 4.6 and 6.3; 2.9   **11.** *Sample answer:* The mean of the data set is 7, while the median is 6.5. The mode is 5. The mode is near the beginning of the data set so it may not be a good representation of the entire data set. The median and mean are very close in value, so either one would make a good choice. 7 would represent the data well as it is the average and near the middle of the data.

13.

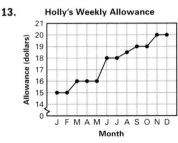

Holly's Weekly Allowance

15. *Sample answer:* Over the course of the year, Holly's allowance increased by one third, from $15 to $20. **17.**

1	2 3 7 8 9
2	0 2 3 5 7
3	0 5 6 6 7 8 8 9
4	1

Key: 3 | 7 = 37

19. $\frac{1}{2}$

21.

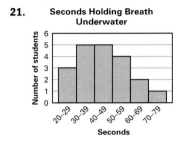

Seconds Holding Breath Underwater

23. Bar graph; since the data is divided into non-numerical categories, a bar graph is the most appropriate display.

Chapter 4

4.1 Getting Ready to Practice (p. 159)

1. *Sample answer:* A prime number has no factors other than 1 and itself, but a composite number has other factors besides just 1 and itself. **3.** composite; $10 = 2 \times 5$ **5.** Prime; it has no factors other than 1 and 43. **7.** Step 1: 1, 2, 3, 5, 6, 9, 10, 15, 18, 30, 45, 90; Step 2: The possible group sizes are 2, 3, 5, 6, 9, 10, 15, 18, 30, 45, and 90. Only 15 meets the criteria of the problem—a group of between 11 and 15 people. Step 3: The only ideal group size that will make equal groups is 15. 11, 12, 13, and 14 are not factors of 90.

4.1 Practice and Problem Solving (pp. 159–161)

9. 1, 3, 5, 9, 15, 45 **11.** 1, 13 **13.** 1, 2, 3, 6, 9, 18 **15.** 1, 2, 3, 6, 9, 18, 27, 54 **17.** 1, 2, 3, 4, 5, 6, 10, 12, 15, 20, 30, 60 **19–27.** Explanations may vary. **19.** Prime; the only factors of 23 are 1 and 23. **21.** composite; $39 = 3 \times 13$ **23.** Prime; the only factors of 67 are 1 and 67. **25.** composite; $99 = 9 \times 11$ **27.** composite; $201 = 3 \times 67$ **29.** 2

31. *Sample answer:* The person making the factor tree stopped too soon. 9 is not prime. It is equal to 3×3. The correct prime factorization is $2^2 \times 3^2$. **33.** Row 2: 26; Row 3: 2, 13; $2^2 \times 13$ **35.** 2×13 **37.** $2^2 \times 17$ **39.** 2^6 **41.** $3^2 \times 5^2$ **43.** $2^2 \times 3^2 \times 17$ **45.** *Sample answer:* When finding the factors of a number, you want to find every possible factor, both primes and composites. Further, you include each factor only once, even if it divides the number more than once. In finding the prime factorization, you only want to find the prime factors, but you also must determine how many times each prime divides the number. **47.** prime **49.** composite **51.** Composite; the sum of the digits in 2019 is 12, which is divisible by 3. So 2019 is divisible by 3, meaning it is a composite number. **53.** $2^2 \times 3^2 \times 7^2$ **55.** $2^4 \times 7 \times 11$ **57.** $3^2 \times 5 \times 7^2$ **59.** 5; 4; 4; 7 **61.** 2 times; I used estimation. The cost of a single visit for this family would be about $140, and so two visits, paying full admission would be about $280, more than the cost of a pass. **63.** divisible by 3 and 5 **65.** divisible by 2, 3, and 6

4.2 Problem Solving Strategies (p. 163)

1. Teams can have 1, 2, 3, 5, 6, 10, 15, or 30 members; 8 different sizes in all. **3.** 12 outfits **5.** 6 is the only perfect number between 1 and 10. **7.** yes **9.** 2 tickets, 2 sodas, and 1 popcorn

4.2 Getting Ready to Practice (p. 166)

1. relatively prime; GCF **3.** 3 **5.** 6 **7.** 9; not relatively prime **9.** 1; relatively prime

4.2 Practice and Problem Solving (pp. 167–168)

11. 1 **13.** 3 **15.** 15 **17.** 6 **19.** *Sample answer:* Write out the prime factorization of each number, using repeated multiplication instead of exponents where needed. Circle pairs of common prime factors between the two factorizations until there are no more pairs to be found. Multiply together one factor from each circled pair. This product is the greatest common factor. **21.** 1; relatively prime **23.** 12; not relatively prime **25.** 15; not relatively prime **27.** 1; relatively prime

29. The GCF of the two numbers is equal to the lesser number. **31.** 13 **33.** 14 **35.** 17 **37.** sometimes **39.** 256; 544 **41.** 19.6 **43.** 6.268 **45.** composite **47.** composite **49.** 6 batches

4.3 Getting Ready to Practice (p. 171) **1.** The numerator and denominator are relatively prime. **3.** no **5.** yes **7.** *Sample answer:* The fraction is still not simplified because you did not divide the numerator and denominator by their GCF. When you notice that the numerator and denominator still have a common factor other than 1, divide both by the common factor. Here, divide both the numerator and denominator by 2, obtaining $\frac{4}{7}$, which is in simplest form. **9.** $\frac{2}{7}$ **11.** $\frac{12}{35}$ **13.** $\frac{35}{50}$; $\frac{7}{10}$

4.3 Practice and Problem Solving (pp. 171–172)
15. $\frac{2}{6}$, $\frac{6}{18}$ **17–21.** Answers may vary. **17.** $\frac{5}{24}$, $\frac{50}{240}$ **19.** $\frac{7}{17}$, $\frac{28}{68}$ **21.** $\frac{7}{8}$, $\frac{21}{24}$ **23.** $\frac{3}{4}$ **25.** $\frac{11}{27}$ **27.** $\frac{6}{22} = \frac{3}{11}$ **29.** $\frac{5}{6}$, $\frac{4}{9}$; not equivalent **31.** $\frac{2}{7}$, $\frac{2}{7}$; equivalent **33–37.** Answers may vary. **33.** $\frac{7}{8}$, $\frac{14}{16}$ **35.** $\frac{9}{28}$, $\frac{18}{56}$ **37.** $\frac{3}{13}$, $\frac{6}{26}$ **39.** $\frac{19}{37}$ min **41.** 7^4 **43.** 8 **45.** 9 **47.** 120

4.1–4.3 Notebook Review (pp. 173–174) **1.** true **2.** true **3.** 2 **4.** 1 **5.** 45 **6.** 16 **7.** $\frac{3}{5}$, $\frac{3}{5}$; equivalent **8.** $\frac{2}{5}$, $\frac{1}{4}$; not equivalent **9.** $\frac{7}{11}$, $\frac{2}{7}$; not equivalent **10.** $\frac{5}{11}$, $\frac{5}{11}$; equivalent **11.** One way is to list all of the factors of each number, and find the largest number in both lists. Another way is to write the prime factorization of each number and multiply together each of the common prime factors.

4.4 Getting Ready to Practice (p. 177) **1.** *Sample answer:* The GCF is the largest number that will divide both numbers; the LCM is the smallest number both numbers will divide into. You can find the GCF by making a list of all of the common factors. The largest one is the GCF. You can find the LCM by making a list of some of the multiples of each number. The smallest number on both lists is the LCM. **7.** 392 **9.** 704 **11.** after 12 min

4.4 Practice and Problem Solving (pp. 177–178)
13. 36 **15.** 330 **17.** 198 **19.** 140 **21.** 644 **23.** 432 **25.** 2028 **27.** 10,800 **29.** 15; 990 **31.** 6; 1188 **33.** 9; 12,960 **35.** 11; 440 **37.** after 52 years **39.** It is the product of the numbers. **41.** w^3 **43.** $4s^4$ **45.** Yes. *Sample answer:* The product of two numbers is always a common multiple of them. But if the two numbers have a greatest common factor other than 1, then this common factor is squared in the product of the numbers when it is only needed to the first power. One way to find the LCM of two numbers is to multiply the numbers together and then divide by their GCF. For example, the GCF of 14 and 21 is 7, so the LCM of 14 and 21 is $(14 \times 21) \div 7 = 42$. If the GCF of two numbers is 1, then this method yields the product of the two numbers as their LCM. **47.** *Sample answer:* $\frac{2}{3}$, $\frac{8}{12}$ **49.** *Sample answer:* $\frac{2}{5}$, $\frac{4}{10}$ **51.** 123 **53.** 1640

4.5 Getting Ready to Practice (p. 183)
1. least common denominator **3.** = **5.** $\frac{3}{10}$, $\frac{1}{3}$, $\frac{11}{30}$, $\frac{2}{5}$ **7.** $\frac{5}{18}$, $\frac{1}{2}$, $\frac{3}{4}$, $\frac{7}{9}$ **9.** $\frac{15}{28}$ **11.** the pumpkin pie

4.5 Practice and Problem Solving (pp. 183–184)
13. > **15.** > **17.** < **19.** > **21.** $\frac{1}{4}$, $\frac{9}{32}$, $\frac{5}{16}$, $\frac{3}{8}$ **23.** $\frac{17}{81}$, $\frac{13}{27}$, $\frac{5}{9}$, $\frac{2}{3}$ **25.** $\frac{5}{12}$, $\frac{19}{36}$, $\frac{3}{4}$, $\frac{7}{8}$ **27.** $\frac{3}{8}$, $\frac{7}{16}$, $\frac{1}{2}$, $\frac{5}{8}$, $\frac{11}{16}$, $\frac{3}{4}$ **29.** $\frac{40}{79}$ **31.** $\frac{19}{30}$ **33.** $\frac{38}{75}$ **35.** $\frac{28}{54}$ **37.** $\frac{18}{35}$; write the two fractions with a common denominator: $\frac{15}{35}$ and $\frac{21}{35}$. The number exactly in the middle of 15 and 21 is 18, so $\frac{18}{35}$ is exactly halfway between them. **39.** 9.07, 9.17, 9.7, 9.71 **41.** 135 **43.** 252 **45.** *Sample answer:* 25,000

4.6 Getting Ready to Practice (p. 187)
1. improper fraction **3.** mixed number **5.** You need to multiply the whole number part times the denominator and then add to the numerator. The new numerator is $(5 \times 3) + 2 = 17$. The improper fraction is $\frac{17}{3}$. **7.** < **9.** > **11.** $\frac{5}{2}$ mi or $2\frac{1}{2}$ mi

4.6 Practice and Problem Solving (pp. 188–189)

13. $\frac{52}{20}$, $2\frac{12}{20}$ **15.** $\frac{30}{7}$ **17.** $\frac{36}{11}$ **19.** $\frac{49}{15}$ **21.** $\frac{91}{8}$ **23.** $\frac{69}{16}$

25. $5\frac{5}{8}$ **27.** $2\frac{2}{11}$ **29.** $24\frac{3}{4}$ **31.** $2\frac{16}{21}$ **33.** $9\frac{15}{16}$

35. 25 quarter-cups **37.** $\frac{40}{40}$, $\frac{22}{20}$, $1\frac{1}{9}$, $\frac{49}{42}$

39. Each of them is 3 and something more. You can ignore the 3's and just order the fractional parts to see what order the original mixed numbers go in. For example, since $\frac{1}{4} < \frac{3}{4}$, $3\frac{1}{4} < 3\frac{3}{4}$.

41. $\frac{28}{3}$, $9\frac{4}{9}$, $\frac{19}{2}$, $9\frac{21}{40}$, $9\frac{11}{20}$

43.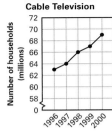

Households with Cable Television

Sample answer: I used a line plot, since the data show a trend over time.

45. $\frac{2}{5}$, $\frac{7}{15}$, $\frac{13}{25}$, $\frac{11}{20}$ **47.** 265 **49.** 1559

4.7 Getting Ready to Practice (p. 192)

1. *Sample answer:* A terminating decimal has a finite number of digits after the decimal point. A repeating decimal has a block of one or more digits that repeats after the decimal point.

3. 1.25 **5.** $0.8\overline{3}$ **7.** 2.4 **9.** $3.\overline{4}$ **11.** $1\frac{1}{4}$ **13.** $\frac{1}{8}$

4.7 Practice and Problem Solving (pp. 193–194)

19. 0.6; terminating **21.** $0.2\overline{7}$; repeating **23.** 7.45; terminating **25.** $0.58\overline{3}$; repeating **27.** $0.\overline{7}$

29. $3.5\overline{8}$ **31.** $\frac{4}{5}$ **33.** $\frac{19}{40}$ **35.** $6\frac{6}{25}$ **37.** $2\frac{49}{200}$

39. *Sample answer:* The mixed number to a decimal; it is easier to compare decimals.

41. $\frac{16}{5}$, $3\frac{2}{3}$, 3.67, $3.6\overline{7}$, $3\frac{4}{5}$ **43.** $\frac{15}{20}$, $\frac{6}{7}$, 0.89, $\frac{9}{10}$, $0.\overline{90}$

45. $\frac{5}{2} = 2.5$, $\frac{4}{3} = 1.\overline{3}$, $\frac{63}{20} = 3.15$ **47.** $5.\overline{432}$; repeating

49. 1.71875; terminating **51.** $\frac{1}{9} = 0.\overline{1}$, $\frac{2}{9} = 0.\overline{2}$, $\frac{3}{9} = 0.\overline{3}$; $\frac{4}{9} = 0.\overline{4}$, $\frac{5}{9} = 0.\overline{5}$, $\frac{6}{9} = 0.\overline{6}$. *Sample answer:* With fractions involving 9 as a denominator, predict that the numerator will be the single repeating digit. **53.** 490,000 **55.** 377,430,000

57. $6\frac{2}{9}$ **59.** 8 h 52 min

4.7 Technology Activity (p. 195)

1. $\frac{3}{8}$ **3.** $2\frac{14}{25}$ **5.** $15.8\overline{3}$ **7.** $6.\overline{6}$

4.4–4.7 Notebook Review (pp. 196–197)

1. least common denominator **2.** 160 **3.** 2970

4. 945 **5.** = **6.** < **7.** < **8.** 2.125 **9.** $7\frac{13}{20}$

10. The product of two whole numbers is always a common multiple of the numbers, but it is not always the least common multiple. If the numbers have a common factor other than 1, then it is not the least common multiple.

Chapter Review (pp. 198–199) 1. prime number
3. improper fraction **5.** least common denominator **7.** composite; 1, 3, 9, 27 **9.** prime; 1, 43 **11.** $2^2 \times 29$ **13.** $3^3 \times 17$ **15.** 6 **17.** 2 **19.** 8 **21.** 48 **23.** 40 bracelets; 7 green beads, 5 yellow beads, and 6 blue beads **25.** *Sample answer:* $\frac{2}{3}$, $\frac{4}{6}$

27. *Sample answer:* $\frac{4}{14}$, $\frac{10}{35}$ **29.** 40 **31.** 30 **33.** 405

35. 1872 **37.** $\frac{3}{4}$, $\frac{11}{13}$, $\frac{49}{52}$, $\frac{25}{26}$ **39.** $\frac{2}{9}$, $\frac{5}{21}$, $\frac{1}{3}$, $\frac{3}{7}$ **41.** <

43. > **45.** $26\frac{1}{3}$ lb, $26\frac{2}{5}$ lb, $\frac{187}{7}$ lb, $\frac{59}{2}$ lb, $\frac{121}{4}$ lb

47. $\frac{3}{50}$ **49.** $3\frac{5}{16}$ **51.** 5.875 **53.** $4.\overline{7}$

Chapter 5

5.1 Getting Ready to Practice (p. 207)

1. least common denominator **3.** $1\frac{3}{10}$ **5.** $\frac{1}{3}$

5.1 Practice and Problem Solving (pp. 208–209)

7. The second sum is the first sum rewritten with a common denominator. **9.** $1\frac{2}{7}$ **11.** $\frac{2}{5}$ **13.** $\frac{2}{3}$

15. $\frac{17}{18}$ **17.** $\frac{1}{6}$ **19.** $\frac{11}{36}$ **21.** *Sample answer:* about $1\frac{1}{10}$ h **23.** Each fraction is $\frac{1}{16}$ more than the previous fraction; $\frac{5}{16}$, $\frac{3}{8}$, $\frac{7}{16}$. **25.** $\frac{1}{8}$ **27.** Yes; if each fraction is greater than $\frac{1}{3}$ then their sum must be greater than 1. *Sample answer:* $\frac{1}{2} + \frac{4}{9} + \frac{5}{9} = 1\frac{1}{2}$.

29. $\frac{7}{9}$ **31.** $\frac{1}{3}$ **33.** $1\frac{1}{60}$ **35.** No; $\frac{1}{4} + \frac{1}{2} + 2 + \frac{3}{4} = 3\frac{1}{2}$, which is less than 4. **39.** 20.67 **41.** 239.707 **43.** $\frac{17}{100}$ **45.** $10\frac{17}{50}$ **47.** 1310.4 **49.** 517.75

5.2 Getting Ready to Practice (p. 213)
1. When the fractional part of the number being subtracted is larger than the fractional part of the number you are subtracting it from. **3.** $4\frac{2}{5}$ **5.** 13 **7.** $11\frac{5}{12}$ **9.** $3\frac{9}{10}$

5.2 Practice and Problem Solving (pp. 213–214)
11. Subtract $\frac{1}{4}$ from $\frac{3}{4}$, obtaining $\frac{1}{2}$, then subtract 1 from 2 obtaining 1. The answer is $1\frac{1}{2}$. **13.** $17\frac{4}{5}$ **15.** 8 **17.** $4\frac{2}{3}$ **19.** $10\frac{17}{18}$ **21.** $17\frac{17}{30}$ **23.** $1\frac{8}{9}$ **25.** Add $\frac{1}{5}$ and $\frac{4}{5}$ to get $\frac{5}{5}$ or 1. Then add $4 + 7 + 1$ to get 12. **27.** $1\frac{19}{21}$ **29.** $1\frac{38}{105}$ **31.** Yes. *Sample answer:* Round $14\frac{4}{5}$ feet up to 15 feet and round $15\frac{5}{6}$ feet up to 16 feet. Since both lengths were rounded up and $15 + 16 = 31$ feet, the two cars will fit in the parking space. **33.** $11\frac{7}{8}$ g **35.** 32.86 ft^2 **37.** $1\frac{2}{11}$ **39.** $\frac{13}{24}$ **41.** 25,811 **43.** 14

5.3 Getting Ready to Practice (p. 218)
1. improper fractions **3.** $\frac{5}{14}$ **5.** 10 **7.** 6 **9.** 6

5.3 Practice and Problem Solving (pp. 218–219)
11. *Sample answer:* Mentally use the distributive property; $1\frac{1}{2} \times \frac{1}{2} = \left(1 + \frac{1}{2}\right)\frac{1}{2} = 1\left(\frac{1}{2}\right) + \left(\frac{1}{2}\right)\left(\frac{1}{2}\right) = \frac{1}{2} + \frac{1}{4} = \frac{3}{4}$. **13.** $\frac{2}{45}$ **15.** 2 **17.** $\frac{1}{3}$ **19.** $\frac{3}{4}$ **21.** 9 **23.** 33 **25.** $2\frac{1}{4}$ **27.** $1\frac{4}{5}$ **29.** 2 **31.** 4 **33.** $1089\frac{3}{8}$ ft^2 **35.** never **39.** < **41.** < **43.** $2\frac{8}{15}$ **45.** *Sample answer:* 4 **47.** *Sample answer:* 8

5.4 Problem Solving Strategies (p. 221) **1.** Yes. *Sample answer:* If you display two of the 4×7's vertically. **3.** 3 blocks east and 9 blocks south **5.** $5 **7.** 4 rolls

5.4 Getting Ready to Practice (p. 224)
1. $\frac{7}{3}$ **3.** 7 **5.** $\frac{9}{13}$ **11.** $\frac{1}{2}$ ft

5.4 Practice and Problem Solving (pp. 225–226)
13. $\frac{4}{7}$ **15.** 1 **17.** $2\frac{2}{5}$ **19.** $\frac{7}{48}$ **21.** $2\frac{10}{11}$ **23.** 14 **25.** $7\frac{1}{2}$ **27.** $2\frac{24}{31}$ **29.** $4\frac{4}{5}$ **31.** 4 times **33.** $\frac{65}{258}$ **35.** 401 gates **39.** kilograms

5.4 Technology Activity (p. 227) **1.** $1\frac{23}{99}$ **3.** $\frac{1}{5}$ **5.** $2\frac{11}{14}$ **7.** $23\frac{2}{3}$ **9.** $\frac{91}{500}$ **11.** $\frac{21}{25}$ **13.** 6 posters; $77.70

5.1–5.4 Notebook Review (pp. 228–229)
1. 1 **2.** $\frac{19}{28}$ **3.** $22\frac{5}{14}$ **4.** $\frac{3}{10}$ **5.** $1\frac{1}{2}$ **6.** $6\frac{1}{4}$ **7.** $10\frac{1}{2}$ **8.** $13\frac{1}{3}$ **9.** $11\frac{11}{12}$ **10.** $10\frac{1}{2}$ **11.** $\frac{1}{10}$ **12.** $5\frac{1}{3}$ **13.** $7\frac{1}{2}$ **14.** *Sample answer:* Multiply the quotient by the divisor. You should get the dividend. $\frac{3}{4} \div \frac{5}{8} = \frac{6}{5}$ since $\frac{5}{8} \times \frac{6}{5} = \frac{3}{4}$. **15.** Less than; you are dividing by a number greater than 1.

5.5 Getting Ready to Practice (p. 233)
1. cup **3.** miles **5.** gallons

5.5 Practice and Problem Solving (pp. 233–234)
7–9. Answers may vary. **11.** $\frac{3}{8}$ lb **13.** $1\frac{1}{2}$ c **15.** ounces **17.** cups **19.** ruler **23.** The scale with pounds divided into fourths. *Sample answer:* Precision improves as the number of markings on a scale increases. **25.** estimate **27.** exact answer **29.** 120 ways; explanations may vary. **31.** $1\frac{1}{2}$

5.6 Getting Ready to Practice (p. 237) **1.** yards **3.** feet **5.** 30 **7.** 12 c 3 fl oz **9.** 5 ft 6 in.

5.6 Practice and Problem Solving (pp. 238–239)
11. To convert from feet to yards, multiply by the conversion fraction $\frac{1 \text{ yd}}{3 \text{ ft}}$. If the answer is not a whole number, express the remainder as a number of feet or as a fraction of a yard. **13.** 60 **15.** 74 **17.** 30 **19.** 2, 2 **21.** 4, 6 **23.** 3 ft 3 in. **25.** Khufu

27. < **29.** < **31.** < **33.** There are approximately $2\frac{1}{2}$ CD widths in 1 inch; since the shelf is 15 inches long, approximately $2\frac{1}{2} \times 15$ or about 37 CDs will fit on the shelf; $15 \div \frac{3}{8} = 40$ CDs. **35.** 3 yd **37.** 2 T **41.** $\frac{f}{5280}$ **43.** 336 **45.** 360 **47.** capacity **49.** 15; 3; 15

5.5–5.6 Notebook Review (pp. 240–241)
1. yard **2.** ounces **3.** inches **4.** $4\frac{1}{4}$ **5.** 684 **6.** 12
7. Multiply by $\frac{4 \text{ qt}}{1 \text{ gal}} \times \frac{2 \text{ pt}}{1 \text{ qt}}$. **8.** Container A.
Sample answer: There are 16 fluid ounces in 1 pint, so there are 44 fluid ounces in $2\frac{3}{4}$ pints. This is more than 36 fluid ounces.

Chapter Review (pp. 242–243) **1.** reciprocal
3. fluid ounce **5.** $\frac{8}{11}$ **7.** $\frac{1}{5}$ **9.** $\frac{1}{24}$ **11.** $\frac{17}{18}$
13. $\frac{1}{2}$ carat **15.** $5\frac{4}{5}$ **17.** $3\frac{11}{12}$ **19.** $10\frac{1}{4}$ **21.** $80\frac{3}{14}$
23. $\frac{1}{8}$ **25.** $2\frac{1}{2}$ **27.** $\frac{3}{7}$ **29.** $\frac{1}{8}$ **31.** $\frac{1}{14}$ of the orchestra
33. $4\frac{3}{4}$ in. **35.** pounds **37.** tons **39.** 12 **41.** $3\frac{1}{8}$
43. 10,560 **45.** 11 gal **47.** 1 T 1113 lb **49.** 0.48 qt, 1.2 qt, $1\frac{1}{2}$ gal, 24 pt, 3840 fl oz

Chapter 6

6.1 Getting Ready to Practice (p. 253)
1. 2675, 0, -56, and 75 **3.** -16; 16 **5.** -15; 15
7. > **9.** > **11.** $-5°F, -2°F, -1°F, 3°F, 9°F$

6.1 Practice and Problem Solving (pp. 253–254)
13–17. Check number lines. Answers may vary.
13. your team's score in a hockey game when they did not make any goals **15.** You owe your parents $9. **17.** a temperature of 3° below zero **19.** <
21. < **23.** > **25.** *Sample answer:* 4, 22 **27.** *Sample answer:* $-13, -20$ **29.** $-28, -17, -12, 0, 7, 18$
31. $-435, -150, -75, 235, 345$ **33–39.** Explanations may vary. **33.** True; -3 is to the left of 2 on the number line. **35.** True; 6 is to the right of -1 on the number line. **37.** False; -7 is to the left of -5 on the number line. **39.** True; 100 is to the right of

0 on the number line. **41.** Syracuse, Carthage, Alexandria, Jerusalem, Byzantium **43.** 100.05
45. 288.7 **47.** 10 gal **49.** 10 ft 7 in. **51.** 112 **53.** 19

Special Topic Exercises (p. 256) **1.** $\frac{1}{36}$ **3.** $\frac{1}{32}$
5. 0.021 **7.** 0.00892 **9.** the width of the sculpture
11. 1×10^{-4} **13.** 9.32×10^{-5}

6.2 Getting Ready to Practice (p. 261) **1.** False; if an integer is positive, its absolute value is equal to the integer, not its opposite, because an absolute value is always positive. **3.** 13 **5.** 43 **7.** 3 **9.** -4

6.2 Practice and Problem Solving (pp. 261–263)
11. $-2 + 3$; 1 **13.** $6 + (-1)$; 5 **15.** 12 **17.** 54
19. 567 **21.** 29 **23.** -14 **25.** -145 **27.** -10
29. -25 **31.** -10 **33.** Absolute value represents a distance, and distances are never negative. **35.** >
37. = **39.** > **41.** 4 **43.** 2 **45.** < **47.** = **49.** 4
51. 5 **53.** -8 **55.** Kyra: $+2$; Mark: $+3$ **57.** Mark
59. always **61.** always **63.** < **65.** > **67.** 14 candles.
Sample answer: Use Draw a Diagram. A diagram is a fast way to find the number of candles arranged according to the directions. **69.** *Sample answer:* 130 **71.** *Sample answer:* 8000

6.3 Getting Ready to Practice (p. 268)
1. opposite **7.** -12 **9.** -14

6.3 Practice and Problem Solving (pp. 268–269)
11. -26 **13.** -11 **15.** 14 **17.** -47 **19.** 60
21. 11,331 ft **23.** -1 **25.** 56 **27.** Mercury: 179°C; Earth: 8°C; Jupiter: -153°C; Saturn: -185°C; Pluto: -236°C **29.** Each number is 3 less than the previous number; $-10, -13, -16$. **31.** 15.12
33. 0.042 **35.** > **37.** = **39.** *Sample answer:* 400; 600 **41.** *Sample answer:* 2400; 3500

6.1–6.3 Notebook Review (pp. 270–271)
1. opposite; absolute value **2.** > **3.** > **4.** < **5.** <
6. 1 **7.** -11 **8.** -13 **9.** -28 **10.** 5 **11.** -9
12. -68 **13.** 17 **14.** The sum of the integers is positive if the absolute value of the positive integer is greater than the absolute value of the negative integer. The sum is negative if the absolute value of the negative integer is greater than the absolute value of the positive integer. **15.** 0

6.4 Getting Ready to Practice (p. 274) **1.** positive
3. 32 **5.** -25 **7.** -54 **9.** 18 **11.** Step 1: multiplication; Step 2: -16; Step 3: $3(-16) = -48°F$

6.4 Practice and Problem Solving (pp. 274–275)
13. 0 **15.** -40 **17.** -30 **19.** 28 **21.** -32 **23.** -45
25. -49 **27.** 25 **29.** 24 **31.** -10 **33.** -60 **35.** 4
37. 10 **39.** -8 **41.** $9(-3) = -27$ ft; 45 ft deep
43.

45. -6 **47.** 49

6.5 Problem Solving Strategies (p. 277) **1.** 75 ft^2
3. $28.36; divide $7,600 by 268 to find the average, instead of the much harder division problem $7,600,000,000 \div 268,000,000. **5.** 3.5 mi
7. 300 mi; Scott drove 140 miles; Dan drove 160 miles.

6.5 Getting Ready to Practice (p. 280) **1.** False; the quotient is only positive if the divisor and dividend have the same sign. **3.** False; division by zero is undefined, so $\frac{-5}{0}$ has no value. **5.** -3
7. -3 **9.** 6

6.5 Practice and Problem Solving (pp. 281–282)
11. -4 **13.** -7 **15.** 4 **17.** -7 **19.** -3 **21.** 0
23. -1 **25.** -5.5 **27.** 0 **29.** $-58°F$ **31.** $-25°C$
33. $26.80 **35.** 320°F **37.** -2 **39.** 9 **41.** -2
43. 14 **45.** When $\frac{9}{5}$ and 32 are rounded to their greatest place value position, they would be 2 and 30, respectively. Therefore, $2C + 30$ is a good estimate of $\frac{9}{5}C + 32$ when converting a Celsius temperature to Fahrenheit; 0°F. **47.** $=$ **49.** $<$
51. $>$ **53.** $>$ **55.** $<$ **59.** $7\frac{7}{9}$ **61.** $1\frac{5}{11}$ **63.** -174
65. 5360 **67.** $\frac{5}{9}$ **69.** $\frac{1}{3}$

6.6 Getting Ready to Practice (p. 286)
1. 1 **3.** 0 **5.** $\frac{2}{5}$ **7.** $\frac{-7}{9}$

9. $3\left(\frac{1}{2}\right)\left(\frac{1}{3}\right)$ [original expression]
$= 3\left(\frac{1}{3}\right)\left(\frac{1}{2}\right)$ [commutative property of multiplication]
$= 1\left(\frac{1}{2}\right)$ [inverse property of multiplication]
$= \frac{1}{2}$ [identity property of multiplication]

11. $7 \cdot 13 \cdot \frac{1}{7}$ [original expression]
$= 7 \cdot \frac{1}{7} \cdot 13$ [commutative property of multiplication]
$= \left(7 \cdot \frac{1}{7}\right) \cdot 13$ [associative property of multiplication]
$= 1(13)$ [inverse property of multiplication]
$= 13$ [identity property of multiplication]

13. $-8\frac{4}{25}, -\frac{631}{100}, -5.87, 1.97$; Southeast; Southwest

6.6 Practice and Problem Solving (pp. 286–287)
15. $\frac{38}{7}; \frac{7}{38}; -\frac{38}{7}$ **17.** $\frac{21}{1}; \frac{1}{21}; -21$ **19.** $-2\frac{2}{3}, -\frac{5}{4},$
$-0.85, 0, 3$ **21.** $-4\frac{7}{8}, -\frac{22}{5}, -4.25, -3, 1$

23. $7(-8)(5)$ [original expression]
$= 7[(-8)5]$ [associative property of multiplication]
$= 7(-40) = -280$ [Multiply -8 and 5, then 7 and -40.]

25. $\frac{1}{2} + \frac{4}{7} + \left(-\frac{1}{2}\right)$ [original expression]
$= \frac{1}{2} + \left(-\frac{1}{2}\right) + \frac{4}{7}$ [commutative property of addition]
$= \left[\frac{1}{2} + \left(-\frac{1}{2}\right)\right] + \frac{4}{7}$ [associative property of addition]
$= 0 + \frac{4}{7}$ [inverse property of addition]
$= \frac{4}{7}$ [identity property of addition]

27. $2(3)(35)$ [original expression]
$= 2(35)(3)$ [commutative property of multiplication]
$= [2(35)](3)$ [associative property of multiplication]
$= 70(3) = 210$ [Multiply 2 and 35, then 70 and 3.]

29. $a + (4.8 + b)$ [original expression]
$= -2.5 + [4.8 + (-6.5)]$ [Substitute -2.5 for a and -6.5 for b.]
$= -2.5 + [-6.5 + 4.8]$ [commutative property of addition]
$= [-2.5 + (-6.5)] + 4.8$ [associative property of addition]
$= -9 + 4.8 = -4.2$ [Add -2.5 and -6.5, then -9 and 4.8.]
31. $<$ **33.** $>$ **37.** 81 **39.** 60 **41.** -16 **43.** 20
45. 300 **47.** $15,000$

6.7 Getting Ready to Practice (p. 290)
1. equivalent **7.** $\$.70(10 + 6) = \$.70(10) + \$.70(6)$

6.7 Practice and Problem Solving (pp. 290–291)
9. $4(4) + 4(5)$ **11.** $8(100) - 8(4)$ **13.** $4\left(\dfrac{3}{5} + \dfrac{2}{5}\right)$
15. 44 **17.** 11 **19.** 31.2 **21.** $20(1 - 0.05); 20 - 1 = \$19$ **23.** 40 **25.** $4(8) + 4(2) = 4(8 + 2)$ **29.** $-9, -8, -5, 7, 8, 9, 10$ **31.** $-\dfrac{16}{3}, -\dfrac{21}{4}, -5, -4.8, -\dfrac{22}{5}$

6.8 Getting Ready to Practice (p. 295)
1. x-axis **3–5.**
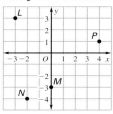
3. on the y-axis
5. Quadrant I

6.8 Practice and Problem Solving (pp. 296–298)
7. $(2, 2)$ **9.** $(-3, -4)$ **11.** $(4, -3)$ **13.** $(0, 2)$
15. $(3, 3)$ **17–23.**
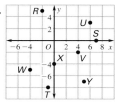
17. Quadrant II **19.** Quadrant III **21.** Quadrant IV
23. the y-axis **25.** $(4, -8)$
27.
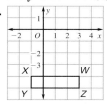
4 units, 1 unit, 4 square units

29.
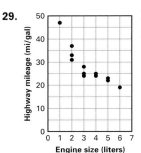
Mileage tends to decrease as engine size increases.

31. Both are positive. **33.** The y-coordinate is zero.
35. x is negative; y is positive. **37.** $(6, -7)$ has the drill move 6 units right and 7 units down, while $(-7, 6)$ has the drill move 7 units left and 6 units up. Both require the drill to move a total of 13 units, 6 one way and 7 another, but the directions of movement are opposites. **39.** V: $(1, -4)$; W: $(-7, 0)$; X: $(-5, 5)$; Y: $(0, -2)$; Z: $(3, 2)$ **41.** A, B, and D are not, C is. **43.** 12 **45.** 13.8 **47.** 4 boxes

6.8 Technology Activity (p. 299)
1–3.
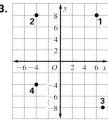
1. Quadrant I
3. Quadrant IV

6.4–6.8 Notebook Review (pp. 300–301)
1. origin **2.** 40 **3.** -48 **4.** 0 **5.** -8
6. $\dfrac{5}{8} \cdot \dfrac{3}{16} \cdot \dfrac{8}{5}$ [original expression]
$= \dfrac{5}{8} \cdot \dfrac{8}{5} \cdot \dfrac{3}{16}$ [commutative property of multiplication]
$= \left(\dfrac{5}{8} \cdot \dfrac{8}{5}\right) \cdot \dfrac{3}{16}$ [associative property of multiplication]
$= 1 \cdot \dfrac{3}{16}$ [inverse property of multiplication]
$= \dfrac{3}{16}$ [identity property of multiplication]
7. $-3(1.2)$ [original expression]
$= -3(1 + 0.2)$ [addition fact]
$= -3(1) + (-3)(0.2)$ [distributive property]
$= -3 + (-0.6) = -3.6$ [Multiply -3 and 1, and -3 and 0.2, then add terms.]

8. $-4(7)(-5)$ [original expression]
$= -4(-5)(7)$ [commutative property of multiplication]
$= [-4(-5)](7)$ [associative property of multiplication]
$= 20(7) = 140$ [Multiply -4 and -5, then 20 and 7.]

9. $4(3.2) + 4(0.8)$ [original expression]
$= 4(3.2 + 0.8)$ [distributive property]
$= 4(4) = 16$ [Add 3.2 and 0.8, then multiply 4 and 4.]

10. $12(10.2)$ [original expression]
$= 12(10 + 0.2)$ [addition fact]
$= 12(10) + 12(0.2)$ [distributive property]
$= 120 + 2.4 = 122.4$ [Multiply 12 and 10, and 12 and 0.2, then add terms.]

11. $-3.7 + 8 + (-4.3)$ [original expression]
$= -3.7 + (-4.3) + 8$ [commutative property of addition]
$= [-3.7 + (-4.3)] + 8$ [associative property of addition]
$= -8 + 8$ [Add -3.7 and -4.3.]
$= 0$ [inverse property of addition]

12–15.

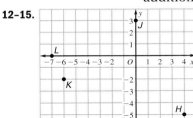

12. Quadrant IV   **13.** on the y-axis   **14.** Quadrant III
15. on the x-axis   **16.** No; $[(-12) \div 6] \div (-2) = [-2] \div (-2) = 1$, while $(-12) \div [6 \div (-2)] = (-12) \div [-3] = 4$.

Chapter Review (pp. 302–303)   **1.** -4 and 4
3. A rational number is any number that can be written as the ratio of two integers.   **5.** The multiplicative inverse of a number has the same sign as the number. When you multiply a number and its multiplicative inverse you get 1. The additive inverse has the same absolute value as the number, but the opposite sign.   **7.** $>$ **9.** $<$
11. $-10, -8, 7, 8, 9, 11$ **13.** -350 **15.** 15   **17.** -10

19. 75   **21.** -38 **23.** 37   **25.** -26 **27.** $-40°C$
29. -100 **31.** -3 **33.** 0   **35.** -54 **37.** $2.4 = \dfrac{12}{5}$,
$-2.1 = \dfrac{-21}{10}, -2\dfrac{4}{5} = \dfrac{-14}{5}, 2 = \dfrac{2}{1}, 2\dfrac{1}{9} = \dfrac{19}{9}$;
ordered: $-2\dfrac{4}{5}, -2.1, 2, 2\dfrac{1}{9}, 2.4$

39. $12 \cdot (-27) \cdot \dfrac{1}{12}$ [original expression]
$= 12 \cdot \dfrac{1}{12} \cdot (-27)$ [commutative property of multiplication]
$= \left(12 \cdot \dfrac{1}{12}\right) \cdot (-27)$ [associative property of multiplication]
$= 1 \cdot (-27)$ [inverse property of multiplication]
$= -27$ [identity property of multiplication]

41. $-\dfrac{1}{4} \cdot 1 \cdot (-4)$ [original expression]
$= -\dfrac{1}{4} \cdot [1 \cdot (-4)]$ [associative property of multiplication]
$= -\dfrac{1}{4} \cdot (-4)$ [identity property of multiplication]
$= 1$ [inverse property of multiplication]

43. $4(0.4 - 0.02)$; 1.52   **45.** $9(2.6 + 5.4)$; 72
47–49.

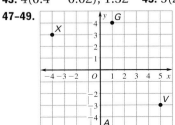

47. Quadrant IV
49. Quadrant I

51.

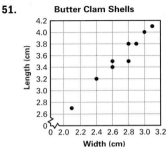

Butter Clam Shells

As the butter clam shell's width increases, its length also increases.

Chapter 7

7.1 Getting Ready to Practice (p. 319)
1. verbal model

7.1 Practice and Problem Solving (pp. 319–321)
7. $-7 + x$ **9.** $\frac{1}{3}x$ **11.** $-50 - x$ **13.** $y + (-9) = 24$
15. $13 = 5 - y$ **17.** $-4x + 3 = 27$ **19–25.** Answers
may vary. **19.** the product of a number and 13
21. 10 divided by a number **23.** 8 more than a
number is 34. **25.** The quotient of 90 and a
number is 1. **27.** $2s$; let s be the team's score.
29. $a - 5$; let a be Ann's height. **31.** $T - 24 = 75$; 99°
33. $b + 30 = 100$; $70 **35.** $t + 15 = 512$; 8 h 17 min
37. $n^2 + 4$ **39.** $\frac{1}{3}n = -8 + n$ **41.** No; suppose you
let n represent the number, then "three less than a
number" is $n - 3$, while "the difference of three
and a number" is $3 - n$. **43.** $(w + 5)w$; 24 in.²

45–47. 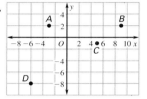 **45.** Quadrant II
47. Quadrant IV

49. 15 houses. *Sample answer:* I used the strategy
Make a List. I listed all of the numbers between
1 and 60 that have a 2 in them, then counted how
many there were. **51.** 14 in.

7.2 Getting Ready to Practice (p. 324)
1. 5, 2; -7, 1; $5z$ and $2z$, -7 and 1 **3.** $24 + 4b$
5. $2(3w) + 2w$; $8w$

7.2 Practice and Problem Solving (pp. 324–325)
7. -4, 5; 10, -8; $-4y$ and $5y$, 10 and -8
9. $12t + 15$ **11.** $-1 + l$ **13.** 19 **15.** $6 - 4j$ **17.** $6b$
19. $2(x + 10) + 2x$; $4x + 20$ **21.** $2(w + 30) + 2w$;
$4w + 60$ **23.** 0 **25.** $5 + 6s$ **27.** $7a - 2 - 2b$
29. $10 + n + 2n$; $10 + 3n$ **31.** no **33.** no
35.

37. *Sample answer:* A number divided by 6
39. *Sample answer:* Twice the sum of a number
and 2 **41.** 2.0706

7.3 Getting Ready to Practice (p. 329) **1.** *Sample answer:* addition and subtraction **3.** 3 **5.** 5
7. -25 **9.** $p - 1.50 = 5.75$; $7.25

7.3 Practice and Problem Solving (pp. 330–331)
11. -30 **13.** -20 **15.** 9.1 **17.** 20.7 **19.** $p - 5 = -17$; -12 **21.** gold: $n + 79 = 197$, 118; silver: $n + 47 = 108$, 61; uranium: $n + 92 = 238$, 146 **23.** R
25. 27.8 **27.** $-\frac{5}{7}$ **29.** $-\frac{1}{35}$ **31.** $4.2 + 5 + 3.9 + x = 21.5$; 8.4 in. **35.** -4 **37.** 4 **39–43.** Sample answers
are given. **39.** The sum of 6 and a number is 22.
41. 200; 250 **43.** 70; 100

7.4 Getting Ready to Practice (p. 335) **1.** division
3. 5 **5.** 3 **7.** 72 **9.** 20 **11.** $300 = 7.5r$; 40 mi/h

7.4 Practice and Problem Solving (pp. 336–337)
13. Divide both sides by -16. **15.** Multiply both
sides by 15. **17.** $\frac{1}{6}$ **19.** -7 **21.** 5 **23.** -12
25. -198 **27.** -154 **29.** -7 **31.** 12 **33.** $7.5w = 45$;
6 m **35.** $2n = -100$; -50 **37.** -1.33 **39.** -0.41
41. 1.36 **43.** 0.75 **45.** $7n = 11,200$; 1600 people/h
47. 64 in.² **49.** 2.3 times **51.** $4(90) = 13.3r$;
27.1 ft/sec **53.** 1.02×10^4 **55.** 1.205×10^7 **57.** -5
59. $-4\frac{1}{2}$ **61.** 150 **63.** 4.25 **65.** 255

7.1–7.4 Notebook Review (pp. 338–339)
1. 15, 4; -6, 13; $15y$ and $4y$, -6 and 13 **2.** $2 + w$
3. $2(w + 4)$ **4.** $w - 8 = -25$ **5.** $\frac{4w}{7} = 6$ **6.** $8x - 4$
7. $17 - 4y$ **8.** $2 - 3g$ **9.** 16 **10.** 14 **11.** 1.8 **12.** 2
13. 16 **14.** 2.86 **15.** *Sample answer:* 12 years from
now your grandfather will be 75. **16.** *Sample
answer:* $2x + 10 + 16x - 3$

7.5 Problem Solving Strategies (p. 341) **1.** $20
3. 45 min **5.** Alex had 20, while Chris and Betty
each had 8. **7.** No. *Sample answer:* If you spent
exactly $15 for the week, that would be an average
of $3 a day. You only exceeded $3 on two days, by
a total of $.40, and you spent $2.50 on Monday.
Since $2.50 + $.40 < $3, the total for the week
must be less than $15. **9.** 55 bricks

7.5 Getting Ready to Practice (p. 344) **1.** the
addition property of equality and the division
property of equality **3.** 2 **5.** 55

7.5 Practice and Problem Solving (pp. 344–345)
7. C, A, D, B   **9.** 5   **11.** 8   **13.** 12   **15.** 64   **17.** 30
19. 3   **21.** $8 + 4n = -4$; -3 **23.** 15 min   **25.** 50 ft
27. $\frac{1}{4}$ **29.** $-1\frac{3}{4}$ **31.** $-2\frac{3}{4}$ **33.** 87   **35.** $>$ **37.** $=$
39. 5   **41.** 35.7   **43.** true

7.6 Getting Ready to Practice (p. 348)
1. The graph of the solution of an inequality is a ray—an infinite set of points. The graph of the solution of an equation is a single point.

3.
$-8 \quad -6 \quad -4 \quad -2 \quad 0$

5.
$0 \quad 2 \quad 4 \quad 6 \quad 8 \quad 10 \quad 12 \quad 14$

7. $b \geq -9$;
$-12 \; -10 \; -8 \; -6 \; -4 \; -2 \; 0$

9. $x < -12$;
$-16 \quad -12 \quad -8 \quad -4 \quad 0$

7.6 Practice and Problem Solving (pp. 348–349)
11. yes   **13.** no   **15.** $n > 2$ **17.** $t \leq 5$

19. $y \geq 18$;
$0 \quad 4 \quad 8 \quad 12 \quad 16 \quad 20$

21. $p \geq 10$;
$-2 \quad 0 \quad 2 \quad 4 \quad 6 \quad 8 \quad 10 \quad 12$

23. $t \geq -14$;
$-16 \quad -12 \quad -8 \quad -4 \quad 0$

25. $e > 22$;
$0 \quad 4 \quad 8 \quad 12 \quad 16 \quad 20 \quad 24 \quad 28$

27. $x \geq 3$;
$-1 \quad 0 \quad 1 \quad 2 \quad 3 \quad 4 \quad 5 \quad 6$

29. $c > 136$;
$130 \quad 132 \quad 134 \quad 136$

31. $s \geq -6$;
$-8 \quad -6 \quad -4 \quad -2 \quad 0$

33. $z > 25$;
$0 \quad 5 \quad 10 \quad 15 \quad 20 \quad 25 \quad 30 \quad 35$

35. $b > 11$;
$0 \quad 2 \quad 4 \quad 6 \quad 8 \quad 10 \quad 12 \quad 14$

37. $x \geq -4$;
$-6 \; -5 \; -4 \; -3 \; -2 \; -1 \; 0 \; 1$

39. *Sample answer:* You already have 3 people riding in your van, which can accommodate at most 10 people, including the driver. x is the number of additional people that can come along.
43. -9 **45.** -35 **47.** 1

7.7 Getting Ready to Practice (p. 352)
1. *Sample answer:* A function is a rule that matches each input value with a unique output value.   **3.** You have switched the values of the inputs with the outputs. When $x = 0$, y is supposed to equal -2, which is backwards from the way the table is set up.

Similarly, when $x = 1$, $y = 1 - 2 = -1$. When $x = 2$, $y = 2 - 2 = 0$. And when $x = 3$, $y = 3 - 2 = 1$. The correct table is

Input x	0	1	2	3
Output y	-2	-1	0	1

7.7 Practice and Problem Solving (pp. 352–353)
5. 10   **7.** 1

9.

Input x	-2	-1	0	1	2
Output y	9	10	11	12	13

range: 9, 10, 11, 12, 13

11.

Input x	-2	-1	0	1	2
Output y	-7.4	-3.7	0	3.7	7.4

range: $-7.4, -3.7, 0, 3.7, 7.4$

13.

Input x	-2	-1	0	1	2
Output y	-2.6	-1.8	-1	-0.2	0.6

range: $-2.6, -1.8, -1, -0.2, 0.6$
15. $y = 5x$ **17.** $y = x - 1.2$ **19.** $m = 12y$; 240 months   **21.** $y = x^2$ **23.** yes; $q = p^2$ **25.** yes; $n = 2m + 1$ **29.** $z > -2$;
$-4 \; -3 \; -2 \; -1 \; 0 \; 1 \; 2$

31–33.

7.8 Getting Ready to Practice (p. 356)
1. A linear function is one whose graph is a line; a nonlinear function has a graph that is not a line.

5.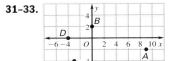
$y = 2x$

7.8 Practice and Problem Solving (pp. 356–358)
7.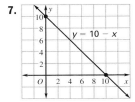
$y = 10 - x$

9.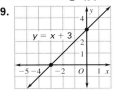
$y = x + 3$

11.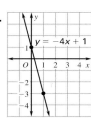

13.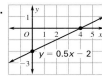

15. $y = 1.5x$;

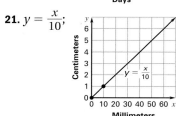

17. *Sample answer:* The distance you travel, driving at a constant rate of speed for a number of hours.

19. $y = \dfrac{x}{7}$;

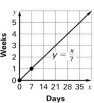

21. $y = \dfrac{x}{10}$;

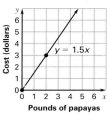

23. It is a function; linear.

25. $y = 3x + 2$;

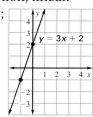

27. $y = -3x + 6$;

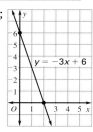

29. 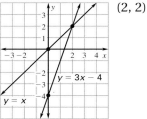 $(2, 2)$

31. 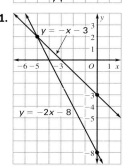 $(-5, 2)$ **35.** $\dfrac{11}{49}$ **37.** $\dfrac{5}{6}$

7.8 Technology Activity (p. 359) **1.** $0.8; 4.2$ **3.** $1; 7$
5. $-0.6; -1.6$ **7.** $(-1, 3); 3 = 2(-1) + 5$ and $3 = -(-1) + 2$

7.5–7.8 Notebook Review (pp. 360–361) **1.** The domain is the set of input values; the range is the set of output values.   **2.** -2 **3.** 29 **4.** -200

5. $y \le -15$;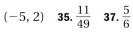

6. $x > 11$;

7. $w < 12$;

8.

Input x	−2	−1	0	1
Output y	−7	−6	−5	−4

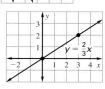

9.

Input x	−2	−1	0	1
Output y	9	6	3	0

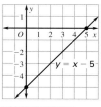

10.

Input x	−1	0	1	3
Output y	$-\dfrac{2}{3}$	0	$\dfrac{2}{3}$	2

11. *Sample answer:* $y = -2x$; $y = x^2 - 5x - 18$

Chapter Review (pp. 362–363)

1. equivalent **3.** domain

5. *Sample answer:* $x < 5$;

7. $m - 9$ **9.** $\dfrac{m}{-5}$ **11.** $16m = 48$ **13.** $-16 + m = 11$

15. $24 = 5 + n$; 19 students **17.** $-6e + 2$ **19.** 21

21. -17 **23.** -33 **25.** -60 **27.** 3 **29.** 2.5

31. $a - 55.4 = 552.3$; 607.7 mi^2 **33.** $x > 1$

35. $x > 12$;

37. $z \geq -3.6$;

39.

Input x	-4	-2	0	2	4
Output y	-1	1	3	5	7

range: $-1, 1, 3, 5, 7$

41.

Input x	-4	-2	0	2	4
Output y	0	1	2	3	4

range: $0, 1, 2, 3, 4$

43. $y = x + 4$

45.

$y = 9 - 2x$

47.

$y = 0.2x + 5$

Chapter 8

8.1 Getting Ready to Practice (p. 371)
1. *Sample answer:* The ratio of boys to girls in my class is $12 : 10$. **3.** $1 : 1$; $\dfrac{1}{1}$; 1 to 1 **5.** $15 : 2$; $\dfrac{15}{2}$; 15 to 2 **7.** $\dfrac{11}{5}$

8.1 Practice and Problem Solving (pp. 371–373)
9. $\dfrac{41}{39}$ **11.** $\dfrac{39}{80}$ **13.** $43 : 13$; $\dfrac{43}{13}$; 43 to 13 **15.** $\dfrac{4}{5}$ **17.** $\dfrac{9}{5}$

19. $\dfrac{2}{3}$ **21.** $\dfrac{1}{2}$ **23.** $\dfrac{5}{2}$ **25.** $\dfrac{6}{1}$ **27.** $\dfrac{1}{6}$ **29.** $\dfrac{84}{5}$ **31.** $=$

33. $\dfrac{21}{4}$ **35.** $1970 : 1.52$; $1998 : 0.75$ **39.** 45 **43.** 9

45. 48 **47.** 868 **49.** 45

8.2 Getting Ready to Practice (p. 376)
1. rate
5. Step 1: 5.8 words per second; Step 2: 4 words per second; Step 3: Sean's rate is slower than that of a "fast talker".

8.2 Practice and Problem Solving (pp. 376–377)
7. $\dfrac{6 \text{ L}}{1 \text{ day}}$ **9.** $\dfrac{\$3.20}{1 \text{ person}}$ **11.** 1.8 cups per pie
13. 1.5 m/sec **15.** 0.5 ft/sec **17.** 6.1 mi/h
19. 2 quarts for \$2.78 **21.** 1.028 g/mL **23.** 240 mi
27–29.

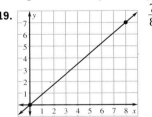

27. on the x-axis
29. Quadrant III
31. $\dfrac{1}{3}$ **33.** $\dfrac{3}{35}$
35. $=$ **37.** $<$

8.3 Getting Ready to Practice (p. 380)
1. rise; run **3.** $\dfrac{3}{4}$ **5.** 4 mi

8.3 Practice and Problem Solving (pp. 381–382)
7. negative **9.** positive **11.** $-\dfrac{2}{3}$ **13.** The graph will show a straight line. The slope of the line is the rate at which you are walking. **15.** \$6/h
17. *Sample answer:* The total number of words typed over a period of steady typing. A good typist will type about the same number of words each minute, and the total number of words typed will be represented by a straight line.

19.

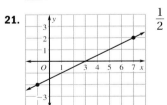

$\dfrac{7}{8}$

21.

$\dfrac{1}{2}$

23.

-3 **25.**

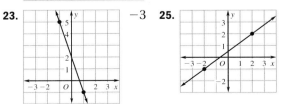

27. The Leatherback turtle; its line is steeper
29. perimeter: 4, 8, 12, 16 **33.** $-\frac{1}{6}$ **35.** 77.7
37. $\frac{2}{5}$ **39.** $\frac{1}{20}$

8.3 Technology Activity (p. 383) **1.** 4 **3.** -3
5. They are the same.

8.1–8.3 Notebook Review (pp. 384–385)
1. unit rate **2.** > **3.** < **4.** = **5.** 2.2 ounce bag
6.
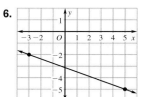
$-\frac{3}{8}$ **7.** 40 mi/h

8.4 Getting Ready to Practice (p. 389)
1. proportion

8.4 Practice and Problem Solving (pp. 390–391)
9. 1 **11.** 20 **13.** 18 **15.** 15 **17.** 3750 words
19. 285 lb **21.** Biscuits: 80; Flour: 3 **23.** $\frac{6}{16} = \frac{z}{40}$; 15
25. 4200 people **31.** 0.1, 0.6, 0.$\overline{6}$, $\frac{6}{7}$, $\frac{12}{5}$
33. 0.$\overline{1}$, 0.15, $\frac{2}{5}$, 1.1 **35.**

37. >

8.5 Problem Solving Strategies (p. 393)
1. between the blue and yellow stripes **3.** 6 people
5. 32 color photos **7.** 6:40 P.M. **9.** blue

8.5 Getting Ready to Practice (p. 396) **1.** 2 · 35
and 7 · 10 **3.** 2 **5.** 9

8.5 Practice and Problem Solving (pp. 396–398)
9. 8 **11.** 35 **13.** 8 **15.** 7 **17.** 6.25 **19.** 4.4 **21.** 108
times **23.** 7.5 g **25.** 30,000 females **27.** do form a
proportion **29.** don't form a proportion **31.** Yes.
Sample answer: 71.4 is 7 times 10.2, and 88.9 is
7 times 12.7. **35.** False. *Sample answer:* $\frac{2}{3} = \frac{6}{9}$, but
$\frac{2}{9} \neq \frac{6}{3}$. **41.** $9n = -54$; -6 **43.** 6 **45.** 3 **47.** 8.68 ft^2
49. 78.288 in.^{2}

8.6 Getting Ready to Practice (p. 402) **1.** True;
the scale gives the ratio of a measurement on the
drawing to the corresponding measurement of
the actual object. **7.** 1 : 12

8.6 Practice and Problem Solving (pp. 402–403)
9. 250 mi **11.** 217.5 mi **13.** *Sample answer:* 14.0 m
15. *Sample answer:* 31.6 m **17.** 5 ft **19.** If a drawing
is not to scale, distances in the drawing are not
in the same proportion as the corresponding
distances in the real world. **21.** about 760 cm or
7.6 m **25.** $\frac{7}{25}$ **27.** $5\frac{1}{40}$ **29.** 0.01

8.4–8.6 Notebook Review (pp. 404–405)
1. proportion **2–9.** Methods may vary. **2.** 25;
equivalent ratios **3.** 2; equivalent ratios **4.** 8;
algebra **5.** 2; algebra **6.** 9; cross products **7.** 25;
cross products **8.** 13.5; cross products **9.** 20;
cross products **10.** 10 months **11.** 9 ft **12.** Yes;
they are equivalent ratios, since $4 \times 9 = 36$ and
$4 \times 26 = 104$.

Chapter Review (pp. 406–407) **7.** $\frac{9}{1}$ **9.** $\frac{4}{7}$ **11.** $\frac{1}{5}$
13. $\frac{12}{1}$ **15.** \$5 per person **17.** \$1.75 per soda
19. 5 brushes for \$2.75 **21.** $-\frac{1}{2}$ **23–29.** Methods
may vary. **23.** 45; equivalent ratios **25.** 7.5; algebra
27. 3; algebra **29.** 2; cross products **31.** $\frac{4}{11} = \frac{10}{p}$;
27.5 **33.** 12 tablespoons **35.** 24 ft **37.** 66 ft

Chapter 9

9.1 Getting Ready to Practice (p. 417)
1. per hundred **3.** $\frac{23}{100}$ **5.** $\frac{1}{5}$ **7.** 52% **9.** 40%
11. 27 **13.** 51

9.1 Practice and Problem Solving (pp. 417–418)
15. $\frac{67}{100}$ **17.** $\frac{23}{25}$ **19.** $\frac{2}{25}$ **21.** $\frac{19}{25}$ **23.** 44% **25.** 32%
27. 15% **29.** 90% **31.** 15 **33.** 6 **35.** 38 **37.** 100
39. 90% have attached garages **41.** $\frac{x}{100}$; 65
43. $\frac{z}{100}$; 10 **45.** $\frac{19}{20}$; $\frac{3}{100}$ **47.** 10 mL **49.** 4 to 5, 81%,
$\frac{41}{50}$ **51.** 33 **53.** 16 **55.** 1 in. : 5 ft or 1 : 60
57. 0.00036 **59.** 119.64852

9.2 Getting Ready to Practice (p. 422)

1. a represents the part, b represents the base, and p represents the percent. **3.** $a = 18$, $b = 30$, p is the unknown percent; 60%. **5.** $a = 30$, b is unknown, $p = 75$; 40. **7.** a is unknown, $b = 200$, $p = 32$; 64. **9.** 25,000 m, or 25 km

9.2 Practice and Problem Solving (pp. 423–424)

11. $\frac{a}{50} = \frac{30}{100}$; 15 **15.** 10% **17.** 300 **19.** 49
21. 30% **23.** 40 **25.** 8 **27.** *Sample answer:* On one side of the proportion is the quantity $\frac{a}{b}$, where a is the part of the whole and b is the base. On the other side of the proportion is $\frac{p}{100}$, where p is the percent. **29.** 48% of the games **31.** 22% **33.** 31%

37.
```
1 | 6 9
2 | 2
3 | 0 1 1
4 |
5 | 1
```
Key: 3 | 1 = 31

39. $\frac{18}{25}$ **41.** $\frac{7}{20}$
43. 1, 9, 17, 25, 102

9.3 Getting Ready to Practice (p. 427)
1. *Sample answer:* 3.05; 0.0003 **3.** 0.03 **5.** 0.0002 **7.** 2.08
9. 64.2% **11.** 0.105% **13.** 1550% **15.** 77.8%
17. 56.3%

9.3 Practice and Problem Solving (pp. 428–429)
19. 0.11 **21.** 2.1 **23.** 0.0015 **25.** 0.0301 **27.** 26%
29. 4.9% **31.** 0.5% **33.** 214% **35.** 73.3%
37. 94.4% **39.** 35.9% **41.** 40.8% **43.** 16; 24; 32.
Sample answer: These are just multiples of 8. For example, 500% of 8 would be $5 \cdot 8 = 40$. **45.** No; at most 100% can respond in the affirmative.
47. Yes; your last score must have been fairly low, and then you scored much better on the next test.
49. about 37,400,000 people **51.** 0.923; $\frac{923}{1000}$
53. 2.52; $2\frac{13}{25}$ **55.** $\frac{877}{10,000}$; 8.77% **57.** $3\frac{13}{100}$; 313%
59. < **61.** = **63.** < **65.** $84.87 **69.** 4 **71.** 27
73. 196 **75.** 84 **77.** *Sample answer:* 105
79. *Sample answer:* 350

9.4 Problem Solving Strategies (p. 431) 1. 6 girls
3. $2 **5.** 8 doughnuts and 8 bagels **7.** 5 h
9. 12 different ways

9.4 Getting Ready to Practice (p. 434) 1. The
part of the base is equal to the percent times the base. **3.** 200 **5.** 90% **7.** 140 **9.** 28 games

9.4 Practice and Problem Solving (pp. 434–435)
11. 30 **13.** 48% **15.** 25 **17.** 17% **19.** 50 **21.** 2
23. $86.25 **25.** 25% of 44 **27.** 65% **29.** 14%
31. 5%; 105 students **33.** 0.992 **35.** 12.6 **37.** $\frac{47}{50}$
39. $\frac{2}{5}$ **41–43.** Check work.

9.1–9.4 Notebook Review (pp. 436–437)
1. Move the decimal point two places to the right, and write the percent sign after the number.
2. $\frac{9}{25}$ **3.** $\frac{13}{20}$ **4.** 8% **5.** 46% **6.** 12 **7.** 70 **8.** 75
9. 0.4% **10.** 63% **11.** 75 **12.** *Sample answer:* In 2000 you earned $89.00 babysitting your little sister. In 2001 you earned 110% of this amount. How much did you earn babysitting your little sister in 2001? $97.90. **13.** Greater than; 55% is greater than $\frac{1}{2}$, which is 50%. Since 60 is one half of 120, 55% will be greater than 60.

9.5 Getting Ready to Practice (p. 442)
1. Change each percent to a decimal and multiply by 360° to find the measure of each angle. Draw a circle, then use a protractor to mark each angle. Label the sections. **3.** 252° **5.** 72°

9.5 Practice and Problem Solving (pp. 443–444)
7. 18% **9.** car **11.** 162° **13.** A good response should include: • both used for categorical data • both show relative size of each category • one is a circle, the other vertical or horizontal bars • bar graph includes a scale that tells the length of each bar • circle graph shows relative size of each section • circle graph often used when data is given in percents

15.

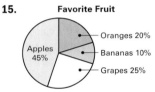

Favorite Fruit
Oranges 20%
Bananas 10%
Grapes 25%
Apples 45%

17.

Favorite Movie Type

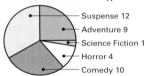

- Suspense 12
- Adventure 9
- Science Fiction 1
- Horror 4
- Comedy 10

21.

Chemical Composition of Earth

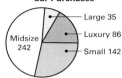

- Iron 34.6%
- Other 8%
- Magnesium 12.7%
- Silicon 15.2%
- Oxygen 29.5%

23. 40.1; 28; 27; 59.9

25. 43.2

27. 0.62; $\frac{31}{50}$

29. 0.23; $\frac{23}{100}$

9.5 Technology Activity (p. 445)

1.

Car Purchases

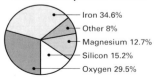

- Large 35
- Luxury 86
- Midsize 242
- Small 142

9.6 Getting Ready to Practice (p. 448)
1. If the new value is greater than the original value, there was a percent increase; if the new value is less than the original value, there was a percent decrease. **3.** increase; about 33.3% **5.** $4000

9.6 Practice and Problem Solving (pp. 448–449)
7. decrease; 58% **9.** decrease; about 72.2% **11.** increase; 30% **13.** 40% **15.** about 1,720,000 mi² **17.** golf: 15%; ice skating: 4%; snowboarding: 199% **19.** No. *Sample answer:* There were many fewer participants in snowboarding as compared to golf. So even though participation nearly tripled over the first ten year period, I wouldn't expect it to surpass golf any time soon.

21.

Participation in Various Sports by 7–17 Year Olds

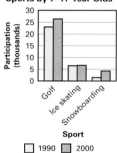

Sport

□ 1990 ▨ 2000

23. $0.41\overline{6}$ **25.** 0.8

9.7 Getting Ready to Practice (p. 452) **1.** 15
3. 15.75 **5.** Step 1: $12; Step 2: A discount; subtract it from the original price. Step 3: $36

9.7 Practice and Problem Solving (pp. 452–453)
7. $82.50 **9.** $51.75 **11.** $19.20 **13.** in-line skates: $164; skateboard: $225; scooter: $126 **15.** No; the 50% markup increased the price to $210. Now the 50% discount is taken from this larger amount, so the sale price will be $105, which is less than $140. **17.** Yes; the total cost of the books is $19.55, which is less than the $20 on your gift card. **19.** $25.50 **21.** 1.92 **23.** 0.1902 **25.** 12.5%

9.8 Getting Ready to Practice (p. 456) **1.** the principal **3.** $24; $124 **5.** $6; $206 **7.** 3 years

9.8 Practice and Problem Solving (pp. 456–457)
9. $9; $459 **11.** $128; $2128 **13.** $1; $401 **15.** $600 **17.** 6 months **19.** $500 **21.** 4 years **25.** 4 **27.** 50 **29.** 1 **31.** < **33.** >

9.5–9.8 Notebook Review (pp. 458–459)
1. interest rate, expressed as a decimal

2. Favorite Color **3.** 5% **4.** $28 **5.** 5 years

- Red 30
- Green 75
- Blue 45

6. A good answer will include: • finding the proportion or percent of each category • using these values to find the angle measure for each category • drawing a circle, and dividing it into sectors • labeling the graph **7.** Divide the amount of tax paid by the price, then convert to a percent.

Chapter Review (pp. 460–461) **1.** percent of change **3.** circle graph **5.** 60% **7.** $\frac{11}{20}$ **9.** Less than; 80 is exactly half of 160. 45% is less than $\frac{1}{2}$, so 45% of 160 would be less than 80. **11.** 90% **13.** 140 **15.** 0.14 **17.** 0.0025 **19.** 70.5% **21.** 0.41% **23.** 27 **25.** 150 **27.** 24 questions

29.

Breakfast Foods

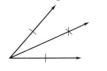

- Cold Cereal 45%
- Eggs 27.5%
- Other 5%
- French Toast 7.5%
- Pancakes 15%

31. 137.5% increase
33. 40% decrease
35. $18   **37.** $50.40
39. $319   **41.** 8.8%

27. 68; 112   **29.** 116; 64   **33.** $6\frac{3}{5}$, 6.64, $6\frac{2}{3}$, $\frac{27}{4}$

35. 60 min. *Sample answer:* Use the strategy Work Backward, since you know how many minutes were left over. Start with this figure, 24, and use the information in the problem to find out how many minutes there were to start with.

Chapter 10

10.1 Getting Ready to Practice (p. 477)
5. *Sample answer:* 32° and 58°

10.1 Practice and Problem Solving (pp. 477–478)
7. straight   **9.** right   **11.** supplementary;
145 + 35 = 180   **13.** neither; 47 + 41 = 88
15. 107°; 17°   **17.** 90°; not possible   **19.** 18°; not possible   **21.** 177°; 87°   **23.** 47°   **25.** The complementary angle. *Sample answer:* An angle complementary to 15° has a measure of 75°, while an angle supplementary to 125° has a measure of 55°.   **27.** never   **29.** 30°   **31.** 60°   **33.** All of the angles have a common vertex at F, and so $\angle F$ would be ambiguous.   **35.** $\frac{7}{25}$ **37.** $\frac{18}{25}$ **39.** $207
41. 45   **43.** 0.25

10.2 Getting Ready to Practice (p. 481)
1. adjacent; vertical   **3.** *Sample answer:* $\angle 1$ and $\angle 2$, $\angle 5$ and $\angle 6$ **5.** 120°

10.2 Practice and Problem Solving (pp. 482–483)
7. $\angle 1$ and $\angle 2$, $\angle 2$ and $\angle 3$, $\angle 3$ and $\angle 4$, $\angle 4$ and $\angle 1$
9. 147°   **11.** Two of the angles have measure 108°, since they each form adjacent supplementary angles to the first angle. The third angle has a measure of 72°, since it is vertical to the first angle.
13. perpendicular   **15.** 123°   **17.** 123°   **19.** 99°
21. always   **23.** always   **25.** 117°   **27.** 90°
29. 127°   **31.** >   **33.** <   **35.** obtuse   **37.** straight
39. 14 m; 10 m²

10.3 Getting Ready to Practice (p. 487)   **1.** False.
Sample answer: If one angle has a measure over 90°, the triangle is an obtuse triangle.   **3.** 33°
5. right   **7.** scalene

10.3 Practice and Problem Solving (pp. 487–489)
9. 96   **11.** 27   **13.** 33.2°   **15.** 20.9°   **17.** 136   **19.** 135°
21. acute   **23.** scalene   **25.** equilateral and isosceles

Special Topic Exercises (pp. 490–491)
3. A sample construction is shown.

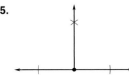

5.

Two lines are perpendicular if they intersect in right angles. A straight angle has a measure of 180°. When you bisect it, you get two angles with a measure of 90°. This means the two lines are perpendicular.   **7.**

10.4 Problem Solving Strategies (pp. 492–493)
1. 6400 ft²   **3.** 88 in.²   **5.** Patrick   **7.** *Sample answer:* 860 pages

10.4 Getting Ready to Practice (p. 496)
1. a rectangle; a square   **3.** polygon; hexagon
5. Steps 1 and 2:   Step 3: 720°

10.4 Practice and Problem Solving (pp. 497–498)
7.   parallelogram

9. Parallelogram; not regular; not all sides and not all angles are congruent.   **11.** Trapezoid; not regular; not all angles and not all sides are congruent.   **13.** triangle; regular   **15.** Check sketches. *Sample answer:* Hexagon, trapezoid, isosceles triangle, rhombus; no; none of the polygons appear to have all sides congruent and all angles congruent.   **17.** True; a square is a parallelogram with four right angles.

19. False; a trapezoid has only one pair of parallel sides.   **21.** 5.75 cm

23.

Polygon	Triangle	Quadrilateral	Pentagon	Hexagon
Sum of angle measures	180°	360°	540°	720°
Measure of each angle in a regular polygon	60°	90°	108°	120°

25. 900°; $128\frac{4}{7}°$ **27.** Square; all squares have four sides of equal length and four right angles, each of measure 90°.   **29.** obtuse   **31.** 9   **33.** 625

10.1–10.4 Notebook Review (pp. 499–500) **1.** An equilateral triangle is also an isosceles triangle because it has at least 2 sides that are congruent. **2.** 105°   **3.** 105°   **4.** a polygon; pentagon   **5.** not a polygon; not made up only of line segments **6.** Since the sum of all three angle measures is 180° and a right angle has a measure of 90°, the measures of the two acute angles must add up to 90° also. So they are complements of one another. **7.** The angles adjacent to the acute angle are supplements of it, so they are obtuse. The other angle is a vertical angle to the first one, so it is congruent to it and must be acute.

10.5 Getting Ready to Practice (p. 504)
1. similar   **3.** $\frac{2}{3}$

10.5 Practice and Problem Solving (pp. 504–505)
5. The corresponding sides are $\overline{FG}$ and $\overline{JK}$, $\overline{GH}$ and $\overline{KL}$, and $\overline{FH}$ and $\overline{JL}$. The corresponding angles are $\angle F$ and $\angle J$, $\angle G$ and $\angle K$, and $\angle H$ and $\angle L$. $m\angle H = 60°$; $m\angle J = 45°$; $m\angle K = 75°$ **7.** similar; $\frac{1}{2}$

9. similar; $\frac{5}{4}$ **11.** False. *Sample answer:* A 2 by 10 rectangle has the same perimeter as a 3 by 9 rectangle, but they are not congruent.   **13.** A good answer should include: • sketches of a rectangle similar to *DEFG* and a rectangle congruent to *DEFG* • all angles are right angles and therefore corresponding angles are congruent

• the ratios of corresponding side lengths for the similar rectangle to the side lengths of *DEFG* being 4 : 5 • the side lengths of the congruent rectangle being 4 inches and 5 inches   **17.** 64 m **19.** divisible by 2, 3, and 6   **21.** divisible by 2

10.6 Getting Ready to Practice (p. 508)
1. proportion   **3.** 4 in.

10.6 Practice and Problem Solving (pp. 508–509)
5. 12 cm   **7.** 30 in.   **9.** 18 ft   **11.** 1.8 m; 1.56 m; 1.38 m   **13.** *Sample answer:* Have a friend stand near the building on a sunny day. Measure your friend's height and the length of his or her shadow. Measure the length of the building's shadow. Set up a proportion using your measurements and the unknown height of the building. Solve for the height.   **15.** 51°   **17.** 15° **19.** $\overline{CD} \cong \overline{RS}$; $\overline{DE} \cong \overline{ST}$; $\overline{CE} \cong \overline{RT}$; $\angle C \cong \angle R$; $\angle D \cong \angle S$; $\angle E \cong \angle T$

10.7 Getting Ready to Practice (p. 513)
1. reflection   **3.** rotation; 90° counterclockwise

10.7 Practice and Problem Solving (pp. 514–515)
5. reflection; *y*-axis   **7.** translation   **11.** *Sample answer:* If you move through 180°, you move halfway around a circle. You end up at the same point whether you move around the circle clockwise or counterclockwise.

13. 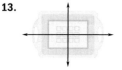 rotational symmetry; 180° clockwise or counterclockwise

15.  no rotational symmetry

17.  rotational symmetry; 120° both clockwise and counterclockwise

19.

Sample answer: Hexagon with rotational symmetry of 180°, square with rotational symmetry of 90° and

180°, both clockwise and counterclockwise

23.

3   **25.** 7 cm

27. 37.625; 21.5; 20; 62

Special Topic Exercises (pp. 516–517)

1. yes;
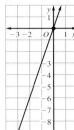

3.

Sample answer: Translate the parallelogram right or left to form a row of parallelograms. Then translate the row up or down.   **5.** Yes; no; no; at each step, rotate the quadrilateral around the midpoint of a side that is bordering empty space. Continue to do so, and you will fill the plane. You cannot form a tessellation using only translations, because you will leave gaps. The copies will not fill the plane. The same thing happens if you try only reflections.   **7.** yes;
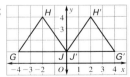

10.8 Getting Ready to Practice (p. 520)

1. image   **3.** $(x, y) \rightarrow (x - 5, y + 1)$
5. $G'(-2, -2)$, $H'(0, 1)$, $J'(2, -2)$;
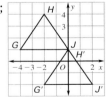

7. $G'(4, 1)$, $H'(2, 4)$, $J'(0, 1)$;
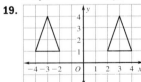

10.8 Practice and Problem Solving (pp. 521–522)

9. $(x, y) \rightarrow (x - 1, y - 2)$

11.
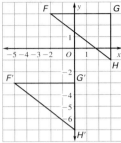
$F'(-5, -3)$, $G'(0, -3)$, $H'(0, -7)$

13.
$F'(1, 9)$, $G'(6, 9)$, $H'(6, 5)$, $J'(1, 5)$

15.

$F'(-2, -3)$, $G'(3, -3)$, $H'(3, 1)$, $J'(-2, 1)$

17. $(x, y) \rightarrow (x - 3, y) \rightarrow (-x, y) \rightarrow (x + 1, y)$

19.
a reflection in the *y*-axis or a translation 6 units to the left

21. $L'(2, -2)$, $M'(-1, -4)$, $N'(-2, -2)$ **23.** $W'(0, 0)$, $X'(-3, -5)$, $Y'(4, -3)$ **27.** 7   **29.** $1.25; $3.75. *Sample answer:* Use the strategy Write an Equation; $x + 3x = 5$, $4x = 5$, $x = 1.25$.   **31.** 890

10.8 Technology Activity (p. 523) **1.** $(6, -2)$
3. $(-2, 2)$

10.5–10.8 Notebook Review (pp. 524–525) **1.** Yes; no. *Sample answer:* To be similar, polygons must be the exact same shape, but to be congruent, they must be the exact same shape and the exact same size. Thus, congruent polygons are similar, but similar polygons do not have to be congruent.
2. 4 cm

3. 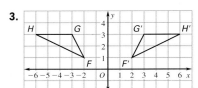 $F'(2, 1)$, $G'(3, 3)$, $H'(6, 3)$

4. Yes. *Sample answer:* Suppose the first translation is given by $(x, y) \rightarrow (x + j, y + k)$ and the second by $(x, y) \rightarrow (x + l, y + m)$. Then the effect of doing the two translations one after the other is to move a point (x, y) to the point $(x + (j + l), y + (k + m))$, which is another translation.   **5.** never

Chapter Review (pp. 526–527) **1.** 180°   **3.** none
5. *Sample answer:* A line of symmetry divides a figure exactly in half, so that if you were to fold the figure along the line, the two halves would match exactly.   **7.** acute; 155°; 65°   **9.** acute; 175°; 85°
11. $\overline{SW}$ and $\overline{TV}$ **13.** *Sample answer:* $\angle 1$ and $\angle 2$
15. 115°   **17.** 132; obtuse   **19.** polygon; pentagon; not regular   **21.** not a polygon; not comprised only of line segments   **23.** similar; 3:2   **25.** 3; one through each vertex, perpendicular to the opposite side; since all three angles and all three sides are congruent, if you were to fold the triangle in half along such a line, the remaining sides and angles would match.

27. 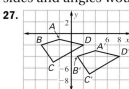 $A'(4, -3)$, $B'(1, -4)$, $C'(3, -7)$, $D'(8, -4)$

29. 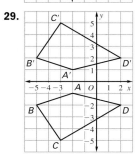 $A'(-2, 1)$, $B'(-5, 2)$, $C'(-3, 5)$, $D'(2, 2)$

Chapter 11

11.1 Getting Ready to Practice (p. 535) **1.** radical expression   **3.** 6   **5.** −12   **7.** ±2   **9.** ±5   **11.** 16 ft

11.1 Practice and Problem Solving (pp. 536–537)
13. 30, −30   **15.** 27, −27   **17.** 100, −100   **19.** 23, −23   **21.** 15   **23.** −18   **25.** −26   **27.** 32   **29.** 7 cm
31. 14 m   **33.** 2   **35.** 4   **37.** −5   **39.** ±12   **41.** ±9
43. ±24   **45.** 1300 m   **47.** 1.5, −1.5   **49.** 0.05, −0.05
51. 2   **53.** 8   **55.** $5\frac{1}{3}$ knots; $10\frac{2}{3}$ knots   **57.** 9 m
59. 147   **61.** 146.55
63. 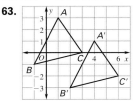 $A'(4, 1)$; $B'(2, -3)$, $C'(6, -2)$

65. *Sample answer:* 440,000; 600,000   **67.** *Sample answer:* 700; 800

11.2 Problem Solving Strategies (p. 539)
1. a score of 173   **3.** 2 balcony seats, 6 floor seats
5. tickets: $12; hot dogs: $3.50   **7.** 720°   **9.** 5 weeks; 7 weeks

11.2 Getting Ready to Practice (p. 542)
1. irrational   **3.** 5; 4.8   **5.** 11; 11.4   **7.** Rational; $\sqrt{1600} = 40$, which is an integer.   **9.** Irrational; 115 is not a perfect square.

11.2 Practice and Problem Solving (pp. 543–544)
11. 6; 5.9   **13.** 8; 7.5   **15.** 11; 11.2   **17.** 14; 14.1
19. A step is missing, it should read: Because 29 is closer to 25, $\sqrt{29} \approx \sqrt{25} = 5$.   **21.** 18.7 ft
23. Irrational; it is a nonterminating, nonrepeating decimal.   **25.** Rational; it is the ratio of two integers.   **27.** Irrational; 21 is not a perfect square.
29. Rational; it is a repeating decimal.   **31.** 9.33
33. 11.83   **35.** Irrational numbers; more numbers are not perfect squares than are perfect squares.
37. $\sqrt{17}$, 4.3, $4.\overline{3}$, $\frac{17}{3}$ **39.** ±3.61   **41.** ±2.24
43. $24 - 4j$ **45.** $6t - 9u$ **47.** ±12   **49.** ±4   **51.** 16
53. 6

11.3 Getting Ready to Practice (p. 548)
1. hypotenuse   **3.** 16 ft   **5.** 1.4 m

11.3 Practice and Problem Solving (pp. 548–549)
7. 9.4 yd   **9.** 2 mm   **11.** 26 ft   **13.** The two values should be about equal.   **15.** 4; 5   **17.** 18.1 ft

21. 30.8°   **23.** $\sqrt{72}$, 8.6, $\sqrt{81}$, 9.2   **25.** 0.3, $1.\overline{3}$, $1\frac{2}{5}$, $\sqrt{3}$
27. 70 m; 250 m^2

11.1–11.3 Notebook Review (pp. 550–551)
1. perfect squares   **2.** ±17   **3.** ±11   **4.** ±4   **5.** 5
6. 7   **7.** 15   **8.** 8 in.   **9.** 3.1 cm   **10.** Take the square
root of the area to find the length of one side, then
multiply this length by 4 to find the perimeter.
Sample answer: If a square has area 3600 square
feet, then the length of one side is $\sqrt{3600} = 60$,
and the perimeter is 4(60) = 240 feet.

11.4 Getting Ready to Practice (p. 554)
1.   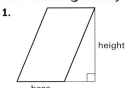   **3.** 18 in.^{2}

5. The height is the length of a perpendicular
segment between the base and the opposite side.
Here, the height is 4 centimeters. The area is
$10 \times 4 = 40$ square centimeters.

11.4 Practice and Problem Solving (pp. 554–555)
7. 32 mm; 45 mm^2 **9.** 19 in.; $14\frac{19}{20}$ in.^{2} **11.** 13 ft
13. 18 in.   **15.** about 72,000 mi^2 **17.** 6 ft
19. *Sample answer:* about 2.59 in.; about 7 in.^{2}
23. 6   **25.** 56   **27.** 150 m   **29.** prime   **31.** composite

11.5 Getting Ready to Practice (p. 560)
1.   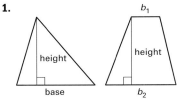   **3.** 170 yd^2
5. 36 cm^2

11.5 Practice and Problem Solving (pp. 561–562)
7. 27.5 m^2 **9.** 6 km   **11.** $9\frac{1}{3}$ mi   **13.** 121 cm^2
15. 44 m^2 **17.** 25 cm   **19.** $7\frac{1}{4}$ in.   **21.** The area is
4 times the original area. *Sample answer:* If a
triangle has a base of 10 inches and a height of
4 inches, its area will be 20 square inches. If you
double the base and height, the base will have a
length of 20 inches and the height will be 8 inches.

Its area will be $\left(\frac{1}{2}\right)(20)(8) = 80$ square inches,
which is 4 times the original area of 20 square
inches.   **23.** 180 m^2 **25.** 1038.395 ft^2 **29.** acute
31. obtuse   **33.** 66.56   **35.** 335.92

11.6 Getting Ready to Practice (p. 565)
1.
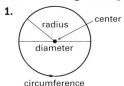
5. The d in the formula means diameter. The
diameter is twice the radius, so the diameter is
10 meters. The correct circumference is $10\pi \approx$
31.4 meters.

11.6 Practice and Problem Solving (pp. 565–567)
7. 28.3 in.   **9.** 20.4 cm   **11.** 3.78 in.   **13.** 9 in.; 4.5 in.
15. 26 mm; 13 mm   **17.** $12\frac{3}{5}$ cm; $6\frac{3}{10}$ cm   **19.** The
circumference is tripled as well. *Sample answer:* If
the diameter is 7 inches, the circumference of the
circle is about 22 inches. If you triple the diameter
to 21 inches, the circumference will be $\left(\frac{22}{7}\right)(21) =$
66 inches, or 3 times 22 inches.   **21.** 5π in., or
about 15.7 in.   **25.** 40%   **27.** 237,600

11.7 Getting Ready to Practice (p. 569)   **5.** 4 m;
50.2 m^2 **7.** 4.5 mi; about 63.6 mi^2 **9.** 113 ft^2

11.7 Practice and Problem Solving (pp. 569–570)
11. 460 cm^2 **13.** 907 mm^2 **15.** 5.31 in.^{2} **17.** 9 ft;
18 ft   **19.** Divide the circumference by 2π to find
the radius. Then, square the radius and multiply
by π to find the area.   **21.** 28.3 m^2 **23.** 7.07 in.^{2}
25. 38.5 yd^2 **31.** 283 km   **33.** 67.2 yd   **35.** $\frac{3}{5}$ **37.** $\frac{12}{25}$

11.7 Technology Activity (p. 571)   **1.** 21.61   **3.** 66
5. 128.81   **7.** 31.01

11.4–11.7 Notebook Review (pp. 572–573)
1. radius   **2.** 63 in.^{2} **3.** 166.5 yd^2 **4.** 107 in.; 907 in.^{2}

5. Find the area of the rectangle: $6 \times 8 = 48$ square inches. Add to this the area of the two right triangles, each with base 4 inches and height 6 inches: $2\left(\frac{1}{2}\right)(4)(6) = 24$ square inches. This gives a total area of 72 square inches.

Chapter Review (pp. 574–575) **1.** radical expression **3.** diameter **5.** irrational **7.** 6 **9.** 7 **11.** 1440 gal/min **13.** ±7 **15.** ±1 **17.** 6; 5.6 **19.** 17; 17.0 **21.** Irrational; 65 is not a perfect square. **23.** Rational; 3.34 is a terminating decimal. **25.** 18 mm **27.** 11.5 cm **29.** 12 in. **31.** 136.5 ft^2 **33.** 176 in.; 2464 in.^{2} **35.** about 18 in.

Chapter 12

12.1 Getting Ready to Practice (p. 585) **1.** faces

12.1 Practice and Problem Solving (pp. 585–587)
7. triangular prism **9.** triangular pyramid
11. square prism **13.** False. *Sample answer:* By definition a prism has two parallel, congruent bases. **15.** true **17.** pentagonal prism; 7 faces, 15 edges, 10 vertices **19.** triangular prism; 5 faces, 9 edges, 6 vertices **21.** Half. *Sample answer:* The figure shows the center of the sphere lying in the circular base. This occurs when a sphere is exactly cut in half. **23.** lines h and k **25.** lines k and j
27. $502.50 **29.** 4% **31.** 9 in.; 18 in. **33.** 21 ft; 42 ft
35. 6 mm; 12 mm **37.** $1\frac{2}{3}$ **39.** $3\frac{4}{7}$

12.2 Getting Ready to Practice (p. 590) **1.** top; side; front **3.** front **5.** side

12.2 Practice and Problem Solving (pp. 590–591)

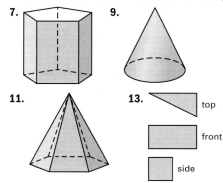

15. 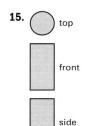 **17.** rectangular pyramid **21.** 0.76
23. 0.001 **25.** sphere **27.** 0.012
29. 270

Special Topic Exercises (p. 593)

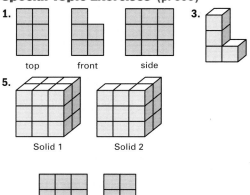

12.3 Getting Ready to Practice (p. 596) **1.** surface area **3.** top and bottom: 8 mm^2, front and back: 4 mm^2, sides: 2 mm^2; surface area = 28 mm^2

12.3 Practice and Problem Solving (pp. 596–597)
5. 312 cm^2 **7.** 1174 mm^2 **9.** 654 ft^2 **11.** 551 ft^2
13. 217.48 m^2 **15.** 5.76 m^2 **17.** 7 in. **19.** 36 square units **21.** 22 mm; 11 mm **23.** 45.5 cm; 22.75 cm
25. 56 **27.** 219.8

12.1–12.3 Notebook Review (pp. 598–599)
1. vertices; faces; edges
2. 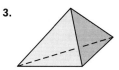 7 faces, 15 edges, 10 vertices

3. 4 faces, 6 edges, 4 vertices

4. 188 ft^2 **5.** 52 m^2 **6.** 384 in.^{2} **7.** B. *Sample answer:* A door is about 3 feet wide and 7 feet tall, so each side has an area of about 21 square feet. The total surface area for both sides is about 42 square feet.

12.4 Problem Solving Strategies (p. 601)
1. 12 in. **3.** 24 triangular pieces, no square pieces
5. 35 cubes; 86 faces are visible. **7.** 400 m
9. 300 mi

12.4 Getting Ready to Practice (p. 604)
1. circles; rectangle **5.** 226 in.^{2}

12.4 Practice and Problem Solving (pp. 604–605)
7. 113 cm^2 **9.** 1360 cm^2 **11.** 2140 in.^{2} **13.** 15 in.
15. 816 mm^2 **17.** 3120 cm^2 **19.** 8 ft **21.** 9 km^2
23. 42 m^2 **25.** 92 ft^2 **27.** 22.4 **29.** 0.081

12.5 Getting Ready to Practice (p. 609)
1. The volume is the space an object fills up. The surface area is the total area of all of its surfaces.
3. 360 in.^{3} **5.** 5832 cm^3

12.5 Practice and Problem Solving (pp. 609–610)
7. 648 m^3 **9.** 4620 ft^3 **11.** 77 mm^3 **13.** 8 ft
17. 6.75 ft^3 **19.** about $20 for 4 bags **21.** *Sample answer:* Keep the sizes of the books in each stack exactly the same. **23.** 4 **25.** 90 **27.** 791 cm^2
29. 3; 2.4; 2; 5.9

12.6 Getting Ready to Practice (p. 613)
1. base; height **3.** 314 m^3 **5.** 2 ft

12.6 Practice and Problem Solving (pp. 613–614)
7. 1610 ft^3 **9.** 452 cm^3 **11.** cylinder D **13.** 1 cm
15. large pool: about 804 ft^3, kiddie pool: about 100 ft^3; $\frac{804}{25} = \frac{100}{x}$, $804x = 100(25)$, $x \approx 3.11$ T
19. 6. *Sample answer:* Use the strategy Guess, Check, and Revise. I started with the value 8, and found out it was too big. The answer has to be an even number, so next I tried 6, and it worked.
21. 210; 5

12.6 Technology Activity (p. 615) **1.** 56.2 in.^{2}; 27.6 in.^{3} **3.** The surface area will be 9 times as great as the original surface area, and the volume will be 27 times as great as the original volume.

12.4–12.6 Notebook Review (pp. 616–617)
1. $S = 2\pi r^2 + 2\pi rh$; $V = \pi r^2 h$ **2.** 1170 in.^{2}
3. 96.7 m^2 **4.** 170 ft^2 **5.** 33 ft^3 **6.** 184 in.^{3}
7. length and width

Chapter Review (pp. 618–619) **1.** solid **3.** volume
5. net **7.** cylinder **9.** triangular prism
11. 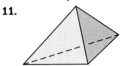 **13.**

15. 150 cm^2 **17.** $2x^2 + 2x^2 + 2x^2 = 6x^2$
19. 31.4 mm^2 **21.** 45 mm^3 **23.** 135 yd^3 **25.** 1 m
27. 2 cm **29.** A, D, B, C **31.** 6 ft

Chapter 13

13.1 Getting Ready to Practice (p. 636)
1. probability

13.1 Practice and Problem Solving (pp. 636–638)
7. $\frac{4}{11}$ **9.** $\frac{2}{11}$ **11.** $\frac{1}{2}$; 0.5; 50% **13.** 0; 0; 0% **15.** $\frac{4}{5}$; 0.8; 80% **17.** 0.47 **19.** *Sample answer:* The hat is not symmetric, so the two outcomes are not equally likely. Also the hat may land on its side, which gives another possible outcome that must have some probability. **21.** $\frac{1}{2}$ **23.** 3 to 7; 7 to 3
25. 20 automobiles **27.** 4 red and 12 blue
29. square **31.** $10\frac{1}{2}$ **33.** $5\frac{1}{7}$

13.2 Getting Ready to Practice (p. 641) **1.** The first branching shows the possible outcomes of the first roll: 1, 2, 3, 4, 5, or 6. Each of these branches into the possible outcomes of the second roll, again 1, 2, 3, 4, 5, or 6.

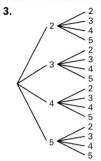
13.2 Practice and Problem Solving (pp. 641–642)

3.
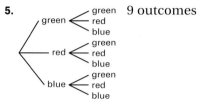 16 outcomes

5. 9 outcomes

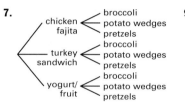

7.

chicken fajita — broccoli, potato wedges, pretzels
turkey sandwich — broccoli, potato wedges, pretzels
yogurt/ fruit — broccoli, potato wedges, pretzels

9. $\frac{1}{5}$

11.

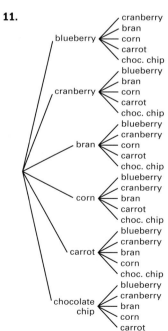

13. $\frac{1}{18}$ **17.** 270
19. 10^4 **21.** x^3

13.3 Getting Ready to Practice (p. 646)

1. the number of different outcomes for the first event followed by the second event **3.** $\frac{1}{40}$

13.3 Practice and Problem Solving (pp. 646–647)

5. 156 **7.** 1140 **9.** 125,000 locker combinations
11. The counting principle says to multiply the number of outcomes for each event together;
$6 \cdot 6 \cdot 6 = 216$. **13.** 12 ways **15.** $\frac{1}{729}$ **17.** 15 in.

19.

5	2
6	
7	5 8
8	5 5 8
9	5 7 7 7
10	1 4 5
11	6

Key: 10 | 1 = 101

13.1–13.3 Notebook Review (pp. 648–649)

1. event **2.** $\frac{1}{6}$

3.

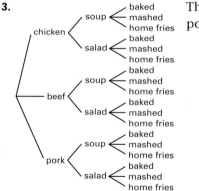

There are 18 possible meals.

4. $\frac{1}{12}$ **5.** *Sample answer:* If you buy a 5th shirt, there will be 3 new outfits, since the new shirt can be combined with any of your 3 pairs of pants. Thus, there are $12 + 3 = 15$ outfits possible.

13.4 Getting Ready to Practice (p. 653)

1. combination

13.4 Practice and Problem Solving (pp. 653–655)

5. 120 **7.** 4845 **9.** 5040 ways **11.** 17,550 ways
13. 10 choices **15.** 3003 choices **17.** 270,725

19. combination; 210 choices **21.** permutation; 10,626 ways **23.** *Sample answer:* Permutation: arranging books on a shelf; combination: choosing a group of CDs to take on a trip. **25.** 120 ways **29.** $\frac{2}{5}$; 0.4; 40% **31.** $\frac{3}{10}$; 0.3; 30% **33.** $\frac{1}{2}$ **35.** $\frac{2}{13}$

13.4 Technology Activity (p. 656) **1.** 93,024 ways

13.5 Getting Ready to Practice (p. 659)
1. Disjoint events have no outcomes in common; overlapping events have one or more outcomes in common. **3.** 0.6 **5.** 0.6 **7.** 0.77

13.5 Practice and Problem Solving (pp. 660–661)
9. disjoint **11.** 0.61 **13.** 44.3% **15.** $\frac{3}{5}$ **17.** 63%
19. 48% **21.** 0.8 **23.** Yes; since there is no overlap, the total probability will be the sum of the three separate probabilities. **25.** $\frac{1}{3}$ **27.** $\frac{1}{3}$ **29.** never
31. No. *Sample answer:* If A and B are disjoint events, then $P(A$ or $B)$ would be $0.7 + 0.9 = 1.6$, and probabilities are never greater than 1. **33.** ±6
35. ±8 **37.** 10; 10; 10; 6 **39.** 3.2; 3.3; 3.6; 1.3

13.6 Problem Solving Strategies (p. 663)
5. about $27 **7.** Take the three toothpicks on the right end. Place one so that it connects the top vertices of the two remaining triangles, and place the other two to form a new triangle with this as its base. There are now 4 identical small triangles arranged in a larger, fifth triangle.

13.6 Getting Ready to Practice (p. 667) **1.** If two events are independent, the fact that one has occurred does not affect the likelihood that the other one has also occurred. If two events are dependent, then the fact that one has occurred does affect the probability of the other having also occurred. **3.** 0.25 **5.** 0.72 **7.** 0.05

13.6 Practice and Problem Solving (pp. 667–669)
9. independent **11.** 0.18 **13.** 0.7 **15.** 0.9 **17.** To make the two choices independent, you must return the first tile to the set and thoroughly mix them up before choosing the second. **19.** 0.3294
21. $\frac{2}{9}$ **23.** dependent events; $\frac{19}{177}$, or about 11%

25. A good answer should include: • the results of the first 25 rolls of a pair of number cubes, recording how many times you got 2 of a kind • the calculation of the experimental probability: $\frac{\text{times you got 2 of a kind}}{25}$ • the fact that the next two rolls are independent • the calculation of the probability both were 2 of a kind, the experimental probability squared **27.** 36.4%
29. 235% **31.** 43% **33.** 8.5 **35.** 21.1

13.4–13.6 Notebook Review (pp. 670–671)
1. permutation **2.** 5040 different PINs **3.** 16%
4. $\frac{5}{14}$, or about 36% **5.** No. *Sample answer:* If two disjoint events have nonzero probabilities, then they are not independent. The probability that the second event occurred given that the first event occurred is zero. Thus, the occurrence of the first event affects the probability of the second event also occurring. This makes them dependent.

Chapter Review (pp. 672–673) **7.** $\frac{3}{8}$; 0.375; 37.5%
9. $\frac{5}{8}$; 0.625; 62.5% **11.** $\frac{1}{10}$ **13.** $\frac{4}{25}$ **15.** $\frac{3}{25}$
17. 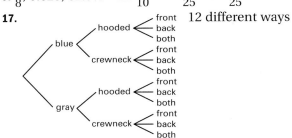 12 different ways

19. 55 **21.** 882 **23.** permutation; 40,320 **25.** 0.9
27. 0.67 **29.** 0.24 **31.** 0.15

Skills Review Handbook

Whole Number Place Value (p. 681)
1. $3 \times 1000 + 8 \times 100 + 2 \times 1$ **3.** $9 \times 100{,}000 + 1 \times 1000 + 3 \times 1$ **5.** 45,097 **7.** 2361

Comparing and Ordering Whole Numbers
(p. 682) **1.** 0, 1, 2, 4, 8, 10 **3.** 0, 6, 9, 11, 19, 29
5. $5 < 12$ **7.** $15 > 11$

Rounding Whole Numbers (p. 683) **1.** 340
3. 28,000 **5.** 9000 **7.** 300,000 **9.** 58,900 **11.** 5210
13. 28,000,000 **15.** 1,500,000

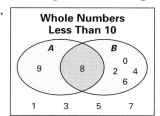

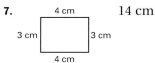

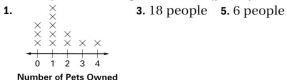

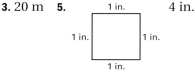

Number Fact Families (p. 684) **1.** 9; 9; 16 **3.** 3; 4; 4 **5.** 56 **7.** 11 **9.** 7 **11.** 10

Divisibility Tests (p. 685) **1.** 2 **3.** 3 **5.** 2, 3, 5, 6, 9, 10 **7.** 3, 5 **9.** 5 **11.** 2, 3, 5, 6, 9, 10 **13.** 2, 5, 10 **15.** 5

Modeling Fractions (p. 686) **1.** $\frac{7}{8}$ **3.** $\frac{2}{7}$ **5.** $\frac{5}{8}$ **7.** $1\frac{1}{8}$ **9.** $1\frac{2}{3}$ **11.** $1\frac{5}{6}$

Using a Number Line to Add and Subtract (p. 687) **1.** 13 **3.** 15 **5.** 8 **7.** 25 **9.** 4

Addition and Subtraction of Whole Numbers (p. 688) **1.** 102 **3.** 290 **5.** 34 **7.** 285 **9.** 4316 **11.** 1918 **13.** 13,111 **15.** 29,921

Multiplication of Whole Numbers (p. 689) **1.** 4806 **3.** 320,016 **5.** 16,700 **7.** 970,000

Division of Whole Numbers (p. 690) **1.** 45 **3.** 23 **5.** 110 R6 **7.** 8

Estimating Sums (p. 691) **1–9.** Estimates may vary. **1.** 720 **3.** 1970 **5.** 14,600 **7.** 2100 **9.** 3600

Estimating Differences (p. 692) **1–7.** Estimates may vary. **1.** 640 **3.** 410 **5.** 2100 **7.** 6800

Estimating Products (p. 693) **1–15.** Estimates may vary. **1.** 200; 600 **3.** 1000; 1800 **5.** 6000; 12,000 **7.** 2000; 6000 **9.** 50,000 **11.** 540,000 **13.** 400,000 **15.** 130,000

Estimating Quotients (p. 694) **1–23.** Estimates may vary. **1.** 30; 35 **3.** 250; 300 **5.** 17; 18 **7.** 50; 60 **9.** 2000; 2500 **11.** 900; 950 **13.** 48 **15.** 600 **17.** 21 **19.** 30 **21.** 4500 **23.** 550

Solving Problems Using Addition and Subtraction (p. 695) **1.** $12 **3.** 44 people **5.** $44

Solving Problems Using Multiplication and Division (p. 696) **1.** 36 pencils **3.** 4 muffins **5.** 13 cards

Units of Time (p. 697) **1.** 300 **3.** 72 **5.** 2 **7.** > **9.** = **11.** =

Solving Problems Involving Time (p. 698) **1.** 2 h 15 min **3.** about 1 h

Using a Compass (p. 700) **3.** The length of the segment should be about $3\frac{3}{4}$ inches.

Basic Geometric Figures (p. 701) **1.** 12 cm **3.** 20 m **5.** 4 in.

1 in. 1 in. 1 in. 1 in.

7. 4 cm 3 cm 3 cm 4 cm 14 cm

Venn Diagrams and Logical Reasoning (p. 702)

1.

3. True; 8 is the only number in both set A and set B.

Reading Bar Graphs and Line Graphs (p. 703) **1.** 5 students **3.** 10 A.M.

Reading and Making Line Plots (p. 704) **1.** **3.** 18 people **5.** 6 people

Number of Pets Owned

Extra Practice

Chapter 1 (p. 705) **1.** Each number is 8 less than the previous number; 25, 17, 9. **3.** Each number is the previous number divided by 2; 100, 50, 25. **5.** 15 **7.** 36 **9.** 11^3 **11.** y^4 **13.** 100 **15.** 0 **17.** 65 **19.** 6 **21.** 7 **23.** 9 **25.** 36 ft; 77 ft^2 **27.** 64 cm; 256 cm^2 **29.** 10 games

Chapter 2 (p. 706) **1.** 0.05, 0.25, 0.5, 5.2 **3.** 6.08, 6.2, 6.28, 6.82 **5.** 0.92 **7.** 738.05 **9.** 19.6 **11.** 1.123 **13.** 2.16 **15.** 0.05476 **17.** 7.7964 **19.** 57.92 **21.** 12.02 **23.** 80 **25.** 0.045 **27.** 20.75 **29.** 5.61

31. 8.2×10^9 **33.** 4.316×10^2 **35.** $422{,}100{,}000$
37. $5{,}376{,}100$ **39.** milliliters **41.** kilogram **43.** 400
45. 0.12 **47.** 0.0361 **49.** $=$

Chapter 3 (p. 707) 1. 31.5; 25.5; 22; 39 **3.** 7; 7; 2
and 7; 10 **5.** Median. *Sample answer:* The mode
is 35, which is also the smallest data value. It is
not very representative of the data set as a whole.
The mean is 44, while the median is 41.5. The
median is the best representative of the data,
since it is close to most of the values. The mean is
a little high because of the one reading of 69,
which is a little bit larger than the other data
values. **7.** *Sample answer:* The amount of money
you earn each week with your paper route

9.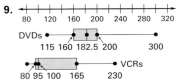

11.

DVD players	Interval	VCRs
0	70–109	7
2	110–149	2
6	150–189	0
3	190–229	2
2	230–269	1
1	270–309	0

13. *Sample answer:* Since there is a break in the
vertical scale, the bar heights appear to differ a lot
more than the data themselves would indicate.

Chapter 4 (p. 708) 1. composite; $1, 3, 5, 15, 25, 75$
3. prime; $1, 83$ **5.** $2^2 \times 3 \times 7$ **7.** 5^3 **9.** 24; not
relatively prime **11.** 4; not relatively prime
13. $\frac{5}{6}$; $\frac{5}{6}$; equivalent **15.** $\frac{3}{4}$; $\frac{7}{9}$; not equivalent **17.** 48
19. 126 **21.** $>$ **23.** $=$ **25.** $>$ **27.** $<$ **29.** $\frac{22}{3}$ **31.** $\frac{49}{9}$
33. $3\frac{4}{7}$ **35.** $4\frac{1}{8}$ **37.** $0.\overline{7}$ **39.** 8.9 **41.** $\frac{17}{25}$ **43.** $5\frac{5}{8}$

Chapter 5 (p. 709) 1. $\frac{3}{4}$ **3.** $\frac{5}{11}$ **5.** $\frac{13}{18}$ **7.** $\frac{2}{3}$ **9.** 7
11. $6\frac{7}{10}$ **13.** $2\frac{4}{5}$ **15.** $\frac{3}{7}$ **17.** $\frac{7}{12}$ **19.** 4 **21.** 2 **23.** $\frac{4}{5}$
25. $\frac{9}{2}$ **27.** $\frac{6}{19}$ **29.** $\frac{6}{7}$ **31.** 9 **33.** feet **35.** gallons
37. pounds **39.** 108 **41.** 64 **43.** 4; 3 **45.** 10 qt
47. 1 T 1700 lb

Chapter 6 (p. 710) 1. $-10, -3, 0, 3, 6$ **3.** $-84,$
$-70, -10, 15, 71, 99$ **5.** -4 **7.** 27 **9.** -4 **11.** 79
13. 72 **15.** -12 **17.** -13 **19.** 3 **21.** $\frac{-9}{10}$; $-\frac{10}{9}$; $\frac{9}{10}$
23. $\frac{-1}{1}$; -1; 1

25. $-6 \cdot 10 \cdot \left(-\frac{1}{6}\right)$ [original expression]

$= -6 \cdot \left(-\frac{1}{6}\right) \cdot 10$ [commutative property of multiplication]

$= \left[-6 \cdot \left(-\frac{1}{6}\right)\right] \cdot 10$ [associative property of multiplication]

$= 1 \cdot 10$ [multiplicative inverses]

$= 10$ [multiplicative identity]

27. $50 \cdot 13 \cdot 2$ [original expression]

$= 50 \cdot 2 \cdot 13$ [commutative property of multiplication]

$= (50 \cdot 2) \cdot 13$ [associative property of multiplication]

$= 100 \cdot 13$ [multiplication fact]

$= 1300$ [multiplication fact]

29. 80 **31.** 6 **33.** $4(\$25 - \$.05) = \$100 - \$.20 =$
$\$99.80$

35–37. 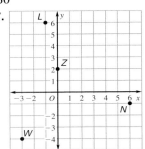 **35.** y-axis
37. Quadrant II

39. Pressure increases as the depth increases.

Chapter 7 (p. 711) 1. $x - 17$ **3.** $\frac{y}{2} = -5$ **5.** 2
7. $2y + 12$ **9.** $-6 - 5x$ **11.** -10 **13.** -2.4 **15.** 7
17. -27 **19.** 6.5 **21.** 3.1 **23.** $x > -7$
25. $b > -6$;

27. $s \le 5$;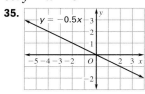

29.

Input x	−4	−2	0	2	4
Output y	−5.5	−3.5	−1.5	0.5	2.5

range: $\{-5.5, -3.5, -1.5, 0.5, 2.5\}$

31.

Input x	−4	−2	0	2	4
Output y	12	10	8	6	4

range: $\{4, 6, 8, 10, 12\}$

33. $y = x - 6$

35. 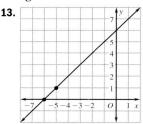 **37.**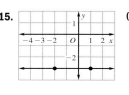

Chapter 8 (p. 712) **1.** 3 to 1 **3.** 3 to 14 **5.** $\frac{1}{4}$
7. $\frac{\$1.45}{1 \text{ gal}}$ **9.** $\frac{36 \text{ words}}{1 \text{ min}}$ **11.** 15 fl oz

13.  1 **15.** 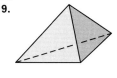 0

17. 25 **19.** 27 **21.** 19.5 **23.** 25.2 **25.** 600 calories
27. 30 ft by 15 ft

Chapter 9 (p. 713) **1.** $\frac{3}{5}$ **3.** $\frac{21}{25}$ **5.** 40% **7.** 25%
9. 64% **11.** 67.5 **13.** 0.02 **15.** 1.06 **17.** 57.5%
19. 0.12% **21.** 45.6 **23.** 31.25%

25.

Work Schedule
at Video Store
- Tuesday: 5 h
- Monday: 3.5 h
- Friday: 2.5 h
- Thursday: 3 h
- Wednesday: 6 h

27. decrease; 6.25%
29. increase; 9.375%
31. $211.20
33. $12.50; $262.50
35. $2.20; $602.20

Chapter 10 (p. 714) **1.** 94°; 4° **3.** 90°; no
complementary angle **5.** 123°; 57° **7.** 38°; 142°
9. isosceles **11.** 1080°

13. Yes; any two squares are similar, since all of
their angles are congruent, each with a measure
of 90°, and each pair of corresponding sides has
the same ratio. Here, the ratio is 4 to 5. **15.** 30 ft
17. 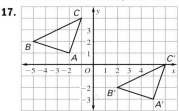 $A'(5, -3)$,
$B'(2, -2)$, $C'(6, 0)$

19. 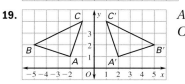 $A'(2, 1)$, $B'(5, 2)$,
$C'(1, 4)$

Chapter 11 (p. 715) **1.** 6 **3.** 13 **5.** 12, −12 **7.** 6, −6
9. 4; 4.4 **11.** 12; 11.6 **13.** Irrational; it is not a
finite or repeating decimal. **15.** Rational; 49 is a
perfect square. **17.** 9 m **19.** 12.8 in. **21.** 8 ft
23. 32 m² **25.** 44 cm² **27.** 264 mi **29.** 157 cm
31. 5024 yd² **33.** 154 ft²

Chapter 12 (p. 716) **1.** sphere **3.** rectangular
pyramid **5.** 4; 6; 4 **7.** 7; 12; 7
9. 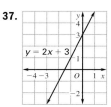 **11.**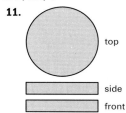

top

side

front

13. 121.2 ft² **15.** 37.7 m² **17.** 245 ft² **19.** 280 in.³
21. 137.5 cm³ **23.** 252 mm³ **25.** 1130 in.³ **27.** 5 ft

Chapter 13 (p. 717) **1.** $\frac{3}{20}$; 0.15; 15% **3.** 72% **5.** $\frac{2}{9}$
7. $\frac{1}{17{,}576}$ **9.** 4060 ways **11.** $\frac{17}{18}$ **13.** $\frac{3}{8} = 0.375$